PN 1995.9 .W6 H26 1998

Hannsberry, Karen Burroughs,
 1962-

Femme noir

DATE DUE

D1596544

DEMCO 38-297

NEW ENGLAND INSTITUTE
OF TECHNOLOGY
LEARNING RESOURCES CENTER

Femme Noir

Femme Noir

Bad Girls of Film

by
KAREN BURROUGHS HANNSBERRY

McFarland & Company, Inc., Publishers
Jefferson, North Carolina and London

11/98

38200225

British Library Cataloguing-in-Publication data are available

Library of Congress Cataloguing-in-Publication Data

Hannsberry, Karen Burroughs, 1962–
    Femme noir : bad girls of film / by Karen Burroughs Hannsberry.
      p.   cm.
    Includes filmographies, bibliographical references and index.
    ISBN 0-7864-0429-9 (library binding : 50# alkaline paper) ∞
    1. Motion picture actors and actresses — United States — Biography.
2. Film noir.   3. Femmes fatales in motion pictures.   I. Title.
PN1995.9.W6H26   1998
791.43'028'082 — dc21   97-42496
                                                      CIP

©1998 Karen Burroughs Hannsberry. All rights reserved

No part of this book may be reproduced or transmitted in any form or by any means, electronic or mechanical, including photocopying or recording, or by any information storage and retrieval system, without permission in writing from the publisher.

Manufactured in the United States of America

McFarland & Company, Inc., Publishers
  Box 611, Jefferson, North Carolina 28640

For my family and friends who never doubted,
always supported, and continue to champion my dreams.

Acknowledgments

For taking the time to share with me their recollections of experiences from the golden age of Hollywood and the realm of the film noir, I offer my heartfelt thanks to Bruce Bennett, Rosemary DeCamp, Richard Fleischer, Sally Forrest, Coleen Gray, Jane Greer, Signe Hasso, Charles Korvin, Victor Mature, David Wilde, Marie Windsor and Robert Wise.

For their assistance with my research, I am most sincerely indebted to Alan David Burroughs, Theresa Henderson Burroughs, Rod Crawford, Stephan Eichenberg, Richard Hegedorn, Evelyn Mildred Henderson, Bob King, Janet Lorenz of the Margaret Herrick Memorial Library of the Academy of Motion Picture Arts and Sciences, Doug McClelland, Randi Massingill, Paul Payne, Phillip Pessar, Bob J. Robison, Dan Van Neste, the staff of the Library of the Performing Arts at Lincoln Center in New York and the staffs of the Beverly Branch Library and the Harold Washington Library in Chicago, Illinois. Part of my research involved viewing each of the 149 film noir features in which the actresses appear, and for aiding me in acquiring these films, I extend great appreciation to Nick Lapetina, Jim Lindsay, and Dan Van Neste.

Finally, for assisting me in locating stills, I am especially grateful to T. Gene Hatcher and Manuel Núñez, as well as Ed Colbert, Robert Pelot, Phil Petras, Carole York, Jim Yurchak, Metro Golden Memories in Chicago, Movie Star News in New York City, Cinema Memories in Key West, Florida, and Jim Shepard of Collectors Book Store in Hollywood, California.

Table of Contents

Introduction

I find more bitter than death
The woman whose heart is snares and nets
And he who falls beneath her spell
Has need of God's mercy.
         — from *Born to Kill* (RKO, 1947)

What could be more unsettling than the statue-like cast of Gene Tierney's face as she coolly observes the drowning of her young brother-in-law in *Leave Her to Heaven?* Or the waves of horror that seem to ripple in Joan Crawford's eyes when she overhears her husband plot her murder in *Sudden Fear?* Or Barbara Stanwyck's unflinchingly composed voice in *Double Indemnity* when she tells her lover that it's "straight down the line, for both of us" in their scheme to murder her spouse?

These actresses are the femmes of film noir — literally translated as "black film" — one of cinema's most popular and widely imitated genres. The movies that fall into this category were initially identified in 1946 by French critics who noticed the darker mood that had begun to appear in films produced in America. Unlike the Western and gangster film genres, however, film noir cannot be unequivocally defined by setting or conflict, but instead is characterized by the more tenuous qualities of tone and mood. Produced primarily between the early 1940s and the late 1950s, these films depict a world of pessimism, corruption and hopelessness, and are distinguished by their dim, shadowy appearance and dark overtones.

Movies from the film noir era are notable for a number of recurring visual characteristics, including rain-swept streets, murkily lit rooms, mirror reflections, looming shadows and foggy nights. In terms of style and technique, these films abound with interior and exterior night scenes that suggest dingy realism, and feature unique lighting that emphasizes deep shadows and accents the mood of fatalism. Aside from visual characteristics, these films contain both heroes and villains who are cynical and disillusioned, inextricably bound to the past and ambivalent about the future.

1

In addition, most films noirs offer portraits of complex female characters who, to some degree, are fundamental to the development of the plot. Some exist as champions for the male protagonists, as in *Phantom Lady* (Universal, 1944), where the relentless determination of Ella Raines' Carol lifts the protagonist from his state of inevitable doom and results in the exposure of the man who framed him for murder. In other noir films, the female is portrayed as an innocent victim, caught up in circumstances beyond her control, such as Keechie (Cathy O'Donnell) in *They Live by Night* (RKO, 1948), who falls in love with a naive petty criminal. Then there are the femmes who are gutsy but sincere, as in *High Sierra* (Warners, 1941), where Ida Lupino's Marie is hard-boiled and implacable, but also possesses a deep sense of compassion and a propensity for true love.

Finally, there is the assortment of film noir females who use their wiles to get their way, as often as not at the expense of their male counterparts. The mystical French figure of *la belle dame sans merci*— the beautiful woman without mercy — is personified by the femmes in these productions. In first-rate, often shocking performances, an array of talented actresses — from such prominent stars as Barbara Stanwyck and Lana Turner, to lesser known actresses including Peggie Castle, Hope Emerson and Helen Walker — portrayed the dark side of the female; women who, in turn, could be avaricious, selfish, possessive, slovenly, calculating, masochistic and callous. While usually possessing a keen intelligence and shrewd cunning, these were women totally lacking in morals, bent on satisfying their own lustful, mercenary or violent desires, utterly aware of their unique feminine tools, and willing to capitalize on them whenever necessary.

I am several decades removed from the generation that witnessed the original release of the movies that feature these actresses, but my fascination with this era is nonetheless ardent and ongoing. I saw my first film noir at the tender age of 14; although the movie had been filmed nearly 20 years before my birth, it did not seem dated, but instead instantly drew me into its shadowy, mystifying world. It was *Double Indemnity* (Paramount, 1944), starring Barbara Stanwyck, Fred MacMurray, and Edward G. Robinson, a dark tale of murder and lust that offered spicy, rapid-fire dialogue, intriguing characterization and an intricate, engrossing plot. As my initiation into the realm of film noir, this movie will always have a special significance for me, for after viewing it, I instantly became, and have since remained, a staunch devotee of this unique era of filmmaking.

With startling clarity, I can remember sitting in front of the television set on the living room floor, an untouched bowl of popcorn in my lap, my rapt attention disrupted only by annoying commercial breaks. A number of the film's subtle nuances did not become apparent to me until many years and many viewings later, but I can still recall the graphic impression of Barbara Stanwyck's hardened beauty, her brassy blond hair offering a dramatic contrast to the gritty, somber look of the movie. I can still remember the atmosphere of sexual desire between Stanwyck and MacMurray, so tangible that the screen fairly crackled and burned. And I can still recollect the seething emotions of betrayal, greed and desperation that were interwoven throughout the gripping plot. The vivid images of this movie remained in my mind long after the pictures had faded from the screen, and have never quite been obliterated.

Femme Noir: The Bad Girls of Film looks at the personal lives and cinematic contributions of 49 actresses who were most frequently featured in the movies of the film noir era. Many of those studied became archetypes of the film noir femme: Gloria Grahame as the impishly sexy masochist; Lizabeth Scott as the duplicitous schemer; Claire Trevor, the ruthless spider woman; Ida Lupino, the hard-boiled dame with a vulnerable core; Audrey Totter, sullen and insidious; and Barbara Stanwyck — perhaps noir's most notorious femme — as the grim, unflinching murderess. Others, such as Marilyn Monroe, Jane Russell and Rita Hayworth, were better known for their roles in Technicolor musicals or romantic comedies, but nonetheless made their mark in a highly regarded assortment of brooding films from this age. While most of the actresses included in this volume appeared in three or more films noirs, there are a number of exceptions, including Lana Turner, Ava Gardner and Jane Greer — these women made few noir appearances, but starred in three of the most acclaimed films of the period: *The Postman Always Rings Twice* (MGM, 1946), *The Killers* (Universal-International, 1946), and *Out of the Past* (RKO, 1947), respectively. All told, the actresses described herein depicted a multiplicity of fascinating femmes who won our admiration in spite of their infamy, devilish dames who enticed our cheers as well as some chills down our spines, and beguiling babes whose identities remain indelibly etched in our minds like blood on a white satin pillowcase.

I invite you now to delve into the world of femme noir, where — in the words of Raymond Chandler — the streets are dark with something more than the night.

Lauren Bacall

Lauren Bacall was the girl with "The Look," a sultry, sensuous beauty with a husky voice and a hard-as-nails facade that let the world know that she was a force to be reckoned with. Perhaps best known for her marriage to actor Humphrey Bogart, Bacall was once described as a combination of Marlene Dietrich, Katharine Hepburn and Bette Davis, with overtones of Veronica Lake and Barbara Stanwyck and undertones of Mae West and Jean Harlow.

Such heady comparisons aside, and notwithstanding an acclaimed performance in her film debut, most of Bacall's screen vehicles were somewhat less than stellar, and many are now all but forgotten. But the indomitable actress enjoyed a monumental career resurgence nearly a half-century after her first screen appearance, continuing to secure feature roles in high-profile films and, at the age of 72, earned her first Academy Award nomination. During her Hollywood heyday, Bacall starred opposite such superstars as Kirk Douglas, Charles Boyer and John Wayne, and her career included starring roles in three top-notch films noirs: *The Big Sleep* (1946), *Dark Passage* (1947) and *Key Largo* (1948).

Bacall was born Betty Joan Perske in the Bronx, New York, on September 16, 1924, the only child of William, of Alsatian descent, and Natalie, who was born in Romania. When young Betty's parents separated in 1932, Natalie assumed the last half of her maiden name, Weinstein-Bacal, and her daughter became Betty Bacal. Betty moved with her mother to Manhattan and attended the Highland Manor school for girls in Tarrytown, where she experienced her first taste of life as a performer in the school's weekly dramatic programs. Next, Betty enrolled at the Julia Richman High School for girls. As the actress wrote in her book *Now*, attending girls' schools and being raised by her mother fostered her belief that "women had the upper hand — got things done — were listened to." This would be a conviction that would typify the star's actions throughout her personal and professional life.

During her high school years, Betty participated in Saturday classes at the New York School of the Theatre, and her high school senior yearbook photo featured the caption, "May your dreams of being an actress overflow the brim." After her graduation, she set about making those dreams come true. She spent a year at the American Academy of Dramatic Arts (while a student there, she dated fellow student and future costar Kirk Douglas), but could not return because her mother was unable to afford the tuition. Instead, she turned to modeling, securing her first job at the age of 16 and earning $30 a week.

While working as a model, Betty spent much of her time pursuing her big break on Broadway. Walgreen's Drug Store on 44th Street was one of her favorite haunts, where she poured through copies of *Actor's Cue*, a publication that included listings of road tours and plays being cast. She also sold *Actor's Cue* outside Sardi's Restaurant, a popular theatrical retreat, boldly making herself known to a variety of notables, including producer Max Gordon, director

Lauren Bacall

George Kaufman and actor Paul Lukas, whom Betty called her "first important friend in the theater." After six months of modeling, Betty got a night
job as an usher, spending her days seeking work in the theater.

Betty's first job on the stage was a walk-on in *Johnny 2 × 4*. (By the time
she'd signed the contract to appear in this play, Betty had added an extra "l"
to her last name, to avoid mispronunciation.) Despite her excitement over
securing her first job in the theater, however, the play closed after eight weeks.
In 1942, she landed her first speaking part in *Franklin Street*, but after tryouts
in Washington and Wilmington, this show, too, was unsuccessful.

Undaunted in the wake of her disappointing entry into the world of the
theater, Betty returned to modeling, landing a job with *Harper's Bazaar* magazine. Her second appearance in the magazine featured the lithe young beauty
in a two-page spread and, although she was incorrectly identified as "Betty
Becall," her pictures attracted the attention of a number of Hollywood big
shots, including David O. Selznick, Howard Hughes and Howard Hawks. A
photo on the magazine's cover led to an offer by Hawks for a screen test in
Hollywood, and on April 3, 1943, Betty boarded the train for California. She
was 18 years old.

Betty's test resulted in her signing a seven-year contract with Hawks,
starting at $100 a week and increasing to $1,250 in the seventh year. Her
mother moved to California where they settled into a small furnished apartment in Beverly Hills. Betty spent the remainder of the year taking singing
lessons, reading aloud for voice training and hounding Hawks' agent, Charlie Feldman, for a screen role. Shortly after Christmas 1943, Howard Hawks
gave Betty what she called "the only present I wanted from life," a test for his
new film, *To Have and Have Not* (1944). She got the part and a new moniker —
which Hawks instructed her to tell the press had been her great-grandmother's
name — and the world was introduced to Lauren Bacall.

In addition to being her film debut, *To Have and Have Not* was also
notable for its introduction of Bacall to her future husband, Humphrey Bogart. From the first day of shooting, Bacall said that Bogart made a special
effort to put her at ease: "He was quite aware that I was a new young thing
who knew from nothing and was scared to death," she stated. The on-screen
rapport between the two soon developed into something more. Although Bogart was married to actress Mayo Methot (together they were called the "Bat-
tling Bogarts" because of their frequent fights — Methot once stabbed Bogart
with a knife and set fire to their house), Bacall and Bogart began seeing each
other off the set. "Anyone with half an eye could see that there was more
between us than the scenes we played," Bacall said.

Despite the difference in their ages — Bacall was 19 and Bogart was 44 —
the couple fell head over heels in love. "We shared so much, understood so
much about each other," Bacall once said. Bogart loved Bacall's fun-loving,
down-to-earth nature ("She's a good joe," Bogart said) and Bacall found Bogart

to be gentle, sentimental, and loving — quite unlike his gruff screen image. After several separations, Bogart and his wife were divorced on May 10, 1945, and he and Bacall were married 11 days later.

Bacall's first film catapulted her to stardom, with one critic raving: "Lauren Bacall has cinema personality to burn.... She has a javelin-like vitality, a born dancer's eloquence of movement, a fierce female shrewdness and a special sweet-sourness ... plus a stone-crushing self-confidence and a trombone voice." And Bacall's wave of popularity continued with her next film, the noir classic *The Big Sleep* (1946). Based on the Raymond Chandler novel, *The Big Sleep* focuses on the efforts of Philip Marlowe (Humphrey Bogart) to find out who is blackmailing Gen. Sternwood (Charles Waldron), the millionaire father of two daughters, Carmen (Martha Vickers), a thumb-sucking nymphomaniac whose compromising photos are the subject of the blackmail, and Vivian (Bacall), the level-headed older sister. Before Marlowe is through, he has been ordered off the job by the district attorney's office, been beaten up by thugs when he doesn't obey, and has tracked murder and blackmail to the door of a gambler. In the end, he gets $500 — and Vivian — for his troubles.

Chock full of colorful characters and logging no less than seven dead bodies, *The Big Sleep* is renowned for its complex plot. In fact, it is perhaps even more confusing than most noirs — the reviewer for *Cue* declared that audiences needed "a geneological chart, a gangsters' glossary, and a plot synopsis to keep you even vaguely informed on what's going on before your unbelieving eyes." Even producer/director Howard Hawks admitted that he "never figured out what was going on."

Bacall was again lauded for her performance, with *Time*'s critic comparing her to an "adolescent cougar" and the reviewer for *Film Daily* noting that she "carries off her part the way audiences expect." But her next screen role, an aristocratic English girl in *Confidential Agent* (1945) with Charles Boyer, brought Bacall's fast rising star plummeting to earth. The film was a disaster and Bacall would later say: "It took me years to prove that I was capable of doing anything at all worthwhile." She was quoted in a 1946 Louella Parsons article as admitting that her success "came too fast. I don't believe there are many girls who are unknown one day and looked upon as a famous star the next. Perhaps it would have been better if I had come up more slowly."

Bacall's fourth film, *Dark Passage* (1947), teamed her again with her husband. This noir thriller begins when Vincent Parry (Bogart), wrongly convicted of his wife's murder, escapes from prison and is picked up on the highway by Irene Jansen (Bacall), a wealthy artist who takes him to her apartment and supplies him with clothes and money. It turns out that Irene had been an avid follower of Vincent's murder trial and had even written scathing letters to local newspapers, decrying their coverage of the crime. "I suspected you were getting a raw deal," Irene explains. "When I get excited about something, I give it everything I have. I'm funny that way."

Following a tip from a good-hearted cab driver, Vincent undergoes plastic surgery, planning to stay with a friend, George Fellsinger (Rory Mallinson), until the bandages can be removed. But when he returns to George's house after the operation, Vincent finds him dead, and seeks refuge with Irene. Meanwhile, he is charged with his friend's murder, manages to elude police, is confronted by a cheap crook who tries to blackmail him, and learns that his wife had actually been killed by Madge Rapf (Agnes Moorehead), his wife's friend and, coincidentally, also a friend of Irene's. When Vincent confronts Madge, she refuses to admit her guilt and dies after accidentally falling from her window. Faced with the hopelessness of his situation, Vincent flees to South America and is later joined there by Irene, where they begin their life together.

Reviewers noted that Bacall made a "definite impression," but the film was dismissed by many as failing to live up to the expectations of a Bogart-Bacall pairing. However, one of the film's most interesting aspects was its use of the first-person point-of-view camera, which showed only Bogart's hands and forearms for the first 40 minutes.

Meanwhile, Bacall continued to display her invincible spirit by refusing to accept roles in films "whose scripts I hated," resulting in her suspension by Warner Bros. on several occasions. Her independence was again exhibited in fall 1947, when she and Bogart became active in a protest against the investigations of Communism in Hollywood by the House Un-American Activities Committee. Along with a number of other notables, including actors Gene Kelly, Danny Kaye and John Garfield, director John Huston and composer Ira Gershwin, Bacall and Bogart traveled to Washington to offer moral support to the writers, directors and actors who were the victims of the Committee's infamous smear campaign. Bacall even penned an article for the *Washington Daily News* which asserted her belief in the right of Americans to freedom of speech and freedom of political persuasion, and stated that she had been "frightened" by the Committee hearings. The investigation resulted in the blacklisting of "The Unfriendly Ten," including writer Dalton Trumbo and director Edward Dmytryk, and although Bacall expressed doubts in her autobiography that the Hollywood protest served as any help, it did further illuminate her personal courage and strong sense of conviction.

Early in 1948, Bacall and Bogart started work on their fourth film together, *Key Largo*, another film noir classic, costarring Edward G. Robinson, Lionel Barrymore and Claire Trevor. Here, Bacall plays Nora Temple, a level-headed war widow who helps operate a hotel in one of the Key Islands off the coast of Florida, owned by her wheelchair-bound father-in-law (Barrymore). The story opens when ex-war hero Frank McCloud (Bogart) visits the hotel to tell Temple of his (Temple's) son's valiant exploits in the war, but his stopover takes a dramatic turn when he encounters a group of thugs led by a vicious gangster, Johnny Rocco (Robinson). Rocco plans to sell a stack of counterfeit bills that he has imported from Cuba, and when the gang takes over the hotel, Frank and Johnny engage in a battle of wills that results in the death of a local policeman, two Indians and Johnny's four henchmen, before Johnny himself is killed by Frank.

The film was another hit for Bogart and Bacall, who recalled it as one of her happiest movie experiences, and a short time later, in January 1949, the Bogarts experienced another joyous event: the birth of their first child, Stephen (named for Bogart's character in *To Have and Have Not*). But professionally, Bacall continued to appear in films that failed to showcase her talent, including *Young Man with a Horn* (1950), costarring her old friend Kirk Douglas, and *Bright Leaf* (1950), with Gary Cooper. As Bacall stated, "I kept receiving terrible scripts and I kept going on suspension."

But as the 1950s unfolded, Bacall's fortunes began to change. In 1952, she gave birth to a daughter, Leslie, named after Bogart's first mentor and long-time friend, actor Leslie Howard, who had been killed during the war. And the following year Bacall won her best part in years, in *How to Marry a Millionaire* (1953), a comedy about three women searching for rich husbands. Co-starring Marilyn Monroe and Betty Grable, the film gave Bacall's career a much-needed boost, and led to an invitation to embed her hand and foot-prints in the forecourt of Grauman's (now Mann's) Chinese Theater in Hollywood. However, in typical maverick Bacall fashion, she declined, becoming the first actress to do so. "There's a difference between notoriety and fame," Bacall said, adding that, to her, Grauman's was "the Hall of Fame of the motion picture industry and the people in it were unforgettables and irre-placeables. I don't think of myself as either."

Bacall's next film, *Woman's World* (1954), a witty tale of three top executives in line for a managerial position, was also a success, but it was followed by *The Cobweb* (1955), which flopped at the box office, despite an all-star cast that included Richard Widmark, Charles Boyer, Lillian Gish and Gloria Grahame. *Blood Alley* (1955) with John Wayne, a fairly routine action picture, was not much better.

In 1955, plans were announced to re-team Bogart and Bacall in *Melville Goodwin, U.S.A.*, which would be their fifth film together. The contracts were signed and wardrobe selection had started, when Bogart began to complain of feeling unwell. Suffering from a sore throat and a chronic cough, he visited a doctor and, shortly afterward, was diagnosed with throat cancer. In March 1956, Bogart underwent an eight-hour surgery, during which doctors removed two inches of his esophagus and lymph glands, raised his stomach 12 inches and excised one rib. But Bogart continued his daily smoking and drinking habits, and his condition gradually weakened. Despite chemotherapy, the cancer spread and on January 14, 1957, the famed actor died, three weeks after his 57th birthday. His body was cremated; inside the urn, Bacall placed a small gold whistle, a symbol of the memorable line she'd delivered to Bogart in their first film together: "If you need anything, just whistle." In his eulogy at Bogart's funeral, director John Huston praised Bacall's bravery throughout the ordeal, stating that "out of the power of her love, she was able to hide her grief and go on being her own familiar self for Bogie — a flawless performance." Of her 12-year union with Bogart, the actress herself would recall: "We didn't have a perfect marriage. We argued. He drank. But we had a relationship. We had love."

Less than a year after Bogart's death, Bacall had a brief affair with crooner Frank Sinatra — she stated in her autobiography that she later realized she had used the relationship in an attempt to obliterate the pain she'd experienced after Bogart's death. The couple had even discussed plans for marriage, but these fell through when news of the impending nuptials was announced in the *Los Angeles Examiner*. According to Bacall, Sinatra was enraged by the leak to the press, and that was "the end of our exciting, imperfect, not-to-be love affair.... I had a wonderful time with Frank, but looking back, I realize I was pretty desperate for companionship."

During Bogart's illness, Bacall made two films, *Written on the Wind* (1956), a glossy soaper starring Rock Hudson and Dorothy Malone, and a comedy with Gregory Peck, *Designing Woman* (1957). In 1958, she played Robert Stack's dying wife in *The Gift of Love*, traveled to London, India and Spain for the filming of *Flame Over India* (1959), then returned to New York to appear in the stage version of *Goodbye Charlie*. While in New York, she began dating actor Jason Robards, whom she described as "quite dazzling," and although Robards was married with three children, Bacall said they "gravitated toward each other immediately ... it was impossible for me to turn away." Robards' wife filed for divorce in October 1960, citing Bacall in the suit, and not long afterward, the actress discovered that she was pregnant. On July 4, 1961, Bacall and Robards were married in Mexico and their baby boy, Sam, was born five months later. But the Robards-Bacall union would not last. Robards was a heavy drinker and Bacall said that although she loved the talented actor, "nothing went smoothly for more than two days at a time.... I'd forgotten how to laugh, to relax, to have any sane social exchange. I had no peace." The marriage ended in 1969.

Meanwhile, in an effort to get her stalled film career on track, Bacall appeared in *Shock Treatment* (1964), a film she described as "truly tacky," playing a psychiatrist who goes mad. She followed it with a featured role in a light comedy with Natalie Wood and Tony Curtis, *Sex and the Single Girl* (1964), and *Harper* (1966), a detective yarn starring Paul Newman. The latter film would be her last screen performance for nearly 10 years, as Bacall returned to her roots on the stage for a two-year run in the highly successful *Cactus Flower*. But her pleasure from this triumph would be tarnished when the movie rights to the play were sold to Columbia Pictures, and Bacall discovered that her role would be played in the film by Ingrid Bergman. "Here I was in a hit play, having achieved a great personal success, and I still hadn't convinced the Hollywood moguls that I was worth putting in the movie," Bacall recalled.

In 1970, continuing her Broadway career, Bacall starred as Margo Channing in *Applause*, the musical version of the Bette Davis vehicle *All About Eve* (1950). For her performance, Bacall won a Tony Award, and the smash-hit production would enjoy a five-year run. Bacall returned to the screen in 1974 for *Murder on the Orient Express*, in a role that she said "saved me, it broke my theater rhythm." And two years later she appeared in *The Shootist*, the last film in the career of veteran actor John Wayne. But Bacall would not be absent from the stage for long. In 1981, she scored another Broadway success in *Woman of the Year*, which ran for two and a half years, and for which she won her second Tony Award. She next starred as Alexandra Del Lago in *Sweet Bird of Youth* in 1985.

In the 1990s, Bacall experienced a phenomenal renaissance of her career. After appearing in the well-received feature film production of *Misery* (1990), starring Kathy Bates and James Caan, Bacall turned to the small screen, co-starring with Gregory Peck in *The Portrait* (1992) and appearing in the remake of *Dinner at Eight* (1993), both for Turner Network Television. In addition, her still-distinctive voice was instantly recognizable in a number of television commercials, including spots for Fancy Feast cat food and Royal Caribbean cruise ships. Then, leading to what Bacall jokingly called "sudden stardom," the actress portrayed Barbra Streisand's feisty mother in the romantic comedy *The Mirror Has Two Faces* (1996), earning a Golden Globe Award, a Screen Actors Guild Award and an Academy Award nomination for Best Supporting Actress. "This is the first time I have ever gotten this kind of attention for my film work," she said. "When I started, I got a different kind of attention, but … nobody's paid attention to me in pictures for a long time. It's extraordinary, and I don't think it's sunk in yet. I don't get it." And the actress was receiving plaudits for her off-screen performances as well — along with fellow actors Martin Landau, Jack Lemmon and Gregory Peck, she earned a Grammy nomination in the category of Spoken Word or Non-Musical Album for "Harry S. Truman: A Journey to Independence" (the award would be won by U.S. first lady Hillary Rodham Clinton for "It Takes a Village").

After her successful performance in *The Mirror Has Two Faces*, Bacall co-starred in *My Fellow Americans* (1996) with Jack Lemmon and James Garner, and the following year appeared in a French film, *Le Jour et la Nuit* (1997), with Alain Delon. Also in 1997, the actress found time to participate in a nationwide celebrity lecture series, "Unique Lives and Experiences," which combined intellectual entertainment with issue-driven discussion. And she topped off the year as one of the honorees at the Kennedy Center Honors Ceremony in December 1997.

In a career that she herself described as having "many more downs than ups," Bacall continues to make an impression as an actress with talent and class, and still in solid possession of "The Look." As she stated in recent years, "I've made a lot of mistakes in my life, and I'm not foolish enough to think I'll never make another one. I've lived well, but I'm not going to sit around. What else could I do — sit around and give soirées for the rest of my life? That's not where my head is at. I've got to keep moving. If I fall on my ass, I'll pick myself up, dust myself off, and go on.

"This adventure is not over."

Film Noir Filmography

THE BIG SLEEP   *Director and Producer:* Howard Hawks. Released by Warner Bros., August 1946. *Running time:* 118 minutes. *Cast:* Humphrey Bogart, Lauren Bacall, John Ridgely, Martha Vickers, Dorothy Malone, Patricia Clarke, Regis Toomey.

DARK PASSAGE   *Director:* Delmar Daves. *Producer:* Jerry Wald. Released by Warner Bros., September 1947. *Running time:* 106 minutes. *Cast:* Humphrey Bogart, Lauren Bacall, Bruce Bennett, Agnes Moorehead, Tom D'Andrea, Clifton Young.

KEY LARGO   *Director:* John Huston. *Producer:* Jerry Wald. Released by Warner Bros., July 1948. *Running time:* 100 minutes. *Cast:* Humphrey Bogart, Edward G. Robinson, Lauren Bacall, Lionel Barrymore, Claire Trevor, Thomas Gomez, Harry Lewis. *Awards:* Academy Award for Best Supporting Actress: Claire Trevor.

References

Bacall, Lauren. *By Myself.* New York: Ballentine Books, 1978.
_____. *Now.* New York: Alfred A. Knopf, 1994.
"Bacall Is Back and Knopf Has Her Book." *Hollywood Studio Magazine,* June 1979.
Colby, Anita. "The Story of Lauren Bacall." *Photoplay,* October 1947.
Crichton, Kyle. "Watch for Bacall." *Collier's,* October 21, 1944.
"Debut in *To Have and Have Not.*" *Life,* October 16, 1944.
Greenberger, Howard. *Bogey's Baby.* New York: St. Martin's Press, 1978.
Hagen, Ray. "Lauren Bacall." *Films in Review,* April 1964.
Hall, Gladys. "The Life of 'The Look.'" *Photoplay,* April 1945.
Hyams, Joe. *Bogart and Bacall: A Love Story.* New York: D. McKay, 1975.
"Journey to Bacall." *Cue,* February 17, 1945.
Kaplan, James. "What Becomes a Legend Most." *The New Yorker,* October 10, 1994.
"Lauren Bacall Talks About Bogart, Sinatra, and Her New Life." *McCalls,* July 1966.
London, Ephraim S. "And So They Are One." *Silver Screen,* September 1945.
"The Love Song of Bogie and His Betty." *Screen Greats,* Summer 1971.
Maksian, George. "Bacall Recalls." *New York Daily News,* March 9, 1990.
Morris, Bob. "Just Shooting the Breeze." *New York Times,* September 19, 1993.
Parsons, Louella O. "In Hollywood with Louella O. Parsons." *Los Angeles Examiner,* January 6, 1946.
Petrucelli, Alan W. "Talking with Lauren Bacall." *Redbook,* June 1988.
Quirk, Lawrence J. *The Films of Lauren Bacall.* Secaucus, N.J.: Citadel Press, 1986.
"Redbook Readers Talk with Lauren Bacall." *Redbook,* July 1966.
Silverman, Stephen M. "Bacall: If I Have a Limo to the Show, I've Earned It." *New York Post,* May 3, 1982.
Smith, Liz. "How Bacall Handles the British Press." *New York Daily News,* July 9, 1985.
_____. "Non-Applause for a Woman of the Year." *New York Daily News,* July 23, 1982.

Stephens, Cliff. "Bacall Steals the Show." *New York Daily News*, January 30, 1983.

"Talents and Tailoring." *Time*, October 23, 1944.

"Talk with a Star." *Newsweek*, March 10, 1958.

Viorst, Judith. "Still Smoldering." *New York Times*, October 9, 1994.

Weintraub, Bernard. "Bacall Still Walks and, Especially, Talks." *New York Times*, December 19, 1996.

Wickware, Francis Sill. "Lauren Bacall." *Reader's Scope*, August 1945.

"Young American Legend." *Vogue*, November 15, 1959.

Zwecker, Bill. "A Star Is Born — Again." *Chicago Sun-Times*, February 2, 1997.

Joan Bennett

Joan Bennett was born to act. The youngest child of a family renowned for its dramatic accomplishments, Bennett began her lengthy career in the shadow of her famous father and her flamboyant sister, but would ultimately emerge to become a star in her own right. Perhaps best remembered by movie-goers as the level-headed matriarch of *Father of the Bride* and its sequel, *Father's Little Dividend*, Bennett left a lasting impression in four highly acclaimed films noirs: *The Woman in the Window* (1945), *Scarlet Street* (1946), *The Scar* (1948), and *The Reckless Moment* (1949).

Bennett, born Joan Geraldine in Palisades, New Jersey, on February 27, 1910, was the last of three daughters of Richard Bennett, a matinee idol, and his stage actress wife, Adrienne. Bennett would later remember her father as "gifted, proud, vain and powerless to be anything else," and as a child, she and her sister Barbara feared Richard's emotional outbursts. It was only the eldest sibling, Constance, who would stand up to their father's rages and match his flare-ups with her own.

Raised in a family that lived and breathed the theater, Bennett would first appear on the stage at the tender age of four, when her father had his daughters join him in a curtain call of his play *Damaged Goods*, adapted from the French play *Les Avariés*. Of the production, which dealt with the effects of syphilis, Bennett would later recall, "I think that's my first remembrance of being in a theater, though the effect of the play's subject matter on the three of us was negligible. Constance couldn't spell it, Barbara couldn't pronounce it, and I couldn't understand it."

The following year, Bennett made her film debut when her father directed and starred in a film version of *Damaged Goods* (1915), whose cast included the entire Bennett family. The three Bennett girls appeared in the prologue and, as Bennett stated, the siblings "danced around looking like refugees from a number three company of Isadora Duncan's." Later that year, the family's Palisades home was destroyed by fire, and Richard Bennett moved his clan to a country house in Park Hill, New York. There, Joan began to hone her budding acting skills as Peaseblossom in *A Midsummer Night's Dream*, produced in the family's backyard. The play, designed to help the country's war effort, was attended by a number of luminaries, including famed showman Florenz Ziegfeld and his wife, actress Billie Burke.

Bennett enjoyed a pleasant, often exciting childhood, frequently being allowed to attend her parents' rehearsals and performances. One of her only trials seemed to be her need to wear glasses because of her nearsightedness: "I thought they made me look ugly," Bennett said, referring to herself as "the mess of the family." She attended Miss Chandor's Day School and Miss Hopkins School for Girls in New York City, and later entered St. Margaret's boarding school in Waterbury, Connecticut. But in 1923, Bennett's happy world came crashing down on her when her beloved parents separated. Her mother Adrienne explained the split: "You see, Mr. Bennett is a genius and geniuses should be segregated." Two years later, charging her husband with "misconduct," Adrienne Bennett would sue for divorce.

Meanwhile, with her sister, Constance, beginning her film career, and Barbara dancing in a Paris revue, 15-year-old Joan found herself disillusioned with boarding school life. She convinced her mother to let her change schools and, in 1925, she enrolled at La Lierre, a finishing school located near Paris. Before beginning her studies there, Bennett sailed to Cherbourg, accompanied by a friend of her mother's, and while on board she met John Marion Fox, who was 10 years her senior. Impressed by the older man's sophistication and flattered by his attentions, Bennett recalled him as "the handsomest man I had ever met.... Jack did drink rather a good deal, but then I thought perhaps it was just a sign of his worldliness."

Upon entering La Lierre in August 1925, Bennett soon grew bored with the school's stifling climate, likening it to "living in a tomb." Escaping over the wall of the school one night, she telephoned Fox for help and accompanied him to London, where he was to produce a musical comedy. While there, Bennett stayed with family friends until her mother enrolled her in another finishing school, L'Hermitage in Versailles. But by then, Jack Fox had proposed marriage to Bennett and, after she completed the term at L'Hermitage, the two were married in London on September 15, 1926. "I wore an ivory gown by Lanvin and carried white orchids," Bennett remembered. "Mother gave away the bride, who was scared stiff and cried all the way down the aisle."

Living in Carlyle Square, London, the 16-year-old bride was delighted with the fact that she was "a married woman, and therefore, an adult." But her dreams of an idyllic existence were soon dimmed by her husband's excessive drinking and his failed theatrical enterprises. The couple later moved to Hollywood, where Bennett gave birth to her first child, Adrienne Ralston Fox (whose name would later be changed to Diana), on February 20, 1928. But the addition to the family did little to salvage Bennett's rapidly deteriorating marriage; Fox continued to drink heavily and subject his family to frequent rages. Feeling that the relationship had become a "graveyard," Bennett divorced Fox later that year.

At only 18 years of age, with a young child to support, Bennett turned to her theatrical roots. She obtained jobs as a movie extra in *Power* (1928), starring William Boyd, and *The Divine Lady* (1929), then appeared on Broadway in her father's new play, *Jarnegan*. Although Bennett played only a small ingenue role, she received favorable notices from several critics, including Richard Watts, Jr., of the *New York Times*, who wrote: "Joan Bennett is both almost unbelievably beautiful and entirely moving." Bennett's performance also attracted the attention of Fox studios, who invited her to make a screen test at their offices in Manhattan. The actress later recalled that the test "must have been forgettable because the studio was mercifully silent." She later made a second screen test, this time for Paramount, arranged by the studio's general manager, Walter Wanger, whom Bennett had met on a date with critic George Jean Nathan. This test, too, led to a dead end, and Wanger reportedly told Bennett's mother, "Your daughter is very sweet, but she'll never photograph."

But Bennett's start in films was just around the corner. While rehearsing for a new play, *Hot Bed*, she was contacted by representatives of Samuel Goldwyn, who were seeking an actress to play opposite Ronald Colman in his first talking picture, *Bulldog Drummond* (1929). Without having to undergo another screen test, Bennett was offered the role, along with a five-year contract with United Artists at $500 a week.

Bennett later admitted that she was initially intimidated by performing with the more-established Colman, but she said that working with the actor was "a wonderful sendoff for any neophyte.... He couldn't have been sweeter or more helpful, and I'll always remember his encouragement at a time when it really mattered." For her role in the film, the petite blonde starlet was noted by the critic for the *New York Times* as being "engaging both as to voice and appearance."

Despite this praise, however, Bennett was released from her contract after her next United Artists feature, *Three Live Ghosts* (1929), and over the next year, she appeared in such fare as *Disraeli* (1929), a Warner Bros. film starring acclaimed actor George Arliss; *Crazy That Way*, a Fox production in which Bennett played the love interest of Kenneth McKenna, Regis Toomey and Jason Robards; and *Moby Dick* (1930), another Warners film. In 1930 she signed a two-year contract with Fox Pictures, but the studio failed to capitalize on her budding talents, casting her in a series of mostly forgettable pictures, including *Scotland Yard* (1930), in which Bennett portrayed the unsuspecting wife of a bank robber, *Hush Money* (1931), starring Bennett as a gangster's former mistress, and *Careless Lady* (1932), which was panned by critics as "too artificial and strained to awaken much interest." Also among her films from this period was *She Wanted a Millionaire* (1932), a dull drama starring Spencer Tracy that was notable primarily because Bennett was thrown from a horse during production, resulting in a fractured hip and three vertebrae. Because of her injury, doctors feared that she might be permanently impaired, but after being confined to bed for three months, Bennett made a successful recovery.

Shortly before her accident, Bennett met and fell in love with Gene Markey, a screenwriter for MGM who was 15 years her senior. Markey wooed the actress through notes, gifts and frequent telephone calls, and during Bennett's recuperative trip to the Panama Canal, Markey spent a great deal of time with her three-year old daughter, becoming "the father she'd never had." On March 12, 1932, Bennett wed Markey, with her sister Constance, now a popular film star, serving as matron of honor.

Following her disappointing run with Fox, Bennett was signed by RKO Pictures, which immediately cast her as Amy, the spoiled, vain sister in *Little*

Joan Bennett in *Little Women* (1933)

Women (1933). Nearly a half-century after the film's release, its director, George Cukor, recalled his selection of Bennett for the role: "I saw her at a party and she was a little tight, and I thought, 'Oh, yes!' She was very sweet and funny, and absolutely right, so we cast her." Bennett would later count the film among her favorites, and her performance was a hit with critics, including Mordaunt Hall of the *New York Times*, who called her "as vital, sympathetic, and full of the *joie de vivre* as one could hope for." The year after her triumphant appearance in *Little Women*, the actress gave birth to her second daughter, Melinda Markey, on February 27, 1934 — Bennett's 24th birthday.

Career-wise, Bennett's future looked bright. Most notably, her performance in *Little Women* had caught the eye of producer Walter Wanger, who years earlier had assured Bennett's mother that her youngest child had no future in films. After viewing Bennett's small but effective portrayal of Amy, Wanger signed Bennett to a term contract and began loaning her out to a variety of film companies. Her first film under Wanger's guidance was *The Pursuit of Happiness* (1934), an engaging comedy set in the 1700s, followed by the oddly titled, *The Man Who Reclaimed His Head* (1935), starring Claude Rains. Bennett next appeared in what she called "the first really challenging and the most dramatic role I'd played up to that time," *Private Worlds* (1935), starring Claudette Colbert. Playing the neurotic, pregnant wife of a doctor, Bennett was lauded by critics, who took particular note of the scene in which her character loses her grip on reality.

For the next two years, Bennett appeared in a series of films that failed to live up to the promise she displayed in *Private Worlds*, including two Bing Crosby vehicles, *Two for Tonight* (1935), and *Mississippi* (1935), in which she sang a duet with the famed crooner; *Wedding Present* (1936), a flimsy screwball comedy; and *Vogues of 1938* (1937), a Technicolor musical highlighted by a lavish fashion show. In her films of this period, Bennett frequently received good notices — her performance in *Big Brown Eyes* (1936) was praised by the reviewer for the *New York Daily News*, who stated that the actress "tosses about the smart cracks ... with deftness that tickles the audience." In the *New York Herald Tribune* review of *Vogues of 1938*, Howard Barnes took note of Bennett's "adept and agreeable performance." Still, most of her roles fell short of showcasing her talents and, as Bennett herself later stated, "With the exception of *Little Women* and *Private Worlds*, I'd played the insipid blonde ingenue."

While her career appeared to be somewhat stagnant, Bennett's home life was not faring much better. In the five years since her marriage to Gene Markey, the couple's relationship had dissolved into "a kind of dull, lusterless routine ... little by little erosion set in and quietly wore away our relationship," Bennett said. In addition, the marriage was further rocked by insistent — and accurate — rumors in Hollywood that producer Walter Wanger harbored more than a mere businesslike interest in Bennett. In June 1937, Bennett filed for divorce, charging that her husband had frequently displayed a violent temper and had abandoned her for more than a month. (Markey would go on to marry, and divorce, actresses Hedy Lamarr and Myrna Loy, winding up with Calumet baking powder heiress Lucille Park Wright.) Walter Wanger continued to pursue Bennett, but neither she nor the recently divorced producer were interested in making their relationship a permanent one.

After her split with Markey, Bennett took a break from filmmaking to replace a pregnant Margaret Sullavan in the national company of *Stage Door*, starring in the role of Terry that had been portrayed that year on screen by Katharine Hepburn. She returned to the screen in 1938, teaming with Henry Fonda in *I Met My Love Again* (panned by the *New York Herald Tribune* as "a hapless and witless yarn"), *The Texans*, a post–Civil War film with Randolph Scott, and *Artists and Models Abroad*, in which Bennett starred opposite Jack Benny as the daughter of a Texas oil millionaire. Again, none of these roles managed to advance her career.

But with her next picture, *Trade Winds* (1938), Bennett received a much-needed boost when the film's director, Tay Garnett, insisted that she don a black wig for her role as an accused murderess. "After that film, everybody liked me in dark hair, so I turned my hair dark," Bennett later said. "It's been that way ever since. The minute I turned brunette, the parts I got were so much better and I then became interested in what I was doing in films."

Bennett's new look caught the attention of producer David O. Selznick, who was then scouring the globe for an actress to play the plum role of Scarlett O'Hara in *Gone with the Wind* (1939). Bennett worked with a dialogue coach to develop a Southern accent and was directed by George Cukor in three tests for the film. Although Bennett seemed to have a good chance at winning the role, however, her hopes were dashed when Selznick's brother Myron met Vivien Leigh, who would later win an Academy Award for her performance. "I always said that if Vivien Leigh hadn't come over to see Larry Olivier, who was working over here at the time in *Wuthering Heights*, I would have gotten the part," Bennett recalled. "It was that close!"

After her disappointment over losing the role of Scarlett O'Hara, Bennett starred in *The Man in the Iron Mask* (1939), which was dismissed by critics as a "slightly stuffy historical romance," *The Housekeeper's Daughter* (1939), a slapstick yarn that flopped at the box office, *Green Hell* (1940), an adventure tale set in the South American jungle, and *The House Across the Bay* (1940), of which the reviewer for the *New York Herald Tribune* overlooked Bennett's acting ability to note her "veritable warehouse of lovely clothes."

After completion of *The House Across the Bay*, the 29-year-old Bennett decided to plunge into marriage for a third time when she accepted the proposal of Walter Wanger, and the two were wed on January 12, 1940: "By then I knew I was in love with Walter and felt I could give him, at last, the settled domestic life he'd never had," Bennett said. But a mere three months after her wedding, the actress claimed that she "was on the point of divorcing [Wanger] for a romantic dereliction," and when she later became ill during one of Wanger's frequent absences, Bennett asked her new agent, Jennings Lang, for assistance with medical help. "I turned to Jennings more often after that with feelings that went beyond our business relationship," she said.

On screen, Bennett starred in *The Man I Married* (1940), as an American woman who discovers that her husband is a Nazi, and *The Son of Monte Cristo* (1940), a swashbuckling tale set in a mythical European kingdom. In

1941, she inked deals with Columbia and 20th Century–Fox, and in her first film under the Fox contract, *Man Hunt*, the actress delivered one of the best performances of her career. For her role as a Cockney prostitute in pre-war London, Bennett was unanimously hailed by critics. Archer Winsten of the *New York Post* claimed that her accent was "so good that you have to look again to remind yourself that it's really Joan Bennett," and the reviewer for the *New York Morning Telegraph* wrote that she offered "the most realistic acting job she ever hired out to pictures."

Once again, however, Bennett followed up a triumphant film with a series of clunkers, including *She Knew All the Answers* (1941) with Franchot Tone, which was panned by critics as a "lightly textured romantic farce with unsophisticated material," *Confirm or Deny* (1941), described by the *Brooklyn Daily Eagle* as "a curious blend of history and commonplace fiction, the credible and the incredible," and *Girl Trouble* (1942), an unfunny comedy that was dismissed as "less than silly — it's plain stupid" by Wanda Hale of the *New York Daily News*.

In 1943, Bennett took a break from the screen when she discovered that she was pregnant again, and on June 26, 1943, her third daughter, Stephanie Wanger, was born. When she resumed her career the following year, Bennett chose an ideal vehicle — the film noir thriller, *The Woman in the Window* (1945).

This Fritz Lang–directed feature centers on Richard Wanley (Edward G. Robinson), a stodgy college professor who is pleasantly surprised as he leaves his men's club one evening and encounters a beautiful dark-haired woman who was featured in a portrait he'd recently admired. After a bit of harmless flirting, the woman in the portrait, Alice (Joan Bennett), invites Wanley home for a drink, but as they enjoy an innocent nightcap, Alice's boyfriend enters her apartment. Wanley and the man, whom Alice knows as "Frank Howard," struggle briefly, then Wanley mortally wounds his attacker with a pair of scissors. Dismissing his original plan to report the self-defense crime to police, Wanley hatches a scheme to dispose of the body, but it is soon discovered and Wanley learns that the dead man was actually a wealthy, well-known financier.

Before long, Alice is contacted by Heidt (Dan Duryea), the financier's bodyguard, who attempts to extort money from her to keep quiet about his alleged knowledge of the crime. After Alice makes an unsuccessful attempt to poison Heidt, Wanley decides that they must turn themselves in but, unable to face the scandal, he prepares to commit suicide. Meanwhile, Heidt is killed in a gun battle with police outside Alice's apartment. When the financier's gold watch is found on Heidt's body, the police assume that he is the killer. Alice telephones Wanley to notify him of this latest development, but the professor has swallowed poison and lacks the strength to answer the call. As Wanley is seen in this unconscious state, an employee of his men's club awakens him, and it is revealed that the entire incident was a dream.

As Alice in *The Woman in the Window*, Bennett was a sensation, depicting a femme caught up in circumstances beyond her control, but well up to the challenge. When Wanley briefly leaves her with the financier's dead body, for instance, Alice has no qualms about rifling the man's pockets, later telling the professor, "It had to be done, didn't it?" Later, when the blackmailing body-guard visits her apartment, Alice displays an unruffled countenance, at one point even accepting his veiled proposal of sex in lieu of payment. After years of playing coquettish flirts and slightly ditzy but harmless dames, Bennett took both critics and audiences by surprise with this alluring portrayal.

After the success of *The Woman in the Window*, Bennett, Wanger, and director Fritz Lang formed an independent film company, Diana Productions, named after Bennett's eldest daughter, and inked a deal for their films to be released through Universal. Following Bennett's appearance as a society dame in *Nob Hill* (1945), the first offering of Diana Productions was Bennett's second film noir, *Scarlet Street* (1946).

This grim tale of lust, greed and murder was the remake of a Jean Renoir movie, *La Chienne* (1931)—"The Bitch"— and reunited Bennett with her *Woman in the Window* costars, Edward G. Robinson and Dan Duryea. The film begins as a mild-mannered cashier, Christopher Cross (Robinson), is being honored by his coworkers for 25 years of faithful service. Later, Cross spies a woman being beaten in the streets, and after gallantly fighting off the offender with his trusty umbrella, Cross joins the woman, Kitty March (Ben-nett), for a drink in a local pub, allowing her to believe that he is a wealthy artist. Encouraged by her con-man boyfriend, Johnny Prince (Duryea), Kitty persuades the unhappily married Cross to establish her in a luxurious apart-ment that he can use as a studio for his painting. Prince finds a market for Cross's unusual artwork, passing Kitty off as the artist and earning her sud-den acclaim. When Cross discovers this deception, he forgives Kitty, but when he learns that she is Prince's lover, he mortally wounds her with an ice pick. Prince is mistakenly arrested for the crime and is ultimately executed, but Cross suffers a different brand of punishment when his guilt from the murder drives him mad.

In *Scarlet Street*, Bennett played her most unsavory character to date, an attractive but slothful dame who carelessly drops gum wrappers and spits grape seeds on the floor of her apartment. Repelled by Cross, she is instead attracted to the abusive Johnny, telling him in one scene: "I hate [Chris] when he looks at me like that. If he were mean or vicious or if he'd bawl me out or some-thing, I'd like him better." But her disdain for her benefactor becomes her undoing when she scoffs at Cross's proposal of marriage: "Oh, you idiot!" she mocks. "How can a man be so dumb? I've wanted to laugh in your face ever since I first met you. You're old and ugly and I'm sick of you. Sick, sick, sick!" This violent and unremittingly bleak example of noir offered Bennett a prime opportunity to again demonstrate that she was up to portraying a femme of less than stellar repute. And although the reviewers from *The New Yorker* and the *New York Times* were less than impressed by her performance, the editor of *The Hollywood Review* hailed Bennett's portrayal of Kitty, claiming that it was her finest screen work: "She is bitterly shrill and sharp as the pitiful nympho ensnared by the worthless Johnny's manhood. And she is every inch the actress again as she turns it on soft and beautifully feminine to trap the meek cashier. There is a dividing line between the two sides of character that few other actresses could walk as straightly as Miss Bennett does."

Next, Bennett was seen as a society reporter in a mildly entertaining comedy, *Colonel Effingham's Raid* (1946), followed by *The Macomber Affair* (1947), in which she was hailed for her portrayal of a selfish, deceitful wife. After playing a seductive wife in *The Woman on the Beach* (1947), she was hailed in *Time* magazine as "one of Hollywood's most efficient players of loose women." She portrayed yet another femme fatale in *Secret Beyond the Door* (1948), the second and final feature produced by Diana Productions, which fizzled out due to artistic differences between Walter Wanger and Fritz Lang.

On July 4, 1948, Bennett gave birth to her fourth daughter, Shelley Wanger, and soon after was seen in her third film noir, 1948's *The Scar* (also known as *Hollow Triumph*). Paul Henreid, who also produced, starred in this ironic tale as Johnny Muller, a con artist and ex-convict who rounds up the members of his old gang for the heist of a gambling hall owned by racketeer Rocky Stansyck (Tom Henry). An unexpected glitch causes the scheme to fail and only Johnny and his friend Marcy (Herbert Rudley) escape alive. Hiding from Stansyck, Johnny discovers that he is a dead ringer for an area psychiatrist, Dr. Victor Bartok, the only difference being a deep scar on the doctor's cheek. After learning that Marcy has been murdered by Stansyck, Johnny hatches a plan to assume the doctor's identity, beginning by romancing the doctor's secretary, Evelyn (Bennett), a world-weary beauty with a tough-as-nails exterior. Despite her hard-nosed demeanor, however, Evelyn falls for Johnny and is devastated when he abruptly ends their brief relationship.

Unbeknownst to Evelyn, Johnny has been painstakingly studying Dr. Bartok's characteristics. To make the deception complete, he shoots a photograph of the doctor and, using a scalpel, makes an incision on his cheek to copy Bartok's. But Johnny is unaware that the negative was unintentionally reversed during printing, and after murdering the doctor and preparing to dump his body, he discovers that he has scarred the wrong cheek. Still, no one notices the discrepancy, and Johnny smoothly takes over the life of Dr. Bartok. He even manages to fool his own brother Fred, who is searching for Johnny to inform him that Stansyck has been jailed and is no longer a threat. Ultimately, Evelyn discovers Johnny's deception and, bitter and disillusioned, prepares to sail to Hawaii. Johnny realizes his love for his one-time girl and makes plans to join her, but as he rushes to the ship, he is waylaid by two men demanding $90,000 in gambling debts that had been accrued by Dr. Bartok. Johnny tries unsuccessfully to explain his real identity, even pointing out the dissimilarity of the scar, but he is shot and killed by the men and dies on the dock, unnoticed by the passing travelers.

Although *The Scar* received mixed reviews, with *Cue* panning its "bad dialogue, awkward dramatic clichés and poor direction," Bennett's performance as the cynical but soft-hearted Evelyn was noted by a number of critics, including Thomas Pryor of the *New York Times*, who thanked her for "helping out in the clinches." Her appearance in this mildly successful thriller was followed by a starring role in her final film noir, *The Reckless Moment* (1949).

This film's opening shots show a pleasant seaside community where well-to-do housewife Lucia Harper (Bennett) lives with her husband, two children and father-in-law. Lucia's serene lifestyle is shattered, however, when she unsuccessfully attempts to circumvent the relationship between her rebellious 17-year-old daughter Bea (Geraldine Brooks) and the unprincipled Ted Darby (Shepperd Strudwick). When Darby accidentally falls to his death after an argument with Bea, Lucia discovers the body and dumps it in the sea to protect her daughter. But revealing love letters penned by Bea are unearthed by a local hood, Nagle (Roy Roberts), and his partner, Martin Donnelly (James Mason), who use the correspondence to extort money from Lucia. Before long, Donnelly finds himself romantically drawn to Lucia and withdraws his blackmailing threat, but the ruthless Nagle insists on following through with the original plan. Finding Nagle at Lucia's house, Donnelly kills him but is involved in an auto accident while fleeing with Nagle's body. Lucia later learns that Donnelly nobly confessed to Darby's murder before succumbing to his injuries.

In recent years, this Walter Wanger–produced film has developed a cult following, and Bennett in particular has been lauded for her portrait of the middle-class matron who breaks the law to protect her family. But at the time of its release, *The Reckless Moment* was not well-received by critics, and its moderate success at the box office was only the beginning of Walter Wanger's troubles. The producer had previously gone into debt in order to finance *Joan of Arc* (1948), an epic flop starring Ingrid Bergman. After this failure, Wanger found it difficult to secure financial backing for his film ventures and, for a time, he moved his family to Rome in an unsuccessful attempt to coax Greta Garbo into making a screen comeback.

In contrast to her husband's woes, Bennett's professional career reached new heights when, graduating from the sultry femme fatale to the sensitive and understanding mother, she starred opposite Spencer Tracy in *Father of the Bride* (1950), a poignant and entertaining comedy. The following year, she reprised her role in the film's sequel, *Father's Little Dividend*, the tenth highest-grossing film of 1951. Also that year, Bennett made her first television appearance, warbling a duet with actor Pat O'Brien on NBC's *Show of Shows;* appeared with her daughter, Melinda, in a stock production of *Susan and God* in Westport, Connecticut; and starred opposite Paul Douglas in a rather dull comedy, *The Guy Who Came Back* (1951).

But at this point, Bennett's personal life abruptly intruded on her professional career, and she would not appear on screen for another three years. With her husband close to involuntary bankruptcy, Bennett's agent and friend Jennings Lang had proposed several money-making ventures, including a possible television series to be produced in Manhattan. Wanger objected, however, considering it to be "a challenge to his position as head of the household," Bennett recalled. Wanger told his wife on several occasions that he would kill Lang if Bennett continued to see him, and in December 1951, he nearly made good on his threat when he shot Lang in the groin. A short time later, Wanger turned himself into police, announcing, "I've just shot the son of a bitch who tried to break up my home." Lang, who made a speedy recovery after emergency surgery, publicly forgave his attacker several days later, but Wanger was charged with assault with a deadly weapon and was sentenced to four months in jail.

Because of the incident, Bennett became a pariah in the Hollywood community and, after a film career that had lasted nearly a quarter of a century, she was unable to find screen work. "It was a slight scandal — today it would have been nothing. In fact, if it happened today, I would be in great demand!" Bennett said several years later. But at the time, she stated, she was "a professional outcast. Everybody sort of thought I was taboo." Instead, she returned to the stage, starring in the national tour of *Bell, Book and Candle* from April 1952 to March 1953. When Wanger was released from jail, he and Bennett resumed living together, but "from then on, our lives were separate," Bennett said. "We preserved the amenities only for the sake of the girls." The couple would stay married until 1965, when Bennett obtained a Mexican divorce.

Bennett's first screen appearance after the shooting incident was in 1954, in the poorly received *Highway Dragnet*, a low-budget picture that *Variety* panned as being "strung on a plot that will not bear close inspection." Still struggling to secure film roles, Bennett starred later that year in *The Man Who Came to Dinner* on CBS's *The Best of Broadway* series. In 1955, however, Bennett's screen career got back on track when she appeared with Humphrey Bogart in *We're No Angels*. "Bogie, who also lived on the same street that I did, insisted that I be in *We're No Angels* or he wouldn't do it," Bennett later said. "That is a good friend."

The following year, Bennett starred in *Navy Wife* (1956) produced by Wanger for Allied Artists, but after appearing with Fred MacMurray and Barbara Stanwyck in *There's Always Tomorrow* (1956), she would again be absent from the big screen, this time for a four-year stretch. In September 1956, Bennett began an 11-month tour in *Janus*, selecting as her costar veteran actor Donald Cook, with whom she had appeared in 1932's *The Trial of Vivienne Ware*. When the tour of *Janus* ended in March 1957, Bennett moved to New

York and over the next two years, she costarred with Cook in a six-week television series, *Too Young to Go Steady*, and two plays, *The Pleasure of His Company* and *Love Me Little*, for which she was commended in the *New York Morning Telegraph* as "deliciously right for the role of the mother." Bennett would later call her friendship with Donald Cook "one of the most important relationships in my life." During this time, Bennett returned to feature films with a small role in *Desire in the Dust* (1960), described in *Variety* as an "essentially pointless tale of greed and lust in the backwaters of the present-day South."

But Bennett experienced a setback in her personal life in 1961, when Donald Cook was suddenly stricken with a fatal heart attack. Befriended by John Emery, an associate of Cook's, Bennett accepted his offer to appear in *The Reluctant Debutante* in Chicago, but two years later, while starring in *Never Too Late* in London, Bennett learned that Emery was dying of cancer. "I accepted no offer of work in order to go about the privileged duties of meeting his daily needs," Bennett said.

After guesting in a variety of television productions, including *Playhouse 90* and *Junior Miss*, Bennett took on a permanent role in 1966 on *Dark Shadows*, a Gothic soap opera for ABC-TV. She was initially scheduled to appear on only a few shows each week, but the program quickly gained widespread popularity, and Bennett's role as Elizabeth Stoddard Collins, matriarch of the Collins clan, was expanded to five shows per week. "I had no idea *Dark Shadows* was going to be such a big success," Bennett said years later. "I still get letters from fans who say they're running it in certain places throughout the country, and write to me that they rush home to watch *Dark Shadows*." The series would last for five years, and in 1970 Bennett reprised her role in a feature film, *House of Dark Shadows*. In the next decade, Bennett published her autobiography, *The Bennett Playbill*, which was cowritten with Lois Kibbee and included a chronology of her family since the 1880s. She also busied herself on a variety of stage, screen and television projects, including *Gidget Gets Married* for ABC-TV and *Butterflies Are Free* at the Pheasant Run Playhouse in Chicago.

On Valentine's Day, February 14, 1978, Bennett was married again, this time to newspaper publisher David Wilde, whom she had first met more than a decade earlier. For the 68-year-old actress, the fourth time was obviously the charm, as her husband recalled in 1996: "We met with instantaneous rapport — lucky me! [She] epitomized for me all the things worthwhile in human relationships. Securely enclosed beneath the epitome of her physical beauty was the most gracious, gentle lady of taste, tolerance, understanding and love. I have been among the luckiest of humans to have been able to share so many enviable years at her side."

Although Bennett never formally retired from performing, her final feature film role was in an Italian production, *Suspiria*, in 1977, and she accepted fewer roles after moving with her husband to Scarsdale, New York. In what would be her last appearance, she was featured in a 1986 television documentary about her *Father of the Bride* costar, Spencer Tracy. Then, on December 7, 1990, just days after she received a Photoplay Lifetime Achievement Award, Bennett suffered a heart failure at her home. According to her husband, Bennett succumbed "in the midst of dinner when her head fell forward on her chest and she was gone. Shocking as it was to be a survivor, I can only say that we can only wish to 'cast off this mortal coil' with as much grace and finality as she did."

With nearly 80 feature films to her credit, as well as numerous stage and television roles, Joan Bennett was not only a star in every sense of the word, but also possessed true acting talent and was well-loved off screen as well. The strikingly attractive woman with the career that spanned nearly 70 years was perhaps best described by Martha Hyer, Bennett's costar in *Desire in the Dust*, who called her "a lovely lady possessed of dignity, charm and humor. She was warm and friendly ... but had just the right amount of reserve and mystery that a star should have."

Film Noir Filmography

THE WOMAN IN THE WINDOW   *Director:* Fritz Lang. *Producer:* Nunnally Johnson. Released by RKO, January 1945. *Running time:* 99 minutes. *Cast:* Edward G. Robinson, Joan Bennett, Raymond Massey, Edmond Breon, Dan Duryea, Thomas E. Jackson. *Awards:* Academy Award nomination for Best Score: Hugo Friedhofer, Arthur Lange.

SCARLET STREET   *Director and producer:* Fritz Lang. Released by Universal, December 1945. *Running time:* 102 minutes. *Cast:* Edward G. Robinson, Joan Bennett, Dan Duryea, Jess Barker, Margaret Lindsay, Rosalind Ivan.

THE SCAR (ORIGINAL RELEASE TITLE: *HOLLOW TRIUMPH*)   *Director:* Steve Sekely. *Producer:* Paul Henreid. Released by Eagle-Lion, October 1948. *Running time:* 82 minutes. *Cast:* Paul Henreid, Joan Bennett, Eduard Franz, Leslie Brooks, John Qualen, Mabel Paige.

THE RECKLESS MOMENT   *Director:* Max Ophuls. *Producer:* Walter Wanger. Released by Columbia, December 1949. *Running time:* 81 minutes. *Cast:* James Mason, Joan Bennett, Geraldine Brooks, Henry O'Neill, Shepperd Strudwick, David Bair, Roy Roberts.

References

Baker, Rob. "Tonight in Manhattan." *New York Daily News*, December 17, 1980.
Bennett, Joan and Lois Kibbee. *The Bennett Playbill*. New York: Holt, Rinehart and Winston, 1970.
Bowers, Ronald. "Joan Bennett." *Films in Review*, June–July 1977.
Briggs, Colin. "Remembering." *Hollywood: Then and Now*, June 1991.
"Calling on Joan Bennett: As Movie Star, Mother, and Wife of Producer, Her Day Is Busy." *Life*, September 9, 1940.
Efron, Edith. "No Tears for Miss Bennett." *TV Guide*, August 26, 1967.

Flint, Peter. "Joan Bennett Dies at 80." *New York Times*, December 9, 1990.

"A 40s Fling: Myrna, Claudette, and Joan." *Life*, June 16, 1972.

Gallagher, John A. "Joan Bennett: Looking Back at a Career That Has Spanned Over Fifty Years." *American Classic Screen*, November–December 1983.

"Glamorous Grandmothers." *Coronet*, February 1951.

Hall, Gladys. "Her Home Life." *Motion Picture*, December 1934.

_____. "Her 10 Commandments for a Mother." *Movie Classic*, January 1937.

Hayes, Barbara. "Hedy Lamarr vs. Joan Bennett." *Photoplay*, November 1939.

"Joan Bennett Ends Marriage of 25 Years." *New York Daily Mirror*, September 22, 1965.

"Joan Bennett Here." *New York Evening Journal*, October 15, 1935.

"Life Goes Calling on Joan Bennett." *Life*, September 9, 1940.

Meyer, Jim. "TV, Films Keep Joan Busy." *The Miami Herald*, June 28, 1970.

Parsons, Harriet. "Her Own Worst Enemy." *Silver Screen*, May 1931.

"Pin-Up of the Past." *Films and Filming*, July 1972.

"Stage, Film Actress Dies." *Newsday*, December 9, 1990.

Wilson, Earl. "Don't Kid the Public." *Silver Screen*, August 1941.

_____. "Experiences She'd Love to Relive." *Silver Screen*, December 1939.

_____. "She Has Everything." *Silver Screen*, February 1936.

Ann Blyth

A petite brunette with soulful blue eyes and a wide, genuine smile, Ann Blyth enjoyed a performing career that spanned more than a half century, but she vanished from the silver screen in the late 1950s, concentrating instead on what she called her "role as a woman in my community and in my home." Still, Blyth distinguished herself as both a talented actress and singer, and showcased her abilities not only in movies, but in radio, television and on stage. During the height of her fame, Blyth held her own opposite such stars as Joan Crawford, Mickey Rooney, Claudette Colbert and William Powell, and while most of her 33 films are now all but forgotten, she delivered a classic "bad girl" performance in one of her two films noirs, *Mildred Pierce* (1945).

Ann Marie Blyth was born in Mt. Kisco, New York, on August 18, 1928. Her Ireland-born parents, Harry and Nan Lynch Blyth, separated when the actress was still a baby, and a short time later, she moved with her mother and older sister Dorothy to a fourth-floor walk-up apartment in New York City. With her mother forced to find work to support her young family, Blyth would later recall that her childhood was "rather meager. The fact that my father left my mother with two daughters to raise is, of course, something many families and children have to face," Blyth said. "My mother faced it, as indeed anyone who knew her and loved her felt she would. And she always saw to it that my sister and I had enough to eat, and clean, pretty clothes on our backs — but I know that wasn't easy for her."

From an early age, Blyth expressed an interest in performing. She made her first appearance when she was only five years old, singing and reciting on New York radio station WJZ. In the years that followed, Blyth honed her talents through study at Manhattan's Professional Children's School as well as private acting and singing lessons. Unlike her peers, Blyth spent little time playing with baby dolls or skipping rope; instead, as the owner of a neighborhood restaurant recalled in a 1957 *Photoplay* article, Blyth's energies were more likely to be focused on arriving on time to her next appearance: "Sometimes she'd want to be out playing with the other kids, but there'd be a radio performance to give, or singing and dancing lessons to go to.... Spaghetti became a strategic necessity. A plate of her favorite dish somehow helped to ease the disappointments." But Blyth's endless hours of coaching paid off— between 1937 and 1940, she joined New York's Children's Opera Company, sang three seasons with the San Carlos Opera Company, and became a seasoned radio performer with appearances on such programs as *The Sunday Show*, *Our Barn Children's Show* and Jean Hersholt's *Dr. Christian* series.

Blyth's introduction to the "big time" came when she was only 13 years old. While the attractive youngster was eating lunch at the Professional Children's School, she was spotted by Broadway director Herman Shumlin and renowned playwright Lillian Hellman. "I saw these two people looking across the room," Blyth recalled. "The [school] principal's secretary came over and said, 'Miss Hellman and Mr. Shumlin would like to speak with you.' And that was the beginning of it. I read for the part, waited to hear the response, then read for them again." Blyth was eventually cast as Paul Lukas' daughter in Hellman's Pulitzer Prize–winning play *Watch on the Rhine*, appearing in the hit production for more than two years, first on Broadway, then on a cross-country tour. "It meant so much for so many reasons," Blyth recalled of her professional stage debut. "It meant that for the first time in years, my mother wouldn't have to work so hard."

Fortune smiled on Blyth again while she was touring with *Watch on the Rhine*. During a run of the play at Los Angeles' Biltmore Theatre, her performance was admired by director Henry Koster, then with Universal Studios, who offered her a screen test. A short time later, she signed a seven-year contract with Universal, and in 1944 made her movie debut in a teenage musical, *Chip Off the Old Block*, starring Donald O'Connor. Playing a talented member of a show business family, Blyth displayed her lilting soprano voice in two numbers, making a favorable impression on critics and audiences alike.

Later that year, Blyth appeared in three more musicals for Universal, but none was as well-received as her first. *The Merry Monahans* (1944) offered a warmed-over retread of the backstage tribulations of a vaudeville family, *Babes on Swing Street* (1944) suffered from a plodding script about a group of youngsters who put on a show to raise school funds, and *Bowery to Broadway* (1944), despite a massive cast that included Jack Oakie, Susanna Foster, and Frank McHugh, did only passable business at the box office. But Blyth continued to be singled out by critics for her melodic voice and pleasing appearance, and would later fondly recall these initial movie roles: "The kinds of films I found myself in were very good learning experiences," she said. "And there's such an innocence and joyfulness about them. They weren't the greatest movies, but the joy expressed is delightful."

By now, movie magazines of the day began featuring Blyth in a variety of articles, including one which predicted that she was "well on her way to stardom," and noted that "wherever she goes, young men from 19 to 90 pause as if struck by moonlight and stand gaping in her wake." But it wasn't until her next movie, Warner Bros.' *Mildred Pierce* (1945), that Blyth would be catapulted to fame. In this picture, her first film noir, Blyth had the plum role of the title character's eldest daughter, described by one critic as "about as spoiled a brat as ever tongued caviar from a silver spoon."

This riveting film tells the story of the title character (Joan Crawford), a housewife who is forced to support her two daughters when she is deserted by her husband Bert (Bruce Bennett). Faced with a mound of unpaid bills, Mildred gets a job as a waitress. Her spoiled eldest daughter Veda (Blyth) is horrified to discover the source of Mildred's income, and Mildred puts into effect her plan to open a restaurant. Later, when her younger daughter dies of pneumonia, Mildred is even more driven to provide the best for Veda, and she expands her business to a successful chain of five restaurants. While

Ann Blyth

building her business empire, Mildred becomes romantically involved with an impoverished playboy, Monte Beragon (Zachary Scott), but she later ends the relationship when Monte becomes a financial drain.

Meanwhile, Veda, in her ongoing pursuit of wealth, secretly marries a rich lad (John Compton), then divorces him, demanding $10,000 for the child she says she is carrying. But Mildred is appalled to learn that Veda lied about her condition. In the film's most riveting scene, Veda maliciously explains her rationale: "You'll never be anything but a common frump whose father lived over a grocery store and whose mother took in washing. With this money, I can get away from every rotten, stinking thing that makes me think of this place or you!" Mildred orders Veda out of the house, but after several months, determined to lure her daughter back home, Mildred proposes marriage to Monte, giving him a third of her business in exchange for setting up house in his mansion. Veda returns, tearfully promising to change her selfish ways, but Mildred is horrified when she later finds Monte and Veda locked in a passionate embrace. After fleeing the house, Mildred hears gun shots and discovers that Veda has murdered her lover, who had told her "he didn't want me around anymore. He told me to get out." Mildred plans to report the crime to police, but is yet again conflicted by her devotion to Veda, and takes the blame for the crime. Following a night-long investigation, however, the police learn that it was Veda who fired the fatal shots. At the film's end, Veda is led off by detectives ("Don't worry about me, Mother," she says stonily. "I'll get by"), and Mildred is reunited with her first husband, Bert.

Blyth was almost unanimously hailed for her portrayal of Veda, with the reviewer for *New Movies* stating that she "interprets the role of the nasty daughter with a brattishness that would get up anyone's dander." The *Hollywood Review* critic proclaimed, "This Blyth child is exquisite in her understanding of one of the most difficult roles ever written. Only the undeniable genius that has made Joan Crawford the great popular star she long since became enables her to keep Ann Blyth from running off with the film." Blyth would later recall the role as one of her favorites, saying that it was "wonderfully written, and I really hadn't been given the opportunity to play that kind of part before. For me, Veda was the quintessential bad person. She was truly evil.... It was a great part to play. I'm delighted to be remembered for it. More and more, in fact, with each passing year. People will come up to me and say, 'I hated you.' But I take that as a compliment."

For her efforts, Blyth received an Academy Award nomination for Best Supporting Actress, making her, at age 17, the youngest actress up to that time to be so honored. Although it was predicted that Blyth would win, the statue went instead to Anne Revere for her touching performance in *National Velvet*. Years later, the veteran character actress would amusingly recall that she herself was surprised to have won: "Little Ann Blyth was the favorite for her performance in Warners' *Mildred Pierce*," Revere said. "My winning was such an upset, some of the papers the next day were still dazed and wrote things like: 'Anne Revere, who played the troublesome teenager in *Mildred Pierce*, won the Best Supporting Actress Academy Award last night.'"

After Blyth's success in *Mildred Pierce*, Warner Bros. borrowed her for a second feature, *Danger Signal* (1945), with Zachary Scott and Faye Emerson. But disaster struck shortly after filming began when Blyth, vacationing at Lake Arrowhead, was thrown from a toboggan sled and broke her back. (She was replaced in the film by Mona Freeman.) Blyth's prognosis following her accident was grim, and doctors suspected that she might never walk again. But after spending seven months in bed, and another seven in a steel brace, she staged a complete recovery. During her recuperation, however, Blyth suffered another blow when her mother died of cancer at the age of 50. Then only 18, Blyth moved in with relatives in the San Fernando Valley, and would later state: "My mother died too young, but I was lucky to have an aunt and uncle who cared and took over. Bless them."

After recovering from her injury, Blyth was cast in her first starring role in Universal's *Swell Guy* (1947). Playing opposite Sonny Tufts, Blyth was hailed for her "highly effective performance" as a rich small-town girl who is compromised by a former war hero. She was also praised for her small role in her second film noir, *Brute Force* (1947), in which she played the sensitive wheelchair-bound girlfriend of a convicted criminal. Of her "good girl" role, the actress's first in three years, Blyth said, "It feels grand, even smug, to be respectable again."

This film primarily takes place in a men's prison and focuses on a group of cellmates, including Joe (Burt Lancaster), Soldier (Howard Duff) and Tom (Whit Bissell). The prisoners are constantly tormented and dehumanized by a cruel guard, Capt. Munsey (Hume Cronyn), and find solace only in gazing at the picture of a pin-up girl in their cell, which reminds them of the women they left behind. In brief flashbacks, the film shows that Tom, a quiet, reflective chap, was imprisoned because he embezzled funds to buy a fur coat for his unhappy wife Cora (Ella Raines). Like Tom, Soldier's crime, too, was related to a woman — his wife, Gina (Yvonne DeCarlo), who, after murdering a military policeman during the war, allows her husband to take the blame. As for Joe, the pin-up photo reminds him of his girlfriend Ruth (Blyth), a sweet, sensitive lass who is confined to a wheelchair because of an undisclosed illness.

Joe's desire to return to Ruth prompts him to organize a prison break, but the sadistic Munsey discovers the plan. In the film's violent climax, Munsey, along with each of the men involved in the attempted escape, is killed. The picture ends with the prison's sympathetic doctor (Art Smith) bleakly telling an inmate: "Nobody escapes. Nobody ever really escapes."

Brute Force was hailed by most reviewers, including Lloyd L. Sloan of the *Citizen News* who wrote, "Everyone who comes before the cameras deserves to be lauded," and *Newsweek* magazine, which termed the film "a forceful, even sadistic melodrama with moments of terrifying action and a climax that will raise the hackles on your neck." After this box office success, Blyth's string of hits continued with a loan-out to MGM for *Killer McCoy* (1947), a boxing melodrama starring Mickey Rooney. She then returned to Universal for *A Woman's Vengeance* (1948), turning in a polished performance as the wife of a man accused of murder, followed by a starring role in *Another Part of the Forest* (1948), which was hailed in *Variety* as "one of the best [performances] she has ever turned in." Blyth would later count this film among her favorites, offering high praise to costars Edmond O'Brien, Dan Duryea and Fredric March. "Wonderful experience!" Blyth said in a 1994 interview in *Scarlet Street* magazine. "If you can't learn from being with people like that, then I don't think it possible to learn anything."

Next Blyth starred opposite William Powell in *Mr. Peabody and the Mermaid* (1948), a fairly amusing comedy in which she plays a mermaid caught by a staid Bostonian. Of this fishy role, Blyth would later recall that it was "physically exhausting, but great fun. And I learned how to swim with that tail. Just keeping warm and having to just stay put, as it were, all day long was the hardest part. But it was one of the more pleasurable films because it was a lovely fantasy." The following year, the actress was kept busy with roles in four features, but each was rather forgettable and failed to adequately showcase her talents. In one of the films, *Once More, My Darling* (1949) with Robert Montgomery, Blyth's performance was panned by the *New York Herald Tribune* reviewer, who stated that her role "requires a solemn, furious enthusiasm delivered in a steady stream of breathless dialogue, and there are mighty few actresses who could prevent this type of thing from becoming irritating. Certainly Miss Blyth is not one of them." The actress fared little better in Paramount's *Top o' the Morning* (1949), a corny comedy starring Bing Crosby and Barry Fitzgerald, or *Free for All* (1949) with Robert Cummings. In the latter film, Blyth was singled out for criticism by one reviewer who said she "looks startled and wide-eyed, which she mistakenly thinks is the only way to play comedy."

Blyth rebounded, somewhat, in RKO's *Our Very Own* (1950), a sentimental soaper costarring Farley Granger, in which the actress portrayed an adopted girl in search of her natural mother. Her high point of the year, however, came during the 1950 Academy Award ceremonies, when Blyth wore a revealing, flaming red dress and sang "My Foolish Heart," a contender for Best Song. Her acclaimed rendition failed to alter her "good girl" screen image, as she'd hoped, but it did result in her winning the role of the title character's wife in MGM's *The Great Caruso* (1951). In this box-office smash starring Mario Lanza, Blyth more than held her own, and one of her two songs in the film, "The Loveliest Night of the Year," became a popular hit nationwide.

For the rest of 1951, Blyth's busiest year since arriving in Hollywood, the actress appeared in four more features, including *Katie Did It*, a mildly entertaining comedy with Mark Stevens, *I'll Never Forget You*, a romantic fantasy starring Tyrone Power, and Universal's *Thunder on the Hill*, which starred Blyth as a wrongly convicted murderess who is defended by a nun (Claudette Colbert). The following year, Blyth appeared in three films of varying quality: *Sally and Saint Anne* (1952), a family oriented comedy about an Irish family's battle to save their home, *One Minute to Zero* (1952), a cliché-ridden Korean war drama, and *The World in His Arms* (1952), an exhilarating actioner featuring Blyth as a Russian countess fleeing from a loveless marriage. After this well-received film, Blyth's contract with Universal expired and she signed with MGM, which promptly starred her with Stewart Granger and Robert Taylor in the box-office hit *All the Brothers Were Valiant* (1953). Blyth would later favorably recall her experience on the film, stating: "Who wouldn't be happy with those two good-looking men around you? It was just lovely. They were both so sure of who they were, there was never an issue of one fighting for more attention than the other. The feeling on the set was just terrific."

Blyth's first film under her new MGM contract would be her sole picture of 1953 — she had more pressing matters to occupy her time. On June 27, 1953, she married an obstetrician, Dr. James McNulty, in a lavish ceremony that included a special benediction from Pope Pius XII, featured more than 600 invited guests, and boasted such celebrated bridesmaids as Elizabeth Taylor, Joan Leslie and Jane Withers. The couple had been introduced three years earlier by McNulty's brother, singer-comedian Dennis Day, and although Blyth admitted that her "heart didn't turn over at first sight of him," she added that it "was probably because I didn't dare let it. I just remember Jim's kind eyes and I was so glad when he called five days later." The couple would go on to have five children (Timothy, Maureen, Kathleen, Terence and Eileen), eight grandchildren (as of 1996), and enjoy one of Hollywood's longest and most successful marriages.

Returning to the screen in 1954, Blyth was not as fortunate in her film appearances as she was in her personal life. Although the actress was applauded for her performance in the big-budget *Rose Marie*, the film suffered in comparison to the popular 1936 Jeanette MacDonald–Nelson Eddy version, and her next film, *The Student Prince* (1954), was nearly shelved when its star, Mario Lanza, dropped out of the production. A suit was filed by MGM against the temperamental singer, but by the time their differences were resolved, Lanza had grown too overweight to play the lead. Lanza was replaced by Edmund Purdom, who lip-synched the words to Lanza's previously recorded songs. While Blyth was again favorably received, the film was a disappointment. Blyth would later say that if Lanza had played his role as originally planned, "things would have been quite different. So much had been written about his problems with the studio that I think everyone was waiting to pounce on the movie."

In the next two years, Blyth would make only three films, *The King's Thief* (1955), a modestly successful costumer in which she was re-teamed with Edmund Purdom; *Kismet* (1955), a lavish, big-budget musical that suffered from Vincente Minnelli's uncharacteristically lackluster direction; and *Slander* (1956), a mildly diverting melodrama about a victim of scandal magazine blackmail. After Blyth's performance in the latter film, the now-declining MGM canceled her exclusive contract at her request, and although the actress agreed to do some films for the studio at a later date, she never did.

Instead, as Blyth's film career spiraled toward its end, she next starred in Paramount's *The Buster Keaton Story* (1957). In this poorly made biopic, Donald O'Connor was inappropriately cast in the title role, and Blyth provided only lackluster support as the comedian's long-suffering wife. Despite passable direction by Sidney Sheldon, and acrobatic gags that were staged by Keaton himself, the film was a box office disaster. But with only one more picture left on her cinematic resumé, Blyth went out with a bang, landing the title role in Warner Bros.' popular feature *The Helen Morgan Story* (1957), costarring Paul Newman.

When the casting calls were announced for the film, Blyth was thought by many to be too "nice" to portray the real-life 1920s torch singer who was nearly destroyed by alcoholism and personal tragedies. A Warner Bros. official reportedly said of Blyth, "This kid can't even smoke — much less act drunk! She's about as sexy as a cream cheese and jelly sandwich." And a well-known critic of the day scoffed: "Little Miss Sweetness and Light as Helen Morgan? Don't make me laugh. Keep her in the featherweight comedies and musicals — that's where she belongs!" Blyth was ultimately chosen for the part over 40 other actresses, but despite her pleasing soprano voice and her extensive singing experience in previous movies, Warner Bros. chose to use singer Gogi Grant to sing the vocals in the film. Blyth later said that she "wasn't hurt by the decision because I felt that dramatically the movie was strong. The music was certainly a major part of the story, but not the entire story. I was disappointed but not heartbroken."

Blyth received mixed reviews for her performance, and was unfavorably compared with actress Polly Bergen, who played Morgan in a *Playhouse 90* television drama that was released shortly before the feature film. Typical of Blyth's reviews was the appraisal from the *New York Post* critic, who stated: "Ann Blyth makes a good pretense of putting forth the songs. Her emotional acting gamut is a narrow one, turning simply from large, rolling, glistening tears, or a set gloomy expression, to the dazzling smile that has long been her trademark. If she doesn't quite convince you she's Helen Morgan, at least she manages to become sufficiently awry-eyed to turn aside suspicions that she might still be Ann Blyth." Such criticisms notwithstanding, *The Helen Morgan Story* has gained acclaim in the years since its release, and remains one of Blyth's most memorable films.

After *The Helen Morgan Story*, at the relatively youthful age of 29, Blyth retired from films, later stating: "The parts just weren't there, and the ones that were weren't very interesting. Making movies was and is wonderful, but if the right parts don't come along, then you do other things." And Blyth did exactly that. Having made her television debut in 1954, playing the Elizabeth Taylor role in *A Place in the Sun*, Blyth went on to make numerous television appearances, including the small screen adaptation of *The Citadel*, and guest spots on such programs as *Wagon Train, The Bell Telephone Hour, The Perry*

Como Show, Quincy and *Switch.* She also acquired a new generation of fans during the 1970s when she appeared in a long-running series of television commercials as the spokesperson for Hostess Cupcakes. "Many people remember me for that," Blyth said in a 1995 interview. "I think to be remembered for something you've done is very comforting."

In addition to Blyth's television work, she returned to her stage roots in the 1960s, and has since performed in numerous musicals throughout the country, including *Show Boat, Carnival, The King and I, South Pacific* and *Kiss Me, Kate.* "Most actors who have done theater dearly love getting back to it," Blyth has said. "Once you start, that's it. Nobody's going to say, 'Cut, let's try it again.' You must continue, but that's part of the excitement. I love it a lot."

In recent years, Blyth has been seen in coast-to-coast "In Person" appearances, and in a musical tour with Bill Hayes, best known for his long-running role in television's *Days of Our Lives.* According to the still-strikingly attractive actress, she has no plans to retire from performing: "Life is so rich," she said. "There's so much to see and do. Life is an ongoing process." And although her big-screen career lasted just 13 years, Blyth still harbors pleasant memories of her days as a Hollywood star: "I had all the opportunities anyone could possibly ask for. I have only a deep love and respect for my profession and for all the joy it has brought me. I consider my husband, my children, my religion, my home, work when I want it, satisfaction enough to be truly fulfilled."

Film Noir Filmography

BRUTE FORCE *Director:* Jules Dassin. *Producer:* Mark Hellinger. Released by Universal-International, June 1947. *Running time:* 95 minutes. *Cast:* Burt Lancaster, Hume Cronyn, Charles Bickford, Ann Blyth, Ella Raines, Anita Colby, Sam Levene, Howard Duff, Art Smith, Roman Bohnen, John Hoyt, Richard Gaines, Frank Puglia, Jeff Corey, Whit Bissell.

MILDRED PIERCE *Director:* Michael Curtiz. *Producer:* Jerry Wald. Released by Warner Bros., September 1945. *Running time:* 113 minutes. *Cast:* Joan Crawford, Jack Carson, Zachary Scott, Eve Arden, Ann Blyth, Bruce Bennett, George Tobias, Lee Patrick, Moroni Olsen. *Awards:* Academy Award for Best Actress: Joan Crawford. Academy Award nominations for Best Picture, Best Supporting Actress (Eve Arden), Best Supporting Actress (Ann Blyth), Best Screenplay (Ranald MacDougall), Best Cinematography (Ernest Haller).

References

Arnold, Maxine. "Angel Face." *Photoplay*, April 1951.
_____. "Her Guardian Angel Kissed Her." *Photoplay*, January 1956.
Blyth, Ann. "Having Fun with Bing and Barry." *Silver Screen*, March 1949.
"Blyth Spirit." *American Magazine*, September 1949.

Corwin, Jane. "She Keeps Hollywood Guessing." *Photoplay*, September 1952.

Ghulam, Lance Erickson. "Ann Blyth: Ann of a Thousand Smiles." *Classic Images*, February 1995.

Harris, Eleanor. "Cake, Ice Cream, and Fame." *Motion Picture*, June 1944.

Hawn, Jack. "A Blyth Spirit from an Earlier Era." *Los Angeles Times*, February 28, 1985.

Lewis, James. "You Don't Know Ann Blyth." *Photoplay*, December 1957.

Lilley, Jessie. "I Remember Mama: Ann Blyth on the Making of *Mildred Pierce.*" *Scarlet Street*, Spring 1994.

Linet, Beverly. "To Love and to Cherish." *Photoplay*, September 1953.

Mulvey, Kay. "Her Valentine's Day Party." *Photoplay*, February 1949.

"New Star Is Born." *Musician*, April 1944.

"Should Teenagers Marry?" *Photoplay*, December 1946.

Slate, Libby. "Playing Their Songs." *The Los Angeles Times*, October 14, 1994.

Waterbury, Ruth. "Ann Blyth's Wonderful Love Story." *Photoplay*, April 1953.

_____. "Blyth Spirit." *Photoplay*, February 1973.

_____. "The Family Ann Married." *Photoplay*, November 1953.

Wilding, Stephen. "Ann Blyth: The Beautiful Survivor — Still a Blyth Spirit." *Hollywood Studio Magazine*, June-July 1985.

Peggie Castle

Peggie Castle was a tall, blonde stunner who began her career with promise, but wound up as a Hollywood tragedy, dying alone at age 45, all but forgotten by the public. Outspoken and ambitious, the actress found a measure of fame in both films and television, but her successes were overshadowed by an often joyless personal life, including reportedly unhappy relationships with her father and her only child, three failed marriages, and the deaths of her mother and her fourth husband within weeks of each other. In front of the camera, however, the actress exhibited a versatility that allowed her to play a wide range of characters, and she made a notable contribution in her three film noir features: *I, the Jury* (1953), *99 River Street* (1953) and *The Long Wait* (1954).

Once described as a "dulcet-voiced doll," the green-eyed actress was born Peggie Thomas Blair in Appalachia, Virginia, on December 22, 1927, the only child of Doyle and Elizabeth Blair. Because of Doyle's job as an industrial efficiency expert for a large corporation, the family traveled frequently and Peggie spent her formative years attending more than 20 schools in cities throughout the country. (The actress would later attribute these frequent moves to her father's competence in his position, saying, "The harder an efficiency expert works, the sooner he's out of a job.") Struck at an early age by a desire to act, Peggie began her dramatic training at age eight while attending a private school in Pittsburgh, where she made her performing debut in a play at the Pittsburgh Playhouse. Several years later, when Peggie was 14, her family settled for a time in Los Angeles, and while a student at Hollywood High School, Peggie falsified her age and earned extra money by being a photographer's model and working as an usher during evenings at the Hollywood Bowl.

After graduating from high school, Peggie enrolled at Mills College in Oakland and studied drama under Madaleine Milhaud, formerly of the Comédie Français in Paris. While at Mills, Peggie took time out from her studies to marry the first of her four husbands, Los Angeles businessman Revis Call, on August 19, 1945. During her second year at Mills, Peggie won the highest scholastic award bestowed by the school, but at the year's end, she quit in favor of a $375 a week job on a radio soap opera, *Today's Children*. Later, Peggie appeared on several pioneer programs on the new medium of television, including *Fireside Theatre, Saturday Night Revue, Screen Director's Playhouse* and *Today's Children*. She also made her unauspicious film debut in a bit part in Columbia's *When a Girl's Beautiful* (1947), billed as Peggie Call.

While managing to obtain steady work, Peggie had yet to achieve her goal of becoming a film actress, but at age 22, her big break was just ahead. Stories differ, however, as to how this opportunity came about. One version has film director Elliott Nugent spotting Peggie on a television show and giving her a bit part in his upcoming film *Mr. Belvedere Goes to College* (1949), while another states that she was discovered and offered a screen test after an appearance on *Lux Radio Theater*. But the actress's official studio biography, which offers a far more interesting account, claims that Peggie was eating a shrimp salad at the Farmer's Market in Los Angeles when a talent scout spotted her and arranged for her to be tested for the *Belvedere* feature. Regardless of the circumstances, Peggie's association with this Clifton Webb comedy would offer a needed boost to her fledgling career. While filming her scene with Webb, the actor reportedly became irritated with Peggie and spoke sharply to her. In an unscripted response, Peggie snapped back and the result was so amusing that it remained in the picture. When the film was released, Peggie's brief appearance attracted the attention of agent Charles Feldman, who took her to Universal Studios. "If I hadn't had a temper, I might not have come to Mr. Feldman's attention at all," she later said. Before long, Peggie signed a contract with the studio and changed her screen name from Call to Castle.

Interestingly, in 1949 Universal introduced the "cheesecake" clause in its contracts, which called for "any feminine star who has special physical charm to display this asset" through the first five years of her contract, both on screen and in publicity stills. According to a spokesman for the studio, "Many young actresses begin screen careers by displaying figures and later refuse to permit this type of exploitation, which seems unfair to their public and to themselves." The first actress to sign with Universal under this new edict was Peggie Castle.

In her first film for her new home studio, Castle was given a small role as a waitress in *Woman in Hiding* (1949), a suspenseful thriller with Ida Lupino and her future husband, Howard Duff. She next appeared briefly as a store operator in *I Was a Shoplifter* (1950), which featured Mona Freeman as a socialite who is caught stealing from a department store, followed by bit parts in *Buccaneer's Girl* (1950), a clichéd pirate romp starring Yvonne DeCarlo, and *Air Cadet* (1951), a Gail Russell starrer notable primarily for its flying sequences. Finally, on loan-out to RKO, Castle was cast in her first important role, playing the rebellious daughter of Bette Davis in *Payment on Demand* (1951). But Castle's performance in this top-notch drama failed to make much of an impact at her home studio, and back at Universal she finished out the year with a pair of forgettable features, *The Golden Horde* (1951), an historical action picture, and *The Prince Who Was a Thief* (1951), an Arabian Nights-type adventure starring Tony Curtis and Piper Laurie.

While Castle was compiling screen credits, she was also busy behind the scenes. She divorced Revis Call in 1950 and the following year, on New Year's Day 1951, she married Universal publicist Robert H. Rains. Castle claimed to have fallen in love with Rains "at first sight," upon seeing him on her initial day at Universal, but the marriage would not last, and after separating on their third anniversary, the couple would divorce in April 1954. In her tearful court testimony, Castle claimed that her husband degraded her talent, saying that her method of emoting "went out with Mary Pickford" and that she "should have taken up typing" instead. Castle also testified that Rains treated her parents as "intruders" when they visited the couple, and that he had once threatened legal action to keep them away.

In 1952, Castle's contract with Universal expired and her option was not renewed. Instead, she turned to freelancing, publicly citing the disadvantages of being a studio contractee. "I used to watch wonderful parts go to outsiders while a lot of us gathered dust," she told columnist Howard McClay. "It seems odd that so many of the studios keep their young talent in the deep freeze instead of turning them loose early. And it isn't a matter of being 'ready' for a part either. I've seen some of my contemporaries being handed roles way above their heads after being bypassed for stuff they could really handle. I wish I could figure it out." On her own, she won her first lead role in Monogram's *Wagons West* (1952), a mediocre horse opera about a wagon train headed for California, followed by two Columbia features, *Invasion U.S.A.* (1952), a crude but provocative picture about an atomic attack on America, and *Harem Girl* (1952), a weak comedy which cast Castle as a princess menaced by an evil sheik.

After playing the second female lead in an above-average Western, *Son of Belle Starr* (1953), Castle won her best role to date in her first film noir, *I, the Jury* (1953). Shot in 3-D but released flat, *I, the Jury* was the first of several film appearances of Mickey Spillane's popular private detective, Mike Hammer. In this first screen incarnation, however, the character was played by the rather ineffectual Biff Elliot. Elliot soon faded into obscurity, despite Castle's effusive description of him as a "cross between Marlon Brando and the late John Garfield."

This fast-moving film begins with the murder of Jack Williams, an insurance investigator, by an unknown assailant. Mike Hammer, a close friend of the victim, sets out immediately to solve the case, focusing on a list of guests who attended a party given by Williams on the night he was killed. Among those questioned by Hammer are George Kalecki (Alan Reed), a fight promoter who dabbles in art collecting; Myrna (Frances Osborne), a former drug addict who was Williams' fiancée; Hal Kines (Robert Cunningham), an art student who lives with Kalecki; sex-starved identical twin sisters Esther and Mary Bellamy (Dran and Tani Seitz); and Charlotte Manning (Castle), a stunning psychiatrist with whom Hammer soon falls in love.

Working in tandem with Police Captain Pat Chambers (Preston Foster), Hammer discovers that the intricately intertwined lives of the party guests are more than what they seem: Kalecki is a racketeer and jewel smuggler, aided in his criminal exploits by Kines, who is having an affair with Mary Bellamy and is also being treated by Dr. Manning. As Hammer delves further into the case, a number of the principal players wind up dead, including Kalecki, Kines, Myrna and Bobo (Elisha Cook, Jr.), a seemingly dim-witted vagrant who was actually one of Kalecki's henchmen. The mysterious case is solved when

Peggie Castle

Hammer learns that his friend was murdered by Charlotte Manning, who had been a participant in Kalecki and Hines' jewel smuggling operation. When confronted by Hammer, Charlotte initially denies her guilt, then tries a different tack, seductively disrobing as she tells him: "My mistake was falling in love with you. Listen to me—you told me you loved me, Mike, you said that yourself. There's so much we could do together. The two of us. The world, Mike — it could be ours." Embracing Hammer, Charlotte reaches for a gun hidden in a potted plant, but Hammer shoots her. Before she dies, the stunned Charlotte asks him, "How could you?" Hammer coolly replies: "It was easy."

For her portrayal of what Mickey Spillane described as "the type of doll who can take off her gloves and make it look like a strip tease," Castle was dismissed by Howard Thompson in the *New York Times* but won high praise in *Variety*, whose critic wrote, "Peggie Castle, a psychiatrist, is the chief sex lure and heavy of the piece, being excellent on both counts." Finally, six years after Castle's screen debut, it seemed that the Hollywood community was beginning to take notice. "You seldom become famous playing good girls," she told a reporter. "I appeared in 20 pictures, mostly as a wide-eyed ingenue, and nobody ever heard of me. Then I did *I, the Jury*. It wasn't exactly the greatest picture ever made. But now people know who I am." With Castle's star seemingly on the rise, it was announced in August 1953 that she had been signed by United Artists to star in *Kiss Me Deadly* (1955), another film based on Mickey Spillane's Mike Hammer. But the film was later made without Castle, who was seen instead as a saloon singer in an Allied Artists Western, *Cow Country* (1953). This tedious, talky oater was a box-office flop, but the actress fared better with a small but meaty role in her next film, *99 River Street* (1953), the second of her three films noirs.

99 River Street stars John Payne as Ernie Driscoll, a frustrated taxi driver whose promising prize fighting career had ended abruptly following a severe eye injury. Ernie's misery is heightened by the constant needling from his shrewish wife Pauline (Castle), who works in a flower shop to make ends meet: "I would have been a star if I hadn't married you," Pauline says in one scene. Later, when Ernie notices her new watch, she nastily retorts, "Rhinestones wrapped around a ten-dollar movement — they might be real if I hadn't married a pug." Unbeknownst to the hapless Ernie, Pauline intends to run away to Paris with her lover, Victor Rawlins (Brad Dexter), a small-time hood who is financing their journey with funds he plans to collect by fencing a stolen cache of jewels.

When Victor and Pauline attempt to sell the stolen jewels, the fence, Christopher (Jay Adler), strenuously objects to Pauline's involvement in the crime and refuses to turn over the agreed-upon amount. Victor decides to rid himself of Pauline and after strangling her, dumps her body in the back of Ernie's cab. (Ironically, Pauline had earlier complained to her husband, "Has it ever occurred to you that when I ride in a cab I would rather it be in the back seat?") When Ernie discovers his wife's lifeless body, he sets out to find the killer, aided by an actress friend, Linda James (Evelyn Keyes). Meanwhile, Victor forces Christopher to fork over $50,000 for the stolen jewels, then heads for a Jersey City bar, located at 99 River Street, where he plans to obtain a false passport and board a freighter bound for France. Christopher and two of his henchmen follow Victor, intent on murder, and they, along with Ernie and Linda, find him at the bar. Ernie is wounded during a shootout, but he manages to subdue Victor until police arrive.

After being commended in the *New York Times* for her "juicy" performance in this top-notch thriller, Castle was seen in a series of dreary films for United Artists, starting with *The Yellow Tomahawk* (1954), a run-of-the-mill Western that was heavy on action but weak on everything else. Next she starred in a stale expedition story, *The White Orchid* (1954), portraying a photographer who treks through the Mexican jungles in search of a lost civilization, followed by two more Westerns, *Overland Pacific* (1954), a formulaic Indians-versus-railroad men tale, and *Jesse James' Women* (1954), a poorly made production featuring Castle as one of the many dames in a small Mississippi town who is romanced by the title character. By far the best of Castle's United Artists features was *The Long Wait* (1954), her final film noir.

Based on a Mickey Spillane novel, this picture stars Anthony Quinn as Johnny McBride, who loses his memory after an automobile accident and returns to his hometown in search of his past life. Once there, Johnny finds himself arrested for the murder of the city's district attorney. Although he is later released because his burnt fingers prevent the use of fingerprints as evidence, Johnny is determined to find the real killer. Johnny's first order of business is to locate his former girlfriend, Vera West, but because she has undergone plastic surgery, he is stymied in his efforts. Among the women Johnny approaches are Venus (Castle), a dress shop owner; Wendy (Mary Ellen Kay), a gambling house waitress; Carol (Shawn Smith), the secretary of local mob boss Servo (Gene Evans); and Troy (Dolores Donlon), Servo's mistress.

As Johnny continues his search for Vera, he becomes certain that Servo is responsible for the district attorney's murder, but as he gets closer to solving the mystery, he is abducted by Servo's men. After being savagely beaten and bound by the mob boss' henchmen, Johnny learns that Venus has been kidnapped as well, and discovers that Servo suspects that she is Vera. As Servo prepares to murder the couple, Venus manages to retrieve a gun from Johnny, kill Servo and free Johnny. Later, Johnny learns that his former employer, Mr. Gardiner (Charles Coburn), was the financier behind Servo's criminal operation and was responsible for the district attorney's murder. After turning Gardiner over to police, Johnny also learns the real identity of Vera — she was the gambling house waitress, Wendy.

Although *The Long Wait* only did moderate business at the box office, Castle's performance was noted by Howard Thompson of the *New York Times*, who singled her out among the film's principal female leads: "Peggie Castle, Mary Ellen Kay, Shawn Smith and Dolores Donlon comprise the luscious, undulating quartet and, in case anybody cares, we'll take Miss Castle."

By now, Castle's personal life once again overshadowed her career when, shortly after her divorce from Robert Rains in 1954, she married husband number three, director-producer William McGarry. Castle and McGarry would go on to have a daughter, Erin, but this union, too, would ultimately end in divorce and, reportedly, Castle would later become estranged from her only child. Meanwhile, on screen, Castle was still working steadily; according to a Warner Bros. studio biography, the actress claimed that she enjoyed acting because "it keeps her busy and constantly affords her the opportunity of meeting new people." (The actress would later state, with a touch of cynicism, that she became an actress because "I enjoy the paychecks.") These paychecks continued to roll in with her seven films during the next two years, including *Tall Man Riding* (1955), a talky Western starring Randolph Scott and Dorothy Malone; *Target Zero* (1955), a Korean war drama featuring Castle as the love interest of Richard Conte; *Quincannon, Frontier Scout* (1956), a United Artists Western which miscast crooner Tony Martin in the role of a rough-and-ready frontiersman; and *Two-Gun Lady* (1956), in which the actress delivered an effective performance as a gun-toting woman who hunts down the three men who murdered her parents (interestingly, the killers were played by the film's executive producer, associate producer and writer).

Between 1957 and 1959, Castle traveled with her husband throughout the British Isles, taking time out to appear on location in England for Warner's *The Counterfeit Plan* (1957), an uninteresting picture featuring Castle as the daughter of a reformed forger, and in Italy for her last screen appearance, MGM's *The Seven Hills of Rome* (1958), in which the actress played an American heiress who is pursued to Rome by Mario Lanza. During this period, Castle was also top-billed in what must have been her worst screen effort, the prophetically titled *Beginning of the End* (1957). Produced and directed by Bert I. Gordon (who went on to make such howlers as *The Amazing Colossal Man*, *Empire of the Ants* and *Food of the Gods*), *Beginning of the End* was a ludicrous film in which radioactive material produces a crop of gigantic grasshoppers that attack Chicago, destroy the city's downtown area and are climactically lured to a drowning death in the waters of Lake Michigan.

In the late 1950s, Castle turned to the medium of television, of which, ironically, she had spoken disparagingly several years earlier. "I hate television," she told a reporter in 1954. "I don't like to watch it and I don't like to act in it. They make those half-hour films so quickly, you can't possibly do a good acting job. And they pay you shoebuttons." But with no film offers coming her way, Castle gladly accepted guest spots in a number of programs, including *Conflict, Cheyenne* and *77 Sunset Strip*. In 1959 she won the continuing role of Lily Merrill on the ABC-TV series, *The Lawman*. Playing the saucy proprietess of The Birdcage, a gambling house and saloon, Castle described her character as "a great woman. If you'll pardon the expression, a wonderful dame. She's all ruffles and spangles, humor and heart. The townspeople frown on her because of her occupation, but her moral behavior is above reproach."

After *The Lawman* was canceled in 1962, Castle seemed to vanish, resurfacing only occasionally in brief mentions in newspapers and magazines. During these lean years, she reportedly became increasingly dependent on alcohol, and by 1970 her 16-year union with William McGarry was over. A short time later, she married her fourth husband, businessman Arthur Morgenstern, but Castle's life was rapidly careening toward a destructive end. With her daughter living with relatives in Huntington Beach, California, and her physical condition deteriorating, Castle suffered a devastating blow in 1973 when both her mother and her husband died within weeks of each other. In a desperate attempt for help, Castle entered the Camarillo State Hospital, but it was too late. A few months after her release, on August 11, 1973, Castle was found dead by her third husband William McGarry, in a shabby apartment above Hollywood Boulevard. According to the Los Angeles coroner, the cause of death was cirrhosis of the liver and a heart condition. She was 45 years old.

With a descent to obscurity that was as rapid as her rise to fame, Peggie Castle had a life that reads like the script for a big-screen tear-jerker. After years of struggling in forgettable roles, Castle managed to gain a measure of fame and appeared to be well on her way to stardom, but her promise was never fulfilled. And off-screen, the actress fared little better, suffering through failed marriages, a reported estrangement from her only child and a drinking habit that would ultimately contribute to her death. Still, while the strikingly attractive actress was never considered a great talent, she demonstrated a natural acting style in such films as *Payment on Demand* and *I, the Jury*, and proved that she deserved more acclaim than she earned.

Film Noir Filmography

I, THE JURY   *Director:* Harry Essex. *Producer:* Victor Saville. Released by United Artists, August 1953. *Running time:* 88 minutes. *Cast:* Biff Elliott, Preston Foster, Peggie Castle, Margaret Sheridan, Alan Reed, Frances Osborne, Robert Cunningham, Elisha Cook, Jr., Paul Dubov, Mary Anderson, Tani Seitz, Dran Seitz.

99 RIVER STREET   *Director:* Phil Karlson. *Producer:* Edward Small. Released by United Artists, October 1953. *Running time:* 83 minutes. *Cast:* John Payne, Evelyn Keyes, Brad Dexter, Frank Faylen, Peggie Castle, Jay Adler, Jack Lambert.

THE LONG WAIT   *Director:* Victor Saville. *Producer:* Lesser Samuels. Released by United Artists, July 1954. *Running time:* 94 minutes. *Cast:* Anthony Quinn, Charles Coburn, Gene Evans, Peggie Castle, Mary Ellen Kay, Shawn Smith, Dolores Donlon.

References

"Actress Peggie Castle Dies." *Los Angeles Herald Examiner*, August 11, 1973.
"Actress Peggie Castle Found Dead at Home." *Los Angeles Herald Examiner*, August 12, 1973.

"Apple of the Marshal's Eye." *TV Guide*, June 4, 1960.

Biography of Peggie Castle. ABC Television Center, September 2, 1960.

Biography of Peggie Castle. Warner Bros. Studios, Burbank, California, circa 1959.

"Criticism of Her Show Wins Actress Divorce." *Los Angeles Examiner*, April 30, 1954.

Crivello, Kirk. "Peggie Castle." *Hollywood Studio Magazine*, December 1973.

King, Loretta. "A New Star Has Arisen, Blonde and Beautiful." *Sunday News*, August 9, 1953.

Lieber, Perry. Biography of Peggie Castle. RKO Studios, 1950.

Manners, Dorothy. "Temper Leads Peggie Castle Into First Movie Contract." *Los Angeles Examiner*, August 23, 1953.

McClay, Howard. "Peggie Castle." *Los Angeles Daily News*, January 11, 1953.

"Peggie Castle Dead; Film and TV Actress." *New York Times*, August 12, 1973.

"Peggie's 'Dead,' but Not Long!" *New York Sun*, June 9, 1954.

"Says Mate Made Her 'Miserable.'" *New York Daily News*, April 30, 1954.

Thomas, Bob. "Peggie Castle Enjoys Acting in Lanza Film." *New Haven Evening Register*, October 8, 1957.

Wilson, Earl. "Money's Not Everything, But ..." *New York Post*, August 9, 1953.

Jeanne Crain

Once described as "eager as a brand new day, confident like the morning sun, and naive yet knowing," Jeanne Crain exuded a wholesome warmth and girlish charm that struck a chord with audiences worldwide. Perhaps best known for her "girl next door" roles (she was labeled "Miss Homespun America" at one point in her career), Crain was the mother of seven children and one of the few Hollywood actresses who successfully combined a film career with an abundant family life. While she never achieved superstardom, the unaffected beauty with the engaging smile was a popular favorite in a number of hit films, including *State Fair* (1945) and *A Letter to Three Wives* (1949), and lent her considerable talents to three films noirs: *Leave Her to Heaven* (1945), *Vicki* (1953) and *The Tattered Dress* (1957).

Born on May 25, 1925, in Barstow, California, Jeanne Elizabeth Crain was the oldest of George and Loretta Carr Crain's two daughters. (Crain's sister Rita, born in 1927, would serve as Crain's stand-in during her films of the mid–1940s.) At one time an aspiring singer, George Crain was an educator who moved with his wife and infant daughter to Los Angeles in late 1925 in order to accept a position as head of the English and language department of Inglewood High School.

When Crain was three and a half years old, she almost died after contracting double pneumonia and emphysema, and after four months in the hospital, she emerged weighing a mere 28 pounds. During her recovery, her beloved Aunt Elizabeth taught her to read, a pastime that Crain would cherish throughout her life. Along with losing herself in tales of Tom Sawyer and other favorite fictional characters, Crain loved to draw and, in fact, planned to make it her vocation until she won the role of a disfigured Indian maiden in *Scarface*, an eighth grade play at St. Mary's Academy. "I was a quiet, introspective child," Crain later said. "I lived in my imagination and my dreams and my books. I came out of my shell in school plays when I could be somebody else but Jeanne Crain."

After St. Mary's, Crain attended Inglewood High School, and although she was shy and reserved, a high school friend recalled that she possessed "a kind of aura which was felt by everyone who met her. She decidedly wasn't the typical American high school girl. She was composed beyond her years. She had great composure, perfect manners, a soft, refined way of speaking. From the moment she entered Inglewood High School she was the talk of the campus."

During her sophomore year, Crain had her first brush with the motion picture industry during a class tour of RKO Studio. Famed "boy wonder" Orson Welles spotted Crain in the studio commissary and had his secretary arrange a screen test for the 15-year-old Crain for a leading role in his new film, *The Magnificent Ambersons* (1942). Welles would later decree that Crain "had something in person that didn't come through on the screen," and gave the part to Anne Baxter, but the experience served to heighten Crain's ambition for film stardom. Throughout her remaining high school years, the fresh-faced student appeared in numerous school plays and earned a variety of honors, including her election as Queen of the Gridiron, taking the dramatic title at the 1941 Interscholastic Shakespearean Contest held at Occidental College, being named "Miss Long Beach of 1941" and "Camera Girl of 1942" and finishing second runner-up in the "Miss America" competition. Her publicity from the beauty pageants led to several modeling jobs, and Crain appeared on the covers of *Coronet, Pic, Ladies' Home Journal* and *True Romance*.

Following her high school graduation, Crain enrolled at the University of California at Los Angeles to study drama and art. While there, she interviewed for a part in Max Reinhardt's stage production of *The Song of Bernadette* and was spotted by Reinhardt's wife, who gave her tickets to another play, *Two on an Island*. When Crain attended the performance, she caught the eye of no less than three talent scouts, including 20th Century–Fox's Ivan Kahn, who arranged for a screen test at the studio. This time, two years after her disappointing experience at RKO, Crain recalled: "I had more poise — and what really helped was that I had a great deal more determination." After the test, Crain was signed to a standard contract with Fox, earning $100 a week. At age 17, Crain was on her way to achieving her dreams of seeing herself on the silver screen.

For the first several months at Fox, Crain was kept idle — her most important assignment from the studio was to escort Monty Woolley to Grauman's (now Mann's) Chinese Theatre. (Photos from the event show Crain and another Fox contractee, Jo-Carrol Dennison, dutifully helping Woolley imprint his whiskers into wet cement.) Finally, five months after signing with the studio, Crain made her first appearance before the cameras in *The Gang's All Here* (1943), starring Alice Faye and Carmen Miranda. Although Crain's role was limited to a walk-on in a swimming pool sequence, her trim figure and striking countenance attracted the attention of Fox head Darryl Zanuck, who cast her in a featured role in *Home in Indiana* (1944). Playing a rough-and-tumble tomboy, Crain was praised by several critics, including Howard Barnes of the *New York Herald Tribune*, who found her "fine as a nice hoyden," and John T. McManus of *PM*, who said that Crain's "cosmeticless charm and naturalness promise a very pleasant screen visit."

Crain was next billed above the title in *In the Meantime, Darling* (1944), a modest programmer directed by Otto Preminger. This time, however, critics were not so kind — the reviewer for *Variety* called her performance "unconvincing," adding that the actress "needs plenty more training and work before she rates the stellar billing Twentieth has given her." But Crain was not put off by this criticism, and instead, worked even harder at her craft, earning the laudable title of "one-take Crain" for her ability to perform her scenes on the first run.

In her third picture of 1944, *Winged Victory*, Crain appeared as a soldier's wife, but her next feature, another World War II drama, was scrapped because the war was coming to an end. However, Crain's disappointment over the studio's decision was short-lived, as she was promptly cast in the color musical *State Fair* (1945), the film for which she is perhaps best known. With her tunes dubbed by singer Louanne Hogan, Crain played a perky young girl who falls in love while visiting the state fair with her parents, and was hailed in *Variety* as a "beaut for whom Technicolor is a smart foil." After the release of the film, which earned the studio more than $4 million, Crain was named a "Star of Tomorrow" by *Motion Picture Herald* and signed a new four-figure contract with Fox.

Off-screen, meanwhile, Crain became involved with Paul Brinkman, who had launched a brief film career as Paul Brook and was once billed as "a second Errol Flynn." After two small roles at RKO, Brinkman abandoned his film aspirations and later found success as head of a missile parts manufacturing company and a helicopter business. Crain spied the handsome Brinkman at a brunch party, and although they did not meet, the actress later admitted that she "knew at once he was the one." Following a two-year courtship, and over her mother's vehement objections, Crain and Brinkman eloped on December 31, 1945. Two years later, Crain gave birth to her first child, Paul Brinkman, Jr., and the couple would go on to have six more children, the last born on Crain's fortieth birthday, May 25, 1965.

After her success in *State Fair*, Crain appeared in her first entry in the realm of film noir, *Leave Her to Heaven* (1945), starring Gene Tierney and Cornel Wilde. In this rare Technicolor noir, Crain portrayed Ruth Berent, the adopted sister of Ellen (Tierney), whose striking beauty cannot mask her possessive nature and her insane jealousy of those she loves. After an impromptu marriage to writer Richard Harland (Wilde), Ellen is vexed by the presence of her husband's invalid brother, Danny, and in the film's most terrifying scene, allows the young boy to drown in the lake near her husband's country lodge. Later, after attempting to salvage her marriage by becoming pregnant, Ellen's jealousy extends to her unborn child, and she causes a miscarriage by throwing herself down a flight of stairs.

Meanwhile, Ellen becomes resentful of the growing friendship between Richard and her sister, and is enraged when Richard dedicates his latest book to "the gal with the hoe," his pet name for Ruth. But after accusing her sister of pursuing Richard, Ellen is confronted with the consequences of her possessive nature: "All my life I've tried to love you, done everything to please you," Ruth tells her. "All of us have—Mother, Father, and now Richard. And what have you done? With your love you wrecked Mother's life, you pressed Father to death, and you've made a shadow of Richard. I don't envy you—I'm sorry for you. You're the most pitiful creature I've ever known." When Ellen is forced to admit her guilt in the deaths of Richard's brother and their unborn child, Richard leaves her, only to return when Ellen ingests a lethal dose of poison. He soon discovers, however, that Ellen has reached from the grave to maintain her hold on him by cleverly making her suicide appear that she was murdered by Ruth. Although Ruth is later acquitted during a court trial, Richard is accused of being an accessory to his brother's death for failing to report Ellen's guilt in the crime, and is sentenced to two years in prison. After his release, he returns to Ruth, who has waited for him.

Although Crain's role in *Leave Her to Heaven* was less flashy than that of the film's star, Gene Tierney, critics were almost unanimous in their praise of the actress, with the reviewer for *Film Daily* saying that Crain "has never been shown to finer advantage." Perhaps the highest acclaim came in the *Citizen News*, whose reviewer wrote that Crain, "always stunning in Technicolor, is more than charming this time out; she makes of her first all-dramatic role a tremendous success."

Crain's first release of 1946 was a musical set in the 1870s, *Centennial Summer*, with her singing again dubbed by Louanne Hogan. The film, which was only moderately successful at the box office, was notable primarily as the last music score written by Jerome Kern, who died soon after completing it. She next starred in *Margie* (1946), a smash hit that *Life* magazine called "the first film that depended on [Crain's] performance for its success or failure. She is completely sweet and captivating." Like *State Fair*, this film grossed over $4 million, and Crain's volume of fan mail increased to 2,000 letters a week, coming in second only to Betty Grable.

In 1948, Crain starred in two features, *You Were Meant for Me*, a pleasant musical that included songs from the 1920s and 1930s, and *Apartment for Peggy*, starring William Holden. Originally titled *Apartment for Jenny* and *Apartment for Susie* before receiving its final designation, the popular comedy-drama focused on the post-war problems of a returning soldier and his young spouse. Departing from her previous quiet, low-key roles, Crain was excellent as the fast-talking, excitable wife, and was applauded by Bosley Crowther of the *New York Times* for her "vivid characterization."

In her three films of 1949, Crain showed audiences that she was capable of playing more mature, sophisticated characters. In the first of these, *A Letter to Three Wives*, Crain delivered what Alton Cook of the *New York World Telegram* called "the most credible performance of her brief but very crowded career." Next, Crain portrayed Lady Windemere in *The Fan*, based on a play by Oscar Wilde, followed by the role of a black nurse who passes for white in *Pinky*. In the latter film, her first major dramatic role, Crain received excellent notices, with the *New York Herald Tribune* review stating that she handled the part with "skill and persuasion" and Archer Winsten of the *New York Post* predicting that the role "should mean the beginning of a new career."

Although many Southern cities refused to book the film because of its theme of racial intolerance, *Pinky* was a hit with moviegoers and made Crain the top box office earner of 1949. The film also earned Crain her only Academy

Award nomination for Best Actress, but she later lost to Olivia de Havilland for *The Heiress*. In connection with the release of *Pinky*, Crain placed her hand and footprints in the forecourt of Grauman's Chinese Theatre in Hollywood, six years after she had assisted Monty Woolley in the ceremony.

On the heels of her success in *Pinky*, Crain signed a four-year contract with Fox, this one providing that she work 40 weeks a year. In her first film under her new contract, Crain returned to playing what she called "the typical Jeanne Crain part ... the kind I don't like to do," portraying the eldest of 12 children in the box-office smash *Cheaper by the Dozen* (1950), and in her next film, *I'll Get By* (1950), a musical starring June Haver and Gloria DeHaven, Crain was seen in a cameo role playing herself.

Because she was pregnant with her third child, Crain missed out on an opportunity to play the role of a lifetime, the title role in *All About Eve* (1950), which would earn a Best Actress Oscar nomination for Anne Baxter. Her condition would also cost Crain the lead role played by Susan Hayward in *I'd Climb the Highest Mountain* (1951). Instead, after the birth of her son Timothy, Crain starred in *Take Care of My Little Girl* (1951), an indictment of college sorority and fraternity life, for which she was commended for her "considerable expressiveness" by the *New York Times*' Bosley Crowther. She next starred opposite Cary Grant in *People Will Talk* (1951), but she received widely divergent notices for her role as a pregnant medical student who marries her professor. A review in the *New York Times* claimed that she displayed "both intelligence and charm" in the film, while the critic for *The New Yorker* found that although Crain "looks pretty and speaks her lines clearly ... her performance is not acting in the traditional sense of the word."

Despite the varied reception by both critics and audiences, Fox chief Darryl Zanuck recognized Crain's ability to portray more grown-up roles, and cast her next in *The Model and the Marriage Broker* (1951), directed by George Cukor. But after this film, Crain was assigned to yet another college student role in *Belles on Their Toes* (1952), the sequel to *Cheaper by the Dozen*. After appearing opposite Farley Granger in the "Gift of the Magi" segment of *O. Henry's Full House* (1952), Crain gave birth to her fourth child, daughter Jeannie, on March 5, 1952, and on the advice of her physician, passed up the starring role in *Something for the Birds* (1952) that would be played by Patricia Neal. Crain also missed out on coveted parts in *With a Song in My Heart* (1952) and *The Robe* (1953) when Fox executives cast Susan Hayward and Jean Simmons, respectively.

As a substitute for these plum roles, Crain was cast in her first Western, *City of Bad Men* (1953), but was termed "just a whisper too noble and pure" in the *New York Times*. Then, after a role in *Dangerous Crossing* (1953) as a wealthy woman being driven mad by unknown assailants, Crain starred in her second film noir, *Vicki* (1953).

A remake of the 1941 Betty Grable vehicle *I Wake Up Screaming*, this film begins with the murder of Vicki Lynn (Jean Peters), a model whose beautiful face is known nationwide. On learning of the crime, New York police detective Ed Cornell (Richard Boone) vehemently insists on heading up the case and he immediately focuses his investigation on Steve Christopher (Elliott Reid), a publicity man who had discovered Vicki working as a waitress and turned her into a star. Insisting that Steve is guilty, Cornell suggests that the publicity man was motivated by his anger when his ambitious protégée secretly negotiated a Hollywood movie deal and planned to leave town. Vicki's sister Jill (Crain), who is in love with Steve, suggests that the killer might be a man she'd seen frequently watching Vicki during her waitressing days, but when she recognizes Cornell as the mysterious peeper, the detective smoothly explains that the restaurant was part of his jurisdiction.

Police believe the case is solved when they begin a search for the missing switchboard operator of Vicki's apartment building, Harry Williams (Aaron Spelling, later the successful producer of such TV series as *Charlie's Angels, Dynasty* and *Melrose Place*). But Cornell later announces that Williams is innocent and continues his unrelenting surveillance of Steve. Overhearing Jill and Steve as they discuss a potentially incriminating note that Steve had sent to Vicki, Cornell handcuffs Steve and plans to beat him into confessing, but Jill knocks the detective unconscious and she and Steve escape. Managing to elude police, Steve begins his own investigation into the murder, which leads him back to Harry Williams. With Jill's help, Steve tricks the switchboard operator into revealing his guilt, and learns that although Williams had previously confessed to Cornell, the detective had told him to keep quiet about the murder. When Steve later goes to Cornell's apartment to confront his tormentor, he finds that the detective's home was a veritable shrine to Vicki, and that he had held Steve indirectly responsible for her death. "You're the one who took her away from me, not him," Cornell says. "I used to hang around that cafeteria at night, just to make sure she got home safe. We had a cup of coffee together. I started to hope we'd get to know each other better — I might even get up the courage to ask her to marry me some day. Why didn't you leave her alone?"

Vicki opened to only mediocre reviews, but Crain's performance was singled out by several critics, including Bosley Crowther of the *New York Times*, who said that the actress, along with costars Peters and Reid, "make the best of Harry Horner's brisk direction to make it look as though they're playing a tingling film. It might be indeed if the story were not so studiously contrived and far-fetched." After this film, Crain was slated to star in *Three Coins in the Fountain* (1954) with Dorothy McGuire and Maggie McNamara, but when her husband objected to required on-location shooting in Europe, the part was given to her *Vicki* costar Jean Peters instead. At this point in her career, when she was earning $5,000 a week, Crain decided to end her ten-year association with Fox, citing her frustration over the image that had been created for her.

"Fox was wonderful to me, but I wasn't happy for the last few years," Crain explained. "I wasn't permitted to go to other studios on loan-outs and other girls were signed for the roles I wanted at my own studio. I asked for singing and dancing roles, but the answer was always 'no.' Now, maybe I'll get my big chance."

As part of her campaign to secure mature, sexy parts, Crain dyed her hair red, notifying the press that she wasn't "the washed-face pigtail type people think I am." But her first film after leaving Fox, Warner Bros.' *Duel in the Jungle* (1954), was noted more for its on-set adversities than any sort of memorable role for Crain. (During filming, a fire in Kruger National Park threatened to destroy thousands of dollars worth of equipment, and a drowning accident later claimed the lives of several crew members.) Still striving to change her image, Crain then signed a five-year contract with Universal Pictures, starring as a morally loose ranch owner opposite Kirk Douglas in *Man Without a Star*. Back at Fox she appeared with Jane Russell in *Gentlemen Marry Brunettes* (1955), the sequel to the Marilyn Monroe starrer *Gentlemen Prefer Blondes* (1953). Although many found that Crain paled in comparison with Monroe's vivacious sexuality, William K. Zinsser of the *New York Herald Tribune* applauded her performance, writing that Crain "has been hiding her light under a pinafore far too long. She turns out to be a fine song and dance girl from head to toe." Crain's final release of the year was *The Second Greatest Sex*, a musical version of Aristophanes' *Lysistrata*, followed in 1956 by another Western, *The Fastest Gun Alive*, costarring Glenn Ford.

With Crain's on-screen career thriving, her life at home seemed to be equally successful. Throughout her marriage to Paul Brinkman, fan magazines delighted in covering the couple's fruitful relationship, publishing articles with such titles as "How to Keep Marriage Romantic" and "Three-Year Honeymoon." In these articles, the Crain-Brinkman union was described as "one of Hollywood's happiest, sweetest, and most romantic," and Crain was recognized as "living proof that today's modern woman can combine home and career successfully without neglecting either." But in spring 1956, it looked as if this thriving marriage had come to an end when *Confidential* magazine published a prominent spread claiming that Brinkman had been pursuing several women on the sly.

The scandalous allegations led to Crain's filing for divorce and accusing her husband not only of seeing other women, but also of physical abuse. Brinkman countered by claiming that Crain was having an affair with millionaire Homer Rhoades, who was quoted as saying that he was going to marry Crain. On August 6, 1956, Crain obtained an interlocutory divorce, but before the end of the year, the couple reconciled, and Crain informed reporters that the break-up was "the result of our first fight. Our religion is one of the main reasons our marriage survived it."

Back on screen following this close call in her marriage, Crain starred in her final film noir, *The Tattered Dress* (1957). Here, the actress portrayed Diane, the estranged wife of James Cordon Blane (Jeff Chandler), an unscrupulous criminal attorney who, by his own admission, specializes in serving as "the mouthpiece for racketeers, dope peddlers and panderers." In a highly publicized case, Blane is hired to defend Michael Reston (Philip Reed), a wealthy resort town resident who is accused of murdering the lover of his trampy wife (Elaine Stewart). The case results in an acquittal for the guilty man, primarily due to Blane's savage cross-examination of the town sheriff, Nick Hoak (Jack Carson). Seeking revenge on the high-powered attorney, Hoak frames Blane by making it appear that he won the case by bribing a juror, Carol Morrow (Gail Russell), who is Hoak's mistress. Diane rallies to her husband's side, and Blane defends himself in the case, ultimately winning an acquittal. As Blane and Diane triumphantly leave the courthouse, Hoak pulls a gun on the attorney, but instead, Hoak himself is shot and killed by his mistress.

Termed by the *New York Times* as a "workmanlike and sometimes absorbing melodrama," *The Tattered Dress* would mark the last film Crain would make for Universal, as the studio cancelled her contract when the birth of Crain's fifth child, Lisabette, prevented her from reporting for her next film. In response to this action, Crain sued Universal the following year for $30,288 in back pay. She next starred with Frank Sinatra in Parmount's *The Joker Is Wild* (1957), a biopic about comedian Joe E. Lewis. This compelling drama was a smash hit at the box office, but it would be Crain's last feature film for three years. During her absence from the screen, the actress turned to television, appearing as Daisy in *The Great Gatsby* (1958), a musical special, and *Meet Me in St. Louis* (1959). She returned to the big screen in the mediocre 1960 film *Guns of the Timberland* starring Alan Ladd and Frankie Avalon, and later told reporters, "No matter how long you're in this business, you can't take some time off without people thinking something has happened. If you allow your name to get out of circulation, it doesn't mean as much. It's a phenomenon."

At just 36 years old, Crain's big box office days were behind her. After giving birth in 1961 to her sixth child, Maria, she was scheduled to star with Victor Mature in *The Trojan War*, and in *Il Brigante* with Rosanno Brazzi, but both projects were cancelled. Instead, she made *Daggers of Blood* (1961), an Italian film that would not be released in the United States for another four years; *Twenty Plus Two* (1961), of which the critic for the *New York Herald Tribune* said Crain "plays an unpleasant minor part unpleasantly"; *Madison Avenue* (1962), an uninteresting cheapie starring Dana Andrews; and another Italian-made picture, *Nefertiti, Queen of the Nile* (1963), costarring Vincent Price.

During the filming of the Italian epics, Crain lived with an Italian family and became fluent in the native language. A short time later, she took another break from the screen, explaining, "I suddenly had the sensation of doing a tango on a treadmill, so I just danced off. I hadn't had time to evaluate

Jeanne Crain

myself as a person. Every actress should try it, now and then." As part of her "self-evaluation," Crain renewed her longtime love for art by taking art classes at UCLA and also studied at a private art school in Los Angeles. During the 1970s, she would utilize this training to exhibit her artwork at the Mascagni d'Italy gallery and the Westwood (California) Art Association, at which a number of her pictures were sold. Crain also busied herself with stage tours of *The Philadelphia Story* and *Claudia*, appeared in several television series, including *G.E. Theatre* and *U.S. Steel Hour*, and starred in a pilot for a new television program, *The Jeanne Crain Show*, in which she portrayed a former model with two children. Although Crain remarked that she "liked the idea and heard the sound of residuals," however, the pilot was not made into a series. On May 25, 1965, Crain gave birth to her seventh child, Christopher.

In her 1967 screen comeback, Crain appeared in another clunker, *Pontius Pilate*, and was criticized by one critic as portraying Pilate's wife "as if in a trance." Later that year, she appeared with Dana Andrews in the dreadful *Hot Rods to Hell*, which Crain herself panned by declaring, "Frankly, I wouldn't go see a film named *Hot Rods to Hell*." Over the next several years, Crain made only two more screen appearances: *Skyjacked* (1972), starring Charlton Heston, and her last feature film to date, *The Night God Screamed* (1974), a dreadful picture in which she portrayed a woman pursued by a hooded murderer after testifying against a group of bloodthirsty religious fanatics.

After this dismal end to her promising screen career, Crain focused her energies on raising her large family. In addition to her responsibilities as wife and mother, Crain also started a clothing line known as "Jeanne Crain of Hollywood" and kept busy indulging in such favorite pastimes as painting, sculpting, cooking and reading. In the mid–1970s, she also starred in *Janus* in Chicago, Illinois, and occasionally appeared in a variety of television commercials and game shows.

Although Crain has all but retired from her performing career, her contributions to such memorable features as *Leave Her to Heaven*, *Pinky* and *Letter to Three Wives* have afforded her a prominent position in the annals of Hollywood film. During a span of 31 years, she offered her talents to nearly 40 films but, ultimately, she found that her life behind the camera was more rewarding than her on-screen career: "You have to decide which is more important to you," she once said, "an armful of babies or a scrapbook full of screen credits."

Film Noir Filmography

LEAVE HER TO HEAVEN *Director:* John M. Stahl. *Producer:* William A. Bacher. Released by 20th Century–Fox, December 1945. *Running time:* 110 minutes. *Cast:* Gene Tierney, Cornel Wilde, Jeanne Crain, Vincent Price, Mary Phillips, Ray Collins.

VICKI *Director:* Harry Horner. *Producer:* Leonard Goldstein. Released by 20th Century–Fox, September 1953. *Running time:* 85 minutes. *Cast:* Jeanne Crain, Jean Peters, Elliott Reid, Richard Boone, Casey Adams, Alex D'Arcy, Carl Betz, Aaron Spelling.

THE TATTERED DRESS *Director:* Jack Arnold. *Producer:* Albert Zugsmith. Released by Universal-International, March 1957. *Running time:* 93 minutes. *Cast:* Jeff

Chandler, Jeanne Crain, Jack Carson, Gail Russell, Elaine Stewart, George Tobias, Edward Andrews, Philip Reed, Edward C. Platt.

References

Brinkman, Paul. "All the Things You Are." *Modern Screen*, June 1948.
_____. On a Pink Cloud With Jeanne Crain." *Photoplay*, May 1950.
_____. "This Is My Wife." *Photoplay*, February 1947.
Colby, Anita. "The Story of Jeanne Crain." *Photoplay*, December 1946.
Deere, Dorothy. "Scenic Wonder." *Photoplay*, February 1946.
Dudley, Fredda. "Seventh Heaven." *Photoplay*, December 1952.
Graham, Sheilah. "C for Circe." *Photoplay*, December 1944.
Hegedorn, Richard. "Jeanne Crain." *Films in Review*, May 1966.
Hopper, Hedda. "Make Way for Youth." *Modern Screen*, June 1949.
"Overnight Rise to Movie Stardom." *Life*, September 4, 1944.
Parsons, Louella. "Fair and Fancy Free." *Photoplay*, December 1945.
Maxwell, Elsa. "Smartest Girl in Town." *Photoplay*, October 1948.
McClelland, Doug. "Jeanne Crain." *Films in Review*, June 19, 1962.
_____. "Jeanne Crain." *Films in Review*, June-July 1969.
McManus, Margaret. "Jeanne Stays Young." *Newark Evening News*, April 1959.
Muir, Florabel. "First Born." *Modern Screen*, July 1947.
"Reconciliation in Hollywood." *New York Herald Tribune*, January 1956.
St. Johns, Elaine. "Dear Baby." *Photoplay*, October 1947.
_____. First Year." *Photoplay*, April 1947.
_____. "One Dream for Two." *Photoplay*, August 1946.
"Science Puts Oomph Into Jeanne Crain's Bubble Bath." *Life*, September 30, 1946.
Skolsky, Sidney. "Hollywood Is My Beat." *New York Post*, January 15, 1961.
_____. "Jeanne Crain, Our Cover Girl ... and Why." *Motion Picture*, April 1948.
"Story of Jeanne Crain." *Life*, October 17, 1949.
Waterbury, Ruth. "Our Baby, Paul Frederick Brinkman, Jr., Is Here." *Photoplay*, July 1947.
_____. "Runaway Bride." *Photoplay*, April-May 1946.
Wheeler, Lyle. "Plot for a Home." *Photoplay*, July 1951.

Joan Crawford

All too often, the mention of Joan Crawford's name evokes images of a monstrous, domineering woman who cruelly abused her children and ruled her home — and, often, her lovers — with an iron will that bordered on psychosis. These charges notwithstanding, Crawford was one of Hollywood's major talents and possessed a prodigious tenacity and drive that catapulted her to superstardom. Appearing in 80 films from the silent era through 1970, Crawford was the recipient of three Academy Award nominations, as well as the Oscar for Best Actress of 1945. The star of such memorable films as *Grand Hotel* (1932), *The Women* (1939) and *Humoresque* (1946), Crawford was also a highlight of four outstanding examples of film noir: *Mildred Pierce* (1945), *Possessed* (1947), *The Damned Don't Cry* (1950) and *Sudden Fear* (1952).

Joan Crawford was born Lucille Fay LeSueur in San Antonio, Texas. (Sources alternately report the year of her birth as 1904, 1906, and 1908, however, and the truth will probably never be known.) Shortly after her birth, her father, Thomas LeSueur, abandoned young Lucille, her older brother Hal and their mother Anna. Anna later married Henry Cassin, a vaudeville theater manager, and the family moved to Lawton, Oklahoma, where Cassin bought an opera house and operated an open-air theater. Lucille adopted the name of Billie Cassin and was introduced by her beloved stepfather to the exciting life of the theater, but her happy existence would not last long. Cassin was charged with gold embezzlement and, although he was acquitted, the family moved to Kansas City, Kansas, to escape the stigma of the allegation.

Shortly afterward, Cassin left his family and in 1915 Anna obtained a divorce. Anna and her two young children were forced to live in a cheap Kansas City motel, and Billie waited on tables in exchange for schooling at St. Agnes Convent. While there, she experienced what may have been lasting scars when she was looked down upon by her fellow classmates, who excluded her from their activities and even their conversations. Her high school years were not much better. Billie enrolled at the Rockingham Academy, where she continued to work for her lessons, but she suffered frequent abuse at the hands of the school's principal.

But Billie's never-say-die spirit carried her through these atrocities, and she emerged all the stronger. After completing her high school studies, Billie spent a short period of time at Stephens College in Columbia, Missouri, then briefly worked as a salesgirl in several department stores. Soon afterward, she determined to seek a dancing career and got a job in the chorus of the Katherine Emerine revue, resuming her given name of Lucille LeSueur. Although the show closed after two weeks, Lucille was undaunted, showing the first signs of the steely determination that would later become an integral part of the Joan Crawford persona.

In 1923, after winning an amateur dance contest, Lucille decided to try her luck in the big city and traveled to Chicago, where she got a job in a chorus at what she described as an "out of the way" café. A week later, she joined a revue in Oklahoma City, and later appeared at the Oriole Terrace in Detroit. Although she was not a great beauty, and was slightly overweight, Lucille exhibited a natural effervescence that drew attention to her. She soon was noticed by theatrical producer J. J. Shubert, who hired her for the chorus of his show *Innocent Eyes* in New York. This job would prove to be the break that the ambitious Lucille had waited for. Harry Rapf of MGM spotted her in the chorus and gave Lucille a screen test. She was offered a five-year contract starting at $75 a week, and on New Year's Day, 1925, Lucille boarded a train for Hollywood.

Once there, Lucille spent the bulk of her time posing for cheesecake publicity photos and taking lessons in elocution, dance, voice and acrobatics. Her first work before the camera was as a double for Norma Shearer in *Lady of the Night* (1925)—an ironic assignment in view of the animosity that would develop between the two stars in the years to come. Her screen debut was as a chorine in *Pretty Ladies* (1925) starring ZaSu Pitts, followed by a bit part in *The Only Thing* (1925) and a slightly larger role in *Old Clothes* (1925), a vehicle for child star Jackie Coogan. By the time the latter film was released, Lucille's name had been changed again, following a contest in *Movie Weekly* magazine that invited readers to select a new moniker for the promising new actress. She reported that she initially hated the name of Joan Crawford, complaining that it sounded too much like "crawfish," but that she later "came to love it." The new Joan Crawford caught the eye of a number of reviewers in *Old Clothes*, including columnist Louella Parsons, who wrote that the young actress was "very attractive and shows promise."

Acting on the advice of her friend, actor William Haines, Crawford began appearing at a number of Hollywood hot spots, including the Cocoanut Grove, the Montmartre and the Garden Court Hotel, often winning contests for her exuberant dancing style. Haines' advice appeared to result in a breakthrough in Crawford's budding career, as she was soon cast in *Sally, Irene, and Mary* (1925), with Constance Bennett and Sally O'Neil. Crawford was noted by critics for her "good" performance and "lovely" appearance, and the following year was named as one of the 13 Wampas Stars for 1926, a group of promising starlets that included Mary Astor, Fay Wray and Dolores Del Rio. Despite this honor, however, Crawford was assigned to a series of bland roles in more than a dozen films, including *The Boob* (1926), which was panned by critics as "a piece of junk," *Tramp, Tramp, Tramp* (1926), where she appeared as the girlfriend of comedian Harry Langdon, *The Unknown* (1927), starring Lon Chaney, whose dedication to acting gave Crawford "the desire to be a real actress," and two vehicles starring matinee idol John Gilbert, *Twelve Miles Out* (1927) and *Four Walls* (1928).

She continued to be noticed by critics for showing "a development far beyond her work," but it wasn't until her role as Dangerous Diana in *Our Dancing Daughters* (1928) that Crawford ascended to the stardom she would enjoy for the next four decades. The movie was a smash hit and critics commended Crawford for the best work of her young career, praising her good looks, charm and dancing talent. Writer F. Scott Fitzgerald proclaimed that Crawford was the "best example of the flapper, the girl you see at smart nightclubs, gowned to the apex of sophistication," and her newfound popularity was rewarded by MGM, who increased her salary to $500 a week and presented her with a new roadster. Years later, Crawford said that after the success of *Our Dancing Daughters*, "I was never again carefree. Before, I had been absolutely sure of myself in a brash and very young way. Now I began to study and observe myself. I was immersed with my own image on the screen ... but I did have sense enough to know I must work, and work hard. I kept setting the goal higher and higher."

But Crawford had been noticed by more than critics and fans — she had also caught the eye of Douglas Fairbanks, Jr., known as "the Crown Prince of Hollywood." She had first met the actor in 1927, when she attended the opening of his play *Young Woodley* (escorted by Paul Bern, who would later commit suicide shortly after his marriage to actress Jean Harlow). Touched by Fairbanks' "sensitive, tender performance," Crawford went backstage to offer her congratulations and, impressed by Crawford's sincerity, Fairbanks asked her for a date. The two soon became one of Hollywood's most famous couples, and although their romance was reportedly opposed by Fairbanks' father, famed swashbuckler Douglas, Sr., and his stepmother, "America's Sweetheart" Mary Pickford, the engagement of Crawford and Fairbanks was announced on October 8, 1928.

However, Crawford felt ill at ease in the world of Pickfair, the palatial home of Fairbanks, Sr., and Pickford. "I was doing fine until I hit Pickfair," she later recalled. "I was out to tear up the world in the fastest, brashest, quickest way possible. Then I saw myself through the Pickfair eyes and every last bit of my self-confidence dropped away from me. Immediately I set out to change myself in every way." Under the guidance of her fiancé, Crawford intently began the transformation from carefree flapper to cultured lady. A *Motion Picture* magazine article stated that Crawford "spoke in a low voice, the raucous laughter was gone, her wardrobe leaned towards softly clinging materials, white gloves and picture hats — outfits obviously planned and more suited to the grounds of Pickfair."

Capitalizing on the couple's fame, MGM starred them in *Our Modern Maidens* (1929), which one reviewer called "silly and juvenile, but the sort of silliness the fans gobble by the carload." In connection with the film's release, Crawford embedded her hand and footprints in the courtyard of Grauman's (now Mann's) Chinese Theater, becoming only the fifteenth star to do so, and joining such impressive company as Charlie Chaplin, Gloria Swanson and Norma Shearer. In June 1929, Crawford and Fairbanks were married, with Fairbanks, Sr., and his wife conspicuously absent.

Meanwhile, talkies had hit Hollywood and, though Crawford was horrified by the first sound of her voice coming from the screen ("That's a man!" she reportedly exclaimed), she successfully made the transition from silent films in *Untamed* (1929), the first of five movies she would make with Robert Montgomery. In 1930, Crawford starred in three films, *Montana Moon*, panned as an "interminable, amateurish" talking picture; *Our Blushing Brides*, her second pairing with Montgomery; and *Paid*, originally intended for Norma Shearer, who had to turn down the role because of her advancing pregnancy.

In 1931, three of her four films teamed her with Clark Gable: *Dance, Fools, Dance*, loosely based on the real-life murder of a Chicago newspaper reporter by organized crimelords; *Laughing Sinners*, for which Crawford was hailed as "seldom looking so radiantly alive and beautiful"; and *Possessed*, a well-mounted production that featured Crawford in the rags-to-riches role that would become so familiar throughout her career. Crawford and Gable proved to be a hit with audiences — and with each other. Although both stars were married (Gable to second wife Ria Langham), they began a steamy love affair that reportedly ended when MGM head Louis B. Mayer intervened. They remained close friends until Gable's death in 1960.

Although Crawford's affair with Gable surely contributed to the demise of her marriage, it is believed that the rift between the budding star and her husband began because of Crawford's mounting boredom with the ritual of visiting Pickfair on Sunday afternoons. Another factor was the increasing difference in the careers of the two stars; while Fairbanks asserted that "movies are not the end-all and be-all of life," Crawford was completely focused on becoming MGM's biggest and brightest star. And Crawford was earning $150,000 a year, with Fairbanks bringing home less than half that amount. Despite a second honeymoon to Europe, the marriage could not be salvaged, and the couple divorced in 1933. Soon afterward, Crawford told a reporter that she would "never marry again as long as I live."

Crawford's career continued to soar with her appearance as Flammchen in the star-studded *Grand Hotel* (1932), with a cast that included Greta Garbo, John and Lionel Barrymore and Wallace Beery. Crawford would later state that *Grand Hotel* was her "first big chance. They told me I wouldn't be able to hold my own with the big boys, against Garbo and the Barrymores. But I proved otherwise." Her next film, *Letty Lynton* (1932), successful in its own right, was also notable for its introduction of the "Crawford look," as designed by Gilbert Adrian, earning it the distinction, according to designer Edith Head, of being the single most important influence on fashion in film history. With *Rain*, her final film of 1932, however, Crawford took a career misstep. In playing the prostitute Sadie Thompson, Crawford was rejected by audiences and critics alike. One reviewer viciously slammed Crawford's performance, writing that she should "wait until she has grown up before attempting a serious role," and Abel Green of *Variety* claimed that the part of Sadie was "beyond her range." Later, Crawford herself would admit that she "did it badly."

In 1933, Crawford starred in *Today We Live* with the man who would become her second husband — Franchot Tone. The picture was a failure, but she rebounded with her next venture, *Dancing Lady* (1933), which re-teamed her with Clark Gable. She then starred again with Tone in *Sadie McKee* (1934), another rags-to-riches potboiler, followed by *Chained* (1934) and *Forsaking All Others* (1934) with Gable and *No More Ladies* (1935) with Robert Montgomery.

On October 11, 1935, Crawford and Tone were married in New Jersey. At the time, Crawford was earning $240,000, while Tone was paid only $1,000 a week. Initially, this disproportion was of no consequence to the newlyweds, but it later would become an issue in the marriage. Tone, an actor with stage origins, encouraged Crawford to break from her established roles of glamourous socialites or hard-working shopgirls, and Crawford agreed, taking on the role of an innkeeper's daughter in the costume drama *The Gorgeous Hussy* (1936). The film was a box office bomb, and critics rightly complained that Crawford's modern face and personality did not correspond with her century-old wardrobe. But Crawford's next film, *Love on the Run* (1936), reunited her with Clark Gable, and fans returned to the theaters in droves. Still, the actress seemed unable to string together a series of successes, and after her next two films, *The Last of Mrs. Cheyney* (1937) and *The Bride Wore Red* (1937), the National Theater Distributors of America voted her "box office poison" along with other stars including Katharine Hepburn, Marlene Dietrich and Mae West. Nevertheless, MGM showed their continuing faith in Crawford and she was given a new five-year contract, at $250,000 a year. Later that year, she starred with Margaret Sullavan and Melvyn Douglas in *The Shining Hour*. Critics praised Crawford's performance but, again, audiences were not impressed.

In 1939, Crawford's marriage to Tone ended; the actress would later attribute it to the disparity in the couple's career, as well as Tone's reported drinking and physical abuse. But Crawford used her career to recover from her personal troubles, starring in *The Women* (1939), a wickedly satirical comedy with an all-female cast. One of Crawford's costars was Norma Shearer, whom Crawford had bitterly viewed as her major rival throughout her years at Metro ("She was married to the boss," Crawford once said, referring to Shearer's husband, MGM executive Irving Thalberg, "and I was just an actress.... Big budget meant Norma, ex-shopgirl meant me"). The two stars clashed several times on the set of the film, and after the production was completed, they never spoke again.

Reviews hailed Crawford's portrayal of a scheming husband-stealer and *The Women* became one of MGM's top-grossing films of the year. Crawford followed this success with *Strange Cargo* (1940), her eighth and final film with Clark Gable, and *A Woman's Face* (1941), delivering what many consider to be her finest performance. However, she then appeared in a series of films that did little for her popularity, including *They All Kissed the Bride* (1942), as a shrewish career woman, *Reunion in France* (1942), playing a spoiled Parisian who discovers that her lover is consorting with the Nazis, and *Above Suspicion* (1943), a confusing spy yarn that would be Crawford's last MGM film for ten years. Of her departure from the studio, Crawford later said: "I left by the back gate. I loved MGM — it was home. But I longed for challenging parts and I wasn't getting them.... If you think I made poor films at MGM after *A Woman's Face*, you should have seen the ones I went on suspension *not* to make!"

In the midst of this decline in her career, Crawford's personal life was certainly not at a standstill. In 1939, she adopted the first of her four children — Christina. Christopher was adopted four years later and two younger sisters, Cathy and Cynthia, would be added to the family in 1947. And in 1942, she married her third husband, actor Phillip Terry, but the union lasted only three years. "I hadn't loved Phillip enough," Crawford later said. "I married because I was unutterably lonely. Don't ever marry because of loneliness."

In 1944, Crawford began work on the film that would lead to one of the most triumphant comebacks in Hollywood history — the film noir classic *Mildred Pierce* (1945). Crawford portrayed the title role, a housewife who is forced to work as a waitress to support her two daughters after being abandoned by her husband, Bert (Bruce Bennett). Mildred is obsessed with providing a luxurious lifestyle for her beautiful but spoiled eldest child, Veda (Ann Blyth), spending the family's meager funds on piano lessons and fancy dresses. When her younger daughter dies of pneumonia, Mildred becomes even more obsessed with providing only the best for Veda and opens a restaurant, which she turns into a fabulously successful chain.

While building her restaurant empire, Mildred falls for impoverished playboy Monte Beragon (Zachary Scott), but the relationship sours when Monte makes a habit of "borrowing" money and charging expensive clothing and jewelry to Mildred. Meanwhile, Veda, in her never-ending quest for more money, secretly marries and divorces a rich lad, Ted Forrester (John Compton), demanding $10,000 for the child she says she is carrying. Horrified to discover that Veda has lied about her condition, Mildred orders her out of the house, but later begs her to return. In order to entice her society-climbing daughter, Mildred returns to her old lover, Monte, and offers him a third of her business if he will marry her and set up house in his mansion. Monte, naturally, agrees, and Veda returns triumphantly, with hollow promises to change her ways. But before long, Mildred discovers that Monte has bankrupted her business, and later learns that he is having an affair with Veda. Confronting the couple at her beach house, Mildred draws a gun on Monte, only to drop it and flee. When Monte scoffs at Veda's ideas for marriage, calling her a "rotten little tramp," she shoots and kills him. Although Mildred tries to take the blame for the crime, Veda is ultimately arrested and Mildred is reunited with her first husband.

Critics were nearly unanimous in their effusive acclaim for Crawford. The reviewer for *Variety* stated that the role of Mildred Pierce "is one which is a constant temptation to melodrama and overplaying and the actress avoids both pitfalls in a smooth performance," and the critic for *Pacific Coast Musician* raved: "Miss Crawford does one of the most monumental portrayals of her career. She has departed from the glamour gal category and has turned into one of the finest actresses in films." Crawford was also commended by her costar, Ann Blyth, who called her "the kindest, most helpful human being I've ever worked with."

It was this movie that introduced Crawford to the term "film noir." "I was being interviewed by a critic of the cinema, which, as you might know, has nothing to do with the movies," she said years later. "He kept talking about this film noir style [in *Mildred Pierce*] and I didn't know what the hell he was talking about. When it came up again sometime later, I called [producer] Jerry Wald and said, 'Darling, what is this film noir they're all talking about?' He explained it to me, which made me appreciate the film even more."

Crawford followed this triumph with the well-received *Humoresque* (1946), starring John Garfield, and her second film noir, *Possessed* (1947), in another widely praised performance. The film opens with Crawford's character, Louise Howell Graham, wandering the streets in a stupor, in search of "David." She winds up at the psychopathic ward of a hospital where doctors give her medication that allows her to tell them the story of the events that led to her catatonic state. As a nurse caring for Pauline Graham (whose character is never seen), a mentally unstable invalid, Louise had harbored an obsessive love for engineer David Sutton (Van Heflin). "I want a monopoly on you, David," Louise tells him in one scene, "or whatever it is that people have when they don't want anyone else to have any of you." Feeling smothered by her affections, David abruptly ends their relationship, an action that triggers Louise's gradual descent into madness. Soon afterward, Pauline Graham commits suicide, having wrongly suspected Louise of having an affair with her husband Dean (Raymond Massey). Asked by Dean to stay on to care for his young son, Louise begins to imagine that she had helped Pauline drown herself. And though she later marries Dean, Louise continues to be consumed by her desire for David, who begins a love affair with Dean's daughter, Carol (Geraldine Brooks). Louise's psychosis further deepens when she hallucinates that she murders Carol, and she grows increasingly unable to distinguish fantasy from reality. When her attempts to destroy David's relationship with Carol fail, Louise confronts him, warning him matter-of-factly: "I explained to you how important it was for you not to leave me again." Finally, after David tells her that he and Carol are to be married, Louise draws a gun and mortally wounds him — the act that led to her complete breakdown.

Crawford offered a striking portrait of a woman consumed by madness, a performance that was undoubtedly aided by her daily visits to a mental hospital to observe patients subjected to straitjackets, shock treatment and truth serums. "Those days taught me compassion for people suffering from emotional and mental illnesses," Crawford stated. "Normally I'm a happy person. But after I finished making that film I was melancholy for two months. Although I was exhausted I knew I had done a good job — had met the challenge. That was important to me. Give me a challenge any time and I'll come out a better person for it. Meeting the challenge of *Possessed* made it my favorite film."

Crawford received her second Academy Award nomination for this role (losing to Loretta Young in *The Farmer's Daughter*) and critics raved about her performance. "Miss Crawford is generally excellent," said James Agee of *Time*, "performing with the passion and intelligence of an actress who is not content with just one Oscar," and Harrison Carroll of the *Herald Express* stated that Crawford was "all too convincing in the most taxing role of her career."

But the actress followed *Possessed* with a string of films that failed to continue the momentum that had built up since her triumphant comeback: *Daisy Kenyon* (1947), a glossy soap opera starring Dana Andrews and Henry Fonda and *Flamingo Road* (1949) with Zachary Scott. *The Damned Don't Cry* (1950) was also panned as "contrived" and "shabby," but it is a film noir entry that holds the viewer's interest until the final reel.

The first scene in the movie is vintage film noir: A car is seen driving through the desert at night. When it stops, two men emerge and toss a lifeless body down a sandy dune. The body, it is later discovered, is that of a notorious mobster. In the dead man's apartment, police find home movies featuring Lorna Hansen Forbes (Crawford), a Texas oil heiress, and a nationwide manhunt for the missing "darling of café society" is launched. A flashback reveals that the wealthy socialite is actually Ethel Whitehead, a small-town housewife who had left her factory worker husband after their son was struck and killed by an automobile. Moving to the big city, Ethel gets a job modeling for a wholesaler and makes money on the side by dating the clients. She befriends a hardworking, idealistic accountant, Marty Blackford (Kent Smith), arranges for him to become a tax consultant for a restaurant owner with underworld connections, and later coaxes him into working for an organized crime syndicate run by a cultivated but unscrupulous gangster, George Castleman (David Brian). "There is such a thing as self-respect," Marty protests. "Don't talk to me about self-respect," Ethel shoots back. "Self-respect is something you tell yourself you've got when you've got nothing else. The only thing that counts is that stuff you take to the bank — that filthy buck that everybody sneers at but slugs to get."

Soon afterward, Marty proposes to Ethel, but she has her eye on bigger fish — George Castleman. The underworld boss finances her transformation into Lorna Hansen Forbes, and when one of Castleman's henchmen is found murdered out West, Lorna is dispatched by Castleman to set a trap for Nick Prenta (Steve Cochran), a renegade member of Castleman's gang. Instead, Lorna falls in love with Nick, and purposely delays the plan to ensnare him. When Castleman senses Lorna's change of heart, he travels West, savagely beats her and kills Nick. Lorna escapes and returns to her home. Marty follows her and warns her that Castleman is hot on her trail, but before they can flee, Castleman arrives and shoots her, then is himself killed by Marty.

Although Crawford's performance in the film was panned in the *New York Times*, with Bosley Crowther saying that "a more artificial lot of acting could hardly be achieved," the actress was applauded by most critics. Dorothy Manners of the *Los Angeles Examiner* called her "a magic personality in front of the camera," the *Los Angeles Times'* Edwin Schallert said Crawford "again sweeps in laurels in the new field of shady living," and the reviewer from *The Hollywood Reporter* wrote, "The picture is Joan Crawford's, lock, stock and barrel. She looks terrific, and her performance is exciting in every phase of its development."

Crawford followed this triumph with *Harriet Craig* (1950), a remake of *Craig's Wife* (1936), which starred the actress in the title role of the overbearing, house-proud wife; *Good-bye My Fancy* (1951) with Robert Young; and *This Woman Is Dangerous* (1952), starring David Brian and Dennis Morgan. But the latter film, dismissed by critics as "a film of many pretenses but little conviction," was a box office disappointment, and after its release Crawford left Warners to star in RKO's classic noir, *Sudden Fear* (1952). Passing up a salary in exchange for a 50 percent interest in the film, Crawford turned in an acclaimed performance that earned her a third Academy Award nomination for Best Actress.

In *Sudden Fear*, Crawford's character, playwright and San Francisco heiress Myra Hudson, falls in love with and marries actor Lester Blaine (Jack Palance). Myra is gloriously happy in her marriage and plans to make a will which provides amply for Lester but is primarily earmarked for a foundation. Shortly before the will is to be signed, Myra discovers that her husband is having an affair with Irene Neves (Gloria Grahame), and that they plan to kill her. Myra spends a sleepless night agonizing over this revelation, but her sorrow soon turns to vengeance, and she conceives a complex scheme to murder Lester and frame Irene for the crime.

While in Irene's apartment, preparing to shoot Lester, Myra loses her nerve and flees, but Lester has figured out the plot and follows her. Coincidentally, Irene is walking in a direction opposite from Myra and is clad in a coat and white scarf similar to Myra's. As Lester searches for Myra, he mistakes Irene for his wife and runs her down with his car, simultaneously killing himself in the accident.

Crawford was almost universally hailed for her portrayal of Myra Hudson, with Ruth Waterbury claiming in the *Los Angeles Examiner* that the film "proves not only why [Crawford] got to the top, but why she has stayed at the top of her profession for more than 20 years," and Milton Luban of *The Hollywood Reporter* saying that the film serves as "a tour de force for Joan Crawford whose truly brilliant performance will make a conversation piece for a long time to come." And although Crawford lost the Academy Award to Shirley Booth in *Come Back, Little Sheba*, she was again riding high on a wave of popularity. She returned triumphantly to MGM for *Torch Song* (1953), in which she showed that, though nearing 50, her body was still in shape and her dancing talent intact. But career-wise, Crawford's heyday had seen its end. Her next six pictures, including the rather bizarre Western *Johnny Guitar* (1954), *Female on the Beach* (1955), another woman-in-peril film starring Jeff Chandler, and *Queen Bee* (1955), in which Crawford portrayed a domineering shrew, did little for her popularity.

Meanwhile, in 1955, Crawford married her fourth husband, Pepsi-Cola executive Alfred Steele, and became heavily involved with the company. By all accounts, this union — Crawford's first with a non-actor — was a joyous one, and the actress would later state in her book, *My Way of Life*: "I achieved, at last, a completely happy marriage." Sadly, Steele died just four years later, in 1959. Crawford was then named to the Pepsi-Cola Board of Directors, and continued to be active in the company's affairs for a number of years.

In 1962, Crawford made another comeback of sorts, starring in the horror film, *What Ever Happened to Baby Jane?* The film was one of the year's biggest box office hits and Crawford was hailed by critics for her "remarkably fine interpretation" of an invalid who is terrorized by her mentally unbalanced sister. But this victory would be short-lived, as her career wound to a close in films such as *The Caretakers* (1963), which was condemned as "shallow, showy, and cheap," *Strait-Jacket* (1964), after which one critic urged Crawford to "get out of those housedress horror B movies and back into haute couture," and *Trog* (1970), her last film, which was panned as "absurd, often laughable." Showing Crawford as a physician who serves as a compassionate caretaker to a prehistoric man, *Trog* represented a shabby conclusion to a remarkably resilient career.

In 1973, Crawford was forced into retirement by the Pepsi-Cola company, whose executives felt she had outlived her usefulness to them. Bitterly referring to the company's CEO as "Fang," she had to learn to live without both Pepsi and her movie career. Her relationship with her two oldest children, Christina and Christopher, had deteriorated, and she became increasingly reclusive, spending much of her time writing between five and ten thousand letters to fans, old friends and others. Crawford's last public appearance was in 1974, as hostess of a party to honor veteran actress Rosalind Russell. After viewing a candid photo taken of her at the event, Crawford stated: "If that's the way I look now, I will no longer be photographed publicly."

Joan Crawford

After several years of declining health, Crawford died of acute coronary occlusion on May 10, 1977, in the apartment where she had spent her final years. None of her four children were at her side. In her will, she left $77,500 each to her youngest girls, Cathy and Cynthia, but the two oldest children were completely cut off, as the will stated, "for reasons best known to them." The following year, Christina Crawford wrote a scathing biography, *Mommie*

Dearest, which detailed Crawford's excessive drinking, neurotic obsession for cleanliness and savage abuse of her children, resulting in a shocking evisceration of Crawford's stellar image.

Despite this sad footnote, it cannot be denied that Joan Crawford was a towering personage of an age gone by, an actress who not only possessed an outstanding and well-acknowledged talent, but also was a star in the true sense of the word. In June 1977, two months after her death, at a memorial service held for Crawford in Beverly Hills, director George Cukor offered a moving tribute that fittingly epitomized the persona of Joan Crawford:

> She was the perfect image of the movie star and, as such, largely the creation of her own, indomitable will. She had, of course, very remarkable material to work with: a quick native intelligence, tremendous animal vitality, a lovely figure and, above all, her face, that extraordinary sculptural construction of line and places, finely chiseled like the mask of some classical divinity from fifth-century Greece. It caught the light superbly, so that you could photograph her from any angle.... The camera saw, I suspect, a side of her that no flesh-and-blood lover ever saw.

Film Noir Filmography

MILDRED PIERCE   *Director:* Michael Curtiz. *Producer:* Jerry Wald. Released by Warner Bros., September 1945. *Running time:* 113 minutes. *Cast:* Joan Crawford, Jack Carson, Zachary Scott, Eve Arden, Ann Blyth, Bruce Bennett, George Tobias, Lee Patrick, Moroni Olsen. *Awards:* Academy Award for Best Actress: Joan Crawford. Academy Award nomination for Best Picture, Best Supporting Actress (Eve Arden), Best Supporting Actress (Ann Blyth), Best Screenplay (Ranald MacDougall), Best Cinematography (Ernest Haller).

POSSESSED   *Director:* Curtis Bernhardt. *Producer:* Jerry Wald. Released by Warner Bros., May 1947. *Running time:* 108 minutes. *Cast:* Joan Crawford, Van Heflin, Raymond Massey, Geraldine Brooks, Stanley Ridges, John Ridgely, Moroni Olsen. Academy Award nomination for Best Actress (Joan Crawford).

THE DAMNED DON'T CRY   *Director:* Vincent Sherman. *Producer:* Jerry Wald. Released by Warner Bros., May 1950. *Running time:* 103 minutes. *Cast:* Joan Crawford, David Brian, Steve Cochran, Kent Smith, Hugh Sanders, Selena Royle.

SUDDEN FEAR   *Director:* David Miller. *Producer:* Joseph Kaufman. Released by RKO, August 1952. *Running time:* 110 minutes. *Cast:* Joan Crawford, Jack Palance, Gloria Grahame, Bruce Bennett, Virginia Huston, Touch [Mike] Connors. *Awards:* Academy Award nomination for Best Actress (Joan Crawford), Best Supporting Actor (Jack Palance), Best Cinematography (Charles B. Lang, Jr), Best Costume Design (Sheila O'Brien).

References

Albert, Katherine. "Glamour Girl Against the World." *Liberty*, Spring 1972.
_____. "With Time and Tears." *Liberty*, Spring 1975.

Asher, Jerry. "Cocktails with Joan." *Silver Screen*, June 1936.

Bowers, Ronald. "Joan Crawford: Latest Decade." *Films in Review*, June-July 1966.

_____. "Joan Crawford's Fiftieth Anniversary." *Films in Review*, January 1975.

Considine, Shaun. *Bette and Joan: The Divine Feud*. New York: E.P. Dutton, 1989.

Crawford, Joan. "I'm An Adopted Mother." *Photoplay*, February 1948.

_____. *My Way of Life*. Simon and Schuster, 1971.

Crichton, Kyle. "Lady in Waiting." *Collier's*, October 28, 1944.

Dudley, Fredda. "Untold Tales About Crawford." *Silver Screen*, December 1945.

Flint, Peter B. "Joan Crawford, Screen Star, Dies in Manhattan Home." *New York Times*, May 11, 1977.

"Good Taste Is Never Old Fashioned." *Picture Show*, January 23, 1960.

Graham, Sheilah. "The House That Joan Built." *Photoplay*, February 1948.

"Her Separation from Douglas Fairbanks, Jr." *Motion Picture*, May 1933

"Hollywood's Once and Only Star." *Time*, May 23, 1977.

"I Couldn't Ask for More." *Ladies' Home Journal*, December 1942.

"Joan Crawford: Her Films, 1927–1959." *Film Fan Monthly*, July-August 1972.

"Joan Crawford Remembered." *After Dark*, March 1978.

"Joan Crawford Retrospect." *Hollywood Studio Magazine*, August 1977.

"Joan Crawford's Other Life." *Time*, November 20, 1978.

"Joan Goes Back to Old Ways." *Life*, November 9, 1953.

"Joan Seizes MGM's Handles of Power." *New York Post*, October 11, 1983.

"Lady in the Dark." *TV Guide*, August 16, 1969.

"Living it Up with Pepsi." *Time*, May 19, 1958.

Lusk, Norbert. "Close-Up." *Modern Screen*, May 1948.

Manners, Dorothy. "The Girl Without a Past." *Photoplay*, October 1935.

_____. "Her First Trip to Europe." *Motion Picture*, December 1932.

_____. "Second Marriage." *Photoplay*, May 1936.

_____. "Will Her Career Wreck Her Marriage?" *Motion Picture*, September 1932.

Maxwell, Elsa. "Mademoiselle la Chandelier." *Photoplay*, February 1947.

Newquist, Roy. "Joan Crawford's Revealing Last Interviews." *McCall's*, August 1977.

Parsons, Louella O. "Joan Crawford." *Los Angeles Examiner*, June 12, 1947.

Quirk, Lawrence J. *The Complete Films of Joan Crawford*. Secaucus, N. J.: The Citadel Press, 1988.

_____. "Joan Crawford." *Films in Review*, December 1965.

St. Johns, Adela Rogers. "Joan Crawford, the Dramatic Rise of a Self-Made Star." *Photoplay*, October/November/December 1937.

St. Johns, Ivan. "She Doesn't Use Lipstick in Public." *Photoplay*, May 1927.

Scrivani, Joan C. "Mildred Pierce." *Scarlet Street*, Spring 1994.

Service, Faith. "The Star Who Never Rests." *Movie Classic*, January 1933.

Springer, John. "Joan Crawford." *Screen Stories*, August 1962.

"Still Going Great." *Screen Greats*, Summer 1971.

"Story of Joan Crawford." *Newsweek*, October 15, 1945.

Thomas, Bob. *Joan Crawford: A Biography*. New York: Bantam Books, 1978.

Waterbury, Ruth. "Joan Crawford." *Photoplay*, August 1939.

_____. "Love Is Laughter." *Photoplay*, October 1942.

_____. "Stormy Passage for Joan and Phil." *Photoplay*, March 1946.

_____. "Un-possessed." *Photoplay*, August 1947.

Wilkinson, Harry. "Looking Hollywood Way." *Good Old Days*, May 1970.

Wilson, Earl. "Crawford Rebels." *Silver Screen*, February 1933.

_____. "First Shots of Rain." *Silver Screen*, August 1932.

_____. "Projections of Crawford." *Silver Screen*, October 1936.

_____. "She's Dancing Again." *Silver Screen*, January 1939.
Zeitlin, Ida. "Why Joan Crawford Remains Great." *Photoplay*, October 1936.

Documentary

"Joan Crawford: Always the Star." Copyright 1996, Wombat Productions. A Division of the CineMasters Group. As seen on "Biography," a presentation of the Arts and Entertainment cable network.

Peggy Cummins

Peggy Cummins, a well-known stage and screen star in Britain, is per-haps best remembered in the United States for two films — 20th Century –Fox's extravagant production of *Forever Amber* (1947) and the film noir cult classic *Gun Crazy* (1950). Despite her association with *Forever Amber*, however, Cummins never appeared in the final print. After a nationwide search that rivaled the hunt for Scarlett O'Hara in *Gone with the Wind*, Cummins was announced for the starring role in *Amber*, only to be summarily dismissed after several weeks of shooting. While this setback might have proved fatal to the career of a lesser personality, Cummins took the experience in stride, making several well-received films in America, and later returning to England where she played leading roles through the 1960s.

Labeled with such lavish descriptors as a "diminutive, deliciously curved charmer" with "elfin allure" and a "cuddly daintiness," Cummins went against type with her sole film noir appearance as a gun-toting murderess in *Gun Crazy*. Critics and the public initially doubted her ability to believably por-tray the ruthlessly corrupt Annie Laurie Starr, but Cummins proved to be an electrifying presence in the production and it remains her best-known Amer-ican film.

The pint-sized blonde with the emerald eyes entered the world as Mar-garet Diane Augusta Cummins on December 18, 1925. Her parents, William Hollywood Cummins, a journalist and music professor, and Margaret Mary Cummins, were residents of Killiney, located just outside Dublin, Ireland. (Cummins, however, was born in Prestatyn, North Wales; the actress's mother, while visiting an aunt toward the end of her pregnancy, was stranded by a storm that made Channel crossings impossible.) The youngest of three children, Cummins was a tomboy as a child and her efforts to keep pace with her two brothers, William and Harry, turned her into an expert swimmer, diver, fence jumper and roof climber.

At an early age, Cummins was bitten by the acting bug and her mother, who had a great love of the theater, encouraged her interest, saying: "What-ever happens, it's your life, so get on with it!" Cummins recalled. When she was seven years old, she began taking dance lessons at the Abbey School of Ballet, and in her performance debut played a boy in *The Duchess of Malfi* at the Gate Theatre in Dublin. In her role, for which she was paid a box of chocolates, Cummins was required to appear behind a silhouette screen in profile, but the assignment didn't sit well with the youngster. "I yelled out: 'Nobody sees my face' and turned right to the audience," Cummins said in 1948. "But the lights were set for a silhouette so I was completely obscured. For my second part — as a boy — I walked on without knowing my lines. Just made them up. But they rehired me."

Shortening her first name to Peggy, Cummins continued to play in a vari-ety of stage productions for the next six years, usually as young boys, includ-ing MacDuff's son in *Macbeth*, the page boy in *Saint Joan* and the young Prince

Albert in *Victoria Regina*. At one point, the busy youngster appeared in two plays simultaneously, changing her costumes in a taxi as she rushed from the Gate Theatre's production of *A Comedy of Errors* to the Abbey Theatre for *On Bailie's Strand*. Finally, at age 11, Cummins got to play a rare female role in *Judgement Day*, where she stood on a covered box in order to portray a 16-year-old witness at a trial.

By this time, news of the talented adolescent had reached London, and a family friend recommended Cummins to famed producer Aubrey Blackburn. Despite Blackburn's initial reluctance to handle another child performer, he was enchanted with Cummins after their first meeting and promptly signed her for her London debut in *Let's Pretend*, which opened on the actress' 13th birthday. Although the play was a flop, Cummins received glowing notices that not only resulted in her being cast as a ballet dancer in a television series called *Coffee Stall*, but also attracted the attention of Hollywood. Before long, the teenager had inked an agreement with Warner Bros. studio, which assigned her to make one British production, *Dr. O'Dowd* (1940), before she was to make the trek to the United States. Playing the demonstrative daughter of a drunken Irish doctor, Cummins scored a hit in her first screen role: "In one scene I fell and cut my knee so badly I cried," Cummins later said. "They kept the cameras going and the London critics said that scene was the dramatic highlight of the picture and I was a wonderfully natural little actress." But on the day that filming completed on the production, war was declared, making trans-Atlantic travel dangerous, and Cummins' contract with Warners was cancelled by mutual agreement.

Shortly after the outbreak of World War II, Cummins' father died and she moved with her mother to London, where she was heard in a number of radio plays including *The Immortal Falstaff* and *The Far-Off Hills*. She also continued her stage work, appearing in *Ah, Wilderness, Sixteen* and *The Moon in the Yellow River*. Also during this time, Cummins appeared in her second film, *Salute John Citizen* (1942), a wartime drama from Britain's most prolific director, Maurice Elvey. She later joined the Women's Voluntary Services, becoming (at age 15) the organization's youngest member. Between her stage performances, Cummins worked with the WVS, serving food, washing dishes and serving as emcee at the Stage Door Canteen, the Rainbow Club and the Variety Band Box.

In March 1943, Cummins opened at the Saville Theatre in London as Fuffy in *Junior Miss*, giving 1,000 performances over the course of the next 20 months. On many occasions, Cummins was required to execute her acting duties to the outside accompaniment of falling bombs and shrieking sirens, but the frightening experience only served to enhance the teenager's poise. "I had some close calls during the blitz. I was scared out of my wits most of the time," she said several years later. "Then, I'd look down at all those faces in the audience — not a soul moving from his seat — all of them looking toward the stage, as if that was where their life hung. Their calm always cured my panic." In addition to her role in *Junior Miss* and her activities with the WVS, Cummins managed to find time to appear in three British films, *English Without Tears* (1943), *Old Mother Riley, Detective* (1944) and *Welcome, Mr. Washington* (1944), in which Cummins stole the picture as a youngster who farms the land left behind by her soldier father.

When *Junior Miss* closed in November 1944, Cummins was signed to play the lead in an eight-week Yuletide season presentation of *Alice in Wonderland* at the Palace Theatre. Critics hailed her performance, labeling her "the most enchanting performer of this decade," and Cummins suddenly found herself courted by America once again. Having seen Cummins in both *Junior Miss* and *Alice in Wonderland*, 20th Century–Fox's London representative beat every other Hollywood talent scout to Cummins' door and, without a screen test, signed her to a long-term contract. With World War II now ended in Europe, the actress was put aboard the first plane available to civilians and on July 25, 1945, Cummins arrived in America. She was 19 years old.

When Cummins landed in Hollywood, the film community was involved in a much-ballyhooed search for an actress to play the title role in Fox's upcoming production of *Forever Amber*, based on Kathleen Winsor's runaway bestseller. Such notables as Vivien Leigh and Margaret Lockwood had been offered the coveted part of the saucy English wench and turned it down, and with more than 200 hopefuls having tested for the role, Paulette Goddard, who'd bleached her brunette locks to a brassy blonde, was reportedly a front-runner. In the midst of this feverish hunt, Cummins was cast in the role of Betty Cream in *Cluny Brown*, but before long, in a massive media blitz, she was being touted as the new Amber.

Journalists nationwide carried the news of Cummins' imminent casting in the role. In November 1945, famed columnist Louella Parsons confidently predicted: "Just as I was the first to tell my readers that Vivien Leigh was chosen as Scarlett, I'll tell you now, without an if, and or but — Peggy will play Amber." By early 1946, this claim was confirmed. Cummins herself would later say she'd learned from the newspapers that she had been cast as Amber: "Then, I was telephoned by the studio. It's a perfectly marvelous opportunity. What a chance for acting!" Actress Helen Walker was cast to replace Cummins in *Cluny Brown*, and plans for Cummins as Amber commenced immediately.

With the announcement of Cummins' casting, a number of journalists questioned her ability to portray the immoral Amber, with one remarking that she "appears less like Amber than Alice in Wonderland, whom she played on the English stage." In response to such naysayers, Cummins tersely declared: "I'm really not at all perturbed at the prospect of playing Amber. I think that an accomplished actress should be willing to tackle anything." The first order of business after Cummins signed on with the production was the title character's lavish wardrobe. Fox costume designer Rene Hubert had already planned Amber's costumes for a more voluptuous figure than the one possessed by the 98-pound, five-foot-one Cummins, causing Hubert to abandon his preliminary designs and create an entirely new wardrobe. By March 1946, the film's entire cast had been decided, including Cornel Wilde as Bruce Carlton, Vincent Price as Lord Harry Aimsbury and Reginald Gardiner as King Charles II. Shooting began in June.

But just two months later, on August 4, 1946, Fox head Darryl F. Zanuck called a halt to the filming, expressing his dissatisfaction both with director John Stahl and Cummins. In a *Photoplay* article released a year later, Zanuck explained his dilemma: "We realized that Peggy could act the role, but could never look it. She was too young. We had spent two years on research for the perfection of the production, but we also wanted perfection in casting. So we decided to start all over again." At a cost of $1 million, Zanuck dismissed Cummins from the role and instead cast Linda Darnell, whom he described as "a star who had not only great beauty and talent, but a sense of sophistication which would convince the public and critics that this was the Amber the author had written about." Along with Cummins, Zanuck also dumped John Stahl in favor of Otto Preminger, and replaced Vincent Price and Reginald Gardiner with Richard Greene and George Sanders.

Although one columnist would report that Cummins' "heart was all but broken" over losing the part, and another said she took the news "lying down — on her tummy and sobbing," the actress seemed to view the experience philosophically. "I can't deny it was like having a lovely jewel, or some other wonderful gift, and then having to give it back," she told *Photoplay* in 1947. "It's hard, but you have a choice. You can let yourself ache over your loss — or you can think instead of how wonderful and exciting it was while you had it. Life is very well balanced. As an unknown, I might have kept *Amber* and met with envy and hostility. I lost it, and found friendship, sympathy and kindness — things that might ordinarily have taken me much longer to earn in a country that was not my own." Released in October 1947, *Forever Amber* earned a whopping $6 million in its first week of release, but it was thoroughly lambasted by critics. Cummins would admit years later, "When I saw it, of course, I just felt relieved."

Cummins' compensation for losing out on *Amber* was a lead role in *The Late George Apley* (1947), a superb comedy which had first been a Pulitzer Prize–winning novel by John P. Marquand, then was adapted by Marquand and George S. Kaufman into a play. Starring opposite Ronald Colman, Cummins earned an award from *Look* magazine as "most promising actress" for her performance, and was hailed by critics, including the reviewer for *Variety*, who wrote: "Peggy Cummins, in her first American film part, plays the daughter excellently. A piquant blonde looker with an elf-like figure, Miss Cummins performs with considerable vigor and authority." Cummins later seemed pleased with the experience of working on her American film debut, telling reporters, "Working with Ronald Colman was exciting, he is such a magnificent actor. And the fact that he is English made things very nice. With Edna Best in the cast, too, I knew we'd always take time out for tea." She added, however, that she'd learned to ice skate for a scene in the film, resulting in a broken toe: "I mastered the sport, and then the whole thing was left on the cutting room floor."

Next, Cummins starred in *Moss Rose* (1947), a tense turn-of-the-century mystery with Victor Mature, Vincent Price and Ethel Barrymore. Praised by one critic as "unusually interesting," Cummins turned in a standout performance as a Cockney singer-dancer, and after the film's release, director Gregory Ratoff forecast that Cummins "is going to be a very big star. Peggy has everything that the doctor prescribed. She has youth, looks, tremendous technique, and also sex appeal. And a woman without sex appeal is like soda water without bubbles. And Peggy Cummins has plenty of bubbles."

In August 1947 it was announced that Cummins would star with Cornel Wilde in *The Black Rose*, but the picture was later released in 1950 with Tyrone Power and Cecile Aubry. Instead, Cummins was cast in *Green Grass of Wyoming* (1948), a lightweight romance about two rival families in the trotting race business, then returned to England to star in her last film for Fox, *Escape* (1948), which starred Rex Harrison as a prison escapee who is reformed by Cummins' love. Back in America, Cummins was next cast in her final Hollywood film and the one for which she is best known: United Artists' *Gun Crazy* (1950).

Before the film's release, John Rosenfield of the *Dallas Morning News* expressed doubt over the wholesome Cummins' ability to portray the corrupt character in *Gun Crazy*. "We haven't seen this movie with its siren, but we have to snicker anyhow. Can makeup and direction erase what appears to be an innate gentility?" Rosenfield queried. "Or will [Cummins] look like Margaret O'Brien wearing Cleopatra's bloomers to a kiddy party?" Cummins would go on to prove that Rosenfield's concerns were unfounded.

Released as *Deadly Is the Female*, this film noir thriller begins by showing young Bart Tare (Rusty Tamblyn), who is so fascinated by weapons that he is sent to a reform school for breaking into a gun store. Years later, the now-grown Bart (John Dall) returns to his hometown, and when he accompanies two boyhood friends to a local carnival, he is drawn by the antics of Annie Laurie Starr (Cummins), who works as a sharpshooter in the carnival's sideshow. When Bart bests Annie in a shooting match, he is hired by the carnival and the two soon are embroiled in a heated affair. ("We go together," Bart says. "I don't know why. Maybe like guns and ammunition go together.") But the couple's happiness is dimmed when carnival's owner (Berry Kroeger), who has designs on Annie, learns of their relationship and fires them.

Bart and Annie marry, but when their meager funds run out, Annie uses her sexual allure to spur her husband into committing a string of small-time robberies. Although Bart is horrified when Annie's trigger-happy methods result in several deaths, he is unable to leave her and continues to be drawn into a life of desperation and inevitable doom. Now sought by authorities, Annie and Bart are forced to abandon their biggest haul in a hotel room when the police close in, and they seek refuge in Bart's hometown. But Bart is shunned by his family. When his two boyhood friends, now sheriff's deputies, come to arrest the couple, they flee into the nearby mountains. As Annie prepares to open fire on the approaching deputies, Bart fatally wounds her just before he himself is gunned down.

Upon its release, *Gun Crazy* received mostly favorable reviews, although Cummins was labeled "unconvincing" in *Variety*, and Howard Thompson of the *New York Times* called the film a "spurious concoction basically on a par with the most humdrum pulp fiction." However, the critic for *The Hollywood Reporter* termed the picture "dramatic and compelling," singling Cummins out for her "commanding performance of the twisted girl," and David Bongard of the *Los Angeles Daily News* wrote that the film was one of the screen's "finer pieces of craftsmanship." Perhaps the best notices came from Philip K. Scheuer of the *Los Angeles Times*, who called the film "a sockdolager of a show" that contains "just about as much continuous excitement as it is possible to cram onto one screen…. As for the cuddly, lethal Miss Cummins, she is permitted to burn up the screen without apologies. She is the female — hence, deadly."

By now, Cummins had been romantically linked with several Hollywood notables, including Cary Grant and millionaire dilettante Huntington Hartford, but after the release of *Gun Crazy*, she moved back to England and on December 14, 1950, she married Derek Dunnett, the scion of England's largest seed business. The couple would go on to have a son and a daughter.

Cummins continued her screen career in England, working almost non-stop in a variety of features, including two directed by her Hollywood champion Gregory Ratoff: *If This Be Sin* (1950), a tawdry tale that showed Cummins' beau being romanced by her mother, played by Myrna Loy, and *Operation X* (1950), a bland melodrama starring Edward G. Robinson as megalomaniacal businessman whose love for money is matched only by his love for his daughter, Cummins. The actress also appeared in a variety of other productions, including *The Passionate Sentry* (1951), an amusing farce based on a highly successful stage play, *The Love Lottery* (1953), a clever British satire on the Hollywood star system, *Always a Bride* (1954), featuring Cummins in a charming portrayal as a con man's daughter, *The March Hare* (1956), starring Cummins as an American who falls for a baron she has mistaken for a horse groom and *Curse of the Demon* (1958), an eerie and suspenseful low-budget supernatural horror movie that has developed a strong cult following.

After only a handful of films in the 1960s, Cummins ended her career

Peggy Cummins

with *Your Money or Your Wife* (1965), an unfunny farce about a woman due to inherit a large sum of money only if she is widowed or divorced. After this picture, Cummins retired from the screen, raising her children in the family's 18th-century mansion in Sussex, England, but two decades later she would express her interest in acting again. "Stage, screen, TV — character part or starring role," she told author Richard Lamparski in 1984. "If I think I could do a good job with it, I'd do it, and I think I still have some very good work left in me." To date, however, Cummins has not resumed her career.

With more than 30 film appearances over a span of nearly a quarter-century, Peggy Cummins enjoyed a successful career both on stage and on the screen. While she never achieved the star status that was anticipated upon her arrival in America, she compiled an impressive array of performances that leave no doubt as to her talent. With her indelible portrayal of the corrupt femme in *Gun Crazy*, she earned a firm place in the annals of film noir, and despite the unpleasant legacy of the *Forever Amber* debacle, Cummins demonstrated that she possessed the inner fortitude that is necessary to overcome a devastating hurdle. Perhaps it was one of the actress' favorite quotes that helped her to succeed: "You have what you give. Just that — if you give out happiness and good, you also keep it."

Film Noir Filmography

GUN CRAZY (Original release title: *Deadly Is the Female*)   *Director:* Joseph H. Lewis. *Producer:* Frank and Maurice King. Released by United Artists, January 1950. *Running time:* 87 minutes. *Cast:* Peggy Cummins, John Dall, Berry Kroeger, Morris Carnovsky, Anabel Shaw, Harry Lewis, Nedrick Young.

References

"Actress Here for Premiere." *San Francisco Examiner*, April 28, 1947.
"*Amber* Role Contender Gets Contract." *Los Angeles Daily News*, December 21, 1945.
"Amber Role to Newcomer." *Los Angeles Examiner*, February 1, 1946.
Biography of Peggy Cummins. 20th Century–Fox Studios, circa 1947.
Brock, Patrick. "Peggy Cummins: An Overnight Success." *Classic Images*, September 1994.
Cook, Alton. "An Irish Miss to Pay Amber St. Clare." *New York World Telegram*, December 24, 1945.
Deere, Dorothy. "Bit of Ireland." *Photoplay*, August 1947.
Dudley, Fredda. "Bernhardt from Britain." *Silver Screen*, June 1946.
_____. "It Was Only a Dented Fender." *Silver Screen*, June 1947.
Fields, Sidney. "Irish Rebel in Hollywood." *New York Daily Mirror*, September 20, 1948.
Fuller, Tyra. "Peggy Cummins, Young British Star, Proves She Is Versatile." *Worcester Sunday Telegram*, April 28, 1946.
Gebhart, Myrtle. "Newest Film Star Is Irish Lass, Product of Dublin Stage." *Boston Sunday Post*, February 24, 1946.
Graham, Sheilah. "Can an Angel Be a Hussy?" *Des Moines Sunday Register*, March 10, 1946.
_____. "98 Pounds of *Amber*." *The Baltimore Sun*, March 10, 1946.
Heffernan, Harold. "Irish Actress Disarmingly Calm Over Being Cast as *Amber*." *Dallas Morning News*, February 12, 1946.
"Her Irish Heart Was Breaking." *American Magazine*, October 1947.
Kauffmann, Stanley. "Not So Crazy." *The New Republic*, June 24, 1991.
"London Actress Arrives Here." *Los Angeles Times*, September 25, 1945.
Mortimer, Lee. "It Could Only Happen in Hollywood." *Sunday Mirror Magazine*, February 3, 1946.
Parsons, Louella. "Peggy Cummins Gets *Moss Rose* Lead, Gregory Ratoff Directing." *Los Angeles Examiner*, September 23, 1946.
"Peggy Cummins: 19-Year-Old Irish Girl May Play Gaudy Heroine of *Forever Amber*." *Life*, November 19, 1945.
Ratoff, Gregory. "This Little Peggy...." *Modern Screen*, July 1947.
Reid, Ashton. "Peggy in Amberland." *Collier's*, May 25, 1946.
Skolsky, Sidney. "Hollywood Is My Beat." *Citizen News*, April 24, 1947.
_____. "Never Amber." *New York Post Week-End Magazine*, May 10, 1947.

Smith, Gary. "The First *Amber*." *Films in Review*, February 1989.
"So This Is Going to Be Amber! British Girl in Coveted Role." *Sunday World-Herald*,
    November 25, 1945.
Woodbury, Mitch. "Mitch Views Exciting Shots in *Forever Amber* Film." *Toledo Blade*,
    March 27, 1948.
Zanuck, Darryl F. "On the *Amber* Spot." *Photoplay*, June 1947.

Rosemary DeCamp

A self-described "goody goody" who is best known for her character roles as a warm and sympathetic mother, Rosemary DeCamp wasn't yet 30 years old when she made her film debut as a 65-year-old matriarch. DeCamp, who was often labeled as "the girl with a hundred faces," began her successful career as a radio personality and later became known to television audiences on such popular programs as *Love That Bob* and *That Girl*. With an illustrious career that included such box office hits as *Hold Back the Dawn* (1941) and *Yankee Doodle Dandy* (1942), DeCamp is one of the most unlikely candidates for the dark realm of film noir, but she was featured in three examples from the era: *Danger Signal* (1945), *Nora Prentiss* (1947) and *Scandal Sheet* (1952).

The veteran character actress was born on November 14, 1910, in Prescott, Arizona, the only child of Marjorie Hinman DeCamp, a pianist, and Val DeCamp, a mining engineer. Originally, her family was from Canada, and her grandfather came to America by sneaking across the border. "His name was DeChamps, but he figured, when he hit the West, that was too fancy a name for a miner, so he called himself DeCamp instead. Which led in time to Rosemary DeCamp. Sounds like a stripper, doesn't it?" the actress laughingly said.

DeCamp's childhood was spent in the mining camps and border towns of Arizona, and she received her first brush with Hollywood during these early years when such stars as Harry Carey and Tom Mix would ride into town to film location shots for their popular westerns. Shy and reticent as a child, DeCamp enjoyed listening to people talk and showed a talent for mimicry that would serve her in the years to come. While attending school in Arizona, DeCamp played her first lead at the age of 14, in a little theater play in Phoenix, *Road to Yesterday*. Her performance was so impressive that she was offered a job with the Marta Oatsman stock company in Los Angeles. But after informing her father of her ambitions to become an actress, DeCamp later remembered being told, "All right, but be a good one. Go to college first. By the time you get out, you'll be old enough to swim, not flounder."

DeCamp declined the offer in favor of her education, and after graduating from high school, majored in drama at Mills College in Oakland, California, becoming a star performer in a variety of campus productions. She went on to earn her Bachelor of Arts and Master of Arts degrees, then remained at the school to teach speech courses. But after a year of teaching a topic about which DeCamp later admitted she was "very vague," the actress gave in to her yen for performing and turned to radio, earning her first job on *One Man's Family* in San Francisco.

A short time later, DeCamp began appearing in a number of productions for the Carmel stock company, participating in a cross-country tour of *The Drunkard* and landing a small role in her Broadway debut in *Merrily We Roll Along* (1935). After the latter play closed, DeCamp was unable to find additional theater work and took on a job as assistant drama editor on the *New*

York Morning Telegraph. But this new career would be short-lived. After scolding the paper's managing editor for cutting her copy, DeCamp was fired: "I was too snooty and thought I knew it all," she recalled.

After performing in several summer stock productions in Ivorytown, Connecticut, DeCamp resumed her radio career and spent the next few years performing a wide variety of roles, from young boys to doddering grandmothers, in programs including *Easy Aces, Gang Busters* and *The Goldbergs*. In 1937, intending to use her performing background to break into the movies, she moved to Los Angeles, but after knocking on the doors of nearly every studio in town, the actress found no success. "I've got a funny nose and I'm not very impressive looking," DeCamp would later say, "but I used to wonder how they could decide by a glance at my face that I couldn't act." Undaunted, DeCamp returned once again to radio, performing in such programs as *Lux Radio Theatre, The Career of Alice Blair* and *The Shadow* (with Orson Welles). She also earned the role of Nurse Judy Price on *Dr. Christian,* starring Jean Hersholt (whom DeCamp described in 1997 as a "dear man"), and would remain with the program for the next 17 years. During most of this long-running series, the cast performed two live shows, three hours apart, before a studio audience. With no summer hiatus, they were heard twice weekly, 52 weeks a year.

Finally, just when it appeared that DeCamp would spend the rest of her career as a talented but faceless radio personality, she got the opportunity that she had so long awaited. When film actress Martha Scott left radio to star in *Cheers for Miss Bishop* (1941), she suggested DeCamp for the role in the picture of a Danish woman. "Martha fought with the producer, director and everyone to give me the part," DeCamp later said. "I kept telling her not to bother, as I had up to that time failed on every interview or test I'd had. But she got me the job. I didn't have to do a thing but sit still and use one of my dearly beloved radio accents." Then, after a bit part in Warner Bros.' *The Wagons Roll at Night* (1941), she earned another chance to utilize her talent for dialects as an Austrian immigrant in *Hold Back the Dawn* (1941), starring Charles Boyer and Olivia de Havilland.

Although she was at last on her way as a film actress, DeCamp's career was overshadowed by her life behind the scenes when she married Judge John Shindler, whom she had first met during her college years, when Shindler was studying law at nearby Stanford. The two had parted ways after DeCamp's graduation, but Shindler contacted the young actress in 1940 after hearing her on a local radio station. A year later, the couple were married and would go on to have four daughters, Margaret, born in 1942, Martha in 1946, Valerie in 1947 and Nita in 1952.

Meanwhile, DeCamp appeared in five films in 1942, including roles as Sabu's mother in *The Jungle Book,* in which she aged from 16 to 30, and George M. Cohan's mother *in Yankee Doodle Dandy*—despite the fact that she was a full decade younger than her on-screen son, James Cagney. After the birth of her first daughter, DeCamp made only one film appearance the following year, in Warner Bros.' musical salute to the war effort, *This Is the Army* (1943). Next, she appeared in back-to-back roles as Ann Blyth's mother in two rather flimsy musicals, *The Merry Monahans* (1944) and *Bowery to Broadway* (1944), followed by *Practically Yours* (1944), a silly Claudette Colbert starrer that flopped at the box office. But her film vehicles began to improve in quality when the actress signed a one-year contract with Warner Bros., appearing first in *Pride of the Marines* (1945), a moving account of a disabled war hero's efforts to adjust to his affliction.

After portraying the mother of George and Ira Gershwin in *Rhapsody in Blue* (1945), DeCamp got a welcome departure from her maternal roles with an appearance in her first film noir, *Danger Signal* (1945). This film begins as a mercenary writer, Ronald Mason (Zachary Scott), is seen escaping from the window of a New York apartment building, leaving behind the lifeless body of a young housewife. Traveling cross-country to Los Angeles, Mason rents a room in the home of Hilda Fenchurch (Faye Emerson), a stenographer who is promptly attracted by Mason's charm. But soon after Mason proposes to Hilda, he learns that her younger sister Anne (Mona Freeman) will come into a sizable inheritance upon her marriage and he craftily transfers his affections to the younger sibling.

Discovering this betrayal, Hilda is unable to convince her naive sister of Mason's ulterior motives and, in desperation, confides in a psychiatrist friend, Dr. Silla (DeCamp). After meeting Mason, Dr. Silla is quickly able to grasp the key to his personality: "An interesting study, that man, rather complicated," she tells Hilda. "He spent his adult life in pursuit of women; at the same time he has no respect for them. Men like that can be fascinating and dangerous. They prey on women and very often the women love it." Determined to prevent Mason from exploiting her sister, Hilda steals a vial of poison from the lab of Dr. Andrew Lang (Bruce Bennett), then tricks Mason into meeting her at Dr. Silla's beach house, later telling him that she has poisoned the food he has just consumed. Meanwhile, having discovered Hilda's theft of the poison, Dr. Lang and Dr. Silla arrive at the beach house a short time later, only to learn that Hilda had been unable to carry out her plans for the murder. Vowing revenge on Hilda, Mason leaves, not knowing that he has been followed by Thomas Turner (John Ridgely), the husband of the murdered New York housewife. Spotting the man, Mason runs, but he trips over an exposed tree root and falls down a cliff to his death.

Singled out by several critics for her striking performance, DeCamp would later say that *Danger Signal* was the favorite of her three film noir appearances, citing her "smart and sophisticated" wardrobe and her enjoyment at playing the clever Viennese psychiatrist. She recalled, however, that the production was plagued with problems, beginning with a back injury sustained by Ann

Rosemary DeCamp

Blyth, who was originally cast in the role of Anne Fenchurch. After Blyth was replaced, Faye Emerson became engaged to Brigadier General Elliott Roosevelt, the son of President Franklin D. Roosevelt. "Every time [Elliott] flew over the sound stage we all had to turn out and wave, falling behind day after day," DeCamp said in 1994. "Then they — Faye and Elliott — went to Arizona for their wedding, adding another four days to the schedule. When filming resumed, our fabulous cinematographer, Jimmy Wong Howe, said he couldn't repair the honeymoon damage and Faye's face had to have a rest. Finally, we had almost caught up when President Roosevelt died, and Faye went off to Washington. In spite of all this, the film turned out very well — clever and interesting."

Never idle for long, DeCamp next appeared in a number of productions of varying quality, including *Too Young to Know* (1945), a limp drama about an Air Force captain who discovers that his ex-wife has given their child away; *Week-end at the Waldorf* (1945), a wildly successful remake of *Grand Hotel* (1932), with a star-studded cast that included Lana Turner, Van Johnson, Ginger Rogers and Walter Pigeon; *From This Day Forward* (1946), a tearjerker starring Joan Fontaine that was trashed by critics but embraced by the public; and *Two Guys from Milwaukee* (1946), an entertaining comedy with Dennis Morgan and Jack Carson.

Then, in her sole film appearance of 1947, DeCamp appeared in her second film noir, *Nora Prentiss*, starring Kent Smith and Ann Sheridan. Here, DeCamp portrays a San Francisco wife and mother of two teenagers who, content with her comfortable, middle-class existence, fails to see that her doctor husband, Richard (Smith), is growing increasingly discontented with his regimented life. While his wife is away on a weekend vacation with the children, Richard encounters a local nightclub singer, Nora Prentiss (Sheridan), and the two soon become embroiled in a torrid affair. But when Nora realizes that Richard will never leave his family, she ends the relationship, planning to take a singing job in New York. Desperate to keep Nora, Richard discovers a solution when a patient conveniently suffers a fatal heart attack in his office. He disguises the man's body as his own, places it in his automobile, sets the car ablaze and sends it plummeting over a cliff. He then joins Nora in New York, satisfied that his ploy has succeeded.

Before long, however, Richard learns that police have uncovered evidence pointing to his murder, and he becomes increasingly paranoid, fearing that he will be recognized. Mistakenly believing that Nora has been unfaithful, Richard attacks her nightclub boss, Phil Dinardo (Robert Alda), fleeing in a panic after he knocks Dinardo unconscious. But in his haste to escape, he becomes involved in a fiery auto accident which leaves his face horribly disfigured. Ironically, after the crash, police tie Richard to the murder of Dr. Talbot, and he is arrested for the death he faked in San Francisco. Tried and convicted, Richard refuses to reveal his true identity and accepts his sentence, grimly telling Nora: "You saw my children in court. You heard them talk about their father — that he was a good man. Their memory of him is a good memory. I want to keep it that way. Don't you see that I'm no possible good to anybody? You, my family, myself. Besides, I am guilty. I killed Richard Talbot."

Upon its release, *Nora Prentiss* was met with widely varying reviews — William R. Weaver of *Motion Picture Herald* stated that "the skill with which the story is unfolded gives it fascination," while the notoriously caustic Bosley Crowther of the *New York Times* labeled it "major picture-making at its worst." And the critic for *Variety*, who found that the film was "never quite believable," stated that "Rosemary DeCamp, as Smith's wife, and others in the cast do their best with limited material." After this film, DeCamp was off-screen for a year following the birth of her daughter, Valerie, then returned in *Night Unto Night* (1949), a talky time-waster starring Viveca Lindfors and Ronald Reagan. She had better luck with her next feature, *The Life of Riley* (1949), an amusing comedy based on the popular radio program. Later that year, she would reprise her role in the television version of *The Life of Riley* opposite Jackie Gleason. "Jackie stayed sober, he dieted, he was nice and he was awfully funny," DeCamp said of her experience with the famed comedian. "He was always so shiny and immaculate and — the odd things that you remember — he always smelled so nice."

In her next big-screen feature, DeCamp returned to her standard maternal role, this time playing Doris Day's mother in *Look for the Silver Lining* (1949), a musical biopic of Marilyn Miller, followed by *The Story of Seabiscuit* (1949), a fictionalized account of the legendary thoroughbred, *The Big Hangover* (1950), a silly box-office flop about a talking dog, *On Moonlight Bay* (1951), a mediocre musical which again cast DeCamp as Doris Day's mother, and *Night Into Morning* (1951), which focused on the lives and loves of university teachers. Although DeCamp played only a small role in the latter picture, she was praised by the reviewer for *Variety*, who said that her "single sequence as the wife is excellent."

The first of DeCamp's two 1952 releases, *Scandal Sheet*, would be her final entry in the realm of film noir, and one of the few negative portrayals of her career. This film focuses on the employees of the *New York Express*, a formerly respectable publication that has been turned into a sleazy but highly successful tabloid by editor Mark Chapman (Broderick Crawford). The paper's employees include Chapman's eager protégé Steve McCleary (John Derek) and his girlfriend, Julie Allison (Donna Reed). Julie objects to Chapman's unethical tactics to increase readership, which include a "Lonely Hearts Ball" where prizes are given to single couples who agree to marry. During the ball, Chapman is recognized by one of the attendees, Charlotte Grant (DeCamp), who insists that the editor meet her later. When he does, it is revealed that Chapman is actually Charlotte's husband, George Grant, who had deserted her 20 years earlier. Now living in a shabby one-room apartment, Charlotte shows her husband the scars from an unsuccessful suicide attempt, and bitterly spurns Chapman's offer of a quiet divorce and a comfortable settlement.

Infuriated when Charlotte threatens to expose his deception, Chapman shoves her, accidentally causing her death when she hits her head on a pipe. Frantic to cover all traces of his crime, he hastily removes the badge from the Lonely Hearts Ball that was pinned to her dress, pockets a pawn shop claim ticket he finds among her effects, then leaves her body in the bathtub, making it appear as if she slipped in the tub and drowned. The incident is later investigated by Steve McCleary, who unearths several clues that point to the woman's murder, and Chapman is forced to hide his guilt by encouraging Steve's efforts. Meanwhile, Chapman's role in the murder is discovered by Charlie Barnes (Henry O'Neill), a Pulitzer Prize–winning reporter whose career was ended by his alcoholism, but Chapman kills him before he can reveal what he has learned. Later, Steve and Julie manage to find the judge who had married Charlotte two decades earlier, and the judge identifies Chapman as her husband. Confronted in his office, Chapman draws a gun and is shot by police. "You remember I told you that someday you were going to have a really big story?" Chapman says to Steve before he dies. "Well, this one ought to do it. Write it up big, kid. It'll sell a lot of newspapers."

As the embittered Charlotte Grant, DeCamp turned in a standout portrayal of a woman scorned that was unlike any role she played before or since. Although she logged less than ten minutes of screen time, she managed to deliver a noteworthy performance, especially in the scene where Charlotte both verbally and physically attacks her erstwhile husband: "Turnabout is fair play," she says nastily. "Everything you worked for, grabbed for, ruined people to get — it's all going to die! I'm going to spread your story all over town. Mark Chapman, the great editor! Wife deserter — living under a false name for 20 years! What else did you cover up living under a phony name? Your public's sure going to love this. And the other papers, they'll cut you to ribbons with this information!" DeCamp would later say that this role was especially memorable for her because of the scene in which she is assaulted by her screen spouse: "I convinced Brod Crawford that he must really strike me in our big, vicious scene to make the whole plot hold together," she said in 1994. "He had hands like hams and hit me off the floor across the room onto a bed. Mother's Day that year came two days after the blow. I had a black eye, a swollen face, and could only turn my head very slowly."

After this role, the actress ended the year portraying the wife of William Powell in *Treasure of Lost Canyon* (1952), a box office disappointment about an orphaned youngster who is taken in by a kindly small-town doctor. This was followed by DeCamp's third appearance as the mother of Doris Day, this time in *By the Light of the Silvery Moon* (1953), an enjoyable musical that was the sequel to their earlier *On Moonlight Bay*. And the following year, in *So This Is Love* (1953), a biopic of soprano Grace Moore, DeCamp played the mother of Kathryn Grayson. "I was everybody's mother," DeCamp would later joke. "I have this non-aggressive motherly look."

By now, DeCamp's screen career was winding to a close and she would only appear in two films during the rest of the decade, *Many Rivers to Cross* (1955), a backwoods comedy that was a hit at the box office but panned by critics, and *Strategic Air Command* (1955), which starred James Stewart as a baseball player who gives up his career to join the Air Force. But this popular feature would be DeCamp's last big screen appearance for the next five years. Instead, she began focusing her energies on her highly successful television career, and from 1955 to 1960 would earn a new generation of fans with her role as the sister of Bob Cummings in *The Bob Cummings Show*. In addition to this program, DeCamp was a familiar presence on television through her commercials for Borax detergent, which aired during the popular Western series *Death Valley Days*. DeCamp's association with Borax, which began in 1952, would last for 25 years.

In 1960, DeCamp briefly returned to feature films in *13 Ghosts*, a silly movie about a family that moves into a haunted house populated by 12 ghosts who are looking to recruit the 13th. Produced and directed by William Castle, the film was notable mainly for a promotional gimmick that allowed audiences to view the film through a visual aid known as "Illusion-O." Several years later, in 1964, DeCamp joined another long-running television series, *That Girl*, on which she played — what else? — the mother of star Marlo Thomas. "I think Marlo is just simply amazing to be in every shot and look good and to hire the people, see all the rushes, and sign the checks," DeCamp told *TV Guide* in 1969. "She was a great producer with taste and know-how."

While continuing in her recurring role on *That Girl*, DeCamp managed to find time for a variety of pursuits. In 1965, she was appointed by President Lyndon B. Johnson to the Board of Governors of USO International, and later traveled to Pakistan, where she lectured on drama and poetry as part of a State Department cultural exchange program. She also authored the highly successful children's book *Here's Duke!* in 1962 and, for a year, wrote a regular column in a legal publication, the *Los Angeles Daily Journal*. Outside of these activities, DeCamp also enjoyed indulging her passion for copper enameling, which she exhibited at several successful shows, including one at the Los Angeles County Museum of Art in 1969. "I work in fields as fleeting as the wind — films, radio, and television — so I suppose my enameling is a striving for an immortality that is probably impossible," the actress explained. "But enamel is as permanent as a steel bridge or a marble statue. Enamels are forever."

Other than a small role in *Tora! Tora! Tora!* in 1969, which DeCamp says was completely cut from the final print, the actress has had only one feature film appearance in recent years, in *Saturday the 14th* (1981), a spoof of the *Friday the 13th* horror films. Her latest television appearance was a small role in the series *Hotel* in 1985, which DeCamp said she accepted "just to let people know I'm still alive." Around this time, the actress began to experience a partial hearing loss, but she viewed this condition with characteristic good humor: "Like most people, I only half-listened to people before this happened to me," DeCamp said. "But I've taught myself to pay strict attention to the other person, and I get along fine. Not so incidentally, I'm a better person because of it." Meanwhile, the talented character actress has not been idle. In 1991, she authored an audio book of her memoirs, entitled *Tales of Hollywood* ("And it's good!" DeCamp said), and as of 1997, she was at work on another book, a family journal called *Twice-Baked Potatoes*.

Although Rosemary DeCamp spent the majority of her career in supporting roles, and more likely than not appeared as someone's mother, she enjoyed a lengthy career that she herself termed as "remarkable."

"I can't believe I had such fun and met so many wonderful people who were kind and generous to me," DeCamp said in 1997. "I've been a character actress from the very beginning, and the only thing remarkable is my survival, as I have seen them come and go," DeCamp said. "I must admit it has been dull at times, but it was easier for me to survive in this business."

Film Noir Filmography

DANGER SIGNAL   *Director:* Robert Florey. *Producer:* William Jacobs. Released by Warner Bros., November 1945. *Running time:* 78 minutes. *Cast:* Faye Emerson, Zachary Scott, Dick Erdman, Rosemary DeCamp, Bruce Bennett, Mona Freeman, John Ridgely.

NORA PRENTISS   *Director:* Vincent Sherman. *Producer:* William Jacobs. Released by Warner Bros., February 1947. *Running time:* 111 minutes. *Cast:* Ann Sheridan, Kent Smith, Bruce Bennett, Robert Alda, Rosemary DeCamp, John Ridgely.

SCANDAL SHEET   *Director:* Phil Karlson. *Producer:* Edward Small. Released by Columbia, January 1952. *Running time:* 82 minutes. *Cast:* John Derek, Donna Reed, Broderick Crawford, Rosemary DeCamp, Henry O'Neill, Henry Morgan.

References

Ames, Walter. "Put Them All Together, Rosemary Spells Mother." *Los Angeles Times*, October 5, 1952.

Biography of Rosemary DeCamp. Columbia Broadcasting System, November 30, 1939.

Biography of Rosemary DeCamp. Universal Studios, January 17, 1944.

Dale, Jerry. Biography of Rosemary DeCamp. Hollywood, California: Alexander Korda Films, Inc., circa 1942.

"Everybody's Mother." *TV Guide*, September 1, 1956.

Hoaglin, Jess. "Rosemary DeCamp, Favorite Actress and Artist." *Hollywood Studio Magazine*, December 1980.

Hobson, Dick. "She Worked with Orson Welles When He Was Thin." *TV Guide*, July 5, 1969.

Schlaerth, J. Don. "A Mother First, Actress Second." *Buffalo Evening News*, July 19, 1969.

Sills, Claire. "Stars of the Late Show." *TV Radio Mirror*, July 1973.

Zeitlin, Ida. "The Girl with a Hundred Faces." *Photoplay*, March 1942.

Yvonne DeCarlo

Yvonne DeCarlo is perhaps best known to today's generation as the ghoulish vampire Lily from the campy television sitcom, *The Munsters*. But in her heyday during the 1940s and 1950s, the gray-eyed brunette was touted as "The Most Beautiful Girl in the World," and was showered with a variety of descriptions, from "an eyeful" to "one in a million." While she may not have been considered one of Hollywood's top talents, DeCarlo was a hit in a number of Westerns and exotic film roles, including the box office smash *Salome, Where She Danced* (1945), and she made her mark in two films noirs, one of which — *Criss Cross* (1949) — is among the finest examples of the era.

DeCarlo was born Margaret Yvonne Middleton on September 1, 1922, in a small town near Vancouver, British Columbia. When the actress — called Peggy by her family — was three years old, her New Zealand–born father left home, and she never saw him again. "As far as I am served by my memory, I had no father," DeCarlo stated in her autobiography, "and there was never a time when I took the void lightly." Peggy's childhood was characterized by poverty. Her mother Marie was frequently forced to go on relief, and they lived in a series of small flats, including one without furniture or even a stove, which rented for five dollars a month. At times they moved in with Marie's parents in Vancouver, where the mischievous youngster with the jet black pageboy would frequently buy penny candy with coins intended for the Sunday collection plate. On one occasion she was nabbed by the neighborhood grocer with several handfuls of treats hidden in her bloomers.

When Peggy was six years old, Marie began teaching her to dance, providing instruction in the Charleston and other popular dances. Herself a frustrated dancer, Marie had great dreams of stardom for her child. But although Peggy first enjoyed the lessons, they soon "became more serious, and far less fun," the actress would later recall. "[My mother] was usually a fun-loving, happy-go-lucky kind of person. But not when it came to my dancing." In addition to her hoofing abilities, Peggy also showed talent in other areas, winning a poetry contest sponsored by the Vancouver *Daily Sun* when she was 11 years old, and frequently writing and staging plays in her backyard. Several years later, Peggy joined the church choir and often gave impromptu concerts for approving family members.

In 1937, Marie and Peggy boarded a bus bound for Los Angeles, in search of an opportunity to start the teenager on the road to fame. Although the trip was unsuccessful, the two would travel annually to California for the next several years. In the meantime, Peggy studied classical dance at the British Columbia School of Dance in Vancouver and at Fanchon and Marco in Hollywood, a popular dance school whose clients included Judy Garland, Betty Grable and Jackie Coogan. During these years, Peggy also secured her first job, at the Palomar nightclub in Vancouver. Prior to her brief one-week run there, she and her mother decided on a new moniker for the budding dancer — Yvonne DeCarlo, derived from her middle name and her mother's maiden name.

It appeared that Marie's unwavering determination might have finally paid off when, at the age of 17, DeCarlo was chosen as first runner-up in the Miss Venice Beach bathing beauty contest. A short time later, she was hired for the chorus line at the Florentine Gardens in Hollywood, with a starting salary of $35 a week. She soon became a featured player, performing an exotic dance to Ravel's *Bolero* and singing the Portugese lyrics of "Babalu," which would later be popularized by Desi Arnaz. The club's owner, Nils T. Granlund, would later remember DeCarlo as "a shy, demure, silent brunette" who came to Hollywood with "looks, intense ambitions, and nothing else.... She remained a sweet, unspoiled kid and continued plodding patiently instead of seeking fame overnight when she saw what happened to the gals who tried to get there the quick way."

While performing at the Florentine Gardens, DeCarlo's dark, exotic looks caught the attention of a number of celebrities, including Franchot Tone, Orson Welles, Burgess Meredith, Sterling Hayden and bandleader Artie Shaw, who urged DeCarlo to quit her job at the Florentine Gardens and seek a career in film. DeCarlo followed his advice, signing with agent Jack Pomeroy, who quickly got her a role as a bathing beauty in *Harvard, Here I Come* (1942), described by DeCarlo as "a dreadful B movie ... but I didn't know it was dreadful." The starlet only had a single line of dialogue, for which she was paid $25, but DeCarlo stated that she was "certain I was hell-bent for stardom."

DeCarlo's brief film debut did little to jump-start her career in pictures, so she returned to the nightclub scene, landing a job with Earl Carroll's show at the Aquarius Theatre. But her stay with Carroll would not last. While working at the Aquarius Theatre, DeCarlo violated her contract by accepting a bit part in *This Gun for Hire*, starring Veronica Lake and Alan Ladd. When Carroll discovered DeCarlo wearing motion picture makeup, she was fired on the spot. "I was scuttled, dumped, banished forever," DeCarlo recalled.

Dejected but not defeated, the actress returned to her former job at the Florentine Gardens, where she was allowed to continue her quest for a film career. She was soon appearing in short subjects for the Soundies Music Corporation, and can be spotted in the background of several feature films, including *Road to Morocco* (1942), starring Bob Hope and Bing Crosby, *Lucky Jordan* (1942), with Alan Ladd, and *Youth on Parade* (1943), a run-of-the-mill musical starring Martha O'Driscoll. She was then signed to a six-month contract with Paramount, which promptly loaned her out to Monogram Studios for *Rhythm Parade* (1943), in which she played — ironically — a Florentine Gardens dancer. She next appeared as a secretary in *The Crystal Ball* (1943) starring Ray Milland, with whom she had a brief affair, and was among a crowd of partygoers in a café scene in *For Whom the Bell Tolls* (1943), with Gary Cooper and Ingrid Bergman.

After several more appearances as an extra, DeCarlo finally won a featured role in her ninth film of 1943, *The Deerslayer*, in which she portrayed an

Indian princess. Of this film, DeCarlo would later state: "There have been several movie versions of *The Deerslayer* and this was probably the least memorable, but at the time I was thrilled to be in it." But after this somewhat promising stint, DeCarlo returned to brief appearances in a variety of films, including a bit as a native girl in *The Story of Dr. Wassell* (1944) and a hatcheck girl in *Bring On the Girls* (1944). In between these parts, DeCarlo was kept busy by the studio posing for cheesecake poses, and being labeled with such laughable titles as "The Girl G.I.s in Italy Would Most Like to Read a Map With."

At the end of 1944, Paramount dropped DeCarlo from her contract, and just when it seemed as if she would never achieve her dreams of stardom, she was given the role she had been waiting for—the title character in Universal Pictures' *Salome, Where She Danced* (1945). The film's producer, Walter Wanger, had been struck by DeCarlo's resemblance to his wife, Joan Bennett and, after two screen tests, awarded DeCarlo the part, along with the distinction of "The Most Beautiful Girl in the World." DeCarlo was promptly signed to a stock contract with Universal at a pay of $150 a week, a figure that she said was "like a fortune to me."

While most critics panned *Salome*, the film was a huge money-maker for Universal and DeCarlo was hailed in a number of publications, including *Variety*, which called her "a looker with lots of talent" and the *Los Angeles Examiner*, whose reviewer wrote that DeCarlo "casts the most torrid shadow in Technicolor of any personality in years. Not only is she completely equipped to inspire wolf whistles, but she is something new in the line of potential stars." Five years after her departure from Vancouver, Yvonne DeCarlo was finally on her way.

With her star on the rise, DeCarlo was given new attention by Universal, which enrolled her with the John Robert Powers modeling organization for lessons on how to "walk, talk, stand, sit, eat and drink," DeCarlo recounted. "I had been taught ... how to choose the right piece of silverware at the right time, how to hold a wine glass, everything—including the proper way to eat soup." She was next cast in the leading role in another box office hit, *Frontier Gal* (1945), and her portrayal of a dance hall hostess was commended by the critic for *Time*, who wrote: "The picture's chief excitement is Yvonne DeCarlo, a vigorous, shapely actress who looks equally luscious in sequins or a fringed deerskin skirt."

Along with her rapidly increasing popularity, DeCarlo's personal life began to heat up as well when she became involved with Howard Hughes, whom she met during "Yvonne DeCarlo Night" at the Palomar, the nightclub where she'd had her first, brief job as a showgirl. DeCarlo said she first found Hughes to be "remarkably sad, [but] didn't take very long at all for me to fall in love with him." But Hughes was also involved with a number of other Hollywood luminaries, including Ava Gardner and Linda Darnell, and although

Yvonne DeCarlo

the actress was eager to marry the eccentric billionaire, she admitted that Hughes "never even publicly acknowledged that we were dating." Over time, their heated romance died, but DeCarlo would always remember him as one of the most important loves of her life.

Career-wise, DeCarlo was next cast as an exotic dancer in *Song of Scheherazade* (1947), which was dismissed by critics as "the worst nonsense that Hollywood has cooked up about a composer." DeCarlo herself fared no better, with one reviewer stating that she "brings very little color to a conventional heroine's role and her dancing is not yet up to standards one would expect from the premiere danseuse of a first-rate production." But DeCarlo's next picture, the film noir thriller *Brute Force* (1947), would take her far from the "sand and sandals" parts that she was becoming known for, and offer the actress her best role to date.

Brute Force is a gritty tale set in a men's prison populated by a motley crew of quirky personages, including an inmate with a life sentence who plans a prison break "every Tuesday." The inmates are continuously brutalized by a sadistic guard, Capt. Munsey (Hume Cronyn), and, no longer able to endure their inhumane treatment, the five inmates of one cell plot an elaborate escape. On the wall of the cell hangs a pin-up girl that reminds each man of the woman he left behind. One of the convicts, Joe Collins (Burt Lancaster), thinks of the sweet wheelchair-bound girl who remained blissfully oblivious to his secret life of crime, while Tom Lister (Whit Bissell) ruefully recalls embezzling company funds so that he could purchase a fur coat for his unhappy wife. And Soldier (Howard Duff) dreams of returning to the small town in Italy where he met his wife, Gina (DeCarlo). A flashback shows Soldier taking food to Gina and her father during the war, when military police show up looking for him. When Gina's father refuses to cover for Soldier, Gina shoots an officer, killing him, and Soldier takes the blame for the crime.

Despite the meticulous planning of the prison break, Capt. Munsey uncovers the plot and the film concludes with a violent climax, in which each of the men are killed, along with Munsey, who is tossed from a tower into a swarm of angry inmates. The film ends with a rueful observation from the prison doctor: "Nobody escapes. Nobody ever really escapes."

During shooting for *Brute Force*, DeCarlo became involved with her on-screen husband, Howard Duff, and although she had little in common with the volatile, heavy-drinking actor, the two were engaged to be married by the time the production ended. But DeCarlo later confessed that "with the little diamond ring on the third finger I began to get that old trapped feeling," and before long, the relationship was over. However, the beautiful actress was not alone for long. Soon after her break with Duff, she fell in love with Prince Abdorezza Pahlavi of Iran, and later said that she "was still young and naive enough to believe in fairy tales and could see nothing to keep my prince and me from riding off into the sunset as man and wife." Although the relationship would last nearly five years, DeCarlo could not imagine living in Iran's politically explosive climate and eventually conceded that marriage to the prince was an "impossible dream."

Meanwhile, after her appearance in the highly acclaimed *Brute Force*, DeCarlo was cast in a series of forgettable pictures, including *Slave Girl* (1947), a desert epic in which she portrayed a mysterious dancer, *Casbah* (1948), a poorly received remake of *Algiers* (1938), and *Calamity Jane and Sam Bass* (1949), of which Howard Barnes of the *New York Herald Tribune* wrote: "Miss DeCarlo is properly swaggering ... but she always looks as though she had just come from a beauty parlor, even when she is shooting it out with the law on a craggy hillside." It wasn't until her starring turn in the film noir shocker *Criss Cross* (1949) that DeCarlo would play a role that would properly showcase her considerable dramatic talents.

The story in this aptly named film unfolds as Steve Thompson (Burt Lancaster) returns to his hometown of Los Angeles, from which he had fled a year earlier following a bitter divorce from his wife, Anna (DeCarlo). Although Steve believes himself immune to his ex-wife's charms, the two soon begin dating again, but their reconciliation ends when Steve learns that Anna has secretly married Slim Dundee (Dan Duryea), a gambler with underworld connections. Confronting Anna with her betrayal, Steve is moved when she tearfully confides her unhappiness with her new spouse, and the two renew their affair in secret.

Before long, Slim catches the couple together in his house, and Steve hastily concocts a tale centering on his plan to rob the armored car company where he works and his need for Slim's assistance. Slim agrees to the scheme, in exchange for half of the profits, but during the robbery, an employee of the armored car company is killed, and Steve kills two of the men in Slim's gang. Although the bankroll in the armored car is not recovered, Steve is hailed throughout the city as a hero. Meanwhile, Anna disappears with the stolen cash. Steve is abducted by one of Slim's underlings, but he bribes the man to take him to a cottage where Anna is waiting. Realizing that the man will inform Slim of their hideout, Anna prepares to leave, taking the money with her; "How far could I get with you?" she asks bluntly. "What do you want me to do, let him get us both? You have to watch out for yourself— that's the way it is, I'm sorry. What do you want me to do, throw away all this money?" Before she is able to flee, however, Slim arrives and shoots them both. Anna and Steve die in each other's arms, and the film closes with the sound of approaching sirens.

Upon the release of *Criss Cross*, the critic for *Variety* wrote that DeCarlo was "perfectly cast as a gal who likes high living and doesn't care who pays for it." And while the reviewer for the *New York Times* labeled DeCarlo's performance as "uneven," he also acknowledged that the actress "is trying something different as Anna, a dangerous dish who wants to have her cake and eat it, too. The change is welcome." But after her appearance in this film, the actress returned to the familiar roles that had been the staple of her career, including an Arabian princess in *The Desert Hawk* (1950), which prompted *New York Times* critic Bosley Crowther to comment: "Somehow we have the feeling we've seen this a hundred times before." Following this film, DeCarlo and Universal reached an agreement that required the actress to appear in only one picture for the studio each year, while allowing her to freelance for other studios and accept nightclub and other musical engagements. DeCarlo promptly took advantage of this new arrangement, appearing in 1950 with Donald O'Connor at a Berlin nightclub and making her operatic stage debut the following year at the Hollywood Bowl. Also in 1951, DeCarlo recorded "Take It or Leave It" for Capitol Records and participated in a nine-performance singing tour in Israel.

But while DeCarlo was engaging in a variety of performing activities, her film choices improved little as a result of her freelancing privileges. Although she considered *Hotel Sahara* (1951), a British comedy with Peter Ustinov, to be one of her favorites, most of DeCarlo's roles during this period were standard fare, including a wagon train singer in *Tomahawk* (1951), a saloon singer in *Scarlet Angel* (1952) and a Polynesian girl in *Hurricane Smith* (1952).

Between films, the comely actress found time to engage in an active romantic life. Her dates during this period included the Ninth Earl of Lanesborough, Spanish actor Mario Cabre (who had previously carried on a much-publicized affair with actress Ava Gardner) and Prince Aly Khan, who had recently separated from wife Rita Hayworth. The French and Italian press made much of her involvement with the prince (one newspaper featured a photo caption reading: "Watch Out Rita, I've Got Your Man"), but DeCarlo would later admit that she "settled for remaining Aly's friend and lover for as long as it was convenient for both of us, happier with it that way because at least I knew where I stood."

In 1953, DeCarlo appeared in four features: *Sombrero*, a big-budget MGM film that flopped at the box office; *Sea Devils*, a mini-epic in which she starred as a British spy; *Fort Algiers*, with the actress playing a French spy masquerading as a nightclub singer; and the best of her releases of the year, *The Captain's Paradise*, a witty comedy for which DeCarlo was praised by *New York Times* critic Bosley Crowther as "wonderfully candid and suggestive." DeCarlo wound up the year with her television debut on NBC's *Ford Theatre*, and later appeared in an episode of the network's *Backbone of America* series.

The following year saw DeCarlo's appearance in another quartet of films: *Border River* (1954), *Passion* (1954), *The Contessa's Secret* (1954) and another of DeCarlo's favorites, *Tonight's the Night* (1954), a slapstick comedy starring David Niven. But by now, with Hollywood concentrating on bombshells like Marilyn Monroe, DeCarlo found herself being offered only minor roles in low-profile films. In 1955, she played opposite two former beaus: Sterling Hayden in *Shotgun* and Howard Duff in *Flame of the Islands*, and in 1956, she continued her performances in forgettable pictures, including *Magic Fire*, a dull drama that was slammed by one critic as "romanticized slush ... overloaded with pretentiousness and bad acting."

DeCarlo's declining career received a much-needed lift when she won the role of Sephora in Cecil B. DeMille's big-budget epic, *The Ten Command-ments* (1956). For her performance as the patient, understanding wife of Moses, the actress was applauded by Bosley Crowther as "notably good in a severe role." After the filming of *The Ten Commandments*, DeCarlo began dating Bob Morgan, a stuntman on the picture who had been recently widowed. After a courtship of less than a year, the two were married on November 21, 1955. The following year, on July 7, 1956, DeCarlo gave birth to her first child, Bruce Ross Morgan. His godfather was Cecil B. DeMille.

DeCarlo's first film after the birth of her son was *Band of Angels* (1957), in which she portrayed the daughter of a Kentucky planter who discovers that her mother was a slave. Featuring a cast that included Clark Gable and Sidney Poitier, the picture was billed as the new *Gone with the Wind*, but it fell far short of expectations and was panned by critics such as William Zinsser of the *New York Herald Tribune*, who wrote, "Fanciers of awful movies won't want to miss this one." *Band of Angels* would mark DeCarlo's last starring role and the irrevocable decline of her film career. During production of the film, DeCarlo became pregnant again, and on November 14, 1957, gave birth to her second son, Michael.

Seeking a boost to her career, DeCarlo formed a production company, Vancouver Productions, and announced plans to make a Western and an outer space comedy. These projects, however, would never get off the ground: "It seemed like a terrific idea at the time," DeCarlo would later explain, "and we had great expectations, but unfortunately expectations are never enough. We couldn't get it all together, and our heralded corporation eventually faded into nothing more than a vague memory." Instead, the actress accepted the role of Mary Magdalene in an Italian biblical picture, *La Spada e la croce* (1959), after which one reviewer referred to DeCarlo as "that ex–most beautiful girl in the world." This clunker was followed by what would be her last film for the next four years, *Timbuktu* (1959), a desert drama blasted in *The Monthly Film Bulletin* for its "leaden-footed performances, the pompous dialogue and the settings of glaring artificiality."

For the next several years, DeCarlo stayed busy playing nightclub engagements, and guesting on a number of television programs, including *Bonanza*, *Adventures in Paradise* and *Follow the Sun*. In 1961, she was scheduled to star in a pilot for a new television series, *Scheherazade and a Thousand and One Nights*, but when these plans fell through, DeCarlo accepted the starring role of Frenchy in a road version of *Destry Rides Again*. Of her performance in the successful play, Virgil Miers of the *Dallas Times Herald* raved, "Miss DeCarlo, it turns out, has been hiding an admirable musical theater voice in a screen career of playing harem beauties and adventuresses. This ... is a vibrant actress with a singing voice that projects, and with fine comedy timing."

Meanwhile, DeCarlo's marriage to Bob Morgan was on shaky ground. The couple quarreled frequently and "seemed incapable of compromise — we just kept knocking our heads together against a wall of incompatibility," DeCarlo said. But in 1962, their failing relationship witnessed its greatest challenge when Morgan was run over by a train while doing stunt work on *How the West Was Won*, suffering the loss of his left leg. Of the fateful accident, DeCarlo would later say: "Just days earlier I had been seriously planning divorce. Now, nothing mattered but for Bob to survive this catastrophe. My friends praised me for standing by Bob during his period of crisis, but to have done anything other than what little I did would have been unthinkable." However, in the years that followed Morgan's tragic accident, their marriage would continued to deteriorate, and in 1974, DeCarlo would file for divorce.

To raise funds for Morgan's costly medical bills, DeCarlo threw herself into her career, accepting small club dates, summer theater performances and a small role in one of her better-received films, *McLintock!* (1963), a Western comedy starring John Wayne. As DeCarlo stated, her "luck began to change for the better" after the Wayne film. She next landed a cameo in *A Global Affair* (1964), earning praise from one critic for playing her role with "oomph," then portrayed a saloon singer in a mediocre Western, *Law of the Lawless* (1964), and was featured in a tour of Carl Reiner's hit Broadway comedy *Enter Laughing*, which DeCarlo said gave her "the kind of prestige and exposure I needed."

Then in September 1964, DeCarlo took on the role that would endear her to a new generation of audiences — the part of Lily Munster, a 156-year-old vampire, in the CBS television series *The Munsters*. DeCarlo stated that she originally had misgivings about playing the role, for which she would wear green makeup, black fingernails and a long black wig with a wide silver streak, "but the money was good, and it was comedy — that was what really clinched it for me." The series was an instant hit, and DeCarlo said she did "whatever was necessary to keep the Munster image alive," including customizing the family car with coffin handles, spiderweb hubcaps and a solid brass wolf's head on the hood. Capitalizing on the popularity of the series, Universal Pictures produced a feature-length version, *Munster, Go Home* (1966), which included most of the cast from the television show, but the film was a box office disappointment. After two seasons on the air, the television series was cancelled. Although there were reports that DeCarlo had become increasingly dissatisfied with her role, she states in her autobiography that "nobody seems to know" why the program was dropped. Despite its short run, the program is still shown in syndication throughout the country.

After *The Munsters* was cancelled in 1966, DeCarlo performed in *Pal Joey* at Melodyland in Anaheim, California, and toured the summer tent theatrical circuit in *Catch Me If You Can*. She next played yet another dance hall performer in *Hostile Guns* (1967), a Western that was notable primarily for the sudden death of silent screen star Francis X. Bushman, who was slated to play a featured role. DeCarlo didn't fare much better in her next two films, *The*

Power (1968), from which her cameo performance was cut when it was released abroad, and *Arizona Bushwackers* (1968), another poorly received Western.

Taking a break from her waning film career, DeCarlo continued to find success on stage, touring the United States and Canada in the title role of *Hello Dolly* and receiving acclaim from *Variety* for her "proper verve for the role." She also starred in a road production of *Cactus Flower* and returned to pictures in 1970, playing a small role in a spy melodrama, *The Delta Factor*, starring Christopher George and Yvette Mimieux.

The following year, DeCarlo was given special billing in *Follies*, a Broadway musical by Stephen Sondheim in which she performed the show-stopper "I'm Still Here." The actress received mostly favorable reviews for her role of an ex-showgirl, and the play ran for 522 performances. During the run of the show, DeCarlo found time to appear in another film, *The Seven Minutes* (1971), a box office flop based on the trashy best-selling novel by Irving Wallace. Of the cast of veteran actors that included John Carradine and David Brian, the critic from the *New Yorker* reported that "only Yvonne DeCarlo emerges unscathed, playing the lovely older movie star she happens to be." After the close of *Follies* in 1972, DeCarlo continued her stage career, replacing Cyd Charisse in *No, No, Nanette* and appearing the following year at the Off Broadway Theatre in San Diego in *Ben Bagley's Decline and Fall of the Entire World as Seen Through the Eyes of Cole Porter*.

Admitting later that her need for money had caused her to become less discriminating in her choice of roles, DeCarlo returned to television in 1974, playing small roles in *The Girl on the Late, Late Show* and *The Mark of Zorro*, and appeared the following year in three feature films: the never-released *Arizona Slim*, *It Seemed Like a Good Idea at the Time*, in which she portrayed the gun-toting mother of Stefanie Powers, and *Blazing Stewardesses*, a tasteless comedy which made much of DeCarlo's ample bosom. She also appeared in *Dames at Sea* in Windsor, Ontario, and *The Sound of Music* in Dallas, Texas. In 1976, she had a cameo in *Won Ton Ton: The Dog Who Saved Hollywood*, joining a cast of Hollywood veterans that included Virginia Mayo, Joan Blondell, Dorothy Lamour, Walter Pidgeon, Johnny Weissmuller, Alice Faye and Rudy Vallee. Later that year, she was featured in an Argentinian-made melodrama, *La Casa de las sombras*.

As the 1970s drew to a close, DeCarlo appeared in a number of low-budget horror films, including *Satan's Cheerleaders* (1977), in which she played the devil-worshipping wife of sheriff John Ireland, *Fuego Negro* (1978), which focused on a voodoo cult, and *The Silent Scream* (1979), where she played a woman who imprisons her insane daughter in her attic. And in 1981, DeCarlo reprised her role as Lily Munster for the NBC-TV movie *The Munsters' Revenge*. More recently, however, she has appeared in films that, while not box office blockbusters, have at least been of higher quality, including *American Gothic* (1987) and *Oscar* (1991), a screwball farce starring Sylvester Stallone.

Between these films, DeCarlo found time to pen her autobiography, *Yvonne*, published in 1987, in which she offered a fascinatingly candid account of her life and loves.

DeCarlo has been off-screen since the early 1990s, but her exotic beauty and vivacious acting style live on. In a screen career that spanned nearly a half-century, the actress demonstrated a flair for comedy as well as drama, appearing in more than 80 films. She may always be best remembered for her over-the-top portrayal of the campy vampire in *The Munsters*, but DeCarlo proved in such films as *Criss Cross* and *The Ten Commandments* that she was more than just a pretty face.

Film Noir Filmography

BRUTE FORCE *Director:* Jules Dassin. *Producer:* Mark Hellinger. Released by Universal-International, June 1947. *Running time:* 95 minutes. *Cast:* Burt Lancaster, Hume Cronyn, Charles Bickford, Ann Blyth, Yvonne DeCarlo, Ella Raines, Anita Colby, Sam Levene, Howard Duff, Art Smith, Roman Bohnen, John Hoyt, Richard Gaines, Frank Puglia, Jeff Corey, Whit Bissell.

CRISS CROSS *Director:* Robert Siodmak. *Producer:* Michel Kraike. Released by Universal-International, January 1949. *Running time:* 88 minutes. *Cast:* Burt Lancaster, Yvonne DeCarlo, Dan Duryea, Stephen McNally, Richard Long.

References

Bawden, J.E.A. "Yvonne DeCarlo." *Films in Review*, April 1977.

Broeske, Pat. "In Search of ... Yvonne DeCarlo." *Los Angeles Times*, January 13, 1991.

Cassa, Anthony. "Yvonne DeCarlo." *Hollywood Studio Magazine*, May 1982.

Crivello, Kirk. "Whatever Happened to the Most Beautiful Girls in the World?" *Film Fan Monthly*, July-August 1970.

DeCarlo, Yvonne. "Mistakes I've Made in Love." *Silver Screen*, April 1949.

_____, with Doug Warren. *Yvonne: An Autobiography*. New York: St. Martin's Press, 1987.

Deere, Dorothy. "Yvonne, Where She Danced." *Photoplay*, March 1946.

Eaton, Harriet. "Blue Jeans and Mink." *Photoplay*, January 1947.

Lopez, Albert. "Yvonne DeCarlo: Hollywood's Bad Girl." *Hollywood Studio Magazine: Then and Now*, June 1989.

"Once and Future Follies." *Time*, May 3, 1971.

"One Man's Mambo." *Collier's*, June 13, 1953.

Roura, Phil and Tom Poster. "The Loves of Yvonne DeCarlo." *New York Daily News*, July 25, 1985.

_____. "People." *New York Daily News*, March 25, 1987.

St. Johns, Elaine. "Dusky Dreamer." *Photoplay*, September 1948.

Faye Emerson

Faye Emerson was probably best known as the daughter-in-law of President Franklin D. Roosevelt and, later, as one of the most popular personalities on television. With her striking features and hint of subtle sexiness, the petite blonde actress was considered one of the more interesting leading ladies at a time when most films were essentially geared toward men. While never a superstar of the silver screen, Emerson appeared in 30 feature films during her career—all but two for Warner Bros.—and was featured in four unique examples from the film noir era: *The Mask of Dimitrios* (1944), *Danger Signal* (1945), *Nobody Lives Forever* (1946) and *Guilty Bystander* (1950).

Born Faye Margaret Emerson, the "First Lady of Television" entered the world in Elizabeth, Louisiana, on July 8, 1917, a date that she, unlike many a screen actress, never tried to conceal. ("No sense in being coy about it," she would later say. "Everybody knows it anyway.") In 1918, Emerson's parents and her four siblings moved to El Paso, Texas, but a year later, when she was only three, her parents divorced. Her father remarried and moved to Chicago, her mother relocated to San Diego, California, and the remainder of Emerson's childhood was spent shuttling between the two. After several years, Emerson was enrolled in the Academy of San Luis Rey, a convent boarding school in Oceanside, California, and later attended Point Loma High School where—despite her ambition to become a writer—she took part in several school plays and was encouraged by a teacher to seek an acting career. By all accounts a popular and vivacious student, Emerson took her instructor's advice and continued acting at San Diego State College, joining the summer stock group at the St. James Repertory Theater in Carmel at age 18. A short time later, she became a member of the San Diego Players, and for her first play with the group, *Russet Mantle* (1935), the budding actress was paid $15 a week.

Over the next several years, Emerson continued to expand her acting repertoire, appearing in such productions as *The Taming of the Shrew, Holiday* and *Tonight at 8:30*. In October 1938, Emerson's professional activities were briefly interrupted when she married William Wallace Crawford, Jr., a San Diego automobile dealer, but although the couple would have a son the following year, the marriage would be over by 1942. Meanwhile, Emerson's stage experience was leading her closer to Hollywood. While appearing in *Here Today* in 1941, at San Diego's Municipal Theatre, she was offered contracts from both Paramount and Warner Bros. Studios, and eventually chose to sign on as a contract player with Warners, where she would remain throughout her screen career.

During the remainder of 1941, Emerson was seen in minor roles in seven films, including *Manpower*, a cliché-ridden drama with a top-notch cast that included Marlene Dietrich, Edward G. Robinson and George Raft; *Bad Men of Missouri*, an action-packed Western starring Dennis Morgan and Arthur Kennedy; and *Affectionately Yours*, a rather dismal comedy with Dennis Morgan and Merle Oberon. Emerson began landing larger roles in 1942, but the films were mostly box office bombs, including *Murder in the Big House*, a tiresome melodrama about reporters who uncover a murder ring inside a state penitentiary, and *Lady Gangster*, considered to be one of the worst pictures of the year, in which Emerson portrayed the title role of a moll who is shown the error of her ways. The latter film was so poor, in fact, that its director, Robert Florey, ordered his name removed from the release, and the directorial credit went, instead, to the fictional "Florian Roberts." Of the actress's next set of releases, the best were *The Hard Way* (1942), the story of a talented stage performer and her ruthlessly ambitious sister, and *Air Force* (1943), one of the most riveting aviation pictures of the period. But the actress was woefully miscast as a native girl in *The Desert Song* (1943), starring Dennis Morgan, and fared little better in *Find the Blackmailer* (1943), an uninteresting programmer starring Jerome Cowan.

Emerson's failure to land starring roles in first-rate pictures could be attributed to the fact that she'd had no agent since arriving in Hollywood and seemed content to accept the assignments given her by studio heads. "I don't believe in promoting myself," she said. "It seems to me that if you have talent and are in a position to get ahead, you shouldn't push your luck. If I knew what I was and what I could do, what power I possess, I would go to the front office and use that knowledge to get better things for myself. But I'm just finding out about my potential worth to the studio. For the time being, I'm satisfied to let them run my career." Although she never lacked for screen assignments, Emerson continued to play a series of secondary roles in films of varying quality, such as *Destination Tokyo* (1944), a box-office smash starring Cary Grant and John Garfield; *In Our Time* (1944), a well-meaning but unsuccessful romance set in pre-war Poland; *Uncertain Glory* (1944), a poorly conceived Errol Flynn vehicle about a condemned Frenchman who becomes a Resistance hero; and *The Mask of Dimitrios* (1944), her first film noir.

This fascinating tale begins in Istanbul, where the body of a murdered man washes up on shore, containing identification which reveals that he is a notorious criminal, Dimitrios Makropoulos (Zachary Scott). When a detective story writer, Cornelius Leyden (Peter Lorre), is shown Dimitrios' dead body, he becomes intrigued and sets out to reconstruct the man's life. Leyden learns that Dimitrios' first crime took place in Smyrna, where he murdered a local merchant, then allowed a beggar to be blamed and executed for the deed. Traveling to Sofia, Leyden is introduced to Irana Preveza (Emerson), who had known and loved Dimitrios 15 years before. ("I've known many men," Irana tells Leyden. "But I've been afraid of only one. Dimitrios.") From Irana, Leyden learns that Dimitrios had been involved with an assassination attempt on the country's premier. Meanwhile, Leyden discovers that he is being trailed by Mr. Peters (Sydney Greenstreet), who had spent time in prison after being betrayed by Dimitrios in connection with a jewelry smuggling ring in Paris. Peters directs Leyden to Paris to meet with Wladislaw Grodek (Victor Francen), who had been double-crossed by Dimitrios in their successful scheme to steal government secrets.

In Paris, Leyden meets again with Peters, who reveals that Dimitrios is still alive and, having faked his own death, is now working in the lucrative position as director of the Eurasian Credit Trust. Seeking revenge on Dimitrios for his betrayal, Peters proposes that they blackmail the criminal for one million francs. Dimitrios delivers the money as promised, but in an attempt to kill his blackmailers, he is murdered by Peters, who tells Leyden, "I did what I had to do."

Although Emerson was praised in the *New York Times* as "good in a minor role" in *Dimitrios*, the actress had begun to tire of her increasingly insipid assignments, and reportedly stormed the front office at Warners to demand better parts. Studio executives responded by casting her in *Hotel Berlin* (1945), which chronicled the fates of a diverse group of people during the last days of World War II, and she was hailed by critics for her warm performance of the resident hostess, Tili Weiler. But her professional career took a back seat to her personal life during the filming of this picture when, on December 3, 1944, on the rim of the Grand Canyon, Emerson married Brigadier General Elliott Roosevelt, the son of Franklin and Eleanor Roosevelt. The two had first met at a Hollywood party in 1943, and found that Emerson's volatile enthusiasm was a favorable complement to the docile Army man. After the marriage, however, Emerson was frequently angered to find marquees advertising "Mrs. Elliott Roosevelt," and heatedly responded to suggestions that she had married the president's son to further her career. "As for my marriage to Elliott doing anything for my career, that's a laugh," she told one reporter. "I was all set for star billing before the marriage. The studio forgot to make the announcement until after the marriage, that's all. I could spit in their eye."

In addition to the aspersions cast on her film career, Emerson also faced criticism in the press following an incident concerning her dog, who displaced three servicemen on a flight from England. The episode caused a furor in the press and even led to a Congressional investigation. "So much was made of the dog incident, and very little was said about our being completely exonerated after the Congressional investigation," the actress said in a 1945 interview. "Such things are rather dismaying, but I, personally, am reconciled to the fact that they must be experienced under these circumstances, and have made up my mind that they will not affect me personally, or the life of Elliott and myself together."

Back at Warners, Emerson appeared in back-to-back films noirs, *Danger Signal* (1945) and *Nobody Lives Forever* (1946). In the first, Emerson portrays Hilda Fenchurch, a stenographer who falls in love with Ronald Mason (Zachary Scott), a charming, urbane writer. Unbeknownst to Hilda, Mason is being sought by the husband of a young housewife who was found dead in a New York apartment. Although a suicide note written by the woman had been found on the scene, her husband suspects Mason of murdering her. Mason proposes to Hilda, but insists that she keep their engagement a secret. Meanwhile, Mason transfers his affections to Hilda's younger sister, Anne (Mona Freeman), when he learns that the girl will inherit a sizable trust fund when she marries.

Before long, Hilda discovers her fiancé's betrayal, but she is unable to convince her impressionable sister that Mason is not all that he appears to be. Desperate, Hilda confides in a psychiatrist friend, Dr. Silla (Rosemary DeCamp), telling her: "All I can think about is how to stop his lying. I've got to destroy what he's done to us. He isn't fit to live." Later, Hilda steals a vial of poison from the lab of Dr. Andrew Lang (Bruce Bennett), then tricks Mason into meeting her at Dr. Silla's beach house, where she tells him that she has poisoned his food. Having discovered Hilda's theft of the poison, Dr. Lang and Dr. Silla arrive at the beach house a short time later, only to learn that Hilda had been psychologically unable to carry out her plans for the murder. Vowing revenge, Mason leaves, but Thomas Turner (John Ridgely), the husband of the New York housewife, has followed him. Mason runs from the man, but trips over an exposed tree root and falls over a cliff to his death.

After being noted for her "realistic" performance in *Danger Signal*, Emerson appeared in her third film noir, *Nobody Lives Forever*, starring John Garfield and Geraldine Fitzgerald. As this feature begins, Garfield's character, a notorious gambler by the name of Nick Blake, is returning to his home in New York after being injured in the war. Eager to see his girlfriend Toni (Emerson), Nick soon discovers that she has used his savings of $50,000 to establish a nightclub with her new lover, Chet King (Robert Shayne). Confronting King at the club, Nick forces the man to return his money, then moves to the West Coast with his sidekick Al Doyle (George Tobias).

In Los Angeles, an old friend, Pop Gruber (Walter Brennan), convinces Nick to join forces with a local hood, Doc Ganson (George Coulouris), in a plan to extort money from a wealthy widow, Gladys Halvorsen (Fitzgerald). Nick ingratiates himself into the widow's life, but he soon falls in love with the sweet, warm-hearted woman and finds that he is no longer willing to carry out the scheme. He plans to use his own money to pay off Doc Ganson, but Toni re-emerges in his life and suspects his motives: "Listen, I know Nick from every angle," she tells Al. "Maybe he can kid you, but not me. Nick paying off with his own dough and passing up a couple of million bucks? That guy hasn't been overseas that long. I can't wait to see Doc's face when he hears about this." True to her word, Toni alerts Ganson, who refuses Nick's payoff money and kidnaps Gladys, holding her for ransom at a deserted pier. Nick, Al and Pop go to her rescue, and Doc is killed during a gun battle, but Pop is mortally wounded as well. After Pop's death, Nick tells Gladys: "I guess his time was up. Nobody lives forever — that's the way he looked at it anyway. He said, 'Nick, life goes by so fast. You wake up one morning and you find you're old.' He was worried about us wasting time."

Although *Nobody Lives Forever* was only mildly successful, Emerson was singled out by several critics, including Bosley Crowther of the *New York Times*, who noted her "showy" role, and the reviewer for *Variety*, who wrote, "Faye Emerson does well as a past love of Garfield's who almost ruins his romance." The actress followed this film with an appearance in *Her Kind of Man* (1946), but after claiming that the film was based on "possibly the worst script ever written," she walked out on her contract. It was reported that her agreement with the studio was canceled "by mutual consent," but Emerson would later tell the press that she "never really liked pictures anyway. Maybe that's why I wasn't such a big success in them."

Leaving Hollywood, Emerson returned to her roots on the stage, appearing in 1947 in *Here Today* and *Profile* at the Cape Playhouse in Dennis, Massachusetts, and making her Broadway debut the following year in *The Play's the Thing*. As the sole female cast member in the latter production, Emerson received mostly favorable reviews, with Brooks Atkinson of the *New York Times* praising her "high spirit and vitality," and William Hawkins of the *New York World Telegram* stating, "She is extremely handsome, plays with authority, and gets the grainy quality of a woman of willful temperament and morals." Also during this period, Emerson was frequently heard on the radio; on September 15, 1946, she and her husband introduced a new regular show, *At Home with Faye and Elliott*, which featured such guests as Lucille Ball and Desi Arnaz, Toots Shor and Martha Scott. .

In December 1948, Emerson was in the news again when she was rushed to a Poughkeepsie, New York, hospital for treatment of what the county sheriff called a "self-inflicted razor slash of the wrist." Released after a two-day stay, Emerson revealed that the injury was an accident caused when she reached into a drawer for an aspirin and struck several razor blades instead, but the press made a field day of the incident and rumors abounded that the couple's marriage was on the rocks.

Meanwhile, Emerson made her television debut on *Tonight on Broadway* in May 1948, and by the following year she had appeared so frequently as a guest artist on quiz programs that *Cue* magazine referred to her as one of the "peripatetic panelists." While continuing her radio stints on such programs as NBC's *My Silent Partner*, Emerson was called on late in 1949 to substitute on the television premiere of *The Diana Barrymore Show* when the program's star showed up drunk at the CBS studios. The first show, with guests ventriloquist Paul Winchell and his "sidekick" Jerry Mahoney, was a smash hit, and led to a contract for Emerson's own weekly television program. The actress's natural charm and wit, combined with her polished delivery, made the show a popular one with audiences. And viewership was no doubt enhanced by the actress's revealing evening gowns, prompting *Life* magazine to report, "Faye Emerson's décolleté makes TV melee." Critics unanimously hailed Emerson's appeal, with Val Adams of the *New York Times* noting her "female charm

Faye Emerson

presented with careful, ladylike discretion," and adding, "Coupled with Miss Emerson's photogenic qualities is a mental alertness not usually expected of glamour girls. She lays no claim to being a wit or a good storyteller, but conversationally she's in the upper brackets."

In 1950, Emerson returned to the silver screen, starring with Zachary Scott in *Guilty Bystander* (1950), her final film noir. Here, Emerson played the ex-wife of Max Thursday (Scott), an ex-cop fired from his job because of his alcoholism. Now working as house detective for a run-down waterfront hotel, Max finds himself embroiled in a desperate search for his kidnapped son. In the course of his quest, Max encounters a shady doctor, a gang of gem smugglers and a double-crossing hotel proprietess known as Smitty (Mary Boland, in a rare non-comedic role). Ultimately, Max learns that the kidnapping was engineered by Smitty, and at the film's end he locates his son and is reunited with his former spouse.

Although *Guilty Bystander* received mixed reviews, most critics agreed on Emerson's performance, with Bosley Crowther writing in the *New York Times* that she "does very nicely as [Scott's] frightened and earnest ex-wife," and the critic for Variety reporting: "Faye Emerson, out of pictures for some time, looks good as [Scott's] divorced wife who does her part in the search for the hoods and the kid."

During the filming of *Guilty Bystander*, Emerson announced to the press that her marriage to Elliott Roosevelt was over. "I am sorry to say that Mr. Roosevelt and I have been separated for some time and I plan a divorce when I have finished my current picture," she stated. "Elliott and I parted on friendly terms." In January 1950, the actress secured a Mexican divorce and less than a year later, in November 1950, she revealed her plans to marry Lyle "Skitch" Henderson, a pianist-conductor. The actress announced her engagement on her television show, for which Henderson served as musical arranger, telling viewers: "Because you are all my friends, I want you to meet the man I am going to marry." The couple wed the following month, but the third time would not be the charm for Emerson, and in 1957 she and Henderson were divorced. Years later, the actress would philosophically state: "[My] divorces were all quiet. ... Bad as divorces are, you can at least have the good manners to be civilized about them!"

Professionally, Emerson starred in the Washington production of *Good-bye, My Fancy* and continued to expand her television resumé, moving from CBS to NBC in early 1950 to star in *Celebrity Time*, then adding two more programs by the end of the year. She also made guest appearances on such shows as *Philco Playhouse*, *Ford Theatre* and *Billy Rose's Playbill*, and in the summer of 1950, managed to find time to return to Broadway for a two-week run of *Parisienne* with Francis Lederer. For her efforts on the small screen, Emerson was nominated for a 1950 Emmy Award as the Most Outstanding TV Personality, but lost to Groucho Marx. In 1951, however, she was given *Look* magazine's first annual TV award, earning the label of "Television's Most Appealing Personality."

In June 1951, Emerson began a new weekly television show, *Faye Emerson's Wonderful Town*, a program described in *Variety* as "saluting a city and presenting guests associated with the locale." During the next several years, she kept up a nearly non-stop schedule, appearing on such television anthology shows as the *U.S. Steel Hour*, and in MGM's *Main Street to Broadway*

(1953), as part of a star-studded cast that included Ethel and Lionel Barrymore, Tallulah Bankhead, Louis Calhern, Lilli Palmer and Rex Harrison.

In 1954, the multi-talented actress began writing a syndicated newspaper column which featured her comments on the world and its inhabitants. The famed Emerson wit was in full force in these columns; an item on pianist Liberace read: "Such dimpling and winking. Such tossing of curls and fluttering of eyelashes and flashing of teeth — such nausea!" Throughout the remainder of the decade, Emerson continued her frequent television appearances, showing up on such programs as *Studio One*, and returned to Broadway in 1955 in *The Heavenly Twins* and *Protective Custody*. When both plays were blasted in reviews and quickly folded, the outspoken actress frankly voiced her opinion of New York critics on nationwide television.

Emerson was again nominated for an Emmy Award in 1956, this time for "Best Female Personality [in a] Continuing Performance on Television," but lost to Dinah Shore. Undaunted, she made a cameo appearance in her final feature film, *The Face in the Crowd* (1957), then returned to the stage, delivering what was considered her best stage performance in *Back to Methuselah* with Tyrone Power and Arthur Treacher. Next, Emerson toured extensively in several plays, including *State of the Union, Biography, The Pleasure of His Company* and *Elizabeth the Queen*.

At this point in her life, Emerson finally started to slow down. After a summer tour of *The Vinegar Tree* and a few television guest spots, she suddenly turned her back on her fame and left the United States. Sailing to Europe in 1963, the actress lived for a time in Switzerland and later moved to a whitewashed hillside house on the island of Majorca. Once there, she contentedly allowed herself to gain weight and her blonde locks to turn silver, and although she continued to be besieged with offers, she never again appeared before a television or film camera. During her years in this peaceful Spanish island, Emerson penned her autobiography, in which the Roosevelt family figured prominently, but the manuscript was never published.

On March 9, 1983, Emerson died in Majorca of cancer, with her only son, William Wallace Crawford, III, at her side. At the time of her death, Emerson had been out of the public eye for two decades, but she will always be remembered for her outstanding cinematic offerings, her sparkling contribution to the television industry and her unparalleled personality that was perhaps best described by a reviewer from the *Washington Post*: "Miss Emerson is all a woman should be. Dimpled, shapely, warm of spirit, witty but not caustic, wise but not overbearing."

Film Noir Filmography

THE MASK OF DIMITRIOS   *Director:* Jean Negulesco. *Producer:* Henry Blanke. Released by Warner Bros., June 1944. *Running time:* 95 minutes. *Cast:* Sidney Greenstreet, Zachary Scott, Faye Emerson, Peter Lorre, George Tobias, Victor Francen, Steve Geray.

DANGER SIGNAL   *Director:* Robert Florey. *Producer:* William Jacobs. Released by Warner Bros., November 1945. *Running time:* 78 minutes. *Cast:* Faye Emerson, Zachary Scott, Dick Erdman, Rosemary DeCamp, Bruce Bennett, Mona Freeman, John Ridgely.

NOBODY LIVES FOREVER   *Director:* Jean Negulesco. *Producer:* Robert Buckner. Released by Warner Bros., November 1946. *Running time:* 100 minutes. *Cast:* John Garfield, Geraldine Fitzgerald, Walter Brennan, Faye Emerson, George Coulouris, George Tobias, Robert Shayne, Richard Gaines.

GUILTY BYSTANDER   *Director:* Joseph Lerner. *Producer:* Rex Carlton. Released by Film Classics, April 1950. *Running time:* 92 minutes. *Cast:* Zachary Scott, Faye Emerson, Mary Boland, Sam Levene, J. Edward Bromberg, Kay Medford.

References

Asher, Jerry. "The Fabulous Fayezie." *Silver Screen*, August 1944.

Deere, Dorothy. "The Girl with Two Lives." *Photoplay*, August 1945.

"Divorce Matter of Time." *New York Herald Tribune*, January 14, 1950.

Emerson, Faye. "The Low-Down on Low-Neck Gowns." *TV Guide*, April 15, 1950.

_____. "TV Hostess." *TV Guide*, January 27, 1951.

"Faye Emerson: Town Crier in a Mink Stole." *TV Guide*, January 21, 1950.

"Faye Emerson Cut by a Razor Blade." *New York Times*, December 18, 1948.

"Faye Emerson Engaged." *New York Times*, November 8, 1950.

"Faye Emerson on TV." *TV Week*, June 9, 1957.

"Faye's Décolleté Makes TV Melee." *Life*, April 10, 1950.

"Faye Sheds a Husband, Sees a Fight." *Life*, January 23, 1950.

"Fayzie's Flabbergasted." *TV Guide*, February 19, 1955.

"If Faye Emerson Were President." *TV Guide*, June 3, 1950.

"Not Too Heavy." *Time*, April 24, 1950.

Prial, Frank J. "Faye Emerson Is Dead at 65; Actress and TV Personality." *New York Times*, March 11, 1983.

Samuels, Charles. "Stars of Tomorrow." *Motion Picture*, February 1945.

Schallert, Edwin. "Quiet Life, Aim of Faye Emerson." *Los Angeles Times*, October 7, 1945.

Torre, Marie. "Faye Emerson Nears Ambition as Producer." *New York Herald Tribune*, October 13, 1958.

"TV, Movie Star, Faye Emerson, 65." *Philadelphia Inquirer*, March 11, 1983.

Weller, Helen. "Let's Pretend You're Mrs. Elliott Roosevelt." *Motion Picture*, October 1945.

Hope Emerson

At six-foot-two, 230 pounds, Hope Emerson enjoyed an often unortho-
dox career that encompassed such stints as shoeing a horse on stage and hoist-
ing veteran actor Spencer Tracy six feet into the air. The original radio voice
of Elsie the Cow, Emerson was a performer for more than 30 years, gaining
prominence in film, on stage, in radio and television, and entertaining audiences with her "hot" piano playing in supper clubs nationwide. Perhaps best
remembered for her Academy Award–nominated performance as the sadistic
matron in *Caged* (1950), Emerson was a versatile actress who played in everything from Greek classics to musical comedy and, in addition to *Caged*, lent
her commanding presence to three additional films noirs: *Cry of the City* (1948),
Thieves' Highway (1949) and *House of Strangers* (1949).

Emerson was born in Hawarden, Iowa, a small town near Sioux City, on
October 29, 1897, the only child of John Emerson, an advertising manager,
and the former Pauline deRosa, a well-known repertory actress in the Mid-
west. Although an MGM studio biography would later claim that Emerson
began her professional career singing and dancing at the early age of three,
the actress said that she started working when she was 12 years old, selling
music in a ten-cent store. "I was so big everybody thought I was 18," she
recalled. "I sat behind the counter and played the piano." Later, Emerson
honed her talents at the keyboard by playing for "every road show that hit town"
at the local opera house owned by her uncle. After her graduation from Des
Moines West High School, Emerson played stock in Omaha, Sioux City and
Denver, then toured in a coast-to-coast vaudeville act called "June and Buck-
eye" with her partner, Ray Shannen.

By the time Emerson was 18, she decided that she was ready for the big
time. "I went to New York, thinking it was time I did a dramatic show on
Broadway, and also dreaming that perhaps Broadway needed me," she said.
"But I soon found out that getting a play was not just a matter of showing up
in a producer's office and telling him you were ready to go on the stage. For
a year Broadway couldn't see me. I got hungrier and hungrier." To make ends
meet, Emerson relied on her piano-playing ability, appearing in local nightclubs and later signing on as an entertainer at Pennsylvania's Buckward Inn, a
popular resort in theatrical circles. It was during her run at the Buckward that
a friend suggested Emerson try out for the Broadway play *Lysistrata*. "Norman Bel Geddes was directing the play, and I heard he was looking for a big
woman for a part," Emerson said. "I wangled an interview with Bel Geddes
[and] he took one look at me and yelled, 'Finally, I've found a big woman.'
The play lasted two years."

Emerson's Broadway debut brought her in contact with some of the country's most highly acclaimed thespians — she played in New York for a year with
Charles Coburn and Fay Bainter, then toured with the play for another year
with Sydney Greenstreet, Miriam Hopkins and Ernest Truex. For Emerson's
role as the leader of the Amazons, critics divided their praise with their

amazement at her ability to make her fellow players look like midgets. "I've been a hem-dropper from childhood on," Emerson once jokingly said of her massive physique.

The following season, Emerson was back on Broadway with Fred Stone in *Smiling Stone*, in which she sang, danced, played the piano and all but stole the show. Next, she toured for two years with Allan Jones in a revival of *Bittersweet*, sang three straight summers with the St. Louis Municipal Opera in such productions as *Show Boat* and *Rose Marie*, and returned to Broadway to play a lady blacksmith in *Swing Your Lady*. To prepare for this role, Emerson studied under a woman blacksmith in Greenwich Village, and in every performance of the play, she actually shoed a horse on stage. "I wore out more horses that way," Emerson said. "More people came to see that show just to see the remarkable resemblance between the horse and me!"

When *Swing Your Lady* folded, Emerson returned to the nightclub scene and was initially hired for a two-night engagement at the Ruban Bleu, an elegant club on New York's East side. "The management thought I was too raucous, but evidently the customers didn't. I played there for the next 46 weeks, and for the next ten years did nothing but work in nightclubs." Around this time, Emerson joined the Jimmy Durante–Garry Moore radio show, portraying a character known as "Toodles Bong-Snook" by day, and playing her piano and singing in clubs at night. Later, she found time to launch her own show, *That's a Good One*, and was also heard on Ed Wynn's radio show, on which she originated the voice of Elsie the Cow for the program's sponsor, Borden.

In the mid–1940s, Emerson returned to Broadway to play a drunken yodeler in *Chicken Every Sunday*, then tried out for the musical version of *Street Scene*, but she found that her size was an obstacle. "They wanted someone who looked like Beulah Bondi who could sing and dance. I was constantly told, 'We want a little girl — you're too big,'" she remembered. "Finally, I got mad and said, 'Just listen to me read. That's all I ask.' So I read for 19 people and met the man who wrote it. 'Size doesn't mean a thing to me,' said he." Emerson won the role of a malicious gossip in the play, in which she sang six operatic arias and, as she remembered, "never missed a show."

Emerson's performance in *Street Scene* caught the attention of a 20th Century–Fox talent scout, who promptly cast her in *Cry of the City* (1948), a taut film noir focusing on a small-time hood, Martin Rome (Richard Conte). At the film's opening, Rome is in the hospital after being wounded during a botched restaurant hold-up that resulted in the death of a policeman. Believing that Rome's death is imminent, an unscrupulous attorney, Niles (Berry Kroeger), urges Rome to confess to a recent jewel robbery, but Rome refuses. Recovering from his injuries, Rome learns that both police and Niles are searching for his innocent girlfriend Teena (Debra Paget, in her film debut), and he escapes from the hospital.

Realizing that Niles is the brains behind the jewel heist, Rome seizes the stolen goods and coerces the attorney into disclosing that the actual theft was committed by his client, Whitey Liggett, and a local masseuse, Rose Given (Emerson). But when Niles pulls a gun on Rome, he is forced to kill the attorney in self-defense. Later, Rome locates Given, whose heartless persona is immediately evident when she learns of Niles' death: "I'm glad you killed him," she says. "He was a bad man, very bad. You're a cute man, Martin. I should've worked with you instead of that fool, Liggett." Rome offers to trade Given the jewels for a car, $5,000 in cash and tickets to South America, and while she appears to willingly agree to the proposal, Given first tries to secure the jewels by strangling Rome in the midst of a massage. Thwarted in this effort, Given goes through with the plan, but Rome double-crosses her and she is arrested by police while trying to collect the jewels from a subway station locker. Rome, meanwhile, is being tracked by Lt. Candella (Victor Mature), who finally catches up to him at a neighborhood church, where he has gone to meet Teena. Candella reveals Rome's unsavory past and Teena abandons him. When the hood tries to escape, Candella guns him down in the street.

Although Emerson's role in *Cry of the City* was limited to only a few scenes, she caught the notice of a number of critics with her performance as the murderous masseuse, including the reviewers for *Variety*, who noted her "standout job," and the *New York Times*, who included her in his praise of the film's "fine supporting roles." Of the memorable scene in which she was required to strangle Conte, Emerson later said that she was fearful of hurting the actor and was jokingly berated by the film's director, Robert Siodmak, for her "lifted pinky" choking technique. Determined to infuse the scene with realism, Emerson "went all the way," causing Conte to seek medical treatment. "I always had my hands around his throat," Emerson said.

Following her successful screen debut, Emerson returned to the stage, touring with Elizabeth Bergner in *The Cup of Trembling*, then was called back to Hollywood to play in 20th Century–Fox's *That Wonderful Urge* (1948), in which she portrayed Tyrone Power's landlady. After taking time out to appear in the CBS television comedy *Kobb's Korner*, Emerson was seen in her second film noir, *Thieves' Highway* (1949), in a small role as a savvy, no-nonsense produce buyer.

Directed by Jules Dassin, this gritty film focuses on 24 hours in the life of war veteran Nick Garcos (Richard Conte), who is bent on retribution against Mike Figlia (Lee J. Cobb), a corrupt merchant responsible for an accident that crippled Nick's father. Teaming up with a local trucker (Millard Mitchell), Nick purchases two truckloads of prized apples and drives across the country to San Francisco, where he leaves his truck in front of Figlia's market. Exhausted, Nick allows himself to be picked up by a local refugee, Rica (Valentina Cortesa), not knowing that Figlia has paid the woman to entice him. While Nick is sleeping in Rica's apartment, Figlia sells his apples, but

Hope Emerson

Nick later forces the merchant to turn over the money he received. Triumphant over this victory, Nick calls Polly (Barbara Lawrence), his fiancée back home, instructing her to travel to San Francisco so that they can marry, but he is later beaten and robbed by two of Figlia's thugs.

Arriving in town, Polly is suspicious of Nick's relationship with Rica and heartlessly terminates their engagement after learning that he is broke. Meanwhile, Nick's partner dies in a fiery accident on the road, and Figlia pays a local trucker to retrieve the dead man's apples. Learning of this affront, Nick goes after Figlia and beats him into confessing that he had caused the truck accident that maimed his father. Figlia is taken to jail, and the film ends on a happy note when Nick proposes marriage to Rica.

Again playing a relatively minor role, Emerson nonetheless gave a memorable portrayal of the crafty fruit buyer whose formidable presence intimidates her fellow merchants, and the film itself was almost unanimously hailed by critics, including Bosley Crowther of the *New York Times*, who noted its "top-form cast" and termed it "one of the best melodramas — one of the sharpest and most taut — we've had this year."

By now, Emerson was becoming well-known in the Hollywood community, but she found that she was frequently confused with two other actresses, Faye Emerson and Hope Hampton. "If I had their looks and Hope's money," Emerson once jested, "I'd be leading a Technicolor life for love, instead of working in a Technicolor picture for dough." Meanwhile, after *Thieves' Highway*, Emerson remained in California, appearing next as the gun-toting Levisa Hatfield in RKO's *Roseanna McCoy* (1949), a fictionalized retelling of the infamous feud between the Hatfields and the McCoys. This picture was followed by a role as an overbearing mother in the actress's third film noir, *House of Strangers* (1949), for which she learned to speak Italian.

A fascinating character study, *House of Strangers* focuses on the lives of the Monetti family, whose close-knit relationship is severed because of a banking scandal. The patriarch of the clan, Gino (Edward G. Robinson), is a bank owner who finds himself in trouble with the law due to his questionable operating practices. Gino's favorite son, Max (Richard Conte), is engaged to Maria, a "nice Italian girl" (Debra Paget), but their relationship fizzles when he falls for a local socialite, Irene Bennett (Susan Hayward). When Gino is put on trial, Max tries to bribe a juror and is betrayed by his eldest brother, resulting in a seven-year prison sentence. Bent on revenge, Max seeks out his siblings after his release, but when a brawl nearly results in Max's death, he manages to escape and leaves the town to start his future with Irene.

For her performance as Maria's stern, uncompromising mother, Emerson was singled out for acclaim in *Citizen News* and *Motion Picture Herald*, and the film itself was praised by the latter publication as "dramatic, punchy, understanding, tender at times, and earthily humorous." Emerson followed this box office hit with a role as an irate landlady who evicts William Powell from his apartment in Fox's musical comedy *Dancing in the Dark* (1949), then played a circus performer in *Adam's Rib* (1949), starring Spencer Tracy and Katharine Hepburn. Featuring Judy Holliday and Jean Hagen in their first significant roles, this sophisticated comedy was highlighted by a courtroom scene in which Emerson was required to lift Tracy several feet off the ground. "We waited a week for him to get up the courage to do that scene," Emerson told columnist Hedda Hopper. "He didn't trust me. I don't blame him — I don't trust myself. We'd never have gotten the scene if there'd been more than one take, but we did it in one take and I damned near broke my arm and my back. Spencer wouldn't have done it again for anything."

After the well-received *Adam's Rib*, the actress was seen in Universal's *Double Crossbones* (1950), a musical comedy starring Donald O'Connor, and Paramount's *Copper Canyon* (1950), a run-of-the-mill Western starring Hedy Lamarr. Emerson's appearance with the glamourous brunette in this film prompted the good-humored actress to quip, "I'm always the contrast gal — the ugly duckling who makes everyone else look like a graceful swan. But with Hedy and me in the same picture, they ought to call it Beauty and the Beast!"

Next, as Evelyn Harper in *Caged*, Emerson's final film noir appearance, the actress played the role with which she is best identified, a sadistic matron described by one critic as "evil incarnate." Also starring Agnes Moorehead as a compassionate warden, *Caged* is set in a women's prison populated by a hodgepodge of inmates, including Marie Allen (Eleanor Parker), a pregnant first-offender, Kitty Stark (Betty Garde), the hard-boiled leader of a shoplifting ring, Smoochie (Jan Sterling), a good-natured, baby-faced prostitute, and Georgia (Gertrude Michael), a Southern belle accused of check forgery.

Demoralized by their circumstances, each of the women experience various transformations during the course of the film, including one who hangs herself after being denied parole. And, after being tormented by Evelyn Harper and suffering a lengthy solitary confinement, Kitty goes mad and murders the cruel matron. Despite the kind efforts of the prison warden, her efforts appear to be in vain at the film's downbeat end, as she acknowledges the conversion of Marie from a naive innocent to a hardened criminal. "Keep her file active," the warden directs a clerk upon Marie's release. "She'll be back."

Labeled by one critic as "vicious and inexorable," Emerson offered an unforgettable performance in *Caged*, creating a character with a steely exterior and a heart to match. Her temperament is evidenced early on, after one inmate severs an artery during an escape attempt. As the woman lies bleeding on the cold prison floor, Harper callously suggests: "The cold hose will quiet her down." And later, she brazenly upbraids the warden for her kind-hearted techniques: "You believe any bull these inmates hand you. You sit there on your big bustle — the big boss — and think you know how to run this place. Do you know how it ought to be run? Break 'em in two if they talk out of turn. Anyone who doesn't toe the mark sits in solitary for one month. Bread and water. One funny move from a girl and I'd clip every hair off of her head. That's the way it used to be run and that's the way it ought to be run. Just like they're a bunch of animals in a cage." Although the critic for the *New York Times* panned the film as a whole for its "cliché-ridden account" of prison life, most reviewers applauded the film and its principal players, especially Emerson, who received an Academy Award nomination as Best Supporting Actress for her efforts (she lost, however, to Josephine Hull for *Harvey*).

Soon after the release of the film, Emerson noted the series of "bad girls" that she had played since her film debut. "For 20 years before I came to Hollywood I did comedy," she said. "Then I got into the worst rut on the screen, killing, choking people and playing jail matrons. Since I got in pictures, people write to ask why I do such terrible things. They all think I'm a sadist and figure my family must be highly abused." But the actress's life off-screen was a far cry from her film persona. Since the death of Emerson's father in 1935, she had taken care of her wheelchair-bound mother, with whom she lived until her mother died. Despite her devotion to her only living parent, however, and her size and weight notwithstanding, Emerson was seldom "beauless," according to the press. Although she would never marry, Emerson was seen most often during the 1950s in the company of Los Angeles jeweler Bob Overjorde who, at six-foot-three, was an ideal physical match for the immense actress. "When we enter a restaurant, everyone looks as though they're afraid we'll literally raise the roof," Emerson cracked, "but they soon get used to us."

On screen, Emerson was seen in MGM's *Westward the Women* (1951), a Robert Taylor starrer about a wagon train full of women who trek across country from Chicago to California, followed by several features for Republic Pictures, including *Belle LeGrand* (1951), a mediocre musical Western, *The Lady Wants Mink* (1953), a mildly amusing comedy about a woman who tries to grow her own mink when her husband can't afford to buy her a fur coat, and *Champ for a Day* (1953), a hard-hitting crime drama starring Alex Nicol as a boxer searching for the men who murdered his manager. During the rest of the decade, Emerson appeared in only four pictures, including two big-budget box office successes, *Casanova's Big Night* (1954), a costume comedy starring Bob Hope and Joan Fontaine, and *Untamed* (1955), an adventure-romance with Tyrone Power and Susan Hayward that was advertised as being "Africolossal" and dubbed by many as the African *Gone with the Wind*. Her last screen appearance would be in *All Mine to Give* (1957), a four-hanky tearjerker about the efforts of an orphan to find homes for his baby siblings on Christmas Day.

During this time, Emerson also reached a new level of fame with roles on two popular television series, *Peter Gunn*, on which she played a nightclub owner known as "Mother," and *The Dennis O'Keefe Show* which featured her as "Sarge." Having conquered every performing medium, Emerson's prolific career subsided in the late 1950s when she was diagnosed with a liver ailment. Then, in the spring of 1960, after driving from Phoenix to California, she entered Hollywood Presbyterian Hospital, where she died a few days later, on April 24, 1960. She was 62 years old.

With a career that spanned four decades, Hope Emerson possessed a unique talent that was equally adaptable to comedy or drama, and an inner fortitude that sustained her even in the bleakest of times. But although the actress would eventually never want for work, and would maintain houses in Iowa, New York and Hollywood, she seemed to never forget the early years of her career when she "starved successfully," and she once claimed that "making money" was her only hobby. "My life was never easy. I have never had time to play," Emerson said. "But I love the work. I have the best time playing the worst part in the world. I work on my voice all the time — I always figure that someday I'll have to go back to nightclubs or some beat-up saloons. But that's my life and I love it. I'll work until I'm so old they'll have to wheel me in."

Film Noir Filmography

CRY OF THE CITY *Director:* Robert Siodmak. *Producer:* Sol Siegel. Released by 20th Century–Fox, September 1948. *Running time:* 96 minutes. *Cast:* Victor Mature, Richard Conte, Fred Clark, Shelley Winters, Betty Garde, Berry Kroeger, Tommy Cook, Debra Paget, Hope Emerson.

THIEVES' HIGHWAY *Director:* Jules Dassin. *Producer:* Robert Bassler. Released by 20th Century–Fox, September 1949. *Running time:* 94 minutes. *Cast:* Richard Conte, Valentina Cortesa, Lee J. Cobb, Barbara Lawrence, Jack Oakie, Millard Mitchell, Joseph Pevney, Morris Carnovsky, Hope Emerson.

HOUSE OF STRANGERS *Director:* Joseph L. Mankiewicz. *Producer:* Sol Siegel. Released by 20th Century–Fox, July 1949. *Running time:* 101 minutes. *Cast:* Edward G. Robinson, Susan Hayward, Richard Conte, Luther Adler, Paul Valentine, Efrem Zimbalist, Jr., Debra Paget, Hope Emerson, Esther Minciotti.

CAGED *Director:* John Cromwell. *Producer:* Jerry Wald. Released by Warner Bros., May 1950. *Running time:* 97 minutes. *Cast:* Eleanor Parker, Agnes Moorehead, Ellen Corby, Hope Emerson, Betty Garde, Jan Sterling, Lee Patrick, Olive Deering, Jane Darwell. *Awards:* Academy Award nominations for Best Actress (Eleanor Parker), Best Supporting Actress (Hope Emerson), Best Original Screenplay (Virginia Kellogg, Bernard C. Schoenfeld).

References

Brand, Harry. Biography of Hope Emerson. 20th Century–Fox Studios, 1949.
"Hope Emerson, Film Star, Dies." *Los Angeles Mirror-News,* April 25, 1960.
"Hope Emerson, 62, Actress in Movies and on TV, Dead." *New York Herald Tribune,* April 26, 1960.
"Hope Emerson, 62, Actress, Is Dead." *New York Times,* April 26, 1960.
Hopper, Hedda. "Big Girl Makes Good!" *Chicago Sunday Tribune,* circa 1953.
Stricking, Howard. Biography of Hope Emerson. MGM Studios, 1951.

Rhonda Fleming

A seductive redhead with emerald-green eyes and a figure that a columnist once said "practically whistles at itself," Rhonda Fleming is perhaps best remembered for her roles in a variety of Technicolor Westerns and costume dramas, in which her distinctive titian-hued tresses were shown to great advantage. Although the actress has been virtually absent from the silver screen since the late 1960s, she has remained in the public eye through her active involvement with a number of charity organizations, and in the 1990s established a clinic at the University of California at Los Angeles for women suffering from cancer. Teamed during the peak of her fame with such stars as Bing Crosby, Burt Lancaster and Dick Powell, this statuesque beauty appeared in more than 40 films during her career and lent her talents to five pictures from the film noir era: *Out of the Past* (1947), *Cry Danger* (1951), *The Killer Is Loose* (1956), *Slightly Scarlet* (1956) and *While the City Sleeps* (1956).

One of only a handful of actresses who can claim Hollywood as their home, Marilyn Louise Louis entered the world on August 10, 1923, the second of two daughters born to Harold, an insurance broker, and Olivia, a musical comedy actress who performed under the name of Effie Graham. As a child, Marilyn was known throughout her Los Angeles neighborhood as a tomboy and received more than her share of bumps and bruises — on one occasion she lost her two front teeth during a bicycle race, and on another, she broke her nose while doing chin-ups on a railing. Her athleticism continued during her years as a student at Beverly Hills High School, where she served as captain of both the basketball and volleyball teams, competed in sandlot baseball and was a member of a championship bowling team.

Her love of sports notwithstanding, Marilyn became interested at an early age in pursuing a singing career: "It was my mother's dream and mine to study for a career in light opera, and I took lessons for ten years as a kid," the actress said. "I always remember singing. Movies just never occurred to me, although we lived right in the movie capital." Despite her indifference to a future in films, however, Marilyn received her first brush with Hollywood while she was still a high school student. Shortly after placing as a semi-finalist, along with future star Linda Darnell, in Jesse Lasky's "Gateway to Hollywood" contest, she was spotted on the street by David O. Selznick's talent scout Henry Willson, who offered her a screen test. More interested in her school activities than a career in pictures, Marilyn declined the test and, after her graduation, performed in a six-week stint as a showgirl in a local musical comedy show, *Blackouts*. The producer of the revue, Ken Murray, would later recall that he selected the future actress from a pool of 100 young hopefuls: "You know how beautiful Rhonda is now," he said in 1960. "Imagine what she looked like as a teenager! She was my first choice."

At this point, at only 16 years of age, Marilyn married the first of her five husbands — a local interior designer, Thomas Wade Lane. The couple would have a son, Kent, born in 1942, but the marriage would end after seven years:

"He was a genius at furnishing homes, but he couldn't completely furnish my life," the actress would later say of Lane. "He was wonderful with the main things, but sometimes the little accessories were missing."

Meanwhile, Marilyn finally decided to give movies a try and signed a six-month contract with 20th Century–Fox in 1943 under the name of Marilyn Lane. But although she made her screen debut as a dance-hall girl in a John Wayne starrer, *In Old Oklahoma*, followed by another bit in *Hello, Frisco, Hello* (1943), Marilyn's talents were all but wasted at Fox and she spent the majority of her time posing for countless publicity shots. Still, it would be her short-lived contract with Fox that would lead to Marilyn's first real break. After a chance meeting in the studio's parking lot with Henry Willson, Marilyn was invited to a luncheon date with David O. Selznick, who was so impressed by her youthful beauty that he sidestepped the usual screen test and signed her to a contract. It was Willson who suggested Marilyn be renamed "Ronda Fleming" and Selznick added the "h," Fleming recalled. To introduce the new Rhonda Fleming to the world, Selznick assigned her to the small role of a dancer in *Since You Went Away* (1944). "Mr. Selznick was a genius to me, always bubbling with ideas," Fleming said years later. "I always regretted that I never worked for him in a string of pictures."

After a bit part in Monogram's *When Strangers Marry* (1944), Fleming was introduced by Selznick to famed director Alfred Hitchcock, who cast her as a neurotic mental patient in *Spellbound*, starring Gregory Peck and Ingrid Bergman. "He said I'd be portraying a nymphomaniac, and I ran home to tell my family," Fleming recalled. "We looked the word up in the dictionary and were pretty shocked. I didn't even know what a nymphomaniac was — that's how naive I was."

Although it was limited to two scenes, Fleming's performance in *Spellbound* did not go unnoticed by moviegoers, and the actress was singled out by columnist Hedda Hopper, who "suggested I could have won an Academy Award nomination for supporting actress had my role been a little bit larger," Fleming said. "That was the biggest thrill I had during those first few years." Capitalizing on the starlet's growing popularity, Selznick loaned her to RKO for the well-received *The Spiral Staircase* (1946), followed by United Artists' *Abilene Town* (1946), a Western starring Randolph Scott, and Paramount's *Adventure Island* (1947), a dull actioner about beachcombers held captive on a tropical island. "Who was I to argue? I needed exposure and Mr. Selznick said they'd be good for my career," Fleming said of the latter two pictures. "But they were pretty mediocre."

Next, Fleming was again loaned to RKO, this time for the classic *Out of the Past* (1947), a complicated film noir that one critic said "may leave many who see it too limp to try to figure it out." This picture starred Robert Mitchum as Jeff Bailey, a small-town gas station owner whose mysterious background is revealed when he learns that he has been found by an associate from his past. As he explains to his wholesome girlfriend Ann (Virginia Huston), Jeff has previously worked as a private detective and was hired by a mobster, Whit Sterling (Kirk Douglas), to locate his girlfriend, who had shot him and stolen $40,000. Jeff tracks down the girlfriend, Kathie Moffett (Jane Greer), in Mexico City, but she convinces him that she is innocent of Whit's allegations of theft, and before long, Jeff falls in love with the sultry brunette. Managing to elude Whit, Jeff and Kathie flee to San Francisco, where they live an idyllic existence until they are tracked down by Jeff's former partner, Fisher (Steve Brodie), who has been hired by Whit to find the pair. To Jeff's horror, Kathie kills Fisher, and he later finds his lover's bankbook which shows that she had indeed stolen the money from Whit.

Disillusioned, Jeff moves to Bridgeport, where he assumes his life as a gas station owner. It is here that the past catches up to the present, as Whit summons Jeff to him again. Arriving at the mobster's estate, Jeff is shocked to see that Kathie has returned to Whit, and discovers that Whit has secured Kathie's loyalty by blackmailing her about Fisher's murder. Whit likewise uses blackmail to force Jeff into obtaining potentially damaging tax records from a turncoat accountant. Reluctantly accepting his assignment, Jeff is referred to Meta Carson (Fleming), who works as the secretary for the accountant, Leonard Eels (Ken Niles). Described by Jeff as "awfully cold around the heart," Meta sets up a meeting with Jeff and Eels and informs Jeff that he is to return later to steal the records from Eels' apartment. Jeff learns that the accountant is actually marked for death and that Whit intends to frame him for the crime, but he is too late to prevent the man's murder. After he manages to obtain the damaging tax records, Jeff confronts Whit, forcing the mobster to agree to reveal Kathie as Fisher's murderer. But Kathie learns of the plan, kills Whit and convinces Jeff to flee the country with her. Jeff agrees to the plan, but he secretly contacts police, who set up a barricade on a nearby road. When they encounter the roadblock, Kathie shoots Jeff. Their car crashes and both are killed.

While Fleming's role was limited to two scenes, she made the most of them, delivering a portrayal of a beautiful but hard-boiled schemer who was not to be trifled with. In one scene, after receiving a physical threat from Jeff, Meta coolly inquires, "Do you always go around leaving your fingerprints on a girl's shoulder? Not that I mind, particularly — you've got nice, strong hands." And although two publications — *The Hollywood Reporter* and *Motion Picture Daily* — both misidentified Fleming as "the small-town girl Mitchum wants to marry," other critics called her performance "commendable" and singled out Fleming for her "brief but effective" portrayal.

Despite her favorable showing in *Out of the Past*, Fleming was absent from the screen in 1948, primarily due to Selznick's increasing concentration on securing film roles for his future wife, actress Jennifer Jones. Determined to jumpstart her flagging career, Fleming arranged a $25,000 buyout of her contract with Selznick and promptly signed a non-exclusive agreement with Paramount Pictures. In her first film under her new contract, Fleming got her long-awaited big break, replacing Deanna Durbin in the Technicolor Bing Crosby starrer *A Connecticut Yankee in King Arthur's Court* (1949). "[Durbin] suddenly decided she didn't want to make any more movies, moved to France and never came back," Fleming recalled. "Paramount gave me a $50,000 test in color and black and white — a lot of money in those days. They also tested 250 other women. But Bing Crosby, who was playing the Connecticut Yankee, liked me. Still it was about two or three months before I knew I had the role. Bing was wonderful. He was like a mother hen. He watched over me and wanted everything just right." This popular film provided the actress with a rare opportunity to display her trained singing voice, and also marked her debut in Technicolor. "Suddenly, my green eyes were *green green*. My red hair was *flaming* red. My skin was *porcelain*," Fleming told *People* magazine in 1991. "There was suddenly all this attention on how I looked rather than the roles I was playing." Still, the actress won raves for her role in the film, with a typical review appearing in *Variety*: "Miss Fleming's Titian beauty shows up well in Technicolor and she wears the costumes of the period with grace. On her vocals she pleases, and her physical charms as Alisande, King Arthur's niece, are expressive enough to illustrate why the Yankee would develop a yen for her."

Later that year, Crosby's frequent costar Bob Hope said, "'If Bing's gonna use her, so am I,'" Fleming recalled, which led to her casting in Hope's *The Great Lover* (1949). A smash hit at the box office, this hysterical comedy was followed by two run-of-the-mill Westerns, *The Eagle and the Hawk* (1950), with John Payne, and *The Redhead and the Cowboy* (1950), starring Glenn Ford. "I'm always invited to those conventions of Western movie buffs," Fleming said in a 1994 interview. "I'm somehow identified with the West." But in her next film, RKO's *Cry Danger* (1951), Fleming proved that she could do far more than jauntily sport a dusty cowboy hat or hang on to a bucking horse.

This picture, Fleming's second film noir, begins as Rocky Malloy (Dick Powell) is released from prison after serving a five-year sentence for a murder and $100,000 robbery that he did not commit. His release was secured after an ex-marine, Delong (Richard Erdman), provided Rocky with an alibi, but Delong actually gave false testimony in hopes of securing a substantial payoff from Rocky. Assuring the affable marine of his innocence, Rocky nonetheless solicits his aid in finding the real killer, in order to gain the release of his friend, Danny Morgan, who was also framed for the crime.

Danny's wife, Nancy (Fleming), soon makes it apparent that she is attracted to Rocky, and repeatedly urges him to abandon his efforts to clear her husband. Nonetheless, Rocky immediately centers his investigation on a local hood, Castro (William Conrad), who had initially asked Rocky and Danny to commit the robbery. As he grows closer to learning the truth, Rocky's life is threatened on more than one occasion. Later, Delong is injured and his girlfriend Darlene (Jean Porter) is killed when they are mistaken for Rocky and Nancy. Finally, in a chilling scene, Rocky corners Castro, continuously firing a gun at his head in "Russian Roulette" fashion. In desperation, the mobster admits that Danny had actually been involved in the robbery and murder, and that Nancy has all along been in possession of Danny's share of the stolen money. But when Rocky confronts her with the truth, Nancy proposes that they take the money and flee. "It's all worked out now," she says. "You're free and we're back together again — that's all that matters. It's always been you and me, Rocky. You know that." Although Rocky admits his love for Nancy, he reluctantly turns her over to police.

After *Cry Danger*, in which the *New York Times* critic said Fleming "turns on the charm effectively," the actress returned to the wild West, starring in *The Last Outpost* (1951), her first of four on-screen teamings with Ronald Reagan. ("He surprised everyone because he never looked in a mirror," Fleming would later say of her costar. "How many actors can you say that about?") The actress followed this popular oater with *Little Egypt* (1951), playing a phony Egyptian princess who tries to bilk a tobacco tycoon out of his fortune, *Crosswinds* (1951), a tired tale about a captain who tries to recover gold from a downed plane in New Guinea, and *Hong Kong* (1951), which focused on an adventurer's efforts to steal a cache of jeweled treasure.

The following year, Fleming focused her energies off screen and in July 1952 married prominent Beverly Hills surgeon Dr. Lewis Morrill, described as being "as attractive as any leading man." The couple was a popular subject for fan magazines — in a typical item, one columnist informed moviegoers, "When the doctor is aroused by midnight summons from his patients, Rhonda gets up too and makes hot coffee." But over the course of their marriage, the couple would experience numerous separations and reconciliations, and the final split came in 1958, with Fleming telling the press, "Let's just say we were incompatible. We should never have married and we shouldn't have stayed married as long as we did."

In 1953, Fleming would enjoy the busiest year of her career, beginning with *The Golden Hawk*, a Technicolor spectacle starring Sterling Hayden, in which she portrayed a well-bred plantation owner masquerading as a lady pirate. "I submit it is very difficult to keep a straight face and make such stories work. If you camp it up, the audience will snigger," Fleming said. "Now, Sterling Hayden may have been tall in the saddle, but on a buccaneer's ship, he waddled — he was bow-legged. I'd look at him and want to giggle, but he was a good sport." The actress's other 1953 releases included *Tropic Zone*, a forgettable story of the struggle between banana plantation owners and greedy shipping magnates, the box office flop *Serpent of the Nile*, which cast a bewigged Fleming as Cleopatra opposite Raymond Burr's Mark Antony, and *Those Redheads from Seattle*, the first 3-D color musical, featuring a weak plot set during

Rhonda Fleming

the Alaskan gold rush. "*Redheads* is a picture people still mention to me and I shiver," Fleming said years later, "because I was always trying to get into another big-budgeted musical and this wasn't it."

The actress didn't fare much better the following year, with starring roles in *Jivaro* (1954), in which she battled the Brazilian jungle and head-hunting Indians in a search for gold, and *Yankee Pasha* (1954), a desert adventure featuring Fleming as a New England damsel who is kidnapped and sold into a

Moroccan harem. But she was shown to decidedly better advantage in her sole release of 1955, *Tennessee's Partner*, set in the raucous atmosphere of the California gold rush. Despite her spate of run-of-the-mill vehicles, however, Fleming remained philosophical about the course of her film career, insisting that she benefitted from freelancing, rather than being tied to a studio contract: "This way I'm master of my own fate," she told columnist Hedda Hopper. "Of course, you don't have studio guidance, so you have nobody to blame but yourself for your mistakes. That makes you careful, not having a patsy. If you are not aware of every angle of the business, you can get snowed under. I try to choose roles that will give me variety."

In 1956, Fleming gained the variety she'd been seeking, appearing in three consecutive films noirs: *The Killer Is Loose, Slightly Scarlet* and *While the City Sleeps*.

In the first, the actress portrayed Lila, the wife of well-respected police detective Sam Wagner (Joseph Cotten) who accidentally shoots and kills the innocent spouse of a bank robber, Leon Poole (Wendell Corey). Convicted and sentenced to prison, Poole vows revenge on Wagner, and escapes three years later, killing a guard in the process. Aware that Poole is bent avenging his wife's death by murdering Lila, police throw out a dragnet over the area, but Poole craftily slips through it, killing a local farmer and stealing his truck. Reluctant to tell Lila of the impending danger, her husband spirits her away to the home of a close friend, planning to wait at his home for Poole to show. When Lila discovers her husband's plan, she returns to him, arriving just as Poole reaches the area, and narrowly avoids being killed by the murderous convict before he is gunned down by police.

Next, in *Slightly Scarlet*, a rare Technicolor film noir, Fleming starred as June Lyons, whose troubled younger sister, Dorothy (Arlene Dahl), is a sex-starved kleptomaniac who has recently been released from prison. Before long, June is contacted by Ben Grace (John Payne), an unscrupulous hood who plans to use Dorothy's prison record as part of a scheme to circumvent the mayoral candidacy of June's boss and fiancé, Frank Jansen (Kent Taylor). But after being humiliated by his boss, Solly Caspar (Ted deCorsia), Ben provides June with incriminating proof that Caspar murdered a prominent newspaperman who is Jansen's top supporter. Later, Jansen is elected to office, and June finds herself falling in love with Ben.

When two of Caspar's underlings are jailed, the mobster flees the country and Ben takes over his operation. Meanwhile, Dorothy sets her sights on Ben, and although June suspects him of infidelity, she appeals to Ben for help when Dorothy is jailed for stealing a string of pearls. Later, Caspar returns to the city and, learning of Ben's betrayal, plans to use Dorothy to entice Ben to his beach house. When Ben arrives, a gun battle breaks out, and Ben is shot several times before police arrive and take Caspar to jail.

While the City Sleeps, Fleming's final film noir, provides a glimpse into the lives and loves of the employees of Kyne Enterprises, including television anchor Edward Mobley (Dana Andrews), newspaper editor John Day Griffith (Thomas Mitchell), wire service manager Mark Loving (George Sanders), photo service editor Harry Kritzer (James Craig) and local reporter Mildred Donner (Ida Lupino). When Walter Kyne (Vincent Price) takes over the company after the death of his father, he devises a gimmick for Mobley, Griffith, Loving and Kritzer to compete for the newly created job of executive director ("Someone to do the actual work," he says). The coveted post will be given to the first one who can solve a series of brutal sex crimes being committed throughout the city by "The Lipstick Killer."

As Dorothy, Kyne's ex–Vegas showgirl wife, and Kritzer's mistress, Fleming offers a portrait of an unscrupulous gold digger who uses her seductive wiles in an effort to win the editor position for her lover: "If I make my husband give you the big prize, you won't be Walter's man — you'll be mine," she tells Kritzer. "And you'll do as I say. And you won't forget that. Ever." Despite Dorothy's influence with Kyne, the case of the "Lipstick Killer" is ultimately solved by Mobley, who sets up his fiancée (Sally Forrest) to act as bait for the killer — a drugstore delivery boy — and captures him in a subway station. Mobley gives the scoop to John Griffith, who is given the job.

Fleming's three films noirs of 1956 were met with varying reactions from critics; Bosley Crowther of the *New York Times* slammed *The Killer Is Loose*, saying "the only thing remarkable about this picture is that it could be so absolutely dull with Mr. Cotten and Mr. Corey in it," and he was equally disparaging about *Slightly Scarlet*, calling it "an exhausting lot of twaddle." Crowther was kinder to *While the City Sleeps*, however, noting that it was "full of sound and fury ... and a fair quota of intramural intrigue," and he included Fleming in his praise of the film's cast, reporting that they "do justice to their assignments."

With most of her best parts behind her, Fleming next played a supporting role to an assortment of chimpanzees, crocodiles and elephants in *Odongo* (1956), set on an animal farm in Kenya and filmed on location in Africa. And the actress sank even lower with her appearance in *Queen of Babylon* (1956), a lavishly costumed action epic and the first of several Italian productions in which Fleming starred. Years later, Fleming would express regret over her appearances in these European productions, which would include *The Revolt of the Slaves* (1961) and *Run for Your Wife* (1966), but, the actress admitted, "My ego demanded it — over there I was still a big star."

After the laughable *Queen of Babylon*, Fleming portrayed what she termed "an extended cameo" in *The Buster Keaton Story* (1957), then briefly returned to her former screen glory in *Gunfight at the O.K. Corral* (1957), considered by many to be one of the best films to depict the legend of Marshall Wyatt Earp and his compatriot, the tubercular Doc Holliday. But after the film's release, Fleming was disappointed to realize that much of her portrayal of a mysterious gambler had been cut from the final print. "I literally had one good, big scene left and I was heartbroken," she recalled. "But the woman was so enigmatic she stuck in the minds of moviegoers and people still ask me about that one."

Fleming's last film of 1957 was also the only picture of her career for MGM — *Gun Glory*, a mediocre horse opera starring Stewart Granger. But her career picked up steam again with performances in three well-received films, *Home Before Dark* (1958), a glossy drama starring Jean Simmons and Dan O'Herlihy, *Alias Jesse James* (1959), an amusing Western spoof which reunited Fleming with Bob Hope, and *The Big Circus* (1959), a behind-the-scenes big top drama that Fleming judged "a far better circus picture than *The Greatest Show on Earth*," which had won the Academy Award for Best Picture in 1952. But this film would be the final high point of Fleming's screen career. Instead, as her movie offers dwindled, the actress turned to television, appearing on such shows as *Wagon Train*, *The Dick Powell Theatre* and *Burke's Law*. "It paid the bills," Fleming said. "But I learned not to get too enthusiastic about television. The regular star always got the best close-ups." During this period, Fleming also launched a brief but successful singing career, which included a stint at the Tropicana Hotel in Las Vegas and a tour with Skitch Henderson entitled *A Night of Gershwin*.

Meanwhile, Fleming made a third trip to the altar, marrying actor Lang Jeffreys on April 30, 1960. Like her previous unions, this one would not last, and in January 1962 the couple divorced, with Fleming testifying in court that her husband failed to support her and made no attempt to obtain employment. "He spent most of his time around the house listening to the radio or watching TV," the actress said. Four years later, in 1966, she would marry again, this time to producer-director Hall Bartlett, perhaps best known for the box office disaster *Jonathan Livingston Seagull* (1973). With her marriage to Bartlett, Fleming all but retired from acting, appearing in only three films between 1966 and 1973, when the couple divorced. "I married Hall Bartlett for love and security. He wanted me to quit my career and I was ready to go along with it," Fleming said in a 1973 interview. "I became completely dependent upon a man for the first time in my life. I relied on him for every dollar. Sometimes I had to beg for money. I put on weight and lost my vivaciousness. I was becoming a dullard, not the woman I was before. I still believe in putting a man first, but my advice to women is to keep your life separate or you're destined for ruin. I know. I've been there. I was one of those women."

After her acrimonious parting from Bartlett, Fleming accepted her first major role in eight years, portraying Miriam Aarons in the Broadway revival of Clare Boothe Luce's *The Women*. Costarring with Alexis Smith, Myrna Loy and Kim Hunter, Fleming told the press, "I need to work — I knew I had to start from the ground up and that nothing I'd done before was important. I'm just happy to be holding my own with these wonderful girls who have never quit. Life has to knock you down to wake you up." Three years later, in 1976,

Fleming starred as Lalume in a special ten-week engagement of *Kismet* at the Los Angeles Music Center's Dorothy Chandler Pavilion, followed by a highly successful one-woman concert at the Hollywood Bowl. Also that year, she returned to the big screen with a cameo in the comedy spoof, *Won Ton Ton: The Dog Who Saved Hollywood*.

Then in 1979, Fleming married millionaire theater-chain magnate Ted Mann, current owner of the old Grauman's Chinese Theater, and for the actress, it appeared that the fifth time was the charm. For the next decade, Fleming and Mann resided in separate "his-and-her" condominiums in Century City, California, finding that their unique living arrangement added to the romance of their relationship. "We both love our privacy and we have a lot of trust in each other," Fleming said in 1991. "And we both have freedom. He has the best of both worlds and so do I." The couple has since built a two-story house where they live under one roof, but they still maintain separate quarters. "We love each other very much," Fleming said. "I'm more fulfilled today than at any time in my life." In 1980, Fleming appeared in her last feature film to date, a box office failure called *The Nude Bomb*, which was executive-produced by her husband, and the following year, on September 28, 1981, her hand and footprints were embedded in the forecourt of Mann's Chinese Theatre, with the inscription: "To my Mann, Ted."

Meanwhile, Fleming began to devote the bulk of her energies to humanitarian causes, including projects with which she had been active for several years, such as City of Hope, Childhelp USA, Olive Crest Treatment Centers for Abused Children and various cerebral palsy organizations. And, in 1991, when her sister, Beverly Engle died after a 19-year struggle with a rare form of ovarian cancer, Fleming and her husband joined forces to establish the Rhonda Fleming Mann Clinic for Women's Comprehensive Care, a center for female cancer patients at the University of California at Los Angeles. "On one wall of the clinic we've inscribed the words 'Communication, Compassion, Caring, Concern,'" Fleming said. "And that's what the clinic is all about. We have some of the finest facilities available to treat women who have cancers of the reproductive system. It's also a place where, when the women come in, people reach out to them and where they really care about them as persons, not just as cancer patients."

Coinciding with the opening of the cancer clinic, Fleming also made a rare appearance in a half-hour syndicated television drama, *Waiting for the Wind* (1991), which told the story of a Kansas farmer dying of cancer. The actress later said that it was her sister's death that prompted her to take on the role of the farmer's matronly, world-weary wife. "I hadn't planned to return to the screen. I'd been away from acting for 20 years and had become involved in so many projects that I simply didn't miss the work," Fleming said. "My sister had died just a few months before I was asked to do the film. She was a fighter. She believed, as I do, that where there's life, there's hope, and where there's hope, there's life. And that's what I felt came through so strongly in this drama, which is why I agreed to do it. When I read this script, I realized if there was going to be a film that would persuade me to return to acting, this was it."

Since her appearance in *Waiting for the Wind*, Fleming has not returned to film or television, but she does not rule out the possibility. "Now that I've worked again, I wonder if that little ember isn't starting to burn inside me," she said. "I doubt I ever really wanted to be a glamour queen. Truth is, I would really enjoy doing another good character part." Until Fleming decides to grace the screen with her luminous gifts, however, she will continue to be appreciated not only for her considerable physical charms, but also for the inner beauty that she exhibits through her ongoing commitment to humanity.

Film Noir Filmography

OUT OF THE PAST   *Director:* Jacques Tourneur. *Producer:* Warren Duff. Released by RKO, November 1947. *Running time:* 96 minutes. *Cast:* Robert Mitchum, Jane Greer, Kirk Douglas, Rhonda Fleming, Richard Webb, Steve Brodie, Virginia Huston, Paul Valentine, Dickie Moore, Ken Niles.

CRY DANGER   *Director:* Robert Parrish. *Producers:* Sam Wiesenthal and W.R. Frank. Released by RKO, February 1951. *Running time:* 79 minutes. *Cast:* Dick Powell, Rhonda Fleming, Richard Erdman, William Conrad, Regis Toomey, Jean Porter, Jay Adler.

THE KILLER IS LOOSE   *Director:* Budd Boetticher. *Producer:* Robert L. Jacks. Released by United Artists, March 1956. *Running time:* 73 minutes. *Cast:* Joseph Cotten, Rhonda Fleming, Wendell Corey, Alan Hale, Jr., Michael Pate, Virginia Christine, John Larch, John Beradino.

SLIGHTLY SCARLET   *Director:* Allan Dwan. *Producer:* Benedict Bogeaus. Released by RKO, February 1956. *Running time:* 99 minutes. *Cast:* John Payne, Arlene Dahl, Rhonda Fleming, Kent Taylor, Ted deCorsia, Lance Fuller.

WHILE THE CITY SLEEPS   *Director:* Fritz Lang. *Producer:* Bert Friedlob. Released by RKO, May 1956. *Running time:* 99 minutes. *Cast:* Dana Andrews, Rhonda Fleming, George Sanders, Howard Duff, Thomas Mitchell, Vincent Price, Sally Forrest, John Barrymore, Jr., James Craig, Ida Lupino.

References

Bacon, James. "If It Takes a Beauty to Recognize One..." *Louisville Courier-Journal*, May 29, 1960.
Bawden, James. "Rhonda Fleming." *Films in Review*, November-December, 1994.
Bell, Arthur. "'Women' Women." *The Village Voice*, April 12, 1973.
Brand, Harry. Biography of Rhonda Fleming. 20th Century–Fox Studios, circa 1952.
Cohen, Charles, and David Marlow. "Queen of the B's." *People*, October 14, 1991.
Colby, Anita. "Have a Beautiful Time." *Photoplay*, July 1950.

Dunn, Angela Fox. "Star House Call." *Star*, October 15, 1991.

Gerard, Lou. "'I Want a New Husband,' Says Rhonda Fleming...." *The National Enquirer*, July 6, 1958.

Groves, Seli. "Rhonda Fleming: Always a Time for Hope." King Features Syndicate, August 26, 1991.

Holland, Jack. "Bing's New Leading Lady." *Silver Screen*, November 1948.

Parsons, Louella O. "Rhonda Fleming." *The New York Journal-American*, February 19, 1948.

"Rhonda Fleming." *Life*, March 14, 1949.

"Rhonda Fleming Gets 3d Divorce." *New York Herald Tribune*, January 12, 1962.

Skolsky, Sidney. "Hollywood Is My Beat." *New York Post*, October 11, 1953.

"Sunday School Teacher." *American Magazine*, March 1946.

Thirer, Irene. "'This Is My Year,' Rhonda Believes." *New York Post*, June 2, 1959.

Wahls, Robert. "Rhonda the Beautiful." *Sunday News*, May 13, 1973.

Nina Foch

Although many a Hollywood hopeful never managed to emerge from the ranks of studio starlet, Nina Foch was not one of these. The chic, blonde beauty suffered through a spate of inferior film vehicles in her early career, but she exuded a classic screen presence and superb acting ability that catapulted her from obscurity to become one of Hollywood's most highly respected actresses. In addition to her Oscar-nominated performance in *Executive Suite* (1954) and critically acclaimed portrayals in such films as *An American in Paris* (1951) and *The Ten Commandments* (1956), Foch was featured in four films noirs: *My Name Is Julia Ross* (1945), *Johnny O'Clock* (1947), *The Dark Past* (1949), and *The Undercover Man* (1949).

The stylish star was born Nina Consuelo Maud Fock in Leyden, Holland, on April 20, 1924, the only child of noted Dutch composer and symphony conductor Dirk Fock and Consuelo Flowerton, an American silent film actress and the famous World War I "Poster Girl." When Nina was only two years old, her prominent parents divorced and she moved with her mother to New York. Once there, at her father's insistence, Nina received an exhaustive musical education. When she was still in her early teens, she made an impressive debut as a concert pianist at Aeolian Hall. She also studied painting and sculpturing at the Parsons School of Design and the Art Student's League, determined to pursue a career as a pianist or a painter. However, as she later stated, "I was a failure in both professions at the age of 16, so I decided to try acting."

In 1942, Nina enrolled in the American Academy of Dramatic Arts, and eventually would study acting with such future notables as Lee Strasberg and Stella Adler. She later recalled, however, that landing her first stage role was difficult. "Everywhere I applied, I was turned down because I had had no experience. One day I changed my tactics," the actress said. When asked by a producer about her prior stage roles, she blithely informed him that she'd been featured in *Life Is Like That*. "It was a big lie. I made up the name on the spot because friends told me I'd have to lie. [The producer] believed me, gave me my first job, summer stock. But the joke is there never was any such play. And what makes it funnier is that a number of biographies have listed that play as the one in which I made my stage debut!"

After appearing with several small theater groups in New York, the actress won a small part in the touring company of *Western Union, Please*, starring Charles Butterworth. However, despite the valiant efforts of the cast to keep it afloat, the play was a flop. "We did everything to keep it going," she said. "We did it in period costume and others. Only thing we missed, Charlie said, was blackface." When the play finally closed, the actress found it difficult to find work, but during these lean times, she was looked after by her "wonderful" agent, Lester Schurr. "He saw to it that I never went hungry for long," she said. "I'd be sitting in his office and he'd suddenly say, 'I think I'll have a sandwich. How about you?' Or he'd give me an urgent call and tell me to meet him in some restaurant. Of course, I understand now that he was taking care of me."

In 1942, the actress finally got her long-awaited break. Just before her agent entered the Army, he secured a six-month deal with Warner Bros. Studios that took her to Hollywood. Although Warners dropped her after only two months, her option was picked up by Columbia, which signed her to a seven-year agreement. Once there, the actress recalled, studio executives wanted her to change her name, but the strong-willed, outspoken beauty steadfastly refused. "I am the granddaughter of the speaker of the Dutch Parliament and the Governor General of the Dutch East Indies," she said in a 1980 *Drama-Logue* interview. "I said, 'I'm not going to change my name for you or anybody.' I did, however, change the 'k' to 'h'—for obvious reasons. My family background made it easier for me to fight those people."

Foch made her screen debut in 1943, in Columbia's *The Return of the Vampire*, a genuinely scary production starring Bela Lugosi as the nocturnal count. In a nearly non-stop filming schedule, she made six more features in the following year, including *Cry of the Werewolf*, in which she received star billing as the gypsy daughter of a deceased New Orleans belle, *She's a Soldier, Too*, an undistinguished wartime drama featuring the actress as a lady cab driver who helps a soldier find the son he left behind, and *Shadows in the Night*, the third of a ten-picture series starring Warner Baxter as the "Crime Doctor."

In Foch's first film of 1945, she was cast as Constantina in *A Song to Remember*, a lavish, big-budget biopic starring Cornel Wilde as composer Frédéric Chopin. After her track record of "B" movie appearances, Foch later said that she was delighted to be in Columbia's top production of the year. But at the other end of the spectrum, Foch's next picture, *My Name Is Julia Ross* (1945), was another "B" production that the actress jokingly said was "shot in about three and a half minutes."

At the start of this film noir thriller, the title character (Foch) accepts a position as live-in secretary to a wealthy matron, Mrs. Williamson Hughes (Dame May Whitty), and her psychotic son, Ralph (George Macready). But after her first night in the Hughes' London home, Julia awakens to find that she has been transported to a mansion overlooking the Cornwall seacoast. Held in a locked room, she is told by the Hugheses that she is Ralph's wife Marion, and that she was recently released from a mental institution. Insisting that she is not Marion Hughes, Julia makes several futile attempts to flee. Mrs. Hughes spreads the word throughout the small village that her daughter-in-law is "balmy."

In a desperate attempt to escape, Julia explains her plight in a letter to her boyfriend, Dennis Bruce (Roland Varno), but she soon learns the reason behind the Hughes' subterfuge: Ralph murdered the real Marion Hughes and disposed of her body in the sea, and now Hughes plans to kill Julia and make her death appear as a suicide so that they can profit from Marion's estate. After thwarting Ralph's attempt to kill her by a fall from the stairs, Julia fakes her own suicide, tossing her dressing gown to the rocks below and escaping through a secret door in her room. When Ralph goes to the coast below to insure that Julia has died, he sees her body move and prepares to finish her off with a rock. But before he can strike the fatal blow, Dennis arrives with police and Ralph is shot and killed trying to escape.

Hailed by reviewers as a "suspenseful sleeper," *My Name Is Julia Ross* provided Foch with "the first [role] that I really liked. I wanted that role and they were very considerate at Columbia and gave it to me," the actress told reporters shortly after the film's release. "I feel that I have accomplished something because they are listening to my other pleas and pleadings about what I like. In fact, I'm taking a stand now about my career, because I feel that it is time."

Foch's well-received performance in *My Name Is Julia Ross* marked what she called "the first time Columbia and our boss, Harry Cohn, paid any attention to me." Still, she was next cast in *Prison Ship* (1945), a trite melodrama set aboard a Japanese tanker, *I Love a Mystery* (1945), in which Foch played a woman trying to provoke her playboy husband into suicide, *Boston Blackie's Rendezvous* (1945), the ninth and one of the better offerings in a 15-episode series starring Chester Morris, and *Escape in the Fog* (1945), a farfetched, undistinguished programmer starring Foch as a Navy nurse who dreams of a man about to be murdered and later saves him from his fate.

After next appearing in *The Guilt of Janet Ames* (1947), a poorly scripted psychological drama starring Rosalind Russell and Melvyn Douglas, Foch appeared in her second film noir, *Johnny O'Clock* (1947), a gritty thriller starring Dick Powell.

Here, Foch portrayed Harriet Hobbs, a hatcheck girl in a casino operated by Johnny O'Clock (Powell) and his partner, Pete Marchettis (Thomas Gomez). Harriet is desperately in love with Chuck Blayden (Jim Bannon), a crooked cop who serves as an enforcer for the casino, and refuses to heed Johnny's warnings that Blayden is no good. "I'm full of mistakes," she admits. "I never knew anything like this could happen to me. It's not over — not for me." Soon after Blayden tries to take Johnny's place as partner in the casino operation, his body is found floating in the river and Harriet is found dead in her apartment from an apparent suicide.

Harriet's showgirl sister Nancy (Evelyn Keyes) arrives in town when she hears of the incident, and quickly falls for Johnny. But Johnny is also being pursued by Marchettis' wife, Nelle (Ellen Drew), with whom he had been involved before her marriage to the wealthy gangster. Meanwhile, when police discover that Harriet was actually murdered, Johnny is suspected, but he soon realizes that Marchettis is responsible. Suspecting him of having an affair with Nelle, Marchettis makes an unsuccessful attempt on Johnny's life, and Johnny makes plans to flee with Nancy. But while at the casino to dissolve the partnership and collect his share of the proceeds, Johnny is confronted by Marchettis and is forced to kill him. Nelle witnesses the killing and views her husband's death as an opportunity to be reunited with Johnny. When he rejects her, she lies to police, saying that Johnny shot her husband in cold blood while trying to rob the casino. Certain that police will not believe his story, Johnny plans to shoot his way out of the casino, but Nancy manages to convince him to turn himself in.

Although Foch turned in a commendable performance as the luckless Harriet, *Johnny O'Clock* received mixed reviews, with the critic from *Motion Picture Herald* terming it "an exciting, expertly acted thriller," and the *New York Times*' Bosley Crowther saying "the slowness and general confusion of the plot for two-thirds of the film does not make for notable excitement." After the film's release, Foch decided to return to the stage, and took a year off to debut on Broadway as the star of *John Loves Mary*. When the production turned out to be the comedy hit of the 1947-48 season, Foch became the toast of New York, a distinction that was particularly gratifying in view of the fact that Columbia executives "never did know what to do with me," Foch said. "In the beginning they said, 'You can act but you're not pretty.' In the years I was at Columbia, I was either the girlfriend of a ghoul or a cold neurotic. The brass said I had no sex appeal: I was too flat-chested and my nose was crooked." But in her New York reviews, a number of critics noted Foch's distinctive beauty and earthy allure, and the actress returned to Hollywood "with a new respect as an actress and got some leads in 'A' movies. The only drawback was that now that my attractiveness had been validated by New York, I got chased around a few desks in Hollywood.... I solved the problem by telling them all that they reminded me of my father!"

After her year-long stint on Broadway, Foch went to Harry Cohn and told the irascible studio head, "You can have me for another seven years, or you can let me go to be a good actor. But I'll never be a good actor if I keep doing these pictures for you. I think I'm more talented than that." Foch later recalled of the incident, "I was scared to death, my knees were knocking.... The next day, he said, 'You're right,' and I went to New York." After returning to Broadway to appear in *Twelfth Night*, Foch resumed her screen career with her third film noir, *The Dark Past* (1949).

A remake of 1939's *Blind Alley*, this film opens as police psychiatrist Andrew Collins (Lee J. Cobb) relates a personal experience in order to explain to a coworker the advantages of psychiatric treatment for criminals. A flashback shows that several years before, Collins had encountered notorious criminal Al Walker (William Holden) during a retreat to his lakeside cabin with his wife and three friends. The pleasant weekend getaway was interrupted by the arrival of Walker, who had recently escaped from prison after murdering two guards and the prison warden. Accompanied by his tough, gun-toting girlfriend Betty (Foch) and two underlings, Walker took over Collins' home, holding the vacationers hostage while his gang awaited the arrival of a boat to take them to safety.

Nina Foch

As the hours wear on, Collins learns that Walker suffers from recurrent nightmares and becomes interested in unearthing the psychological basis for Walker's criminal behavior. Eventually, Collins is able to induce Walker's recollection of betraying his father to police as a child, and then watching as he was gunned down. Later, when police surround the cabin, Walker finds that this revelation from his past has rendered him unable to kill again, and he is recaptured. "With proper attention earlier in life, perhaps [Walker] never would have killed at all. Only it was too late," Collins says at the film's conclusion. "All some of them need is a break. A little understanding and guidance — maybe we can salvage some of this waste."

Praised in the *New York Times* for her "competently unrestrained job as the gangster's moll," and in *Motion Picture Herald* for her "near-perfect performance," Foch followed *The Dark Past* with her fourth and final film noir, *The Undercover Man* (1949), which was inspired by Al Capone's arrest for tax evasion. In this feature, the actress played the rather thankless role of Judith Warren, the wife of IRS tax investigator Frank Warren (Glenn Ford), one of several undercover agents working to expose the crimes of a notorious mob boss referred to in the film only as the "big fellow." Warren's initial lead in the case comes from a potential informant named Emanuel Zanger (Robert Osterloh). When Zanger is gunned down in the street before he can turn over the needed information, Warren and his coworkers, George Pappas (James Whitmore) and Stan Weinburg (David Wolfe), begin a grueling six-month quest to unearth evidence that will lead to a conviction of the "big fellow" on tax evasion charges.

During the investigation, Warren is savagely beaten by henchmen of the "big fellow," but he continues to doggedly pursue the case, eventually persuading Zanger's partner, Salvatore Rocco (Anthony Caruso), to turn over valuable information. But Rocco, too, is murdered, and Warren decides to leave the agency after a high-powered mob attorney intimates that Warren's wife is in danger. But before Warren can resign, he is urged by the immigrant mother of Salvatore Rocco to remain on the case. The woman gives Warren a ledger found in her son's belongings that contains the evidence needed to indict the "big fellow," and the mobster, along with his underlings, are sent to jail.

Although *The Undercover Man* was labeled as an "exciting, fast-paced film" in *Motion Picture Herald*, and dismissed as "drearily static," in the *New York Times*, Foch received mostly favorable notices for her understated performance, and starred next in a diverting crime drama, *Johnny Allegro* (1949), playing opposite George Raft as the wife of a crime boss. This film, her last under her Columbia contract, was followed by another stint on Broadway in *A Phoenix Too Frequent* and Shakespeare's *King Lear*.

When she returned to Hollywood, Foch signed with MGM, appearing in *An American in Paris* (1951), which starred Gene Kelly and Leslie Caron and was acclaimed as the studio's great artistic triumph of the year. Next, she was loaned to United Artists for *St. Benny the Dip* (1951), a mediocre tale starring crooner Dick Haymes as a con man who impersonates a priest and hides from the law in a Bowery mission. Although the film was not a box office success, Foch was singled out for her performance by the critic for *Variety*, who wrote, "Miss Foch is excellent as the romantic interest who finally reforms Haymes through marriage. She's the only important femme in the cast." Foch then returned to MGM for *Young Man with Ideas* (1952), an amusing light comedy starring Glenn Ford; *Scaramouche* (1952), an entertaining Stewart Granger starrer that scored high at the box office; *Sombrero* (1952), an overly complicated romantic drama that flopped despite a cast that included Vittorio Gassman, Yvonne DeCarlo and Ricardo Montalban; and *Fast Company* (1953), a horse-racing saga with Howard Keel and Polly Bergen.

In 1954, Foch ended her agreement with MGM with *Executive Suite*, an absorbing drama about the professional and private lives of a company's board members. The film, which boasted a top-notch cast including Barbara Stanwyck, Fredric March, William Holden, Shelley Winters, Walter Pidgeon and June Allyson, featured Foch in a small role as a loyal and efficient secretary. Foch had to be talked into taking the role by producer John Houseman, and although it consisted of only ten lines, Foch turned in a performance that earned her an Academy Award nomination for Best Supporting Actress (she lost to Eva Marie Saint for *On the Waterfront*). "There was really no part there," Foch said in a 1979 interview in *The Hollywood Reporter*. "If it worked, it's because there was acting and there was training to turn those few lines into a real person. I'm not saying that I'm so good," she added modestly. "I'm just saying that I'm well trained."

In Foch's second 1954 release, she appeared in Universal's *Four Guns to the Border* (1954), a Technicolor Western that told the story of four financially strapped cowboys who rob a bank. The film was unpopular with audiences, but Foch later said she enjoyed her role as the wife of the town sheriff: "This woman is a strong character, righteous and mean when her temper is worked up by her enemies," the actress said. "She is no glamour girl. The role was a challenge, an experiment, and I liked playing her very much." Also that year, Foch joined the American Shakespeare Festival at Stratford, Connecticut, portraying Isabella in *Measure for Measure* and Katharine in *The Taming of the Shrew*. "My agent almost killed me," Foch said of her decision to participate in the annual festival. "'What are you doing that for?' he asked. Well, because I wanted to play Stratford sometime in my life."

Between her film and stage appearances, Foch somehow managed to find time for a personal life. On June 12, 1954, following a long engagement, she married James Lipton, then-star of the CBS-TV soap opera *The Guiding Light*. Several months after the wedding, Foch said of her husband, "We enjoy the same things, we love each other. Better still, we like each other. Two years of being together as constantly as my work permits assured us that we can put up with each other's faults." Despite her confident words, however, the marriage ended five years later.

Back on screen, Foch was seen next with Dean Martin and Jerry Lewis in Paramount's *You're Never Too Young* (1955), and opposite Edward G. Robinson in *Illegal* (1955), her first film for Warner Bros., the studio that had dropped her more than a decade before. Meanwhile, having debuted on television in the late 1940s on *Outward Bound* with Lillian Gish and Mary Boland, Foch added a wide variety of guest appearances to her hectic performing schedule and during the next several decades would appear on hundreds of programs, including *Climax, Playhouse 90, Studio One, Route 66, Bonanza, The Wild Wild West, McCloud, Name of the Game, Gunsmoke, Hawaii Five-O* and *Owen Marshall, Counselor at Law.* In addition to her guest roles, Foch also served as moderator for an NBC debate program, *Let's Take Sides* and as a frequent panelist on *It's News to Me.* In 1980, she was nominated for an Emmy Award for her portrayal of a fragile Hollywood recluse on *Lou Grant.* "I love TV; it's a good, tough, hard profession with some very nice people working in it," Foch said. "Nobody has any personal ego to be buttered. The standards of acting in TV are better than any other medium. TV shows the actor's true worth. It separates the men from the boys."

In her sole film of 1956, Foch turned in a sensitive and memorable performance in Cecil B. DeMille's epic *The Ten Commandments*, portraying the Egyptian pharaoh's sister who finds the baby Moses in the bullrushes and raises him as her own. Reportedly, DeMille selected Foch for the role after spotting her in *Sombrero*, which he was viewing in order to appraise actress Yvonne DeCarlo, who would be cast as Sephora, the long-suffering wife of Moses. "Don't ask me why he wanted me in the picture. He could have had others more suitable," Foch said shortly after filming ended on the picture. "I'm not exactly everybody's idea of an Egyptian — I'm blonde and blue-eyed. Wigs and brown contact lenses took care of that though. The lenses, by the way, were a problem in themselves. They gave the effect of very dark sun glasses and I couldn't see to the left or right, only straight ahead. I spent considerable time tripping over things on the set." The difficulties with her contact lenses aside, Foch would be highly critical of the popular film many years later, calling it "a terrible film" and lamenting her participation in it: "I did the DeMille picture in a year when I was very hot. What a stupid thing to do to tie myself up for 28 weeks with Cecil B. DeMille in a rotten picture," she said in a 1980 interview for *Drama-Logue.* "I knew it was going to be rotten ... and I'll always be remembered for it. I can't go anywhere without people falling over dead, 'Oh I remember you in *The Ten Commandments.*'"

The following year, Foch appeared in *Three Brave Men* (1957), a passable 20th Century–Fox drama starring Ray Milland and Ernest Borgnine. But at the relatively young age of 33, the actress found that her screen offers were dwindling. "I leave it to you to decide what a person like me is to do at this stage of my career," she told Joe Hyams of the *New York Herald Tribune.* "Now I've come to this point in a society that doesn't admire being just old. I can at last do the things I'm no longer asked to do. I can play 12-year-olds or 90-year-olds or glamour girls ... but no one knows what to do with me." Undaunted, the actress continued her numerous appearances on the small screen, including an acclaimed performance on *Alcoa Theatre* in the televised version of "A

Double Life," and in 1958 became an assistant to director George Stevens on *The Diary of Anne Frank*. In this capacity, she worked closely with each of the film's actors, particularly Millie Perkins, who portrayed the title role, helping to polish their performances and gain a deeper understanding of their roles. "I'm trying this kind of position out for size," Foch said at the time. "My dream of being successful is one of personal satisfaction that will come only with fulfilling my own ideals as an artist, and that includes helping someone else realize their art, too."

In addition to her coaching duties and television appearances, Foch found time to indulge the passion for painting that she'd harbored since childhood, staging an exhibition of her artwork in Beverly Hills and holding two one-woman shows in New York, where more than half of her paintings were purchased by patrons. The following year, 1960, Foch returned to the big screen in Warner Bros.' *Cash McCall*, which starred James Garner as a financial whiz-kid who is nearly destroyed because of his business ventures, and Universal's *Spartacus* (1960), joining a star-studded cast that included Kirk Douglas in the title role, Laurence Olivier, Jean Simmons, Charles Laughton, Peter Ustinov and Tony Curtis.

After returning to Broadway in 1960 for *A Second String*, Foch married for the second time, to television writer Dennis Brite. Two years later, at age 38, Foch gave birth to a son, Schuyler Dirk Brite, but she and Brite divorced in 1963. Four years later, she would marry again, this time to producer Michael Dewell. Throughout the 1960s, Foch continued her numerous television appearances, and from 1966 to 1968 she served as adjunct professor on the faculty of the University of Southern California. After an absence from feature films of more than a decade, she appeared in Otto Preminger's *Such Good Friends* (1971), a mediocre comedy in which Foch stood out as a prim, pushy mother. In 1974 she appeared in *Salty*, a little-seen film by the producers of the *Flipper* and *Gentle Ben* television series.

Since then, Foch has concentrated primarily on serving others with her considerable talents. She has served as artist-in-residence at several institutions, including the University of Ohio at Columbus and the University of North Carolina at Greensboro and worked as a faculty member for the American Film Institute's Center for Advanced Film Studies. In 1975 she founded the Nina Foch Studio, where she provided private coaching to actors, pop artists, producers, directors and screenwriters, as well as consulting services for trial lawyers, corporate executives and government officials in preparation for their public appearances. "The reason I'm a good teacher is because I love it and because I'm tough," Foch said. "There's not that much difference between acting for films, TV, or the stage. I've done them all…. Whatever differences there are, I can teach in 20 minutes."

In recent years, Foch has been seen in supporting roles in a number of films, including *Rich and Famous* (1981), *Indian Summer* (1986), *Skin Deep* (1989),

Morning Glory (1993), *It's My Party* (1996), *'Til There Was You* (1997) and *Hush* (1998), and in 1996 served as consultant for *Moll Flanders,* which starred Liam Neeson and Morgan Freeman. And with a career under her belt that has spanned more than a half century, the actress shows no signs of stopping. "I think you must be fiercely disciplined in every part of your life," Foch has said. "You can't indulge in anything less than perfection. Everything you do must be done with enormous personal pride. In fact, if you look at the people who last, you know I've been around long enough to notice who's here still, only the strong survive."

Film Noir Filmography

MY NAME IS JULIA ROSS   *Director:* Joseph H. Lewis. *Producer:* Wallace MacDonald. Released by Columbia, November 1945. *Running time:* 64 minutes. *Cast:* Nina Foch, Dame May Whitty, George Macready, Roland Varno, Anita Bolster, Doris Lloyd, Leonard Mudie, Joy Harrington, Queenie Leonard.

JOHNNY O'CLOCK   *Director:* Robert Rossen. *Producer:* Edward G. Nealis. Released by Columbia, March 1947. *Running time:* 95 minutes. *Cast:* Dick Powell, Evelyn Keyes, Lee J. Cobb, Ellen Drew, Nina Foch, Thomas Gomez, John Kellogg, Jim Bannon.

THE DARK PAST   *Director:* Rudolph Maté. *Producer:* Buddy Adler. Released by Columbia, December 1948. *Running time:* 74 minutes. *Cast:* William Holden, Nina Foch, Adele Jergens, Stephen Dunne, Lois Maxwell, Berry Kroeger, Steven Geray, Wilton Graff, Robert Osterloh.

THE UNDERCOVER MAN   *Director:* Joseph H. Lewis. *Producer:* Robert Rossen. Released by Columbia, April 1949. *Running time:* 85 minutes. *Cast:* Glenn Ford, Nina Foch, James Whitmore, Barry Kelley, David Wolfe, Frank Tweddell, Howard St. John, John F. Hamilton, Leo Penn, Joan Lazer, Esther Minciotti, Angela Clarke, Anthony Caruso, Robert Osterloh, Kay Medford.

References

Barnes, Edward. "Nina Foch Fibbed Her Way to Broadway." *New York Inquirer,* May 26, 1957.

Biography of Nina Foch. Paramount Pictures Corporation, circa 1971.

Braun, Katherine. "Nina Foch Has a Technique for Survival in a 'Tough Business.'" *The Hollywood Drama-Logue,* April 10-16, 1986.

"Consuelo Flowerton Dies; Follies Beauty, Film Star." *New York Herald Tribune,* December 22, 1965.

Danzig, Fred. "Cologne Bath Her Recipe for Acting." *New York World Telegram,* December 2, 1957.

Fields, Sidney. "Nina Foch: In and Out of the Nile." *New York Daily Mirror,* May 27, 1955.

Friedman, Stan L., and Associates. Biography of Nina Foch. Los Angeles California, circa 1980.

Galligan, David. "Nina Foch Dissects Directors." *The Hollywood Drama-Logue,* August 28–September 3, 1980.

Hyams, Joe. "Nina Foch Tries a New Job." *New York Herald Tribune*, July 8, 1958.

Knight, Arthur. "An Actor Prepares: Nina Foch." *The Hollywood Reporter*, August 24, 1979.

Leamy, Edmund. "How Old Is Nina?" *World Telegram and Sun Saturday Magazine*, circa 1952.

McClelland, Doug. "Nina Tries Again." *Newark Sunday News*, October 9, 1955.

Minoff, Philip. "Elementary for Nina." *Cue,* April 28, 1951.

"Nina Foch: Shakespeare Above Money." *TV Guide,* June 15, 1957.

"Nina Foch Stages Own Art Exhibition." *Newark Evening News*, October 15, 1959.

Pollock, Arthur. "Nina Foch: From Gun Moll to a Bourgeoise Widow." *The Daily Compass*, April 19, 1950.

Schallert, Edwin. "Nina Foch Career Gains New Luster." *Los Angeles Times*, December 30, 1945.

"Son Born to Nina Foch." *New York Times*, October 31, 1962.

Torre, Marie. "Nina Came Hither, Films Took a Look." *New York World Telegram,* April 25, 1949.

Sally Forrest

In the annals of Hollywood, the name Sally Forrest is not one that is readily recognized. But while her film career spanned less than a decade, this attractive blonde with the distinctive blue eyes was a highly regarded talent during her heyday in the 1940s and 1950s, and she appeared on screen with many of the era's top stars, including Claire Trevor, Mickey Rooney, Burt Lancaster and Dana Andrews. Once described as possessing "dancing feet and stardust in her eyes," Forrest has not graced the big screen with her presence since 1957, but she appeared in close to 20 films during her brief career, including three multifaceted examples of the film noir era: *Mystery Street* (1950), *The Strip* (1951) and *While the City Sleeps* (1956).

Born Katherine Sally Feeney on May 28, 1928, in San Diego, California, the actress with the effervescent personality was the third child of Ireland-born Michael James Feeney, a career boatswain's mate in the U.S. Navy, and his wife Karolina. Young Sally's parents were what she termed "awfully good" ballroom dancers, which perhaps led to her early interest in dance. Although the family did not have the money for lessons ("We couldn't afford anything," she said), Sally was able to enroll in a series of inexpensive summer courses in dance, and made her performance debut at the age of five. "I played the triangle in a kindergarten recital," the actress recalled. "But I was not happy about it—I wanted to play the castanets." Still, with this initial appearance under her belt, the youngster seemed to be irrevocably aimed toward a career in the arts. "It was always there," she said of her desire to perform. "I can't remember a time when it wasn't."

Because her father's navy job forced the family to frequently move from town to town, Sally was educated in several West Coast cities, including Long Beach and Bremerton ("I seemed to change schools every year"). But when Sally was 12, the Feeney family settled in San Diego, where the already attractive adolescent would begin charting her course to Hollywood. Her trek was initiated by Marguerite Ellicott, the teacher from one of Sally's summer dance courses and one of the early founders of Starlights, San Diego's Civic Light Opera Company. "She was really, really wonderful—a fantastic teacher," the actress said. "She saw me and my mother on the street one day and she said I should pursue career in dance." Ellicott offered to give Sally lessons and, in exchange, Sally would assist in teaching classes to younger students.

During her high school years, Sally honed her performing skills by appearing in "everything they had in school," and earned extra money by modeling for a local photographer. But fate stepped in during her last year in high school when she was taken under the wing of a San Diego couple who were involved in show business. "They were really a big part of helping me get into my career," Sally said. "They brought me up here to Hollywood, took me around to the studios, and I got a job right out of high school as a chorus girl at Metro, which in those days was extremely rare—and really nice."

Upon her arrival in Hollywood in 1945, the actress billed herself as Cary

Gibson, acting on the advice of a female agent. "[The agent] thought it was a very interesting name, but I suppose I didn't feel like a Cary," she said. Instead, she retained her middle name and chose the name Forrest after randomly selecting it from a telephone book. Many years later, after learning that her family's original Irish name was O'Phaerna, Forrest would lament her name change: "That's a terrible thing that I'll regret forever," she said. "Sally O'Phaerna — I would have loved that name."

Before long, Forrest had secured dancing roles in several movies, including her film debut in *Till the Clouds Roll By* (1946), a box office smash about the life of composer Jerome Kern. She also worked as assistant to studio choreographer Robert Alton on such major MGM musicals as *The Kissing Bandit* (1948). But after two years, Forrest was among the casualties when MGM dropped all its dancers as part of a retrenchment program. Undaunted, Forrest found work as a private dancing coach, and fortune smiled on her again when she applied for a job teaching Spanish dances to actor Anthony Dexter, who was preparing for a role as Rudolph Valentino in an upcoming biopic for Columbia Studios. While visiting the studio, Forrest recalled, she was unaware that a young agent by the name of Milo Frank had his eye on her. "I got the job and on my way out, I went into several offices by mistake," the actress said, adding that she literally bumped into Frank. "I asked him how to get out and we started talking. I told him my name was Sally Feeney, and he said that must be my real name, because nobody would choose a name like that. I thought he was awful cute. He told me, 'You can't be just a dancer in this town, you have to be an actress.' And he was right."

Before long, Forrest became Frank's client and steady date, and under his direction, she won her first starring role. As one of 250 hopefuls, Forrest was given the lead in *Not Wanted* (1949), the first film directed by actress Ida Lupino. "It was absolutely extraordinary, of course," Forrest said of her "discovery" by Lupino. "I had expected to be successful, and this was the beginning. [The film] was very controversial then because it was about an unwed mother. Now, it wouldn't even raise an eyebrow." Made on a shoestring budget of less than $200,000, *Not Wanted* was a box office hit, and Forrest received glowing reviews. The actress would later credit her performance to Lupino's direction: "She was an absolutely wonderful person, multi-talented. She wrote, directed, produced, and I even wore her clothes in this picture, so she was an all-around girl. She gave me a wonderful basis, a wonderful beginning."

Forrest's performance in *Not Wanted* was noticed by a number of critics, including famed columnist Louella Parsons, who bestowed on the actress a special citation for the best performance by a newcomer. "The characterization she projects with such poignance is such a demanding one," Parsons wrote. "She is innocent, enraptured, hurt, lost, resigned, and finally happy, as the script demands, and never once does she reveal that she has barely said a line before this picture."

The following year, Forrest was cast in Lupino's *Never Fear* (1950), co-starring Hugh O'Brian and Keefe Brasselle. Again, Forrest was well-received for her portrayal of a young dancer who faces adjustment problems when she contracts polio. Meanwhile, MGM was searching for an actress who combined youth, good looks and talent for their upcoming film *Mystery Street* (1950). Forrest was the 89th actress who interviewed for the role — and the last. Upon receiving the part, she signed a contract with the studio that had released her several years earlier. Forrest said that she was thrilled to be given the part: "I was always ecstatic. It was always the best thing in the world."

In *Mystery Street* (1950), Forrest's first film noir, she portrayed Grace Shanway, whose luckless husband, Henry (Marshall Thompson), has been arrested for the murder of Vivian Heldon (Jan Sterling), a flashy cocktail waitress. Henry assures Grace of his innocence, admitting that Vivian had stolen his car after he'd gotten drunk in a bar, and that he'd never seen her again. Arresting officer Peter Morales (Ricardo Montalban) begins to doubt Henry's guilt, but continues to search for evidence, incurring the ire of Grace: "I had measles and whooping cough — a couple of tickets for parking in a no-parking zone. Honeymooned in Niagara Falls — I stole a towel from the hotel there. Maybe you'd like to arrest me, too," she says bitterly. "No? Maybe my husband's mother. She comes from Kansas. That's where they raise wheat. I'm sure there must be a law against that somewhere!"

After further investigation, Morales learns that Vivian had been romantically involved with a wealthy married man, James Harkley (Edmon Ryan). Meanwhile, Harkley is being blackmailed by Vivian's landlady, Mrs. Smerrling (Elsa Lanchester), who stole Harkley's gun after realizing that he murdered Vivian. Harkley visits Mrs. Smerrling's apartment in an effort to recover the weapon, but he kills her when she refuses to produce the claim check that he needs to retrieve it from the local train station. Followed closely by Morales, Harkley convinces the station baggage claim attendant to turn over the suitcase containing the gun, but he discovers that the gun's clip has been removed and he is later cornered by Morales and arrested.

After the release of *Mystery Street*, Forrest was hailed for her "solid" performance, and was later named in a *Photoplay* Magazine poll as "The Newcomer Most Likely to Become a Star." Years later, the actress stated that she was "knocked out" to receive the honor: "Howard Keel was the opposite man, and I got many more votes than he," she said. "I just knew I was on my way then." In 1951, Forrest continued her successful ride to film fame, appearing in *Bannerline*, an newspaper drama with Lewis Stone and Lionel Barrymore, *The Strange Door*, an eerie tale starring Charles Laughton as a crazed French nobleman, *Excuse My Dust*, a Red Skelton vehicle about the dizzy inventor of a horseless carriage, and the Ida Lupino–directed *Hard, Fast and Beautiful*. In the latter film, the actress played a promising tennis player thrust into the limelight by her ambitious mother (Claire Trevor), and earned high praise in

Variety, whose reviewer stated: "Miss Forrest adds another strong credit to her growing list. With continued good assignments, the young actress has the makings of a name."

Also in 1951, Forrest starred in her second film noir, *The Strip*, with Mickey Rooney and William Demarest. Here, she portrayed Jane Tafford, a nightclub dancer and aspiring actress who, as one character says, "only likes to get mixed up with people who can do her some good." Jane is initially indifferent when the club's new drummer, Stanley Maxton (Mickey Rooney), falls for her, but she later encourages his affections when she learns that one of Stan's associates, Sonny Johnson (James Craig), has "connections" to the film industry. A ruthless racketeer with no intentions of furthering Jane's career, Sonny seduces the young dancer, and when Stan tries to warn Jane, he is beaten by Sonny's underlings and ordered to leave town. Angered by Sonny's tactics, Jane accidentally kills him during an argument, but not before she is herself seriously wounded during the struggle for the gun. Later, Stan tries to protect Jane by saying that he killed Sonny, but shortly before she dies in custody, Jane admits her guilt. Stan unhappily returns to his job at the nightclub.

Upon its release, *The Strip* was judged as merely mediocre by most critics; *Variety* panned the performances as "generally ineffective, as characters are not real enough to be believable." Forrest, however, did earn acclaim for her dance numbers in the film, which were labeled "excellent" in *Variety*.

Despite her nearly non-stop film schedule, Forrest managed to find time for her personal life. On August 5, 1951, she and agent Milo Frank were married, with Ida Lupino serving as matron of honor, and the couple would go on to enjoy one of Hollywood's longest and most successful unions. That year was also notable for the release of *The Daring Miss Jones*, an exploitation film featuring Forrest. The actress, along with future television star Betty White, had appeared in the film several years earlier, while both were working as chorus girls at Metro. "After I made a name for herself, a lawyer who was a bad egg bought [the film]," Forrest remembered of the effort to cash in on her new-found celebrity. "It was just this stupid little thing. There was no reason to release it."

But this low-budget bomb had no effect on Forrest's career. In 1952, when Milo Frank accepted an executive post with CBS Television, the actress moved with her husband to New York, working in summer stock and later playing on Broadway in *The Seven Year Itch* opposite Tom Ewell. The year-long run was "just a wonderful experience," Forrest said. "And Tom was so wonderful. He was a pro beyond the pro. He did a lot of smoking in the show and one night the sofa caught fire. Without missing a beat, he went over, got the seltzer bottle, and put out the fire. No one knew but us."

The following year, the actress returned to the big screen in *Code Two* (1953) featuring Ralph Meeker and Keenan Wynn. But this tepid drama about motorcycle police in training would complete Forrest's contract with MGM and, as quickly as her cinematic star had risen, she found that her services were no longer in demand. Next Forrest appeared with Dale Robertson and Lili St. Cyr in RKO's *Son of Sinbad* (1955), a box office flop that suffered from major censorship problems and was condemned by the Catholic Legion of Decency. Forrest had inked an agreement with RKO because studio head Howard Hughes "liked to have girls under contract," but after *Son of Sinbad*, the actress was offered no further film roles by the studio. Before long, she told RKO executives that she "wanted a new picture or out of her contract," Forrest recalled. "Needless to say, I got out of it — after howling and yowling for a long time."

Meanwhile, Forrest continued her stage career, playing to excellent reviews in *Damn Yankees* in Vancouver, British Columbia; *Remains to Be Seen* with Roddy McDowall in San Francisco; and *Bus Stop* in LaJolla, California, opposite Lee Marvin. She also appeared on numerous television variety programs, including *The Ed Sullivan Show*, *The Dinah Shore Show*, *The Red Skelton Show*, *Ford Star Jubilee*, *Lux Video Theatre* and *Front Row Center*.

Back on screen, Forrest starred in her final film noir in 1956, RKO's *While the City Sleeps*, a complex tale that centers on the employees of a powerful news organization, including television anchor Edward Mobley (Dana Andrews), newspaper editor John Day Griffith (Thomas Mitchell), wire service manager Mark Loving (George Sanders), photo service editor Harry Kritzer (James Craig) and reporter Mildred Donner (Ida Lupino). After the death of the company's owner, the organization is taken over by the amateurish Walter Kyne (Vincent Price), who forces the company's top staff members to compete for the newly created job of executive director — he will award the post to the first man who is able to unravel the mystery behind a series of violent sex murders.

In an effort to secure the coveted job, each of the men shamelessly exploits the woman in his life — Kritzer, who is having an affair with Kyne's wife (Rhonda Fleming), asks his mistress to use her influence to sway the job in his favor; Loving seeks help from his girlfriend Mildred to obtain information from Mobley, who, in turn, sets up his fiancée, Nancy (Sally Forrest), to act as bait for the killer. Although Nancy first balks at the idea ("You don't want a wife — you want an illiterate, common law woman," she tells Mobley), she later agrees to her fiancé's scheme, resulting in the capture of the killer, a mentally unbalanced delivery boy. Mobley gives the scoop to John Griffith, who is given the job, and Mobley and Nancy wind up together.

Forrest and her costars were praised in the *New York Times* for "doing justice to their assignments," but the actress next appeared in Columbia's *Ride the High Iron* (1956), a tedious soaper starring Don Taylor and Raymond Burr that was originally made for television and quickly disappeared soon after its theatrical release. Forrest's portrayal of a poor little rich girl would be her final screen role, not necessarily by design, but definitely with no regrets. In 1960,

Sally Forrest

Forrest was signed to a two-week stint at the New Frontier Hotel in Las Vegas with George Chakiris. "George and I had just done a television variety show, *The Ford Star Theatre*," Forrest said in a 1984 *Drama-Logue* interview. "We were celebrating at Chasen's when a phone call came from these Las Vegas producers who had seen the show and wanted us to open in Vegas. That's the kind of thing that usually doesn't happen." The two-week gig wound up being held over for the next three months: "It was the most marvelous thing," Forrest said.

After her Las Vegas appearance, Forrest was away from performing for the next two decades, spending much of her time traveling to Europe and the Orient with her husband, who had become a consultant to the international communications industry. "My life went on," Forrest said. "When you're traveling as much as I have, you cannot do them both. I'm a happily married person, so I don't have to worry about things. When you've done it when you're young, you don't have that terrible gnawing, 'oh I've got to do it.' I've done it."

But in 1984, following a 24-year absence from the stage, Forrest starred in *No, No, Nanette* at the Starlight Theatre in San Diego. For her role as Sue Smith, the actress had to learn tap dancing for the first time, but she rose to the challenge, telling the press, "It's hard work and so different from ballet where I was always used to being on the ground. I'm glad I got the chance to learn." Since her well-received performance in *No, No Nanette*, Forrest has again been out of the spotlight, writing television commercials for political figures for whom her husband served as consultant, and is working on a novel that she describes as "based on fact and people I've known in Asia — some pretty amazing people."

Forrest looks back with fond memories on her relatively brief but exciting film career, stating that she now concentrates on "living and being happy and gardening. I still dance every day. I live a good life. Early on, I wanted to be Greta Garbo, but now I feel it was just right. I had enough of it and it was fun, but my life is good.

"And I'm still here."

Film Noir Filmography

MYSTERY STREET   *Director:* John Sturges. *Producer:* Frank E. Taylor. Released by MGM, July 1950. *Running time:* 94 minutes. *Cast:* Ricardo Montalban, Sally Forrest, Bruce Bennett, Elsa Lanchester, Marshall Thompson, Jan Sterling, Edmon Ryan, Betsy Blair. *Award:* Academy Award nomination for Best Original Screenplay (Leonard Spigelgass).

THE STRIP   *Director:* Leslie Kardos. *Producer:* Joe Pasternak. Released by MGM, August 1951. *Running time:* 84 minutes. *Cast:* Mickey Rooney, Sally Forrest, William Demarest, James Craig, Kay Brown, Tommy Rettig, Tom Powers. *Award:* Academy Award nomination for Best Song (Bert Kalmar, Harry Ruby, Oscar Hammerstein II).

WHILE THE CITY SLEEPS   *Director:* Fritz Lang. *Producer:* Bert Friedlob. Released by RKO, May 1956. *Running time:* 99 minutes. *Cast:* Dana Andrews, Rhonda Fleming, George Sanders, Howard Duff, Thomas Mitchell, Vincent Price, Sally Forrest, John Barrymore, Jr., James Craig, Ida Lupino.

References

Asher, Jerry. "Love Walked Right In." *Photoplay*, February 1951.
Chandler, David. "It Pays to Get Fired." *Collier's*, January 21, 1950.
Hyams, Joe. "Sally Forrest May Replace Jane Russell with RKO." *New York Herald Tribune*, March 1, 1954.

Mulvey, Kay. "The Forrest Party Plan." *Photoplay*, January 1951.

"On Her Way." *New York World Telegram and Sun*, July 1962.

Parsons, Louella O. "Cosmopolitan's Citation for the Best Performance by a Newcomer." *Cosmopolitan*, September 1949.

"Sally's Up in the Air." *Weekend Picture Magazine*, November 7, 1954.

Skolsky, Sidney. "Hollywood Is My Beat." *New York Post*, October 1950.

Steckling, Larry D. "Tapping Home with Sally Forrest." *Drama-Logue*, August 2–8, 1984.

Strickling, Howard. Biography of Sally Forrest. MGM Studios, circa 1951.

"The Turning Point." *Parade*, August 1951.

"What's Become of Sally ... Look!" *New York Journal American*, May 1954.

Ava Gardner

Labeled "the most beautiful animal in the world," Ava Gardner possessed a significant talent that was often dismissed because of her smoldering looks, or overshadowed by her marriages to three of the nation's most well-known men. Although she enjoyed a successful film career that spanned nearly a half-century, Gardner was far from the typical Hollywood star. She was instead a free spirit who defied convention, "like a child let loose in a candy store," as a friend once said. Her off-screen exploits notwithstanding, Gardner offered a number of highly acclaimed performances in such films as *The Barefoot Contessa* (1954) and *Night of the Iguana* (1964). She made her first cinematic splash in her sole film noir appearance, *The Killers* (1946).

The youngest of seven children, Ava Lavinia Gardner was born on December 24, 1922, in Grabtown, North Carolina. Her father was a sharecropper on a tobacco farm and, along with her siblings, Gardner worked in the fields. In her autobiography, she stated that she disliked school, particularly because it required her to force her feet into shoes and she loved going barefoot: "It's a special kind of freedom," she stated.

In 1929, the Depression caused tobacco prices to plummet, forcing the Gardner family to abandon the home that had been theirs for 30 years. The family was "dirt poor," Gardner said, and she and her mother Mollie were forced to move to Newport News, Virginia, where Mollie took in boarders. After Ava's father died a few years later, the family moved back to North Carolina, this time to the rural community of Rock Ridge.

At the age of 17, Gardner enrolled in the Atlantic Christian College in Wilson, North Carolina, where she studied business education and secretarial science. But her career plans went in a new direction the following summer when she visited the New York home of her eldest sister, Beatrice — known as Bappie — and her husband, Larry Tarr, the owner of a photography studio. After Tarr placed a picture of Gardner in the window of his studio, it caught the attention of Barney Duhan, a clerk for the legal department of MGM. At Duhan's request, Tarr delivered a dozen portraits of Gardner to MGM's New York offices, which ultimately led to her first screen test. Shortly afterward, the studio expressed interest in offering Gardner a contract, and as Gardner later stated: "Movies may not have been a dream of mine, but I admit, straight away, that when I compared the idea of a secretarial job in Wilson, North Carolina, with the chance of going to Hollywood and breathing the same air as Clark Gable — well, the choice was not hard to make."

On August 23, 1941, Gardner and her sister arrived in Hollywood, but her introduction to the film capital was memorable more for personal (rather than career-related) reasons. While taking a tour of the sound stage for the musical *Babes on Broadway*, she met Mickey Rooney, who immediately asked the stunning starlet to dinner. Although the actress said she was initially "stunned" by Rooney's diminutive stature, she soon found him to be "charming, romantic and great fun — the original laugh-a-minute boy ... so different from me. He was enthusiastic and sure of himself, and me, I was still a tongue-tied country girl." After a whirlwind romance, the two became man and wife on January 10, 1942.

After signing a contract for $50 a week, Gardner spent most of her time posing for cheesecake photos (including one seated on a block of ice with an ice cream cone in hand) and participating in lessons in elocution, drama and voice projection, successfully ridding her of her thick North Carolina accent. But her first screen appearance did little to show the results of her studies. It was a one-day bit in the Norma Shearer vehicle *We Were Dancing* (1942), in which Gardner strolled across a hotel lobby. Next, in *Joe Smith—American* (1942), Gardner can be seen in a background shot as a German spy groupie.

Despite her new status as Mrs. Mickey Rooney, Gardner continued to appear in mediocre roles, including a walk-on in *Reunion in France* (1942) starring Joan Crawford, and her first speaking part as a waitress in *Kid Glove Killer* (1942). In a 1951 magazine article, Gardner credited her husband as refining her talents during these years: "Mickey was so patient, so kind ... he showed me how to walk, to stand, what to do with my hands, how to ignore the camera. If I ever do anything big, I'll owe a lot of it to Mickey, bless him." In striking contrast, however, Gardner stated in her autobiography that Rooney did little to further her burgeoning career: "The plain facts are that being Mrs. Rooney never gave me a single boost in the direction of stardom. Mickey never tried to make me an actress, never taught me anything and never got me an acting job." According to Gardner, Mickey spent most of their honeymoon playing golf, and the bulk of their marriage "loving booze, betting and girls." After a year, Gardner called it quits. The couple's divorce was granted on May 21, 1943 — the same day that Gardner's mother died of breast cancer.

For the next three years, Gardner was featured in a series of forgettable movies, including *Ghosts on the Loose* (1943), starring the Dead End Kids and Bela Lugosi; *Swing Fever* (1943), with Kay Kyser; *Maisie Goes to Reno* (1944), starring Ann Sothern; and *She Went to the Races* (1945), a comedy featuring James Craig and Edmund Gwenn. During these years, she was linked romantically with billionaire Howard Hughes, but their often rocky relationship would not be a permanent one. Instead, there was another man on the horizon — musician Artie Shaw. The couple was introduced by the wife of actor Van Heflin, and eight months after they began dating, Gardner moved into Shaw's Beverly Hills home, making her one of the first women in Hollywood to live openly with a man who was not her husband. Gardner called Shaw "the first intelligent, intellectual man I'd ever met and he bowled me over."

The couple's union was legalized on October 17, 1945, but as Shaw later said, "Marrying Ava was purely an act of propriety — we should not have gotten married. We had the best of our lives when we lived together." By all accounts, the two were simply mismatched, with Shaw trying to transform the country girl into an intellectual, hiring a Russian grandmaster to teach her chess, plying her with books by Sinclair Lewis, Dostoyevsky and Aldous Huxley, and introducing her to the works of Mozart and Beethoven. The marriage would only last a year and a week.

Professionally, Gardner's career was at a standstill, as MGM failed to capitalize on its beautiful asset. As stated by Sidney Guilaroff, Gardner's hairdresser and longtime friend, "MGM didn't even know what they had. They thought nothing of her. She just portrayed parts, little things — a girl, a hatcheck girl. Stock shots that didn't matter a thing. And she got nowhere. Not until she was loaned out. Other studios saw something in her that MGM didn't." In one such loanout, United Artists' *Whistle Stop* (1946), Gardner starred opposite George Raft, and her next film, Universal's *The Killers*, catapulted the actress to stardom.

Viewed as a quintessential noir film, *The Killers* featured Gardner as Kitty Collins, a ruthless femme fatale that she counted among her favorite screen roles. "Until I played the role of Kitty Collins in *The Killers*, I had never worked very hard in pictures, nor taken my career very seriously," Gardner said two years after the film's release. "Certainly I never fussed over the unimportant roles that came my way, and I felt no burning ambition to become a real actress. I was just a girl who was lucky enough to have a job in pictures; after I played Kitty I began to feel that I might have a little talent."

As *The Killers* begins, two professional gunmen enter a diner in the small town of Brentwood, New Jersey, and announce their intention to kill "the Swede" (superbly portrayed by Burt Lancaster in his debut role), a gas station attendant and frequent visitor to the diner. But their victim does not show up, and after they leave, the diner's owner sends a warning to the Swede, who admits only that he "got into some trouble once," and waits for his fate without resistance. After the murder, an insurance investigator, Jim Reardon (Edmond O'Brien), checking on the dead man's policy, undertakes to unsnarl the tangled threads of the Swede's past. Through interviews with a maid in New Jersey, a Philadelphia detective, a former sweetheart and three hoods who participated in a payroll robbery, Reardon unearths a pattern of greed, lust and murder.

Reardon's investigation reveals that the Swede, a former prizefighter, was lured into a life of petty crime by Kitty Collins, the girlfriend of gangleader Big Jim Colfax (Albert Dekker). From the first moment the Swede sees Kitty, clad in a form-fitting black dress, he seems unable to tear his gaze from her, like a moth fatally drawn to a flame. Kitty convinces him to take part in an elaborate armored car robbery, and later urges him to double-cross Colfax and take all of the money. The Swede goes along with the plan, but in the end, Kitty and Colfax escape with the loot. Reardon, in an effort to see justice done, sets himself up as a decoy to catch the Swede's killers. The two gunmen are shot by police, and Colfax is later murdered by one of the members of his own gang. Colfax dies in Kitty's arms as she screams hysterically, and in vain, for him to clear her name.

Gardner received high praise for her performance in *The Killers*, winning the *Look* magazine award for the most promising newcomer of 1947 (five years and 22 films after her arrival in Hollywood). Later, Gardner would credit producer Mark Hellinger with casting her in the part: "Mark saw me as an actress, not as a sexpot. He trusted me from the beginning, and I trusted him. I knew he was a genius. He gave me a feeling of the responsibility of being a movie star which I had never for a moment felt before."

Next, Gardner starred with Clark Gable and Deborah Kerr in The *Hucksters* (1947). Halfway through filming, however, she staged a brief walkout, which resulted in the increase of her salary to $1,250 a week. She signed a three-year contract, which included the promise of a $10,000 bonus at the satisfactory completion of the third year, and the right to borrow up to $25,000 from MGM, at the rate of four percent, for the purchase of a house. Despite this profitable agreement, *The Hucksters* was followed by a series of lightweight films including *Singapore* (1947), in which she was miscast as a sweet, young amnesia victim; *One Touch of Venus* (1948), featuring the actress as a statue of the goddess Venus come to life; *The Bribe* (1949), a box office flop starring Robert Taylor; *East Side, West Side* (1949), a predictable soaper with Gardner portraying the "other woman"; and *My Forbidden Past* (1951), which Gardner herself described as "melodramatic mishmash." During these years, Gardner kept up a spirited lifestyle of nightclub dancing and late hours, and drifted in and out of flings with a number of notables, including Howard Duff, Robert Taylor, Peter Lawford and a second whirl with Howard Hughes. But her most famous — and intense — relationship was yet to come, with crooner Frank Sinatra.

Gardner and Sinatra began their love affair in 1949, when Sinatra was still very much married to his wife and mother of his three children, Nancy. But Gardner was powerless to fight her feelings for Sinatra. "Oh, God, it was magic," she wrote in her autobiography. "I truly felt that no matter what happened, we would always be in love — and God almighty, things did happen." During the first few months of the affair, the couple were careful to avoid being seen together in public, but news of their affair exploded in the press after Gardner attended one of Sinatra's singing engagements, at the Shamrock Hotel in Houston. Within weeks, Gardner began receiving scores of hate mail calling her a "scarlet woman" and "homewrecker," a number of newspaper columnists turned on her, and the Legion of Decency threatened to ban her movies. In typical Gardner fashion, the actress declared, "I decided from the first that I had the right to act according to my own principles, and if mine clashed with theirs, and they didn't like it, that was not going to be my problem."

Meanwhile, the relationship between Gardner and Sinatra heated up in dramatic fashion, characterized by frequent arguments, jealous accusations and suicide threats. In 1950, Gardner traveled to Spain for filming on *Pandora and the Flying Dutchman* (a film that she ranks as one of her "most obscure"), and news quickly reached the United States that Gardner had

Ava Gardner in *The Killers*

become involved with Mario Cabre, a bullfighter turned actor who played one of Gardner's three lovers in the film. Sinatra responded by being photographed on the town with his former flame, actress Marilyn Maxwell, then flew to Spain, where he and Gardner spent five tense days together. Despite the publicity given to the affair, Gardner contended in her autobiography that her relationship with Cabre was limited to a one-night stand and that the bullfighter was "a Spanish pain in the ass, better at self-promotion than either bullfight-ing or love." Gardner left Spain — and Cabre — behind, and her combustible relationship with Sinatra continued to heat up.

In May 1951, Nancy Sinatra's attorneys announced that she had agreed to a divorce, and Gardner and Sinatra were married six months later. But the union would be a turbulent one. "They adored each other — fought the whole time," said Gardner's friend and costar Stewart Granger. For the next two years, the couple endured accusations of infidelity, physical altercations and separations caused by their careers. In addition, although she and Sinatra wanted children, Gardner underwent two abortions because, as she stated, she and her husband "didn't even possess the ability to live together like a nor-mal married couple." Two years after their marriage, the couple split, and on October 29, 1953, MGM's publicity director issued the following statement: "Ava Gardner and Frank Sinatra stated today that having reluctantly exhausted every effort to reconcile their differences, they could find no mutual basis on which to continue their marriage. Both expressed deep regret and great respect for each other. Their separation is final and Miss Gardner will seek a divorce."

Though her private life was in disarray, Gardner's acting career contin-ued to soar. After *Pandora*, she starred in the musical *Showboat*, in which she portrayed a half-caste Southern girl. While Gardner stated that the role of Julie was "one of the few I rather liked," she never forgave the studio for dub-bing another singer's voice for her two songs in the film. Next, she starred opposite Clark Gable in *Lone Star* (1952), followed by *The Snows of Kiliman-jaro* (1952) with Gregory Peck and Susan Hayward. In the latter film, Gard-ner played Cynthia, which she called the first role "I understood and felt com-fortable with, the first role I truly wanted to play." The following year, Gardner was again teamed with Clark Gable, this time in *Mogambo*, a remake of the Jean Harlow vehicle *Red Dust* (1932), for which Gardner received her only Academy Award nomination. (She lost to Audrey Hepburn in *Roman Holiday*.)

After appearing in *Knights of the Round Table* (1954), which Gardner termed "a typical piece of historical foolishness," she starred in the role with which she is perhaps best associated — Maria Vargas in *The Barefoot Contessa* (1954). As a poor Italian dancer who becomes an international movie star, Gardner was mesmerizing, particularly in the scenes in which she demon-strated her new proficiency in flamenco dancing. And Gardner's personal life continued to make headlines as well, with widely publicized affairs with Span-ish bullfighter Luis Miguel Dominguin and Italian actor Walter Chiari. But at this point, having never truly fit into the superficial and stifling Hollywood scene, Gardner left the United States for good in 1955 and settled in Spain. "Being a movie star in America is the loneliest life in the world," she explained. "In Europe they respect your privacy. No one believes me when I say I'm going to Europe to live, but I am, and I won't be back." Although she would travel back to Hollywood to film several movies, Gardner made good on her vow.

Gardner's stardom increased with her roles in *Bhowani Junction* (1956), as a half-caste beauty; *The Sun Also Rises* (1957), touted in advertisements as a story "so daring — so delicate — it could not be filmed until now"; *The Naked Maja* (1959), the film which marked the end of her MGM contract; and *On the Beach* (1959), starring Gregory Peck. Of her performance in the latter film, Peck later said Gardner was "quite magnificent. The role suited her — the role of a girl who has lived some, and been around some, few men in her life, been knocked around a little. She had experience to draw on."

After appearances in several films of little note, Gardner starred in 1964 with Richard Burton in *Night of the Iguana*, and critics raved about her performance, calling her "absolutely splendid" and claiming that she "all but runs away with the picture." Two years later, she appeared as Sarah in *The Bible*, and began an affair with costar George C. Scott. However, Scott was a heavy drinker and, according to Gardner, "could go berserk in a way that was quite terrifying." Although he was married at the time to actress Colleen Dewhurst, Scott was reportedly jealous of Gardner's friends and frequently flew into rages that turned violent. After a number of such episodes, one which resulted in Gardner suffering a detached retina in one eye, their relationship abruptly ended. Gardner would later say that the relationship so affected her that merely seeing Scott on television would make her "start to shake all over again."

In 1968, Gardner left Spain and moved to London, continuing to act despite her feeling that "being a film star is a big, damn bore. Given this, why do I keep doing it? For the loot, honey, always the loot." During the next several years, Gardner appeared in a dozen films, including *Mayerling* (1969) with Omar Sharif; *Earthquake* (1974), a disaster film starring Charlton Heston; and *The Sentinel* (1977), an odd horror film starring Cristina Raines and Burgess Meredith. Time, however had caused her fame to fade, and she would never recapture the superstar status that she had held for so many years. Her last film was the 1986 release *Harem*. Later, she would make a number of television appearances, including *Knots Landing* (1985), *The Long Hot Summer* (1985) and *Maggie* (1986).

In 1986, Gardner suffered a stroke and, after a long illness, died in London on January 25, 1990, at the age of 67. But the magic spell that she wove on screen lives after her. As described in a 1992 documentary by her friend, actor Roddy McDowall, "She was like a queen with the soul of a peasant." It is that spirit that Gardner leaves as her legacy.

Film Noir Filmography

THE KILLERS   *Director:* Robert Siodmak. *Producer:* Mark Hellinger. Released by Universal, August 1946. *Running time:* 105 minutes. *Cast:* Edmond O'Brien, Ava Gardner, Albert Dekker, Sam Levene, John Miljan, Virginia Christine, Vince Barnett,

Burt Lancaster, Charles D. Brown, Donald MacBride, Phil Brown, Charles McGraw, William Conrad. *Awards:* Academy Award nominations for Best Director (Robert Siodmak), Best Original Screenplay (Anthony Veiller), Best Editing (Arthur Hilton), Best Score (Miklos Rozsa).

References

Arnold, Maxine. "Lonesome on Top of the World." *Photoplay*, February 1954.
"Ava and Her Times." *Newsweek*, November 24, 1942.
"Ava Gardner — Beauty." *Vogue*, February 1, 1954.
"Ava Gardner Plays the Gypsy." *Colliers*, July 23, 1954.
"Ava Wants Out." *Modern Screen*, September 1952.
"Beautiful, but Wise." *Lions Review*, December 1944.
Caldwell, Rowena. "Twilight of a Goddess." *Ladies' Home Journal*, July 1972.
Corwin, Jane. "Cease Fire." *Photoplay*, December 1953.
"End of the Affair." *Time*, June 21, 1954.
"Farmer's Daughter." *Time*, September 3, 1951.
Flamini, Roland. *Ava.* New York: Coward, McCann & Geoghegan, 1983.
Gardner, Ava. *Ava: My Story.* New York: Bantam Books, 1990.
"Glamour in Africa; Filming *Mogambo*." *Look*, June 2, 1953
Graves, Robert. "A Toast to Ava Gardner." *New Yorker*, April 26, 1958.
Higham, Charles. *Ava: A Life Story.* New York: Delacorte Press, 1974.
"Hometown Girl." *Good Housekeeping*, April 1950.
"How Ava Gardner Fooled Hollywood." *Photoplay*, October 1951.
Hyams, Joe. "Private Hell of Ava Gardner." *Look*, November 27, 1956-December 11, 1956.
Mann, Roderick. "Ave Ava: A Maverick's Homecoming." *Los Angeles Times*, February 17, 1985.
"Man Who Wouldn't Look at Ava." *Look*, October 6, 1953.
"Many Passions, No Regrets." *People*, February 12, 1990.
Martin, Pete. "Tarheel Tornado." *Saturday Evening Post*, June 5, 1948.
Mathews, Leone. "Take it Easy, Ava." *Screenland*, May 1953.
Maxwell, Elsa. "The Gardner-Sinatra Jigsaw." *Photoplay*, July 1951.
"My Acting Makes Me Want to Die." *Motion Picture*, January 1950.
"New Light on Ava." *Life*, April 12, 1954.
Scott, Vernon. "Ava." *Ladies' Home Journal*, November 1974.
"The Strange Fears of Ava Gardner." *Modern Screen*, July 1950.
"Untamed." *Photoplay*, April 1973.
Vincent, Mal. "Ava Gardner." *Films in Review*, June-July 1965.
Waterbury, Ruth. "Ava Gardner's Dry Tears." *Photoplay*, April 1957.
_____. "The Life and Loves of Ava Gardner." *Photoplay*, February 1952.
Wayne, Jane Ellen. *Ava's Men: The Private Life of Ava Gardner.* Oxford: Clio Press, 1990.
"We Fight but We Love It." *Modern Screen*, August 1952.
"Why Is a Movie Star?" *Look*, February 10, 1943.
Wilson, Earl. "My Pal Ava." *Silver Screen*, June 1953.
"You Ought to Be in Pictures." *Lions Review*, April 1944.

Documentary

"Ava Gardner." Robert Guenette Productions. Copyright 1992, Home Box Office, Inc. As seen on "Crazy About the Movies," a presentation of Cinemax, a Time Warner Company.

Gloria Grahame

Perhaps the definitive film noir bad girl, Gloria Grahame was once described as "sexy in a strange way. Like a woman who's begging you to wallop her in the mouth, 'cause she'd just love it." With her expressive eyes and sulky countenance, she possessed an on-screen presence that almost always suggested more than a passing acquaintance with the wrong side of the tracks. But off-screen, Grahame suffered a series of sometimes scandalous, often tragic, personal experiences that frequently eclipsed her promising film career. Nonetheless, as an Academy Award nominee after only four years in Hollywood, and an Oscar winner for *The Bad and the Beautiful*, Grahame added a formidable contribution to almost every picture in which she appeared, and was a striking addition to seven films noirs: *Crossfire* (1947), *In a Lonely Place* (1950), *Macao* (1952), *Sudden Fear* (1952), *The Big Heat* (1953), *Human Desire* (1954) and *Odds Against Tomorrow* (1959).

The sultry actress was born Gloria Grahame Hallward in Los Angeles, California, on November 28. (Sources vary on the year of her birth, from 1923 to 1933, but most agree that she entered the world in 1925.) Gloria was a descendant of royalty — the antecedents of her father, Reginald Michael Hallward, were the Plantagenet kings of England, and her mother, Jean, a former actress, descended from Dougall, King in the south Isles and Lord of Lorn in Scotland. Her regal background notwithstanding, Gloria and her older sister Joy enjoyed a normal, fun-filled childhood, and theirs was the house on the block where all the neighborhood children would come to play. An industrial designer who later found success as the author of children's books, Reginald Hallward moved his family to San Diego when Gloria was still a child, then later to Pasadena, where he was stymied by the Depression in his efforts to find employment. Before long, perhaps due in part to Reginald's failure to support his family, the Hallwards were divorced and Reginald moved to Massachusetts, where he would later remarry and have a son, Peter. This rupture in the Hallward household would have a profound effect on the family. To support her children, Jean taught at the Westridge School, where Gloria was a student, gave private lessons in drama and forensics, and directed productions at the Pasadena Playhouse. Joy added to the family income by working as a secretary, and even Gloria contributed by taking odd jobs after school, including selling potted plants door to door.

Following in her mother's theatrical footsteps, Gloria made her stage debut at the age of nine, playing a fairy in *The Bluebird*, and later entered various forensic contests, twice being named a West Coast Forensics League Champion. In the late 1930s, in order to give Gloria the opportunity to seek an acting career, the family moved to Hollywood, where Gloria was enrolled at the Guy Bates Post School of dramatic art and later at Hollywood High School. Once there, it didn't take long for Gloria to land a role in her first professional production, *Maid in the Ozarks*, which played at the Los Angeles Grand Playhouse for more than a year.

In spring 1942, Gloria appeared in a senior class play, *Ever Since Eve*, and was noticed by the critic for the *Citizen News*, who wrote that she "had all the proper curves in all the proper places, plus a pair of legs that made the movie makers at the senior play goggle their eyes — like air raid wardens." Her performance also caught the attention of Howard Lang, producer of the road company of *Good Night, Ladies*, who offered Gloria a walk-on and understudy role in his play. Arranging to complete her high school degree by mail, Gloria accepted the job and toured with the play to San Francisco and Chicago. After the play closed, Gloria and her mother moved to New York, where the budding actress quickly found work as Miriam Hopkins' understudy in *The Skin of Our Teeth*, and as a 14-year-old ingenue in the out-of-town tryout of *Stardust*. In this play, Gloria's understudy was future star Marie Windsor, who later stated, "Gloria and I became friends. I liked her and she always seemed a little nicely off-the-wall to me."

Gloria's next play, *The World's Full of Girls*, flopped after only a week, but she was mentioned in at least three reviews, including the *Daily News*, which found her to be a "flamboyant and amusing floozy." And a short time later, in *A Highland Fling*, Gloria would be handed the break that she had been patiently awaiting. In her role as a saucy barmaid, Gloria was spotted by Dudley Wilkinson, a talent agent from MGM's New York office. Gloria declined Wilkinson's offer for a screen test (years later she explained, "I knew that if it turned out badly, it would queer my chances not only with MGM but also with whatever studio might borrow the test and run it"). But even without it, she was signed to a seven-year contract with the studio, starting at $250 a week. The head of MGM, Louis B. Mayer, felt that Gloria's given name was too theatrical, and determined that her middle name, Grahame, was more suitable to the glamourous MGM image. Gloria Grahame was "born."

After spending her first three months posing for cheesecake photos and participating in drama lessons, Grahame made her screen debut as a flirtatious maid in *Blonde Fever* (1944), a marital comedy starring Mary Astor and Philip Dorn. Prior to the release of this modest moneymaker, Grahame was featured in a spread in *Look* magazine, which informed readers that "your reaction will help decide her career." However, despite the swiftness with which Grahame received her first screen role, she spent most of the next year participating in endless photo shoots, and only appeared in one film, a Spencer Tracy–Katharine Hepburn starrer, *Without Love* (1945).

To fill the idle months between assignments, Grahame signed up for war bond and USO tours, and on one of these treks, the actress met Stanley Clements, a 20th Century–Fox contract player who had enlisted in the army at the start of World War II. After a whirlwind courtship, the two were married in a civil ceremony in Wichita Falls, Texas, on August 29, 1945. But the idyllic relationship began to deteriorate under the weight of Clements' penchant for drinking and gambling, coupled with his failing film career and extreme jealousy where his attractive young wife was concerned. A close friend of Grahame's, actress Jeff Donnell, would recall that Grahame often provoked her impetuous young husband: "There was a need to have lots of intrigue in her life, plenty going on…. Whether she cheated on Stanley or not, she knew his possessiveness, his jealous temperament, and deliberately made things worse. It was as if she needed all of that to confirm his interest in her and her own sense of worth."

During the next two years, the volatile couple would twice separate and twice reconcile, with the final split coming on November 12, 1947, when Grahame sued for divorce. Claiming that she had lost 15 pounds because of her husband's abusive behavior, Grahame told a reporter from the *Herald Examiner*: "He became jealous if I would talk to a man. When I was working on a picture he was jealous of any man who was connected with the picture. Finally, it got to the point where he refused to allow me to shake hands if I was introduced to a man." A month later, Grahame was awarded an interlocutory decree, and the union was ended. (Ironically, Stanley Clements would die just days after Grahame's death in 1981, reportedly after being informed of his first wife's passing.)

Professionally, Grahame appeared in her third feature film in 1946, Frank Capra's RKO classic *It's a Wonderful Life*. The legendary director spotted Grahame in a screen test and borrowed her from MGM for the part of Violet Bick, the town flirt who is saved from a life of disrepute by the film's hero, portrayed by James Stewart. Although it was a small role, Grahame made the most of her screen time, and MGM quickly cast her in three features, *It Happened in Brooklyn* (1947), a lavish musical spectacle with Frank Sinatra and Jimmy Durante; *Merton of the Movies* (1947), a Red Skelton starrer in which Grahame portrayed a Hollywood siren; and *Song of the Thin Man* (1947), the sixth and final entry in the popular William Powell–Myrna Loy series. In this film, she portrayed a hard-boiled torch singer who is murdered because of information she possesses; it would be the first of her many on-screen demises.

As Grahame began to see success in her career, she reportedly developed an obsession with her physical appearance that would last throughout the remainder of her life. Viewing her small imperfections as atrocious deficiencies, she had the first of many plastic surgeries in 1946. Her niece Vicky Mitchum would later explain, "Over the years, she carved herself up, trying to make herself into an image of beauty she felt should exist but didn't. Others saw a beautiful person, but she never did, and crazy things sprang from that…. Gloria's sense of self-worth came from her beauty because she had no sense of interior self worth."

After her role in *Song of the Thin Man*, Grahame was again loaned to RKO, for *Crossfire* (1948), a move that would represent an enormous boost to her career. In this picture, her first film noir, Grahame portrayed Ginny, a world-weary dance hall girl who befriends a soldier accused of murder.

The film begins with the savage beating of Joseph Samuels (Sam Levene), a Jewish ex-serviceman, then shows two men leaving his apartment, their faces obscured by shadows. Headed by police detective Finlay (Robert Young), an investigation reveals that Samuels had met several soldiers at a bar on the evening of his death, including Arthur Mitchell (George Cooper), Floyd Bowers (Steve Brodie), Montgomery (Robert Ryan) and Leroy (William Phipps). According to Montgomery, a blustering, arrogant sort, he, along with Mitchell and Floyd, later visited Samuels' apartment for a drink. When he and Floyd left, Montgomery explains, they left Mitchell with Samuels.

While relating his story to police, Montgomery speaks disparagingly of the dead man: "I've seen a lot of guys like him," he tells Finlay. "Guys that played it safe during the war. Scrounged around keeping themselves in civvies. Got swell apartments, swell dames — you know the kind. Some of them are named Samuels, some of them have got funnier names." With help from Keeley (Robert Mitchum), Mitchell's best friend and roommate, Finlay discovers that Montgomery and Floyd Bowers were responsible for the murder of Samuels, and that Montgomery later killed Bowers in order to insure his silence. Confronted with the evidence against him, Montgomery tries to escape and is gunned down in the street by Finlay.

Directed by Edward Dmytryk in 20 days, *Crossfire* was the first Hollywood drama to broach the subject of anti–Semitism, and included a number of candid indictments against this form of discrimination. Perhaps most eloquent was a statement by Robert Young's character: "This business of hating Jews comes in a lot of different sizes. There's the 'you can't join our country club' kind. And 'you can't live around here' kind. Yes, and the 'you can't work here' kind. And because we stand for all of these, we get Monty's kind. He's just one guy, we don't get him very often, but he grows out of all the rest.... Hate — Monty's kind of hate — is like a gun. If you carry it around with you, it can go off and kill somebody."

For her role as Ginny, Grahame received her first nomination for an Academy Award for Best Supporting Actress, but lost to Celeste Holm for *Gentleman's Agreement*, another film with an anti–Semetic theme, released several weeks after *Crossfire*. Although her part was a small one, the actress was singled out by several reviewers, including the critics from the *New York Herald Tribune*, who said she "does a brilliant turn as a tired man-hating dance hall hostess," and *Variety*, who wrote, "Gloria Grahame as a floozy should get much audience (and RKO studio) attention."

After Grahame's outstanding performance in *Crossfire*, MGM released her from her contract, allowing her to sign with RKO. Her first film under her new agreement was *Roughshod* (1949), a low-budget but above-average Western starring John Ireland and Robert Sterling, followed by *A Woman's Secret* (1949), in which she played a petulant singer who is accidentally shot during a struggle with her benefactress. This often-confusing picture, which starred Maureen O'Hara and Melvyn Douglas, was a flop at the box office, but it was memorable for another reason. During production, Grahame fell under the spell of the man who would become husband number two — the film's director, Nicholas Ray.

Grahame was almost immediately attracted to the handsome and creative Ray, and on June 1, 1948, the day on which her divorce to Stanley Clements became final, she and Ray were married in Las Vegas. Ray would later claim that he married Grahame only because she was pregnant, and their son, Timothy, was born five months after their wedding, on November 12, 1948. (Press reports of the day maintained that the baby had been due in February 1949 and was born prematurely.) However, the union was a rocky one from the start, and Grahame's sister Joy would later state that Ray was "married to drinking, gambling, and drugs." By 1951, the couple had separated, with Ray telling the press, "I think we made a good try. In fact, we tried over and over again, but it just didn't come off." In August 1951, Grahame testified in court that her husband had beaten her on several occasions, and that he was "sullen and morose and would go into another room when my friends came to the house. This made me so unhappy I lost weight and it hurt my acting." The divorce was granted.

Meanwhile, Grahame's career was nearly as unstable as her private life. After *A Woman's Secret*, she was suspended on two occasions for failing to report for *Terror* and *Carriage Entrance* (which was eventually released as *My Forbidden Past* in 1951), and was devastated when RKO chief Howard Hughes refused to make her available for the coveted role of Billie Dawn in Columbia's *Born Yesterday* (1950). The part was played to much acclaim by Judy Holliday, who won an Academy Award for Best Actress for her portrayal. Instead, Grahame starred in her second film noir, *In a Lonely Place* (1950), directed by her soon-to-be-ex-husband Nicholas Ray.

This intriguing tale focuses on Dixon Steele (Humphrey Bogart), a Hollywood screenwriter notorious for his quick temper and heavy drinking. One night, in order to avoid having to read a lengthy book he is considering for development, Dix hires a hatcheck girl (Martha Stewart) from a local bar to tell him the story. He takes her to his home, then listens to her humorous retelling of the dramatic tale. "I think it'll make a dreamy picture — what I call an epic," she says. "You know, a picture that's real long and has lots of things going on." Afterward, he sends her home in a taxi, only to learn from police the next morning that the girl has been found dead. During questioning, Dix's alibi is confirmed by his alluring neighbor, Laurel Gray (Grahame), who states that she saw the girl leave his apartment alone. Instantly attracted to the woman, Dix pursues her, and before long they fall in love. Still, police continue to suspect Dix of the murder and even call Laurel into the station to show her Dix's extensive arrest record, describing him as a "violent, erratic man." Despite Laurel's initial belief in Dix's innocence, she begins to doubt him after an incident in which Dix nearly kills a young man who sideswiped his car.

Tormented by her conflicting emotions, Laurel begins taking sleeping pills and is visibly reluctant when Dix insists that they get married. Having confided to Dix's kindhearted agent (Art Smith) that she fears Dix and cannot marry him, Laurel reaches the final breaking point when Dix slaps his agent during dinner at a crowded restaurant. Laurel flees the restaurant, but when Dix follows her to apologize, he finds that she is no longer wearing her engagement ring and that she is planning to leave town alone. Enraged, he starts to strangle her, but stops when a telephone call from police reveals that the real murderer of the hatcheck girl has been arrested. This news, however, has come too late. "Yesterday this would have meant so much to us," Laurel says. "Now it doesn't matter. It doesn't matter at all." Mournfully, Laurel watches Dix leave and whispers goodbye.

The reaction of the critics to Grahame's performance in this film may have served to mollify the actress somewhat for losing out on the role in *Born Yesterday*. She rated "kudos" in *Variety*, was singled out in the *New York Times* for her "smoldering portrayal," and the reviewer for *Screen Album* gushed: "When [Grahame] looked, she really looked, and when she listened, she really listened, and her appearance in a scene guaranteed that scene a certain mood value and vitality. As an actress, she's well trained; as a woman, she has an original quality which sets her apart from a good many of the young blonde starlets that infest Hollywood. In a melodramatic situation she quite admirably refuses to be melodramatic, and when she's in love, you trust her, and when she's in trouble, you're worried."

After this film, however, Grahame was again disappointed when she was prevented by Howard Hughes from accepting the role in George Stevens' *A Place in the Sun* that would eventually be played by Academy Award nominee Shelley Winters. Hughes instead assigned Grahame to a small role in *Macao* (1952), her third film noir.

This complex thriller takes place in "a fabulous speck on the earth's surface, just off the coast of China ... often called the Monte Carlo of the Orient, it has two faces — one calm and open, the other veiled and serene." Into this mysterious setting enter three Americans — Nick Cochran (Robert Mitchum), an ex-serviceman escaping a minor criminal charge in the United States, Lawrence Trumble (William Bendix), a New York police detective posing as a traveling salesman, and Julie Benson (Jane Russell), a singer who seems to be existing on her wiles as she drifts throughout the Orient. Trumble is the fourth New York detective to come to Macao in an attempt to collar Vincent Halloran (Brad Dexter), the owner of the city's largest gambling house, The Quick Reward. But Halloran, having ordered the murders of the previous officers, mistakenly believes that Cochran is a detective and offers him $6,000 to leave town. Meanwhile, Trumble solicits Cochran to sell a large diamond to Halloran, which is actually a ploy to lure the gambling house owner beyond the borders of Macao where he can be arrested. Recognizing the diamond as part of a necklace he'd attempted to sell in Hong Kong, Halloran orders his henchman to kill Cochran.

Cochran is captured and held by Halloran's men, but he is set free by Halloran's girlfriend, Margie (Grahame). The gangsters pursue him to a dark wharf, but they inadvertently kill Trumble, who was tailing Cochran. Before he dies, Trumble assures Cochran that his criminal record in America will be dismissed if he can lure Halloran beyond the Macao border. Concocting an elaborate scheme, Cochran succeeds in capturing the gangster, and he and Julie plan for a life together in the United States.

Unlike her most recent films, Grahame's role in *Macao* was a relatively superfluous one. Her character delivers a number of snappy one-liners, however, as in the scene when Halloran spots Margie admiring a bracelet and informs her that "diamonds would only cheapen you." Margie promptly rejoins, "Yeah, but what a way to be cheap." Still, in light of her outstanding portrayals in *Crossfire* and *In a Lonely Place*, Grahame's minor role in this film certainly did little to further her career. But with her next venture, the suspenseful *Sudden Fear* (1952), Grahame hit the jackpot.

In this top-notch offering from the film noir era, Grahame portrayed Irene Neves, a captivating vixen who is having an affair with Lester Blane (Jack Palance), the newly married husband of San Francisco playwright and heiress Myra Hudson (Joan Crawford). When Irene learns that Myra is planning to change her will to leave the majority of her fortune to a charity foundation, she goads her lover into murder. "You thought you were playing it so smart — not taking anything from her. No presents, no jewelry, no handouts, no nothing!" Irene says, revealing that Myra is slated to sign the new will on the following Monday. "Suppose she isn't able to sign it ... suppose something happens to her between now and Monday. Who'd get her money?"

While Irene and Lester are conspiring her demise, Myra inadvertently discovers their plans when she hears a recording of their conversation on her office dictaphone machine. After recovering from her initial shock, Myra develops an elaborate scheme to kill Lester and frame Irene for the crime. But later, just moments before she is to shoot her husband, Myra loses her confidence and flees, with Lester in close pursuit. By chance, Irene is walking on a street nearby, dressed in a coat and scarf nearly identical to Myra's. In his desperate search for Myra, Lester mistakes Irene for his wife and runs her down with his car, simultaneously killing himself in the process.

As the thoroughly avaricious and conscienceless Irene, Grahame delivered a riveting performance and was hailed by critics, including Ruth Waterbury of the *Los Angeles Examiner*, who called her "just plain wonderful," and Howard McClay of the *Los Angeles Daily News*, who said, "There are few lasses in the business who can compete with this blond ball of fire in the predatory female department." And the film's director, David Miller, would later join the chorus of praise for Grahame's depiction of Irene, saying, "Best of all was her restraint. She knew how to reach without reaching, how to express without being overt."

After three frustrating years with RKO, Grahame parted with the studio, appearing next in Cecil B. DeMille's all-star circus spectacular *The Greatest Show on Earth* (1952), in a cast that included James Stewart, Charlton Heston, Betty Hutton, Cornel Wilde and Dorothy Lamour. Playing Angel, the elephant girl, Grahame performed her own stunts, including one heart-stopping feat in which a two-ton elephant places its foot just inches from her face. In a 1973 interview with Rex Reed, she recalled, "I was petrified. You know there was one retake on the scene. The elephant came so close he left a smudge on my nose." This box office smash, which won an Academy Award for Best Picture, was followed by *The Bad and the Beautiful* (1952), a highly acclaimed drama about the rise and fall of a Hollywood producer. In this film, Grahame played a novelist's Southern belle wife who is killed in an airplane crash while traveling with an actor she has been seeing on the sly. For her cunning, sexy and comic portrayal, Grahame won an Academy Award for Best Supporting Actress, beating out Thelma Ritter in *With a Song in My Heart*, Jean Hagen in *Singin' in the Rain*, Terry Moore in *Come Back, Little Sheba* and Colette Marchand in *Moulin Rouge*.

But Grahame's Oscar win was shrouded with controversy. When the actress's name was announced, she tripped on the way to the podium and uttered an epithet, causing a rumor that she was drunk. "People said I was drinking, but, of course, I wasn't," Grahame later told the *Herald Examiner*. "I don't drink. I think I was emotionally drunk." She caused another stir after the ceremony when she refused to give interviews, and made matters worse when she first left her Oscar lying around the set of her latest film, then gave it to her son to play with. When she finally did submit to press interviews, Grahame spent most of her time explaining her behavior: "I know I made a mistake in not seeing people, but I only did it because I was working so hard to do a good job in my new picture and I thought my work was more important than an interview.... I am not uncooperative, and I didn't realize I was hurting people's feelings by refusing interviews."

A week after the Academy Awards, Grahame was paid $5,000 for her television debut on *The Eddie Cantor Colgate Hour*, but the Maxi the Taxi sketch in which she appeared was panned by *Variety* as "slowed by long speeches and Mrs. Grahame's uneasy foiling for [Cantor's] comedy lines." On screen, she was seen in an odd mixture of films that ranged from quirky and offbeat to downright shoddy. The first of these, *The Glass Wall* (1953), told the story of a Hungarian immigrant's efforts to enter the United States, and primarily consisted of a protracted chase scene between authorities and the film's hero, portrayed by Vittorio Gassman. Grahame then signed a multi-picture agreement with 20th Century–Fox and starred as the shrewish wife of a circus owner in *Man on a Tightrope* (1953), which was critically acclaimed but a disappointment at the box office. This film was followed by *Prisoners of the Casbah* (1953), a trashy mini-epic that *Variety* panned as "a minimum of entertainment, even for the least discriminating filmgoer."

But Grahame's career received a much-needed boost when she appeared in her fifth film noir, *The Big Heat*, starring Glenn Ford and Lee Marvin. Described by one critic as a "sizzling nest of vipers melodrama," this fast-paced picture begins with the suicide of a New York police officer, Lt. Duncan. Retrieving a letter penned by Duncan to the district attorney, his wife (Jeanette Nolan) immediately contacts Mike Lagana (Alexander Scourby), a notorious gangster. Meanwhile, when police detective Dave Bannion (Ford) uncovers evidence that may link Lagana to the policeman's death, a bomb is planted in Bannion's car, killing his wife. Distraught over his wife's death and believing that the police commissioner himself has ties to Lagana, Bannion quits the force and begins a one-man vendetta to find his wife's killer. His primary suspect is Lagana's top henchman, Vince Stone (Marvin), whose girlfriend Debby (Grahame) is a fun-loving, outspoken coquette whose chief personality trait is her habit of admiring herself in the mirror. After encountering Bannion in a local bar, Debby invites herself to his hotel room for a drink, where she reveals her reasons for staying with the sadistic, brutish Vince: "Most times it's a lot of fun — expensive fun. You gotta take the bad with the good. Clothes, travel, expensive excitement — what's wrong with that? The main thing is to have the money. I've been rich and I've been poor — believe me, rich is better."

Wrongly suspecting Debby of revealing vital information to Bannion, Vince attacks her when she returns home and, in one of film noir's most memorable scenes, throws a pot of scalding coffee in her face. After being treated at a hospital, Debby returns to Bannion, giving him the details about the deaths of the policeman and Bannion's wife. It turns out that the key to the investigation is Mrs. Duncan, the dead policeman's widow, who is using her husband's letter to the district attorney in order to extort money from Lagana. When Bannion is unsuccessful in getting Mrs. Duncan to confess, Debby goes to the woman's home and shoots her, knowing that with her death, "the big heat will fall" and Lagana will be exposed. Next, Debby goes to the home of Vince and, as he enters, she throws coffee in his face. "It'll burn for a long time, Vince. It doesn't look bad now. But in the morning your face will look like mine," Debby says, snatching off her bandage to reveal the damaged skin beneath. "Look at it. It isn't pretty, is it?" When Debby reveals that she has killed Mrs. Duncan ("The lid is off the garbage can," she taunts), Vince shoots her. Seconds later, Bannion arrives, and after a gun battle, Vince is captured. After the arrest, Bannion comforts Debby as she breathes her last. "I don't want to die," she says, covering the scarred side of her face with her mink coat. "Vince shouldn't have ruined my looks. It was a rotten thing to do."

Praised by *Newsweek* for her "highly effective performance" in *The Big Heat*, Grahame herself would later discuss her role in *Silver Screen* magazine: "If

Gloria Grahame

I had a title ... perhaps I should be called Miss Obituary of 1953, or any other year," she said. "Seriously, though, I dote on death scenes, or any kind of Spillane-type manhandling, because it is those scenes which linger in an audience's memory. I don't want to be typed as a woman with a face nice enough to look at, but I am interested in roles that sometimes turn a cinema-goer away in horror. So I didn't mind having my face horribly scarred because my gangster boyfriend threw a pot of boiling coffee over me. Being glamorous in movie roles all the time is not only artificial but horribly monotonous."

Grahame next appeared in *The Good Die Young* (1954), a British thriller with Laurence Harvey and Richard Basehart; *Naked Alibi* (1954), playing a gangster's moll who helps police investigate a series of murders; and her sixth film noir, *Human Desire* (1954). In this feature, Grahame portrayed Vicki Buckley, a sexy young housewife whose husband Carl (Broderick Crawford) has been fired from his job as the assistant yard master at the local railroad. Vicki manages to restore Carl's position by appealing to a wealthy shipper, John Owens (Grandon Rhodes), for whom Vicki's mother had worked as a housekeeper, but Carl suspects his wife's methods. He forces Vicki to pen a note to Owens, suggesting a rendezvous aboard a train, then murders Owens in a jealous rage and pockets the note. "This letter is going to keep us together," Carl tells her.

After the murder, Vicki finds herself attracted to Jeff Warren (Glenn Ford), an off-duty railroad engineer, and before long, the two are embroiled in a passionate affair. Meanwhile, when Carl refuses to destroy the incriminating letter, Vicki convinces Jeff to kill her husband. Jeff follows Carl to the railroad yard and retrieves the letter, but he is unable to commit the murder. "You couldn't kill him," Vicki says derisively. "You tried and you couldn't ... I guess it's only people like Carl who can kill for something they love." Jeff gives Vicki the letter and leaves, knowing their relationship is over. The following day, Vicki is seen taking a train out of town. Carl, having lost his job again, follows her to her compartment, expressing his love for her and vowing to destroy the letter. Vicki scoffs at him: "You haven't got it. You haven't got me or the letter or a job or anything." Enraged by Vicki's mockery, and believing that she is running away with her lover, Carl kills her.

Although Bosley Crowther of the *New York Times* panned Grahame's performance in *Human Desire*, saying her portrayal of Vicki Buckley was "as wholly devoid of fascination as a lush on a stool in a saloon," the film's director Fritz Lang took a far different view: "Gloria Grahame is definitely on the way up," he said. "Like all stars, she is a personality with her own individuality. She represents today's femme fatale. While this type changes with the period, their power over men always comes from a combination of a calculating nature and a glamourous body."

Grahame's first film role of 1955, for which she received a career-high salary of $100,000, would be the most uncharacteristic portrayal of her career. As Ado Annie in the Rogers and Hammerstein musical *Oklahoma!*, Grahame was "the girl who can't say no," and her offbeat, comedic performance earned her several favorable notices, including one from William K. Zinsser of the *New York Herald Tribune*, who said that Grahame "steals the acting honors.... Her subtle performance is one of the movie's biggest treats." Despite this acclaim, however, the film would turn out to be the turning point in Grahame's career. Prior to her appearance in *Oklahoma!*, items had been seen in the press about Grahame's conduct, describing her as sometimes difficult, often insecure, and nearly always inconsistent in her actions. An article in *Silver Screen* reported that "people either like her or dislike her intensely," and on the set of *Oklahoma!* the actress reportedly alienated nearly every member of the cast and crew. "She did terrible things," costar Gene Nelson later said. "[She] would step on my feet or on [Eddie Albert's] lines, and would do all sorts of physically gimmicky things, like playing with her gloves, to draw attention away from him.... The dancers and crew all had horror stories too." Because of Grahame's behavior on the set, Nelson claimed, "she was blackballed all over town ... it haunted her until the day she died."

By now, Grahame was deeply involved in a relationship with the man who would become her third husband, radio and television writer Cy Howard. The two began dating in April 1952, and although the courtship was by all accounts a stormy one, Grahame and Howard were married while *Oklahoma!* was still in production, on August 15, 1954. The guest list of the couple's lavish wedding included such Hollywood luminaries as Gary Cooper, Lauren Bacall, Kirk Douglas, Tyrone Power, Dean Martin and Jerry Lewis, and shortly after the nuptials, Howard told the press, "This is not going to be a typical Hollywood marriage. It will be a marriage of love, respect and dignity."

This lofty claim notwithstanding, the *New York Herald Examiner* ran an article in February 1955 about a rowdy argument between the couple at a Naples restaurant, and later that year, the *Examiner* revealed that Grahame, during a tour of Europe with her husband, "took a pair of scissors and cut up Cy Howard's suits, shirts, ties, everything he owned." Although the couple would have a daughter, Marianna Paulette (later called Paulette), born on October 1, 1956, they separated and reconciled on several occasions, and a year after their daughter's birth, the marriage was over. Years later, actor John Ireland would observe, "Gloria thought mostly of her work, and maybe Cy put that in the wrong perspective and was jealous of it. If that was the case, why marry an actress?"

Careerwise, Grahame followed *Oklahoma!* with the star-studded *Not as a Stranger* (1955), playing the "other woman" in a cast that included Robert Mitchum, Olivia de Havilland and Frank Sinatra. Although the film was a smash hit, critics were nearly unanimous in their unfavorable reviews for Grahame. In her next film, *The Cobweb* (1955), she didn't fare much better, frequently causing difficulties because of her continued fixation on her looks. Producer John Houseman later recalled, "Gloria gave us problems on *Cobweb*. She became obsessed with a passionate desire to be sexy, and to achieve it through cosmetic surgery, which made her self-conscious and defensive.... In fact, she showed up for the first day's shooting with stitches in the lip, which threw people into a minor panic.... She looked awful." Next, in her final film for 20th Century–Fox, *The Man Who Never Was* (1956), Grahame received mixed reviews, with the *New York Times'* Bosley Crowther calling her performance "so very poor," and the critic for the *New York Times Mirror* stating that her "makeup is nothing short of horrible. She is seen as an oily skinned, dark-haired attraction." Grahame then appeared in *Ride Out for Revenge* (1957), a small-budget Western that is now all but forgotten, and her final film noir, *Odds Against Tomorrow* (1959).

This fascinating picture focuses on an elaborate scheme to rob a bank in upstate New York, planned by ex-cop David Burke (Ed Begley). To carry out his plot, Burke solicits the help of Earl Slater (Robert Ryan), a racially prejudiced ex-convict, and Johnny Ingram (Harry Belafonte), a black singer. Despite their initial reluctance, both Slater and Ingram agree to participate in the scheme, Slater because his pride can no longer allow him to be supported by his hard-working wife (Shelley Winters), and Ingram due to a $7,000 debt owed to a ruthless bookie who has threatened to harm Ingram's ex-wife and daughter.

Although Slater is angered that Burke "didn't say nothing about the third man being a nigger," the plans for the robbery proceed as scheduled. But the well-designed plot goes wrong from the start, characterized by the underlying racial tension between Slater and Ingram. ("I know how to handle him," Slater says of Ingram in one scene. "I've been handling them all my life. He's no different 'cause he's got him a $20 pair of shoes.") The men manage to successfully steal the cash from the bank, but Burke is wounded by police and Slater and Ingram escape with the police in hot pursuit. Atop a pair of oil storage tanks, the two men turn on each other and after a shootout, both die in a fiery blaze. The following day, with the corpses laid out side by side, one fireman asks another, "Which is which?" In a reply tinged with irony, his colleague tells him, "Take your pick."

Grahame appeared in only two scenes in *Odds Against Tomorrow*, but although her minor part was an odd inclusion in the film, the actress displayed her usual talent and was praised in the *New York Times*, along with Shelley Winters and Kim Hamilton as "fine in small incidental roles." Discussing Grahame's performance, the film's director, Robert Wise later said that she was "a good actress, but needed to be carefully cast to be effective on the screen. She was a little withdrawn and hard, really, to know, and took a bit more work in blocking out scenes, but when she felt comfortable she could be quite effective."

With her once-promising film career now rapidly declining, Grahame became involved in 1958 with actor-producer Tony Ray, the 20-year-old son of her second husband, Nicholas Ray. Despite the gap in their ages, Grahame and Ray were married in Tijuana, Mexico, on May 13, 1960, and Grahame's sister Joy would later say the pair were "just like a couple of teenagers together." Although the union would become Grahame's longest marital relationship, producing two children (Anthony, Jr., on April 30, 1962, and James, September 21, 1965), the couple would divorce in 1975.

During her marriage to Tony Ray, Grahame returned to her roots on the stage, appearing in 1960 in a Los Angeles production of Chekhov's *The Three*

Sisters, and in a variety of plays over the next two years, including *The Marriage-Go-Round* in Milwaukee, Wisconsin, *Laura* in Traverse City, Michigan, and *The Country Girl* in Ann Arbor, Michigan, in a cast that included John Ireland and Grahame's husband, Tony Ray. Grahame also tried her hand in the medium of television, appearing on *G.E. Theater, The Outer Limits, The Fugitive, Harrigan and Son, The New Breed* and *Sam Benedict*.

Although it appeared that Grahame's life was finally on an even keel, things began to take a turn for the worse in 1964. The first blow occurred when her eldest son Timothy chose to leave Grahame's house to live with his father, Nicholas Ray. Next, Grahame's third husband, Cy Howard, sued her for custody of their daughter Paulette, objecting to the manner in which the child was being raised. The lawsuit, in part, charged, "A part of the unhealthy home atmosphere stems from the unusual and highly embarrassing marital relationship of the plaintiff. Plaintiff has remarried and is presently living with her fourth husband, a man 15 years her junior. Her fourth husband is the son of her second husband by another marriage…. The marriage between the plaintiff and her present husband has been unstable and has been characterized by open conflict between them and physical separation."

Howard's lawsuit led to a flurry of negative press reports that included details of the relationships between Grahame, her husbands and her children, and the actress was reportedly devastated by the coverage. Soon after the lawsuit was filed, Grahame collapsed on stage while rehearsing for a play in Milwaukee, and was hospitalized, receiving a series of shock treatments to relieve her fragile emotional condition. During her hospitalization, Cy Howard was awarded custody of their daughter, and although Paulette would be returned to the actress two years later, the protracted battle would not only adversely affect Grahame, but the child as well. A physician's report submitted to the court in July 1968 stated that Paulette "has a difficult reality problem in view of the chaotic family situation, and is need of a great deal of support and therapeutic effort aimed at helping her make use of her assets. She overemphasizes her beauty, intelligence and charm, and overreacts with suspicion, withdrawal and emotional outbursts."

As the 1960s drew to a close, Grahame focused her energies on raising her children, making only one film, *Ride Beyond Vengeance* (1966), a low-budget feature starring Chuck Connors and Bill Bixby, and appearing only sporadically in such television shows as *Daniel Boone, Then Came Bronson* and *The Name of the Game*. But in 1971, Grahame returned to the big screen, making such forgettable pictures as *The Todd Killings* (1971), starring Richard Thomas of *The Waltons* fame, and *Blood and Lace* (1971), a low-budget horror film in which Grahame portrayed the murdering head of an orphanage for girls. Although the latter film was a box office disaster, Grahame's performance was singled out by the reviewer for *Variety*, who said that she "makes some brave stabs at cutting through the silliness."

Also that year, Grahame was seen in three television movies —*Escape*, the pilot for a series that never materialized, *Black Noon*, a Western with an underlying occult theme, and *Chandler*, a detective story starring Leslie Caron and Warren Oates. After her appearances in these productions, Grahame stated, "It's hard to get a good script. Maybe I should just keep doing housework and not try to come back at all, you know what I mean?" During the next several years, Grahame was seen in a variety of offbeat films, including *Julio and Stein* (1972), a motorcycle film which featured the actress as the waitress mother of a misunderstood teen, and *Mama's Dirty Girls* (1974), in which she portrayed a mother who lures wealthy men to marry her daughters, then murders them for their money. She also played a small role in the stage production of *The Time of Your Life*; her costar Henry Fonda would later say, "The highlight of my recent tour, at least for me, was the ten-minute scene I played with Gloria Grahame. She's a most riveting actress."

In the midst of this "comeback," Grahame discovered a lump in her breast that was diagnosed as inoperable breast cancer. But six months later, after Grahame underwent radiation treatments and adhered to a strict diet regime, the tumor shrank and disappeared. Now divorced from Tony Ray, she returned to her acting career, and throughout the remainder of the decade kept busy in films, television and stage productions, including *Mansion of the Doomed* (1975), a cheapie horror film starring Richard Basehart; *Melvin and Howard* (1980), a quirky picture about Howard Hughes and the mechanic who claimed to be his beneficiary; *Rich Man, Poor Man*, a highly acclaimed television miniseries; and the stage presentations of *The Price* in Milwaukee, Wisconsin, *Bell, Book, and Candle* in New Jersey and *The Merry Wives of Windsor* in Los Angeles.

In 1980, Grahame made what would be her final feature film, *The Nesting*, a cheap horror picture in which she portrayed a vengeful ghost. Later that year, her breast cancer recurred, but Grahame seemed to function as if in denial, continuing to appear in such television series as *Tales of the Unexpected* with Robert Morse and *Mr. Griffin and Me*, a movie with Burgess Meredith. But after several months, the ravages of her disease began to catch up with Grahame, who could no longer ignore the fact that she was dying. In August 1981, ignoring the warnings of her family and physicians, she flew to Lancaster, England, to rehearse for the stage production of *The Glass Menagerie*. But just days before the play's scheduled opening, her condition had deteriorated so that she had to be flown back to New York, where she was admitted to St. Vincent's Hospital. Refusing any life-sustaining procedures, Grahame died shortly after she entered the hospital, on October 5, 1981, with her children at her side.

Hampered by her off-screen exploits and, according to some, "jinxed" by her Academy Award win, Gloria Grahame never truly attained the recognition that her talent deserved. Still, in a career that lasted nearly four decades, she was the highlight of a series of top-notch films noirs, and an outstanding contributor to some of the screen's best-known productions. With her pouty lips, smoldering gaze and come-hither demeanor, it was perhaps Grahame herself who best described the reason for her appeal: "It wasn't the way I looked at a man," she said, "but the thought behind it."

Film Noir Filmography

CROSSFIRE   *Director:* Edward Dmytryk. *Producer:* Adrian Scott. Released by RKO, July 1947. *Running time:* 85 minutes. *Cast:* Robert Young, Robert Mitchum, Robert Ryan, Gloria Grahame, Paul Kelly, Sam Levene, Jacqueline White, Steve Brodie, George Cooper, Richard Benedict. *Awards:* Academy Award nomination for Best Picture, Best Director (Edward Dmytryk), Best Supporting Actor (Robert Ryan), Best Supporting Actress (Gloria Grahame), Best Original Screenplay (John Paxton).

IN A LONELY PLACE   *Director:* Nicholas Ray. *Producer:* Robert Lord. Released by Columbia, May 1950. *Running time:* 94 minutes. *Cast:* Humphrey Bogart, Gloria Grahame, Frank Lovejoy, Carl Benton Reid, Art Smith, Jeff Donnell, Martha Stewart, Robert Warwick.

MACAO   *Director:* Josef von Sternberg. *Producer:* Alex Gottlieb. Released by RKO, April 1952. *Running time:* 81 minutes. *Cast:* Robert Mitchum, Jane Russell, William Bendix, Thomas Gomez, Gloria Grahame, Brad Dexter, Edward Ashley.

SUDDEN FEAR   *Director:* David Miller. *Producer:* Joseph Kaufman. Released by RKO, August 1952. *Running time:* 110 minutes. *Cast:* Joan Crawford, Jack Palance, Gloria Grahame, Bruce Bennett, Virginia Huston, Touch [Mike] Connors. *Awards:* Academy Award nomination for Best Actress (Joan Crawford), Best Supporting Actor (Jack Palance), Best Cinematography (Charles B. Lang, Jr.), Best Costume Design (Sheila O'Brien).

THE BIG HEAT   *Director:* Fritz Lang. *Producer:* Robert Arthur. Released by Columbia, October 1953. *Running time:* 90 minutes. *Cast:* Glenn Ford, Gloria Grahame, Jocelyn Brando, Alexander Scourby, Lee Marvin, Jeanette Nolan, Peter Whitney.

HUMAN DESIRE   *Director:* Fritz Lang. *Producer:* Lewis J. Rachmil. Released by Columbia, August 1954. *Running time:* 90 minutes. *Cast:* Glenn Ford, Gloria Grahame, Broderick Crawford, Edgar Buchanan, Kathleen Case, Diane DeLaire, Grandon Rhodes.

ODDS AGAINST TOMORROW   *Director and Producer:* Robert Wise. Released by United Artists, October 1959. *Running time:* 96 minutes. *Cast:* Ed Begley, Harry Belafonte, Robert Ryan, Shelley Winters, Gloria Grahame, Will Kuluva, Mae Barnes, Carmen DeLavallade.

References

"Actress Gloria Grahame Dies." *Los Angeles Times*, October 7, 1981.

Agan, Patrick. "Gloria Grahame: Hollywood's Bad Time Girl." *Hollywood Studio Magazine*, May 1982.

Bell, Arthur. "Gloria Grahame: On the Steamy Side." *The Village Voice*, October 29, 1979.

Buckley, Michael. "Gloria Grahame." *Films in Review*, Part I, December 1989.

_____. "Gloria Grahame." *Films in Review*, Part II, January-February 1990.

"Budding Star." *Life*, October 21, 1946.

Curcio, Vincent. *Suicide Blonde: The Life of Gloria Grahame*. New York: Morrow, 1989.

"Gloria Grahame, 55, Motion Picture Actress, Dies." *New York Times*, October 8, 1981.

Goodman, Dean. "Gloria Grahame: The Tart with a Heart." *Films of the Golden Age*, Winter 1996.

Hale, Wanda. "Gloria Admits Paris Had Her Spellbound." *Sunday News*, May 1959.

"Hollywood's New Generation." *Life*, May 24, 1948.

Hyams, Joe. "Gloria Grahame, Back and Pouting." *New York Herald Tribune*, May 1959.

"Local Girl Makes Good." *Lions Review*, February 1945.

Masters, Dorothy. "Gloria Doing Better by Freelancing." *Sunday News*, August 1952.

Osborne, Robert. "Oscar Winner Gloria Grahame, 57, Loses Battle with Cancer." *The Hollywood Reporter*, October 9, 1981.

Reed, Rex. "This Is Your Life ('Whoops'), Gloria Grahame." *Southland Sunday*, July 29, 1973.

Coleen Gray

With a film career that spanned four decades, and a personal life that managed to steer clear of the stereotypical Hollywood pitfalls, Coleen Gray has enjoyed an existence that she appropriately describes as "luckier than anybody I know." Gray, a petite beauty with soft, fawn-like eyes and a winsome smile, was seen most often in Westerns and crime dramas, in which she exhibited her talent for portraying a wide variety of characters. Although she admits to receiving more fan mail for her campy starring role in *The Leech Woman* (1960) than for any other, Gray was teamed during her career with such screen luminaries as Tyrone Power and Bing Crosby, and was featured in five of film noir's finest offerings: *Kiss of Death* (1947), *Nightmare Alley* (1947), *The Sleeping City* (1950), *Kansas City Confidential* (1952) and *The Killing* (1956).

Gray began her life as Doris Bernice Jensen in Staplehurst, Nebraska, on October 23, 1922, the second of two children born to Arthur Jensen, a farmer, and his wife Anna. Although her years as a popular Hollywood film actress were little more than a distant dream, young Doris made her performance debut at the tender age of four, singing such popular ditties as "Golden Slippers" and "Ain't She Sweet?" on the radio. "My father played violin in a group called The Home Orchestra," the actress recalled. "I don't know how they dragged me into it, but I could remember the words and I sang on pitch."

In 1929, the family moved to Hutchinson, Minnesota, where Arthur Jensen had purchased a 40-acre dairy farm, and it was while attending the small town's junior high school that Doris first expressed her desire to seek a career in acting. "Our English teacher had each person voice their ambition in life, and most of the girls wanted to be a teacher or a nurse or a housewife. That's about all anybody's imagination was at that time in rural America," she said. "I said I wanted to be a movie star and they laughed at me — boy did they laugh. So I never said it again, ever." Instead, following her graduation from high school, Doris entered Hamline University in St. Paul, Minnesota, with plans to become a public school music teacher. Attending college on a scholarship and equipped with only the $40 that her father had borrowed against an insurance policy, Doris worked her way through school in a variety of jobs, including waiting tables and mowing lawns.

Despite her teaching goals, however, Doris did make one attempt to revive her suppressed acting ambitions during her freshman year at Hamline. "I was going to try out for a play," the actress explained. "I waited my turn to audition, but I was so overcome with the talent and the confidence of the other students that I just slunk away." But in her senior year, Doris took another shot at her dream, this time winning the second lead in a university production of *Letters to Lucerne*.

After graduating summa cum laude from Hamline in 1943, Doris traveled to San Diego, California, intent upon visiting a young serviceman to whom she had become engaged. Before long, however, the relationship ended, and Doris moved on to Los Angeles where, she said, "I hoped to make the world a better place. I had a social conscience." But working at a local YWCA was the best Doris could do, and after suffering through positions as a typist and a receptionist, the future actress turned to the want ads. To her delight, she discovered that a little theater group, the Carl Heins Roth Players, was casting for a play, *Letters to Lucerne*— the same production in which she had appeared in college. "I auditioned and [Roth] gave me the lead," she said. "It was fun and it fulfilled my dreams, my imagination. The work at the YWCA was really boring and I was not saving the world. This was my relief."

While continuing to support herself by working at the YWCA, Doris next appeared in Roth's productions of *Night Must Fall* and *Brief Music*. Her starring turn in the latter play was noticed by Hollywood agent Jack Pomeroy, who was impressed by the young woman's poise and talent and signed her to a contract. Making the rounds with Pomeroy at several studios, Doris finally made an impact at 20th Century–Fox where, on July 14, 1944, she gave an impromptu reading of several scenes from *Brief Music* for a roomful of studio representatives that included Rufus LeMaire, head casting director, his assistant James Ryan and Ivan Kahn, head of talent. "There were a couple of speeches from the play — one was very happy and upbeat, and I segued from that into another scene that was full of tears. I did very well on that, apparently, because several of the guys were blowing their noses," the actress recalled. "I was signed to a contract that day."

Doris promptly quit her job at the YWCA, but the agreement she had signed with Fox was only a contract to make a screen test, which would not be filmed until October 1944. During the ensuing three months, the budding actress was forced to make ends meet by working at a local drug store, earning $.25 an hour. "On the day I finally tested, I felt as if I had swallowed an electric light bulb of magnificent proportion and I could do nothing wrong," she recalled. Following her successful test, Doris inked a seven-year pact with the studio, starting at $150 a week.

The first order of business for the studio's newest contract player was a name change. "I chose it myself," the actress said. "To me, the name Coleen sounded like water going over stones, and I took out one 'l' just to be different. And I selected the last name because I was considering something short that could be on a marquee in lights at Grauman's Chinese Theater." And so, at the age of 22, Coleen Gray was prepared to take on Hollywood.

A short time later, Gray married Rodney Amateau, a studio staff writer who had penned the material for the actress's screen test. A daughter, Susan, would be born to the couple on June 10, 1946, but three years later, they would divorce. Meanwhile, in 1945, Gray had her screen debut, a bit part in Fox's popular musical *State Fair* (1945), followed by a loan-out in a small but showy role in the John Wayne starrer *Red River*, released in 1948. "It was an absolutely marvelous experience," Gray said. Having filmed her part in 1946, just months after giving birth to her daughter, Gray laughingly recalled that she agonized over still having a "little bit of a pot belly." Fortunately, her anxieties were eased by costar Montgomery Clift: "At that time, thin was the big thing in Hollywood and I remember Clift — bless his heart — he said he liked little tummies. He said it was very feminine," Gray remembered. "He made me feel better."

Gray's next picture was her first in the realm of film noir. Starring Victor Mature and Brian Donlevy, *Kiss of Death* (1947) also featured the screen debut of Richard Widmark who, in one of film noir's most famous scenes, gleefully shoves a wheelchair-bound woman down a flight of stairs to her death. Gray's character, Nettie, serves as narrator of the film, and as it opens, she introduces Nick Bianco (Victor Mature), a career criminal who knocks over a jewelry store along with two other hoods. As his partners make their escape, Nick is wounded by police and captured, but he turns down an offer from the assistant district attorney (Brian Donlevy) to inform on his pals in exchange for a reduced sentence. Later, Nick changes his mind when he learns his wife has committed suicide and that his two young daughters have been placed in an orphanage.

Released on parole after providing damaging information on several criminals, Nick is then asked to unearth information on a murder committed by Tommy Udo (Widmark), a sadistic hoodlum with a high-pitched giggle whom Nick had known during his years in prison. After marrying Nettie, an old friend of his family, Nick regains custody of his beloved daughters and settles into a life of normalcy. But the reformed criminal finds his life in jeopardy when Udo is acquitted on the murder charge. Fearing Udo's revenge, Nick devises an elaborate ruse to trap the psychotic killer. Nick's plan works almost too well, as Udo shoots him several times before being gunned down himself by police. But despite the severity of Nick's injury, Nettie's voice at the end of the film reveals that there is a happy ending: "The Assistant District Attorney got what he wanted," she says, "Nick got what he wanted, and I got what I always wanted — I got Nick."

In her largest role to date, Gray more than held her own as the devoted Nettie — she was singled out by the reviewer for the *New York Times*, who stated, "Coleen Gray, another newcomer, is attractive and competent as the girl who helps Bianco to make a new life," and the critic for *Variety* opined, "Brian Donlevy and Coleen Gray justify their star billing." But the actress admitted that she was slightly nervous about working on the film because of the reputation held by director Henry Hathaway. "He was known for being a mean director — that in itself was terrifying," Gray said. "Everything went pretty well at first, but one day I couldn't seem to please Mr. Hathaway. He spoke harshly to me and I burst into tears. I was crying away in my dressing room and Mr. Hathaway came up and said, 'Don't cry honey, I'm sorry, forgive me.' He was just a bowl of Jell-O — like a big teddy bear. We got along beautifully after that."

Next, in what some consider to be the best role of her career, Gray starred as Molly in the film noir classic *Nightmare Alley* (1947). But while the actress viewed the role as one she was "born to play," she almost didn't get the part at all. Scheduled to renew her contract with Fox, Gray was told she would be given the role only if she re-signed with the studio without the promised incremental raise in salary. "I could have said yes, but I didn't," Gray said. "I cried about it, but I wasn't going to sign, even if I didn't get to play the part. Finally, after a period of threatening and bullying, [Fox executives] gave in to my legitimate point of view and I was able to have Molly."

Winning the coveted role had an added perk for Gray — the opportunity to costar opposite screen heartthrob Tyrone Power, on whom the actress admitted having a crush since her high school years. "That was sheer heaven. He was the most handsome man, I think, that had ever been in motion pictures," Gray recalled. "He had this charisma of nobility. I had the feeling that when he walked, he was an inch or two off the floor. I held him in utmost respect. He was a joy to work with and, of course, being in his arms and being kissed by him was just unbelievable."

In *Nightmare Alley*, Power portrayed Stanton Carlisle, an unscrupulous carnival barker with aspirations of greatness. As the film unfolds, the carnival's mélange of characters is introduced, including Zeena (Joan Blondell) and her alcoholic husband Pete (Ian Keith), who perform a mind reading act; Bruno (Mike Mazurki), the dim-witted strongman; and Bruno's girlfriend Molly, who specializes in a sideshow attraction in which she appears to be infused with thousands of bolts of electricity. Stan's showmanship and personal magnetism make him a natural for the carnival business — as he tells Zeena in one scene: "I was made for it. The crowds, the noise ... you see those yokels out there — it gives you a sort of superior feeling, as if you were in the know and they were on the outside looking in." But Stan isn't satisfied with being a mere barker. Sparking a romance with Zeena, he tries to convince her to develop a new mind reading act with him, using a secret code that had once made Zeena and Pete a top vaudeville act. Zeena declines, having been warned of impending doom by a deck of tarot cards. Soon afterward, Pete is killed when he drinks a quart of wood alcohol accidentally given to him by Stan.

With Pete out of the way, Stan is taught the secret code by Zeena, but their plans to move on to bigger pastures are altered when it is discovered that Stan is secretly involved with Molly. Forced by Bruno to marry the wholesome youngster, Stan incorporates his new wife into his act and finds huge success in Chicago as "The Great Stanton," wowing crowds with what appears to be an uncanny mind reading gift. During one performance, Stan meets Dr. Lilith Ridder (Helen Walker), a beautiful psychologist who is fascinated by his act. Before long, Ridder is providing Stan with confidential details about the lives of her patients, which he uses for financial gain by making them believe he is in contact with their deceased loved ones. Seeking the promise of still-greater rewards, Stan even persuades his reluctant wife to portray the long-dead sweetheart of one of the patients, but his fortunes topple when Molly is unable to continue the charade. With his profitable hoax now exposed, Stan sends Molly back to the carnival and turns to the bottle, quickly becoming a hopeless alcoholic. Stan's swift descent appears to be complete when he tries to get work at a carnival. Not knowing that Molly is also employed there, Stan accepts the degrading job as "the geek," where his chief duty is biting the heads off of live chickens. In the film's final scene, Stan is seen running wildly through the carnival grounds in a state of near-madness, but before he can be restrained, he is spotted by Molly. "I've been waiting for you," she tells him, seemingly blinded to his deteriorated condition. "Everything's going to be all right now. I'll look after you."

After the release of *Nightmare Alley*, Gray was praised by one critic for her "appealing" portrayal, and singled out in *Variety* as "sympathetic and convincing." Next, she was re-teamed with Victor Mature in *Fury at Furnace Creek* (1948), which told the story of two brothers who fight to clear the name of their court-martialed father, followed by *Sand* (1949), a horse story that was praised in *Variety* for its "expert scripting, excellent direction, and agreeable cast." Then, late in 1949, Gray turned her sights toward Broadway when she was offered a role in *Leaf and Bough*, costarring Charlton Heston. "It was exciting to be on the stage in New York — it was another pinnacle," Gray said. Although the play closed after only three performances ("*Leaf and Bough*— it bowed and left," the actress quipped), Gray was not disappointed for long. While still in New York, she received word from Hollywood that famed director Frank Capra wanted her for his newest film, Paramount's *Riding High* (1950), a musical comedy with a top-notch cast that included Bing Crosby, William Demarest, James Gleason and, in a rare non–Laurel and Hardy bit, Oliver Hardy. "It was unbelievable, fabulous good fortune to be in this movie," Gray said. "How lucky can you be to have a beautiful script, an incredible director, and all these wonderful people to work with?" For her standout performance in the film, Gray earned raves in *Variety*, whose critic stated, "Coleen Gray, a relative newcomer to top Paramount roles, shows up very effectively.... She handles both the dramatic end and some musical tomfoolery with Crosby almost equally well."

After this triumph, Gray appeared opposite William Holden in a pleasant comedy from Columbia, *Father Is a Bachelor* (1950), then portrayed one of her rare "bad girl" characters in *The Sleeping City* (1950), her third film noir. "I was always goody two-shoes," Gray said. "I wanted to be sexy, I wanted to be seductive, but I was always wholesome, sweet, good, the kid from the farm. I was thrilled to play a villainess in this picture."

Filmed on location at New York's Bellevue Hospital, *The Sleeping City* begins with the jolting murder of a doctor, who is shot in the face at point-blank range while taking a break from his rounds. In an effort to crack the

Coleen Gray

case, Detective Fred Rowan (Richard Conte) is assigned to work undercover as a hospital intern. As part of his duties, Rowan is teamed with Ann Sebastian (Gray), a conscientious worker who is preoccupied with the illness of her paralyzed young niece.

Rowan soon finds himself attracted to Ann, but within weeks of his arrival at the hospital, a second doctor commits suicide, and the detective begins to believe that this incident is connected to the murder. He is also suspicious of Pop Ware (Richard Taber), an elderly elevator operator who continuously hustles the young interns into placing bets for horse races. When he becomes one of Ware's chief bettors, Rowan discovers that the two dead doctors had been forced to steal and sell drugs in order to cover their gambling debts. Further investigation reveals that Ware was the kingpin of the operation as well as the killer of the first doctor, and that he was not working alone. Equally guilty was Ann Sebastian, who signed the prescriptions necessary to obtain the drugs. "I couldn't help myself," Ann tells Rowan, begging him not to arrest her for the crime. "I needed the money. Not for me — for the kid. To help pay for treatments." Although Rowan has fallen in love with Ann, he reluctantly turns her over to police at the film's end.

In addition to offering the unusual setting of a hospital as the site of corruption and murder, *The Sleeping City* featured a unique prologue, in which Richard Conte assured audiences that the film was not set in Bellevue or in New York City. Reportedly, Universal agreed to insert this prologue when the city's mayor voiced objections to the film's depiction of New York. The preface to the film not only contained this disclaimer, but also featured a glowing tribute to the employees at Bellevue: "On behalf of our entire company," Conte earnestly tells the camera, "we salute the magnificent professional skill and highest devotion to duty known throughout the world that mark each of Bellevue's 1,300 doctors and 1,100 nurses."

Praised in the *New York Times* for her "crisp" performance in *The Sleeping City*, Gray next starred with George Raft in *Lucky Nick Cain* (1951), a slightly above-average crime adventure, and with Stephen McNally in *Apache Drums* (1951), a well-received Western, then returned to film noir in *Kansas City Confidential* (1952). This fast-paced, action-packed picture focuses on an armored car robbery meticulously planned by an embittered former Kansas City police captain, Timothy Foster (Preston Foster), who blackmails three felons into carrying out the crime. Throughout the planning and during the actual heist, Foster insists that the men wear masks to conceal their identities from each other, and always dons a mask himself to remain anonymous.

Meanwhile, Joe Rolfe (John Payne), a rehabilitated ex-convict, is arrested for the crime when he is seen leaving the area in a delivery van identical to the one used in the heist. He is later released but, angered by his brutal treatment by police, sets out to find the real criminals. Joe's search leads him to Mexico, and when one of the felons is gunned down by local police, Joe assumes the dead man's identity. Meeting up with the other hoods in a resort town, Joe makes the acquaintance of Timothy Foster, who is posing as a vacationing fisherman, and Foster's daughter Helen (Gray), a captivating law school student. Joe soon finds that Foster plans to turn the men over to police, collect the sizable reward money and embarrass his former department by proving them incapable of solving the crime. This scheme is thwarted when the men turn on each other. A shootout leaves two of the men dead, and Foster is mortally wounded. To shield Helen from learning of her father's lawless past,

Joe clears Foster's name, telling police that the former captain was responsible for cracking the case.

Although Gray's role in *Kansas City Confidential* was a relatively small one, she made the most of each of her scenes in the film, rendering a character who was vulnerable yet tenacious, flirtatious but keenly perceptive. Despite her law background, Helen is coolly efficient when she finds and returns a gun that Joe unwittingly lost by the swimming pool; in another scene, when Joe angrily warns her away from him, Helen is unfazed: "Now I'm supposed to be hurt. Maybe even cry," she says calmly. "But I won't. I think you're in trouble and I'm going to help you."

Gray's dauntless law student in *Kansas City Confidential* was followed by quite a different character in her next film, *Models, Inc.* (1952), in which she portrayed a gold digger who is killed at the film's end. But after this fairly entertaining picture, she starred in *The Vanquished* (1953), a dull oater about a Civil War officer who returns home to investigate civic corruption, and *The Fake* (1953), a forgettable British production starring Dennis O'Keefe. Between films, Gray began appearing on numerous television shows, including *Armstrong Theater, Pulitzer Prize Playhouse, Bonanza, Perry Mason*, and *Adam 12*. Over the next two decades, Gray would log more than 200 television appearances, including a long-running role on the daytime soap opera *Days of Our Lives* in the late 1960s.

Despite her nearly non-stop schedule, Gray managed to find time for romance. Since her divorce in 1949, the actress had dated numerous Hollywood notables — including actor John Payne and producer Stanley Rubin — but she longed for a more secure, lasting relationship. And in June 1953, she got her wish. While receiving a massage at the home of popular Hollywood masseuse Louise Long, Gray was introduced to a visitor — Lockheed executive William Bidlack. After their brief meeting, Gray said, Bidlack called Long into the next room. "Apparently, he asked Louise if I was married. Louise said 'no,'" Gray recalled. "And Bill said, 'Well, she's going to be.' A month later, we were married." The following year, Gray and Bidlack had a son, Bruce, born on June 1, 1954, and they would remain happily married until Bidlack's death from leukemia in 1978.

Meanwhile, Gray continued her busy performing docket over the next few years, appearing in a number of films of varying quality, including *Arrow in the Dust* (1954), a weakly directed horse opera that was salvaged by the performances of Gray and her costar, Sterling Hayden; *Las Vegas Shakedown* (1955), a run-of-the-mill drama that featured a casino as the backdrop for a hodgepodge of characters and situations; and *Tennessee's Partner* (1955), a lively and entertaining Western with John Payne and Ronald Reagan. But by far the best of Gray's pictures from this period was one of film noir's most highly acclaimed offerings, *The Killing* (1956).

Released near the end of the film noir era, *The Killing* focuses on a race track robbery, carefully designed by Johnny Clay (Sterling Hayden), a petty criminal who has recently been released from prison. Assisting Johnny in the caper are a mixed bag of characters, including Randy Kennan (Ted deCorsia), a police officer who owes money to the mob, George Peatty (Elisha Cook, Jr.), a weak-kneed race track cashier whose spouse, Sherry (Marie Windsor), is a gorgeous gold-digger, and Mike O'Reilly (Joe Sawyer), a good-hearted bartender with an invalid wife. But, as Johnny tells his longtime girlfriend Fay (Gray), none of the men "are criminals in the usual sense. They've all got jobs, they all live seemingly normal, decent lives. But they've got their problems and they've all got a little larceny in them."

Despite the painstakingly devised blueprint for the crime, it ultimately falls apart. A sharpshooter hired to create a distraction at the racetrack by killing a horse is gunned down by police after fulfilling his role. Later, Sherry Peatty's young lover (Vince Edwards) tries to steal the money when the gang meets to split their ill-gotten gains, but his attempt fails miserably, resulting in a shocking shootout. When the smoke clears, all the men are dead except Johnny, who had been delayed, and George Peatty, who manages to live long enough to stagger home and kill his wife. And the final blow comes at the airport, where Johnny and Fay are preparing to board a flight out of town. Having stuffed a large suitcase with the loose bills, Johnny is forced to watch helplessly when the bag breaks open and the bills scatter in the wind. At the film's end, Johnny waits with resignation as the police close in.

As with *Kansas City Confidential*, Gray's role in *The Killing* was a minor one — in fact, the actress admitted, "I have always been embarrassed about getting costar billing because Marie Windsor was so much more deserving. She was certainly the female star of that picture." Still, as the less flashy Fay, Gray presented a well-drawn portrait of one of the few "good girls" in film noir who is devoted to her mate despite her knowledge of his criminal activities. "You know I'll go along with anything you say — I always have, ever since we were kids," Fay tells Johnny in one scene. "I'm no good for anybody else. I'm not pretty and I'm not very smart, so please don't leave me alone anymore."

After *The Killing*, Gray was featured in *Frontier Gambler* (1956), a low-budget oater with John Bromfield and Jim Davis; *The Black Whip* (1957), in which she played one of four women ousted from a Western town for setting free a notorious outlaw; *Destination 60,000* (1957), a test pilot drama that was notable mostly for its striking aerial sequences; and *The Vampire* (1957), a horror film about a doctor who begins attacking his colleagues when experimental pills turn him into a scaly looking bloodsucker. "I always had this fear that I'd never work again, so I took just about everything that was offered to me," Gray said, explaining her appearance in the latter film. "It's better than staying at home wishing that you were working."

As the 1950s drew to a close, Gray was seen in only a handful of pictures, including *Hell's Five Hours* (1958), a mediocre thriller about a disgruntled rocket fuel factory employee who threatens to blow up the plant, and *Johnny Rocco* (1958), a slightly clichéd but entertaining crime drama starring Richard Eyer and Stephen McNally. Then, in 1960, Gray portrayed the title role in *The Leech Woman*, a campy horror film that has become a cult classic. In this howler, Gray is a scientist's wife who goes on a killing rampage when she discovers that she can preserve her youth by extracting the pineal fluid of males. "I was offered the part, and nobody else was asking," Gray said. "No matter what I did, I did it with utmost sincerity — I put my heart and soul into that part. But it was so much fun. The director had a wild sense of humor. Sometimes we had to stop the camera to stop laughing."

Like *The Leech Woman*, Gray's next film, *The Phantom Planet* (1962), has also developed a cult following. A strange science fiction tale about an astronaut who discovers a race of tiny people when he crash-lands on an asteroid, the picture featured an appearance by former silent film star Francis X. Bushman. With her movie career now winding down, Gray would only appear in five more films, including *P.J.* (1968), a violent and often confusing melodrama starring George Peppard and Raymond Burr, and *The Late Liz* (1971), a cliché-ridden film about an alcoholic society woman who is saved from the bottle through the guidance of a minister. Gray also had roles in two films during the late 1970s, *Forgotten Lady* and *Mother*, but neither were released. "The negative of *Forgotten Lady* was ruined somehow," Gray said. "I'm very sorry about that — it had some worth."

In recent years, the high-spirited actress has kept busy indulging in a variety of pastimes such as painting, organic gardening, traveling, gourmet cooking, swimming, jogging, and entertaining. She also performs in Cantori Domino, a 50-member singing group that stages several concerts each year. And in 1979, she married for the third time, to businessman Fritz Zeiser. "We had an old-fashioned courtship," Gray said. "And we've lived happily ever after. We have a wonderful time — this is the happiest period of my life. We are the envy of the geriatric set."

Since her appearance in *Cry from the Mountain* in 1986, Gray has been absent from the big screen, although she has turned down several roles. "They were so gross that I couldn't believe anybody would have the bad taste to do them," she said. "I'm open to [acting], but I don't pursue it. I would rather spend time with Fritzie. I'm very grateful to have had the privilege of being in motion pictures at the time that I was. And I'm also grateful that I have other interests in my life. I don't feel deprived because I'm not acting. That's one aspect of life, but I'm sorry when people are consumed by their careers. Life can be very rich.

"And I've had a charmed life."

Film Noir Filmography

KISS OF DEATH   *Director:* Henry Hathaway. *Producer:* Fred Kohlmar. Released by 20th Century–Fox, August 1947. *Running time:* 98 minutes. *Cast:* Victor Mature, Brian Donlevy, Coleen Gray, Richard Widmark, Karl Malden, Taylor Holmes, Mildred Dunnock. *Awards:* Academy Award nominations for Best Supporting Actor (Richard Widmark), Best Original Screenplay (Eleazar Lipsky).

NIGHTMARE ALLEY   *Director:* Edmund Goulding. *Producer:* George Jessel. Released by 20th Century–Fox, October 1947. *Running time:* 110 minutes. *Cast:* Tyrone Power, Joan Blondell, Coleen Gray, Helen Walker, Taylor Holmes, Mike Mazurki, Ian Keith.

THE SLEEPING CITY   *Director:* George Sherman. *Producer:* Leonard Goldstein. Released by Universal-International, September 1950. *Running time:* 85 minutes. *Cast:* Richard Conte, Coleen Gray, Peggy Dow, John Alexander, Alex Nicol, Richard Taber, James J. Van Dyk, Hugh Reilly.

KANSAS CITY CONFIDENTIAL   *Director:* Phil Karlson. *Producer:* Edward Small. Released by United Artists, November 1952. *Running time:* 98 minutes. *Cast:* John Payne, Coleen Gray, Preston Foster, Dona Drake, Jack Elam, Neville Brand, Lee Van Cleef.

THE KILLING   *Director:* Stanley Kubrick. *Producer:* James B. Harris. Released by United Artists, May 1956. *Running time:* 84 minutes. *Cast:* Sterling Hayden, Coleen Gray, Vince Edwards, Jay C. Flippen, Marie Windsor, Ted deCorsia, Elisha Cook, Jr., Joe Sawyer, Timothy Carey, Jay Adler.

References

Biography of Coleen Gray. Paramount Pictures, June 1949.

Brand, Harry. Biography of Coleen Gray. 20th Century–Fox Studios, circa 1947.

Briggs, Colin. "The Unsung Fox Heroines." *Hollywood: Then and Now*, October 1990.

Cassa, Anthony. "Hollywood's Forgotten Daughters." *Hollywood Studio Magazine*, October 1980.

"Charm of Coleen." *Photoplay*, December 1947.

"Coleen Gray Has Scored in Another Field." *TV Guide*, April 1959.

"Farmer's Daughter." *American Magazine*, March 1948.

Gray, Coleen. "I Had a Lulu of an Inferiority Complex." *Silver Screen*, August 1951.

_____. "What Men Should Mean to You." *Silver Screen*, August 1951.

Harris-Kubrick Pictures. Biography of Coleen Gray. Hollywood California, November 21, 1955.

Kendall, Robert. "Mini-Interview with Coleen Gray." *Hollywood Studio Magazine*, September 1980.

Raddatz, Leslie. "Right Soap Opera — Wrong Coleen." *TV Guide*, October 14, 1967.

"A Stripped Gear of the Star System." *TV Guide*, April 18, 1959.

Jane Greer

Jane Greer, a raven-haired, husky-voiced beauty, was one of a number of actresses from Hollywood's Golden Age whose full potential was never quite realized. While she racked up favorable notices for a variety of film roles and starred opposite such stars as James Cagney, Gary Cooper and Robert Mitchum, the comely actress seemed more intent on nurturing her career as a mother than promoting her ambitions toward movie stardom. Still, Greer enjoyed a film career that spanned nearly a half century, and is perhaps best known for her deadly femme fatale in *Out of the Past* (1947), considered by many to be the ultimate film noir.

Along with her twin brother Donne, Bettejane Greer was born on September 9, 1924, to Charles and Bettejane Greer. A native of Washington, D.C., Greer began cultivating her acting career at an early age, participating in talent contests, beauty pageants and professional modeling. At Western High School she was president of the dramatics club, but her budding interest in the arts appeared to be forever thwarted when she awoke one morning, at the age of 15, to find that the left side of her face was completely paralyzed. She was diagnosed with Bell's palsy, a neurological disorder from which few recover. Determined to overcome this obstacle, she later stated, "I had always wanted to be an actress, and suddenly I knew that learning to control my facial muscles was one of the best assets I could have as a performer." She was cured by undergoing strenuous physical therapy, and by age 16 had resumed her modeling activities.

In her senior year, Greer left high school to take a job with the Ralph Hawkins band for $100 a week, and later sang Spanish songs with Enrico Mandriguera's orchestra and participated in his nightly radio program. When America became involved in World War II, Greer took an assignment modeling uniforms for the Women's Army Auxiliary Corps. Her appearances in a recruiting poster, a photo layout for *Life* magazine and a Paramount newsreel proved to be the first steps toward her career as an actress.

Paramount's talent department viewed the newsreel and gave Greer a screen test, but the studio later informed her, "'We have so many of your type,'" she recalled. Meanwhile, her exposure through the newsreel and magazine layout caught the attention of singer Rudy Vallee, who obtained Greer's telephone number and offered to sponsor her film career. But as Greer was only 17 years old at the time, Vallee's offer was rejected. Several months later, Greer was tested in New York by producer David O. Selznick, but he was beaten to the punch by Howard Hughes, who had also seen Greer's test and immediately signed her to a contract.

While Greer participated in lessons in drama, poise and coordination, she again came in contact with Rudy Vallee, and before long was singing at the crooner's Coast Guard band appearances. On December 2, 1943, following a brief courtship, the 19-year-old Greer and the 41-year-old Vallee were married. But the union was doomed from the start. Less than a year later, in

July 1944, the two were divorced, with Greer testifying that Vallee said she was "stupid and had the mind of a child." In the newspapers of the day, Vallee took responsibility for the breakup, saying: "Bettejane is one of the finest persons I have ever known and one who has asked for nothing from me but her freedom and a chance for happiness. I sincerely hope she will find that happiness."

Meanwhile, Greer's professional life was at a standstill, and after a year under contract to Hughes, she had not appeared in a single film. Ultimately, she bought out her contract and signed with RKO, where she appeared in her first film, *Two o'Clock Courage* (1945), starring Tom Conway and Ann Rutherford. Her seventh-billed role made little impression on the public, however, and Greer herself stated, "My mouth was much too large, my eyes turned out, and my legs were toothpicks. Aside from that, I was numb." For the next two years, Greer appeared in a series of minor pictures, including *Pan-Americana* (1945), *George White's Scandals* (1945), *The Bamboo Blonde* (1946) and *Sunset Pass* (1946). In a 1984 *Los Angeles Times* article, Greer recalled that the studio consistently typed her in these films as a "bad girl" because of her dark-colored locks: "I dyed my hair black, parted it in the middle, wore masses of white makeup and very dark lipstick," she said. "I was trying to look exactly like Hedy Lamarr."

While she caught the attention of some critics, it was not until her role in the film noir *They Won't Believe Me* (1947) that Greer was catapulted into stardom. Starring Robert Young and Susan Hayward, *They Won't Believe Me* tells the story of Larry Ballentine (Young), who is on trial for the murder of his wealthy wife. Larry, who married for money, is shown engaging in several affairs, including one with New York magazine writer Janice Bell (Greer).

When his wife learns of his involvement with Janice, she buys Larry an interest in a brokerage firm in California, but he later falls for a secretary in the firm, Verna Carlson (Hayward), and plans to leave his wife to marry her. When Verna is killed in an auto accident, she is mistaken for Larry's wife, giving Larry the idea of murdering his wife for her money. But before he can carry out his plan, Larry finds that his wife has committed suicide and he is arrested for her murder. Before the jury is to return its verdict, Larry tries to escape and is killed by police. Moments later, the jury's verdict is read: Not guilty.

Janice, one of Greer's most sympathetic roles, is not the typical film noir female; she is instead, as described by Larry's wife, "a nice girl, attractive, smart." After the film's release, Greer's career skyrocketed, and critics were unanimous in their praise of her performance, with the reviewer for *Photoplay* declaring the actress a "young hopeful with plenty to back up any hopes," and Jack D. Grant of *The Hollywood Reporter* calling her "just as captivating as all of the more expansive claims made for her capabilities. This girl is star material." Although the often underrated *They Won't Believe Me* is an excellent offering from the film noir era, Greer later stated that, at the time the movie was made, she did not realize that film noir existed. "It was just a marvelous part — the best I had been given at the time," she said in 1994. "When the film

Jane Greer

was completed, both Robert Young and Susan Hayward told [the producer] to give me equal billing with them. What great news!"

Next, in the film noir classic *Out of the Past* (1947), Greer portrayed Kathie Moffett, a role that she described as "a real Alan Ladd part, where people talk about someone in such intriguing terms that when this little five-feet-three guy finally appears, you're too sold to notice that maybe he's not really the biggest, toughest guy in town. That's what happened in *Out of the Past.*"

In a typically complex noir plot, *Out of the Past* is framed within a flash-back, beginning with gas station owner Jeff Bailey (Robert Mitchum) explain-ing his past to his naive and innocent girlfriend Ann (Virginia Huston). Years before, as a private detective, Jeff had been hired by a mobster, Whit Sterling (Kirk Douglas), to locate his girlfriend Kathie, who had shot him and stolen $40,000. As Whit tells Jeff, the money is unimportant: "I just want her back. When you see her, you'll understand better." And Jeff does. He tracks down Kathie in Mexico City, and promptly falls in love with the seductive dame, believing her plaintive claim that she did not steal the money from Whit. The two flee to San Francisco and live an idyllic existence until they are tracked down by Fisher (Steve Brodie), Jeff's former partner, who was hired by Whit to find the pair. During a struggle, Jeff is horrified when Kathie shoots Fisher, mortally wounding him: "You wouldn't have killed him," Kathie says calmly. "You would have beaten him up and thrown him out. You wouldn't have killed him. He'd have been against us." Soon afterward, Jeff finds Kathie's bankbook, discovering that she had indeed stolen the $40,000 from Whit.

Disillusioned, Jeff moves to Bridgeport, where he assumes his life as the gas station owner. It is here that the past catches up to the present, as Whit summons Jeff to him again, and Jeff learns that Kathie has returned to her for-mer lover. Blackmailing Jeff regarding Fisher's murder, Whit forces Jeff to obtain potentially damaging tax records from a turncoat accountant who for-merly worked for him. When Jeff learns that Whit actually plans to frame him for the accountant's murder, he tries — but fails — to prevent the crime. Later, he confronts Whit and gets the mobster to agree to reveal Kathie as Fisher's murderer. Learning of this plan, Kathie kills Whit, and convinces Jeff to flee the country with her: "You're no good for anyone but me," Kathie tells him. "You're no good and neither am I. We both deserve each other." While Jeff appears to agree to Kathie's plan, instead he secretly phones police, who set up a barricade on a nearby road. When Kathie discovers the roadblock, she shoots Jeff. Their car crashes and both are killed.

To date, *Out of the Past* remains Greer's favorite film. "Was I lucky to have Bob Mitchum and Kirk Douglas working with me. Wow!" she said. "It was a wonderful acting experience." With her appearance in the film, Greer's pop-ularity continued to skyrocket, earning praise in *The Hollywood Reporter* as "excellent, indeed," and in *Variety* for delivering her "most effective job to date." Greer's performance was also noticed by RKO executive Dore Schary, who renegotiated her contract from $750 a week to $1,000 a week.

Later that year, Greer wed her second husband, wealthy producer Edward Lasker, son of the multimillionaire Albert Lasker. The couple would have three sons: Alex, born on June 23, 1948; Lawrence, on October 7, 1949; and Steven, on Mother's Day, May 9, 1954. By 1963, however, the Greer-Lasker union was over.

Career-wise, Greer next starred in the Western drama *Station West* (1948), in which, in a role originally intended for Marlene Dietrich, she portrayed a gaming hall hostess who doubled as the head of a gold-robbing gang. She followed up this film with a re-teaming with Robert Mitchum in *The Big Steal* (1949), and later that year *The Saturday Evening Post* named her (along with Ava Gardner, Ruth Roman, Elizabeth Taylor, Audrey Totter and Shelley Winters) as one of the six promising actresses of the future.

But at this stellar point in her career, Greer made the decision to search for more varied roles: "I didn't want my children to grow up and, when asked what their mother did, say: 'Oh, Mom's a gun moll in the movies.'" Her determination in this regard turned out to be the beginning of the end of her promising future in film. She played second fiddle to Lizabeth Scott in the plodding prison melodrama *The Company She Keeps* (1951), then was loaned to 20th Century–Fox for *You're in the Navy Now* (1951), an unfunny comedy starring Gary Cooper, and *Down Among the Sheltering Palms*, a weak musical that was shelved for two years before its release in 1953. During the early 1950s, RKO head Howard Hughes appeared to be more focused on promoting the careers of Jane Russell and Faith Domergue, paying little attention to Jane's interests. As a result, a settlement to her RKO contract was negotiated and Greer bought out of her pact.

Greer next signed with MGM, which all but wasted her talents, assigning her to roles in such lightweight fare as *You for Me* (1952), an engaging screwball comedy that did little business at the box office, *The Prisoner of Zenda* (1952), in which she received fifth billing, and her final film for MGM, *The Clown* (1953), a pale remake of Wallace Beery's *The Champ* (1931). Following her disappointing year-long experience with MGM, Greer did not appear in another movie for three years. Returning to the screen in 1956, she told reporters, "I like the role of being a mother and a wife very much. But it got to be sort of monotonous. But more importantly, I began thinking of myself as a typical drab housewife. I decided to do something about it and here I am."

Greer's "comeback" film was *Run for the Sun* (1956) with Richard Widmark, in which she received favorable reviews for her portrayal of a magazine writer. Her next outing was the distinguished *Man of a Thousand Faces* (1957), starring James Cagney as Lon Chaney. But while the film was lauded for its many merits, Greer's role as Chaney's second wife was rather nondescript, and she was overshadowed by Dorothy Malone, who had the juicier role of the neurotic first Mrs. Chaney.

Another seven years would pass before Greer's next screen appearance. In the meantime, she focused her energies on raising her children ("I guess I am a mother first," she later stated), acting only sporadically in a variety of television roles. In 1964, she returned to the screen in *Where Love Has Gone*, loosely based on the torrid romance between Lana Turner and Johnny Stompanato. The film was panned by one critic as managing to "make every dramatic line ... sound like a caption to a *New Yorker* cartoon," and Greer's small role went generally unnoticed. The following year, she appeared as Patty Duke's mother in the musical-comedy, *Billie* (1965). Although the *New York Herald Tribune* noted that Greer "comes off best" in the film, it added little to her career resumé.

For the next 20 years, Greer only appeared in one film, the little-seen *The Outfit* (1973), starring Robert Duvall and Karen Black. After this film, though, Greer made it clear in the press that she was not on the comeback trail but was merely returning to her professional chores. Her next role, ironically, was in *Against All Odds* (1984), a reworking of *Out of the Past*, starring Rachel Ward in the Kathie Moffett role. In the newer version, Greer portrayed Ward's mother, a role that did not exist in the original. And in recent years, Greer has continued to act in various productions, including two feature films, *Just Between Friends* (1986), in which she portrayed the mother of Mary Tyler Moore, and *Immediate Family* (1989), starring Glenn Close and James Woods. She has also guested on several television series, including *Twin Peaks* and *Murder, She Wrote*. Of the latter program, Greer said: "I got a terrific role playing Angela [Lansbury's] roommate during World War II. I don't do three-camera shows because audiences terrify me. Doing *Murder* was great because I'm not nervous doing film." In addition, Greer participated with Robert Mitchum in a parody of *Out of the Past* on NBC's *Saturday Night Live*. Currently, she has plans to appear in a small budget film for two friends, Carrie and Karl Armstrong.

Although her film career was all too frequently fraught with wasted opportunities and unrealized possibilities, Greer's choice to devote her energies to her family has paid off in the successful careers of her three sons. She proudly points out that her oldest son Alex is an Oscar-nominated writer with a number of successful films to his credit, including *Firefox* (1982) and *Beyond Rangoon* (1994). Lawrence has been writer/producer of such films as *WarGames* (1983), *Awakenings* (1990) and *Sneakers* (1992) and Steven is a Grammy winning record producer.

Greer now lives a quiet life in Los Angeles, out of the glare of the Hollywood spotlight that she once enjoyed, but movie lovers can still rejoice in the riveting performances that the actress offered during the peak of her fame. It is in a line from the highlight film of her career, *Out of the Past*, that may provide the best representation of Greer's appeal: "There was still something about her that got me — a kind of magic..."

Film Noir Filmography

THEY WON'T BELIEVE ME   *Director:* Irving Pichel. *Producer:* Joan Harrison. Released by RKO, July 1947. *Running time:* 95 minutes. *Cast:* Robert Young, Susan Hayward, Jane Greer, Rita Johnson, Tom Powers.

OUT OF THE PAST *Director:* Jacques Tourneur. *Producer:* Warren Duff. Released by RKO, November 1947. *Running time:* 96 minutes. *Cast:* Robert Mitchum, Jane Greer, Kirk Douglas, Rhonda Fleming, Richard Webb, Steve Brodie, Virginia Huston, Paul Valentine, Dickie Moore, Ken Niles.

References

Archerd, Army. "Just for Variety." *Variety*, July 7, 1983.
"Betty Jane Greer to Sue Rudy Vallee for Divorce." *Los Angeles Examiner*, March 7, 1944.
Brand, Harry. Biography of Jane Greer. 20th Century–Fox Studios, circa 1951.
Broeske, Pat H. "Jane Greer." *Drama-Logue*, March 22-28, 1984.
Dolven, Frank. "The Most Beautiful Bad Girl of the Movies." *The Big Reel*, May 1992.
Greer, Jane. "It's Good to Have Bob Back Again." *Silver Screen*, July 1949.
_____. "No Equal Rights for Me." *Silver Screen*, October 1950.
_____. "The Seven Deadly Sins of Romance." *Silver Screen*, April 1952.
Gross, Linda. "Jane Greer: Out of Her Past." *Los Angeles Times*, March 4, 1984.
"Jane Greer." *Life*, June 2, 1947.
"The Lemon-Drop Kid." *New York Herald Tribune*, September 18, 1949.
Marshall, Jim. "Jaunt with Janie." *Collier's*, May 22, 1948.
Maxfield, James F. "Out of the Past: The Private Eye as Tragic Hero." *New Orleans Review*, Fall and Winter, 1992.
McClelland, Doug. "Jane Greer." *Film Fan Monthly*, November 1967.
Parsons, Louella O. "Film Star Jane Greer Weds Edward Lasker at Las Vegas." *Los Angeles Examiner*, August 21, 1947.
Pasta, Elmer. "Jane Greer." *Hollywood Studio Magazine*, July 1975.
"Rudy Vallee Wife Is Given Divorce." *Los Angeles Herald*, July 27, 1944.
Schallert, Edwin. "Woman Puts Jane Greer on Ladder to Film Fame." *New York Times*, circa 1947.
"Vallee Called Her Stupid, Says Wife in Divorce." *Los Angeles Times*, July 28, 1944.
Wilson, Earl. "Let's Be Frank and Cozy." *Silver Screen*, March 1949.

Jean Hagen

Jean Hagen's best-known roles — a self-centered silent screen star in *Singin'
in the Rain* (1952) and a pitifully devoted girlfriend in the film noir classic *The
Asphalt Jungle* (1950)— couldn't be more dissimilar. The versatility Hagen displayed in portraying these divergent characters should have been this statuesque
beauty's ticket to Hollywood stardom, but her wide-ranging abilities actually
worked against her. Without a definitive screen persona such as those retained
by such notables as Lana Turner, Rita Hayworth and Joan Crawford, Hagen's
considerable talents were mishandled by studios, and she languished in a series
of "B" films that are now all but forgotten. Nonetheless, Hagen demonstrated
her expansive acting gifts not only in films, but on stage, radio and television
as well. In addition to *The Asphalt Jungle*, she was a standout in two other outstanding films noirs: *Side Street* (1950) and *The Big Knife* (1955).

The outspoken, often feisty actress was born on August 3, 1923, in
Chicago, Illinois, as Jean Shirley Ver Hagen. (After shortening her name, she
would later lament, "I wish I'd kept it Ver Hagen.") She was one of five children — two girls and three boys — born to Marie and C. M. Ver Hagen, a
native of Holland who came to the United States at age 25 to study opera.
Although Ver Hagen's hoped-for opera career never transpired, he undoubtedly influenced his young daughter with his cultural background, and by an
early age Hagen was determined to become an actress. "I always wanted to
act, ever since I could remember," she said.

At the age of 12, Hagen moved with her family to Elkhart, Indiana, and
after graduating from the local high school, she returned to Illinois, where she
attended Lake Forest College. To help pay for her schooling, Hagen got her
first professional job during her freshman year at Lake Forest, portraying an
eccentric teenager on a popular radio program, *That Brewster Boy*. She also
worked in a little theater group in Lake Forest and later enrolled at Northwestern University, majoring in drama. While at Northwestern (where her
roommate was another aspiring actress, Patricia Neal), Hagen continued part-
time work on a variety of radio shows.

Following her graduation from Northwestern in 1945, Hagen decided
she was ready for Broadway and she headed for New York, moving into an
apartment with her college chum Neal, who had left the school a year earlier.
But after several months of pounding on producers' doors, Hagen was unable
to secure a stage role. Instead, she returned to her roots in the radio, working on such series as *Grand Central Station, Hollywood Story* and *Light of the
World*. The actress supplemented her meager income by selling cigarettes at a
nightclub and ushering at the Booth Theatre, where she would get her first
big break. The play on stage at the Booth was *Swan Song*, authored by Ben
Hecht and Charles MacArthur, and one night Hecht asked the attractive usherette what she thought of the play. "'It stinks,' I told him quite frankly,"
Hagen recalled. "He argued with me, and asked me how I would like to appear
in it. Did I!" Hagen was promptly given a small part in the play, replacing a

departing cast member, but before she was able to assume the role, she contracted appendicitis and was hospitalized. After her recovery, she took over the part, making her Broadway debut in 1946.

In November 1946, just two months after the closing of *Swan Song*, Hagen was seen in her second Broadway production, Lillian Hellman's *Another Part of the Forest*, in which she portrayed a brassy trollop, Laurette Sincee. The play, which starred Patricia Neal as Regina, opened to excellent reviews and both Hagen and Neal were hailed by the *New York Sun* critic for their "superb" performances.

The following year, Hagen was introduced by her roommate to Tom Seidel, a television actor who would later become an actor's agent, and before long the two were planning a fall wedding. But while performing in a summer stock production of *Dear Ruth*, Hagen fractured her leg in a fall, and the couple pushed up their wedding date to July 3, 1947. Ever the good sport, Hagen spent her honeymoon hobbling around the picturesque sites in Montreal, Canada. Three years later, on August 26, 1950, Hagen gave birth to her first child, Patricia Christine, named after her old friend Patricia Neal.

Professionally, Hagen won a part as Judy Holliday's understudy in the uproarious Garson Kanin play *Born Yesterday*, and got a rare opportunity to take over the role while Holliday vacationed for a month in late 1947. Then, in 1948, Hagen earned a leading part in *Ghosts*, but her notices were mixed — Brooks Atkinson of the *New York Times* called her role "well-played," but Richard Watts wrote in *The New York Post*: "I cannot say that Jean Hagen as Regina and Robert Emhardt as Engstrand offer exactly subtle performances." After just five days, the play closed. But the actress fared better with her next Broadway appearance, in *The Traitor* (1949), and it was this production that would lead to her career on screen. While determining location shots in New York for their upcoming MGM film *Side Street* (1950), producer Sam Zimbalist and director Anthony Mann spotted Hagen in *The Traitor* and immediately scheduled her for a screen test. Days later, she was signed to an MGM contract and assigned to the role of a dipsomaniac nightclub singer.

Side Street, a fast-paced offering from the film noir era, starred Farley Granger and Cathy O'Donnell as Joe and Ellen Norson, struggling young marrieds with a baby on the way. During his rounds as a part-time letter carrier, Joe suffers a brief moral lapse and steals a file folder from the office of Attorney Victor Backett (Edmon Ryan). Believing the folder to contain $200, Joe is shocked to find that it is actually filled with $30,000 in cash. Conflicted about his crime, Joe lies to his trusting wife about a new job out of town, leaves the money with Nick, a bar-owner friend, and hides out in a cheap hotel. While there, he comes to regret his impulsive act and decides to return the money to Backett. But, suspecting that Joe has been sent by police, Backett denies any knowledge of the money, which was a blackmail payoff involving the murder of an attractive "B" girl, Lucille "Lucky" Colner (Adele Jergens).

Joe later learns that Nick has fled with his money, but when he tracks the man to a run-down apartment, he discovers that he has been murdered. While there, Joe is spotted by a neighbor and is soon wanted by the police in connection with the deaths of both Nick and Lucky. Meanwhile, Joe confesses his crime to Ellen, but he ignores her pleas to turn himself in to the authorities and goes in search of the real criminals. His hunt leads him to Harriet Sinton (Hagen), the ex-girlfriend of George Garsell (James Craig), who was Backett's partner in the blackmail scheme. A heavy-drinking nightclub singer, Harriet promises to give Joe information about Garsell, but she double-crosses him and takes him instead to an apartment where George is waiting. For her efforts, however, Harriet is murdered by George, who gives her a kiss ("One for the road," he says), then strangles her. With police hot on their trail, George and his sidekick Larry (Harry Bellaver) take Joe on a high-speed chase which leaves George and Larry dead and Joe injured. As he is placed in an ambulance, Joe is reunited with Ellen, and the film's narrator assures the audience that Joe "is going to be all right."

As Harriet Sinton, Hagen offered a memorable portrayal of a pitiable woman whose need for love leads to her demise. She is desperate to regain George's affections, despite the fact that he deserted and even abused her: "You like poetry, hon?" she asks Joe. "George hated poetry. He hit me once when I recited Robert Burns. He hit me right in the eye. George was no good. George had no manners at all." Although Hagen's role was a minor one, she was singled out by a number of reviewers, including the critic for *Variety*, who wrote, "Jean Hagen scores as the alcoholic, torch-singing girl of Craig."

Before *Side Street* could be released, Hagen was seen in her screen debut, *Adam's Rib* (1949), starring Spencer Tracy and Katharine Hepburn as opposing attorneys. In this hilarious courtroom comedy, Hagen played "that tall job" who is responsible for disrupting the marriage of Tom Ewell and Judy Holliday, but her saucy performance was somewhat overlooked by reviewers in favor of fellow-newcomer Holliday. Next, after playing a restless pioneer in a top-notch Western, *Ambush* (1950), Hagen was cast in the film noir classic *The Asphalt Jungle* (1950), portraying the first of the two roles for which she is best remembered.

Here, Hagen portrayed Doll Conovan, the would-be girlfriend of a countrified hoodlum, Dix Handley (Sterling Hayden), who is involved in an intricate jewel robbery masterminded by an aging criminal, Doc Riedenschneider (Sam Jaffe). With the financial backing of an unprincipled attorney, Alonzo Emmerich (Louis Calhern), Doc assembles an assortment of local hooligans to carry out the crime which, in addition to Dix, includes Gus Minissi (James Whitmore), a sensitive hunchback who is responsible for driving the getaway car, and Louie Ciavelli (Anthony Caruso), a safecracker who is devoted to his wife and infant daughter. Despite Doc's careful planning, however, the plot fails after a series of ill-fated incidents, including Emmerich's attempt to double-cross Doc and his gang, and Louie's death after being shot by a misfired gun.

When Emmerich's plot is unearthed, he is confronted by Doc and Dix. Dix kills a private detective hired by the lawyer to sabotage the fencing operation. Dix is wounded in the exchange of gunfire and later, while trying to skip town, Doc is arrested when he makes the mistake of stopping at a local café to watch a young girl dance. Doll and Dix manage to escape to Dix's beloved boyhood home in Kentucky, but he dies there in a farm field, surrounded by the horses he loved.

Hagen's depiction of Doll Conovan was filled with sensitivity and pathos, bringing to life a character propelled by a love that can only lead to tragedy. After her outstanding performance, the film's director, John Huston, would say he selected her for the role "because she has a wistful, down-to-earth quality rare on the screen. A born actress." But while the picture was almost universally hailed by critics (including the *New York Times'* Bosley Crowther, who termed it "electrifying"), most reviews overlooked Hagen in favor of the flashier Marilyn Monroe, who portrayed the attorney's childlike mistress. In subsequent years, with Hagen's appearance in the film all but forgotten, the actress would quip, "There were only two girl roles, and I obviously wasn't Marilyn Monroe."

Despite her compelling performance in *The Asphalt Jungle*, Hagen was next cast in a series of forgettable features. In the first, *A Life of Her Own* (1950), she played the minor role of Lana Turner's friend, followed by another small part as a fly-by-night girl who falls for Ray Milland in *Night Into Morning* (1951). But she scored in her next film, a quickie entitled *Shadow in the Sky* (1951), playing the girlfriend of a war-shocked veteran, and in the low-budget *No Questions Asked* (1951), Hagen was praised for her portrayal of a woman who falls for an unscrupulous lawyer. "It is Jean Hagen who is responsible for the one real performance in the picture," wrote the reviewer for the *New York Herald Tribune*. "With little or nothing to work with, she manages to make the sincere girl both believable and sympathetic."

Then, in 1952, Hagen was seen in the second of her most memorable roles, Lina Lamont in MGM's first-rate musical *Singin' in the Rain*. Playing an egomaniacal, screechy-voiced silent film star, Hagen delivered a wildly funny caricature that all but stole the picture and earned her an Academy Award nomination for Best Supporting Actress (she would lose to Gloria Grahame for *The Bad and the Beautiful*). Even after this acclaimed performance, however, MGM seemed uncertain what to do next with their newest star, and cast her in the thankless role of James Stewart's understanding wife in *Carbine Williams* (1952).

The birth of Hagen's second child, Aric Philip, on August 19, 1952, prevented her from starring as a disagreeable farm wife in *My Man and I* (1952); instead, she played Lana Turner's secretary in *Latin Lovers* (1953), a weak semi-musical about a rich girl living the high life in Rio. After this clunker, she portrayed the wife of a pathetic clown in *Arena* (1953) and played second fiddle to Red Skelton in a mild comedy, *Half a Hero* (1953). Hagen's contract with MGM expired after the latter film, and it would be her last for the prestigious studio.

After Hagen's disappointing four-year run with MGM, she rose to a new level of fame when, on September 29, 1953, she premiered as the wife of Danny Thomas in his popular ABC-TV series, *Make Room for Daddy*. As Margaret Williams, Hagen offered audiences a likable character described in *TV Guide* as a "long-suffering gal with a neat ability to launch a scathing wisecrack." Over the course of her association with the series, Hagen would twice be nominated for an Emmy, but after just a year, she began to display an increasing dissatisfaction with her role. "I chose this part instead of doing my own TV series so I wouldn't be so typed, I thought," she said in 1954. "Understand, I haven't a thing in the world against Margaret Williams, except she's not the type you'd call Peggy. Margaret Williams is a dear, but I can't see her raising any male blood pressure."

The following year, Hagen became even more vocal with her complaints, telling *TV Guide* that she was growing weary of playing "the same role for two solid years and under the most confining circumstances." Seeking a respite from her role as Danny Thomas' faithful sidekick, Hagen returned to the big screen in 1955, accepting a small role in her third film noir, *The Big Knife*.

Dismissed by one critic as "too unrelentingly morbid to appeal to a sizable viewing audience," this grim feature centers on the life of motion picture star Charlie Castle (Jack Palance) who, as the film begins, is unhappily estranged from his wife of nine years, Marion (Ida Lupino). On the condition that Charlie reject a long-term contract offer from his studio, Marion returns to her husband, but Charlie is forced to sign the agreement when his sadistic studio head, Stanley Hoff (Rod Steiger), threatens to expose Charlie's guilt in a drunk driving accident in which a child was killed. Tormented by Hoff's tactics, Charlie allows himself to be seduced by Connie Bliss (Hagen), the wife of his press agent.

Charlie's dilemma worsens when he learns that Dixie Evans (Shelley Winters), a starlet who was in the car on the night of the accident, intends to disclose the truth as a payback for her shabby treatment by studio execs. Charlie tries unsuccessfully to dissuade Dixie from her plans, but he draws the line when Hoff's associate (Wendell Corey) hatches a scheme for Charlie to permanently silence Dixie by poisoning her. Charlie's failure to follow orders evokes the fury of Hoff, who threatens to ruin the actor, but ironically, Dixie is killed in a freak car accident while crossing the street. No longer able to cope with his bleak existence, Charlie commits suicide, and the film's last reel finds Marion screaming despondently for help.

In her efforts to distance herself from her home-spun TV role, Hagen couldn't have chosen a better role than Connie Bliss, a nymphomaniac with what the actress termed "vague ideas about virtue." In one scene, the immoral

Jean Hagen

Connie blatantly propositions Charlie, her insatiable appetites only increasing when he violently pushes her away: "That hurts, boyfriend. You hurt me,
darling," she purrs. "I'm not a girl—I wish I could say I didn't like it." And
later, Connie frankly reveals her freewheeling character when Charlie asks her
what she believes in. "Fun, Charlie," she promptly responds. "Not gloomy

thoughts.... Perfume and staying young, and secrets and locked doors, and doing the wildest things that come to my mind."

After this brief but exceptional performance, Hagen returned to *Make Room for Daddy*, but in 1956 she disappointed her legion of fans by leaving the hit series. "I just became bored with playing the same character week after week," she explained. "They tried to talk me out of it when I told them I wanted to leave. They even told me I could come in just twice a week and I still said no. If I'm going to do something then I'll do it all the way. So, they were left without a wife, but I didn't leave them stranded by any means." Following her departure, Hagen's character was killed off, and the following season, the "widowed" Danny Thomas married Hagen's replacement, Marjorie Lord.

Off-screen for the next year, during which she guested on a variety of television programs, Hagen returned to feature films in *Spring Reunion* (1957), but this dismal Betty Hutton starrer about the attendees of a high school reunion did little to revive Hagen's diminishing career. In 1959, she starred as Fred MacMurray's wife in Walt Disney's *The Shaggy Dog*, followed by an unrewarding role as the devoted secretary of Franklin D. Roosevelt in *Sunrise at Campobello* (1960). After portraying Ray Milland's wife in *Panic in Year Zero!* (1962) and an aging social butterfly in *Dead Ringer* (1964), Hagen retired from pictures.

Meanwhile, after 16 years, Hagen's relationship with Tom Seidel was coming to an end. In the early 1950s, Seidel had abandoned his career as an agent to become a successful building contractor, and in 1959 Hagen lightheartedly announced that the couple's marriage was better than ever since Seidel's career change. "All in all and everything being equal, I think an actress is better off with a non-acting husband," she said. "On the other hand, an actress married to a man who knows the business has a husband who understands her problems, and that's an advantage. Tom, for example, never gets upset when I'm kept late working on the set, and he understands why I have to leave the house before he's even up some mornings." But six years after this pronouncement, in 1965, Hagen and Seidel divorced.

Not long after the split, Hagen fell ill and was eventually hospitalized at the Motion Picture Country House and Hospital in Woodland Hills, California, where, in the early 1970s, she was diagnosed with throat cancer. "I didn't cry," Hagen said. "I was just totally incensed that it happened to me." During the next several years, the actress underwent radiation treatments and two operations in her valiant battle against the disease. In 1974, she would indicate her hope to return to acting, telling author Richard Lamparski, "Acting is all I've wanted to do since I was a kid.... I want more than anything else to work again and with the help of God I will." For a while, Hagen was able to fulfill this desire, and during a period of remission played character roles on such popular television series as *Starsky and Hutch* and *The Streets of San Francisco*.

In the spring of 1977, she appeared in what would be her last performance, in the made-for-TV movie *Alexander: The Dawn of a New Day*. Later that year, according to her ex-husband Tom Seidel, Hagen traveled to West Germany to obtain treatments of Laetrile, a controversial drug that was banned in the United States. But Hagen's life-saving efforts were unsuccessful, and two months after her trip to West Germany, she died at the Motion Picture Hospital on August 29, 1977. She was 54 years old.

Although Jean Hagen demonstrated her ability to play drama or comedy with equal facility, she appeared in only 19 films in 15 years, and her versatile talent failed to secure for her a rightful spot as one of Hollywood's best-known personalities. Still, while most of her features were seldom better than average, the outspoken actress managed to imbue each of her performances with an unequaled style, whether she was playing a gin-soaked sexpot or a sympathetic companion. As the actress herself stated, "I always tried to give everything my best. Maybe I didn't always succeed — but I tried."

Film Noir Filmography

THE ASPHALT JUNGLE   *Director:* John Huston. *Producer:* Arthur Hornblow, Jr. Released by MGM, June 1950. *Running time:* 112 minutes. *Cast:* Sterling Hayden, Louis Calhern, Jean Hagen, James Whitmore, Sam Jaffe, John McIntire, Marc Lawrence, Barry Kelley, Anthony Caruso, Terese Calli, Marilyn Monroe. *Awards:* Academy Award nominations for Best Director (John Huston), Best Supporting Actor (Sam Jaffe), Best Original Screenplay (Ben Maddow, John Huston), Best Cinematography (Harold Rosson).

SIDE STREET   *Director:* Anthony Mann. *Producer:* Sam Zimbalist. Released by MGM, March 1950. *Running time:* 83 minutes. *Cast:* Farley Granger, Cathy O'Donnell, James Craig, Paul Kelly, Edmon Ryan, Paul Harvey, Jean Hagen, Charles McGraw, Ed Max, Adele Jergens, Harry Bellaver, Whit Bissell.

THE BIG KNIFE   *Director and Producer:* Robert Aldrich. Released by United Artists, November 1955. *Running time:* 111 minutes. *Cast:* Jack Palance, Ida Lupino, Wendell Corey, Rod Steiger, Jean Hagen, Shelley Winters, Ilka Chase, Everett Sloane, Wesley Addy, Paul Langton.

References

Briggs, Colin. "The Short and Curly's." *Hollywood: Then and Now*, September 1991.
"Good Girl Gone Right." *TV Guide*, June 18, 1955.
Hagen, Ray. "Jean Hagen." *Film Fan Monthly*, December 1968.
Hall, Prunella. "Screen Gossip." *Boston Post*, June 24, 1952.
Hoaglin, Jess. "Where Are They Today?" *The Hollywood Reporter*, January 30, 1974.
Humphrey, Hal. "Jean Hagen Fights Type-Casting Evil." *New York World Telegram*, July 24, 1954.
"Jean Hagen, a TV and Film Actress." *New York Times*, September 1, 1977.
Kleno, Larry. "Versatile Jean Hagen." *Hollywood Studio Magazine*, November 1974.

Maney, Richard. Biography of Jean Hagen. New York, circa 1946.

Maynard, John. "TV's Perfect Wife Would Rather Be S-e-x-y." *Los Angeles Examiner*, October 17, 1954.

Obituary. *New York Daily News*, August 31, 1977.

Obituary. *New York Post*, August 31, 1977.

Obituary. *Variety*, September 7, 1977.

Reddy, Joe. Biography of Jean Hagen. Walt Disney Productions, circa 1959.

"She's Sick of Goodies." *TV Guide*, July 23, 1955.

Van Horne, Harriet. "A Masquerade Touches Heart." *New York World Telegram*, February 3, 1959.

Dorothy Hart

Once described as "the most beautiful actress in Hollywood today," Dorothy Hart had an all-too-brief screen career and is little remembered by modern audiences. At the peak of her popularity in the 1950s, however, the dark-haired actress with the emerald eyes was hailed as America's answer to Ingrid Bergman. This distinguished comparison notwithstanding, Hart was never consumed by an all-encompassing desire to achieve film stardom and, dissatisfied with the course of her career, abandoned Hollywood after just five years. Although she left the big screen with only 14 films to her credit, Hart was cast in leading roles in the majority of her pictures and was featured in three films noirs: *The Naked City* (1948), *I Was a Communist for the FBI* (1951) and *Loan Shark* (1952).

Dorothy Hart was born on April 3, 1923, in Cleveland, Ohio, and from an early age, she was determined to pursue a career as a performer. After high school, she enrolled at Western Reserve University and, exhibiting a purposefulness that would come to typify her future career, completed her coursework in just two and a half years. "I wanted to get to Broadway before I was too old," she explained. "I knew I wanted to become an actress, but I felt I needed a college education first. Four years seemed a long time to spend getting a degree, so I studied twice as hard." During her relatively brief college stay, Hart was recognized for her brains as well as her beauty, not only earning a pin for highest scholarship, but also winning such titles as Homecoming Queen and Queen of the Air for the National Air Races.

After receiving her Bachelor of Arts degree, Hart took dramatic and vocal lessons and honed her burgeoning talents through lead roles in several productions at the Cleveland Playhouse, as well as in performances on local radio programs. During this time, she also worked as an assistant for an oral surgeon, salting away her pennies for a planned move to New York. But in 1944, the actress was entered in the National Cinderella Cover Girl Contest sponsored by Columbia Studios and, out of a pool of 22,000 entrants, she emerged the winner. As part of her prize, Hart spent a luxurious two weeks at a Park Avenue hotel in New York, was interviewed on numerous radio broadcasts and was offered a contract by Columbia. But, fearful of becoming "just another stock actress," Hart turned down the offer, frankly stating, "I knew I wasn't ready for it." Instead, she settled in New York and began modeling, landing on several national magazine covers. "Of course, I would have got here eventually on my own," she said later. "But it was a lot easier to be a Cinderella and I'm grateful for my good luck."

Before long, Hollywood came calling on Hart again and, after receiving no less than six studio offers, she signed with Columbia. "I insisted on inserting a clause providing that I appear only in 'A' pictures," the ambitious actress said. In her screen debut, she was cast in a lead role opposite Randolph Scott in *Gunfighters* (1947). Featuring Barbara Britton, Bruce Cabot and Charley Grapewin, this Western did brisk business at the box office, but Hart wasn't happy, and promptly obtained a release from Columbia. "I wasn't satisfied with my progress," she said. "I want to be an actress, not a glamour girl."

To make ends meet after her abrupt departure from Columbia, Hart worked in a local department store, but she soon signed a contract with Universal Studios. In her first film for her new studio, Hart was seen in *Larceny* (1948), an interesting story about ruthless con men starring John Payne and Dan Duryea, followed by her first film noir and the picture for which she is perhaps best known, *The Naked City* (1948).

Narrated by producer Mark Hellinger in his last film before his unexpected death, *The Naked City* opens as two men murder a young woman, Jean Dexter. Lt. Dan Muldoon (Barry Fitzgerald), a seasoned police veteran, and his rookie assistant Jimmy Halloran (Don Taylor) quickly center their investigation on Frank Niles (Howard Duff), a friend of the deceased who baffles the officers with his easily exposed falsehoods. Although Niles continues to deny his involvement with the murder, the detectives discover that he had been part of a jewel theft ring involving the dead girl and a former wrestler, Willie Garzah (Ted deCorsia). When Niles finally admits that the murder was committed by Garzah, police corner the crafty strongman on a tower of the Williamsburg bridge. After a gun battle, Garzah falls to his death.

As the unsuspecting fiancée of Frank Niles, Hart had little to do in *The Naked City* but express a sense of heightened incredulity as her lover's crimes are exposed. She did, however, have one particularly good scene, in which she physically attacks Niles after discovering that he was having an affair with the murdered girl. Interestingly, the character seems more dismayed by Niles' infidelity than by his criminal tendencies, but Hart would later claim that she was more interested in less virtuous characters. "I'm the good girl, Kathy," the actress said of her role in the film. "I'd much rather play Kates than Kathys."

With her first three pictures in release, Hart finally seemed pleased with the course of her career. "All three were box office successes, for which I am grateful, because very few pictures are these days," she said. "I have a feeling that Lady Luck is following me. I made a test for *Time Out of Mind*, but didn't get the part — and *Time Out of Mind* was not exactly a box office success!" But "Lady Luck" deserted the actress in her next vehicle, *The Countess of Monte Cristo* (1948), intended as a comeback vehicle for skating sensation Sonja Henie after a four-year absence from the screen. Despite the film's lavish ice skating numbers, audiences stayed away in droves and the film would be Henie's last American picture.

After this disappointment, Hart was seen in five more Universal features over the next two years, beginning with *Calamity Jane and Sam Bass* (1949), in which she portrayed one of two women vying for the affections of Howard Duff. This mediocre Western was followed by a dreary prison melodrama, *The Story of Molly X* (1949), of which the critic for *Variety* wrote, "Dorothy Hart gets her first real chance to show. She photographs exceptionally well, though

her performance is inclined to be a little monotonous." Next, in a mildly interesting "B" thriller, *Undertow* (1949), Hart played a woman who frames her
fiancé for murder, followed by *Take One False Step* (1949), featuring Hart as
the wife of William Powell, and *Outside the Wall* (1950), advertised as "one of
the strangest stories ever told," and starring Hart as a nurse who helps reform
an ex-convict.

Despite her hectic filming schedule, Hart was growing increasingly discontented with her screen roles, and in 1950 terminated her agreement with
Universal in favor of a Warner Bros. contract. "I was doing ingenues largely
and that didn't fit in with my plan to become a dramatic actress," she declared.
"At Warner Bros., my first role fits into my plan perfectly. I'm on the road now."

In Hart's initial assignment with Warners, an above-average oater entitled *Raton Pass* (1951), she played the second female lead, supporting Patricia
Neal's greedy wife who battles with her husband for ownership of their large
ranch. Portraying a spirited girl of Spanish descent, Hart described her character in *Raton Pass* as one who was "capable of a variety of emotions — the girl
is gentle and yet fiery. It is the first time I have really understood a character
and that's important to me." Hart followed this film with a minor role in *Inside
the Walls of Folsom Prison* (1951) which, despite its well-worn plot, was another
box office hit. In her last film of 1951, she starred with Frank Lovejoy in her
second film noir, *I Was a Communist for the FBI.*

This picture offered the actress one of the most interesting characters of
her career, a devoted schoolteacher who is lured and later disillusioned by the
tenets of Communism. Based on the *Saturday Evening Post* memoirs of a steel
worker, the film focuses on the exploits of Matt Cvetic (Frank Lovejoy), who
has worked for nine years as an undercover government agent infiltrating the
Pittsburgh branch of the Communist party. Estranged from his brothers and
teenaged son Dick (Ron Hagerthy) because of his apparent Communist loy-
alties, Cvetic is elevated to the post of chief party organizer and uses his new
position to gather valuable information on the Reds.

Cvetic, disheartened over his son's rejection, writes him a letter explaining his undercover activities, but the correspondence is found by Eve Merrick
(Hart), a schoolteacher at Dick's school who has informed Cvetic that she is
a card-carrying member of the party. Although Eve has been instructed by
party heads to spy on Cvetic, she conceals her knowledge of Cvetic's FBI connection and later renounces her membership: "I joined the Communist Party
because I thought Communism was an intellectual movement," she says. "I've
found out that its only object is to gain complete control of every human mind
and body in the world. Communism is a mockery of freedom." With her disloyalty thus exposed, Eve finds her life in danger, and Cvetic helps her to
escape, killing two Communist thugs in the process. Managing to convince
his superiors of his continued loyalty, Cvetic obtains further damaging evidence
against the Communists and later testifies at a hearing of the House Un-American

Dorothy Hart

Activities Committee in Washington, D.C. With his reputation restored, Cvetic reunites with his son and brothers at the film's end.

For her performance, Hart was labeled as "good" in *Variety* and singled out by the *New York Times'* Bosley Crowther, who termed her "pretty and conventional as the decent American schoolteacher who has swallowed the Communist line." The film itself was a box office hit but, straying from her string of successes, Hart took a misstep with her next role, starring opposite Lex Barker in RKO's *Tarzan's Savage Fury* (1952). This picture, one of the least interesting in the long-running Tarzan series, was panned by one critic as "a series of unexciting jungle heroics," but the reviewer for *Variety* did acknowledge that "Barker, Miss Hart, [Patric] Knowles and [Charles] Korvin do what they can with the cliché dialog and stock situations." But Hart rebounded from this clunker with a lead role in her final film noir, *Loan Shark* (1952), starring George Raft.

This film begins as Joe Cargen (Raft) is released from prison following a three-year stint for assault. Moving in with his sister Martha (Helen Westcott) and her husband Ed (William Phipps), Joe is interviewed for a job at the local tire factory that employs most of the town's men. But Joe is dismayed to learn that the general manager, F. L. Rennick (Charles Meredith), wants to hire him to infiltrate a gang of loan sharks that has ensnared many of the factory's workers. When Joe's brother-in-law is murdered by the gang, he agrees to Rennick's offer, and soon learns that one of the gang's chief operators is a manager in the factory (Russell Johnson, who would later gain fame as the Professor on TV's *Gilligan's Island*).

Keeping his undercover activities a secret from his sister and his girlfriend Ann Nelson (Hart), Joe goes to work for the loan sharks, alienating his loved ones as he rises in the ranks of the organization. One of the gang's top henchmen, Donelli (Paul Stewart), eventually discovers that Joe is a spy, but Joe subdues him during a fight, later learning that the gang is actually run by an unassuming accountant, Walter Karr (Larry Dobkin). After a gun fight in an abandoned movie theater, Joe kills Karr and is later reunited with Ann.

Although Hart was praised in *Variety* as "attractive and able in meeting [the] demands of the role opposite Raft," the actress was once again growing restless. Abruptly, and with as much determination as she had began it, she turned her back on her film career. "By this time, I was actually a pretty good actress," she said several years later. "But I noticed—in meeting older, better, and much more famous actresses—that there wasn't any real happiness in their smiles. That, I think was what made me decide that a movie career, even the most successful one, simply wasn't what I wanted."

Instead, Hart turned to television, appearing on virtually all of the medium's most popular dramatic shows. Around this time, she experienced a dramatic change in her personal life as well. In February 1955, nearly a decade after complaining that there are "very few men [who] are ever really sympathetic with a girl's desire for a career," Hart married Fred Pittera, an industrial research consultant. Moving with her new husband to an East End Avenue apartment in New York, Hart began focusing most of her energies on volunteer work with the United Nations. Hart's interest in public service had initially been sparked in the 1950s when she was a passenger in a small plane that developed landing gear trouble over Long Beach, California: "I knew there was a very good chance we'd crash," Hart said. "As we circled the field, we could see the ambulance and fire trucks racing to the edge of the flight strip. I was frightened, sure, but even more than that, I was heartsick about all the important things in my life that I'd left undone." Foremost in Hart's thoughts during these scary moments was the notion that she should have done something during her life to achieve world peace, she recalled. Later, after the plane's safe landing, she became an active speech-maker and recruiter in U.N. causes, and also traveled to Geneva as a U.S. observer at the meeting of the World Federation of United Nations Associations.

Meanwhile, after several years of appearing on live television dramas, Hart abruptly stopped seeking roles in these programs. "The agonies of uncertainty that I go through just before every performance make the whole thing too painful," she said. "My nervous system just isn't cut out for it." Instead, she began guesting on several game shows, including *Take a Guess* and *I'll Buy That*, and in the late 1950s gained a new level of popularity with a featured role on the CBS-TV program *Pantomime Quiz*. In this popular series based on the game Charades, Hart used what one journalist called her "quick, creative mind and Venus-like physical attributes" as both an "acter-outer" and a guesser. "It's a ball all the way," she said in 1957. "It's the kind of thing I'd cheerfully do for nothing if necessary."

When *Pantomime Quiz* went off the air, Hart vanished from the limelight, and was virtually out of the public eye for the next two decades. Then, in August 1979, it was announced that she had filed a $60 million lawsuit against the publishers and author of *The Editor*, claiming that the novel had libeled her by depicting a character called Dorothy Hart as a bisexual Hollywood "sex machine." The suit, which charged libel and invasion of privacy, specifically cited the book's cover, which stated, "Dorothy Hart was one of the most popular and notorious sex-bombs Hollywood has ever spawned." The actress further charged that the book's publishers traded on public assumptions that she was the actual model for the book's character, and of acting with "actual malice and the design to injure, defame and destroy [her] good name and reputation." When the lawsuit was later settled out of court, Hart once again settled into obscurity and has since remained out of the public eye at her home in Asheville, North Carolina.

Unlike most hopefuls who manage to make it in Hollywood, Dorothy Hart was a rare breed. Never satisfied to merely be on screen, she insisted from the start of her career on appearing in top-quality vehicles, and refused to be entangled by unsatisfactory contractual agreements that were not in her best interests. From her five-year stopover in Hollywood, to her brief second career on television, Hart demonstrated a single-minded resoluteness that her life would be controlled only by herself. As she once stated, "I can't stand mediocrity. As long as I feel I'm learning and progressing, fine — but if ever I realize I can't be a really fine actress, I'll quit the business and do something else. There are too many wonderful things to do with one's life."

Film Noir Filmography

THE NAKED CITY   *Director:* Jules Dassin. *Producer:* Mark Hellinger. Released by Universal-International, March 1948. *Running time:* 96 minutes. *Cast:* Barry Fitzgerald, Howard Duff, Dorothy Hart, Don Taylor, Ted deCorsia, House Jameson. *Awards:* Academy Awards for Best Cinematography (William H. Daniels), Best Editing (Paul Weatherwax). Academy Award nomination for Best Story (Malvin Wald).

I WAS A COMMUNIST FOR THE FBI   *Director:* Gordon Douglas. *Producer:* Bryan Foy. Released by Warner Bros., May 1951. *Running time:* 84 minutes. *Cast:* Frank Lovejoy, Dorothy Hart, Philip Carey, Dick Webb, James Millican, Ron Hagerthy, Paul Picerni. *Awards:* Academy Award nomination for Best Documentary Feature.

LOAN SHARK   *Director:* Seymour Friedman. *Producer:* Bernard Luber. Released by Lippert, May 1952. *Running time:* 79 minutes. *Cast:* George Raft, Dorothy Hart, Paul Stewart, Helen Westcott, John Hoyt, Henry Slate, William Phipps, Russell Johnson.

References

"The Face and Fortune of Dorothy Hart." *Esquire*, June 1945.
"Former Actress Dorothy Hart Files $60 Mil 'Editor' Suit." *Variety*, August 21, 1979.
Minoff, Philip. "TV's Queen of the Charades." *Cue*, August 17, 1957.
Scheuer, Philip K. "Beautiful Starlet Would Save World." *Los Angeles Times*, circa 1948.
Scott, John L. "Resolute Dorothy Hart Keeps Aim Straight and Hits Bull's-eye." *Los Angeles Times*, September 3, 1950.
"Sweet Hart." *TV Guide*, September 10, 1955.

Signe Hasso

With her composed beauty, glacial countenance and stately bearing, Signe Hasso was always considered less a star than a true actress. Although she appeared in fewer than 25 American-made films, the regal Swedish actress starred opposite some of Hollywood's most romantic leading men, including Gary Cooper, Ronald Colman and Cary Grant, and established herself as a solid screen actress with a career that spanned more than six decades. An accomplished author and songwriter in addition to her dramatic talents, Hasso proved to be most memorable on screen in her four films noirs: *The House on 92nd Street* (1945), *Johnny Angel* (1945), *Strange Triangle* (1946) and *A Double Life* (1947).

Signe Eleonora Cecilia Larsson began her life in Stockholm, Sweden, on August 15, 1915, the eldest of three children born to businessman Kefas Larsson and his wife Helfrid, an earnest but unsuccessful artist and writer. Her earliest years were happy ones, but when Signe was four years old, her father died of tuberculosis of the brain, leaving his family penniless. Initially, the family (which included Signe's grandmother, one of Sweden's premier female artists) remained in their large, elegant apartment by taking in boarders, but after two years they were forced to move to a one-room, six-floor walk-up in a Stockholm housing project. "One room for five people — all I remember is beds everywhere. Four families shared an outside toilet," the actress recalled. "My father had been quite well off. He was 38 when he died. He was so young, it never occurred to him to put away any money. And there was no insurance. We were so poor you couldn't believe it." To support her family, Signe's mother sold baked waffles from a street stall, but the three Larsson children were able to attend exclusive private schools paid for by wealthy relatives.

Although the actress remembered attending school in "patched, welfare clothes," it was her expensive education that would lead to her first acting experience. When Signe was 11 years old, a schoolmate appearing in *La Malade Imaginaire* at the Royal Dramatic Theater fell ill, and suggested that the stage manager call the Larsson household for a replacement. "Mother flipped a coin and I was sent to the theater instead of my sister Helfrid," the actress said. "I didn't want to do it. I wanted to be a doctor when I grew up. I threw myself on the rug and drummed my heels and screamed that my sister should be in the play, not I. Then my mother said, 'There's money in it — they will pay you, and I'll give you an orange if you do this.' An orange was very rare. We never had treats like that. So I went to the theater — with the orange in my pocket."

Portraying a nine-year-old in the play, Signe was an overnight sensation, and her original salary of five crowns a night was soon increased to 15. This debut performance led to a scholarship at the Royal Dramatic Theatre in Stockholm, and over the next several years the actress appeared in numerous Shakespearean productions, as well as in plays by O'Neill, Ibsen and Strindberg. In 1933, she made her screen debut in *Tystnadens Hus*, and the following year, Signe won the prestigious Anders de Wahl Award for her performance as Manueloa in *Maids in Uniform*.

At age 18, in the midst of her burgeoning career, the actress married Harry Hasso, a theater director-inventor. Although the union would produce a son, Henry, born June 14, 1934, the marriage would end in divorce in 1940. Still, the actress would retain her married name, and thereafter was known as Signe Hasso. (The pronunciation of her name — Seen-yah Hah-so — would cause a bit of confusion in years to come, prompting the actress to jokingly declare, "You can pronounce it any old way — it means 'Bless you' in Swedish.")

Meanwhile, Hasso continued to excel as an actress of the stage as well as the screen, appearing in *Haxnatten* in 1937, and later that year earning the Swedish equivalent of the Academy Award, the "Guld Bagge," for her performance in *Karriar*, becoming the first female to receive this coveted honor. In 1939, after her appearances in *Pengar Fran Skyn, Vi Iva* and *Emilie Hogqvist*, Hasso was awarded the first Stockholm Stage Award.

The following year, Hasso appeared in five more Swedish films, but by now America had started to beckon. After offers from several Hollywood film executives, the actress signed with RKO and arrived with her son in Los Angeles in August 1940. Once in Hollywood, however, the actress found that the studio had no film assignments for her. Instead, she went to New York where she landed a role on Broadway in *Golden Wings* (1941). Although the play closed after only a week, Hasso caught the attention of famed theater critic George Jean Nathan, who termed her "the most attractive new foreign actress in America."

Back in Hollywood, the idle actress began to occupy her free time by writing. "When I left Stockholm, one of the newspapers quoted me as saying that I was going to write a column from the United States," Hasso recalled. "I hadn't said that, and I was furious. I called the paper and said, all right, I was going to take them up on it. They said that all I had to do was write a post card and sign my name and that they would write the column. 'I will write it, and you can't change a word, and I will charge you a lot of money,' I said, and I did." In addition to serving as a weekly Hollywood correspondent for the Stockholm newspaper, Hasso also honed her writing talent during this period by penning several short stories for a British publication.

Disillusioned by her treatment at RKO, Hasso signed a contract with MGM and was given a small role in what is commonly known as her American screen debut, *Journey for Margaret* (1942), a heart-tugger set in wartime Britain. But Hasso's part in the picture was completely cut out. "I took too much interest away from [costars] Margaret O'Brien and Laraine Day," the actress maintained. "So, that was not my first film." Instead, she was first seen in a prominent role in MGM's *Assignment in Brittany* (1943), the story of a Free French soldier in Nazi-occupied France. Later that year, Hasso was loaned to 20th Century–Fox for *Heaven Can Wait*, a delightful fantasy comedy helmed by Ernst Lubitsch. The actress later recalled that she was cast in the role shortly after being invited to lunch by the renowned director: "I arrived at his office just as he had to leave for a few minutes," she said. "On his desk I noticed that the script for *Heaven Can Wait* was opened, so I started to read. It was at the point where the racy but funny French maid enters. When he came back, he said, 'That's the part I want you to play.' He had purposely left so that I would read the part. Naturally I said yes."

Again on loan-out, Hasso was next cast as a Dutch nurse in Paramount's *The Story of Dr. Wassell* (1944), which focused on the real-life Navy doctor who rescued nine wounded men in Java and coordinated their safe passage to Australia. Years later, Hasso called the production a "fantastic film," praising both Gary Cooper (who played the title role) and director Cecil B. DeMille. "Mr. DeMille was the one who made me a blonde," the actress said. "He said to play a Dutch nurse I had to be a blonde. We got along marvelously and had a wonderful time." Back at MGM, Hasso starred opposite Spencer Tracy in *The Seventh Cross* (1944), a highly acclaimed anti–Nazi film with a top-notch cast that included Hume Cronyn and Jessica Tandy in their first film collaboration.

Hasso's first film of 1945, Fox's *The House on 92nd Street*, was her introduction to the realm of film noir. Based on actual FBI files, this film begins as a college senior, William Dietrich (William Eythe), is recruited by Nazis to act as a spy for the Germans. After notifying the FBI, Dietrich agrees to become an undercover agent for the agency, and sets up an office in New York where he receives valuable information from the Nazis and transmits it to federal authorities. Dietrich's chief contact is Nazi spy Elsa Gebhardt (Hasso), who is a principal figure in Germany's effort to acquire the United States' secret formula for the atomic bomb. Through Gebhardt, Dietrich tries to ascertain the identity of the leader of the spy ring, Mr. Christopher.

Dietrich is marked for death when he is exposed as an undercover agent, but the federal authorities arrive in time to rescue him and arrest the spies. Determined to deliver a final batch of material to Germany, the zealous Elsa attempts to flee, telling a comrade, "Nothing matters except getting this information through, our lives — nothing. It may mean the lives of every single one of us, but this information must be on its way to Hamburg tonight!" Changing into a man's suit and hat, Elsa escapes through a window, but returns minutes later when she encounters FBI agents. Mistaking her for the authorities, one of Elsa's co-conspirators fatally shoots her, and at the film's end, it is revealed that she was "Mr. Christopher."

Critics were nearly unanimous in their praise for Hasso's performance — the *New York Times* reviewer labeled her "first-rate," the critic for *The Hollywood Reporter* stated that Hasso and costar Lydia St. Clair were "two of the best 'nastiest' women yet to get on the screen," and Dorothy Manners raved in the *Los Angeles Examiner:* "One of the most interesting actresses on the screen is Signe Hasso and here she rates one of her most interesting roles. She is beautiful, menacing and compelling." After the release of the film, Hasso received a letter from FBI chief J. Edgar Hoover congratulating her for her portrayal of the spy master in this film, and the actress later recalled that the picture "started a trend for crime films shot entirely on actual locations — semi-documentaries they were called then. At first, Darryl Zanuck, who ran the studio, 20th Century–Fox, didn't think too much of the project, and gave the producer, Louis de Rochemont, only a small amount of money to make it. When Henry Hathaway said he wanted to direct it, Zanuck increased the budget considerably."

Hasso's second film of the year was also her second film noir, *Johnny Angel* (1945), described by one critic as "grade B melodrama and an oddly inert one at that." Released by RKO, the studio that had originally brought the actress to Hollywood, this film involves the efforts of the title character (George Raft) to unravel the mystery surrounding the death of his ship captain father and his crew. Angel, also the captain of a ship, is angered to find that Gustafson (Marvin Miller), the weak-willed head of the shipping line he works for, seems unconcerned about the incident, as does Gustafson's secretary and devoted former nurse, Mrs. Drumm (Margaret Wycherly).

Johnny's search leads him to Paulette (Hasso), a young Frenchwoman who had been aboard his father's ship. From Paulette he learns that the ship had been carrying a cargo of $5 million in gold, which was removed by smugglers during the ship's journey from Casablanca to New Orleans. All of the crew members, along with Johnny's father, were murdered by the smugglers, Paulette tells him, but after removing the gold, the smugglers were killed by a man she could not identify. Later, it is revealed that the culprit was Gustafson, who had stolen the gold in an effort to please his avaricious wife Lilah (Claire Trevor). When Lilah stabs Gustafson in order to have the gold for herself, Gustafson attempts to kill her, but he is stopped by Mrs. Drumm, who shoots him before he can carry out the deed.

Hasso, who earned praise for her "wistful" performance in *Johnny Angel*, was next cast in MGM's *Dangerous Partners* (1945), a mystery thriller with Edmund Gwenn and Mabel Paige, then was loaned again to 20th Century–Fox for her third film noir, *Strange Triangle* (1946), playing an emotionless femme who inspires robbery and murder. As the film opens, newspaper headlines show that a local bank executive, Sam Crane (Preston Foster), is being held in the "Strange Triangle murder." Employing the use of flashback, the film shows the events that lead to Sam's predicament, which began shortly after his return from the war. With Sam unwilling to resume his prewar job as a bank investigator, his old boss Harry Matthews (Roy Roberts) promotes him to the post of district supervisor and suggests that he first take a week off with pay to "have some fun." Following Harry's advice, Sam visits a bar where he is attracted to a beautiful patron (Hasso). The woman flirts with him, but refuses to tell Sam her name and after a three-day fling, she vanishes from Sam's life. "It sure was wonderful while it lasted," Sam recalls. "Then she disappeared. Checked out without saying goodbye or leaving a forwarding address. No dame ever hit me so hard and so fast."

Endeavoring to forget about the woman, Sam starts his new job, stopping first in Santa Rosita, where Harry's brother Earl (Shepperd Strudwick) is the manager of the local bank. Once there, however, Sam is shocked to discover that Earl's wife Francine is the mysterious woman from the bar. Sam is determined to steer clear of the captivating Francine, but before he can leave town, he learns that Earl has stolen $3,000 in bank funds, hoping to make a bundle in the stock market in order to support his luxury-loving wife. Later, Francine coerces Earl into stealing more money from the bank but, suspecting Francine's motives, Sam contacts a friend with the FBI and learns that his ex-lover has an extensive criminal record. Sam confronts Francine as she is preparing to flee. When Earl learns of his wife's unsavory past, he hands over the briefcase full of money to Sam. It is later discovered, however, that Francine had removed the cash from the briefcase, and when Earl returns to retrieve it, a struggle ensues. Francine pulls a gun on her husband and in order to save Earl, Sam fatally shoots her and is arrested for the crime. But in the film's final scene, Earl arrives to admit his role in the crime and Sam is cleared.

As the glacial, manipulative Francine, Hasso offered a memorable performance, clearly revealing her outlook on life when she states, "A girl has to keep her head one step ahead of her heart if she wants to get along." And later, in one of the film's best scenes, Francine craftily convinces her husband to steal: "You made a lot of money for the bank. And what have you got to show for it — nothing. You took the other money, didn't you? I didn't ask you to steal it. What's the difference? Three thousand dollars or a hundred thousand? You're in the same boat."

After this top-notch performance, Hasso starred opposite George Sanders in United Artists' *A Scandal in Paris* (1946), an entertaining comedy-drama about a notorious French thief who became Prefect of Police in Paris, followed by *Where There's Life* (1947), starring Bob Hope as a New York disk jockey who discovers he is the long-lost heir of a European monarch. For her performance in the latter film, Hasso was hailed by the reviewer for *Variety*, who wrote: "Miss Hasso brightens proceedings considerably as the fascinating general. Eye-appeal is strong and talent excellent, which makes the assignment count." Then, in her second picture of 1947, Hasso starred in the outstanding *A Double Life*, her final film noir.

In this George Cukor–directed feature, Hasso portrayed Brita, a Broadway actress who is still teamed on-stage and off with her ex-husband Anthony John (Ronald Colman). When Brita learns of Tony's plan to star in a new production of *Othello*, she objects to appearing with him in the tragic tale of murder and betrayal: "You know Tony," she tells her husband's press agent, Bill (Edmond O'Brien). "When he's doing something gay, it's wonderful to be with him, but when he gets going on one of those deep numbers.... Listen — we

Signe Hasso

were engaged doing Oscar Wilde, broke it off doing O'Neill, got married doing Kaufman, and divorced doing Chekhov." And Brita is not the only character concerned with Tony's state of mind. Even the play's director refers to Tony's habit of "becoming someone else, every night, for just a few hours — so completely. Don't tell me that his whole system isn't affected by it."

Nonetheless, the play goes into production and after a year, it is still playing to packed houses. But the effects of playing the murderous Venetian general take their toll on Tony, who becomes so enmeshed in his character during one performance that he actually chokes Brita, causing her to require medical attention. As Tony becomes further consumed by his character, he goes to the home of Pat Kroll (Shelley Winters), a waitress with whom he had had a brief affair shortly before the play opened. With his mind confusing Pat with the character of his on-stage wife, Tony murders her. Meanwhile, the press agent, Bill, suspects that Tony is guilty of the crime and arranges for a local actress to disguise herself as the dead waitress. When she confronts Tony in a restaurant, his shocked reaction confirms Bill's suspicions. Later that night, Bill arrives at the theater with a police detective and, sensing that he has been exposed, Tony plunges a dagger into his own heart during the performance. In the wings, Tony tells Bill with his dying breath: "In the papers, don't let them say I was a bad actor."

During production of *A Double Life*, Hasso later recalled that life imitated art when the principal actors were filming the scene where her character is strangled by Tony John. Throughout an entire afternoon, Hasso said, Ronald Colman was reluctant to choke her, but director George Cukor insisted. "Mr. Colman tried again and this time I watched his eyes change as his hands dug deep into my throat. I was gasping when he let me go.... They had to run for a nurse. My throat was black and blue. It had to be covered with make-up for days." For her troubles, Hasso was almost universally praised by critics, including Bosley Crowther of the *New York Times*, who said the actress was "remarkably and charmingly nimble."

Hasso appeared in only one film in 1948, Columbia's *To the Ends of the Earth*, a $2 million production that initially faced strong opposition from the Production Code Administration. Concerns about the film's glamorized spin on opium-smuggling turned out to be groundless, however, and the result was a tightly directed melodrama starring Dick Powell as a courageous Treasury agent. Hasso was off-screen during 1949, but returned in 1950 for the role of a gangster's wife in *Outside the Wall*, starring Richard Basehart. Described in advertisements as "one of the strangest stories ever told," the picture was actually a rather humdrum affair concerning the efforts of an ex-convict to go straight. But she fared better in her next film, *Crisis* (1950), a gripping Cary Grant starrer about an ailing dictator and the American surgeon who is forced to operate on him. Also that year, Hasso returned to her native Sweden for her first film there since her departure a decade earlier, starring in *Sånt Händer Inte Här*.

In 1952, Hasso married for the second time, but her husband died four years later. "I still really don't know if I've ever been in love," Hasso said later. "I thought I was. But maybe they were infatuations. If my second husband had lived I would have stayed with him.... It has been easy for me to be infatuated. And when I am infatuated, I'll do anything for a man. I do too much."

Career-wise, Hasso was back on screen in 1953 in another Swedish film,

Maria Johanna, and in 1954 appeared in *Die Sonne von St. Moritz* in Germany and *Taxi 13* in Sweden. And in 1955 she starred in her first American film to be made in Sweden, *The True and the False,* and in *Den Underbara Lögnen* in Sweden. Meanwhile, the actress also appeared in several stage productions, including *Love from a Stranger, Uncle Vanya* with Franchot Tone and the successful revival of George Bernard Shaw's *The Apple Cart.*

But in 1957, during production of *The Apple Cart,* tragedy struck Hasso's life when her son Henry was killed in an automobile accident. The 22-year-old had been ill for several years but had recovered shortly before the accident and was planning to appear in his first film, Hasso said. The actress would later state that she had no regrets about her less-than-perfect relationship with her son, but she did admit that she was pained by the memories. "What's the use of regretting now?" she asked philosophically. "Regret that I wasn't a better mother? That I didn't forgo my career? That I couldn't spend time with my son? But yes, those memories hurt me, and most of all that I couldn't be there when he needed me most, when he was sick. And I didn't earn a lot of money when he needed it. I had given it away…. I still think, 'Jesus, why did I give that fool so-and-so that money instead of my son?'"

In spite of her loss, Hasso gamely continued her stage appearances, starring with Gale Sondergaard in *Anastasia* and touring England and Scotland in *The Key of the Door.* During this period, Hasso also began guesting on a variety of television shows, and during the next several decades would make appearances on such programs as *Route 66, Alcoa Theatre, The Interns, Ghost Story* and *Trapper John, M.D..*

Throughout the 1960s, Hasso concentrated mainly on her stage career, returning early in the decade to Sweden for *The Final Moment.* Soon after, she starred in her first one-woman show at Club Berns, a massive nightclub in Stockholm, and later recalled, "This was something I'd never done before — to sing. I have no singing voice, but I can give the illusion of it. How do I belt out a song? That's something else. I just pray and belt!" Other stage productions included the title role in Edward Albee's *Tiny Alice,* which the actress called her favorite part, *Hedda Gabler, The Tender Heel* with Chester Morris and Kay Medford, and *Cabaret,* opposite Leo Fuchs.

By now, the multi-talented actress had written more than 40 songs in English, Swedish and German, and in 1965, wrote lyrics for 12 folk songs performed by a famous Swedish singer, Alice Babs. The songs were recorded for an album, "Scandinavian Folk Songs — Sung and Swung," which went on to win the Grand Prix Edison International Award, the most coveted prize in the European record industry. Of her songwriting efforts, Hasso later said, "English is easiest, Swedish is tough, and German easier than Swedish. When I start to work, I lie down, turn on my side in bed, and pray to Goethe, Schiller and other poets. It works, and I write my song." In addition to songwriting, Hasso began a second career as a novelist, writing her first in the mid–1970s and entering it in a contest. "There were six hundred and four authors and I won the second prize," she recalled. Since then, she has written a book of poetry and six novels, the last of which was the third volume of her autobiography, published in Sweden in 1990. "It's more or less about my life," the actress explained, "but it's not a kiss and tell story. It actually reads like a novel."

After a 16-year absence from the American screen, Hasso had a cameo role in *Picture Mommy Dead* in 1966, and the following year was seen overseas in Universal's *Code Name: Heraclitus* (1967), which was actually two spliced-together episodes from Hasso's appearance on television's *Bob Hope Chrysler Theatre*. In her latest screen roles to date, Hasso appeared in *A Reflection of Fear* (1973), *The Black Bird* (1975) and *I Never Promised You a Rose Garden* (1977).

In recent years, Hasso has continued to make occasional television appearances, including episodes of *Murder, She Wrote*, and spends most of her time pursuing her writing interests. She has also continued to garner a number of prestigious awards — in 1989, she was named Swedish-American of the Year by the Vasa Order of America (becoming only the third woman in 30 years to receive the honor, and the only woman in the arts), and in 1996 she won the Swedish American Chamber of Commerce Award. Despite her numerous accomplishments, however, the still-strikingly attractive actress has stressed that she is not yet ready to retire: "I haven't fulfilled what I came to do. I have much to finish," Hasso said. "You must fulfill your talents in life, because if you leave them idle, they are taken away. If you don't use a battery, then it goes dead."

Film Noir Filmography

THE HOUSE ON 92ND STREET   *Director:* Henry Hathaway. *Producer:* Louis de Rochemont. Released by 20th Century–Fox, September 1945. *Running time:* 89 minutes. *Cast:* William Eythe, Lloyd Nolan, Signe Hasso, Gene Lockhart, Leo G. Carroll, Lydia St. Clair, William Post, Jr., Henry Bellaver. *Awards:* Academy Award for Best Original Screenplay (Charles G. Booth).

JOHNNY ANGEL   *Director:* Edwin L. Marin. *Producer:* Jack Gross. Released by RKO, December 1945. *Running time:* 76 minutes. *Cast:* George Raft, Claire Trevor, Signe Hasso, Lowell Gilmore, Hoagy Carmichael, Marvin Miller, Margaret Wycherly.

STRANGE TRIANGLE   *Director:* Ray McCarey. *Producer:* Aubrey Schenck. Released by 20th Century–Fox, 1946. *Running time:* 65 minutes. *Cast:* Signe Hasso, Preston Foster, Anabel Shaw, Shepperd Strudwick (credited as John Shepperd), Roy Roberts, Emory Parnell, Nancy Evans.

A DOUBLE LIFE   *Director:* George Cukor. *Producer:* Michael Kanin. Released by Universal-International, December 25, 1947. *Running time:* 103 minutes. *Cast:* Ronald Colman, Signe Hasso, Edmond O'Brien, Shelley Winters, Ray Collins, Philip Loeb, Millard Mitchell. *Awards:* Academy Awards for Best Actor (Ronald Colman), Best Score (Miklos Rozsa). Academy Award nominations for Best Director (George Cukor), Best Original Screenplay (Ruth Gordon, Garson Kanin).

References

Biography of Signe Hasso. RKO Radio Pictures, circa 1940.

"Lady Luck." *Lions Review*, July 1944.

McClelland, Doug. "Signe Hasso." *Films in Review*, November 1967.

Nielsen, Ray. "Signe Hasso: *The Story of Dr. Wassell.*" *Classic Images*, April 1991.

Scheuer, Philip K. "Cameras Use FBI Haunts for Adventure in Reality." *Los Angeles Times*, July 22, 1945.

Skinner, Olivia. "Actress Signe Hasso: Even Waiters Are Charmed." *St. Louis Post-Dispatch*, March 23, 1969.

"Stars of Tomorrow." *Lions Review*, July-August 1942.

"Swedish Hunch." *American Magazine*, September 1944.

Swire, Sydney. "Acting Is One of Many Roles That Signe Hasso Performs." *Larchmont Chronicle*, September 1991.

"Zing Girl." *Lions Review*, April 1943.

Susan Hayward *in Paramount Pictures*

P2553-C597

Susan Hayward

Susan Hayward was a mass of contradictions. She was labeled as aloof, temperamental and "as cold as a polar bear's foot," yet she was unfailingly loyal to her few close friends. Her acting gift was often underrated, but her film performances earned her a total of five Academy Award nominations. She once took an overdose of pills in an attempt to end her life, but she possessed an innate strength that made her a survivor.

While she is most highly regarded for her roles in such "women's pictures" as *My Foolish Heart* (1949) and *I'll Cry Tomorrow* (1955), Hayward nonetheless made a lasting impression in four films noirs: *Among the Living* (1941), *Deadline at Dawn* (1946), *They Won't Believe Me* (1947) and *House of Strangers* (1949). In each, she used her striking looks and worldly wise air to create characters who were fascinating and unforgettable.

Born Edythe Marrenner on June 30, 1918, the woman with the flashing hazel eyes and infectious smile grew up in a tenement in the Flatbush section of Brooklyn, where her father worked as a Coney Island barker. Whenever the family's meager earnings allowed, she would spend hours in darkened movie theaters, entranced by the images that flashed on the screen before her, and yearning to be a part of that world filled with magic, fantasy and make-believe. By her own admission years later, Edythe was born with an active imagination and a natural talent for lying — two perfect ingredients for acting, she said — and she once stated that she couldn't remember a time when she didn't want to be an actress.

It was at the age of seven that young Edythe's inner strength and determination seemed to first rise to the surface. Returning home after a visit to the corner candy store, she was struck by a car which fractured her hip. Despite doctors' grim forecast that she would probably never walk again, Edythe refused to give in to her infirmity. After only six months, she was able to get about on crutches, and after a year she returned to school. Because of improper traction, however, her hip did not heal properly and she was left with one leg that was an inch and a half shorter than the other. As a result, she wore a lift in one shoe, and she stoically endured her classmates' taunts about her odd way of walking — a walk that was later to develop into the sexy strut that became a Hayward trademark.

Her first real acting experience was at Girls Commercial High School, where she acted in numerous school plays, always opting for the "meatier" roles like the toothless witch, rather than the coquettish ingenue. These experiences were an ideal training ground for the emotionally charged performances she would deliver in later years. After graduation from high school, Edythe got a job making designs for a handkerchief factory, a position that soon grew too tedious for the stardom-bound young woman. She abruptly quit the job to take a course at Manhattan's Feagan Drama School. Later, in need of money, she joined the Walter Thornton Agency to pursue a full-time modeling career. With her engaging smile, slightly upturned nose and expressive eyes, she was a natural in front of the camera, and can be seen in a number of magazines from the day, advertising a variety of products, from Ritz crackers to toothbrushes, pedicure scissors to tea, and girdles to Noxema skin cream.

It was shortly after her 20th birthday that Edythe got the break for which she had been waiting. She was asked to appear in an eight-page spread in the *Saturday Evening Post* titled "The Merchant of Venus," which detailed a day in the life of a model. Shortly after the magazine hit the stands, Edythe signed a test contract with Selznick Studios and was asked to audition for the coveted role of Scarlett O'Hara in *Gone with the Wind*. It is not known for certain whether it was director George Cukor, producer David O. Selznick or Selznick's wife Irene who started the wheels of Edythe's career in motion — suffice it to say that in November 1937, Edythe boarded a train for California, and eventual stardom. But she was no overnight success.

Of course, Edythe did not win the role of Scarlett — she was judged too young and inexperienced. Disappointed but undaunted, she engaged an agent, was given a six-month contract at Warner Bros. studio and assumed the persona of Susan Hayward, a name given to her by Warners talent executive Max Arnow. During this time, she appeared in several films as an extra or a bit player, including the 1938 Bette Davis vehicle *The Sisters*, where Hayward's back can be seen at a switchboard with a row of telephone operators.

At the end of her contract term, Hayward's option was dropped by Warners and she signed up for a seven-year stint with Paramount Studios, where she first appeared in the classic 1939 version of *Beau Geste*. Although most of her scenes were cut from the film, the few minutes that remained were enough to make her the new sensation of the Paramount lot. After assignments in two programmers, *Our Leading Citizen* (1939) and *$1,000 a Touchdown* (1941), Hayward was cast in a featured role in her first film noir, *Among the Living* (1941). Released at the beginning of the film noir era, and characterized by Southern Gothic overtones, *Among the Living* tells the story of a millionaire who is accused of a series of murders that were actually committed by his insane identical twin brother, who was thought to have died as a child.

Hayward portrayed Millie Perkins, the daughter of a boarding house owner. Openly flirtatious and fully aware of her charms, Millie meets and befriends Paul Raden (Albert Dekker), the insane brother, when he rents a room at the boarding house. Millie almost immediately displays her predatory nature when she literally licks her lips with anticipation as Paul flashes a wad of cash. Within seconds, she cajoles him into giving her money for a new outfit, explaining that the one she is wearing is "practically falling apart." Later, unaware of Paul's identity, Millie convinces him to assist her in finding the sought-after murderer in order to collect the $5,000 reward. Like Lady Macbeth in a polka dot dress, she questions his manhood when Paul hesitates: "You afraid of those ghosts they're all talking about? I guess I made a mistake. I thought you were a man. Sorry." Seconds later when Paul gives in, Millie purrs, "Well that's more like it. I knew you were only kidding."

On a hunch, Millie takes Paul to Radenhouse, the mansion where he spent years hidden away from the world. When Millie enters the room that had once belonged to his mother, Paul attacks her. Townspeople arrive soon afterward and Paul is shot, but he manages to flee and his twin brother John (also played by Dekker) is mistaken for the killer. The enraged townspeople prepare to lynch the innocent brother, led by Millie, who seems to derive an almost sexual excitement from the chaotic, bloodthirsty crowd. John is saved only when he escapes and trips over the dead body of his brother.

For her role as the avaricious Millie, Hayward was singled out in the *New York Herald Tribune* as being "especially good" and in *Variety* as "plenty sharp." During the next several years, she continued to make a name for herself in a variety of roles, including *Reap the Wild Wind* (1942), a sea yarn directed by Cecil B. DeMille; *I Married a Witch* (1942) starring Veronica Lake and Fredric March; *Young and Willing* (1943), an much-overlooked but highly entertaining comedy with William Holden and Eddie Bracken; and *The Fighting Seabees* (1944), a war propaganda movie which, at the time, was Republic's most expensive film.

In 1944, in the midst of her heightening career, Hayward took on a monumental role in her personal life when she married actor Jess Barker, a coupling that turned out to be stormier and more dramatic than any screen role she would ever portray. Only two months after the wedding, Hayward walked out on her husband, even after finding out that she was pregnant. She later returned to Barker, giving birth on February 19, 1945, to twin boys. For the next several years, the union seemed peaceful, although magazines observed that while Hayward's career was soaring, her husband's was at a standstill. By 1952, in fact, Hayward reported earnings of over $350,000, but Barker's income was a meager $665.

While Hayward served as the breadwinner and Barker, in effect, played "Mr. Mom," the pressures in their marriage continued to increase, reaching a head when, just a few days after their ninth anniversary, Hayward and Barker became embroiled in such a nasty physical altercation that their neighbors called the police. According to newspapers, Barker slapped Hayward, then dumped her into their swimming pool completely nude. It was also reported that Hayward tried to put out a cigarette in Barker's eye, and that she herself emerged with a black eye that she concealed behind dark glasses for several days. Divorce proceedings were initiated soon after, and the marriage was officially ended on August 18, 1954. Afterward, Hayward stated, "I married for love and security. I didn't get either."

Hayward's last film under her Paramount contract was the popular soap opera *And Now Tomorrow* (1944), in which she played a bewitching vixen who steals the fiancé of her deaf sister (Loretta Young). Declining to renew her contract with Paramount, Hayward opted instead to sign with producer Walter Wanger (then-husband of actress Joan Bennett), which turned out to be perhaps the most propitious move of her professional life.

Her initial film under her contract with Wanger was *Deadline at Dawn* (1946), the first movie for which she received top billing. An excellent example of film noir that captures the dark desperation of New York City, *Deadline at Dawn* is peopled with an odd mixture of personalities, including Hayward's character June Goth, a cynical dance hall girl with the proverbial heart of gold.

June is reluctantly drawn into a night of intrigue and suspense when she meets Alex Winkley (Bill Williams), a naive young sailor on a 24-hour leave. When Alex discovers that he inadvertently took some money from a woman he was with while drunk, he enlists June's aid in returning the cash, only to find that the woman is dead. The remainder of the film involves the duo's frantic search to find the killer, who turns out to be a kindly taxi cab driver (Paul Lukas) who had aided the couple during the night. In the film, Hayward does an excellent job in realistically transforming June from a jaded, emotionless young woman to one capable of love and compassion. *Screen Guide* stated that Hayward scored an "acting hit" and another reviewer claimed that she was "better than usual" in this role.

In 1947, Hayward exploded into the theaters of America in the film that would earn her the first of five Academy Award nominations, *Smash Up: The Story of a Woman.* In this top-notch feature, Hayward portrayed Angelica Evans, a nightclub singer who gives up her career in favor of her crooner husband, then turns to the bottle as he skyrockets to fame. Although she lost the Academy Award to Loretta Young in *The Farmer's Daughter,* Hayward continued to ride the wave of success with a showy role in *They Won't Believe Me* (1947), her third film noir.

This film opens in a courtroom where Larry Ballentine (Robert Young) is on trial for murder. In flashback, the film reveals the events that led to Larry's arrest, showing him as a loafer who has married for money and who has no intention of forsaking his financial security for the sake of the ladies he continues to charm. He gives up one girlfriend in New York when his wife buys him an interest in a brokerage firm in California, and when forced to choose between his wife's money and Verna Carlson (Hayward), a secretary in Los Angeles, he accepts his wife's ultimatum and moves to a remote ranch. His love for Verna eventually overcomes his avarice, but while driving with Larry to Reno to obtain his divorce, Verna is killed and mistaken for Larry's wife. Larry returns home with the intent to murder his wife, but finds that she has committed suicide. When her body is later found, Larry is arrested for her murder. Back in the present, moments before the jury is to return its verdict, Larry tries to escape and is killed by police, never to know that the verdict was not guilty.

For her memorable portrayal of a gold digger redeemed by love, Hayward was praised in *Silver Screen* magazine for having learned to "project an intense personality," and noted by another reviewer for her "arrestingly flashy style."

Susan Hayward

She next steamrolled her way through a variety of films, including *The Lost Moment* (1947), in which Hayward portrayed an unbalanced woman who succumbs to nocturnal trances. Despite Hayward's top-notch performance, it was a box office disappointment; the actress herself would later say: "It was a disastrous film. As miserable a failure as you've ever seen. Their name for it may have been *The Lost Moment*, but after I saw it I called it *The Lost Hour and a Half.*" Hayward followed this feature with *Tap Roots* (1948), a grandiose Civil

War drama starring Van Heflin; *The Saxon Charm* (1948), the backstage tale of a ruthless producer; *Tulsa* (1949), her last film with Wanger, who sold her contract to 20th Century–Fox; and Fox's *House of Strangers* (1949), her final entry into the realm of film noir.

Strangers tells the story of the Monetti family, which is torn apart following a banking scandal. The father of the clan, Gino Monetti (Edward G. Robinson), owns a bank which he operates with total disregard of the rules of banking. Gino's four sons all work in the bank for meager salaries, but he shows real affection for only one, Max (Richard Conte). Although Max is engaged to a "nice Italian girl," he falls in love with Irene Bennett (Hayward) when she comes to him for legal advice. The tensions in the Monetti family reach the boiling point when Gino is arrested for his illegal practices. Although Max begs his brothers to aid their father, they refuse, and Max is later jailed for trying to bribe a juror. When he is released from prison seven years later, a bitter man seeking revenge on his siblings, Max's brothers try to murder him. He escapes and later moves away with Irene to make a new start.

Hayward's Irene is strong-willed and passionate, the diametric opposite of Max's unassuming fiancée, portrayed by Debra Paget. This is vividly illustrated in Irene's first meeting with Max, when she barges into his office and finds him on the telephone. "Doors are made to knock on," Max tells her. "I haven't got time," Irene replies. "Whoever it is, say you'll call them back." Max does. Although Irene is initially portrayed as a rich girl who has bought her way through life, she later does a complete about-face, even putting her own life on hold until Max's release from prison, and using their love for each other to dissuade him from his vengeful designs on his brothers.

Again, Hayward received favorable reviews from the press. The critic for *Variety* wrote that she was "wholly convincing and lends an arresting presence to the film," and the *Citizen News* reviewer reported that her "beauty and acting ability … help tremendously." Hayward followed her success in this film with *My Foolish Heart* (1949), for which she earned her second Academy Award nomination (losing to Olivia de Havilland for *The Heiress*); *I Can Get It for You Wholesale* (1951), an entertaining story about the garment industry; *David and Bathsheba* (1951), a sweeping Biblical drama costarring Gregory Peck; and *With a Song in My Heart*, (1952), which brought in Hayward's third Oscar nomination. Although she lost the Academy Award to Shirley Booth for *Come Back, Little Sheba*, Hayward was acknowledged by *Photoplay*, receiving the magazine's Gold Medal as "the nation's most enjoyed actress of 1952," and was named the "World's Favorite Actress" by the Foreign Press Association. During this period, she was also immortalized at Grauman's (now Mann's) Chinese Theater in Hollywood, and her footprints were coated with gold dust to represent the queen she portrayed in *David and Bathsheba* (1951).

In the midst of her triumphs on screen, Hayward's personal life swept into the depths when she was rushed to the hospital after swallowing a handful of sleeping pills on April 26, 1955. The incident took place just hours after a stormy meeting with her ex-husband, and less than a week after the deaths of her agent Ned Marin and a close friend, Martha Little, whose cancer treatments Hayward had financed. Only two days after the incident, however, Hayward emerged from the hospital, her hair beautifully coiffured, wearing a bright print dress and white gloves, looking more like a woman who had just returned from a restful vacation than one who had tried to take her own life. Asked by a reporter why she took the pills, Hayward replied that it was "between me and God. And don't let anyone ever tell you that there is no God. There is."

The following week, Hayward plunged into rehearsals for MGM's *I'll Cry Tomorrow* (1955), the story of singer-actress Lillian Roth, who fell prey to alcoholism, but escaped through her courage and will to live. Singing all her own songs for the film, Hayward was hailed for her "shattering, intense performance," and garnered another Academy Award nomination for Best Actress, but she lost yet again, this time to Anna Magnani for *The Rose Tattoo*. After this fourth consecutive failure to earn the Oscar, Hayward later commented, "I managed not to shed any tears until everything was over. Then I sat down and had a good cry and decided that losing was just part of the game."

Hayward's next film, RKO's *The Conqueror* (1956), was a laughable $6 million epic starring John Wayne as Genghis Khan. The picture was a box office disaster and would later be included among the "50 Worst Films of All Time," but this distinction was the least of its lamentable results. A number of the film's scenes were shot less than 200 miles from Yucca Flat, Nevada, where atomic bomb testing had taken place for several years. After the exteriors of the picture were filmed in nearby St. George, Utah, several tons of Utah soil were shipped to Hollywood for scenes shot inside the RKO studios. Years later, a large number of birth defects and cancers were reported in St. George, and many of those involved with *The Conqueror* would be struck down as well, including character actor Pedro Armendariz, director Dick Powell, art director Carroll Clark, makeup chief Webb Overlander and character actresses Agnes Moorehead and Jeanne Gearson. In addition, the film's star, John Wayne, would die from cancer in 1979, and Hayward herself would develop a brain tumor. It would not be until decades later that the link between these tragic deaths and the nuclear testing in Nevada would be discovered.

But the misfortune caused by Hayward's connection with *The Conqueror* was years away. Meanwhile, at a Christmas party in December 1955, Susan Hayward met the man who would become her second husband and the true love of her life — Floyd Eaton Chalkley, a wealthy attorney and ex–FBI man from Carrollton, Georgia. Chalkley and Hayward started dating soon after their introduction, and eloped in February 1957, moving to Chalkley's home in Georgia. The following fall, after turning down numerous screen offers, Hayward accepted Walter Wanger's offer to star in *The Barbara Graham Story*, the true-life tale of a 32-year-old woman condemned to the gas chamber in

California for a crime that she may not have committed. Retitled *I Want to Live!* (1958), the film was directed by Robert Wise, who later said that in motion pictures, "Susan Hayward is as important a figure as Sarah Bernhardt was to the stage." It came as a surprise to no one when, on Academy Award night, Hayward finally received the award that she had coveted for so many years.

After winning the Oscar, the quality of the roles offered to Hayward declined, although she was as unforgettable as always in a number of box office successes, including *Ada* (1961), a glossy soap opera starring Dean Martin; *Back Street* (1961), the third filming of the Fannie Hurst classic; and *Where Love Has Gone* (1964), a thinly veiled account of the tragic affair between Lana Turner and Johnny Stompanato. However, while her relationship with her husband Eaton Chalkley had continued to thrive, their idyllic marriage ended in January 1966, when Chalkley died after being stricken with hepatitis. After his death, Hayward, a consummate professional, completed the movie she was working on — *The Honey Pot* (1967) — then went into seclusion for the remainder of the year. She emerged to play a small role in *Valley of the Dolls* (1967), after which she stated that she had returned to films because she had "itchy feet.... Now, however, I don't think I'd want to do a full-length role again. I'm glad I had the bulk of my career when you didn't have to take your clothes off."

For the next year or so, Hayward tried to keep her mind off the sorrow that threatened to overtake her after her husband's death, and she spent much of her time fishing, motorcycling and taking long trips to Africa. She was lured back to performing by producer Martin Rackin in mid–1968, who offered her the title role in *Mame*, which she played in Las Vegas for two months before retiring from the show because of a throat ailment. In 1971, after scorning television for years, she performed in a made-for-TV movie, *Heat of Anger*, and later filmed *Say Goodbye, Maggie Cole* (1972), which was to be her final performance.

In early 1973, the news broke that Susan Hayward had been hospitalized because of a serious illness of an unknown nature. Several months later, her son Tim revealed that she was suffering from several inoperable brain tumors and was not expected to live more than six months. But like the little girl who was struck by an automobile and never expected to walk, Hayward's indomitable spirit refused to let her go down without a fight. Approximately a year later, she appeared as a presenter at the April 1974 Academy Awards ceremony, and was also seen at the Governor's Ball, chatting with friends. And in October 1974, she lapsed into a coma, only to come out of it four days later, prompting a nurse to comment that Hayward "simply refused to die."

Even her will to live could not ultimately overcome the disease that had taken over her body, however, and on March 14, 1975, at age 56, Susan Hayward died. She was laid to rest in Carrollton, Georgia, next to her beloved husband, Eaton Chalkley.

Susan Hayward was one of the last true stars of an age in the history of movies that will never again be seen. She did not possess the flawless beauty of Greta Garbo, nor the acclaimed acting prowess of Bette Davis, but her unique looks and remarkable talent, combined with the personal struggles that she fought to overcome, created a personage who deserves a prominent place in the annals of film. Perhaps it was Walter Wanger who summed up the woman known as Susan Hayward when he described her in one brief, simple statement:

"She has real fire inside."

Film Noir Filmography

AMONG THE LIVING   *Director:* Stuart Heisler. *Producer:* Sol Siegel. Released by Paramount, September 1941. *Running time:* 67 minutes. *Cast:* Albert Dekker, Susan Hayward, Harry Carey, Frances Farmer, Gordon Jones, Jean Phillips.

DEADLINE AT DAWN   *Director:* Harold Clurman. *Producer:* Sid Rogell. Released by RKO, April 1946. *Running time:* 83 minutes. *Cast:* Susan Hayward, Paul Lukas, Bill Williams, Joseph Calleia, Osa Massen, Lola Lane, Jerome Cowan, Marvin Miller.

THEY WON'T BELIEVE ME   *Director:* Irving Pichel. *Producer:* Joan Harrison. Released by RKO, July 1947. *Running time:* 95 minutes. *Cast:* Robert Young, Susan Hayward, Jane Greer, Rita Johnson, Tom Powers.

HOUSE OF STRANGERS   *Director:* Joseph L. Mankiewicz. *Producer:* Sol Siegel. Released by 20th Century–Fox, July 1949. *Running time:* 101 minutes. *Cast:* Edward G. Robinson, Susan Hayward, Richard Conte, Luther Adler, Paul Valentine, Efrem Zimbalist, Jr., Debra Paget, Hope Emerson, Esther Minciotti.

References

"Actress Around the World." *Cue*, April 16, 1955.
Andersen, Christopher P. *A Star, Is a Star, Is a Star!* Garden City, NY: Doubleday, 1980.
Arnold, Maxine. "Brooklyn Goes to Bat." *Photoplay*, March 1950.
Barker, Jess. "My Life with Susan." *Silver Screen*, March 1950.
"Brooklyn Bombshell." *Coronet*, April 1956.
Corwin, Jane. "Jeff's Other Love." *Photoplay*, January 1954.
_____. "Smashup." *Photoplay*, November 1953.
"Count Ten and Die." *Newsweek*, November 17, 1958.
Froman, Jane. "She Lived My Life." *Photoplay*, July 1952.
"The Girl on the Cover." *Cue*, March 14, 1942.
Graham, Sheilah. "Only Four More Movies, Says Susan." *New York Mirror*, March 8, 1959.
Hipp, Edward Sothern. "Pioneer Life." *Newark Evening News*, June 11, 1959.
Holland, Jack. "Life with the Barkers." *Silver Screen*, October 1946.
"If You Knew Susan." *Look*, July 14, 1953.
Lamb-Davis, Virginia. "Why Susan Did It." *Motion Picture Magazine*, July 1959.
Linet, Beverly. *Susan Hayward: Portrait of a Survivor*. New York: Berkley Books, 1980.
McClelland, Doug. "The Brooklyn Bernhardt." *Films and Filming*, March 1965.
_____. "Susan Hayward." *Films in Review*, May 1962.

Moreno, Eduardo. *The Films of Susan Hayward*. Secaucus, New Jersey: The Citadel Press, 1979.
Pryor, Thomas. "Susan Hayward Gets Film Role." *New York Times*, May 30, 1957.
"Sex Was Not Enough." *New York Mirror*, May 17, 1959.
"Susan Hayward Bids for an Academy Award." *Look*, December 13, 1955.
"Susan Hayward's Story." *Modern Screen*, June 1954.
Underhill, Duncan. "You Have to Use Your Elbows." *New York World Telegram*, March 29, 1941.
"Waterbury, Ruth. "This Is Susan Hayward." *Photoplay*, May 1951.
Wilson, Earl. "Not So Sweet Susan." *Silver Screen*, December 1947.
"A Woman Is a Woman and a Man Is a Man." *Photoplay*, February 1972.
Zeitlin, Ida. "Three Loves Has Susan Hayward." *Photoplay*, November 1952.

Rita Hayworth

Rita Hayworth was a flame-haired love goddess whose incandescent beauty and smoldering sensuality catapulted her to superstardom during the Second World War. Fans worldwide flocked to her films, whether she was portraying a bubbly, carefree dancer or a mysterious femme fatale, and the personal life of the oft-married star filled page after page of fan magazines. But behind the silver screen, Hayworth's life was a tragedy characterized by failed relationships, controlling male figures, battles with alcohol and the debilitating disease that would ultimately cause her untimely death, Alzheimer's. Still, Hayworth's striking presence lives on in such popular films as *Blood and Sand* (1941) and *You'll Never Get Rich* (1944), as well as three entries in the realm of film noir: *Gilda* (1946), *The Lady from Shanghai* (1948) and *Affair in Trinidad* (1952).

Hayworth was born Margarita Carmen Cansino on October 17, 1918, in New York, to Eduardo, a well-known dancer from of Seville, Spain, and Volga, a former Ziegfeld Follies showgirl. Although Eduardo was reportedly disappointed that his first child was a girl, it soon became apparent that she had inherited her father's dancing talent. From the age of four, Margarita's days were filled with grueling dance lessons. "Rehearse, rehearse, rehearse — that was my girlhood," she would later recall.

Margarita's first stage experience was as part of her family's vaudeville act, the Dancing Cansinos, which included her father, his sister Elisa and several of his brothers from Spain. Added to the act when she was seven years old, Margarita's role was to appear at the end of the act, perform a few steps and play her castanets. She would play a similar part a year later when she made her inauspicious film debut in a Vitagraph short subject designed to showcase internationally traditional dances.

In the late 1920s, Eduardo Cansino turned from performing to teaching. He moved his family — which now included sons Vernon and Eduardo, Jr. — to Hollywood, where he opened a dance studio and found work as a choreographer for several major studios. Among his students were future stars Betty Grable, Lupe Velez, James Cagney and Jean Harlow. But Eduardo's career plans would change again in 1932, when he arranged for his 14-year-old daughter to perform a flamenco dance at the opening night of the movie *Back Street*. After watching her performance, Eduardo would later tell reporters, "Wow! She has a figure! She ain't a baby no more." Abandoning his teaching duties, Eduardo developed a new Dancing Cansinos team, featuring himself and Margarita. Because Margarita was too young to work in California nightclubs where liquor was served, Eduardo accepted engagements in Tijuana and Agua Caliente, a posh resort in Mexico, where the Dancing Cansinos were an instant sensation. But while the voluptuous teen was becoming a seasoned on-stage performer, she had few friends and led a sheltered life. Although Margarita came to resent her stifling lifestyle, she always followed the dictates of her overbearing father — a quality that would come to typify the future star's relationships with men throughout the rest of her life.

Before long, Margarita was spotted by a representative of Columbia Pictures, who used her as an extra in *The Devil's Cross* (1935). While performing in Agua Caliente, Margarita also caught the attention of Winfield Sheehan, then vice president in charge of production of the Fox Film Corporation. Famed columnist Louella Parsons, a dinner guest of Sheehan's, later wrote, "When [Margarita] came to our table she turned out to be painfully shy. She could not look at strangers when she spoke to them and her voice was so low it could hardly be heard. Hardly, it seemed to me, the material of which a great star could be made."

But Sheehan had seen something special in Margarita's graceful demeanor and sultry Latin looks and, after arranging a screen test, he signed her to a standard long-term contract. Sheehan shortened her name to Rita Cansino and arranged for the teenager to engage in a rigid program of acting classes and diction lessons, as well as a strict diet regime to lose her excess weight. The actress would later recall, "I developed a burning ambition — as only a too-fat 17-year-old can burn — to become a good actress.... It didn't require my being a genius to realize Fox was spending a great deal of time and money on my behalf and I intended for them to get their money's worth!"

Rita's first speaking part was a bit in *Under the Pampas Moon* (1935) with Warner Baxter, followed by another small role in *Charlie Chan in Egypt* (1935). She next appeared in *Dante's Inferno* (1935) starring Spencer Tracy, who years later would call the film "one of the worst pictures made anywhere, anytime. The fact that Rita survived in films after that ... is testament enough that she deserves all the recognition she's getting." She also appeared in *Paddy O'Day* (1935), a programmer with Jane Withers, and *Human Cargo* (1936), a Claire Trevor vehicle.

It appeared that Rita's big break had come when Sheehan tapped her for the title role in the remake of *Ramona*, which had been a silent hit for Dolores Del Rio. Rita worked fervently on learning the script for her part, and spent hours on costume fittings and makeup tests. But the star-making role was not to be. When Fox Studios merged with 20th Century Pictures, the newly formed studio was taken over by Darryl Zanuck, Sheehan found himself out of a job and, after being replaced in *Ramona* by the more-established Loretta Young, Rita was dropped from her contract. "It was the worst disappointment of my life," the actress recalled. "I cried my eyes out — but it didn't do any good.... I vowed I would show those people that they had made a terrible mistake. I determined I would become successful and famous in films and they would be sorry."

The opportunity to make good on this promise came in the form of Edward Judson, a 40-year-old ex-gambler and foreign car salesman, who tracked Rita down after seeing a copy of her Technicolor screen test for *Ramona*. Despite an age difference of nearly 30 years, Rita's father gave his enthusiastic permission for Judson to court his daughter, and the charming hustler immediately set about transforming her into a star. "The more I thought of what could be done with a girl like Rita," Judson later said, "the more intrigued I became with the idea of being a masculine fairy godmother to this little Cinderella."

Through Judson's contacts with studio executives, he arranged for her to appear in a small role in *Meet Nero Wolfe* (1936), starring Edward Arnold, as well as four forgettable Westerns, *Rebellion* (1936), *Trouble in Texas* (1937), *Old Louisiana* (1937) and *Hit the Saddle* (1937). Next, Judson convinced Columbia Studios mogul Harry Cohn to sign Rita to a seven-year contract, and he Americanized her Latin name by adding a "y" to her mother's maiden name of Haworth. Thus, at the age of 18, Rita Hayworth was "born."

On May 29, 1937, Hayworth's parents were shocked to learn, by telegram, that their daughter had eloped with Judson to Yuma, Arizona. Only later would Hayworth learn that she was the third Mrs. Judson, and that she had escaped her tyrannical father only to be joined to an equally controlling husband. Hayworth would later recall, "I married him for love, but he married me for an investment. From the beginning he took charge, and for five years he treated me as if I had no mind or soul of my own."

But Judson's take-charge temperament would lead to Hayworth's rise to fame. He instructed her on how to walk, advised her to lower her voice tone, insisted that she lose more weight, selected her clothing and hired a press agent to insure that her name frequently appeared in newspaper gossip columns. Judson also arranged for his wife to undergo electrolysis treatments to raise her hairline and had her dark brown hair lightened to its trademark auburn color. Judson's efforts soon paid off as Columbia executives cast the actress in a series of "B" pictures, including *Criminals of the Air* (1937), the first of six screen appearances with Charles Quigley; *Who Killed Gail Preston?* (1938), in which she portrayed the ill-fated title character; and *There's Always a Woman* (1938), starring Joan Blondell and Melvyn Douglas. And in late 1938, Hayworth won her breakthrough role as a pilot's unfaithful wife in *Only Angels Have Wings* (1939), a Cary Grant–Jean Arthur vehicle directed by Howard Hawks. Although the starlet claimed to be nervous and insecure in the company of her established costars, her natural sensuality came through on screen, prompting one reviewer to gush, "She's a good-looking girl with an ahvoom chassis."

Before the film's release, Hayworth's press agent Henry Rogers concocted a story for *Look* magazine, claiming that the budding star had spent her entire salary of $15,000 a year on clothes and that she had been named the year's best-dressed off-screen actress by the fictional Fashion Couturiers' Association of America. *Look* bought the story and Hayworth wound up on the magazine's cover. "Once the ball got rolling," Rogers later said, "it accelerated by itself. It was self-generating."

With her first magazine cover and her success in the box office hit *Only*

Angels Have Wings, Hayworth was on her way. After favorable roles in *Music in My Heart* (1940) with Tony Martin, and *Blondie on a Budget* (1940), she was loaned to MGM for the George Cukor–directed *Susan and God* (1940), starring Joan Crawford. She next appeared in *The Lady in Question* (1940), the first of four successful teamings with Glenn Ford; *Angels Over Broadway* (1940), in a performance that one critic called "far better than anything she has ever done before"; *The Strawberry Blonde* (1941), an escapist comedy starring James Cagney and Olivia de Havilland; and *Affectionately Yours* (1941), a mildly amusing screwball comedy. But Hayworth would be firmly set on the road to stardom with her next film, the 20th Century–Fox hit *Blood and Sand* (1941). Returning in triumph to the studio that had unceremoniously dropped her years before, Hayworth won the part of an aristocratic Spanish seductress over 37 other actresses. Of her performance, Robert Dana of the *New York Herald Tribune* wrote that Hayworth was "a devastating female menace, lovely and cruel," and *Variety* claimed, "Rita Hayworth takes another stride toward her assured position among the stars in demand."

Columbia capitalized on Hayworth's growing fame by casting her in the classic musical *You'll Never Get Rich* (1941) opposite Fred Astaire, who commended Hayworth's "trained perfection and individuality" and would later say that she was his favorite dance partner. Coinciding with the release of the film, Hayworth was seen in a satin and lace nightgown on the cover of *Life* magazine, kneeling on a bed while gazing seductively over one shoulder. The shot would become her most famous photo, and would provide her with a solid place in the circle of Hollywood's most glamourous stars.

But while Hayworth's star was on the rise, her homelife was becoming increasingly strained. Throughout their marriage, Judson had treated his wife with a Svengali-like dominance and became known around the Hollywood community as a "pimp." According to Hayworth's press agent Henry Rogers, Judson "would leave no stone unturned to have his wife become successful. And if that meant that he had to close his eyes while she went to bed with a film executive or an important male star, I believe that he would do it. I never saw him put his arms around her and kiss her — they seemed to have a business relationship." And Rogers' wife Roz, a friend of Hayworth's, recalled: "She was always afraid of what she would say in front of him, that she wouldn't say the right thing." But as Hayworth advanced in her career, Judson gradually lost his powerful hold over her, and in 1942 Hayworth filed for divorce. In the settlement, Judson received nearly all of the couple's jointly owned property, 200 shares of common stock in Columbia Pictures, 200 shares of preferred stock in 20th Century–Fox and $12,000 dollars in cash. Years later, Hayworth would bitterly state that Judson "helped me with my career and he helped himself to my money."

Despite her acrimonious parting from her first husband, Hayworth continued to further her film career with the splashy Technicolor musical *My Gal*

Rita Hayworth in *Gilda*

Sal (1942), costarring Victor Mature, followed by the star-studded *Tales of Manhattan* (1942), which featured the actress in one of five separate vignettes. (One of the film's stars was Ginger Rogers, whose aunt was married to Hayworth's uncle.) In connection with the release of *Tales of Manhattan*, Hayworth — along with Henry Fonda, Charles Laughton, Edward G. Robinson and Charles Boyer — placed her hand and footprints in the forecourt of

Grauman's (now Mann's) Chinese Theater in Hollywood. Hayworth next appeared in another musical with Fred Astaire, *You Were Never Lovelier* (1941), which again scored big at the box office.

Around this time, Hayworth became involved with the man she would later call the great love of her life — actor/producer/director Orson Welles. Reports vary as to the occasion of their first meeting — some say they were introduced at a party given by Joseph Cotten, while others claim that the couple met at Lucy's, a favorite haunt of the film elite. Nevertheless, it was obvious that Hayworth and Welles were almost immediately attracted to each other and the relationship soon became serious.

Tagged by newspapers as "Beauty and the Brain," the beautiful star and the highly acclaimed creator of *Citizen Kane* (1941) were married on September 7, 1943, with Welles' friends Joseph Cotten and Jackson Leighter as witnesses. By all accounts, Hayworth revered her educated husband, and soon after their wedding she set about improving her mind, visiting museums and listening to classical music. Author Jim Bacon stated, "For all her fame and beauty, Rita was very insecure. She was in awe of Orson's genius and found it hard to believe that one of the great talents in the movies could actually fall in love with her." And Hayworth herself admitted, "He's a genius, and let's face it, I'm no Einstein — but I'm willing to learn. Orson's the most stimulating man I've ever known."

Meanwhile, in keeping with Columbia chief Harry Cohn's decree that Hayworth appear in only one picture per year, she starred in 1944 in *Cover Girl*, with Gene Kelly, and the following year in *Tonight and Every Night* (1945), a lavish musical about wartime London. Shortly after filming began, Hayworth discovered that she was pregnant, and on December 17, 1944, she gave birth to her first child, Rebecca. Although Hayworth was delighted with her new daughter, her joy was dimmed a month later when her mother Volga died suddenly of peritonitis.

The following year, Hayworth starred in the movie that would forever insure her place in the annals of film. In the title role of *Gilda* (1946), the actress portrayed a strikingly beautiful femme who was at once sensual and amoral, vengeful and sensitive. The picture, Hayworth's first film noir, offered an often unfathomable plot, but its spicy dialogue and fascinating characterizations made it riveting from beginning to end.

The story begins as Johnny Farrell (Glenn Ford), a two-bit gambler, wins a bundle playing with loaded dice in a street game. After leaving with his winnings, he is accosted at gunpoint, but is saved by a mysterious stranger with a dagger hidden in his cane. The man is Ballin Mundson (George Macready), owner of a high-class gambling joint and, Johnny later learns, the head of a Nazi-controlled cartel. Johnny proposes that he manage Mundson's casino, and the men soon develop a close and mutually exclusive friendship. But this relationship is fractured when Mundson returns from a trip with a new wife,

Gilda. It turns out that Gilda and Johnny were once intimately involved, but their obviously acrimonious parting is made clear by Gilda, who pastes on an aloof smile as she appears to struggle with her former lover's name: "Johnny is such a hard name to remember," she says coolly, "and so easy to forget."

Although Johnny tries to mask his feelings with open hostility, it soon becomes clear that he and Gilda are still in love. "You do hate me, don't you, Johnny?" Gilda asks him. "Hate is a very exciting emotion. I hate you too, Johnny. I hate you so much that I think I'm going to die from it." After this pronouncement, the couple succumb to their emotions, unaware that their embrace is being observed by Mundson. When Johnny realizes that they have been seen, he follows his employer to an airfield, watching in horror as Mundson's airplane takes off and crashes in the ocean. A short time later, Johnny marries Gilda, but keeps her a virtual prisoner to punish her for being unfaithful to Mundson. They later reconcile, but Mundson, who had faked his death, reappears with plans to murder the couple. His scheme is thwarted when he is killed by the casino's washroom attendant, and Johnny and Gilda are free to begin their future together.

The reviews for *Gilda* ranged from acclaim to censure, with the *New York Herald Tribune's* Howard Barnes calling it "boring and slightly confusing," and Ruth Waterbury of the *Los Angeles Examiner* labeling it an "exciting, glamorous, rich, ruddy melodrama." Still, it was one of the year's most commercially successful features and, if for no other reason, it will always be remembered for Hayworth's sensual striptease to the tune of "Put the Blame on Mame." Hayworth followed this hit with another box office smash, *Down to Earth* (1947), in which she portrayed Terpischore, the mythical goddess of dance. (A print of this popular fantasy-musical, along with other examples of 20th century Americana, was encased in a time capsule to be opened in the year 2047.)

Hayworth's fame continued to grow when, in July 1946, her famous *Life* magazine photo was used to adorn the side of the first atomic bomb tested after World War II. But while the press reported that the actress burst into tears of gratitude upon learning this news, her reaction was actually quite the opposite: "It was Harry Cohn's idea to put my picture on that bomb," Hayworth later revealed. "I was under contract, and they threatened to put me on suspension if I put up a fuss…. That whole bomb thing made me sick to my stomach."

By now, Hayworth's marriage to Orson Welles had begun to deteriorate. Despite her plans for improving her mind, she remained intellectually insecure and reportedly turned to alcohol to cope with her suspicions that Welles was unfaithful. And in 1945, Hayworth herself had a fling with crooner Tony Martin, with whom she had costarred in *Music in My Heart* (1940). By 1946, the couple had formally separated, but Hayworth still decided to fulfill her promise to star in Welles' next project, *The Lady from Shanghai* (1948). "I made an agreement and I'll stand by it," she told the press. "I owe it to Orson."

In this picture, Hayworth's second film noir, the star portrayed Elsa, the beautiful but amoral wife of Arthur Bannister (Everett Sloane), a psychologically and physically impaired lawyer touted as "the world's greatest criminal attorney." The film is narrated in voice-over by Michael O'Hara (Welles), an Irish seaman who says of Elsa, "Once I'd seen her, I was not in my right mind for quite some time. Here was a beautiful girl, all by herself, and me with plenty of time and nothing to do but get myself into trouble." O'Hara first encounters Elsa as she is enjoying a carriage ride in the park and he later gallantly comes to her aid when three men try to mug her. When she learns of O'Hara's vocation, Elsa offers him a job as a crew member on her yacht, telling him, "I'll make it worth your while."

O'Hara accepts Elsa's proposal, but during a lengthy pleasure trip to the Caribbean, he encounters a number of bizarre characters, including Sidney Broom (Ted deCorsia), whom Bannister has hired to spy on his wife, and Bannister's partner George Grisby (Glenn Anders), a shifty-eyed sort who secretly lusts after Elsa. O'Hara soon falls under the spell of the mysterious Elsa and plans to spirit her away from her husband when the trip ends. Before he can accomplish this deed, however, O'Hara finds himself mired in a complex scheme that results in his arrest for the murders of Broom and Grisby. O'Hara is defended in court by Bannister, who intends to insure that the seaman is convicted, but O'Hara escapes and later realizes that it was Elsa who had murdered Grisby. In the film's famous climax, O'Hara confronts his lover in a House of Mirrors at an abandoned amusement park. When Bannister locates the couple there, he and Elsa engage in a lengthy gun battle that ends in both their deaths.

Although *The Lady from Shanghai* seems to improve with subsequent viewings, it was a financial disaster upon its release, and was panned by critics who not only objected to Hayworth's close-cropped blonde hair, but also to the film's convoluted plot. Bosley Crowther of the *New York Times* said that Orson Welles "has a strange way of marring his films with sloppiness," and Welles himself would later state that the picture was "an experiment in what not to do."

On November 10, 1947, shortly after production ended on *The Lady from Shanghai*, Hayworth was granted a divorce from Welles, telling the press: "I'm tired of being a 25 percent wife. Night after night he left me alone.... He's interested in everything about himself and nothing about his wife." After the divorce, Hayworth starred in another well-received feature, *The Loves of Carmen* (1948), then embarked on a European vacation, telling reporters that she was going "just to roam, to live for a year like the natives in each country." But the trip would not be the restful idyll that Hayworth envisioned. Instead, she would meet and fall in love with the man who would become her third husband, Prince Aly Khan.

The screen's love goddess was introduced to the wealthy prince at a party given on the Riviera by international party-giver Elsa Maxwell. At the time, Aly Khan was estranged from his wife, the British heiress to the Guinness brewery millions, and he and Hayworth were soon inseparable. But by early 1949, various church and women's groups had begun to malign Hayworth for her relationship with the married prince, and one organization, the General Federation of Women's Clubs of America, voted to boycott the star's films because of her unbecoming behavior. "I don't believe Miss Hayworth should be given another chance to make other movies unless she improves her conduct," a spokeswoman for the organization stated. In addition, British newspaper columnists criticized Hayworth for allowing her daughter to accompany her on her "irresponsible jaunts," and a column in the influential *Hollywood Reporter* urged that the movie industry "wash its hands of Miss Hayworth." Making matters worse were the growing rumors that Hayworth was pregnant with Aly Khan's child.

Meanwhile, Hayworth's professional reputation was suffering as well. Scheduled to star with William Holden in a Columbia Western, *Lona Hanson,* Hayworth failed to show up for the start of the film's location shooting in Arizona. Hayworth's action held up production on the film, and Harry Cohn placed her on indefinite suspension, resulting in a forfeiture of Hayworth's $248,000 annual salary. A short time later, the Hollywood Women's Press Club named Hayworth the "Least Cooperative Actress of the Year."

In the midst of these slanders on Hayworth's character, it was reported early in 1949 that Aly Khan's wife had filed for divorce and that he and Hayworth would be wed later that year. With the blessing of the prince's father, the spiritual leader of the Ismali Muslim sect, the couple were married in a lavish ceremony in Cannes on May 27, 1949. Aly Khan's many gifts to his new bride included four racehorses, an Alfa-Romeo car and a variety of diamonds and rubies. Seven months later, on December 28, 1949, Hayworth gave birth to her second daughter, named Yasmin. (While Aly Khan insisted to reporters that the baby princess had been born seven weeks premature, the obstetrician who delivered her refused to confirm the prince's statement, stating that he could not discuss matters "of a professional nature.")

For three months after the birth of Yasmin, Hayworth and Aly Khan enjoyed a quiet, idyllic existence in a rented chalet in Gstaad. But Hayworth grew depressed and unhappy after the couple moved to the prince's château on the Riviera, and the marriage was further eroded by the prince's passion for horse racing and gambling, his reported dalliances with other women and his tendency to disappear for hours or even days at a time. In an effort to appease his wife, the prince arranged for a second honeymoon trip to Africa, but instead of a small, intimate excursion, the trip was filmed for a documentary released in 1952, and included an entourage of four Moslem millionaires, two cooks, a valet, two pilots, two aides, three secretaries and a variety of French socialites.

Unable to tolerate what she called her husband's "playboy habits," Hayworth left Aly Khan in Nairobi, collected her two daughters from Cannes and returned to the United States. In a newsreel showing her April 1951 return to New York, Hayworth appeared slightly ill at ease and spoke with a faint British accent: "I'm thrilled to be back home again, and I'm most grateful for the very warm reception that you all have given me," she told reporters. "And the first thing I'm going to do is go out and get a hot dog. I can't wait." The following month, Hayworth drove to Reno, Nevada, to establish the six-week residence required to file a divorce. The final divorce decree would not be finalized until 1953, when Hayworth was awarded full custody of daughter Yasmin.

Meanwhile, Hayworth's first film after returning to America was her third and final film noir: *Affair in Trinidad* (1952), again starring Glenn Ford. A rather uninteresting re-tread of *Gilda*, this film focuses on the efforts of a Trinidad nightclub dancer to expose her husband's killer. As the film starts, Neil Emery is found dead of a bullet wound, and although police originally rule the death a suicide, an inspector (Torin Thatcher) later discovers that the man was murdered. In an effort to trap the suspected killer, local gangleader Max Fabian (Alexander Scourby), the inspector enlists the help of the dead man's wife, Chris (Hayworth). Meanwhile, Neil's brother Steve (Glenn Ford) arrives in Trinidad, having received a letter of invitation from his brother, written on the day of his murder. Steve and Chris fall in love, but Steve becomes jealous over Chris' intimate relationship with Fabian; Chris, under orders from police, is unable to reveal her attempts to unmask Fabian as Neil's murderer. Ultimately, the proof is found, Steve kills Fabian, and Chris and Steve return to America together.

Although *Affair in Trinidad* was one of 1952's top-grossing films, it was slow-moving and tedious, and featured clichéd situations and near-laughable dialogue. In one scene, a Trinidadian maid, Dominique (Juanita Moore), tells Chris, "You cannot live on grief. Yesterday is yesterday, tomorrow is tomorrow. Today is already yesterday." And later, Dominique offers more pearls of wisdom when she announces, "When one day is over, another day begins." While audiences flocked to the film, critics were less than enthused, with *Cue* calling the picture "unwittingly comic rather than dramatic," and the *Los Angeles Examiner* comparing it to a "1930s poverty-row predecessor that was refined, rewritten and remade." Even Hayworth herself later said that *Affair in Trinidad* "wasn't really a movie. It was a culmination of compromises made by everyone from the gateman at Columbia right up to Harry Cohn himself."

After this film, Hayworth played the title roles in *Salome* (1953), a lavish Biblical epic, and *Miss Sadie Thompson* (1953), the third screen remake of the Somerset Maugham short story. But although *Salome* was dubbed by one critic as "Gilda goes to Galilee," and Hayworth herself would later count "*Salome* and her stupid seven veils" among her least favorite films, the picture grossed more than $4 million, proving that Hayworth was still a favorite with moviegoers. *Miss Sadie Thompson* proved to be a moneymaker as well, with reviewers praising Hayworth's "strikingly good performance."

During the filming of *Miss Sadie Thompson*, Hayworth became involved with a man known by many in the movie industry as "Mr. Evil" — singer and film actor Dick Haymes. When he met Hayworth in 1953, Haymes' once-promising career was on the skids, and he was in deep financial trouble, having reportedly squandered as much as $4 million in earnings from his records, nightclub appearances and film work. The Argentine-born actor also had a deportation case pending against him from the U.S. Immigration Office for using his Argentine citizenship to avoid service in World War II, was in trouble with the Internal Revenue Service over $100,000 in back taxes, and was in the process of divorcing his third wife, Nora Eddington Flynn. By all accounts, Haymes viewed the vulnerable Hayworth as the answer to his financial problems and Hayworth, far from being repelled by the troubled actor, felt sympathy for Haymes, and loyally stuck by him as his hardships increased.

On September 23, 1953, Hayworth married Haymes, forging a union that was later characterized in *Photoplay* as "predestined to failure before the ink was dry." While the marriage forestalled Haymes' risk of being deported, the couple's problems were far from over — after only a month, Haymes was arrested for defrauding on his alimony payments to his second wife, actress Joanne Dru. A short time later, when Hayworth left her daughters in the care of a baby-sitter while traveling to Florida, the Westchester Society for Prevention of Cruelty to Children charged the star with child neglect and brought a sensationalized court case against her. Rallying to Hayworth's defense, ex-husband Orson Welles stated that the actress "has always been a most devoted mother to both girls," and a judge later ruled that she would retain the care and custody of her children. Ironically, despite the fervor with which Hayworth fought to keep her children, her relationship with her eldest, Rebecca, would diminish somewhat in the years to come. Some, including Hayworth's friend and choreographer Hermes Pan, would claim that Hayworth showed favoritism to Yasmin, and Rebecca herself would state, "I'm not saying I'd rather not be the child of my parents. I just wish some things had been different." Many years later, when Rebecca married an artist in Tacoma, Washington, neither of her famous parents were in attendance.

Hayworth's misfortunes continued when she walked out on her next film, *Joseph and His Brethren*, and, under her husband's management, formed her own company, Crystal Bay Productions. However, she was still contractually bound to Columbia Pictures, which prevented her from entering into agreements with any other studios, and effectively stymied her professional career. Meanwhile, the hard-drinking Haymes had reportedly become both verbally and physically abusive to his wife. After an incident at the Cocoanut Grove in Beverly Hills, during which Haymes allegedly blackened Hayworth's eye in front of shocked onlookers, the star left her husband and filed for divorce.

Hayworth would later tell the press, "I stood by him as long as he was in trouble, but I can't take it anymore."

Struggling to restart her stalled career and put her bitter relationship with Haymes behind her, the 37-year-old Hayworth reached an agreement with Columbia to make two final films at a total salary of $300,000. After a four-year screen absence, Hayworth's first picture under the agreement was *Fire Down Below* (1957), starring Robert Mitchum and Jack Lemmon. However, while the actress was hailed for her "solidly realistic performance" of a world-weary woman with a shady past, the film was a failure at the box office. She fared better with her next feature, *Pal Joey* (1957), and although many critics noted Hayworth's fading beauty (with one stating she was "no longer the dewy young belle"), the picture was a blockbuster for Columbia and a fitting swansong for Hayworth's long and often antagonistic association with the studio.

After her appearance in *Pal Joey*, Hayworth began to be noticed for what she had always longed to be — a serious actress. Her next film served to enhance this impression. As a vain and selfish socialite in *Separate Tables* (1958), Hayworth showed that was capable of expressive dramatic acting, and critics enthusiastically included her in their praise of the cast's outstanding performances.

In addition to providing a showcase of Hayworth's acting talents, *Separate Tables* was also the film on which Hayworth met her fifth husband, the picture's producer, James Hill. The 41-year-old Hill was a well-educated, wealthy man who had made the Hollywood "most eligible bachelor" list for a number of years. After dating for over a year, Hayworth and Hill married on February 2, 1958, but the producer would later admit that he "wound up as anxious to use her as all the rest." In typical Hayworth fashion, the star placed her professional life in the hands of her husband. After giving first-rate performances in *They Came to Cordura* (1959) and *The Story on Page One* (1960), she formed a production company with Hill, making *The Happy Thieves* (1962), a box office flop. The couple next began preproduction on *I Want My Mother!*, in which Hayworth was to play the mother of a death-row killer, but the project was later cancelled. In addition to these professional disappointments, Hayworth and Hill's married life was deteriorating into a blur of drinking and physical violence. Hayworth's longtime friend Hermes Pan recalled an occasion when he dined at the couple's house: "There was a candelabra on the table. And [Hayworth] just took the candelabra and threw it at Hill! It just missed his forehead. He said, 'Oh, you shouldn't have done that.' But Rita didn't say a word. She just sat there." Hayworth's daughter Yasmin would later recall: "My mother's marriage to James Hill was at first a wonderful, supportive, loving relationship and then, over a period of time, it turned into an alcoholic, drinking partnership."

Hayworth would also suffer a blow when, on May 12, 1960, her third husband, Prince Aly Khan, was killed in an automobile accident in Paris. Hayworth reportedly collapsed after hearing the news, and later told reporters: "For both Yasmin and myself, I can only say at this time how deeply moved we are at the news of Aly's death. It will be a tremendous loss to Yasmin, who has always been most attached to her father."

In June 1961, Hayworth and Hill separated, and three months later, Hayworth filed for divorce, telling the court, "My husband was more concerned with his own career than his family life with me. When he would come home he would be very distant, very aloof, and go off by himself for hour after hour." She also stated: "[Hill] said I was not a nice woman in too loud a voice."

Another two years would pass before Hayworth's next screen appearance, during which time she was involved in a highly publicized romance with actor Gary Merrill, the ex-husband of Bette Davis. The couple drank heavily, argued publicly, and were frequently seen clad in blue jeans and walking barefoot. By now, signs of Hayworth's as-yet-undiagnosed Alzheimer's disease were beginning to surface. In January 1962, she and Merrill were scheduled to costar in the Broadway production *Step on a Crack*, but Hayworth appeared to be nervous and distracted during rehearsals, and after one week, she checked into a hospital. Several days later, she told reporters, "I just want to rest," and pulled out of the play.

After her volatile relationship with Gary Merrill ended, Hayworth was seen in a glorified cameo in *Circus World* (1964), playing the mother of Claudia Cardinale. During production of this John Wayne vehicle, Hayworth exhibited violent mood swings and lapses of memory that were attributed to her increased alcohol intake. Her agent Bud Moss would later recall: "Looking back on it now, the one thing which was very sad was that when the word 'drinking' came up, nobody realized that this was all Alzheimer's. Nobody had any idea. Whenever she would go into her lapses or what people used to think were drunken stupors, it was Alzheimer's setting in."

Two years later, Hayworth was re-teamed with her old friend Glenn Ford in their final film together, *The Money Trap* (1966). Hayworth received a number of favorable reviews, with the critic for *Time* saying, "Rita at 47 has never looked less like a beauty, or more like an actress," and Kevin Thomas of the *Los Angeles Times*, writing, "It is Rita Hayworth who is best of all." But not all critics were so kind. *Film Daily's* reviewer stated, "One might think it would be nice to have Miss Hayworth back again after a long absence. But the role is a thankless one and Rita would have been better advised to wait for a part that did something for her. Here she appears as washed out as the picture." Later that year, Hayworth had a small part in *The Poppy Is Also a Flower* (1966), originally released as a special on ABC-TV and dismissed by the critic for *Time* magazine: "The very best that can be said about this picture is that it's junk."

Over the next four years, Hayworth appeared in four films: *The Rover* (1967), with Anthony Quinn; *Sons of Satan* (1969), which was never released in the United States; *Road to Salina* (1971), in which she delivered a fine performance as an anguished mother; and *The Naked Zoo* (1971), of which one reporter advised, "Miss Hayworth — older, wrinkled and edematous — is seen to such disadvantage that it would be a kindness to her to avoid the film.... The entire affair is abysmal." Also in 1971, Hayworth made several television appearances, including guest spots on *The Carol Burnett Show* and *Laugh-In*. But later that year when she was slated to replace Lauren Bacall in the Broadway hit *Applause*, the actress had trouble learning her lines and dropped out of the play, explaining that a bout with the flu had caused her to miss a week of rehearsals.

Hayworth's final film would be *The Wrath of God* (1972) starring Robert Mitchum and Frank Langella. During the film's production, Hayworth's memory lapses and difficulty with her lines escalated, and Langella later said, "Everything had to be written on cue cards for her, and she couldn't remember a line past the cue of it." Yasmin Khan also recalled this painful period in her mother's life: "She was really a broken person ... totally, totally helpless. I just understood her to have a drinking problem ... at the time I didn't know it was Alzheimer's."

Hayworth managed to finish filming on *The Wrath of God* and, although the picture was panned by critics, the fading star was favorably singled out in the *Los Angeles Times*: "Thankfully, Rita Hayworth, elegant and beautiful, fares pretty well. It is unfortunate she is not on screen more often, because she lends *The Wrath of God* a note of dignity it so desperately needs." In late 1972, Hayworth was signed to appear in a British production, *Tales That Witness Madness*, but after working on the film for just four days, she quit without explanation, and returned to Hollywood.

It would be another eight years until Rita Hayworth was diagnosed with Alzheimer's disease. In that period of time, the debilitating disease continued to manifest itself in her increasingly bizarre behavior. Yasmin Khan recalled, "She would hallucinate in the house, think that she would hear voices outside in the middle of the night, and would call the police ... there would be no one. She did this quite often." Actress Ann Miller related an incident when she arrived at Hayworth's house for dinner: "When [Hayworth] came to the door, she had a butcher knife in her hand and said, 'I'm not signing any autographs today! Who are you?' She didn't know who we were!" The extent of Hayworth's disintegration became public knowledge in 1976 when photographs showed her being escorted from an airplane at London's Heathrow Airport, her hair disheveled and a confused, frightened look in her eyes.

In 1980, it was announced that Hayworth was suffering from the incurable Alzheimer's disease, and Yasmin Khan would later say she received this news with "a sense of relief.... So much embarrassment and heartache could have been saved if at that time it had been known that Rita Hayworth was ill and not guilty of any misconduct." A year later, Yasmin was legally appointed her mother's conservator, as her condition continued to worsen: "She would pace the room, she would shuffle her feet and pace the room, and wring her hands," Yasmin recalled. "She would stop and look in the mirror and talk to herself in a language that was totally ... something that I couldn't understand." Eventually, Hayworth became bedridden and lost the ability to communicate.

In May 1985, Yasmin married Basil Embriricos, of a renowned Greek shipping family, and gave birth to a son, Andrew, later that year. When the marriage later broke up, Yasmin and her son took up residence in an apartment next to Hayworth. Abandoning her own dreams of a singing career, Yasmin began devoting her time to increasing public awareness of the affliction that had claimed her mother's mind and body, and became a spokesperson for the Alzheimer's Disease and Related Disorders Association, for which she continues to organize annual fundraising events.

After years of suffering from the debilitating effects of Alzheimer's disease, Rita Hayworth died at age 69 on May 14, 1987. The pallbearers at her funeral included former costars Glenn Ford and Tony Franciosa. Despite the disease that stole the last years from her life, she can be remembered through her films, as a legendary love goddess who possessed a regal bearing, an unfeigned smile and an elegant sensuality that seems to reach through the silver screen. In paying tribute to Hayworth, the Gordons screenwriting team perhaps described her best: "When Rita Hayworth walked on, she lighted up the screen. There was some spark of personality — today we might call it charisma — that no scientist can ever pin down, no sociologist ever satisfactorily explain ... she was adored by a cult of millions."

Film Noir Filmography

GILDA   *Director:* Charles Vidor. *Producer:* Virginia Van Upp. Released by Columbia, May 1946. *Running time:* 110 minutes. *Cast:* Rita Hayworth, Glenn Ford, George Macready, Joseph Calleia, Steven Geray, Joe Sawyer, Gerald Mohr.

THE LADY FROM SHANGHAI   *Director and Producer:* Orson Welles. Released by Columbia, June 1948. *Running time:* 86 minutes. *Cast:* Rita Hayworth, Orson Welles, Everett Sloane, Glenn Anders, Ted deCorsia, Erskine Sanford, Gus Schilling.

AFFAIR IN TRINIDAD   *Director and Producer:* Vincent Sherman. Released by Columbia, 1952. *Running time:* 98 minutes. *Cast:* Rita Hayworth, Glenn Ford, Alexander Scourby, Valerie Bettis, Torin Thatcher, Juanita Moore. *Awards:* Academy Award nomination for Best Costume Design (Jean Louis).

References

Banks, Harold K. "Rita Hayworth Seeks Happiness — In Vain." *Pictorial Review*, October 26, 1952.
"Carmen Hayworth." *Newsweek*, August 23, 1948.
Corwin, Jane. "The Not-So-Private Life of Rita Hayworth." *Photoplay*, October 1952.
"Cover Girl; Rita Learns New Role." *Life*, January 18, 1943.

Crichton, Kyle. "Rita the Rage." *Collier's*, May 3, 1941.
"Dancing Cansinos." *Dance*, March 1947.
Deere, Dorothy. "Rita Hayworth Lives Here." *Photoplay*, November 1947.
Drew, Bernard. "Heartbreak Hollywood." *American Film*, June 1977.
Holland, Jack. "Dancing with Joy." *Silver Screen*, October 1952.
Kilgallen, Dorothy. "Loves of Rita." *Modern Screen*, June 1948.
Kobal, John. "Rita Hayworth: The Time, the Place and the Girl." *Focus on Film*, Summer 1972.
Leaming, Barbara. *If This Was Happiness: A Biography of Rita Hayworth*. New York: Viking, 1989.
Liebling, A.J. "The Wayward Press." *The New Yorker*, June 11, 1949.
"The Love Goddess in America." *Life*, November 10, 1947.
Maxwell, Elsa. "The Fabulous Life." *Photoplay*, October 1949.
_____. "Love Affair." *Photoplay*, February 1949.
_____. "The Princess Abdicates." *Photoplay*, August 1951.
_____. "Transatlantic Call to Rita and Aly." *Photoplay*, April 1949.
Morella, Joe, and Edward Z. Epstein. *Rita: The Life of Rita Hayworth*. New York: Delacorte Press, 1983.
Muir, Florabel. "She's the Marrying Kind." *Photoplay*, October 1953.
"Nevada Wedding." *Life*, October 5, 1953.
"Onward and Upward." *Time*, May 7, 1951.
"Oui, Oui." *Time*, June 6, 1949.
Parsons, Louella O. "Ask the Boss." *Photoplay*, March 1948.
_____. "Cinderella Princess: The Life Story of Rita Hayworth." *New York Journal American*, June 5, 1949.
_____. "I Saw Rita Hayworth Marry Aly Khan." *Photoplay*, August 1949.
_____. "Intermission for Romance." *Photoplay*, May 1946.
_____. "It's Like This." *Photoplay*, July 1947.
"Prominent Couple Married." *Life*, June 6, 1949.
"Return of a Love Goddess." *Cosmopolitan*, April 1953.
Ringgold, Gene. *The Films of Rita Hayworth: The Legend and Career of a Love Goddess*. Secaucus, N.J.: The Citadel Press, 1974.
"Rita, Rebecca, and Yasmin." *Newsweek*, May 3, 1954.
"Rita Tells All!" *Modern Screen*, September 1952.
"Rita Without Glamour." *Life*, October 26, 1959.
"Rita's Baby Has World Premiere." *Life*, January 16, 1950.
Riumoldi, Oscar. "Rita and Glenn." *Hollywood Studio Magazine*, October 1984.
"Rumors of Marital Trouble." *Photoplay*, November 1941.
Sheppard, Gene. "Rita Hayworth: They All Went to Bed with Gilda, and Woke Up with Me." *Hollywood Studio Magazine*, November 1988.
Stanke, Don. "Rita Hayworth." *Films in Review*, November 1972.
"The Strange Case of Rita Hayworth." *Modern Screen*, March 1973.
"Transition." *Newsweek*, January 1950.
"Unfrumptious Wedding." *Time*, October 5, 1953.
Waterbury, Ruth. "The Romance Hollywood Doesn't Like." *Photoplay*, November 1942.
Wilson, Earl. "The Regal Rita." *Silver Screen*, May 1953.

Documentary

"Rita Hayworth: Dancing into the Dream." Copyright 1990, Home Box Office, Inc. King Arthur Productions. As seen on "Crazy About the Movies," a presentation of Cinemax, a Time Warner Company.

Virginia Huston

Virginia Huston, who was often noted for her likeness to stars Joan Fontaine and Carole Lombard, is perhaps best-remembered for her role as the fifteenth film mate of Tarzan the Ape Man. Hers, however, is a name that is seldom recognized by today's audiences, and her screen vehicles were seldom of the quality necessary to catapult her to lasting fame. Still, Huston was cast in prominent roles from the start of her arrival in Tinseltown, and made a brief but triumphant comeback after an automobile accident threatened to end her career. With appearances alongside such screen luminaries as George Raft, Robert Mitchum and Joan Crawford, Huston was featured in four films noirs: *Nocturne* (1947), *Out of the Past* (1947), *The Racket* (1951) and *Sudden Fear* (1952).

The only daughter and oldest of three children, Virginia Huston was born in Omaha, Nebraska, on April 24, 1925, to Mary Agnes and Marcus Huston, who would later become an executive with American Airlines. Early on, Huston was determined to become an actress and, according to a studio biography, at the age of five she casually invited her mother to attend a school presentation of *Helen of Troy*. It was the first that Mary Agnes Huston had heard of the production, and she was stunned to find that her daughter not only had the title role in the play, but that she was able to read long pages of dialogue without faltering. Several years later, Huston made her professional debut after being asked by a friend to read a radio script. After her impressive dramatic interpretation, she was given a role on a popular local radio program, *Calling All Cars*. The aspiring actress later gained experience on more radio programs and while a student at Duchesne, a Catholic school for girls, she appeared in several plays at the Omaha Community Playhouse. Later, at the age of 18, she starred in the title role of *Janie*, by special request in a performance at the Playhouse in a benefit for handicapped children.

In April 1945, Huston decided that she was ready for Hollywood and, with her parents' blessings, she moved to California, determined to take the film capital by storm. Unlike many a would-be starlet, Huston didn't have long to wait before making it the big screen. Upon arriving in Los Angeles, she hired an agent, who arranged for a screen test at RKO Studios. Although the test would later lead to a contract offer from the studio, Huston remembered it as a near disaster. "I find playing roles easier than taking tests," she said in 1947. "I'll never forget my first camera test. Right at the start, the director had me go through a hysterical scene, which came off very well, if I do say so. Then he told me to walk over to a table and pick up a letter. Do you know I couldn't, for the life of me, do this apparently simple job correctly. Over and over we tried the scene. Finally I really got hysterical. Then the director relented, saying others have had the same trouble. In other words, it's hard to do what should come naturally."

In her screen debut, Huston appeared in a bit part in RKO's *From This Day Forward* (1946), a sappy Joan Fontaine starrer that was a box office hit despite its blasting from critics. Later that year she was seen in a minor role in *The Bamboo Blonde* (1946), a dreary wartime musical starring Frances Langford. But after these two brief screen appearances, Huston was cast in a prominent role in her first film noir, *Nocturne* (1947).

This film's first scene shows a composer, Keith Vincent (Edward Ashley), playing his piano with a woman, whose face is not seen, seated nearby. With unfeeling indifference, Vincent breaks up with the woman — referring to her as "Dolores" — but as he is talking, he is shot in the head and killed. When powder burns are found on Vincent's head and hands, his death is ruled a suicide. However, detective Joe Warne (George Raft) suspects murder and begins an investigation. Warne begins by questioning the series of women whose photographs adorn Vincent's walls, but he runs into a dead end when he not only discovers that the philandering composer called all of his girlfriends by the name of Dolores, but also that each of the women has an alibi for the night of the murder. Warne's superiors warn him off the case after several of the women complain about his tactics, but he stubbornly doubles his efforts, focusing on Frances Ransom (Lynn Bari), a bit actress whose photograph had been removed from Vincent's wall.

When Frances' alibi turns out to be false, Warne continues to harass her, despite the fact that he finds himself drawn to the attractive brunette. Warne is further convinced of Frances' involvement after meeting her nightclub singer sister, Carol Page (Huston), who "accidentally" reveals that Frances was with Vincent on the day of the murder. Stymied in his efforts to identify the killer, Warne gets a break when he is contacted by the photographer who took the pictures of all of Vincent's girlfriends, but he later discovers that the photographer has been killed. Finding Frances' name written on a pad at the photographer's studio, Warne goes to her house, and is shocked when it appears that she has attempted suicide, leaving behind a typewritten note admitting her guilt in the deaths of Vincent and the photographer. After reviving Frances, Warne spots a photograph of Carol with dark hair instead of her current blonde, and he confronts the singer at her nightclub, accusing her of Vincent's murder. Carol admits that it was she, not Frances, who was involved with Vincent, but she denies killing him: "Maybe I should have killed him. Maybe I would have if I had a gun. But I didn't. I thought you'd heard," she adds sarcastically, "he killed himself." Just before Carol is arrested, the club's pianist, Ned "Fingers" Ford, admits that he is Carol's husband, that he had murdered Vincent and the photographer, and that had tried to kill Frances as well.

Although *Nocturne* was dismissed in the *New York Times* as being "as intriguing as the arrest of a peeping Tom," Huston's performance was singled out by the reviewer for *Variety*, who wrote: "Virginia Huston is interesting as Miss Bari's songstress sister and sings three tunes ... all are tuneful." But Huston's next feature, *Out of the Past* (1947), was far better received. This intricately plotted film, Huston's second film noir, begins as Jeff Bailey (Robert Mitchum), a small-town gas station owner, is summoned to appear at the home of Whit Sterling (Kirk Douglas), a mobster with whom he had been associated several years earlier. Compelled to explain his past to his trusting girlfriend Ann (Huston), Jeff reveals that in his former vocation as a private detective, he had been hired to find Whit's girlfriend Kathie (Jane Greer), who had shot Whit and reportedly absconded with $40,000. Tracking Kathie to Mexico City, Jeff soon falls for the sultry beauty, instantly believing her when she denies stealing the money from Whit. Jeff and Kathie flee to San Francisco, but they are discovered by Jeff's partner Fisher (Steve Brodie), who was hired by Whit to find the pair. Jeff is horrified when Kathie shoots and kills Fisher during a struggle, and he is further disheartened to discover that Kathie had indeed stolen the money from Whit.

The disillusioned Jeff settles in a small community, where he buys a gas station and begins his uncomplicated relationship with Ann. Having revealed his past to Ann, Jeff meets with Whit as planned, learning that Kathie has returned, and that she is being blackmailed by Whit about Fisher's murder. Using false evidence that also implicates Jeff as Fisher's killer, Whit forces Jeff to perform one more job — to obtain potentially damaging tax records from Leonard Eels, a former employee of Whit's. Jeff soon learns, however, that Whit actually intends to have the accountant killed and frame him for the murder. After trying, without success, to prevent the crime, Jeff later obtains the tax records, using them to secure Whit's agreement to turn Kathie in for Fisher's murder. Learning of Whit's plan, Kathie kills him, then insists that Jeff flee the country with her. Jeff appears to agree, but secretly contacts police, and when the couple encounter a roadblock, Kathie realizes Jeff's betrayal and shoots him. Their car crashes, killing them both. Devastated by Jeff's death, Ann seeks out a young mute boy, Jimmy (Dickie Moore), who was a close friend of her dead lover: "You can tell me. You knew him better than I did. Was he going away with her? I have to know." Realizing that Ann will be forever locked into the past if she knows the truth, Jimmy lies to her, indicating that Jeff was indeed planning to flee with Kathie. Stoically receiving this news, Ann is able to spurn Jeff's memory, feeling that she is better off without the man she loved.

As the sensitive, trusting Ann, Huston's role was the diametric opposite of the murderous Kathie, but she nonetheless managed to make a significant impact in the film. For her efforts, she was hailed in *Variety* for her "impressive trouping," and included in *The Hollywood Reporter's* praise of the film's "splendid supporting cast."

By now, more than one newspaper columnist had pointed out Huston's striking resemblance to two of Hollywood's most famous actresses, Joan Fontaine and the late Carole Lombard, but Huston seemed to take the comparisons in stride. "It probably depends on my hairdo, so you see I'm not worried, although everyone says I should develop a distinctive personality. But how do you go about doing that? [One] Hollywood custom, going out with

Virginia Huston

one's leading man for publicity purposes, won't give me that distinctive personality people in pictures keep talking about. I'll try to develop it on the studio sets."

Huston made a step toward acquiring the distinction she sought when she was loaned to Warner Bros. for the second female lead in *Flamingo Road* (1949), starring Joan Crawford. In this potboiler, Huston did a commendable job as a spoiled rich girl whose husband's obsession with former carnival coochie dancer Crawford leads to his eventual suicide. Huston followed this film with another loan-out, this time to Columbia for an above-average Western, *The Doolins of Oklahoma* (1949), which featured the actress as the love interest of Randolph Scott, the leader of one of the Southwest's last real-life outlaw gangs. Next, Huston received the first and only top-billing of her career, in Republic's *Woman from Headquarters* (1950). Unfortunately, the film was a laughable timewaster, showing Huston as a tough but pretty super-cop who manages to triumph over a series of far-fetched situations.

Aside from her appearance in the sub-par *Woman from Headquarters*, Huston now had several eye-catching roles to her credit, and it appeared that she might be well on her way to achieving the stardom that had been predicted after her appearance in *Nocturne*. But her rise to fame was abruptly halted in 1950 when she was involved in a serious automobile accident which left her paralyzed for several weeks with a broken back. Only months later, however, it was announced that Huston would become the fifteenth actress to take over the role of Jane in the latest Tarzan adventure, *Tarzan's Peril* (1951).

With some amusement, Huston reported that people were shocked to learn that her new film would show her engaging in such stunts as climbing trees and riding elephants. "Jane is the perfect answer," Huston explained. "I run through the jungle practically barefooted. I wear a brief costume and that makes my doctor happy, too." Frankly discussing her injuries with the press, Huston also revealed that the accident had not only affected her physically, but psychologically as well. "A broken back wasn't all I got. It seems your nervous system is involved in an injury like that. My emotions got all mixed up for a while. I'm okay now, but the doctor says I should avoid any great emotional stress. And you know how simple those Tarzan scripts are. All action, practically."

In *Tarzan's Peril*, Huston portrayed her second starring role, appearing opposite Lex Barker in his third appearance as Tarzan. Considered one of the better episodes in the long-running series, the well-crafted *Tarzan's Peril* showed the Ape Man thwarting the efforts of a pair of gunrunners to pit two African tribes against each other. Unfortunately, Huston's role was overshadowed by that of singer Dorothy Dandridge, who played the queen of a tribe that is saved by Tarzan. In the next Tarzan episode, *Tarzan's Savage Fury* (1952), Huston was replaced by Dorothy Hart, and would never again appear in the series.

Instead, the actress starred with Cameron Mitchell and Arthur Franz in *Flight to Mars* (1951), which focused on a group of scientists who crash-land on Mars. One of the last films produced by Monogram studios before their name-change to Allied Artists, this feature turned out to be a weak programmer. Back at her home studio, Huston rebounded with a higher-quality feature, *The Racket* (1951) but, as the pregnant wife of a zealous police officer, her role was a minor one.

The Racket, Huston's third film noir, stars Robert Mitchum as Capt.

McQuigg, a rare honest cop in a city full of corruption. McQuigg's nemesis is a middle-level hood, Nick Scanlon (Robert Ryan), who is known for his penchant for violence. When a police informant is found murdered in McQuigg's district, the crusading captain places one of his best officers, Johnson (William Talman), on special duty in an effort to prove that Scanlon was behind the hit. Later, when Scanlon pays a visit to McQuigg at the police station, he gets into a scuffle with Johnson and kills him. But Scanlon is arrested after being identified by a reporter who witnessed the crime. While attempting to escape, Scanlon is killed, but the film ends on a typically pessimistic noir note as McQuigg tells a colleague: "Tomorrow it starts all over again."

After Huston's small role in *The Racket*, she appeared in another minor part in her final film noir, RKO's *Sudden Fear* (1952). A tautly scripted and directed thriller, this picture starred Joan Crawford as playwright and San Francisco heiress Myra Hudson, who falls in love with and marries actor Lester Blaine (Jack Palance). Deliriously happy with her groom, Myra plans to make a will that amply provides for Lester's future but is primarily earmarked for a heart foundation. But before she can sign the new document, Myra learns that her husband is having an affair with an attractive local girl, Irene Neves (Gloria Grahame), and that they together are plotting her death. Quickly conquering her grief and horror at this discovery, Myra crafts an intricate scheme to murder Lester and frame Irene for the crime. Later, while waiting in Irene's apartment to shoot Lester, she loses her nerve and flees. Lester, meanwhile, has figured out her plot and follows her in his car. Coincidentally, Irene is walking in a direction opposite from Irene and is clad in a coat and white scarf similar to Myra's. As Lester searches for Myra, he mistakes Irene for his wife and runs her down with his car, simultaneously killing himself in the accident.

In *Sudden Fear*, Huston portrayed the rather superfluous role of Myra Hudson's efficient secretary, logging a total screen time of less than five minutes, and earning a brief mention in *Variety* as merely "okay." The film would be her last for RKO. But Huston had other matters to occupy her time. In August 1952, she married Manus Paul Clinton, II, a real estate broker and Korean War veteran, and moved with her new husband to Malibu. She would later return to Hollywood for a small role in Paramount's *Knock on Wood* (1954), a spy comedy starring Danny Kaye. Following this feature, Huston retired from films and faded into obscurity.

After fewer than 15 films over a span of nine years, Virginia Huston has the distinction of having one of Hollywood's briefest screen careers after one of its most promising starts. Hard-pressed to overcome comparisons to more famous actresses, and perhaps hampered after her severe back injury, Huston nonetheless demonstrated an obvious talent during her stay in Tinseltown, particularly in such features as *Out of the Past* and *Flamingo Road*. It is regrettable that her tenure on screen was so brief.

Film Noir Filmography

OUT OF THE PAST   *Director:* Jacques Tourneur. *Producer:* Warren Duff. Released by RKO, November 25, 1947. *Running time:* 96 minutes. *Cast:* Robert Mitchum, Jane Greer, Kirk Douglas, Rhonda Fleming, Richard Webb, Steve Brodie, Virginia Huston, Paul Valentine, Dickie Moore, Ken Niles.

NOCTURNE   *Director:* Edwin L. Marin. *Producer:* Joan Harrison. Released by RKO, November 1946. *Running time:* 87 minutes. *Cast:* George Raft, Lynn Bari, Virginia Huston, Joseph Pevney, Myrna Dell, Edward Ashley.

THE RACKET   *Director:* John Cromwell. *Producer:* Edmund Grainger. Released by RKO, December 1951. *Running time:* 88 minutes. *Cast:* Robert Mitchum, Lizabeth Scott, Robert Ryan, William Talman, Ray Collins, Joyce MacKenzie, Robert Hutton, Virginia Huston, William Conrad.

SUDDEN FEAR   *Director:* David Miller. *Producer:* Joseph Kaufman. Released by RKO, August 1952. *Running time:* 110 minutes. *Cast:* Joan Crawford, Jack Palance, Gloria Grahame, Bruce Bennett, Virginia Huston, Touch [Mike] Connors. *Awards:* Academy Award nominations for Best Actress (Joan Crawford), Best Supporting Actor (Jack Palance), Best Cinematography (Charles B. Lang, Jr.), Best Costume Design (Sheila O'Brien).

References

Lieber, Perry. Biography of Virginia Huston. RKO Radio Studios, circa 1951.

MacPherson, Virginia. "Just What Doctor Ordered!" United Press International, circa 1951.

Scott, John L. "Blond Will Battle Resemblances." *Los Angeles Times*, October 6, 1946.

"Star Virginia Huston Will Become Bride." *Los Angeles Times*, July 18, 1952.

Adele Jergens

Once described by a columnist as "a lissom, winsome, blondelicious cel-
luloidish with an oo-la-la personality," Adele Jergens was a sleek stunner with
classical features and a statuesque physique. The actress, who was also an
accomplished singer and dancer, proved to be an adept comedienne in such
features as *The Fuller Brush Man* (1948), but she was more often cast as the
"shady lady," and appeared in a succession of films as gangsters' molls, husband stealers, schemers and even the occasional murderess. Before retiring
from the screen in the late 1950s, Jergens would appear in more than 50 films,
and lend her talents to four films noirs: *The Dark Past* (1948), *Side Street* (1950),
Armored Car Robbery (1950) and *Try and Get Me* (1950).

The striking actress, alternately labeled during her career as "The Champagne Blonde," "The Eyeful" and "The Girl with the Million Dollar Legs,"
was born Adele Louisa Jurgens on November 26, 1917, in Brooklyn, New York.
(Years later, a New York columnist would say that wherever the actress went,
people insisted on spelling her last name with an "e," so she "threw her hands
up in despair and adopted Jergens as her stage name.") As the youngest of
four children and the only girl, Jergens was a typical tomboy, enjoying a childhood that was focused more on sandlot baseball than on baby dolls and sewing.
From an early age, Jergens was determined to pursue a career as a newspaper
reporter but, surprisingly, her parents were against the idea. "They wanted me
to become a dancer and actress. That's contrary to the usual story," Jergens
said. "It didn't take me long to find out that my parents were right."

At the age of seven, Jergens began taking dancing lessons, and when she
was 14, she won a scholarship to the Albertina Rasch Dance School in Manhattan: "I was all wrapped up in my dancing," she said. "I used to go to the
dancing school every day during the summer and three times a week the rest
of the year. I never went out with boys. They used to think I was conceited
but, actually, I was shy." One year after enrolling at the Rasch studios, Jergens made her professional debut, appearing in a Broadway musical show during her summer vacation. "I remember very well the first $35 I ever earned,"
the actress recalled. "I was 15 years old and I bought my first tailored suit.
Nothing could hold me back after that."

Following her graduation from Rockville Center High School, Jergens
found work as a Powers model during the day, appearing in ads for everything
from stockings to refrigerators. At night, she worked in local clubs and eventually became one of New York's top showgirls in the chorus of such productions as *Jubilee* (1935) and *DuBarry Was a Lady* (1939). Later, responding to
her longing for travel, Jergens registered with an agency that booked overseas
cabaret shows, and appeared at Grosvenor House and the Savoy Hotel in London, Les Ambassadeurs and Le Toquet in Paris, and the Casino and the
Copacabana in Rio de Janeiro. Upon her return to New York, she entered and
won a contest at the 1939 World's Fair, earning the title "Miss World's Fairest."
The resulting exposure attracted the attention of Hollywood and the actress

promptly signed a contract with 20th Century–Fox, but after languishing for a year in bit parts, she returned to Broadway.

It was while working as understudy to Gypsy Rose Lee in *Star and Garter* (1942) that Jergens finally received her big break. "You know how those jobs are," the actress said later. "All I did was to stand around backstage just in case Gypsy became ill. But those things, I thought, only happened in the movies, where the understudy proves to be a hit." But real life imitated art when Lee missed a show and Jergens performed in her place. As luck would have it, she was spotted by a talent scout from Columbia Studios and placed under contract.

For her first assignment at her new studio, Jergens was given a small role in *Together Again* (1944), an endearing comedy starring Irene Dunne and Charles Boyer, followed by a bit part in *Jane Eyre* (1944) and a lead in the Western serial *Black Arrow* (1944). After another minor role in *Tonight and Every Night* (1945), an entertaining Rita Hayworth starrer, Jergens was treated to a huge publicity campaign for her part as the Princess of Baghdad in *A Thousand and One Nights* (1945). Costarring Cornel Wilde and Evelyn Keyes, this amusing spoof of the Arabian Nights was a box office hit, and Jergens' performance made the Hollywood community sit up and take notice. Noted by critics for her "torrid beauty," the actress also became an instant favorite with World War II servicemen who, according to one article, wrote the actress nearly 16,000 letters "announcing that if they ever were cast away on a coral isle, Miss Jergens is the girl they would love to be cast away with."

Despite Jergens' overnight success, Columbia failed to capitalize on the popularity of their newest starlet, casting her in *She Wouldn't Say Yes* (1946), a trite, predictable comedy starring Rosalind Russell and Lee Bowman. Although her vehicles varied in quality, she appeared in six films for the studio the following year, the best of which, *Down to Earth* (1947), offered the actress the first of her many bad-girl roles. Her other films of 1947 included *I Love Trouble*, a respectable thriller with Franchot Tone, Tom Powers and Lynn Merrick; *The Corpse Came C.O.D.*, a mediocre feature starring George Brent and Joan Blondell as rival newspaper reporters who join forces to solve a murder mystery; and *Blondie's Anniversary*, the 22nd episode of the popular series, for which Jergens was singled out in *Variety*: "Miss Jergens' physical appurtenances lend belief to the shakedown role, and she also has the ability to sell it histrionically."

But Jergens fared better with her first picture of 1948, *The Dark Past*, which also marked her initial entry into the realm of film noir. Starring William Holden, Lee J. Cobb and Nina Foch, this psychological thriller begins as police psychiatrist Andrew Collins (Cobb) relates a personal experience to a colleague in order to illustrate the value of psychiatric rehabilitation for criminals. Three years before, while vacationing at his lakeside cabin with his wife, son and three friends, Collins had encountered a recent prison escapee, Al Walker (Holden). Along with his gun-toting girlfriend (Foch) and two

Adele Jergens

henchmen, Walker held the vacationers hostage while waiting for a boat to carry his gang to freedom. During the night-long ordeal, Collins manages to unearth the psychological roots of Walker's criminal disposition, learning that as a child Walker had been responsible for the death of his father. Walker's recollection of the event renders him unable to kill again, and later, when police surround the cabin, he is forced to surrender.

As Laura Stevens, one of the vacationers at the cabin, Jergens portrayed a philandering wife whose attraction for her husband is revived when he stands up to the hoods holding them captive. In her best scene, Laura boldly defends her spouse when Walker's girlfriend delivers a disparaging remark: "What kind of woman are you, anyway? How can you stand there with your hands covered with blood and joke about it? You're so mean and miserable, I feel sorry for you." After the film's release, Jergens and several other supporting cast members were mentioned in *Motion Picture Herald* for their "near-excellent performances," and in the *New York Times* for their "unobtrusive but neat characterizations."

Next, Jergens starred in *Ladies of the Chorus* (1948), a dreary musical in which she portrayed — of all things — Marilyn Monroe's mother, and *The Prince of Thieves* (1948), a variation on the Robin Hood legend that suffered from limp direction. But she rebounded with *The Fuller Brush Man* (1948), a hilarious slapstick comedy starring Red Skelton, and *The Woman from Tangier* (1948), in which Jergens excelled a café singer who helps an investigator solve a double murder. She continued her non-stop shooting schedule in 1949, appearing in *Make Believe Ballroom*, a fairly entertaining musical featuring Frankie Laine, Jimmy Dorsey and Gene Krupa; *Slightly French*, starring Dorothy Lamour as a cooch dancer who is passed off as a classy French actress; and *The Mutineers*, of which the critic for *Variety* wrote, "*The Mutineers* hasn't much to recommend it, except the sexy presence of Adele Jergens in a few scenes.... The actors perform with a singular lack of enthusiasm. All, that is, save Miss Jergens, who comes out quite well as a loose wench who frankly likes men."

Up to now, Jergens' busy professional life seemed to leave little time for romantic pursuits, but her studio publicists assured the public, "Miss Jergens believes in marriage and having a family but wants to be sure she has picked the right man before she walks to the altar and hopes it will be for life." And during filming of *Treasure of Monte Cristo* (1949), Jergens found "Mr. Right" in her costar, Glenn Langan. Featured in such top-notch films as *Dragonwyck* (1946), *Forever Amber* (1947) and *The Snake Pit* (1948), Langan is often best remembered for his portrayal of the title role in *The Amazing Colossal Man* (1957). Jergens and Langan wed on October 6, 1949, had one son, Tracy, and remained married until Langan's death in 1991.

Meanwhile, when Jergens' contract with Columbia expired, she turned to freelancing, and in 1950 appeared in a whopping ten films. But some of her choices were not always of the highest quality, including *Radar Secret Service*, a silly programmer about agents who track down a ring of thieves through the use of radar; *Travelling Saleswoman*, a lifeless and unamusing comedy which featured Jergens as a shapely saloonkeeper; and *Everybody's Dancin'*, a mediocre musical designed to showcase television country and Western star Spade Cooley. But also in 1950, Jergens would appear in three excellent examples from the film noir era: *Side Street, Armored Car Robbery* and *Try and Get Me.*

In the first, *Side Street,* Jergens played the brief but memorable role of Lucille "Lucky" Colner, whose blackmail of her former lover provides the set-up for this taut thriller. After successfully securing the $30,000 payoff, Lucky is killed by her boyfriend, attorney Victor Backett (Edmon Ryan), and his accomplice, George Garsell (James Craig). The blackmail money, hidden inside a file folder, is later stolen from Backett's office by mail carrier Joe Norson (Farley Granger), who believed the folder contained only $200. Stunned to discover the folder's actual contents, Joe tells his young, pregnant wife Ellen (Cathy O'Donnell) that he has landed a high-paying job out of town, then leaves the money with a friend, Nick, and hides out in a cheap hotel. Joe ultimately decides to return the cash to Backett, but the attorney denies any knowledge of the money, suspecting Joe has been sent by police.

Joe later learns that Nick has fled with the money, but when he tracks him to a run-down apartment, he finds that his friend has been murdered. After being spotted near the apartment by a neighbor, Joe is soon sought by police for the murders of both Nick and Lucky. Meanwhile, Joe reveals his misdeeds to his wife, but he disregards her pleas to turn himself in, and instead goes in pursuit of the real criminals. His search leads him to Harriet Sinton (Jean Hagen), Garsell's ex-girlfriend, but she double-crosses Joe and delivers him to Garsell. Beaten and abducted by Garsell and his sidekick, Larry Giff (Harry Bellaver), Joe is led on a high-speed chase from police which leaves George and Larry dead and Joe injured. At the film's end, Joe is reunited with Ellen, and the audience is assured by the film's narrator that he "is going to be all right."

Although Jergens' appearance in *Side Street* was limited to two scenes, her role was a pivotal one and she made the most of her time on screen. She was particularly vivid in her scene with her married ex-lover Emil Lorrison (Paul Harvey), who shows up at her apartment claiming to have only half of the expected $30,000. "Take a look at yourself, Grandpa," Lucky says sarcastically. "First you sell yourself I'm nuts about you — crazy for your manly charms. And now you think this is bargain day. Well, go on down to Gimbel's bargain basement — you're in the wrong department. Take that other 15 grand out of your pants or get out."

The actress followed this picture with her next film noir, *Armored Car Robbery,* playing a showgirl married to a small-time hood while having an affair with his cunning boss. The action in this fast-paced film begins with the robbery of an armored car at a Los Angeles ballpark, orchestrated by a cold-blooded criminal, Dave Purvis (William Talman), and carried out with the help of Benny McBride (Douglas Fowley), Ace Foster (Gene Evans) and Al Mapes (Steve Brodie). But police arrive on the scene sooner than expected and while making their getaway, the thieves are confronted by police detectives

Cordell (Charles McGraw) and Phillips (James Flavin). During a shootout, Phillips is killed and Benny is severely wounded. Disguising themselves as oil field employees, the men bluff their way through a roadblock, making their way to a waterfront hideout. But when Benny pulls a gun on Purvis, insisting on seeking medical treatment, Purvis disarms him and ruthlessly murders him. When police close in, Foster is shot and killed, Mapes flees in a boat and Purvis manages to escape with the briefcase full of cash.

Later, police nab Mapes when he tries to visit Benny's showgirl wife, Yvonne LeDoux (Jergens), in an effort to obtain his share of the stolen money. Police then learn that Yvonne is Purvis' mistress, and rookie detective Ryan (Don McGuire) poses as Mapes in an effort to learn Purvis' whereabouts from Yvonne. But the quick-witted showgirl tips off Purvis, who abducts Ryan and shoots him, leaving him in a deserted alley. Ryan manages to notify Cordell that Purvis and Yvonne are planning a getaway, and the couple are pursued to a nearby airport. Attempting to flee with the stolen cash, Purvis is struck by a departing airplane and dies as the bills scatter around his lifeless body.

Described in the film as "a lot of woman" and "strictly high-rent," Jergens' character was as hard-boiled and crafty as her artful lover, as demonstrated early on when her estranged husband, Benny, attempts a reconciliation. "What would you say if I told you I was about to hit the big time?" Benny asks, to which Yvonne coolly replies, "I wouldn't know what to say—it'd be such a shock." And later, after learning of her husband's death, Yvonne is totally unaffected. "How does it feel to be a free woman?" Purvis asks her. And Yvonne casually responds: "Just the same." Jergens' performance was mentioned in a number of reviews, including *Variety*, whose critic wrote that she "attracts as a stripteaser."

Jergens next played another flashy role in *Try and Get Me*, her final film noir. This gripping tale of murder and mob violence tells the story of Howard Tyler (Frank Lovejoy), a luckless war veteran who is unsuccessful in his repeated efforts to find employment. Desperate to find the means to support his wife and son, Howard nonetheless hesitates when an acquaintance, Jerry Slocum (Lloyd Bridges), proposes that Howard join him in a series of small-time robberies. But Jerry soon convinces Howard, sardonically asking him: "Anybody else make you any better offer lately? You guys kill me—they kick you in the teeth and the more they kick you, the better you like it." Lying to his wife about securing a lucrative night job, Howard earns substantial cash from gas station and grocery store hold-ups, and he reluctantly participates in Jerry's scheme to kidnap a wealthy local man, Donald Miller (Carl Kent). But when Jerry kills the man unnecessarily, Howard is horrified and begins to unravel emotionally.

After drinking heavily during a double date with Jerry's girlfriend Velma (Jergens) and her friend Hazel (Katherine Locke), Howard becomes unglued when Hazel finds a gold tie clip belonging to Donald Miller. He hysterically admits his role in the crime, and Hazel later reports him to police, leading to Howard and Jerry's arrest. Meanwhile, public emotions are ignited by a series of inflammatory newspaper articles penned by Gil Stanton (Richard Carlson), and a mob of angry local citizens gather around the courthouse where Howard and Jerry are jailed. Despite police efforts to restrain them, the mob breaks into the courthouse and Howard and Jerry are brutally beaten to death. Later, Stanton comes to regret his role in the incident, concurring with his psychologist friend who warned, "Violence is a disease caused by moral and social breakdown. And it must be solved by reason, not by emotion — with understanding, not by hate."

As Velma, Jergens presented a memorable portrait of a money-loving dame who craved life's finer things and didn't care how she got them. In her first scene, she airily informs Hazel that she soon plans to quit her tiresome hairdresser job: "Jerry's got some kind of deal on," she says. "He won't tell me about it, but from the way he acts, I know it's big. He keeps sending plenty — giving me this, and giving me that. He's nature's gift to women and that's no foolin'.'" Jergens caught the notice of several critics who praised her brief, showy performance, and the film itself was a box office hit.

By now, Jergens' film choices were significantly improving, and she was seen in a variety of pictures, including *Sugarfoot* (1951), a talky Western that was redeemed by the performances of Jergens and costar Randolph Scott; *Showboat* (1951), MGM's lavish version of the Edna Ferber novel; *Abbott and Costello Meet the Invisible Man* (1951), an amiable comedy that scored big at the box office; and *Somebody Loves Me* (1952), an entertaining musical biopic about the life of famed vaudevillian Blossom Seeley. But the attractive blonde took a misstep with *Aaron Slick from Punkin Crick* (1952), a highly touted musical that was a dull, uninspired disappointment. During this period, Jergens also became a fixture on the new medium of television, serving as a regular on Mike Stokey's weekly game show *Pantomime Quiz*.

Off-screen in 1953 following the birth of her son, Jergens returned the following year for *The Miami Story* (1954), a fast-paced, tightly scripted crime melodrama starring Barry Sullivan; *The Big Chase* (1954), Jergens' second film appearance with husband Glenn Langan; *Overland Pacific* (1954), a slightly above-average Western with Jack (later Jock) Mahoney and William Bishop; and *Fireman Save My Child* (1954), a slapstick comedy starring Hugh O'Brian and Buddy Hackett (who replaced Abbott and Costello when the latter fell ill). Although Jergens continued to receive film offers, she had discovered that her home life was more enticing than the further pursuit of her career; over the next three years, she would appear in only eight more pictures. While the pictures were widely varied in quality, the most disappointing was MGM's *The Cobweb* (1955), a dull drama that flopped at the box office despite direction from Vincente Minnelli and a top-notch cast that included Lauren Bacall, Richard Widmark, Charles Boyer, Gloria Grahame and Lillian Gish.

Toward the end of her film career, Jergens accepted a role in *Day the World Ended* (1956), a low-budget affair focusing on the survivors of a nuclear holocaust; Jergens was memorable in her role of a one-time stripper. After next appearing in *Runaway Daughters* (1956), a torrid drama about three teenagers who flee their homes and head for Hollywood, Jergens retired from the screen.

In the 1970s, after a number of appearances in television commercials, Jergens announced her plans for a comeback: "Now that I've spent so many years in retirement, I have the urge to get back into the acting profession." Sadly, the actress' intent to resume her career never materialized. Still, although her career spanned less than 15 years, the famed "Champagne Blonde" demonstrated her talent and versatility in a wide range of roles, firmly establishing herself as a "bad girl" supreme, and ensuring that hers is a name that should always be remembered.

Film Noir Filmography

THE DARK PAST   *Director:* Rudolph Maté. *Producer:* Buddy Adler. Released by Columbia, December 1948. *Running time:* 74 minutes. *Cast:* William Holden, Nina Foch, Adele Jergens, Stephen Dunne, Lois Maxwell, Berry Kroeger, Steven Geray, Wilton Graff, Robert Osterloh.

SIDE STREET   *Director:* Anthony Mann. *Producer:* Sam Zimbalist. Released by MGM, March 1950. *Running time:* 83 minutes. *Cast:* Farley Granger, Cathy O'Donnell, James Craig, Paul Kelly, Edmon Ryan, Paul Harvey, Jean Hagen, Charles McGraw, Ed Max, Adele Jergens, Harry Bellaver, Whit Bissell.

ARMORED CAR ROBBERY   *Director:* Richard Fleischer. *Producer:* Herman Schlom. Released by RKO, June 1950. *Running time:* 67 minutes. *Cast:* Charles McGraw, Adele Jergens, William Talman, Douglas Fowley, Steve Brodie, Don McGuire.

TRY AND GET ME   *Director:* Cyril Endfield. *Producer:* Seton I. Miller. Released by United Artists, December 1950. *Running time:* 90 minutes. *Cast:* Frank Lovejoy, Kathleen Ryan, Richard Carlson, Lloyd Bridges, Katherine Locke, Adele Jergens, Art Smith.

References

Biography of Adele Jergens. Paramount Studios, May 1951.
Creelman, Eileen. "Adele Jergens, the Princess of *1001 Nights*, Talks of Making *She Wouldn't Say Yes.*" *The New York Sun*, January 5, 1946.
Hall, Prunella. "Screen Gossip." *Boston Post*, circa 1951.
Hoaglin, Jess. "Where Are They Today: Adele Jergens." *The Hollywood Reporter*, July 20, 1971.
_____. "Where Are They Today: Adele Jergens." *The Hollywood Reporter*, October 22, 1976.
Lieber, Perry. Biography of Adele Jergens. RKO Studios, circa 1950.

LoBello, Nino. "Community Calvalcade." *Ridgewood Times*, circa 1948.

Marshall, Jim. "SRO on a Coral Isle." *Collier's*, November 24, 1945.

McCarthy, Julia. "Adele Jergens, Film Beauty, Now Plays the Field in Love." *New York Daily News*, January 6, 1946.

Mortimer, Lee. "Adele's Success Recipe: Don't Work!" *Sunday Mirror Magazine*, circa 1945.

Peck, Ira. "Meet Miss Adele Jergens." *PM*, September 29, 1946.

Evelyn Keyes

With flashing blue eyes and appealing features, a significant dancing talent, and a flair for both comedy and drama, Evelyn Keyes was almost a shoe-in for fame and fortune. But despite the heights of stardom she reached during her career, the ladylike beauty often gained as much notoriety for her marriages to Hollywood luminaries as for her performing abilities. Still, Keyes, perhaps best remembered for her role as Scarlett O'Hara's sister Suellen in *Gone with the Wind* (1939), made a decisive mark in the realm of film noir, starring in four pictures from the era: *Johnny O'Clock* (1947), *The Killer that Stalked New York* (1950), *The Prowler* (1951) and *99 River Street* (1953).

Evelyn Louise Keyes was born on November 20, 1919, in Port Arthur, Texas, but after the death of her oilman father, Keyes moved with her mother, brother and three sisters to Atlanta, Georgia. The actress later recalled that she grew up watching her mother make ends meet by baking pies, selling corsets and raising canaries for a pet shop. Her vivid imagination offered her an escape from her dreary surroundings, and by the age of 13, Keyes had decided that she would seek a career as an actress. During her high school years, Keyes took dance classes three times a week and performed on the weekends for local organizations including the Masons and the American Legion.

Although legend has it that Keyes' trek to Hollywood was initiated when she won a beauty contest sponsored by Universal Studios, she states in her autobiography that she financed her own fare to California by scrupulously saving her salary from the dancing gigs she'd accepted during her high school years. Once in Los Angeles, Keyes moved into the Hollywood Studio Club, a boardinghouse for young film hopefuls, but her ambitious rounds to the various studios — including screen tests for RKO and Universal — proved fruitless. It wasn't until she met Jeanie MacPherson, a one-time silent screen actress and screen writer for famed director Cecil B. DeMille, that Keyes would get the break that she'd been seeking. MacPherson introduced the aspiring actress to DeMille who, after instructing her to lose her Southern accent, signed her to a seven-year contract beginning at $50 a week. It seemed that Keyes was on her way.

After participating in acting classes and taking voice lessons to eliminate her drawl, Keyes was cast in DeMille's epic *The Buccaneer* (1938), starring Fredric March. Although her screen debut amounted to a total of only three lines, Keyes recalled that she was completely disconcerted by the "bright lights, the hubbub of voices, the boom through the microphone." Still, she managed to complete her scene and went on to appear in minor roles in four more films in 1938: *Men with Wings, Sons of the Legion, Dangerous to Know* and *Artists and Models Abroad*.

In late 1938, Keyes was interviewed for the role of Scarlett O'Hara in David O. Selznick's sweeping tale of the old South, *Gone with the Wind*, but she admitted that she was a "nervous wreck," and was promptly dismissed. But a short time later, Keyes was informed that she was being considered for the role of Scarlett's sister Suellen, and by January 1939, the part was hers. As the spoiled younger sister of the main character, Keyes made a minor impact in the film, but she was frustrated to find that many of her scenes were missing from the final release. "I thought I was getting a wonderful break when Mr. Selznick agreed to let me play the role of Suellen in the year's biggest picture," Keyes said. "But Suellen, in spite of her importance in the novel, meant little in the finished movie."

Despite this disappointment, Keyes had more than just her budding film career to occupy her time — a roommate at the Hollywood Studio Club had introduced her to Barton Leon Bambridge, a handsome architect and owner of a swimming pool corporation, ten years Keyes' senior. In 1938, after a whirlwind romance, Keyes and Bambridge were married by a justice of the peace in Yuma, Arizona, but the union was rocky from the start. Bambridge's flagging business enterprises added little to the family coffers, and his penchant for heavy drinking led to frequent battles in the couple's North Hollywood home. After one argument, during which Bambridge threatened his wife with a gun, Keyes moved back to the Hollywood Studio Club. Two years later, shortly after his separation from Keyes was formalized, Bambridge committed suicide.

Careerwise, Keyes' option was dropped by Cecil B. DeMille, and she signed a seven-year contract with Columbia Studios, starting at $150 a week. Her first job with her new studio was a small role in *Lady in Question* (1940), a charming comedy that was a vehicle for Columbia's budding star, Rita Hayworth. The picture was helmed by Charles Vidor, a Hungarian director described by Keyes as "physically attractive and with a most bewitching foreign accent, hinting of drama, intrigue and Orient Express." Before long, although Keyes was still married at the time to Barton Bambridge, and Vidor was legally bound to actress Karen Morley, the two began an affair.

At Columbia, Keyes was kept busy in such films as *Before I Hang* (1940), a mildly interesting bit of science fiction starring Boris Karloff; *Beyond the Sacramento* (1940), a routine Western yarn; and *The Face Behind the Mask* (1941), a downbeat box office flop in which Keyes portrayed a blind girl who falls for a horribly scarred Hungarian. But Keyes' best role to date came in a well-mounted fantasy starring Robert Montgomery and Claude Rains, *Here Comes Mr. Jordan* (1941). For her performance in the film, Keyes received excellent notices, and she followed this triumph with a small but well-acted role of a maid in *Ladies in Retirement* (1941), starring Ida Lupino and directed by Charles Vidor. But because Rita Hayworth had now become Columbia's top star, Keyes found herself assigned to a series of minor films that failed to showcase her talents, including *Flight Lieutenant* (1942), in which, Keyes said, she "stood about to wave hello and goodbye" to the male stars of the film.

Keyes' string of mostly forgettable "B" movies continued over the next two years with roles in *Dangerous Blondes* (1943), a low-key thriller; *The Desperadoes* (1943), a formulaic Western starring Randolph Scott and Glenn Ford;

There's Something About a Soldier (1944), a docudrama about five cadets at an officer's training school; *Nine Girls* (1944), a fairly entertaining whodunit with Ann Harding and Nina Foch; and *The Strange Affair* (1944), in which Keyes portrayed the wife of an amateur detective.

With her career still languishing in the shadow of Rita Hayworth's stardom, Keyes' personal life once again took center stage. After Charles Vidor obtained a divorce from his wife, he and Keyes were married in February 1944. But it didn't take long for Keyes' second union to collapse. After discovering her husband's affair with a budding starlet, and herself engaging in a brief fling, Keyes filed for divorce after only a year.

Soon after her split from Vidor, Keyes starred in *A Thousand and One Nights* (1945), playing what she described as a "modern, wisecracking genie" opposite Cornel Wilde and Phil Silvers. This amusing Arabian Nights spoof was followed by *The Thrill of Brazil* (1946), a pleasant romantic comedy starring Keenan Wynn; *Renegades* (1946), a standard Western that was notable primarily for its filming in Technicolor; and *The Jolson Story* (1946), a box office smash in which Keyes was cast in one of the best roles of her career. In this highly fictionalized biography, Keyes portrayed the first wife of crooner Al Jolson, offering a performance that earned her the Gold Medal Award from *Photoplay* magazine.

By now, Keyes' career was once again overshadowed by her personal life. After dating such notables as Sterling Hayden, Robert Stack and Peter Lawford, Keyes met John Huston, son of veteran actor Walter Huston and director of the classic *The Maltese Falcon* (1941). Keyes would later recall that while she found Huston to be "not beautiful at all, if anything, almost ugly," she was instantly attracted to the charismatic director. Less than a month after their meeting, Keyes impulsively proposed to Huston, and in July 1946 the two were married in Las Vegas. But like her previous marriages, Keyes' third union was bound for failure. The hard-drinking Huston engaged in several highly publicized affairs, and the often-rocky marriage improved little when the couple adopted a 12-year-old Indian orphan whom they had met on the set of Huston's film *The Treasure of the Sierra Madre* (1948).

Keyes' relationship with her third husband improved briefly in fall 1947, when she and Huston joined a protest against the House Un-American Activities Committee's (HUAC) investigations of Communism in Hollywood. Keyes and Huston, along with a variety of screen stars including Humphrey Bogart, Lauren Bacall and John Garfield, chartered a plane to Washington to lodge their complaints against the Committee's notorious attacks against many of Hollywood's most well-known writers, directors and actors. But Keyes found that their group was made to look "like stupid children interfering with grown-up problems," and the investigation finished the careers of numerous artists, including Larry Parks, who had shot to superstardom after his performance opposite Keyes in *The Jolson Story*.

But their unified front against the HUAC investigations would not be enough to salvage the marriage of Keyes and Huston. The fiery director had added the vice of gambling to his habit for heavy drinking; Keyes also vehemently objected to the menagerie of animals that Huston maintained on their San Fernando Valley ranch, which included wild horses, monkeys, goats and a burro named Socrates. And the final straw came when Huston became openly involved with Enrica Soma, an 18-year-old ballet dancer. After four years, Keyes told the press: "John is the best director and the worst husband." On February 10, 1950, Huston obtained a Mexican divorce; the following day he married Enrica Soma, who would give birth in 1951 to Huston's daughter, future star Anjelica Huston.

Back on screen, Keyes starred in 1947 in her first film noir, *Johnny O'Clock*, starring Dick Powell in the title role. Johnny is a ruthless small-time gangster who runs a gambling casino with his partner Pete Marchettis (Thomas Gomez). Despite Johnny's hard exterior, however, he has a soft side, as evidenced by his fondness for Harriet Hobbs (Nina Foch), the young casino hatcheck girl who is hopelessly in love with one of Johnny's associates, Chuck Blayden (Jim Bannon). A crooked policeman who acts as an enforcer for the casino, Blayden cruelly mistreats Harriet, and reveals his duplicitous nature when he tries to replace Johnny as Marchettis' partner. Later, Blayden's lifeless body is found floating in the river and Harriet is found dead in her apartment, an apparent suicide.

Harriet's showgirl sister Nancy (Keyes) arrives in town when she hears of the incident, and blames herself for abandoning her vulnerable sibling for the sake of her career. Nancy and Johnny soon experience a mutual attraction, but there is another woman on the horizon — Johnny is also being vigorously pursued by Marchettis' wife, Nelle (Ellen Drew). When police discover that Harriet had been murdered, Johnny is suspected of the crime, but he learns that the culprit was Marchettis, who was also responsible for the death of Blayden. Suspecting Johnny of having an affair with Nelle, Marchettis makes an unsuccessful attempt on his life, and Johnny plans to leave town with Nancy. He first stops at the casino to collect his money, but Marchettis confronts him with a gun and after a shoot-out, Marchettis is killed. Witnessing the crime, Nelle sees her opportunity to finally be with Johnny, but when he rejects her, she lies to police, saying that Johnny shot her husband in cold blood while trying to rob the casino. Johnny is cornered in the casino by a police detective and plans to shoot his way out, but he changes his mind after an impassioned plea by Nancy. "I haven't had enough tears — I want more," she says. "I want to be able to say, 'Do you know who I'm crying for? Johnny O'Clock. You know who he was. The smartest man in the world. I know because he told me so. Johnny O'Clock's no fool, he said.' That's why he's dead. Because he's no fool!"

After earning praise for her "charming" and "appealing" performance in

Johnny O'Clock, Keyes appeared in a series of films of varying quality, including *The Mating of Millie* (1948), an agreeable, if routine, comedy with Glenn Ford; *Enchantment* (1948), a sweeping romance with David Niven and Teresa Wright that flopped at the box office; and a rousing adventure tale, *Mrs. Mike* (1949), which featured Keyes as the wife of a Canadian mountie. Keyes was acclaimed for her portrayal in the latter film, with a typical review appearing in *Variety*: "The performances are splendid. Evelyn Keyes particularly shines in the title role with a portrayal that has excellent emotional depth and just the right touch of humor."

Keyes began 1950 with a starring role in her second film noir, *The Killer That Stalked New York*, her last picture under her Columbia contract. Set in New York City, this fascinating film begins with its narrator announcing: "Death didn't sneak into town riding the rods or huddled in a boxcar. It came in on a streamliner, first class, extra fare, right into the Pennsylvania station, big as life." Arriving in New York is Sheila Bennet (Keyes), having just returned from Cuba, where she stole $50,000 in jewels and mailed them, as directed, to her husband Matt (Charles Korvin). Unbeknownst to Sheila, however, she has also brought back with her the deadly smallpox virus. After feeling ill, Sheila is given a tonic by a local physician, Dr. Ben Wood (William Bishop), but while at Wood's clinic, she encounters a little girl and passes the disease to her.

Sheila later reunites with her husband, not knowing that he has been carrying on an affair with her younger sister Francie (Lola Albright). When the coveted diamonds arrive, Matt retrieves them and skips out on his wife, planning to sell them and leave town. But he is informed by local jeweler Moss (Art Smith) that Sheila is being sought by a Treasury Agent and that Matt must wait ten days before the jewels can be sold. When Sheila learns of Matt's affair, she confronts her sister and, in despair, Francie commits suicide. Fueled by the need to avenge her sister's death, Sheila goes in search of her husband. By now, several smallpox cases have been diagnosed, including the little girl from the clinic, the train station porter who carried Sheila's bags and the milkman from Matt's apartment. A citywide vaccination effort is announced, while health department officials frantically search for the original carrier of the disease. Later learning that the Treasury Department is searching for the same woman, officials nearly catch up to Sheila at a flophouse owned by her brother, but she escapes shortly before they arrive. Now gravely ill, Sheila finally catches up to Matt and plans to kill him, but he tries to escape through a window and falls to his death. Moments later, health officials arrive and Sheila is taken in. It is too late for her, however, and she soon dies, but the smallpox epidemic is safely under control.

For her performance in the film, Keyes earned mixed reviews, with Bosley Crowther saying in the *New York Times* that she "manifests great discomfort and distress, but she is no more than a melodramatic cipher in a loosely organized

Evelyn Keyes

chase." But years later, her costar Charles Korvin would call her "maybe the actress I loved to work with most in films. She was considerate and always gave the best in order to get the best from her *vis-à-vis*."

After the release of *The Killer That Stalked New York*, Keyes broke her contract with the studio where she had worked for more than a decade, and quickly accepted roles in two films for Universal Studios, both starring Jeff Chandler — *Smuggler's Island* (1951), a routine melodrama that Keyes called "a junk movie," and the boxing tale, *Iron Man* (1951), which was highlighted by the impressive appearance of newcomer Rock Hudson. Keyes followed these features with a standout performance in her third film noir, *The Prowler* (1951), which she later called "the best picture I ever made." Here Keyes portrayed Susan Gilvray, a housewife who is disturbed by prowlers near her home. She notifies police and one of the officers who investigates her complaint, Webb Garwood (Van Heflin), is instantly attracted to Susan. Although Susan is married to a local late-night radio personality, she and Webb are soon embroiled in a passionate affair.

Susan ends the relationship when her husband John grows suspicious, but a short time later, Webb responds to another call about a prowler at Susan's house. When her husband emerges with a gun, Webb kills him, then shoots himself in the arm with John's gun. Although Susan suspects Webb of deliberately murdering her husband, she refuses to reveal their affair during an inquest and the killing is ruled justifiable. Afterward, Webb convinces Susan that he is innocent and two get married, using Susan's money to purchase a motel in Las Vegas. On their wedding night, Susan reveals that she is four months pregnant, but Webb fears that the baby will be used as evidence of their affair. The couple decides to move to a ghost town in the Nevada desert for the child's birth, but complications arise during the birth, and Webb goes to a nearby doctor for help. After the birth of the baby, Susan learns that the doctor has recognized them and realizes that Webb plans to kill him. She also discovers that Webb's shooting of her husband was no accident. Susan warns the doctor, who leaves with the baby, and when Webb tries to follow him, he is stopped by police, who fatally shoot him as he tries to run.

For her portrayal of Susan Gilray, Keyes was hailed in the *New York Times* for her "unvarnished characterization" and by the critic for *Variety*, who wrote, "She turns in an excellent performance, somewhat overshadowing Heflin." (Given Keyes' earlier protest against the Hollywood Communism investigations, it is ironic that the screenplay for *The Prowler* was penned by Dalton Trumbo, who had been blacklisted and jailed after his appearance before the House Un-American Activities Committee. In order for the film to be released, producer Sam Spiegel was forced to credit another writer for the screenplay.)

Keyes next appeared in a tedious comedy, *One Big Affair* (1952), in which she portrayed a daffy American schoolteacher vacationing in Mexico, and *Shoot First* (1953), a murkily plotted espionage tale. Then, in her last picture of 1953, she starred opposite John Payne in her final film noir, *99 River Street*.

This drama focuses on Ernie Driscoll (Payne), a taxi cab driver whose promising shot at a boxing championship was cut short because of a severe eye injury. Ernie's unhappiness over his thwarted career is compounded by his shrewish wife Pauline (Peggie Castle), who works in a flower shop to make ends meet. Dissatisfied with her husband's lowly status, Pauline is embroiled in an affair with a ruthless hood, Victor Rawlins (Brad Dexter), and after Rawlins steals $50,000 in diamonds, the two plan to flee the country. But Rawlins is unable to sell the jewels as planned to his fence Christopher (Jay Adler), who strenuously objects to Pauline's involvement. Deciding to rid himself of Pauline, Victor strangles her and dumps her body in the back of Ernie's taxi cab, then forces Christopher to give him $50,000 for the diamonds.

Meanwhile, Ernie discovers Pauline's body and sets out to find her killer with the assistance of a friend, Linda James (Keyes). At the same time, Christopher and two of his henchmen also go in search of Victor, who is later found at a bar in New Jersey, located at 99 River Street. When Victor emerges, the gangsters follow in their car, but after a shoot-out, the car crashes. Ernie continues the chase and is wounded by Victor, but he manages to capture him and subdue him until police arrive.

Although *99 River Street* stands up today as a taut thriller, it was not well-received upon its release, and was slammed by the reviewer for the *New York Times*, who wrote: "To say that this film is offensive would be kind; to point out that it induces an irritated boredom would be accurate." The *Times* critic dismissed Keyes' performance as well, saying that she acts "as though she were animated by electric shocks."

Off-screen, Keyes had remained relatively unattached following her third divorce, engaging only in brief relationships with actor Kirk Douglas and an Argentinian diplomat. But during preparation for *99 River Street*, Keyes became involved in an intense, lengthy affair with producer Mike Todd. Keyes later recalled that her first impression of the larger-than-life Todd was far from favorable: "I didn't like the way he looked at all," she stated in her autobiography. "He had on yesterday's pin-striped gangster suit. Shoes with perforated toes. And ... long, slicked-down, patent-leather style hair that even George Raft had stopped affecting years before. And a perfectly monstrous cigar in his mouth." But Keyes was soon won over by Todd's arduous courtship: "What Mike Todd wanted, Mike Todd usually got," she said.

Before long, Keyes was fielding inquiries from the press about the couple's possible marriage, but she was reluctant to wed for a fourth time, telling gossip columnist Sheilah Graham, "I'm not marrying Mike or anybody else just now. Don't you think I've done enough of that sort of thing to last me awhile?" Still, Keyes and Todd were a highly visible couple over the next three years, frequently appearing at Hollywood's hottest nightspots, and traveling to Italy, London, Cuba, Spain, and Russia. Although the relationship was often stormy, Todd proposed marriage in 1956, promising the actress a 15-carat diamond engagement ring. Keyes accepted, but the marriage would never be. During the 1956 filming of Todd's star-studded *Around the World in 80 Days* (in which Keyes played a cameo role), the producer fell in love with Elizabeth Taylor and two months later, by telephone, informed Keyes that their

relationship was over. While Keyes later admitted that she had "been delivered a knockout punch," she philosophically concluded: "You play around with
the big time, the rewards are high. So you have to be prepared to take your
lumps." (Todd and Elizabeth Taylor married on February 2, 1957, following
her divorce from Michael Wilding, but the marriage would be short-lived.
Todd was killed in the crash of his private airplane in March 1958, several
months after Taylor gave birth to their daughter, Liza.)

During her lengthy affair with Todd, Keyes had appeared in four pictures, including *Top of the World* (1955), which Keyes described as "some foolish thing," and *The Seven Year Itch* (1955) with Tom Ewell and Marilyn Monroe. Keyes' brief role in *Around the World in 80 Days* was her last screen
appearance for many years; she later said that her film career "just fizzled away,
as things are apt to do if you don't give them sufficient tender, loving care."

With her acting career behind her, Keyes still managed to stay in the public eye. Soon after her breakup with Todd, she met bandleader Artie Shaw,
whose seven previous wives included Lana Turner, Ava Gardner and Kathleen Winsor, the author of *Forever Amber*. Keyes was impressed by Shaw's
musical talent and his obvious intellect, and the two were soon an item: "When
your prince comes along, you know it," the actress said. The couple were married in 1957 and moved to Shaw's house in Spain, but Keyes soon grew disillusioned with her husband's quick temper and fastidious nature. Later, against
Keyes' wishes, the couple returned to the United States, purchasing a large
house in Lakeville, Connecticut. But the marriage continued to deteriorate,
helped along when Shaw began an affair with an attractive young dancer.
"This sort of put a crimp into the happy-ever-after business for Artie and
Evelyn," the actress said wryly.

Entering a separation from Shaw that would last for several years, Keyes
returned to performing, appearing in the late 1960s in a London play for television, *A Matter of Diamonds*, and a movie for ABC-TV, *The Ugliest Girl in
Town*. She also turned her talents to writing, and in 1971 penned her first
novel, *I Am a Billboard*. The following year Keyes began touring in a revival
of *No, No, Nanette*, joining a cast that included Don Ameche and Ruth Donnelly. Although critics seemed to make a point of noting her age, with one
referring to her as "the non-youngster," Keyes received favorable reviews and
found the year-long experience to be "fun, plain fun."

After the *No, No, Nanette* tour, Keyes began working on her autobiography, making visits to countless old friends and coworkers to stimulate her recollections. Published in 1977, *Scarlett O'Hara's Younger Sister* was an instant
best-seller, enthralling readers with Keyes' candid accounts of her acting career
and her many romantic exploits. While working on her third book, a historical novel, Keyes resumed her acting career, appearing with Betty Garrett and
Jan Sterling in a play produced by Ross Hunter, and guest-starring on various television programs, including *The Love Boat* and *Murder, She Wrote*. Of

her appearance on the latter program in the late 1980s, Keyes said, "I did a couple of shows because they paid me, and it was delightful. It's a terribly professional experience. Everyone comes in to work, there are no jokes on the set. There's no strain, everyone cares, from the drivers up to the top people."

During this period, Keyes was also seen in a film documentary about her fourth husband, *Artie Shaw: Time Is All You've Got* (which won an Academy Award for Best Documentary), returned to the big screen in two horror films, *A Return to Salem's Lot* (1988) and *Wicked Stepmother* (1989), and authored a regular column in the entertainment section of the *Los Angeles Times*, "Keyes to the Town." Then, in 1991, Keyes published her second autobiography, *I'll Think About That Tomorrow*.

Keyes has been away from acting since the late 1980s, but she leaves behind an impressive career of close to 50 films over a span of more than five decades. Although her life behind the scenes was often more fascinating than the characters she portrayed, the actress demonstrated an adeptness for both comedy and drama, and remains one of Hollywood's most entertaining and versatile performers.

Film Noir Filmography

JOHNNY O'CLOCK   *Director:* Robert Rossen. *Producer:* Edward G. Nealis. Released by Columbia, March 1947. *Running time:* 95 minutes. *Cast:* Dick Powell, Evelyn Keyes, Lee J. Cobb, Ellen Drew, Nina Foch, Thomas Gomez, John Kellogg, Jim Bannon.

THE KILLER THAT STALKED NEW YORK   *Director:* Earl McEvoy. *Producer:* Robert Cohn. Released by Columbia, January 1951. *Running time:* 79 minutes. *Cast:* Evelyn Keyes, Charles Korvin, William Bishop, Dorothy Malone, Lola Albright, Barry Kelley, Carl Benton Reid.

THE PROWLER   *Director:* Joseph Losey. *Producer:* Sam Spiegel. Released by United Artists, July 1951. *Running time:* 92 minutes. *Cast:* Van Heflin, Evelyn Keyes, John Maxwell, Katharine Warren, Emerson Treacy, Madge Blake.

99 RIVER STREET   *Director:* Phil Karlson. *Producer:* Edward Small. Released by United Artists, October 1953. *Running time:* 83 minutes. *Cast:* John Payne, Evelyn Keyes, Brad Dexter, Frank Faylen, Peggie Castle, Jay Adler, Jack Lambert.

References

Baskette, Kirtley. "Pixie from Dixie." *Modern Screen*, July 1947.
"Catching Up with Evelyn Keyes." *Modern Screen*, April 1972.
Creelman, Eileen. "Good Scripts Rare, Evelyn Keyes Finds." New *York World Telegram and Sun*, October 30, 1950.
Howe, Herb. "Beauty in Bedlam." *Photoplay*, July 1948.
Keyes, Evelyn. *I'll Think About That Tomorrow*. New York: Dutton, 1991.
_____. *Scarlett O'Hara's Younger Sister*. Secaucus, NJ: Lyle Stuart, 1977.

"Keyes Back from 'Tax Cure.'" *New York Morning Telegraph*, March 23, 1953.

McCarthy, Julia. "Horse Here to Stay, Miss Keyes Feels." *New York Daily News*, June 19, 1942.

McClelland, Doug. "Thinking About Evelyn Keyes." *Hollywood Then and Now*, September 1991.

McPherson, Virginia. "Deaf Ear to Praise, Says Star." *New York Morning Telegraph*, May 11, 1950.

Skolsky, Sidney. "My Romance with Evelyn Keyes." *Photoplay*, July 1947.

_____. "Rising Star." *New York Post*, October 4, 1947.

"True Confessions of Evelyn Keyes." *New York Post*, August 6, 1977.

"Trying Her Luck for 13 G's." *New York Mirror*, October 30, 1960.

"What's My Type?" *American Magazine*, November 1947.

Wilson, Earl. "Men on Her Mind." *New York Post*, November 12, 1950.

Veronica Lake

The life of Veronica Lake was the stuff of which cinematic tragedies were made. Forever to be remembered more for her golden tresses than her acting talent, Lake was one of the most popular stars of her era, but hers was a cinematic flame that ignited swiftly, burned brightly, and flickered out to darkness. Once described as possessing a "figure like a dream, looks to kill, a flair for clothes, and sophistication like champagne," Lake ultimately became known as a hard-drinking troublemaker who befriended few and alienated many. But in front of the camera, her emotionless veneer made her an ideal on-screen partner for the equally deadpan Alan Ladd, and the two were teamed in three film noir classics: *This Gun for Hire* (1942), *The Glass Key* (1942) and *The Blue Dahlia* (1946).

Constance Frances Marie Ockleman was born on November 14, 1922, in Brooklyn, New York, where, the actress recalled, she was the "toughest broad on the block." While she claimed in later years that she never possessed a penchant for acting, she was seen at the age of eight in a grade school production of *Poor Little Rich Girl*— a title that would turn out to be somewhat prophetic, given the course of Lake's life. Her father, a seaman of German-Danish extraction, was killed on a ship in 1932 when Constance was 12, and within a year, her mother married a staff artist for the *New York Herald Tribune*, Anthony Keane, whose last name Constance adopted.

Frequently moving because of Anthony Keane's lung problem, the family spent time in Canada, New York and Florida, where Constance completed her education at Miami High School. On a whim, she entered the Miss Miami beauty contest, winning third place. One of the judges was Broadway celebrity Harry Richman (noted, among other escapades, for his "engagement" to Clara Bow), who suggested that Constance shoot for a career in Hollywood. Constance also entered the Miss Florida contest and won, only to have the title taken from her when judges learned that she was underage.

In 1938, at the age of 16, Constance moved to Hollywood with her mother, stepfather and cousin, Helen Nelson. Once there, mostly due to urging from her ambitious mother, she enrolled in the Bliss Hayden School of Acting on Wilshire Boulevard. Among other activities, Constance practiced diction and walking with books balanced on her head, but later acknowledged that she began her lessons "convinced I would not become a movie star."

Constance got her first taste of filmdom in 1939 when she accompanied a school friend, Gwen Horn, to the RKO Studios, where Gwen hoped to land a bit part in an Anne Shirley vehicle, *Sorority House* (1939). Both girls were given roles as extras, with Lake billed as Constance Keane. She was soon given other bit parts in *All Women Have Secrets* (1939), *The Wrong Room* (1939), a three-reeler with Leon Errol, and *Forty Little Mothers* (1940), an MGM film starring Eddie Cantor. Of her appearances in these films, the actress admitted, "I was so lousy that you could put all the talent I had into your left eye and still not suffer from impaired vision. I was that bad."

In *Forty Little Mothers*, directed by famed musical director Busby Berkeley, Constance was given the role as a schoolgirl who delights in playing pranks and prouncing about as a tomboy. Her fine blond hair constantly fell over one eye, and Berkeley took note of it, decreeing — over Eddie Cantor's objections — that it remain that way. However, no one really noticed Constance, or her soon-to-be-trademark hairstyle.

After *Forty Little Mothers*, Constance made it a point to be seen around town — an effort that paid off when she was spotted by MGM junior executive Freddie Wilcox, who suggested that she make a screen test. But Constance's nervousness turned the test into a disaster ("I was terrible," she recalled). Instead, her presence on the MGM lot had another impact — she attracted the attention of John Detlie, a Metro art director who was 16 years her senior. The two began dating in early 1940, and before the year was out, they would become husband and wife.

Career-wise, things were finally looking up for Constance. She signed with the William Morris Agency, and when Paramount producer Arthur Hornblow, Jr., was preparing his film *I Wanted Wings* (1941), Morris convinced him to test Constance for the role of Sally Vaughn, a nightclub singer. Of her test, Lake later recalled, "My hair kept falling over one eye and I kept brushing it back. I thought I had ruined my chances for the role.... But Hornblow was jubilant about that eye-hiding trick. An experienced showman, he knew that the hairstyle was something people would talk about."

Before the release of *I Wanted Wings*, Constance was renamed Veronica Lake, a fitting moniker for the cool, unflappable image that the mention of her name would ultimately summon. Her new identity was reportedly due to Hornblow, who borrowed the name "Veronica" from his secretary Veronica Grusling, and added the surname because "her eyes are calm and blue like a lake." After the release of *I Wanted Wings*, the entire nation knew of the tiny blonde with the sultry voice and the peek-a-boo hairdo. In fact, her hairstyle so sparked the interest of moviegoers that entire magazine articles were devoted to it. Even *Life* magazine got into the act, utilizing a three-page spread to inform readers of the 150,000 hairs on Lake's head, and the Nulava shampoo-Maro oil-vinegar combination that she used to wash and rinse her locks. Paramount's publicity department fueled the fire by constantly promoting Lake's hairdo and inventing a variety of catchy names for it, including the "Detour Coiffure" and the "Peeping Pompadour."

It was during the making of *I Wanted Wings* that Lake launched the bad-girl off-screen image that was to plague her throughout her career. It was reported that she had "personality clashes" with costar Constance Moore, who said of Lake years later, "This was a girl who was handed stardom on a silver platter ... and in a short time she had blown it all. Her lack of professionalism was evident even during *I Wanted Wings*, her big break. She held up production several times. She'd simply disappear, run off here and there. Veronica

Lake was her own worst enemy. She would goof up on personal appearance tours, make enemies. And worst of all, her drinking."

But Lake's slide into film oblivion was more than a decade away, and in the early 1940s, her star continued to shine. Her next role, in the 1941 Olivia de Havilland vehicle *Hold Back the Dawn*, was unbilled and lasted only a few seconds, but opposite Joel McCrea in *Sullivan's Travels* (1941), she soared to superstardom. In this brilliant comedy-drama directed by Preston Sturges, Lake was hailed by critics as giving a first-rate performance. And, apparently, Lake's personal life was sailing along as well, as she gave birth to her first child, Elaine, shortly after filming completed.

The following year saw Lake's first film noir appearance and her initial screen teaming with Alan Ladd. In *This Gun for Hire* (1942), an early film noir entry, Lake portrayed Ellen Graham, a cabaret performer whose life becomes intertwined with a psychologically disturbed assassin by the name of Raven (Ladd). Graham becomes an agent for federal authorities in their hunt for a Nazi spy, and meets Raven on a train to Los Angeles, where Raven plans to murder the people who double-crossed him. Ellen is first used by Raven as a tool to escape police, but later sympathizes with the sweet-faced killer. Ultimately, Raven is shot and killed by police, but not before he exacts his revenge on his betrayers.

The noir plot was typically complex, and even a little far-fetched, but it was a hit with audiences who seemed fascinated by Lake's enigmatic smile and half-lidded glances. And with good reason. Early in the film, when Ellen Graham warbles "Now You See It, Now You Don't," an onlooker offers a line that might apply to Lake as well as her character, saying that she is "audience-proof ... gets 'em bug-eyed." However, most reviewers failed to note that Lake possessed any real acting talent. Edwin Schallert in the *Los Angeles Times* remarked that the actress "remains definitely a personality, and as always evidences interesting repression," and the reviewer for *Life* wrote that Lake "certainly adds to her reputation, if not as an actress, certainly as a personality." (It is interesting to note that Lake recalled in her autobiography that her character cradled Raven as he died, and even the critic from *Variety* magazine commented, "Better men have died with their heads in less pleasant places." However, in the film, Lake stands beside Ladd during this final scene.)

Regarding her performance, even Lake admitted that her appeal was due more to her presence than any sort of dramatic talent. When asked by a reporter to discuss her acting abilities, she replied, "I don't think I'm outstanding, in fact, I don't believe it is necessary to being a star. The audience doesn't want that, they don't want the best acting on the screen. What they want is personality, something new, something different."

Paramount, eager to capitalize on the icy magnetism between Lake and Ladd, rushed them into production on *The Glass Key* (1942), Lake's second excursion into the realm of noir. In this film she portrayed Janet Henry, a fiercely loyal woman whose strong-willed personality is first displayed when she encounters Paul Madvig (Brian Donlevy), a crude political boss who has bad-mouthed her father in the press. Overhearing Madvig's disparaging remarks, Janet slaps his face, only afterward informing him that the blow was "for talking about decent people … you cheap crook." Later, however, Janet becomes engaged to Madvig, in the hopes of gaining his support for her father's political aspirations.

Meanwhile, Janet finds herself attracted to Madvig's chief aide Ed Beaumont (Ladd), but out of loyalty to his boss, Beaumont rejects her advances. Later, Janet's spendthrift brother, who has been having an affair with Madvig's sister, is found murdered, and Madvig is implicated in the crime. Beaumont guesses the killer's real identity but has police arrest Janet for the crime, a ploy that prompts her father to admit that it was he who accidentally killed his son. The film concludes when Madvig discovers that Janet and Ed "got it bad for each other" and gives them his blessing.

Although the critic for the *New York Times* remarked that Lake had "little more than a sullen voice and a head of yellow hair," most reviewers agreed that the petite bombshell had scored another hit, with the critic from the *Brooklyn Daily Eagle* gushing, "Even without her voice and without her sense of timing in speech and action, and without her ability to cast a spell over her audience by her sheer modernity, Miss Lake would undoubtedly pass for a good actress just by making her appearance in a scene. A girl with her surplus of charms is bound to get herself across anyway — but Veronica Lake is a fine actress as well."

After another smash hit, *I Married a Witch* (1942) with Fredric March and Susan Hayward, Lake was next seen singing "A Sweater, a Sarong, and a Peekaboo Bang" in *Star Spangled Rhythm* (1942), where, along with Paulette Goddard and Dorothy Lamour, she parodied the trademark that had made her famous. And in *So Proudly We Hail* (1943), Lake amazed critics with her portrayal of an emotionally distraught nurse during World War II, prompting one reviewer to rave, "Veronica not only gives the finest performance of her youthful career, but steps out in front as one of the Hollywood greats."

Although Lake was now at her peak of popularity, her marriage to John Detlie was beginning to erode. Objecting to being referred to as "Mr. Lake," Detlie joined the army and moved his family to Fort Lewis in Seattle, insisting that they live off his salary. Detlie also disapproved when Lake participated in a bond-selling trip to New York, and the marriage suffered yet another blow when Lake returned to Hollywood for *So Proudly We Hail*. It appeared that the relationship could be salvaged when Lake became pregnant with their second child, but during production of her next film, *The Hour Before the Dawn* (1944), Lake tripped over a cable on the set and the baby boy was born prematurely. Seven days later, Lake's son died — and so did the marriage. Lake and Detlie were divorced in December 1943, with Lake testifying that her

Veronica Lake

husband "objected to my career and couldn't understand why I had to travel about the country on tours. He also objected to my friends so much that I finally had no friends at all. He'd telephone me and insult me and then send me flowers."

Meanwhile, Lake was becoming known in the Hollywood community as a troublemaking rebel. In a 1944 article in *Click*, she was described as "one of the most acute problems in Hollywood" with a "time-bomb mind." She was notorious for being hot-tempered, frequently insulted her costars, began drinking heavily and reportedly even stole the change that her fans had sent her for her autograph, refusing to sign. Then, after a whirlwind romance, she married director André De Toth, a hard-drinking Hungarian with an explosive, often violent, temperament.

During the next two years, Lake's private exploits caused her popularity to wane, and she appeared in a series of films that failed to reverse this trend, including *Bring on the Girls* (1945), a poorly received piece of fluff in which Lake portrayed a nightclub cigarette girl, and *Out of This World* (1945), which featured Lake in a dull role as an agent's secretary. But in 1946, Paramount again teamed Lake with Alan Ladd, in the noir thriller *The Blue Dahlia*, and Lake — if only briefly — was back on top again. In this film, Ladd portrays Johnny Morrison, a war veteran who returns from service to discover that his wife has been carrying on an affair with a nightclub owner, Eddie Harwood (Howard da Silva). When she is murdered, Johnny is implicated and searches for the real culprit, meeting up with Joyce Harwood (Lake), the nightclub owner's estranged wife. The film's conclusion finds that the murder was committed by a hotel detective who was blackmailing Harwood.

The Blue Dahlia was well received by moviegoers and critics alike — Jack Grant of *The Hollywood Reporter* stated that Lake was "warmer and more polished than she usually is" — but this film was to be the last high point of Lake's contract with Paramount. She would appear in only seven movies over the next six years, none of which managed to boost her sagging career, including *Variety Girl* (1947), a star-studded musical whose cast included Gary Cooper, Barbara Stanwyck and William Holden; *Isn't It Romantic?* (1948), a box office bomb that was referred to as a "poor man's *Meet Me in St. Louis*"; *Saigon* (1948), her final teaming with Ladd, which was panned as "a weak programmer"; and *Slattery's Hurricane* (1949), notable chiefly because it was directed by Lake's husband, André De Toth.

Lake's personal life was hitting the skids as well. Although she gave birth in 1945 to a son, Michael, and in 1948 to a baby girl, Diana, her marriage to de Toth was fraught with constant problems. The free-spending de Toth was notorious for frivolous purchases, including horses, yachts, new automobiles and even a small commercial airplane. And in 1948, the press went wild when Lake's mother sued her for failing to uphold weekly payments based on a 1943 agreement in which the actress promised to repay her parents for backing her career ("My daughter has tossed me off like an old shoe," Mrs. Keane told the press). The matter was ultimately settled out of court, but it represented yet another devastating blow to Lake's slowly decaying existence.

In November 1948, Lake was informed that Paramount would not be renewing her contract. A year later, she and her husband were deeply in debt, and Lake began selling off her jewelry in a futile attempt to keep the family afloat. But her efforts were to no avail — in April 1951, Lake and de Toth were forced to declare voluntary bankruptcy, listing debts of $156,000, and itemizing nearly 100 creditors with claims ranging from a few dollars to several hundred. The couple's ranch in Chatsworth was seized by the IRS for unpaid income taxes and soon afterward, Lake and De Toth separated. Their divorce became final in June 1952.

Following the divorce, Lake rejected offers to star in a number of low-budget features, stating, "I really didn't want to go back through the grind of playing sexy sirens in grade-B thrillers all for the silk purses of the studio management." Instead, she left Hollywood, spending the next several years appearing on stage in *The Voice of the Turtle*, *The Curtain Rises* and *Peter Pan*, as well as stock versions of *Cat on a Hot Tin Roof* and *The Gramercy Ghost*. In addition, she was seen on a variety of television programs, including *Somerset Maugham TV Theatre*, *Tales of Tomorrow* and *Philco Television Playhouse*. The actress explained her absence from the silver screen by saying that she was not "mad at Hollywood or show business.... I simply lost my personal identity and wanted to get it back."

Lake made news again in August 1955 when she remarried, this time to songwriter Joe McCarthy, in Traverse City, Michigan, where she was appearing in a local play. But although Lake later said the couple "did share moments of relative peace and even flashes of happiness," she and McCarthy seemed to be bound mainly by their affinity for alcohol. By 1959, the marriage was over. Although Lake demanded alimony payments of $13,000 a year, the courts awarded her only $65 a week. A short time later, Lake was evicted from her New York apartment when she fell behind in her rent, and her life seemed to have hit rock bottom.

In 1961, Lake found a job pasting felt flowers on lingerie hangers in a small South Broadway factory, and the following year, the press had a field day when she was discovered living at the Martha Washington Hotel in Manhattan, paying a rent of seven dollars a day, and working as a barmaid in the hotel's cocktail lounge. Insisting she was "not destitute," Lake told newspapers: "I just fell into this job. What brought me here? I happen to live here and I like people. But then, how do you explain me to anybody?" When the story broke, fans around the world took pity on Lake, sending her letters and even money, but she returned every dime, claiming, "I still have some pride."

While working at the hotel, Lake became involved with Andy Elickson, a Wisconsin merchant seaman who had never heard of the pint-sized screen siren. Between Elickson's trips, Lake lived with him, and it appeared that her life was finally on the upswing. In 1962 she accepted a job to host *Festival of Stars*, a television program in Baltimore, on which she introduced old movies and offered comments on the Golden Age of Hollywood. The following year she appeared in the off-Broadway revival of *Best Foot Forward*, playing, ironically, an aging movie star struggling for a comeback.

But following this role, Lake dropped out of sight for several years, resurfacing again in the press in April 1965 when she was arrested for drunkenness after beating on the doors of St. Mary's Cathedral in Galveston, Texas. Following her release, she told reporters, "I was sitting around and got to feeling sorry for myself and so I went to the rectory of Father O'Connell. I just wanted to talk to him."

Although Lake's romance with Elickson had become the high point of her life, this relationship ended when the robust seaman fell ill with disorders of the liver, spleen, kidneys and bladder. He died in September 1965, leaving Lake alone once again. By now the grandmother of three, Lake continued to work sporadically, appearing in *Goodbye Charlie* in Miami, Florida, in May 1966. Her arrival there was covered by the press, who described her disheveled appearance: "Her hair was knotted on top of her head in a dark blonde tangle. Flesh-colored band-aids were taped to several fingers. The only makeup on her face was a touch of lipstick and her complexion looked pasty in the bright sunlight." The show lasted just two weeks, and Lake eventually was forced to sue the producer for $2,849 in uncollected salary.

After settling in Miami, Lake returned to the screen in 1966 in the low-budget horror film *Footsteps in the Snow*, followed two years later by *Flesh Feast*, in which she portrayed a physician who had been recently released from a mental institution. *Flesh Feast*—which was released three years after it was filmed and lasted only three days in Los Angeles—would mark Lake's final appearance on the screen.

In 1969, Lake relocated to Ipswich, England, a port city on the eastern coast of England, where she enlisted Donald Bain to help write her autobiography. Titled *Veronica*, the book was published in Britain in 1969, leading to a renewed interest in the actress. Soon afterward, she took on the roles of Lady Louise Peverall in the English version of *Madame Chairman* and Blanche DuBois in *A Streetcar Named Desire*, receiving favorable comments from critics for both. When her book was published in the United States two years later, it met with rave reviews and Lake returned to Hollywood in June 1971 for promotional appearances. During her visit, she told talk show hostess Virginia Graham that she would have "ended up like Alan Ladd and Gail Russell—dead and buried by now" if she had remained in Hollywood: "That rat race killed them and I knew it eventually would kill me so I had to get out. I was never psychologically meant to be a picture star."

In June 1972 Lake was married for the fourth time, to Robert Carlton-Munro, a sea captain with the Royal Navy. But this marriage, characterized by drinking bouts and fights, ended in divorce the following year. By now, years of heavy drinking had taken a toll on Lake's health, and during a visit to friends in Vermont in June 1973, she was hospitalized with acute hepatitis. She died there on July 7, at the age of 53, penniless and alone.

At the end, Lake had appeared to be turning her life around, but it was too late for the sultry temptress who had once held the world in her hands. In one of her last interviews before her death, she had confidently announced her plans for the future: "I fully intend to see the year 2000.... I shall continue to work at my career. The world owes me nothing, but I owe it a great deal and before I get much older I intend to deliver the goods."

Film Noir Filmography

THIS GUN FOR HIRE   *Director:* Frank Tuttle. *Producer:* Richard M. Blumenthal. Released by Paramount, May 1942. *Running time:* 80 minutes. *Cast:* Alan Ladd, Veronica Lake, Robert Preston, Laird Cregar, Tully Marshall.

THE GLASS KEY   *Director:* Stuart Heisler. *Producer:* Fred Kohlmar. Released by Paramount, October 15, 1942. *Running time:* 85 minutes. *Cast:* Brian Donlevy, Veronica Lake, Alan Ladd, Bonita Granville, Joseph Calleia, Richard Denning, Moroni Olsen, William Bendix.

THE BLUE DAHLIA   *Director:* George Marshall. *Producer:* John Houseman. Released by Paramount, April 1946. *Running time:* 98 minutes. *Cast:* Alan Ladd, Veronica Lake, William Bendix, Howard da Silva, Doris Dowling, Tom Powers, Hugh Beaumont. Academy Award nomination for Best Original Screenplay (Raymond Chandler).

References

"All This, and Veronica Too." *Cue*, October 24, 1942.
Biography of Veronica Lake. Paramount Studios, August 1940.
Biography of Veronica Lake. Paramount Studios, June 1948.
"Blonde Heavy Shatters Old Film Tradition." *Paramount News of Hollywood*, circa 1940.
Braun, Eric. "Veronica Lake: Hollywood Comet." *Films and Filming*, May 1974.
"Cadet Flyers Show Their Wings to Defense Film Star." *Life*, April 14, 1941.
Carle, Teet. Biography of Veronica Lake. Paramount Studios, January 29, 1942.
_____. "The Girl with the Peek-a-Boo Bang." *Hollywood Studio Magazine*, December 1972.
Carroll, Harrison. "Actress to File Suit for Divorce." *New York Express*, October 4, 1943.
De Toth, André. "Marriage Is Such Fun." *Photoplay*, April 1948.
"Film Actress Veronica Lake to File Divorce Action Here." *Los Angeles Times*, October 5, 1943.
Flagg, James Montgomery. "What's in a Name Better Than Constance?" *The Sunday Star*, October 12, 1941.
"Her Hair." *Life*, November 24, 1941.
Hopper, Hedda. "Heartbreak for Veronica Lake." *Photoplay*, September 1934.
Lake, Veronica. "Are You a Woman Without a Man?" *Photoplay*, January 1934.
_____. "I Almost Gave Up." *Photoplay*, August 1941.
_____. "You Wouldn't Know Me." *Photoplay*, October 1945.
_____, as told to Niven Busch. "I, Veronica Lake." *Life*, May 17, 1943.
_____, with Donald Bain. *Veronica: The Autobiography of Veronica Lake*. New York: Citadel, 1971.
"Like Women and Make Them Like You." *Cosmopolitan*, June 1943.

"Paramount's Bid for Year's Best Glamour Starlet." *Life*, March 3, 1941.

Parsons, Louella O. "Veronica Lake Weds Director." *Los Angeles Examiner*, October 2, 1940.

Schroeder, Carl A. "Veronica Lake: Rebel." *Click*, December 1944.

Sheppard, Gene. "Veronica Lake: The Peek-a-Boo Blonde." *Hollywood Studio Magazine*, April 1985.

Skolsky, Sidney. "Short for Ronni." *Photoplay*, May 1943.

_____. "Tintypes — Veronica Lake." *Citizen News*, June 24, 1941.

"Star's Mate Waives Rights." *Los Angeles Examiner*, November 6, 1943.

"That Odd Miss Lake." *The New Yorker*, May 13, 1942.

"Veronica Lake." *Life*, April 7, 1947.

"Veronica Lake Awarded Decree from John Detlie." *Los Angeles Examiner*, December 3, 1943.

"Veronica Lake Free to Wed Andre de Toth." *Citizen News*, December 7, 1944.

"Veronica Lake of the Tresses Becomes Bride." *Los Angeles Times*, December 14, 1944.

"Veronica Lake Tells Court of Ordeal and Wins Divorce." *Los Angeles Times*, December 3, 1943.

"Veronica Lake to Sue." *Los Angeles Examiner*, October 5, 1943.

"Veronica Lake Weds Film Art Director." *Citizen News*, October 2, 1940.

Waterbury, Ruth. "What's Wrong with Veronica Lake?" *Photoplay*, October 1944.

Wilson, Earl. "What Love Can Do." *Silver Screen*, April 1948.

Ida Lupino

Never a conventional beauty, nor one of Hollywood's glamour queens, Ida Lupino was nevertheless one of Tinseltown's finest talents and one of the few to achieve distinction as an actress and behind the camera as well. Lupino, a "theater thoroughbred" known for her easygoing professionalism, was a standout in such classics as *They Drive By Night* (1940) and *The Sea Wolf* (1941), and was the archetypal film noir dame in seven pictures from the era: *High Sierra* (1941), *Road House* (1948), *On Dangerous Ground* (1951), *Beware, My Lovely* (1952), *Private Hell 36* (1954), *The Big Knife* (1955) and *While the City Sleeps* (1956).

The actress who referred to herself as a "poor man's Bette Davis" was born in London on February 4; although sources disagree on the year of her birth, ranging from 1914 to 1918, most state that she entered the world in 1918. From the start, it seemed as if little Ida was destined for a theatrical career — her parents Stanley and Connie Emerald Lupino were comedy players on the British stage, her paternal great-grandfather Alfredo Lupino was an acrobatic ballet dancer and singer, and her great-uncles Mark and Harry were stage headliners. Thus, it was assumed by Stanley Lupino that his first-born daughter (Ida's sister Rita would be born two years later) would set her course in the theater.

During the frequent absences of her touring parents, Lupino was introduced to the arts by her grandfather George, a semi-invalid who taught her how to sing, compose music, paint and recite Shakespearean passages. When Lupino was seven years old, her grandfather died and she was sent to school at Clarence House at Hove, where she demonstrated her budding talent by writing, producing and starring in her first play, *Mademoiselle*. She also acted in improvised scenes with her sister at home, to the delight of her parents and visiting friends, and in 1930 she made her first professional stage appearance at London's Tom Thumb Theatre, acting out parodies of works by Shakespeare and enacting segments from the latest musical comedies.

At the age of 13, Lupino enrolled in the Royal Academy of Dramatic Arts, appearing in a variety of roles in student productions, including *Pygmalion* and *Julius Caesar*. Before long, Lupino engaged an agent and her cousin, comedy actor Lupino Lane, helped her to gain work as a screen extra. Her first big break in films came when she was cast as the ingenue in *Her First Affaire* (1932), guided by American director Allan Dwan. Dwan later recalled that Lupino's mother Connie had originally tested for the part, and was accompanied to the interview by her 14-year-old daughter: "[Connie] and her agent went on with their spiel about why she'd be good in it, and I'm looking at the kid," Dwan stated. "I said, 'What about her — can she act? ... That's whom I want — I want her.' Well, they were shocked — everybody was when the word went out I was insisting on this girl whose mother had come for the job. Finally they bent over my way and I got her. She was Ida Lupino. And she was great."

Playing a young girl in love with a married romance novelist, the platinum blonde Lupino was billed as "the English Jean Harlow" and received favorable reviews for her performance. After this triumphant debut, Lupino was flooded with offers and soon accepted a role in an action film about motorcycle racing, *Money for Speed*, the first of her five releases in 1933. Her other films that year included *High Finance*, in which she portrayed a selfish, money-hungry vamp; *I Lived with You*, for which the critic for *Picturegoer* applauded her "remarkable talent"; and *Prince of Arcadia*, her last British film.

By now, Hollywood had begun to beckon, and in July 1933, Lupino signed a six-month contract with Paramount Studios, which announced possible plans to cast the actress in the title role of *Alice in Wonderland*. Despite her misgivings ("It was frightening going to a place with the terrifying name of Hollywood," the actress later said), she set sail for America with her mother the following month. But after makeup and wardrobe tests at the studio, it was determined that Lupino's mature voice and sophisticated manner were totally unsuitable for the role of the innocent Alice, and she was instead cast in *Search for Beauty* (1934), a comedy about Olympic champions who find themselves involved with con men. This lightweight picture was followed by *Come On, Marines* (1934), a rowdy romp in which a shipwrecked bevy of glamour girls are rescued by the Marines. Of this film, Lupino would later recall: "We were either in satin pajamas dancing on tabletops, or wearing those undies with the lace that were all in one."

After only two Hollywood films, Lupino began to display her spirited temperament through bold comments in the press. She told one reporter: "I cannot tolerate fools, won't have anything to do with them. I only want to associate with brilliant people," and to another she scoffed at the notion that she had come to America to play the role of Alice in Wonderland: "You cannot play naive if you're not." After months of impatiently awaiting a role that would better suit her talents, Lupino was cast as the roguish daughter of a flamboyant actress in *Ready for Love* (1934), followed by *Paris in Spring* (1934), a comedic farce in which she played a French lass who contemplates committing suicide from the Eiffel Tower, and *Smart Girl* (1935), portraying a rich girl who goes broke and is forced to work for a living. She was working steadily, but Lupino was becoming increasingly disillusioned with her film assignments, and complained: "If I don't get a part I can get my teeth into, I'm going back home." Shortly after this declaration, she was given five lines in *Cleopatra*, starring Claudette Colbert, and was ordered to stand behind the star waving a large palm frond. When Lupino refused the tiny role, she was placed on suspension — the first of many.

But in May 1935, it was announced in *The Hollywood Reporter* that the feisty actress had won a role in the prestigious *Peter Ibbetson* (1935), starring Gary Cooper and Ann Harding. Appearing in only two scenes, Lupino caught the attention of Andre Sennwald of the *New York Times*, who stated she was "excellent in a brief part." As a result of her performance, Paramount renegotiated Lupino's contract, inking a 52-week pact at a weekly salary of $1,750.

Still, despite her new contract and her favorable showing in *Peter Ibbetson*, Lupino was next assigned to yet another comedy, *Anything Goes* (1936), with a star-studded cast that included Ethel Merman, Bing Crosby and Charles Ruggles. The film was all but stolen by Ethel Merman, who belted out such memorable show-stoppers as "You're the Top" and "I Get a Kick Out of You," while Lupino's role was summed up in *Variety*: "The no. 2 femme is called upon to register adoration while Crosby sings, and that's a thankless task at best." Lupino didn't fare much better on loan-out to United Artists for *One Rainy Afternoon* (1936), a weak comedy starring Francis Lederer. Lupino followed this film with *Yours for the Asking* (1936), a trifling tale about gamblers, then was loaned again to United Artists for *The Gay Desperado* (1936), opposite opera singer Nino Martini. After the release of this comedy about Mexican bandits, Lupino was hailed by the *New York Herald Tribune* for her "comically effective" performance. The film's director Rouben Mamoulian stated: "I have worked with many stars in my time — this Lupino child is the finest trouper of them all. What an actress she is."

Despite the critical and financial success of *The Gay Desperado*, Lupino next found herself in two forgettable loan-outs. In the first, *Sea Devils* (1937), her performance as the daughter of a wild and woolly serviceman prompted Frank Nugent to write in the *New York Times* that Lupino "sparkles whenever an essentially dull role gives her a chance." Her second loan-out of the year was *Let's Get Married* (1937), a plodding tale about a politician's efforts to elevate his daughter's suitor into the higher echelons of Congress. Returning to Paramount, Lupino was cast in *Artists and Models* (1937), playing yet another comedic role that she found to be beneath her dramatic talents. Although the film was a box office hit, Lupino declared that she didn't "care a fig about being pretty-pretty on the screen," and asked to be released from her contract. Paramount not only complied, but took the additional step of banning her from the lot.

Lupino's departure from the studio that had brought her to Hollywood would prove to be a turning point in her career. After appearing in RKO's *Fight for Your Lady* (1937), a musical farce panned so savagely that the studio pulled it from theaters, Lupino decided to retire for a year in order to study acting. At the same time, on the advice of Hedda Hopper (a fellow cast member in *Artists and Models*), Lupino sought a more natural look by allowing her bleached blonde hair to return to its original auburn and letting her pencil-thin eyebrows grow in. During her absence from pictures, Lupino stayed busy with a number of projects, including performing in "The Thirty-Nine Steps" on *Lux Radio Theatre* and composing a musical score, "Aladdin's Lamp," which was performed by the Los Angeles Philharmonic in the summer of 1937.

Meanwhile, Lupino had become involved with Louis Hayward, a handsome, debonair actor who would be best known for his title role in *The Man in the Iron Mask* (1939). The two had first met in 1933, on the set of Lupino's film *Money for Speed*. After their initial encounter, Lupino recalled, the actor "bored me to extinction. It was strange, but the dislike for each other ... amounted to contempt." But despite this first impression, Lupino later fell in love with Hayward and on November 1, 1938, the couple were married. While Lupino would insist in the press that she was content to be "simply" a housewife, she later explained that her husband was not "the kind who liked to paint houses and that sort of thing. He thought I should have a career, so he talked me into getting back into harness again."

After a 16-month absence, Lupino returned to films in Columbia's *The Lone Wolf Spy Hunt* (1939), the first of a nine-picture series in which Lupino was panned by *Variety* as being "at times, ridiculous." Lupino followed this inauspicious comeback with peripheral roles in *The Lady and the Mob* (1939) with Fay Bainter and Lee Bowman and *The Adventures of Sherlock Holmes* (1939), starring Basil Rathbone as the London detective. But her fourth picture of 1939, *The Light That Failed*, provided the determined young actress with the role that she had been waiting for. Although the film was produced by Paramount, the studio that banned her only two years earlier, Lupino's powerful screen test for director William Wellman convinced studio heads to rescind their edict. As Bessie, a hot-tempered Cockney streetwalker, Lupino played to rave reviews, with Howard Barnes of the *New York Herald Tribune* calling her performance "extremely fine," and Frank S. Nugent writing in the *New York Times* that Lupino's portrayal of Bessie was "another of the surprises we get when a little ingenue suddenly bursts forth as a great actress."

Lupino achieved an even bigger success the following year with her appearance in Warner Bros.' *They Drive by Night* (1940), with George Raft and Ann Sheridan, portraying a shrewish wife whose love for a truck driver leads her to murder and eventual madness. Critics were unanimous in their praise for the actress, and she was hailed in *Newsweek* magazine for her "arresting performance." After the release of the picture, Warner's signed Lupino to a contract, starring her next in her first film noir, *High Sierra* (1941).

In this film, Lupino portrays Marie Gossett, a former dime-a-dance girl who falls hopelessly in love with notorious ex-convict Roy Earle (Humphrey Bogart), recently released from prison after an eight-year stretch. Wasting no time in resuming his criminal activities, Earle teams up with a former associate, Big Mac (Donald MacBride), and two minor-league hoodlums, Red (Arthur Kennedy) and Babe (Alan Curtis), to rob a resort hotel in California. On his arrival at the gang's hideout in the mountains, Roy is angered to find that Babe has brought Marie along, but he comes to admire her level-headed, unflappable demeanor. For her part, Marie finds in Roy the man she has been searching for all her life. "Remember what you were saying the other day about prison? And the way you kept from going crazy by thinking all the time about a crash-out? Well, that's the way it's been with me. I've been trying to crash out ever since I can remember," Marie tells him. "I thought Babe was the right guy — I guess I was never really hooked up with any guys that wasn't wrong, so I had nothing to go by. Until I met you."

Roy, meanwhile, has made the acquaintance of Pa and Ma Goodhue (Henry Travers and Elisabeth Risdon), whose granddaughter Velma (Joan Leslie) suffers with a clubfoot. Touched by the young girl's innocence, Roy falls for Velma, pays for an operation to correct her condition, and makes plans to marry her. But after the successful surgery, Velma rejects the aging Roy for another man, and Roy comes to realize that Marie is really the woman for him. Sadly, Roy and Marie's happiness is short-lived. During the resort hotel heist, Roy is forced to shoot a security guard, Babe and Red are killed in an automobile accident, and Roy becomes the focus of a statewide manhunt. He puts Marie on a bus to Las Vegas with plans to meet her the following day, but he is later cornered by police in the High Sierra mountains. Marie returns to the mountains when she hears radio reports of Roy's imminent capture, but her lover is gunned down by police and she cradles him in her arms as he dies.

Singled out by the *New York Times'* Bosley Crowther as "especially impressive" in *High Sierra*, and now being proclaimed as "Hollywood's Hottest Star," Lupino next starred with Edward G. Robinson and John Garfield in *The Sea Wolf* (1941), a memorable film about the sadistic sea captain of a scavenger ship. She followed this top-notch production with another film with Garfield, *Out of the Fog* (1941), which focused on the exploits of a petty hoodlum who terrorizes and robs two elderly men. For her role in this film, Lupino was commended by Howard Barnes of the *New York Herald Tribune*, who wrote, "Ida Lupino, as I have said so many times in the past, is one of the great actresses of the screen, and she does not fall down in this instance."

Lupino's last film of 1941, Columbia's *Ladies in Retirement*, was one she would later term her favorite. Appearing with her husband, Louis Hayward (who reportedly was added to the cast to appease the actress), Lupino was hailed for her role of a murderous housekeeper, and the film was a commercial success. Following this triumph, Lupino renegotiated her contract with Warner Bros., securing a salary of $3,000 a week and the right to appear in four pictures for other studios. But only months later, she was suspended by the studio for rejecting parts in *Kings Row* and *Juke Girl*, both of which would later be played by Ann Sheridan. Still, Lupino refused to be intimidated by the powerful studio heads, and before long she was allowed to appear in the star-studded tribute to the British war effort, *Forever and a Day* (released in 1943, two years after its completion).

Next, following a loan-out to 20th Century–Fox for the lukewarm *Moontide* (1942), Lupino offered a first-rate performance in Warner Bros.' *The Hard Way* (1942), with Joan Leslie, Dennis Morgan and Jack Carson. Although she was troubled during the midst of production by the death of her father, Lupino turned in a stellar performance as the domineering woman who ruthlessly advances her younger sister's show business career, and was again acclaimed

Ida Lupino

by critics. The reviewer for the *New York World Telegram* stated that she "joins Ruth Chatterton and Bette Davis in the right to be a Great American Actress," and the *New York Herald Tribune*'s critic claimed that "the chief asset of the film is the acting of Ida Lupino." The following year, Lupino was awarded the New York Film Critics' Award as Best Actress of 1943 for her performance in the film. Inexplicably, the actress herself would later say, "The other actors in it were magnificent, but my own performance was incredibly bad."

In her follow-up to *The Hard Way*, Lupino starred in the 20th Century–Fox production *Life Begins at 8:30* (1942), playing the crippled daughter of a drunken ex-actor. Lupino was next seen in the star-studded musical *Thank Your Lucky Stars* (1943), followed by *In Our Time* (1944), a poorly received romance set in pre-war Poland, and *Hollywood Canteen* (1944), yet another all-star film dedicated to the war-time effort, with a cast that included Bette Davis, Joan Crawford, Barbara Stanwyck, Eddie Cantor, John Garfield and Peter Lorre.

While Lupino was sailing along professionally, however, her personal life was not as successful. Her husband's film career had floundered for several years, and after his service in World War II, he reportedly became moody and withdrawn. In late 1944, the couple separated, and on May 11, 1945, they were divorced. The following year, in *Silver Screen* magazine, the actress would claim that the marriage ended with no bitterness: "When we parted … it was not because we were incompatible but, curiously, because we were too compatible. Too much alike in every way. But as friends, we were, and we are, and we will continue to be."

Lupino appeared in only one picture in 1945, *Pillow to Post*, a corny comedy in which she portrayed a traveling saleslady. She followed this film with *Devotion* (1946), a costume drama that was panned by the *New York Times'* Bosley Crowther as "a ridiculous tax upon reason and an insult to plain intelligence"; *The Man I Love* (1946), where she starred as a blues singer with a tough exterior and a vulnerable heart; *Escape Me Never* (1947), a box office flop costarring Errol Flynn; and *Deep Valley* (1947), in which she superbly portrayed a shy country girl with a speech disability. One of the many accolades for Lupino's performance in the latter production came in *Variety*, whose critic raved, "Ida Lupino … chalks up one of the finest performances she has ever turned in, tellingly carrying audience sympathy and interest from her opening scene to the finale." Between films, the actress continued to exhibit her versatility in other areas — along with Barbara Reed, she collaborated on a screenplay, *Miss Penington*, which was optioned to RKO for $5,000, and by 1945 she had composed dozens of songs, many of which were recorded and broadcast on the radio.

Following *Deep Valley*, Lupino turned down Warner Bros.' proposal of a high-paying, seven-year agreement that would prohibit her from appearing in films for other studios. Seeking artistic freedom, she terminated her contract and began a partnership with Benedict Bogeaus, an independent producer. Together, they formed Arcadia Productions, but the company's first acquisition, *Early Autumn*, would never be produced, and Arcadia was later dissolved. Instead, Lupino accepted a starring role in *Road House* (1948), her second film noir.

In this successful film, Lupino portrayed Lily Stevens, a hard-as-nails, straight Scotch–drinking singer who is hired by Jefty Robbins (Richard

Widmark) to perform in his road house located near the Canadian border. The club is managed by Pete Morgan (Cornel Wilde), who objects to Lily's high salary and insists that she return to her home in Chicago: "Every time Jefty leaves town, he gets drunk and brings somebody back," Pete says, driving Lily to the train depot. "You see, Jefty gets tired easily, and it's up to me to do the dumping. I don't like it, but if I have to I can get rough." But Lily is unfazed by Pete's emphatic declaration. "Listen, when I want to leave I'll let you know," she declares. "I came out here with a contract — I needed the dough. And I'm going to collect every nasty little cent of it, maybe more. Who knows, before I'm through, you might be running for the depot." And, as if to underscore her meaning, Lily forcefully slaps Pete's face. "Silly boy," she adds.

Despite their rocky beginnings, Lily and Pete soon fall in love and plan to marry. But Jefty has eyes for Lily as well, and when the couple plan to leave town together, Jefty has Pete arrested for theft. Pete is ultimately convicted of the crime, but Jefty persuades the judge to release Pete into his custody, then proceeds to belittle and degrade Pete to the point where he considers escaping across the border to Canada. Finally, Jefty exacts the ultimate revenge when he insists that Lily and Pete accompany him on a trip to his cabin in the woods, along with Susie Smith (Celeste Holm), the good-hearted road house cashier. Once there, Jefty provokes a fight with Pete, who knocks Jefty unconscious and escapes with Lily. Susie, meanwhile, uncovers evidence proving Pete's innocence, but when Jefty revives, he goes after the fugitive couple, intent on killing them both. He catches up to them at the edge of a lake, but while struggling with Pete, he is shot and killed by Lily. "I guess it couldn't be helped," Pete says at the film's end. "It was either Jefty or us."

The popularity of Road House notwithstanding, the actual filming of the picture was physically demanding on Lupino, who was left heavily bruised after one scene, and suffered a pulled neck tendon and a painful back injury in another. Lupino's costar Cornel Wilde later recalled that the actress was "so real, offbeat, and just lots of fun." For her performance in the film, the actress was hailed in Motion Picture Herald for turning in "one of her best screen performances to date," in the New York Times for her "expertly brittle and passionate" portrayal, and in Variety, whose critic raved, "Miss Lupino's standout performance is highlighted by her first-rate handling of a brace of blues numbers.... Her gravel-toned voice lacks range but has the more essential quality of style, along the lines of a femme Hoagy Carmichael."

In her personal life, Lupino had become involved with the man who would become her second husband, Collier Young, a Columbia Studios executive and a close friend of Louis Hayward. Lupino was instantly attracted to Young's charming and sophisticated manner and he, in turn, was impressed by the actress's sharp wit and unpredictability. Soon after they began dating, Young was hinting at an engagement, and the two were wed on August 5, 1948, less than two months after Lupino became an American citizen. The couple later formed an independent company, Emerald Productions, and worked together in the production of *Not Wanted* (1949), a film about illegitimate birth that would become a milestone in Lupino's career. When the picture's original director, Elmer Clifton, suffered a mild heart attack, Lupino took over the reins, astounding all involved with her directorial skill. Although reviews for the film were mixed — with *The Hollywood Reporter* saying it was "done with taste, dignity and compassion," and the *New York Times* terming it "dramatically limp"— the picture was a huge success.

Lupino returned to acting in *Woman in Hiding* (1949), earning acclaim in *Variety* for "one of her most lucid performances as the newlywed who finds out about her mate's conniving just in time." The film was to originally star Ronald Reagan, but when the actor suffered a fractured thigh, he was replaced by newcomer Howard Duff. Lupino would later state that initially she and Duff "couldn't stand each other," and Duff would admit that the actress "scared" him. But Lupino's contempt for the handsome, virile actor began to fade after she received a bouquet of white orchids with a card reading: "From Howard Duff to Ida Lupino — whether you hate me or not." As the attraction between the two performers grew, Lupino's marriage to Collier Young became strained. The couple, who had by now changed the name of their company to Filmakers, frequently clashed on their artistic ventures, and after *Never Fear* (1950), which was also directed by Lupino, Young told the press, "It's pretty hard to have an argument over a script at five-thirty ... and be romantic and husband-and-wifely at six-thirty."

The relationship suffered its biggest blow when Young inked a deal to affiliate Filmakers with RKO Studios, which had been recently acquired by Howard Hughes. As a result, Filmakers gained much-needed financial backing from the studio, but Lupino and Young were forced to surrender complete control to Hughes. This act, combined with Lupino's affair with Howard Duff, signaled the end of the marriage. On October 20, 1951, Lupino divorced Young in Minden, Nevada, and the following day she married Duff. Six months later, on April 23, 1952, the couple's daughter, Bridget Mirella, was born. Surprisingly, Collier Young, who had maintained his business partnership with Lupino, was named the child's godparent, along with his soon-to-be-wife, actress Joan Fontaine.

Back on screen, Lupino appeared in two films noirs, both costarring Robert Ryan — *On Dangerous Ground* (1951) and *Beware, My Lovely* (1952).

In *On Dangerous Ground*, Ryan portrayed Jim Wilson, an embittered police sergeant who lives alone in a bleak apartment and is frequently provoked to excessive violence by the lawbreakers with whom he comes in contact. After a particularly vicious attack on a murder suspect, Jim is assigned to a case in upstate New York, where a young girl has been molested and killed. Tracking the suspect to a remote farm house, Jim meets Mary Malone (Lupino), a blind woman who comes to feel a kinship with the cynical lawman.

Mary confides that her young brother Danny (Sumner Williams) is guilty of the crime and is assured by Jim that Danny will not be harmed, but the emotionally disturbed teen falls to his death from a snow-covered hill while trying to escape. Jim attempts to comfort Mary, but she rejects him: "You're feeling sorry for me. And I don't want anyone feeling sorry for me. The way you are, I don't see how you can help anybody." Dispirited, Jim heads back to New York, but he later returns to Mary, realizing the transformation that she has made in his life. The film's end shows Mary accepting Jim's outstretched hand.

Although both Lupino and Ryan turned in laudable performances, *On Dangerous Ground* was only moderately successful at the box office, with most critics agreeing with *Newsweek*'s assessment of the film that "the resolution is plausible enough, and the acting throughout is effective, but the film never achieves the dramatic intensity to match its good purposes."

In Lupino and Ryan's next teaming, *Beware, My Lovely*, the actress portrayed Helen Graham, a widow who hires an itinerant handyman, Howard Wilkins (Ryan), to help clean the boarding house she operates. Howard proves to be a conscientious worker, but he soon succumbs to paranoia as he believes that Helen is spying on him. Provoked further by Helen's bratty niece, who chides him for doing a "woman's job," Howard becomes completely unbalanced and locks the doors of the house. For the next several hours, he keeps Helen captive, but in a period of lucidity, he confides the source of his plight: "You don't know what it means like I do to find myself in the middle of a room, in the middle of a busy street, or in some house I'm working in ... and wonder where I am, and what I'm doing," he tells the increasingly horrified Helen. "And then sometimes I'm looking down at someone. Someone who's been hurt. And they've been hurt very badly. And I wonder if I've done it."

Despite Helen's numerous efforts, she is unable to escape from Howard, who continues to drift in and out of reality. Finally, after Howard tries to strangle her, Helen faints, and when she comes to, Howard is preparing to leave, completely unaware of the day's events. When a telephone repairman arrives at the house, Helen arranges for him to turn Howard over to police and, without further incident, the mentally unstable handyman departs peaceably.

Although *Beware, My Lovely* was an above-average suspenser, like *On Dangerous Ground*, it was not popular with moviegoers. The critic for *The Saturday Review* offered a theory for the film's failure to catch on with the public, saying "just too many things keep happening at the wrong time, and the final explanation of the hero's mental aberration is altogether too naive for belief."

While continuing her acting career, Lupino was fast becoming one of Hollywood's premier female directors. In the span of three years, she directed as many pictures: *Outrage* (1950), the story of a rape victim; *Hard, Fast and Beautiful* (1951), which involved a tennis champion who is forced into success by her ambitious mother; and *The Hitch-Hiker* (1952), the tale of two businessmen who pick up a murderous passenger while on a fishing trip. She also directed and starred in *The Bigamist* (1953), becoming the first woman to direct herself in a major motion picture. The film, produced by Lupino's former husband Collier Young and costarring Young's then-wife Joan Fontaine, caused many a raised eyebrow due to the relationships of those involved in its production. But Young casually explained, "We want to be grown-up about it all. I don't know how people in Kansas feel about this ... but after our divorce, Ida and I decided to stay in business because our company was a good thing. Since the divorce, the quality of our movies has actually improved." Although *The Bigamist* received mixed reviews, Lupino was singled out for praise by the *New York Times*, whose critic said she "keels the action with such mounting tension, muted compassion and sharklike alacrity for behavior, the average spectator may feel he is eavesdropping on the excellent dialogue." However, because Collier Young had convinced Lupino that Filmakers should assume the costs of their own distribution, the film was not a financial success.

Around this time, Lupino continued to broaden her creative horizons, making her television debut in *Four Star Playhouse* and later appearing in two episodes of *Ford Theater*. Then, after the completion of *The Bigamist*, plans were announced for Lupino to direct her husband in *The Story of a Cop*. But before production began, Duff announced that he wanted a legal separation. It marked Duff's second split from his wife, who told columnist Louella Parsons, "This time he means it. I don't want to get a divorce because I love Howard and he's really a fine person.... It's just that I don't believe Howard likes being married." Both Lupino and Duff were known for their stubborn natures and volatile tempers, but they surprised the Hollywood community by reconciling and purchasing a sprawling ranch home near Sunset Boulevard.

A loving couple once more, Lupino and Duff continued their plans for *The Story of a Cop*, now renamed *Private Hell 36* (1954), Lupino's fifth film noir. To avoid possible clashes with her husband, however, she opted not to direct, instead choosing Don Siegel to take her place. Years later, Siegel would bemoan his experience on the film, saying "there was too much alcohol in the air and I thought the people I was working for were pretentious — talented but pretentious. They'd talk, talk, talk, but they wouldn't sit down and give me enough time. They wouldn't rehearse."

Siegel's complaints notwithstanding, *Private Hell 36* is a fascinating drama that begins with an unsolved crime in New York City — a murder and theft of $300,000 from a bank's night depository. A year later, a $50 bill from the heist surfaces in Los Angeles and detectives Cal Bruner (Steve Cochran) and Jack Farnham (Duff) are put on the case. They track the bill to a nightclub singer, Lili Marlowe (Lupino), who'd received the bill as a tip from a patron. When more bills from the robbery turn up at a local race track, the detectives secure Lili's help in searching for the man, and after several days of tedious surveillance, she spots him driving out of the track's parking lot. Bruner and Farnham give swift chase, but the man is killed when he drives his car over an embankment. In the dead man's car, the detectives find a steel box containing more than $200,000, but instead of turning over the entire amount, Bruner pockets $80,000 and leaves it in a small trailer — Number 36 — in a nearby trailer park.

Although Farnham objects to the theft, Bruner convinces him to split the cash, citing the wife (Dorothy Malone) and small child that Farnham must support. For his part, Bruner has become involved with Lili, and he is driven by a desire to fulfill her material pursuits. The detectives' superior, Capt. Michaels (Dean Jagger), does not appear to suspect them regarding the missing money, but Farnham begins exhibiting signs of guilt over his role in the crime. Meanwhile, Bruner is blackmailed into turning over the money by a man claiming to the partner of the man killed in the car crash. Bruner has no intention of giving up the cash, but Farnham insists, and when the two show up at the trailer to meet with the blackmailer, Bruner shoots Farnham in the back. He in turn is fatally wounded by police, and Capt. Michaels emerges to tell Farnham that there never was an accomplice to the robbery. As the film ends, its narrator intones: "A policeman, unlike most men, lives close to evil and violence. He can, like all men, make his own private hell. The good pass through it with minor burns. The evil stumble and fall, and die in strange places."

Although *Private Hell 36* was dismissed in the *New York Times* as "just an average melodrama about cops," Lupino won praise for her role as the wise-cracking Lili Marlowe, with the critic for *Variety* labelling her "properly brassy." But with Filmakers' profits continuing to be eaten up by distribution costs, *Private Hell 36* turned out to be the company's last film. Lupino would later state that she had opposed Filmakers' venture into distribution, but "I was out-voted and pretty soon we were out of business." After the loss of her company, Lupino focused her energies on acting, starring in Columbia's *Women's Prison* (1955), in which she portrayed a cruel prison warden, followed by *The Big Knife* (1955), an especially grim example from the film noir era.

As this picture begins, Lupino's character, Marion Castle, is separated from her husband, Charlie (Jack Palance), who has changed over the years from an idealistic stage actor to a heavy-drinking, philandering film star. Although Charlie has begged Marion to reconcile, she has refused, specifically citing the seven-year contract he plans to sign at the request of his studio head, the sadistic Stanley Hoff (Rod Steiger). Marion manages to convince Charlie to reject the contract and leave Hollywood with her, but the weak-willed actor is later forced into the agreement by Hoff, who threatens to reveal that it was Charlie — and not his press agent, Buddy Bliss (Paul Langton) — who was responsible for a drunk driving accident in which a child was killed. Once again abandoned by Marion, and distraught over his situation, Charlie gets drunk and has a one-night dalliance with his press agent's wife (Jean Hagen).

Meanwhile, Marion is being courted by Hank Teagle (Wesley Addy), a close friend of Charlie's, but she is unable to ignore her love for her husband and again reconciles with him: "No matter how many times I leave, I always go back," she tells Hank. "He's a part of me. The most terrible thing he can do to me is better than not having him." Still, their future seems doomed when Marion learns that a local starlet, Dixie Evans (Shelley Winters), who was with Charlie on the night of the car accident, is planning to expose the truth. Matters reach a climax when Hoff's associate, Smiley Coy (Wendell Corey), hatches a scheme for Charlie to poison the starlet, thereby permanently insuring her silence. Charlie refuses, and Hoff heatedly vows to ruin his life: "You threw away a kingdom today," he tells Charlie. As a final blow, Charlie is angrily confronted by Buddy Bliss, who has discovered Charlie's indiscretion with his wife. In despair, Charlie locks himself in his bath and slits his wrists, but in an ironic twist, Smiley later reveals that Dixie Evans has been struck by a car and killed. He then plans to report Charlie's death as a heart attack, but he is fended off by Hank Teagle, who insists, "I'll tell the story. He killed himself ... no man had a greater reverence for life, a greater zest for living. Yes, he was wrong. But he just couldn't go on hurting those he loved."

Although one critic rejected *The Big Knife* as "too unrelentingly morbid to appeal to a sizable viewing audience," the film won third prize at the Venice Film Festival in late 1955. Later that year, in December 1955, Lupino joined the cast of television's *Four Star Playhouse*, and early the following year she wrote and directed her first television drama, for NBC's *Screen Directors Playhouse*. Despite her growing affinity for the medium of television, Lupino also continued her screen appearances, starring next in *While the City Sleeps* (1956), her final film noir.

This film focuses on a hodgepodge of characters employed at Kyne Enterprises, including television anchor Edward Mobley (Dana Andrews), newspaper editor John Day Griffith (Thomas Mitchell), wire service manager Mark Loving (George Sanders), photo service editor Harry Kritzer (James Craig) and local reporter Mildred Donner (Lupino). When the amateurish Walter Kyne (Vincent Price) takes over Kyne Enterprises after the death of his father, he creates the position of executive director ("Someone to do the actual work," he says), and announces that the post will be given to the man who solves a series of brutal sex murders.

Each of the men use the women in their lives in an effort to secure the coveted job — Mobley sets up his fiancée (Sally Forrest) to act as bait for the killer; Kritzer employs his mistress (Rhonda Fleming), who is also Kyne's wife, to sway the job in his favor; and Loving seeks help from his girlfriend Mildred to obtain information from Mobley. Ultimately, Mobley catches the killer — a drugstore delivery boy — and gives the scoop to John Griffith, who is given the job.

Along with her costars, Lupino was praised in the *New York Times*, whose

reviewer stated, "Although they are enacting variants of familiar roles, the performers do justice to their assignments." After this film, Lupino accepted a
cameo role in *Strange Intruder* (1956), the story of a mentally unbalanced veteran of the Korean War. It was her last appearance on the silver screen for
over a decade. Instead, turning her sights to television, Lupino continued her
frequent appearances on *Four Star Playhouse*, then debuted in 1957 with
Howard Duff on the couple's new television comedy series *Mr. Adams and Eve*.
Working together on the popular series seemed to bring a much-needed sta-
bility to their relationship and for a while, at least, all was well in the Duff
household.

Meanwhile, after 66 episodes and an Emmy nomination for Lupino (she
lost to Jane Wyatt of *Father Knows Best*), *Mr. Adams and Eve* was cancelled.
Following the series' end, Lupino and Duff gradually resumed their familiar
pattern of frequent disputes, but the couple continued to appear together on
various television programs, including a guest spot on *The Lucy-Desi Comedy
Hour* in 1958. Over the next several years, Lupino also guested on a number
of television series, including *Bonanza* and *The Virginian*, and directed episodes
of *Alfred Hitchcock Presents, The Untouchables* and *The Twilight Zone*, becoming the only woman ever to direct an episode of the famed series. One of only
53 female directors belonging to the 3,000-member Directors Guild of America, Lupino would later say that she "never planned to become a director. The
fates and a combination of luck — good and bad — were responsible."

In 1966, Lupino directed what would be her last feature film, *The Trouble with Angels*, a delightful comedy starring Rosalind Russell and Hayley
Mills, and three years later, she returned to acting on the silver screen in a
low-budget feature, *Backtrack* (1969). But her career, both as a director and
an actress was now on the decline. Although she continued to make guest
appearances on such television shows as *The Mod Squad* and *Family Affair*, she
would only make five more — mostly forgettable — feature film appearances.
One of these, *The Devil's Rain* (1975), in which Lupino portrayed a satanic
slave, was panned as "inept and foolish," and another, *Food of the Gods* (1976),
was a low-budget horror film in which Lupino's character is devoured by a
giant rat.

Off screen, it appeared as if the stormy Lupino-Duff marriage had finally
reached an end in the early 1970s, when Duff left his wife yet again, informing her that he was in love with a young stage actress. After 20 years of marriage, the relationship had suffered its final blow. Still, Lupino and Duff would
not divorce for more than ten years and, according to an article in *Hollywood
Studio Magazine*, Lupino kept a photograph of Duff hanging on the front door
of her home, asking him to come back. The couple finally divorced in 1983,
and Duff married his longtime girlfriend, with whom he remained until his
death in 1990.

With Lupino's final television role in a 1977 episode of the popular series

Charlie's Angels, and her final film appearance the following year, the career of the talented actress came to an abrupt halt. During the years that followed, Lupino became somewhat of a recluse, once telling reporters that she was "happier now, leading more of a peaceful existence.... I have retreated from the whole Hollywood scene." A decade later, however, she did admit that she would be willing to appear before the camera again if presented with a challenging role or "it pays one hell of a lot of money."

In June 1995, after several years of declining health, Lupino was diagnosed with cancer, and following a stroke a month later, she died in August 1995, at her home in Burbank, California. Although the career of the talented actress and director had ended before she reached the age of 60, Lupino's name has continued to be synonymous with professionalism. As one of the first great women directors, her pioneering influence will continue to be felt for generations to come, and she will always be remembered for that unique quality she offered on screen — that special shimmer in her eye, the brusque quality of her speech, and the hint of intensity that let her audience know that she was giving them her all.

Film Noir Filmography

HIGH SIERRA   *Director:* Raoul Walsh. *Producer:* Hal B. Wallis. Released by Warner Bros., January 1941. *Running time:* 100 minutes. *Cast:* Humphrey Bogart, Ida Lupino, Alan Curtis, Arthur Kennedy, Joan Leslie, Henry Hull, Barton MacLane, Henry Travers, Elisabeth Risdon, Cornel Wilde.

ROAD HOUSE   *Director:* Jean Negulesco. *Producer:* Edward Chodorov. Released by 20th Century–Fox, November 1948. *Running time:* 95 minutes. *Cast:* Ida Lupino, Cornel Wilde, Celeste Holm, Richard Widmark, O.Z. Whitehead, Robert Karnes.

ON DANGEROUS GROUND   *Director:* Nicholas Ray. *Producer:* John Houseman. Released by RKO, February 1952. *Running time:* 82 minutes. *Cast:* Ida Lupino, Robert Ryan, Ward Bond, Charles Kemper, Anthony Ross, Ed Begley, Ian Wolfe, Sumner Williams.

BEWARE, MY LOVELY   *Director:* Harry Horner. *Producer:* Collier Young. Released by RKO, August 1952. *Running time:* 76 minutes. *Cast:* Ida Lupino, Robert Ryan, Taylor Holmes, Barbara Whiting, James Williams, O.Z. Whitehead.

PRIVATE HELL 36   *Director:* Don Siegel. *Producer:* Collier Young. Released by Filmakers, September 1954. *Running time:* 81 minutes. *Cast:* Ida Lupino, Steve Cochran, Howard Duff, Dean Jagger, Dorothy Malone.

THE BIG KNIFE   *Director and Producer:* Robert Aldrich. Released by United Artists, November 1955. *Running time:* 111 minutes. *Cast:* Jack Palance, Ida Lupino, Wendell Corey, Rod Steiger, Jean Hagen, Shelley Winters, Ilka Chase, Everett Sloane, Wesley Addy, Paul Langton.

WHILE THE CITY SLEEPS   *Director:* Fritz Lang. *Producer:* Bert Friedlob. Released by RKO, May 1956. *Running time:* 99 minutes. *Cast:* Dana Andrews, Rhonda Fleming, George Sanders, Howard Duff, Thomas Mitchell, Vincent Price, Sally Forrest, John Barrymore, Jr., James Craig, Ida Lupino.

References

"Catching Up with Ida Lupino." *Modern Screen*, November 1972.

Crichton, Kyle. "Career Girl." *Collier's*, June 26, 1937.

"Director Only?" *Films and Filming*, January 1955.

Dixon, Wheeler Winston. "Ida Lupino: Director." *Classic Images*, February 1996.

Donati, William. *Ida Lupino: A Biography*. Lexington, Ky.: The University Press of Kentucky, 1996.

"A Fourth for TV." *TV Guide*, December 3, 1955.

Graham, Sheilah. "Duff-Lupino: Cast Subject to Change Without Notice." *Sheilah Graham's Hollywood Romances*, 1954.

Hall, Gladys. "Ida Lupino." *Motion Picture*, November 1937.

_____. "Ida Lupino Reads Her Tea Leaves." *Silver Screen*, November 1945.

Hayward, Louis, as told to Jack Holland. "What Divorce Has Taught Me." *Motion Picture*, October 1945.

"How Mr. and Mrs. Hayward Live." *Photoplay*, December 1941.

Kelly, Bill. "Ida Lupino: Gem of the Emerald Isle." *Hollywood Studio Magazine*, February 1983.

Lupino, Ida. "Me, Mother Directress." *Action*, May-June 1967.

_____. "My Fight for Life." *Photoplay*, February 1946.

_____. "New Faces in New Places." *Films in Review*, December 1950.

Minoff, Philip. "Non-Private Lives?" *Cue*, January 19, 1957.

"Mr. Duff and Ida." *TV Guide*, June 1, 1957.

"Mother Lupino." *Time*, February 8, 1963.

Natale, Richard. "Lupino Dies at 77." *Variety*, August 7, 1995.

"A New Twist." *TV Guide*, July 13, 1957.

Vermilye, Jerry. "Ida Lupino." *Films in Review*, May 1959.

Waterbury, Ruth. "Home of Ida Lupino." *Photoplay*, February 1949.

"What Directors Are Saying." *Action*, September-October 1969.

Dorothy Malone

While Dorothy Malone spent years languishing in lightweight "pretty girl" roles, she would ultimately prove beyond all doubt that she possessed a dramatic talent to be reckoned with. Along the way, she experienced numerous peaks and valleys, both professionally and personally, from winning an Academy Award to experiencing a literally heart-stopping brush with death. And while she never reached the heights that her acting abilities merited, Malone more than held her own with such highly touted stars as Humphrey Bogart, James Cagney, Rock Hudson and Frank Sinatra, and earned a new generation of fans through her starring role on TV's popular nighttime soaper *Peyton Place*. With her sensuous, full lips and come-hither gaze, Malone was a natural for film noir, and appeared in six pictures from this era: *The Big Sleep* (1946), *Convicted* (1950), *The Killer That Stalked New York* (1950), *Loophole* (1954), *Pushover* (1954) and *Private Hell 36* (1954).

The star of film and television was born Dorothy Eloise Maloney on January 30, 1925, in Chicago, Illinois, the oldest of three children and the only girl. (Her youngest brother Will would die in 1955 at the age of 16, after being struck by lightning.) Before Dorothy was a year old, her family moved from the "Windy City" when her father was transferred to Southern Bell Telephone in Dallas, Texas. There, Dorothy began participating in dancing classes at the age of three, and perhaps received her first taste of the spotlight when she served as Queen of the May at the Ursuline Convent school when she was eight.

Showing her versatility early on, Dorothy modeled clothes for Neiman-Marcus, won prizes for the showing and handling of dogs and performed in a variety of school plays. She was also class president for six successive years and, based on her high academic scores, served as salutatorian at her eighth grade graduation. At Highland Park High School, Dorothy added to her list of accomplishments, winning awards for her athletic activities. She served as parliamentarian of the student council and vice-president of the school chapter of the National Honor Society, and for two years she was selected as best actress in an area competition. "School was fun," the actress would say years later. "Those blue ribbons I won for swimming and horsemanship were fun, even grades were fun."

After earning scholarships to five Eastern girls' colleges and one midwestern college, Dorothy chose to continue her education at a local school, the Hockaday School for Girls, and later attended Southern Methodist University, where she majored in languages and minored in drama. While there, Dorothy won the lead in a school play, *Starbound*, in which she portrayed a star-struck girl living in a Hollywood boarding house, awaiting her big break. It was a role that would soon mirror Dorothy's own life. While appearing in the production, she was spotted by Edward Rubin, a talent scout for RKO Studios, who gave Dorothy a screen test in her mother's living room. A short time later, Dorothy was on her way to Hollywood. She was 18 years old.

After signing a term contract with RKO, Dorothy moved into the

Hollywood Studio Club, a rooming house for young film hopefuls, much like the one occupied by her character in *Starbound*. For the next year, the brown-haired beauty spent most of her time studying dancing and diction, but she failed to log any screen time. Finally, in 1943, she was cast in an unbilled role in her debut film, *The Falcon and the Co-Eds*, and the following year was assigned bit parts in *Show Business* (1944) starring Eddie Cantor, *Seven Days Ashore* (1944), a musical comedy featuring a cast of virtual unknowns, and *Youth Runs Wild* (1944), a preachy melodrama about the evils of juvenile delinquency. On loan-out to Columbia Studios, she was billed for the first time (using her real name of Dorothy Maloney) in *One Mysterious Night* (1944), the fifth episode in the long-running Boston Blackie series, starring Chester Morris.

After this film, Dorothy was released from her RKO contract, but fate stepped in when she portrayed a Spanish dancer in *Ladies Unmasked*, a showcase production at the Hollywood Studio Club. In the audience were a number of scouts and casting directors, including Solly Boiano of Warner Bros. Impressed by Dorothy's performance, Boiano arranged for a screen test, and just days later, the attractive starlet inked a five-year agreement with Warners. In her first assignment with her new studio (again billed under her real name), she appeared briefly in *Hollywood Canteen* (1944), joining a star-studded cast that included Bette Davis, Joan Crawford, Barbara Stanwyck, Ida Lupino, Eddie Cantor, Jack Benny and Jack Carson. It was for her sole screen appearance of 1945, *Too Young to Know*, that the fledgling actress finally dropped the "y" from her last name, becoming Dorothy Malone. Despite her name change, the actress failed to make much of an impact in this wearisome Joan Leslie starrer, nor did she fare much better as Robert Hutton's former flame in *Janie Gets Married* (1946), or as Cary Grant's sister in the musical biopic of Cole Porter, *Night and Day* (1946). But in her next screen appearance, *The Big Sleep* (1946), Malone caused critics and audiences alike to sit up and take notice.

This complex feature, Malone's first film noir, stars Humphrey Bogart as Phillip Marlowe, a private detective hired to identify the blackmailer of a wheelchair-bound invalid, Gen. Sternwood (Charles Waldron). Sternwood is the father of two girls, Carmen (Martha Vickers), a heavy-drinking nympho-maniac whose compromising photos are the basis of the blackmail, and her unflappable older sister, Vivian (Lauren Bacall), who falls in love with the hard-boiled detective. Despite being ordered off the investigation by the district attorney's office, and twice being beaten by thugs involved in the blackmail plot, Marlowe's quest leads him to a ruthless gambler, Eddie Mars (John Ridgely). In the film's dramatic climax, Marlowe forces a confession from Mars, then causes the gambler to be murdered by his own men.

Although Malone appeared in only one scene, she managed to attract attention with her portrayal of a brainy bookstore proprietess who changes from lackluster to gorgeous during a rainy afternoon with Marlowe. After being singled out by several critics, Malone was assigned to bigger — but not necessarily better — roles, starting with *To the Victor* (1948), a well-intentioned but contrived drama about an American black-marketeer who falls for the wife of an ex-collaborator. Malone followed this box office disappointment with *Two Guys from Texas* (1948), a formula musical starring Jack Carson and Dennis Morgan, and *One Sunday Afternoon* (1949), a Technicolor remake of the musical *The Strawberry Blonde* (1941), with Malone, Dennis Morgan, and Janis Paige assuming the roles played in the earlier version by Olivia de Havilland, James Cagney and Rita Hayworth. Both films were directed by Raoul Walsh, but the latter suffered in comparison. Next, Malone was featured in *Flaxy Martin* (1949), an entertaining gangster melodrama starring Virginia Mayo; *South of St. Louis* (1949), an action-packed adventure story set during the Civil War; and her last film under her Warners contract, *Colorado Territory* (1949), an effective remake of *High Sierra* (1941), starring Joel McCrea.

Throughout her years at Warners, Malone managed to participate in a variety of off-screen activities that were reminiscent of her busy elementary and high school years. On one occasion she was sent by the studio on a public relations tour to Mexico and on another, she was presented to the king and queen of England. After covering this event in a series of photographs for *Photoplay* magazine, the actress also visited Scotland, Wales, Paris and Switzerland, where her college studies came in handy during an interview by 14 French-speaking newsmen. And, as if these activities weren't time-consuming enough, Malone also found time to enroll in a number of classes at the University of Southern California.

Meanwhile, Malone turned to freelancing, appearing in Columbia's *The Nevadan* (1950), a better-than-average Western in which she was featured as the love interest of Randolph Scott, and *Convicted* (1950), her second film noir. This film stars Glenn Ford as Joe Hufford, a luckless brokerage firm employee whose fistfight inadvertently leads to the death of a prominent local boy. Although the district attorney, George Knowland (Broderick Crawford), sympathizes with Hufford, he is forced to prosecute and Joe is sentenced to prison. Three years later, Knowland is appointed as warden, and tries to make amends for his prosecution of Joe by making him the prison chauffeur. But when Joe refuses to implicate his cellmate, Malloby (Millard Mitchell), in the murder of a notorious prison stoolie, Knowland reluctantly places Joe in solitary confinement.

Taunted by a sadistic guard, Capt. Douglas (Carl Benton Reid), Joe maintains his silence, even though it causes him to be suspected of the murder. But Malloby later stabs Capt. Douglas and, before being gunned down by guards, he confesses to the murder of the stoolie. After Joe is released from solitary, Knowland uses his influence to gain Joe's parole and the convict is freed. As Knowland's level-headed daughter, Malone turned in an impressive performance, portraying a woman who is forced to mask her growing feelings for her father's imprisoned chauffeur. The reviewer for *Variety* stated that Malone "does well" in her role, and the would-be romance between Malone and Ford was praised in *Variety* for being "kept within believable bounds."

After *Convicted*, Malone went over to MGM for *Mrs. O'Malley and Mr. Malone* (1950), a top-notch comedy-thriller starring Marjorie Main and James Whitmore, then returned to Columbia for her third entry in the realm of noir, *The Killer That Stalked New York* (1950). As this thriller begins, Sheila Bennet (Evelyn Keyes) is seen returning to New York from Cuba, after stealing a cache of jewels and mailing them back home. Sheila is not only unaware that she is being tailed by a Treasury Department official, but she also unknowingly contracted the deadly smallpox virus. After reuniting with her husband Matt (Charles Korvin), Sheila infects several citizens with whom she comes in contact, including a train porter, a little girl and her husband's employer. When the stolen jewels arrive in the mail, Matt retrieves them and skips out on his wife as well as her sister, Francie (Lola Albright), with whom he was having an affair. Devastated by Matt's defection, Francie commits suicide and Sheila goes in search of him, vowing revenge.

With the number of smallpox cases increasing, health department officials institute a citywide vaccination effort and frantically hunt for the carrier of the disease. The health officials and Treasury Department authorities realize they are searching for the same woman, but shortly before they locate her, she catches up to Matt. Attempting to flee from a window, Matt falls to his death, and Sheila is apprehended. She later dies, but with the original carrier secured, the smallpox epidemic is restrained.

After playing the rather thankless role of a health department nurse in this film, Malone appeared in only two pictures in the next two years — *Saddle Legion* (1951), a fairly respectable horse opera, and *The Bushwackers* (1952), a simply constructed but well-acted Western in which she played the daughter of a newspaper publisher. Her shooting schedule picked up in 1953, however, when she was seen in four features: *Torpedo Alley*, portraying a nurse caught in a love triangle; *Scared Stiff*, a profitable but overly silly Dean Martin-Jerry Lewis romp; *Law and Order*, a bland Western starring Ronald Reagan; and *Jack Slade*, which told the highly fictionalized story of a real-life gunslinger. And the following year, the busiest of her screen career, Malone was seen in seven pictures, including three films noirs: *Loophole* (1954), *Pushover* (1954) and *Private Hell 36* (1954)

Malone's best role came in the first of these, *Loophole*, in which she plays the wife of a man wrongly suspected of theft. Described by one critic as a "mighty respectable little melodrama," this film begins as chief bank teller Michael Donovan (Barry Sullivan) discovers a cash shortage of $49,000, not realizing that his cage was robbed by a man posing as a bank examiner. Waiting two days to report the deficit, Donovan is instantly suspected by Gus Slavin (Charles McGraw), a former cop and an investigator with the bank's bonding company. Despite Slavin's bullying tactics, Donovan continues to maintain his innocence and even passes a lie detector test, but when the bonding company cancels his policy, his boss is forced to fire him.

Although police are convinced of Donovan's innocence, Slavin increases his harassment, causing Donovan to lose four successive jobs. Donovan and his steadfast wife Ruthie (Malone) are forced to sell their house, but Donovan is finally able to keep a job as a taxi cab driver. Meanwhile, during a chance encounter at a local bank, Donovan spots the real thief, an unassuming teller named Herman Tate (Don Beddoe). Donovan nearly captures Tate and his accomplice Vera (Mary Beth Hughes) at their apartment, but the couple escape and lure Donovan to a remote beach house. Vera shoots Donovan, but he manages to subdue them both until police arrive and is later reinstated at his bank job. After its release, *Loophole* was applauded in the *New York Times* for its taut direction and plausible screenplay and, along with costars Sullivan and McGraw, Malone was singled out for a "good performance [that blends] in the other ingredients into an enjoyable whole."

Malone's next film noir, *Pushover*, starred Fred MacMurray and Kim Novak (her film debut) in what one critic called "a mild facsimile" of MacMurray's *Double Indemnity* (1944). Here, as Paul Sheridan, MacMurray is a police detective who tries to locate a bank robber through his attractive moll, Lona McLane (Novak), but winds up falling in love with her instead. After Sheridan's initial contact with Lona, he engages in a round-the-clock stakeout of her apartment, along with coworkers Rick McAllister (Phil Carey) and Paddy Dolan (Allen Nourse). Lona later reveals her knowledge that Sheridan is a policeman, but surprises him with a proposal that they kill her boyfriend, Harry Wheeler (Paul Richards): "We could have that money Paul — you and I," she says. "Harry's going to die no matter what we do. So what difference will it make if he shows up and he's killed? Think what that money could mean to us, Paul — me and you."

Sheridan first declines Lona's offer, but his growing obsession with her causes him to agree, and he later kills Wheeler when he shows up at Lona's apartment. Sheridan's carefully planned scheme begins to unravel, however, and he is later forced to shoot Dolan, who had witnessed Wheeler's murder. Seen leaving Lona's apartment by her neighbor Ann (Malone), Sheridan attempts to flee by using Ann as a hostage, but he is later gunned down in the street, and as Lona emerges from hiding he plaintively remarks, "We didn't really need that money, did we?"

Although it suffered in comparison with *Double Indemnity*, *Pushover* was viewed as "creditable" in the *New York Times*, and praised in *Variety* as a melodrama that "holds up nicely." And Malone, along with several of her costars, was singled out for "providing competent support." She followed this feature with her third film noir of 1954, *Private Hell 36*.

This taut thriller focuses on the investigation into an unsolved bank robbery and murder in New York City that is revived a year later when a $50 bill from the $300,000 heist surfaces in Los Angeles. Two detectives, Cal Bruner (Steve Cochran) and Jack Farnham (Howard Duff), trace the bill to a nightclub singer, Lili Marlowe (Ida Lupino), who had received the money as a tip from a patron. Securing Lili's help in identifying the man, Bruner and Farnham finally locate him at a race track, but the man is killed after a chase when he drives his car over an embankment. The detectives find more than $200,000 in the dead man's car, and over Farnham's objections, Bruner pockets $80,000 and leaves it in a small trailer — Number 36 — in a nearby trailer park.

Citing Farnham's financial responsibilities for his wife (Malone) and small child, Bruner convinces his partner to keep quiet about the theft, and despite questioning by their superior, Capt. Michaels (Dean Jagger), the officers appear to have gotten away with their crime. But later, Bruner is contacted by a man claiming to the partner of the man killed in the car crash, who blackmails him into turning over the money. Farnham insists on giving up the cash, but when the detectives show up for the meeting with the blackmailer, Bruner shoots Farnham in the back. He in turn is fatally wounded by police, and Farnham learns that there never was an accomplice and that their superior had known all along of their theft.

Although it stands up today as a well-conceived tale of greed and murder, *Private Hell 36* opened to mediocre reviews, with the critic for *Variety* terming it good but "occasionally slow-paced," and Bosley Crowther of the *New York Times* finding it to be "just an average melodrama about cops." And for her incidental role as Farnham's understanding wife, Malone was barely mentioned.

Despite her busy film schedule, Malone found time for television work, appearing on *Lux Video Theatre, Dr. Kildare, Fireside Theatre, Dick Powell Theatre, The Jack Benny Show* and *The Untouchables.* By now, she had moved from studio starlet to a respected actress, delivering commendable performances in each of her varied roles. She continued this trend in her films of 1955, but often in such mediocre fare as *Five Guns West*, a so-so Western about a Confederate officer who leads a band of prisoners in their search for Union gold. At this point, Malone took matters into her own hands. She switched agents, lightened her hair to its current blonde, and scored a hit with an appearance in *Battle Cry* (1955), a predictable but highly entertaining war drama. Despite a large cast that included Van Heflin, Aldo Ray, Tab Hunter and Anne Francis, Malone was a standout, receiving the best reviews in the film. And Malone herself would later credit this film with serving as the turning point in her career: "Up until then I was only the sweet, girl-next-door type," she said. "When I changed hair color, I though I'd get some strange fan mail reaction. But strangely enough, I received only perfectly lovely letters."

Still, Malone's triumph was short-lived. After *Battle Cry*, her series of run-of-the-mill pictures continued with *Tall Man Riding*, a Randolph Scott

Dorothy Malone

starrer about a tough guy's vendetta against a cattle baron; *Sincerely Yours*, a box office bomb featuring Liberace as a concert pianist who loses his hearing; and *Pillars of the Sky* (1956), a dreary sagebrush actioner starring Jeff Chandler. But Malone's cinematic fortunes were about to change. Because of her outstanding turn in *Battle Cry*, she earned the role of a tortured nymphomaniac in Douglas Sirk's *Written on the Wind* (1956), a torrid tale of a high-powered Texas oil family starring Rock Hudson, Lauren Bacall and Robert Stack. Malone's sexy performance — which included a suggestive strip-tease — was the highlight of the film, earning her an Academy Award nomination for Best Supporting Actress. When the golden statuettes were handed out, Malone walked away with the top honors, beating out Mildred Dunnock in *Baby Doll*, Mercedes McCambridge in *Giant* and Patty McCormack and Eileen Heckart in *The Bad Seed*. It appeared that Dorothy Malone had finally arrived.

After appearing in RKO's *Tension at Table Rock* (1956), a moody Western that suffered from plodding direction and a hackneyed plot, Malone played another highly acclaimed role, as the mentally disturbed wife of James Cagney's Lon Chaney in *Man of a Thousand Faces* (1957). But it soon became apparent that Malone's Academy Award victory was not the career-booster that it should have been. She next starred in *Tip on a Dead Jockey* (1957), a disjointed smuggling yarn that suffered at the box office; *Quantez* (1957), an overly talky Western that was panned by one critic as "static, turgid claptrap"; and *The Tarnished Angels* (1957), which told the story of a romance between a reporter and the wife of an ex–World War I flying ace. In the latter film, producers attempted to capitalize on the success of *Written on the Wind* by reteaming Malone with costars Rock Hudson and Robert Stack, but the results were disastrous.

In Malone's sole feature of 1958, *Too Much, Too Soon*, she received the first top-billing of her career, but nearly every scene in this colorless biography of John Barrymore was stolen by costar Errol Flynn, and Malone was dismissed as "a winsome, earnest protagonist — but no Susan Hayward." After this box office disappointment, industry insiders began to speculate that Malone was incapable of carrying a successful film and that her few well-received pictures were merely flukes. But Malone seemed to take her less than consistent career path in stride: "Some of my parts have been good, some bad — the others we won't even mention," she said in *Photoplay* magazine. "I know now that it is my fate to take what comes along and not make myself miserable as a result. After I won my Academy Award, practically everyone advised me to now hold off. They enumerated the reasons why it was so important to go from one award picture to another, but how can you bank on a myth? You can't always judge a part in advance, so sometimes you must take on a part as a challenge."

Despite Malone's dauntless words, she would only make three movies in the next three years. Of these, the best was *Warlock* (1959), a dramatic, character-driven Western starring Henry Fonda and Richard Widmark. But her next feature, *The Last Voyage* (1960), was an overblown disaster saga set aboard a ship, and *The Last Sunset* (1961), despite a stellar cast that included Kirk Douglas and Joseph Cotten, turned out to be a routine Western that evoked only mild interest due to its theme of incest.

While Malone's career seemed to be suffering a rapid descent, she wasn't faring much better in her personal life. Throughout her years in Hollywood, she had been linked with a variety of notables, including Frank Sinatra, Tab Hunter, Scott Brady and producer Roger Corman. But while shooting on location in Hong Kong for *The Last Voyage*, Malone surprised the Hollywood community by marrying handsome French actor Jacques Bergerac, the ex-husband of

Ginger Rogers. Despite Bergerac's reputation as a ladies' man, Malone told the press that she was attracted to his gentle, soft-spoken demeanor, proclaiming him as "a man with that rare quality, the courage of his convictions." It seemed at first that the couple were ideally suited, and they appeared soon after their wedding in Malone's stage debut, *Once More with Feeling*, in Chicago. But the union (which produced two daughters, Mimi in 1960 and Diane in 1962) was a stormy one, and the actress later stated that Bergerac underwent a transformation after their marriage: "He went back to the old freedom-loving ways. After knowing so many winners, I picked a loser." In 1964, Malone sued for divorce and was granted custody of their children, but bitter court battles with Bergerac over visitation rights and child support would continue for several years to come.

Career-wise, Malone's next appearance was in *Beach Party* (1963), the first of the innocuous beach movie series starring Frankie Avalon and Annette Funicello. Playing the long-suffering girlfriend of a scientist observing teen sexual behavior, the nearly 40-year-old Malone still showed flashes of her earlier allure, but the demeaning role scarcely served to showcase the talents of the former Academy Award winner. But after an unbilled guest appearance in Fox's drama *Fate Is the Hunter* (1964), Malone's career took an unexpected upswing when she was given the lead role of Constance MacKenzie in ABC-TV's *Peyton Place*. The series, which costarred Mia Farrow, Ryan O'Neal and Barbara Parkins, was an instant hit and Malone was back on top again. "I loved the part of Constance when I first read it," she told *TV Guide*. "She's a full-blown woman, with conflicts and guilts, but trying to break out of her shell. I can put a lot into that." A year later, however, Malone suffered another crisis in her personal life. In the fall of 1965, she was rushed to the hospital and underwent more than seven hours of surgery to remove clots from blood vessel leading to her lungs. Several times during the grueling operation, Malone's heart stopped beating and, at one point, last rites were administered by a priest.

Luckily, Malone survived this brush with death and after several years of follow-up treatments, she was judged completely cured. After a lengthy absence, she resumed her role on *Peyton Place* but before long, she began complaining about her dissatisfaction with the series. "All I seem to do is wear dowdy clothes and sell books in my bookstore," she said. "I'd rather they'd kept me owning a dress shop, as first suggested. At least I'd get to wear exciting clothes." Finally, in 1968, Malone was written out of the show, after which she sued the show's producers for $1.6 million, claiming that her part had been diminished in an effort to coax her into quitting. Ultimately, an out-of-court settlement was reached. Shortly after the lawsuit was filed, a former coworker from *Peyton Place* told *Photoplay* magazine, "What people do not understand is that Dorothy is still a child. She is beautiful. She is highly intelligent. She has won fame and earned a tremendous amount — but she has not grown up."

After leaving *Peyton Place*, Malone returned with her daughters to her childhood home; "I went away desperate for peace of mind," she said later. "When I went to Dallas, I never gave a thought to whether I'd ever come back to pictures or not. I felt friendless and alone." For a time, Malone worked in the real estate field, then returned to performing, first in an Italian film, and next in *The Pigeon*, an Aaron Spelling movie for ABC-TV. On the set of *The Pigeon*, Malone was introduced to New York businessman Robert Tomarkin, who immediately invited the actress to lunch. "He's a darling. A dear person, a real person, not a personality boy, which may seem unusual for me, I know," Malone said. "Outspoken, but serious and sensitive." Just three weeks later, on April 3, 1969, Malone and Tomarkin were married at the Silver Bell Wedding Chapel in Las Vegas, and the actress appeared to have found the contentment she had so desperately sought. "Two people in love is what life's all about," she told reporters. "Dear people are hard to come by and life is short. I never dreamed this could happen to me. I usually ponder and ponder every decision and give myself time, but I've discovered you don't need time to fall in love. You can know how you feel in one instant."

But Malone would come to regret her impulsiveness. Just weeks after her elopement, the actress filed for an annulment, claiming that Tomarkin had tried to bilk her out of her savings. (Several years later, Tomarkin would be sent to prison for 40 months for his involvement in a scheme to cheat a New York bank out of $2 million.) And two years later, Malone's spate of bad luck continued when she married Huston Bell, a Dallas motel chain executive. At the start of their relationship, Malone again appeared to have at last found her ideal man, telling *Photoplay* magazine, "He has all the qualities. He reminds me of every boy I was ever crazy about, and yet he's different, himself, a unique character with a fabulous brain. And he's so trustworthy. When he says he'll do it, it's done." The two were married in a garden ceremony with a guest list that included such Hollywood notables as Frank Sinatra, Oscar Levant, Jim Nabors, *Peyton Place*'s Ed Nelson, Helen Morgan and Malone's long-time former beau, Scott Brady. But this union, too, would not last. "He never loved me," Malone told a reporter in 1976. "He didn't marry me for love but for what I could do for him. For the first time in my life, I'm completely free of serious emotional ties to any man. I must say it's kind of peaceful."

Professionally, Malone returned to the big screen in *Carnal Circuit*, a low-budget affair starring John Ireland that was filmed in 1970 but received only scant release in 1974. She also appeared in *The Man Who Would Not Die* (1974), a confusing mystery with Aldo Ray and Keenan Wynn, and *Abduction* (1975), a dreadful would-be thriller in which Malone portrayed the mother of a kidnap victim. But her career received a boost in 1976 when she played the wife of Van Johnson in the highly acclaimed ABC-TV mini-series, *Rich Man, Poor Man*. "I've always liked Van Johnson," Malone said during production. "When I first came out here, he was the one movie star I wanted to meet. The other day, when we played a scene together, I told him, 'You know, this is a lifelong dream for me.'"

Although she has continued to live in Dallas, Malone has made several television and feature film appearances in the last two decades, including two made-for-television movies in which she reprised her Constance MacKenzie character, *Murder in Peyton Place* (1977) and *Peyton Place: The Next Generation* (1985). Of her big screen features, the best was *Winter Kills* (1979), an interesting political thriller with an all-star cast that included Jeff Bridges, John Huston, Anthony Perkins, Sterling Hayden, Elizabeth Taylor and Eli Wallach. And in her most recent feature film role to date, Malone had a surprise cameo appearance in *Basic Instinct* (1992), a box office hit starring Michael Douglas and Sharon Stone.

Although Malone suffered through setbacks and disappointments both on and off the screen, she has proven to be a survivor. During her heyday in the 1940s and 1950s, she consistently exhibited her depth as a performer and her ability to breathe a spark of life into even the dreariest Hollywood projects. While her Academy Award triumph seemed to serve as more of a jinx than a boon to Malone's career, the strong-willed actress has appeared in recent years to view her career with philosophical bemusement: "People think if you win an Oscar you're set for life on Easy Street. Forget it. Fame is a kick, but it's fleeting."

Film Noir Filmography

THE BIG SLEEP   *Director and Producer:* Howard Hawks. Released by Warner Bros., August 1946. *Running time:* 118 minutes. *Cast:* Humphrey Bogart, Lauren Bacall, John Ridgely, Martha Vickers, Dorothy Malone, Patricia Clarke, Regis Toomey.

CONVICTED   *Director:* Henry Levin. *Producer:* Jerry Bresler. Released by Columbia, August 1950. *Running time:* 91 minutes. *Cast:* Glenn Ford, Broderick Crawford, Millard Mitchell, Dorothy Malone, Carl Benton Reid, Frank Faylen, Will Geer.

THE KILLER THAT STALKED NEW YORK   *Director:* Earl McEvoy. *Producer:* Robert Cohn. Released by Columbia, January 1951. *Running time:* 79 minutes. *Cast:* Evelyn Keyes, Charles Korvin, William Bishop, Dorothy Malone, Lola Albright, Barry Kelley, Carl Benton Reid.

LOOPHOLE   *Director:* Harold Schuster. *Producer:* Lindsley Parsons. Released by Allied Artists, March 12, 1954. *Running time:* 79 minutes. *Cast:* Barry Sullivan, Charles McGraw, Dorothy Malone, Don Haggerty, Mary Beth Hughes, Don Beddoe.

PUSHOVER   *Director:* Richard Quine. *Producer:* Jules Schermer. Released by Columbia, July 1954. *Running time:* 88 minutes. *Cast:* Fred MacMurray, Kim Novak, Phil Carey, Dorothy Malone, E.G. Marshall, Allen Nourse.

PRIVATE HELL 36   *Director:* Don Siegel. *Producer:* Collier Young. Released by Filmakers, September 1954. *Running time:* 81 minutes. *Cast:* Ida Lupino, Steve Cochran, Howard Duff, Dean Jagger, Dorothy Malone.

References

Andrews, Phillip. "It Took So Long to Say I Love You." *Photoplay*, January 1972.
Biography of Dorothy Malone. Paramount Studios, March 1955.
"Catching Up with Dorothy Malone." *Modern Screen*, February 1976.
Dern, Marian. "Her Address Is Peyton Place." *TV Guide*, March 20, 1965.
Hall, Gladys. "What Really Goes On with Scott Brady and Dorothy Malone." *Photoplay*, August 1952.
"Hollywood's Strangest Divorce." *Photoplay*, February 1965.
Houser, Mervin. Biography of Dorothy Malone. RKO Radio Studios, circa 1956.
"How I Told My Children About My Divorce." *Photoplay*, October 1972.
Parish, James Robert, Jr. "Dorothy Malone." *Film Fan Monthly*, July-August, 1968.
Posner, Carl. "The Strange Case of Dorothy Malone." *Photoplay*, January 1958.
Riley, Nadia. "Six Days Later, I Said Yes!" *Photoplay*, July 1969.
Samuels, Charles. "Stars of Tomorrow." *Motion Picture*, March 1945.
Scott, Brooke. "How Dorothy Malone Lost All Her Money and the One Man She Loved." *Photoplay*, January 1969.
Waterbury, Ruth. "How She Lost Her Man." *Photoplay*, January 1969.
"Who Is Dorothy Malone?" *Photoplay*, July 1957.

Marilyn Monroe

There are few stars whose fame grants them recognition by their first name only — Marilyn is one. Renowned for her steamy sexuality, reported relationships with John and Robert Kennedy, battles with drugs and alcohol, and her mysterious death, Marilyn Monroe was a true love goddess whose acting ability took a back seat to her celebrity. Still, she demonstrated a distinct flair for comedy in such vehicles as *How to Marry a Millionaire* (1953) and *Some Like It Hot* (1959), and showed a dramatic prowess as well in four films noirs: *The Asphalt Jungle* (1950), *Clash by Night* (1952), *Don't Bother to Knock* (1952) and *Niagara* (1953).

Marilyn Monroe was born Norma Jeane Baker on June 1, 1926, in Los Angeles, California. (The baby's first name was taken from Norma Talmadge, one of the Talmadge sisters of silent film fame.) Her mother Gladys was a film cutter, but there is some question as to the identity of the baby's father; some sources report that he was Martin Edward Mortenson, Gladys's second husband, while others believe that Norma Jeane was fathered by C. Stanley Gifford, a coworker of Gladys's with whom she was having an affair. Like many other facets of Marilyn Monroe's life, the truth will, in all probability, never be known.

Shortly after Norma Jeane's birth, Gladys returned to her job at Consolidated Film Industries, leaving her infant daughter in the care of mail carrier Albert Wayne Bolender and his wife Ida, who lived in Hawthorne, California. The devoutly religious couple became Norma Jeane's foster parents and cared for her for the next seven years, receiving the sum of five dollars a week from Gladys.

Although Gladys — whose family had a history of mental illness — had been plagued for years with bouts with depression, she reclaimed her child in 1933, and she and Norma Jeane moved to a small bungalow in Hollywood. Gladys rented the house to a British couple and leased two rooms from the couple for Norma Jeane and herself. But their stay would not be a happy one. Over the next year, Gladys's depression escalated, and in January 1934, she was committed to Norwalk State Hospital. This action would lead to years of instability in Norma Jeane's life. Grace McKee, a friend of Gladys's, was named Norma Jeane's guardian, but because Grace was unmarried, Norma Jeane remained in the care of the British couple for more than a year. When the couple left the country, Norma Jeane was taken into the home of Harvey Giffen and his wife, who were neighbors of Grace McKee's. Although the Giffens later expressed an interest in adopting Norma Jeane, Gladys would not allow it.

In September 1935, Norma Jeane was placed in the Los Angeles Orphans' Home Society, where she remained until June 1937, then lived in several foster homes — some sources say as many as 12. Meanwhile, Grace McKee married Doc Goddard, a research engineer, and the couple took Norma Jeane into their home in 1938. For a time, it appeared that Norma Jeane's unsettled life would finally be stabilized. She was greatly influenced by Grace's aunt Ana

Lower, whom the actress would later call "the first person in the world I ever really loved."

Norma Jeane enrolled in Emerson Junior High School, and later attended Van Nuys High School. But she would not graduate. In 1942, Doc and Grace Goddard decided to move to the East Coast and, not wishing to take Norma Jeane along, encouraged her budding relationship with Jim Dougherty, a 22-year-old neighbor. In June 1942, Jim and Norma Jeane were married, less than three weeks after her 16th birthday, and although the actress later claimed that the marriage was one of convenience, Jim insisted that the two were in love: "Our marriage may have been made in some place short of heaven ... but there was no pretense in how Norma Jeane and I felt about each other once we'd formed that partnership."

In 1943, Dougherty joined the Merchant Marines. The following year, he was called overseas, and his pretty young wife began working at Radio Plane Company, a plant that made aircraft for target practice. It was this job, inspecting parachutes and spraying fuselages, that would lead to Norma Jeane's first big break. She was spotted in 1944 by David Conover, an army photographer, who was visiting the plant to take pictures for *Yank* magazine of women engaged in war work. Conover later said that Norma Jeane's "eyes held something that touched and intrigued me" and he offered her five dollars an hour for further freelance work. Her photos were shown by a friend of Conover's to Emmeline Snively, head of the Blue Book Model Agency, who convinced Norma Jeane that she was wasting her time and talents working in the defense plant. Norma Jeane signed with the agency in 1945 and was soon one of the studio's busiest models, appearing on the covers of such men's magazines as *Pic, Laff, Salute* and *Sir*. A short time later, she quit her job at Radio Plane.

But although her newfound career was in full swing, Norma Jeane's marriage was deteriorating and she filed for divorce on July 5, 1946. Soon afterward, Norma Jeane had her dark blonde hair lightened and moved into the Studio Club, a residential hotel for struggling actresses. In mid–July, she took her first step toward fame by going to the office of Ben Lyon, head of new talent at 20th Century–Fox.

Immediately struck by the young woman's vibrant beauty, Lyon arranged for a color screen test of Norma Jeane which, he said, "lived up to everything I had hoped." Leon Shamroy, the cinematographer who shot the test, was even more effusive in his praise, stating, "This girl had something I hadn't seen since silent pictures. She had a kind of fantastic beauty like Gloria Swanson, when a movie star had to look beautiful, and she got sex on a piece of film like Jean Harlow." Lyon offered her a contract and renamed her Marilyn, after 1920s Broadway star Marilyn Miller. The new starlet took her last name from her grandmother, Della Monroe Grainger, and, at the age of 20, Marilyn Monroe was "born."

Like most contract players, Monroe spent her early days at the studio posing for publicity photos (including one in a potato sack!) and taking part in voice, drama and body movement classes. After six months, she was given a small part in *Scudda Hoo! Scudda Hay!* (1948), starring June Haver, but the studio pronounced her "unphotogenic," and most of her scenes ended up on the proverbial cutting room floor. Monroe was next given the role of a wait-ress in the all-but-forgotten *Dangerous Years* (1947) starring Billy Halop, a former Dead End Kid. By the time the film was released, Monroe had been unceremoniously dropped from her contract at Fox.

Monroe went on unemployment insurance, resumed her modeling activ-ities and enrolled at the Actor's Laboratory, a spin-off of the New York–based Group Theater acting ensemble. Later that year, she won her first stage role in *Glamour Preferred*, a comedy in which she played the second lead. Shortly afterward, she got her screen career back on track when she was given a con-tract at Columbia Pictures (some say, due to the efforts of Fox executive Joseph Schenck, whom Marilyn had met in early 1947, and with whom she may have had a sexual relationship).

Monroe's first screen role at Columbia was in *Ladies of the Chorus* (1948), a musical starring Adele Jergens and Rand Brooks (best known for his role as Scarlett O'Hara's hapless first husband in *Gone with the Wind*). In an effort to polish Monroe's limited acting abilities, the studio's talent chief assigned her to work with Natasha Lytess, the head drama coach at Columbia. A refugee from Nazi Germany, Lytess later recalled her first impression of Monroe: "[She was] totally unsure of herself ... she was inhibited and cramped; she could not say a word freely." Similarly, actress Shelley Winters, with whom Monroe would share an apartment in 1951, stated that the budding star had "very lit-tle self-worth. She didn't trust that she could do something by herself. And so very early in her career, she began to get coaches." Lytess soon became a central — and controversial — presence in Monroe's life.

Ladies of the Chorus was not much of a movie, but Monroe was noticed by Tibor Krekes of *Motion Picture Herald*, who called her "one of the brightest spots ... she is pretty, and with her pleasing voice and style, shows promise." But this promise would not be realized for two more years. She was dropped from her Columbia contract, and had a role in the Marx Brothers vehicle *Love Happy* (1949), which amounted to approximately one minute of screen time. (Her appearance in this film, however, did lead to the brief label of the "Mmmm Girl," so-called because in Detroit, where a sneak preview of *Love Happy* was being held, some of the people in the crowd couldn't whistle, so they said, "Mmmm.") She also appeared in *A Ticket to Tomahawk* (1950) starring Dan Dailey and Anne Baxter, but the role did little to advance her stalled career.

However, Monroe received a significant boost from Johnny Hyde, one of the nation's most influential agents, who was impressed by her brief appear-ance in *Love Happy* and took her on as a client. He also fell in love with her, left his wife of 20 years and their four sons, and moved out of the family home.

Hyde and Natasha Lytess clashed almost immediately, with Lytess bitterly declaring, "It was Johnny who broke the rules, by falling in love at the age of 53 with a girl ... who did not love him and never could." The one-sided nature of the affair notwithstanding, Hyde began an intense campaign to promote Monroe's career. He arranged for cosmetic surgery to remove two blemishes from her chin, hired hairdressers to regularly bleach her hair, bought her gowns and shoes from Saks Fifth Avenue in Beverly Hills, and escorted her to numerous events where she could be seen by Hollywood's most influential luminaries. Hyde's efforts proved to be successful when Monroe won her breakthrough role as Angela Phinlay, a corrupt lawyer's mistress in the film noir classic *The Asphalt Jungle* (1950), directed by John Huston. Despite Hyde's influence, however, Huston insisted that Monroe won her role "because she was damned good."

The Asphalt Jungle tells the story of Doc Riedenschneider (Sam Jaffe), an aging criminal who masterminds a sophisticated jewel robbery with the financial assistance of a crooked attorney, Alonzo Emmerich (Louis Calhern). To carry out the crime, Doc assembles a group of local hoods including Dix Handley (Sterling Hayden), a trigger-happy hooligan who longs to return to the Kentucky horse farm where he grew up, Gus Minissi (James Whitmore), a sensitive hunchback who specializes in driving the getaway car in petty crimes, and Louie Ciavelli (Anthony Caruso), a safecracker whose conversation generally focuses on the antics of his infant daughter. Despite careful planning, Doc's intricate scheme fails due to a series of ill-fated circumstances, including Emmerich's plan to double-cross Doc and his gang, and Louie's death after being shot by a misfired gun.

When Emmerich's plot is uncovered, he is confronted by Doc and Dix, who kills a private detective that the lawyer hired to sabotage the fencing operation. In the exchange of gunfire, Dix is wounded, and he and Doc briefly hide out at the home of Dix's would-be girlfriend, Doll (Jean Hagen). Doc is later apprehended by police when he makes the mistake of stopping at a local café to watch a young girl dance. Though Dix manages to drive to Kentucky, he dies there in a farm field, surrounded by the horses he loved.

As Emmerich's mistress, Monroe was featured in the small but showy role of a childlike woman whose innocent sexuality is best revealed when she discusses a planned trip to Cuba: "Imagine me on this beach here in my green bathing suit.... Run for your lives, girls, the fleet's in! Yipes!" Of her performance, the critic for *The People* rightly proclaimed, "Marilyn Monroe would fetch the wolves out of any jungle, asphalt or otherwise." In March 1950, primarily due to Hyde's efforts, 20th Century–Fox re-signed Monroe to a seven-year contract, starting at $500 a week. Her first role under the new agreement was a minor part in *All About Eve* (1950), a highly acclaimed drama starring Bette Davis. Monroe appeared as Miss Caswell, the dimwitted mistress of a theater critic and "a graduate of the Copacabana School of Dramatic Art." Although she appeared with such standouts as Davis, Anne Baxter, George

Marilyn Monroe

Sanders and Gregory Ratoff, Monroe more than held her own during her brief screen time. But it may have been during the filming of *All About Eve* that Monroe first began to exhibit the habit for tardiness that would soon become a familiar trait. (Years later, the actress would blithely explain: "It's not really me that's late. It's the others who are in such a hurry.")

Sadly, the man who had such influence over Monroe's career did not have long to live. In December 1950, after a series of heart attacks, Johnny Hyde died in Cedars of Lebanon Hospital, with Monroe at his side. Several days after his funeral, Monroe reportedly attempted suicide and was found by Lytess, who saved her by extracting a wad of undissolved sleeping pills from her mouth.

During the next two years, Monroe appeared in six forgettable films, including *Right Cross* (1950), in an unbilled part as Dick Powell's nightclub date; *The Fireball* (1950), as one of Mickey Rooney's rollerskating groupies; and *Let's Make It Legal* (1951), a weak comedy starring Claudette Colbert. However, her first film of 1952, and her second film noir, *Clash by Night*, offered Monroe her most significant role to date.

Clash by Night is only one of a handful of films noirs that does not involve a crime of violence; it is, however, infused with a typically noir sense of fatalism and doom. As the film opens, Mae Doyle (Barbara Stanwyck) is returning to her home town of Monterey, California, after a long absence. She attracts the attentions of Jerry D'Amato (Paul Douglas), a rugged, honest fisherman she knew in her youth, and Earl Pfeiffer (Robert Ryan), Jerry's cynical friend, who works as a film projectionist. Other characters in this drama include Vince (J. Carrol Naish), Jerry's vagabond uncle, and Peggy (Monroe), who is engaged to Mae's brother, but is unsatisfied with her job in a fish cannery and longs for the exciting life that she believes that Mae led during her years away from home. Despite her independent, outspoken nature, however, Peggy later allows herself to be tamed: "Joe came to the house and was going to kick the door down," she tells Mae. "I never thought I'd like a guy that pushed me around."

Although Mae is drawn to Earl, she decides to marry the stable but unexciting Jerry, and later gives birth to a baby girl. But over time, she grows bored with her life of domesticity and begins an affair with Earl. When Jerry discovers Mae's plan to leave him, he takes his infant daughter and hides her away from Mae aboard his boat. But Mae soon realizes that she cannot sustain a meaningful relationship with the caustic and selfish Earl, and returns home to her family.

Although many reviewers hailed Monroe's performance in *Clash by Night* (with Alton Cook of *The New York World Telegram and Sun* calling her a "gifted new star, worthy of all that fantastic press pageantry"), she did not have an easy time on the set. She was visibly nervous in the company of such accomplished actors, and flubbed so many lines that numerous retakes were required. For a time, Natasha Lytess was allowed to coach Monroe on the set, but she was ejected by director Fritz Lang when it was discovered that she was actually directing the budding star from the sidelines. And costar Barbara Stanwyck later noted Monroe's growing habit for tardiness: "She couldn't get out of her own way. She wasn't disciplined, and she was often late, and she drove Bob Ryan, Paul Douglas and myself out of our minds." Despite these difficulties, the film resulted in Monroe's most favorable exposure to date, and she later won the 1952 *Look* Magazine Achievement Award for Most Promising Female Newcomer.

Several months after production ended on *Clash by Night*, it was revealed that Monroe had posed nude for a calendar in 1949. The press went wild over the story. In an effort to diffuse the scandal, Monroe admitted that she'd posed for the photos, but claimed she had done so because she had no money to pay the rent. Her explanation resulted in a surge of public sympathy, her career received an unlikely boost, and pictures from the famous calendar are still being sold today.

After *Clash by Night*, Monroe appeared in *We're Not Married* (1952), a lightweight comedy about five couples who discover that their marriages are invalid. Monroe was chiefly noted for her striking appearance — Otis L. Guernsey, Jr., of the *New York Herald Tribune* wrote that she "looks as though she had been carved out of cake by Michelangelo." And next, in her third film noir, *Don't Bother to Knock* (1952), Monroe was given her first starring role.

A dark film focusing on mental illness, *Don't Bother to Knock* tells the story of Nell Forbes (Monroe), who had attempted suicide following the death of her lover in a plane crash. Nell's uncle Eddie (Elisha Cook, Jr.) arranges a baby-sitting job for her in the hotel where he works as an elevator operator, and when the child's parents leave for a hotel banquet, Nell passes the time by dressing up in the woman's jewelry and negligee. As she waltzes around the room in her finery, she is spotted by Jed (Richard Widmark), a hotel guest across the courtyard who has just been dumped by his girlfriend Lyn (Anne Bancroft, in her film debut). Jed invites himself — and a bottle of booze — to Nell's room, soon discovering that she is not a vacationing socialite, but a baby-sitter with scars on her wrists.

Nell, growing increasingly distressed, confuses Jed with her dead lover, and accuses her charge, Bunny, of coming between them. Jed later sneaks out of the room, but the situation spirals out of control when the girl's mother returns to check on her child, only to find that Nell has bound and gagged her in the bedroom. Nell and the girl's mother struggle, and Nell wanders, dazed, to the lobby, asking the elevator operator to "tell them I didn't mean it." She buys a razor blade from the hotel counter, but is cornered by hotel employees. Jed and Lyn make their way through the crowd and convince Nell to surrender to police. As the film ends, Jed's experience with Nell has transformed him from a selfish cad to a compassionate soul, and he and Lyn are reunited.

Although Monroe offered an impressive portrait of a woman consumed by madness, the reviews for *Don't Bother to Knock* were mixed. The *Los Angeles Times* critic claimed that Monroe's portrayal was "reinforced by virtually no acting resources whatsoever," and Bosley Crowther wrote in the *New York Times*: "All the equipment that Miss Monroe has to handle the job are a childishly blank expression and a provokingly feeble, hollow voice." However, a handful of critics felt that Monroe gave a top-notch performance, and she was cited in *Variety* for giving an "excellent account of herself in a strictly dramatic role which commands certain attention." Monroe was also commended by

Bancroft, who stated that her experience with the actress was "one of those very few times in all my experiences in Hollywood, when I felt that give and take — that can only happen when you are working with good actors."

Monroe's next two films, *Monkey Business* (1952), in which she played a sexy secretary, and *O. Henry's Full House* (1952), with Monroe in a bit part as a prostitute, did little to further her burgeoning career. But with the release of her fourth and final film noir, *Niagara* (1953), her fame was secured.

As *Niagara* begins, Ray and Polly Cutler (Casey Adams and Jean Peters) are arriving in Niagara Falls for a belated honeymoon. Once there, the couple encounter George Loomis (Joseph Cotten), a brooding, unstable man, and his beautiful young wife, Rose (Monroe). Rose's obvious contempt for her husband is shown early in the film when she feigns sleep as he approaches her bed, flashing a disdainful smile when he reluctantly retires for the night.

While on a sightseeing jaunt to the Falls, Polly spots Rose kissing another man, and it is revealed that Rose and her lover are planning to murder George. Later, when George is reported missing, Rose is called to the morgue to identify his body, but she faints when she discovers that the dead man is her lover. Meanwhile, Polly discovers that George is still alive, and realizes that he intends to murder Rose. She warns police, but she is too late — George hunts Rose down and strangles her with her scarf. Fleeing from police, George steals a boat, not knowing that Polly is aboard. When the boat runs out of gas, it is caught by the churning waters that lead to the Falls. George manages to help Polly to safety, moments before he plummets over the Falls to his death.

After the release of *Niagara*, Monroe skyrocketed to superstardom. Although critics varied in their view of the film, most agreed about Monroe's impact on screen. While the *New York Times'* critic acknowledged that "perhaps Miss Monroe is not the perfect actress at this point," he also noted that the film's producers "have caught every possible curve in both the intimacy of the boudoir and in equally revealing tight dresses. And they have illustrated pretty concretely that she can be seductive — even when she walks." And Ruth Waterbury gushed in the *Los Angeles Examiner*: "Here is the greatest natural star since Jean Harlow. She has more intelligence than Harlow. She out-lures Lana. She makes any other glamour girl you care to name look house-wifely."

Monroe's fame continued to soar with her return to comedy in *Gentlemen Prefer Blondes* (1953), a musical with Jane Russell. After its release, she was invited, along with Russell, to place her handprints and footprints in the forecourt at Grauman's (now Mann's) Chinese Theater in Hollywood. Reportedly, Monroe initially suggested that she leave an imprint of her rear, rather than her hands and feet, but this idea was vetoed. Instead, she used a rhinestone to dot the "i" in her name, but the stone was later pried out by an overexuberant fan and replaced with white frosted glass. According to columnist Sidney Skolsky, the actress waited two days and nights for her prints to dry, then "around two A.M., Marilyn got out of her brass bed, walked from her apartment, and, with no one watching her, she stood in her footprints — alone. It was like hearing all the applause in the world."

Her successful turn in *Gentleman* was followed by *How to Marry a Millionaire* (1953), in which Monroe all but stole the picture from her costars Lauren Bacall and Betty Grable. But Monroe took a slight career misstep with her dramatic turn in *River of No Return* (1954), a rather tedious Western that Monroe herself later called a "Z cowboy movie in which the acting finishes third to the scenery and CinemaScope." And though her rendition of one of Irving Berlin's songs in *There's No Business Like Show Business* (1954) prompted the composer to comment that it "took Marilyn's interpretation to make me see how sexy it was," the film did little to showcase Monroe's acting talents. But with her first film of 1955, *The Seven Year Itch*, Monroe was back on top. In a comedic *tour de force*, Monroe was praised in her role as Tom Ewell's fantasy lover as "just about perfect."

While her career was climbing toward its stellar heights, Monroe's personal life was heating up as well. In March 1952, she had her first date with the man who would become her second husband — baseball great Joe DiMaggio, who had retired from the game the previous year. After spotting Monroe's photo in a newspaper, the "Yankee Clipper" arranged for a friend to set up a blind date, and the two were soon inseparable. As with Johnny Hyde, however, Natasha Lytess took an instant disliking to Monroe's new beau, stating disdainfully: "I doubt very much that he has ever read a book in his life." In addition to Lytess' objections, Monroe and DiMaggio seemed to have little in common. DiMaggio shunned publicity while Monroe thrived on it. Monroe loved to dance — DiMaggio did not. While Monroe favored revealing clothes with plunging necklines, DiMaggio preferred that his attractive lover dress more conservatively.

Despite these differences, and after several changes of heart by Monroe, she and DiMaggio were married on January 14, 1954, with the blonde goddess telling the press, "I couldn't be happier. I'm looking forward to being a housewife, too…. I want six babies." But the union seemed doomed from the start. The couple frequently quarreled, with DiMaggio reportedly becoming violent on several occasions. DiMaggio objected to Monroe's sexy on-screen image, and Monroe would later state that he was "insanely jealous." And while DiMaggio was a popular public figure, his celebrity paled next to Monroe's.

The final straw of the marriage may have resulted from one of Monroe's scenes in *The Seven Year Itch*, shot on location in New York. In the famous scene, Monroe is wearing a white dress with a pleated skirt, and as she stands above a subway grating, the wind from below blows her skirt up above her thighs. Thousands of fans cheered as they watched the filming, but DiMaggio is said to have been appalled by the spectacle. After Monroe and DiMaggio returned to their room at the St. Regis hotel, neighboring guests reported hearing shouting and weeping from inside. When Monroe returned to Los

Angeles, she filed for divorce and testified in October 1954: "[DiMaggio] didn't talk to me. He was cold. He was indifferent to me as a human being and an artist. He didn't want me to have friends of my own. He didn't want me to do my work. He watched television instead of talking to me." (Despite her harsh words, Monroe would remain friends with DiMaggio for the rest of her life; in fact, after her death, DiMaggio made the arrangements for her small funeral service and ordered that a black vase filled with fresh roses — "twice a week, forever" — be placed at Monroe's crypt.)

After her success in *The Seven Year Itch*, Fox offered Marilyn a role in *How to Be Very, Very Popular*, which she rejected. (The part ultimately went to actress Sheree North.) Fox promptly suspended her, and Marilyn moved to New York, an act that would lead to a number of substantial changes in her life. In January 1955, in an effort to secure more serious roles, she announced the formation of Marilyn Monroe Productions, her own independent film production company. In a televised interview with veteran journalist Edward R. Murrow in April 1955, the actress stated that the company was formed "primarily to contribute to making good pictures ... it's not that I object to doing musicals or comedies — in fact, I rather enjoy it. But I would like to do dramatic parts, too."

After the formation of Monroe's company, Fox executives threatened that she would never work in Hollywood again. And the press had a field day with Monroe's lofty plans, publicly deriding her with such labels as "The Bernhardt in a Bikini." Nonetheless, the reality of Monroe's high-grossing box office receipts forced her to be taken seriously, and in August 1955, Fox negotiated a seven-year contract with Marilyn Monroe Productions, granting her director approval, story approval and cinematographer approval, as well as a salary increase to $100,000 per picture.

Despite the pummeling she had received in the press, Monroe refused to abandon her goal of becoming a serious actress, and was introduced in spring 1955 to Lee Strasberg, the artistic director of the Actors Studio in New York, whose famous alumni included Marlon Brando, James Dean, Montgomery Clift, Geraldine Page, Maureen Stapleton and Paul Newman. For three months, Monroe was given private instruction by Strasberg, then began participating in regular classes at the Actors Studio, which encouraged actors to get in touch with their emotional memories and experiences in order to enhance their acting. Monroe abruptly dropped Natasha Lytess as her coach and embraced the "Method" acting that was promoted by Strasberg. In addition to serving as her acting mentor, Strasberg was also responsible for convincing Monroe to enter psychoanalysis, which served as a complement to her acting training. According to John Springer, who would become Monroe's publicist in the early 1960s, "For the first time, Marilyn took her life as an actress seriously because somebody had great faith in her as an actress ... she had never been treated like anything but a kind of beautiful, idiot child."

Meanwhile, Monroe had become involved with playwright Arthur Miller, whom she had met in 1950 shortly after the death of Johnny Hyde. Although the two had experienced an instant mutual attraction, any possibilities for a future together were hampered by the fact that Miller was married with two children. But by 1955, Miller's marriage was collapsing, and he resumed his relationship with Monroe when she moved to New York.

Monroe's first film after joining with the Strasbergs — and the first film made in association with Marilyn Monroe Productions — was 20th Century–Fox's *Bus Stop* (1956), in which Monroe delivered what many believe was the best performance of her career. She was guided through the film by Paula Strasberg, Lee's wife, who worked with Monroe on the movie set. Without exception, critics raved about Monroe's performance in the role of Cherie, a world-weary singer; even the notoriously acerbic Bosley Crowther advised his *New York Times* readers to "Hold onto your chairs ... and get set for a rattling surprise. Marilyn Monroe has finally proved herself an actress in *Bus Stop* ... she gives a performance in this picture that marks her as a genuine acting star, not just a plushy personality and a sex symbol, as she has previously been." And although Monroe was frequently late to work and reportedly did not get along well with her *Bus Stop* costar Don Murray, the actor would later praise Monroe's ability: "She had learned tremendous dramatic and comedy techniques that didn't depend just on her personality, but she could really get into a character and play it with great truth as well as humor."

On June 11, 1956, Arthur Miller was granted a divorce from his wife. He and Monroe were married in a civil ceremony less than a month later, and on July 1, 1956, they participated in a double-ring, Jewish ceremony during which Lee Strasberg gave the bride away. Dubbed "The Egghead and the Hourglass," the newlyweds honeymooned in Roxbury, Connecticut, and flew to England two weeks later for Monroe's role in *The Prince and the Showgirl* (1957) — the first independent film produced under the Marilyn Monroe Productions banner. But filming would be an unpleasant affair for all concerned. Monroe caused expensive delays with her now-characteristic lateness and absences, and her costar and director, Lawrence Olivier, reportedly resented the constant presence of Paula Strasberg on the set. Also, while in England, Monroe discovered a journal that Miller had been keeping which included unfavorable entries about Monroe and indicated that Miller was disappointed in her as a wife. This, according to some, marked the beginning of the end of their marriage.

While Monroe's next film, *Some Like It Hot* (1959), was her most popular, it, too, was plagued with problems. Monroe was chronically late and constantly flubbed her lines. Costar Tony Curtis stated that Monroe was "as mad as a hatter" and publicly denounced her chronic lateness: "Look, if we had a nine o'clock A.M. call, she'd make it by 11. That was on her good days. On her bad days, she didn't show up until after we came back from lunch. She had days when she didn't make it till three." (It should be noted, however, that in a 1996 television interview, Curtis' view of the actress had considerably softened, and he referred to her as a "lovely young woman.") Billy Wilder likened his experience with Monroe to a trip to the dentist: "It was hell at the time, but after it was over, it was wonderful." And Monroe herself resented the fact that she was playing another "dumb blonde" in a film whose plot revolved around other characters. Despite these issues, however, the film was a smash hit, with critics hailing Monroe's "combination of sex appeal and timing that just can't be beat." For her portrayal, Monroe won a Golden Globe Award for best actress in a comedy.

The following year, Monroe became involved in an affair that would signal the end to her marriage to Arthur Miller. During the filming of *Let's Make Love* (1960), she and Miller stayed in a Beverly Hills Hotel suite next to the one shared by her costar Yves Montand and his wife, actress Simone Signoret. When Miller returned to New York, and Signoret flew to Rome for a film commitment, Monroe and Montand engaged in a widely publicized tryst. By the time Miller returned, his marriage to Monroe was over.

Let's Make Love was one of Monroe's weaker films, and was not well-received by critics or audiences. And her next movie — *The Misfits* (1961) — turned out to be her last (as well as that of costar Clark Gable, who suffered a fatal heart attack ten days after filming was completed). Written by Miller and directed by John Huston, *The Misfits* was, like most of Monroe's later films, fraught with difficulties. Although Monroe and Miller had agreed to stay together through the filming of the movie, their relationship had grown increasingly hostile. Also, Marilyn suffered from insomnia and was so heavily under the influence of drugs and alcohol that Huston prophetically stated: "If she goes on at the rate she's going, she'll be in an institution in two or three years, or dead." Production was shut down on more than one occasion, once when Monroe suffered a physical and emotional breakdown and spent ten days in the hospital, prompting columnist Louella Parsons to write that she was "a very sick girl, much sicker than at first believed."

The reviews for *The Misfits* were mixed. One reviewer said that Monroe's role "expresses no more than a neurotic individuality and symbolizes little," while, at the other end of the spectrum, she was hailed for putting forth the best work of her career. Shortly after the film's release, Monroe voluntarily entered the Payne Whitney Psychiatric Clinic in New York, but soon after, she contacted Joe DiMaggio and four days later, he arranged for her discharge. Although Monroe told the press that she felt "wonderful" following her brief clinic stay, her life was careening toward destruction. In early 1962, she purchased a modest three-bedroom dwelling in Brentwood, California, which cost less than $90,000. The inscription before the front door was in Latin: "Cursum Perficio," which means, ironically, "My journey is over." And it soon would be.

In April 1962, Monroe was to begin work with Dean Martin on her thirtieth film, *Something's Got to Give*, a remake of the 1940 Cary Grant–Irene Dunne vehicle, *My Favorite Wife*. But she failed to appear during the first scheduled week of shooting, calling in sick with a virus and sinusitis, and by early May, she had missed 16 of the first 17 shooting days. Then, on May 17, after several days of successful work, Monroe flew to New York to attend the birthday party of President John F. Kennedy at Madison Square Garden, where she delivered a shockingly sensual rendition of "Happy Birthday." This action forced the film to be shut down for two days, leading to increased tension on the set.

A high point of the production took place when Monroe filmed the famous scene in which her character swam nude in her husband's swimming pool. Monroe originally began the scene wearing a flesh-colored bikini, but when a cameraman reportedly complained that the line of her bra was visible, she slipped out of the suit and did the scene *au naturel*. Her skinny-dip, the first by a major American star, was big news, and her photographs appeared in publications in 32 countries. But filming would go downhill from there. On June 1, 1962, Monroe's 36th birthday, she was given a small party at the end of the day's shooting, but her stand-in, Evelyn Moriarty would later state: "There was a pall over it.... it was a pretend celebration." The scenes that were shot that day would be the last of her career. The following week, on June 8, 1962, Monroe was fired from the production, and the film's producer, Henry Weinstein, announced: "The studio does not want her anymore. Marilyn's absence has cost the studio more than half a million dollars.... The fact is that the studios cannot operate with stars who do not report for work."

On the day after her firing, Fox announced that Monroe would be replaced with actress Lee Remick, but Dean Martin, whose contract gave him right of approval over his costars, rejected the substitution. Headlines of the day announced his action: " 'No Marilyn, No Picture' Martin tells Fox." And several weeks later, Fox quietly rehired Monroe, agreeing to pay her more than twice her original salary.

But Monroe would never work again. In the early morning hours of August 5, 1962, according to police reports, Monroe was found dead of a drug overdose in the bedroom of her home in Brentwood, California, lying face down on her bed with a telephone receiver in one hand. Following her death, the Los Angeles coroner told the press: "Miss Monroe has suffered from psychiatric disturbance for a long time. Mood changes were abrupt and unpredictable. In our investigation, we have learned that Miss Monroe had often expressed wishes to give up, to withdraw, and even to die.... On the basis of all the information obtained, it is our opinion that the case is a probable suicide." This official ruling notwithstanding, much conjecture has been made about the cause and manner of Monroe's demise, including the possibility that she may have been murdered, and a connection between her death and her alleged affairs with John F. Kennedy and his brother Robert.

Despite the piteous decline toward the end of Monroe's life, and the mystery surrounding her death, her screen work lives on as a testament to her shining beauty and unquestionable talent. In his eulogy at Monroe's funeral on August 8, 1962, Lee Strasberg described her best: "She had a luminous quality—a combination of wistfulness, radiance, yearning—to set her apart and yet made everyone wish to be part of it, to share in the childish naiveté which was at once so shy and yet so vibrant."

Film Noir Filmography

THE ASPHALT JUNGLE   *Director:* John Huston. *Producer:* Arthur Hornblow, Jr. Released by MGM, June 1950. *Running time:* 112 minutes. *Cast:* Sterling Hayden, Louis Calhern, Jean Hagen, James Whitmore, Sam Jaffe, John McIntire, Marc Lawrence, Barry Kelley, Anthony Caruso, Terese Calli, Marilyn Monroe. *Awards:* Academy Award nominations for Best Director (John Huston), Best Supporting Actor (Sam Jaffe), Best Original Screenplay (Ben Maddow, John Huston), Best Cinematography (Harold Rosson).

CLASH BY NIGHT   *Director:* Fritz Lang. *Producer:* Harriet Parsons. Released by RKO, June 1952. *Running time:* 104 minutes. *Cast:* Barbara Stanwyck, Paul Douglas, Robert Ryan, Marilyn Monroe, J. Carrol Naish, Keith Andes.

DON'T BOTHER TO KNOCK   *Director:* Roy Ward Baker. *Producer:* Julian Blaustein. Released by 20th Century–Fox, July 1952. *Running time:* 76 minutes. *Cast:* Richard Widmark, Marilyn Monroe, Anne Bancroft, Donna Corcoran, Jeanne Cagney, Lurene Tuttle, Elisha Cook, Jr., Jim Backus.

NIAGARA   *Director:* Henry Hathaway. *Producer:* Charles Brackett. Released by 20th Century–Fox, January 1953. *Running time:* 92 minutes. *Cast:* Marilyn Monroe, Joseph Cotten, Jean Peters, Casey Adams, Dennis O'Dea, Richard Allan, Don Wilson, Lurene Tuttle.

References

"Behind the Yves Montand, Marilyn Monroe, Arthur Miller Triangle." *Photoplay*, October 1960.
Corwin, Jane. "Orphan in Ermine." *Photoplay*, March 1954.
"Dostoyevsky Blues." *Time*, January 24, 1955.
Dougherty, James. "Marilyn Monroe Was My Wife." *Photoplay*, March 1953.
Durgnat, Raymond. "Myth: Marilyn Monroe." *Film Comment*, March-April 1974.
"Early, Too Early, for Once." *Newsweek*, August 13, 1962.
"End of Famous Marriage." *Life*, November 21, 1960.
"Girl Who Became Marilyn Monroe." *Reader's Digest*, August 1956.
Guiles, Fred Lawrence. *Legend: The Life and Death of Marilyn Monroe.* New York: Stein and Day, 1984.
Haspiel, Jim. "Extra Appearances." *Films in Review*, December 1974.
"A Look Back in Adoration." *Life*, September 8, 1972.
Mailer, Norman. "Big Bite." *Esquire*, November 1962.
"Marilyn on the Town." *Life*, September 27, 1954.

"Marilyn's New Role." *Time*, February 17, 1961.
"Merger of Two Worlds." *Life*, January 25, 1954.
Miller, Arthur. "My Wife Marilyn." *Life*, December 22, 1958.
"Mr. and Mrs. Joe DiMaggio." *Newsweek*, January 25, 1954.
Odets, Clifford. "To Whom It May Concern." *Show*, October 1962.
"Olivier and Monroe." *Look*, October 3, 1956.
"Remember Marilyn." *Life*, August 17, 1962.
Riese, Randall, and Neal Hitchens. *The Unabridged Marilyn: Her Life from A to Z.* New York: Congdon and Weed, 1987.
Roman, Robert. "Marilyn Monroe." *Films in Review*, October 1962.
Skolsky, Sidney. "Marilyn Monroe's Honeymoon Whirl." *Photoplay*, May 1954.
_____. "260,000 Minutes of Marriage." *Photoplay*, August 1954.
Steinem, Gloria. "Growing Up with Marilyn." *MS*, August 1972.
"Still Magic." *Time*, August 7, 1972.
"Storybook Romance." *Time*, January 25, 1954.
Summers, Anthony. *Goddess: The Secret Lives of Marilyn Monroe.* New York: Macmillan, 1985.
"They Fired Marilyn: Her Dip Lives On." *Life*, June 22, 1962.
"Thrilled with Guilt." *Time*, August 17, 1962.
"The Unquiet Ghost of Marilyn Monroe." *People*, April 29, 1974.
"Unveiling of the New Marilyn Monroe." *Life*, August 27, 1956.
"Will Acting Spoil Mrs. Miller?" *Saturday Evening Post*, August 18, 1956.
Wilson, Earl. "The Things She Said to Me." *Photoplay*, May 1956.
Zolotow, Maurice. "After the Fall." *TV Guide*, December 7, 1974.

Documentaries

"Marilyn Monroe: Beyond the Legend." Copyright 1986, Wombat Productions. A Wombat Production in association with Devilier/Donegan Enterprises. As seen on "Crazy About the Movies," a presentation of Cinemax, a Time Warner Company.
"Marilyn: Something's Got to Give." Copyright 1990, Fox Entertainment News, Inc.
"Marilyn: The Last Interview." Copyright 1992, Kunhardt Productions, Inc.

Agnes Moorehead

One of Hollywood's premier character actresses and the recipient of four Academy Award nominations, Agnes Moorehead is probably best known to modern audiences as the mischievously meddlesome mother-in-law in the popular television series *Bewitched*. But during the height of her fame in the 1940s and 1950s, Moorehead turned in a variety of outstanding performances that began with her debut in Orson Welles' *Citizen Kane* (1941), and included prominent roles in three films noirs: *Journey into Fear* (1942), *Dark Passage* (1947) and *Caged* (1950).

Agnes Robertson Moorehead was born December 6, 1906, in Clinton, Massachusetts, the only child of John Henderson Moorehead, a Presbyterian minister, and his wife, Mary Mildred. At the age of three, Moorehead made her first stage appearance, singing "The Lord Is My Shepherd" on a church program. She would later state that she inherited her voice from her father, who "taught me to speak clearly from babyhood."

A redhead with striking green eyes, Moorehead was such a talented and imaginative youngster that her mother would greet her each day with the question: "Well, Agnes, who are you today?" Her family moved to St. Louis in 1910, and by the time she was 11, she had made her professional debut in the ballet and the chorus of the St. Louis Opera and acted with the Forest Park Stock Company. (Years later, Moorehead would neither confirm nor deny publicity releases that stated she had also once ridden an elephant in a circus act and performed aboard a Mississippi River showboat during her childhood years.)

By the time she graduated from high school in 1919, Moorehead knew that she wanted to pursue a career as an actress. Although her father voiced no objections to Moorehead's decision, he insisted that she complete her education, and she dutifully followed his advice. Over the next several years, she obtained a Bachelor of Arts degree in biology from Ohio's Muskingum College, which was founded by her uncle, a Master's degree in English and public speaking from the University of Wisconsin, and a doctorate in literature from Bradley University. Along with her rigorous studies, she maintained her interest in the performing arts by appearing in several class plays.

To earn additional tuition money, Moorehead taught public speaking and English in 1925 at Central High School in Soldier's Grove, Wisconsin, and later graduated with honors from the American Academy of Dramatic Arts. One of her classmates there was future star Rosalind Russell, who would remain a lifelong friend and later said, "Even then, I knew she had greatness in her — not only as an actress, but as a human being." While a student at the Academy, Moorehead also formed another significant relationship — with fellow student John Griffith Lee. Moorehead and Lee would marry in 1930, but 22 years later, in 1952, the couple would divorce, with the actress testifying that her husband was a heavy drinker and had physically abused her.

After the Academy of Dramatic Arts, Moorehead headed for Broadway, winning a small role in the Theatre Guild production of *Marco Millions*, which opened on January 9, 1928. She also appeared in the stage productions of *Courage* (1928), *Soldiers and Women* (1929) and *Candlelight* (1929) with Gertrude Lawrence. But stage roles soon began to diminish because of the effects of the Depression, tossing the young actress into a financial bind that she would describe several decades later in *Guideposts* magazine: "To make my money last, I ate almost nothing: hot water for breakfast, a roll for lunch, rice for dinner. It was hungry work, making the rounds of casting agents, mile after mile on the unyielding sidewalk, and I used to wonder fervently just how God was going to provide manna in this man-made wilderness."

To make ends meet, the versatile actress turned to radio, a medium with which she would be associated throughout the remainder of her life, appearing on nearly 70 programs in a wide variety of roles. Her first major break came when she was hired for 20 weeks on the *Seth Parker Family Hour* in 1930. She later was heard on the *Evening in Paris* program as Cousin Anna and *The Armour Hour*, on which she performed comedic monologues as "Mrs. Sarah Heartburn." During these years, she also appeared on several broadcasts with actress Helen Hayes, who arranged for Moorehead to interview with a talent agent for motion picture work on the East Coast. But after meeting with Moorehead, the agent reportedly told her, "Sorry, afraid you're not the type."

Undaunted, Moorehead resumed her radio career, starring in 1934 as "Min Gump" in the serialized version of the comic strip *The Gumps*. Himan Brown, producer and director of the program, would later recall Moorehead's talent and professionalism: "She was one of the finest actresses I ever worked with. She could pick up a script and her first reading was good enough for taping." Throughout the remainder of the decade, Moorehead sometimes appeared in as many as six shows a day, including *Way Down East* (1936), *Joyce Jordan, Girl Intern* (1937) and *The Shadow* (1937) opposite Orson Welles, with whom she became fast friends. Welles left the series the following year, but when he founded his Mercury Theater Company, he chose Moorehead as one of his original players, along with Joseph Cotten, Everett Sloane and Ray Collins. On July 1, 1938, Moorehead was featured on the acclaimed troupe's debut broadcast of *Dracula*.

For the next three years, Moorehead continued her varied radio appearances, starring in frequent episodes of the *Cavalcade of America* and *Dreams of Long Ago* programs. In 1939, nearly a decade after her unsuccessful attempt to break into the movies, she accompanied Welles and the other members of the Mercury troupe to Hollywood. Two years later, she made her film debut in Welles' masterpiece, *Citizen Kane* (1941), and although she played only a small role as the title character's mother, Moorehead made a significant on-screen impact. The following year, in Welles' *The Magnificent Ambersons* (1942), Moorehead was given the role of a neurotic spinster aunt, delivering a performance that the critic for *Sight and Sound* said "confirmed the scope of her talents," and which Howard Barnes of the *New York Herald Tribune* called "brilliant and thoughtful." For her efforts, Moorehead won the Best Actress award from the New York Critics, and was nominated for her first Academy Award for Best Supporting Actress. Although she would lose to Teresa Wright for *Mrs. Miniver*, Moorehead had demonstrated that hers was an acting talent to be reckoned with.

In another Welles production, Moorehead next appeared in her first film noir, *Journey into Fear* (1942), starring her Mercury Theater colleague, Joseph Cotten, who also wrote the screenplay. As this film opens, Cotten's character, Howard Graham, is introduced as a munitions expert who is visiting Istanbul with his wife Stephanie (Ruth Warrick). Taken to a nightclub by a local representative from his company, Graham barely escapes being felled by an assassin's bullet. Later, Graham is informed by Col. Haki (Orson Welles), the head of the secret police, that he is the focus of a Nazi conspiracy and that his life is in danger. In an effort to ensure Howard's safe return to America, Haki installs him aboard a cargo ship populated by an assortment of odd characters, most of whom are not what they appear to be. A tobacco salesman named Kuvetli (Edgar Barrier) is actually an agent of the Turkish police assigned to oversee Graham's safe passage. A writer, Dr. Fritz Haller (Eustace Wyatt), who describes himself as a "good German," is in reality Muller, the architect of the Nazi plot. And a man posing as a salesman is actually Banat (Jack Moss), the hired assassin who attempted to kill Graham in the Istanbul nightclub.

Shortly before the ship docks in Batumi, a port on the Black Sea, Graham discovers that Kuvetli has been murdered. Captured by the Nazis, Graham manages to escape and briefly reunites with his wife at a local hotel. He also learns that Col. Haki is on the premises as well, but Graham is quickly found by Muller and Banat. In the midst of a driving rainstorm, the men pursue Graham onto the ledge of the building, where Muller is shot and killed by Haki. Empowered by his growing anger at his plight, Graham turns the tables on Banat and pursues the assassin until he falls from the rain-slick ledge to his death.

After winning praise from the reviewer from the *New York Times* for her "exacerbating portrait of a shrewish woman" in *Journey Into Fear*, Moorehead appeared in *The Big Street* (1942), a Damon Runyon story about a crippled, selfish nightclub entertainer, portrayed by Lucille Ball in one of her few unsympathetic performances. After this film, Moorehead signed a five-year, nonexclusive contract with MGM, and appeared in 1943 as a meddlesome governess in *The Youngest Profession*. Although her part was a small one, Moorehead was noted in the *New York World Telegram* for continuing "her habit of becoming the dominant person of the picture in a minor role."

Also in 1943, Moorehead starred in the radio production of *Sorry, Wrong Number*, playing a role that had been written especially for her. For her portrayal of a high-strung invalid who overhears men plotting her murder on the tele-phone, *Variety* stated that Moorehead "gave one of the memorable perfor-mances of radio history ... [Her] playing of this extraordinary role has rarely, if ever, been equaled on the air." Moorehead would go on to repeat the role on numerous occasions throughout the next nine years, giving *Sorry, Wrong Number* the distinction of holding the record for the dramatic program most frequently aired. Despite Moorehead's acclaimed performance, when Para-mount Pictures produced a film based on the script in 1948, the lead role went to Barbara Stanwyck, earning the actress an Academy Award nomination. Moorehead was understandably disappointed, and years later told the press: "Of course I wanted to play the Stanwyck part.... It had been written for me by Lucille Fletcher and I must have played it on radio about 18 times. I went to Hal Wallis at Paramount when they were casting it to put my hat in the ring, but he said he owed Barbara a picture and that I could have a support-ing role. I said 'no.' I'm not bitter about it. Let the chips fall where they may and go on from there."

The following year saw Moorehead's appearance in six films: *Jane Eyre* (1944), the well-received film version of the Charlotte Brontë novel; *Since You Went Away* (1944), which told the story of an average American family's suffering through World War II; *Dragon Seed* (1944), in which Moorehead por-trayed a devious Chinese peasant wife; *The Seventh Cross* (1944) an escape-from-the-Nazis drama starring Hume Cronyn and Jessica Tandy in their first film collaboration; *Tomorrow the World* (1944), the tale of an American cou-ple who adopt a young German boy; and *Mrs. Parkington* (1944), a smash-hit that told the epic rags-to-riches story of the title character. Moorehead would later recall that she won the role of the film's warm and sympathetic Baroness Aspasia Conti, "only because I put up a fine battle to get it. After playing a series of women who were either strained, neurotic, or mousy, I was eager for a good, normal role, and this was it." Hailed for her "brilliant" portrayal, Moorehead won her second Academy Award nomination, but would lose again, this time to Ethel Barrymore, for *None but the Lonely Heart*. Between films, Moorehead moved with her husband to the West Coast, where four years later the couple would buy a 14-room Italian villa in Beverly Hills. (After Moorehead's 1952 divorce from John Griffith Lee, she would name the house "Villa Agnese.")

Moorehead next appeared with Lana Turner and Laraine Day in *Keep Your Powder Dry* (1945), a rather stale story about the Women's Army Corps in World War II, and *Our Vines Have Tender Grapes* (1945), a top-notch depiction of rural American life starring Edward G. Robinson. She then starred in *Victory in Europe* (1945), a five-and-a-half minute short subject about a woman who learns of her husband's death just as her hometown begins to celebrate the end of the war, followed by *Her Highness and the Bellboy* (1945), a tedious Cin-derella-like story starring Hedy Lamarr and Robert Walker, and *The Beginning or the End* (1947), an engrossing drama about the development of the first atom bomb. In the latter film, the actress portrayed a real-life German scientist who had escaped to Sweden. When a release from the still-living scientist could not be obtained, Moorehead's appearances in the film were deleted.

Next, playing a role described as "a definitive portrait of bitchery," Moorehead appeared in her second film noir, *Dark Passage* (1947). This film opens with the prison escape of Vincent Parry (Humphrey Bogart), who was wrongly convicted of the murder of his wife. While on the highway, he is given a ride by Irene Jansen (Lauren Bacall), who takes Vincent to her apartment and provides him with clothes and money. Admitting that she had followed his trial with great interest, Irene confides that she suspected Vincent was "getting a raw deal." Vincent later undergoes plastic surgery, with plans to stay with a friend, George Fellsinger (Rory Mallinson), until the bandages can be removed. But after the operation, Vincent finds that George has been murdered and, realizing that he will be a prime suspect, seeks refuge with Irene.

As Vincent and Irene grow closer, Vincent learns that both his wife and George had actually been killed by Madge Rapf (Agnes Moorehead), his wife's friend and, coincidentally, also a friend of Irene's. Infuriated by Vincent's rejection of her, Madge had killed his wife in a jealous rage and offered the testimony in court that had ultimately resulted in his conviction. Vincent confronts Madge, prevailing upon her to sign a confession, but the shrewish, manipulative murderess refuses, revealing her fury over Vincent's relationship with Irene. "She wants you very badly, doesn't she?" Madge sneers. "She's willing to run away with you and keep on running and ruin everything for herself. But she wouldn't care because she'd be with you, and that's what she wants. Well, she doesn't have you now, and she'll never have you — nobody will ever have you and that's the way I want it!" Ironically, just moments after this explosive outburst, Madge turns to flee from Vincent and falls to her death from her apartment window. Faced with the hopelessness of his situation, Vincent flees to South America and is later joined there by Irene, where they begin their life together.

Although *Dark Passage* paled in comparison to previous Bogart-Bacall teamings, Moorehead's unsympathetic role was singled out in several reviews and one critic termed her character "one of the most poisonous termagents the screen has presented in some time." After this film, she returned to the stage, portraying Lady Macbeth in Orson Welles' production of *Macbeth*, presented at Utah's 1947 Centennial Celebration in Salt Lake City. The following year, Moorehead was asked to reprise her character for Welles' film version of the play, but her busy schedule would not allow it and the role went instead to Jeanette Nolan. Moorehead ended the year portraying a 105-year-old woman in *The Lost Moment*, an moody psychological drama. Although the film was rejected by critics and audiences alike, one reviewer, Cecelia Ager of *PM*, noted: "Moorehead's eloquent voice ... all by itself achieves a distinguished, complete characterization."

Agnes Moorehead

Moorehead was next seen in her first color feature, *Summer Holiday* (1948), a musical version of Eugene O'Neill's *Ah, Wilderness!*, followed by *The Woman in White* (1948), for which the actress was praised for her "sinister and lunatic" portrayal of a con man's wife, and *Station West* (1948), a first-rate Western starring Dick Powell and Jane Greer. In her last film of 1948, Moorehead appeared in *Johnny Belinda*, portraying the kindly but reserved aunt of a deaf mute girl. Her stellar performance earned Moorehead a third Academy Award nomination for Best Supporting Actress, but this time she lost to Claire Trevor for *Key Largo*.

In 1949, Moorehead portrayed the title character's mother in the box office hit *The Stratton Story*, starring James Stewart and June Allyson, and a vulture-like pawnshop owner in *The Great Sinner*, a gloomy drama whose star-studded cast included Walter Huston, Melvyn Douglas, Gregory Peck, Ava Gardner and Ethel Barrymore. The following year, she appeared in *Without Honor* (1950), an odd, mostly forgettable film starring Franchot Tone and Laraine Day, and *Caged* (1950), her third and final film noir.

In *Caged* Moorehead portrayed Ruth Benton, the compassionate warden of a women's prison populated by a mixed bag of inmates, including Marie Allen (Eleanor Parker), a pregnant first-offender, Kitty Stark (Betty Garde), the hard-boiled leader of a shoplifting ring, Georgia (Gertrude Michael), a Southern belle accused of check forgery who speaks longingly of her beloved rose garden, and Emma (Ellen Corby), a slightly batty dame who brags about her photograph appearing in the local newspaper after she murdered her husband.

Debased by their circumstances and tormented by sadistic matron Evelyn Harper (Hope Emerson), each of the women experience various transformations during the course of the film. Georgia tries to escape and is transferred to a mental ward, another inmate hangs herself after being denied parole, and Kitty, after experiencing a grueling solitary confinement, goes mad and murders Evelyn Harper. Throughout these episodes, the warden works to champion the prisoners and obtain state funds for rehabilitation programs, but her efforts appear to be in vain when Marie is paroled at the film's end, converted from a naive, innocent young woman to a hardened adult. Sorrowfully, Ruth Benton watches Marie's departure and directs a clerk to keep her file active, saying: "She'll be back."

After earning acclaim from critics for her "splendid" performance in *Caged*, Moorehead appeared the next year in *Fourteen Hours* (1951), a tense drama based on the true story about a mentally disturbed man who threatens suicide from a hotel window ledge; *Showboat* (1951), a musical based on Edna Ferber's novel of life on the Mississippi; *The Blue Veil* (1951), a box office smash about a governess who dedicates her life to caring for other people's children; and *Adventures of Captain Fabian* (1951), in which Moorehead, portraying a pipe-smoking octoroon, was compared by one critic to "Al Capp's Mammy Yokum."

Between filming, Moorehead found time to star in the First Drama Quartette stage production of *Don Juan in Hell* with Charles Laughton, Sir Cedric Hardwicke and Charles Boyer. After favorable responses to their performances in Stockton, California, and Washington, D.C., the troupe began an extensive tour that included Chicago, New Orleans, New York and England. Critics unanimously hailed Moorehead's performance as Donna Ana, with William

Hawkins of the *New York World-Telegram* writing that she "has the crisp, clean elegance of a lily. She falls into exquisite poses and moves like a self-appointed queen, to give the play its chief visual attraction." And in her personal life, this busy year was highlighted by Moorehead's adoption of her only child, Sean. (Little is known about her son, however, and according to the actress's obituary in *Variety*, Sean was "believed to have vanished" several years prior to her death.)

In Moorehead's next film, *Captain Black Jack* (1952), she portrayed a socialite dope peddler, followed by *The Blazing Forest* (1952), a routine story of logging and forest fires; *The Story of Three Loves* (1953), a box office disappointment in spite of a cast that included Kirk Douglas, James Mason and Ethel Barrymore; *Scandal at Scourie* (1953), a tedious period drama in which Moorehead portrayed a French nun; *Main Street to Broadway* (1953), notable primarily for the appearances of such stars as Tallulah Bankhead, Lionel Barrymore (in his last film), Shirley Booth and Louis Calhern; and *Those Redheads from Seattle* (1953), the first 3-D color musical, with a flimsy plot set during the Alaskan gold rush.

During this period, Moorehead married her second husband, actor-turned–television director Robert Gist, who was 12 years her junior. She first met Gist on the set of *The Stratton Story*, in which he had a small part, and in early 1953, the two were wed. But by July 1954, the couple were separated and five years later, the union would end in divorce. The collapse of the marriage was perhaps due in part to Moorehead's hectic performing schedule, of which she would later state, "It's really the loneliest sort of life. Sure, it's terribly exciting, but when I'm making a film or traveling in stock, how long am I in one place to make good friends? Mostly, it's just cold hotels. But that's the wandering minstrel's life. I'd love to just stay home and be married again, to have someone take care of me, but I've never been that fortunate."

Meanwhile, in 1954, Moorehead appeared in *Magnificent Obsession*, a glossy soaper starring Jane Wyman and Rock Hudson, but she spent the majority of the year touring the United States, Israel, India and other countries in a one-woman show originally titled "An Evening with Agnes Moorehead," and later changed to "The Fabulous Redhead." The highly acclaimed revue included selected readings from works by a number of noted authors, including Ring Lardner, Edna St. Vincent Millay and James Thurber, and excerpts from *Sorry, Wrong Number*. Of her extensive tour, Moorehead would later say, "There are marvelous audiences all over the country. I always say you haven't played an audience until you've played Stillwater, Oklahoma."

Returning to the screen the following year, Moorehead continued to appear in a wide variety of roles, including a hearty Irish pioneer in *Untamed* (1955), a fun-loving chicken rancher in *Meet Me in Las Vegas* (1955), a dowager queen in *The Swan* (1956) and the mother of Genghis Khan in *The Conqueror* (1956). The latter production, a $6 million box office flop, has been included among the "50 Worst Films of All Time," but it is better known for the tragic circumstances connected with its filming. A number of the film's scenes were shot near a site in Yucca Flat, Nevada, where extensive atomic bomb testing had taken place. Several years later, along with Moorehead, many of those involved with *The Conqueror* would be struck down by various forms of cancer. The shocking link between these deaths and the nuclear testing in Nevada would not be discovered for several decades.

In addition to Moorehead's screen roles in the late 1950s, the actress also turned her talents to the medium of television, making her debut in the 1956 presentation of "Greybeards and Witches" on NBC's *Matinee Theatre*, and appearing the following year on the *Schlitz Playhouse* production of "The Life You Save" with Gene Kelly and Janice Rule. And just when it appeared that Moorehead had no further fields to conquer as an artist, she directed a production of *Don Juan in Hell* starring Ricardo Montalban, Reginald Denny and Mary Astor. (Astor would later recall in her 1959 autobiography, "I liked Agnes Moorehead — Aggie, as we called her. A fine actress, now she proved to be an excellent director.")

Throughout the remainder of the decade, Moorehead continued her hectic schedule of appearances on film, stage, television and radio, including a 72-city tour in *The Rivalry* during 1957 and 1958, appearances on television's *DuPont Show of the Month* and *Shirley Temple Storybook Theater*, and seven films that included *Raintree County* (1957), the sweeping tale about the effects of the Civil War on an Indiana town; *Jeanne Eagels* (1957), which told the tragic story of the famed 1920s actress; and *The Tempest* (1959), an epic drama of old Russia. Despite her frequent performances, however, Moorehead would later say that being an actress was a "terribly discouraging business, a sorrowful business, a critical business…. You have to keep on developing and maturing and being sincere in your work, and just go right on whether audiences or critics are taking your scalp off or not."

During the early 1960s, Moorehead appeared in a mixture of box office flops and critically acclaimed films, from *Twenty Plus Two* (1961), a confusing story about the murder of a devious agent, to *Hush … Hush, Sweet Charlotte* (1964), portraying a slovenly but devoted housekeeper. For her performance in this Bette Davis starrer, Moorehead earned her fourth Academy Award nomination, and although she lost to Lila Kedrova for *Zorba the Greek*, the actress maintained, "The greatest award an actor or actress can achieve is the chance to do another good part…. I'd rather get memorable roles than live on remembered awards which others don't remember. I'm just as happy knowing that I have the respect of the fellow members of my profession. I just want the opportunity to get good parts and do them justice."

Also in 1964, Moorehead landed the role of Endora in the television situation comedy *Bewitched*, playing a meddlesome witch who constantly plagues the life of her daughter (Elizabeth Montgomery) and son-in-law (first portrayed by Dick York and later by Dick Sargent). Years later, Moorehead recalled how she came to take on the role in the long-running series: "I was trapped. I was sent the pilot film script. I looked it over and it was charming and had no violence in it. It was clean and had a smile in it, and a little fantasy and a little romance ... and since they offered me a good sum to make the pilot, I did it. Then I went out on the road to do my one-woman show, and when I came back they told me it was sold ... and I was committed to it." As the acid-tongued Endora, Moorehead endeared herself to television audiences and received six Emmy nominations over the course of the series' seven-year run. Although she never won television's highest honor for this role, she was awarded an Emmy in 1967 for her guest appearance in an episode of *The Wild Wild West*, in which she portrayed a regal Washington hostess who was involved in a series of murders.

Throughout her run on *Bewitched*, Moorehead continued her appearances on stage and in film (she once stated, "It's great to get off the broomstick once in a while!"), including the musical play *High Spirits* (1965), *The Singing Nun* (1966) starring Debbie Reynolds, and the title role in *Dear Dead Delilah* (1972), a Southern-gothic suspense film. John Farris, the writer and director of the latter film, said that he met Moorehead shortly after he completed writing the script for the film: "She spent three hours with me going over every scene, cutting, cutting, cutting. I know she would have been an outstanding director if she'd had more opportunity. As for the work she did in the film, a great many people feel it was one of her best roles.... We were lucky to get her."

After *Bewitched* went off the air, Moorehead guested on a variety of television programs, including *Laugh-In, Marcus Welby, M.D.* and *The Mike Douglas Show*. In 1973, she completed work on the animated Hanna-Barbera feature *Charlotte's Web*, in which she had the role of a stuttering goose. It was her last film performance.

Late in 1973, Moorehead began a strenuous 25-week tour as Aunt Alicia in *Gigi*, stating that if she hadn't accepted the role, "I'd go out and do something else. I'd pick up my grip and go teach a seminar or coach. I can't just sit around. I can't be bothered with that." But after several months, Moorehead's health began to deteriorate. Her condition was exacerbated when, during an outdoor performance in St. Louis, she was required to lie on a wet couch as part of the stage action. Soon after, she was forced to give up the role and was replaced by Arlene Francis. Her condition improved after a brief stay in the Methodist Hospital in Rochester, Minnesota, and she moved to her family farm in Ohio to recuperate. (The 320-acre farm, called Kitchen Middens, had been deeded to Moorehead's grandparents by presidents Monroe and Tyler.) But in spring 1974, Moorehead entered the Mayo Clinic in Minnesota, where she died several weeks later, on April 30, 1974.

At the time of her death, at the request of the actress, hospital officials declined to reveal the cause of Moorehead's death, and only later was it learned that she had suffered from lung cancer. Moorehead's reluctance to inform the public of her ailment perhaps stemmed from the actress' desire to preserve the fascinating aura of the performer: "I think an artist should be kept separated to maintain glamour and a kind of mystery," Moorehead wrote in a 1965 newspaper column. "Otherwise it's like having three meals a day. Pretty dull. I don't believe in the girl-next-door image. What the actor has to sell to the public is fantasy, a magic kind of ingredient that should not be analyzed."

Film Noir Filmography

JOURNEY INTO FEAR *Director:* Norman Foster. *Producer:* Orson Welles. Released by RKO, March 1943. *Running time:* 71 minutes. *Cast:* Joseph Cotten, Dolores Del Rio, Orson Welles, Ruth Warrick, Agnes Moorehead, Everett Sloane, Jack Moss, Jack Durant, Eustace Wyatt.

DARK PASSAGE *Director:* Delmar Daves. *Producer:* Jerry Wald. Released by Warner Bros., September 1947. *Running time:* 106 minutes. *Cast:* Humphrey Bogart, Lauren Bacall, Bruce Bennett, Agnes Moorehead, Tom D'Andrea, Clifton Young.

CAGED *Director:* John Cromwell. *Producer:* Jerry Wald. Released by Warner Bros., May 1950. *Running time:* 97 minutes. *Cast:* Eleanor Parker, Agnes Moorehead, Ellen Corby, Hope Emerson, Betty Garde, Jan Sterling, Lee Patrick, Olive Deering, Jane Darwell. *Awards:* Academy Award nominations for Best Actress (Eleanor Parker), Best Supporting Actress (Hope Emerson), Best Original Screenplay (Virginia Kellogg, Bernard C. Schoenfeld).

References

Bolton, Whitney. "Agnes Moorehead Salutes the Road, Decries Method." *Philadelphia Inquirer*, October 7, 1962.

Bowers, Ronald L. "Agnes Moorehead." *Films in Review*, May 1966.

Cook, Alton. "A Woman Giving Devil His Due." *New York World Telegram*, April 7, 1952.

"Four Hollywood Veterans Go to Hell on Broadway." *Life*, November 5, 1951.

"Four-Star Chat." *New Yorker*, April 19, 1952.

"A Good Scout at Heart." *Lions Review*, December 1944.

Harbison, Janet. "Agnes Moorehead, Minister's Child." *Presbyterian Life*, July 15, 1963.

Hopper, Hedda. "Happiest in Role of 'Nasty' Woman." *The Baltimore Sun*, November 26, 1944.

Jewell, James. "Mrs. Kane Gets a Valentine." *The World of Yesterday*, December 1979.

"Moorehead's Makeup." *Life,* June 9, 1947.

"Right Number Agnes." *Newsweek*, February 3, 1947.

"She Bewitched Us with Her Charm and Talent." *Photoplay*, August 1974.

Sherk, Warren. *Agnes Moorehead: A Very Private Person.* Philadelphia: Dorrance, 1976.

"*Sorry, Wrong Number*: Agnes Moorehead Stars in Repeat Performance of Radio Melodrama." *Life*, September 24, 1945.

Skolsky, Sidney. "Tintypes — Agnes Moorehead." *New York Post*, August 2, 1964.

"Sparring Ladies and Clashing Mountains." *New York Times*, November 11, 1956.

Stumpf, Charles K. "Versatility: A Tribute to Agnes Moorehead." *The World of Yesterday*, December 1979.
"They've Got Her Number." *Norfolk Virginian-Pilot*, December 12, 1948.
Thirer, Irene. "Movie Spotlight." *New York Post*, March 5, 1959.
Ward, L.E. "Agnes Moorehead." *Classic Images*, October 1986.

Cathy O'Donnell

A delicate brunette with doe-like eyes and a wistful smile, Cathy O'Donnell began and ended her brief career with outstanding features that won Academy Awards for Best Picture. Although O'Donnell would become one of the screen's best representatives of the idealized "girl next door," most of her films were low-budget "B" productions that were panned by critics and have all but faded into obscurity. Theories abound as to why O'Donnell failed to live up to her cinematic promise, but she did manage to achieve a measure of fame during her heyday, and made an outstanding contribution to three excellent offerings from the film noir era: *They Live by Night* (1949), *Side Street* (1950) and *Detective Story* (1951).

O'Donnell entered the world as Ann Steely on July 6, 1925, one of two children born to Ora and Henry Grady Steely. A native of Siluria, Alabama, a tiny town with approximately 700 residents, Ann had two favorite pastimes — writing poetry ("Not poetry of the moon and June kind, but little word-pictures that capture my fancy," she would later explain) and visiting the local movie theater operated by her schoolteacher father. During the Depression, Ann lived with an aunt in Greensboro, Alabama, and her dreamy, sensitive nature would be demonstrated when she spoke in later years of the time she spent there: "It was a beautiful town," she told *PM* in 1946. "Nobody struggles there, nobody fights. Nobody was trying to get any place particularly."

Following the death of her father when she was 12, Ann moved with her mother and brother to Oklahoma City where, on her 16th birthday, she saw the movie that she later said made the greatest single impact on her life — *Wuthering Heights*. "I had never thought of motion pictures as art," the actress said, "but now I saw what had been done on the screen with this one picture, and what had been done could be done again."

After graduating from high school, Ann attended Hills Business College for six months, then took a secretarial job at the Army Induction Center in Oklahoma City. But her position at the induction center reportedly ended one day when, engrossed in poetry writing during her lunch break, she failed to return at the appointed hour. Undaunted after her abrupt loss of employment, Ann enrolled at Oklahoma City University, where she appeared in several student productions including *Romeo and Juliet*, *Letters to Lucerne* and *Brief Music*.

Determined to earn enough money to make her way to Hollywood, Ann got a job as a stenographer with a local linoleum company, but she later admitted, "I didn't like office work. It was torture. I got to thinking I'd just as soon die if I had to stay in it much longer." After just a few months, she had saved enough to finance her trip and, along with a friend, Clarice Townsend, the actress rented a furnished room for $40 a month near the Sunset Strip. "I only had enough money to last for a couple of weeks," she recalled. "If I didn't break into the movies by then, I was going to have to go back home to Oklahoma City."

But the aspiring actress didn't have long to wait. Shortly after her arrival in California, she was "discovered" by agent Ben Medford while sitting at the counter of Schwab's Drug Store. "It was in September and we'd only been in Hollywood for about two days," she said. "We'd heard that Schwab's Drug Store was where the stars went for things, so we went there, too, for a sandwich. There weren't any stars there that afternoon, but the little man sitting next to me gave us a big laugh when he asked if I were in pictures. I told him no, I wasn't, but that I was going to be. He said that was fine, that he was an agent and he'd introduce me to Sam Goldwyn."

True to his word, Medford took Ann to see Goldwyn, who was impressed with what he saw and instantly ordered a screen test. "I answered questions, and I was nervous," the actress remembered. "My coiffure was awful. I wore a funny-looking dress — very elaborate, with a huge pattern on it. And I was quite fat." Despite this assessment, Goldwyn offered Ann a contract without even viewing the test and promptly ordered a name change. Ann herself chose the name Cathy, after the heroine in her favorite film, *Wuthering Heights*, and Goldwyn's wife Frances selected O'Donnell "because she said the public loves Irish names," the actress explained. And so, at the age of 19, Cathy O'Donnell was ready to take Hollywood by storm.

Goldwyn's first order of business with his newest discovery was to assign her to dramatic study with Natasha Lytess, who would later gain fame as the controversial coach of Marilyn Monroe. While O'Donnell worked to lower her voice and get rid of her Southern accent, Goldwyn used his influence to have her cast as Beth in a production of *Little Women* (1944) at the Pasadena Playhouse. Later, O'Donnell was sent to New York, where she was enrolled in the American Academy of Dramatic Arts. "I cried because I wanted to stay in Hollywood," O'Donnell recalled. "All the time I was there I wanted to come back, and I used to telephone Mr. Goldwyn long distance, but he always said 'no.'" After an extensive training course with Eddie Goodman, who had formerly coached stage veteran Katherine Cornell, O'Donnell was cast in *Life with Father* (1945), and it was her performance in this play that led to her screen debut. Touring with the production in the ingenue role of Mary, O'Donnell was reportedly spotted in Washington by director William Wyler, who cast her in his upcoming film, Goldwyn's *The Best Years of Our Lives* (1946).

In this highly acclaimed post-war drama, O'Donnell played the sensitive and understanding girlfriend of Harold Russell, an actual veteran who lost both hands during the war. O'Donnell was praised by critics for her first screen appearance and held her own with such stars as Fredric March, Myrna Loy and Dana Andrews, but she later recalled her fears at the start of production. "I was very frightened and shy," she said. "But Mr. Wyler, he has this wonderful sympathy for you. He got me over this shyness by being mean. As soon as he was mean I was all right. He wouldn't let me get away with anything. He sort of made me stand on my own feet, which was good."

After *Best Years*, which won seven Academy Awards including Best Picture,

O'Donnell was loaned to the Eagle-Lion studio for two low-budget features, *Bury Me Dead* (1947), a well-done mystery which saw O'Donnell cast in the unusual role of a nymphomaniac suspected of murder, and *The Spiritualist* (1948), also known as *The Amazing Mr. X*, which starred Turhan Bey as a bogus mentalist trying to con a wealthy woman out of her money.

Behind the scenes, O'Donnell had found a man who met her very specific requirements for the ideal man: "I want someone very intelligent, an artist in some way or other, and a very good one," she said in 1946. "Someone who won't want to be with too many people all the time, someone kind and sensitive. I like him to have a lot of strength — inner strength. And I would never like an actor. They're too conceited. Most actors are a little too interested in how they look. I don't care how a man looks particularly. And I'll marry a man much older than I am. Young men are too insensitive." The man who fit the bill was William Wyler's older brother Robert, a writer and associate producer, whom O'Donnell had met during production of *The Best Years of Our Lives*. A gray-haired, bespectacled man of middle age, Robert Wyler was everything O'Donnell had been searching for, and on April 11, 1948, the two eloped to Las Vegas. Despite an age difference of a quarter century, the marriage would be a happy one, and would last until O'Donnell's death in 1970.

But O'Donnell's joyous personal life may have had an adverse affect on her career. Sam Goldwyn had reportedly been feuding with director William Wyler and, incensed at his protégée's marriage to Wyler's brother, Goldwyn cancelled her contract. Although she promptly signed an agreement with David O. Selznick, the famed *Gone with the Wind* producer failed to assign her to a single picture during their two-year contract, and it would be her last association with any studio or producer. Still, in her first picture after parting with Sam Goldwyn, O'Donnell scored a hit with *They Live by Night* (1949), costarring Farley Granger.

In this top-notch film noir offering, Granger portrays Arthur "Bowie" Bowers, a young convict who escapes from prison with two hardened fellow inmates, Chickamaw (Howard da Silva) and T-Dub (Jay C. Flippen). When the escapees hide out at the home of Chickamaw's alcoholic brother Mobley (Will Wright), Bowie is drawn to Mobley's daughter Keechie (O'Donnell), and shares with her his plans to seek a pardon and "get myself squared around." Keechie, however, berates Bowie for his continued association with Chickamaw and T-Dub: "Fine way to get squared around — teaming with them. Stealin' money and robbin' banks. You'll get in so deep trying to get squared they'll have enough on you to keep you in prison for two lifetimes."

Despite Keechie's warning, Bowie joins with Chickamaw and T-Dub in a local bank robbery, but Bowie is injured in an auto accident during their getaway and Chickamaw shoots and kills a police officer who offers to help. Keechie nurses Bowie back to health, and the two later get married, settling in a remote mountain cabin. After several months of an idyllic existence, however, they are found by Chickamaw, who forces Bowie to take part in another bank robbery. But the gang's luck has run out. T-Dub is killed during the robbery, Chickamaw is later shot while trying to break into a liquor store, and Bowie becomes the focus of a nationwide manhunt, labeled "Bowie the Kid." With Keechie now pregnant, she and Bowie go on the run, hiding out at a motel run by T-Dub's sister Mattie (Helen Craig). Unwilling to further expose Keechie and his unborn child to danger, Bowie plans to continue his getaway alone, but Mattie double-crosses Bowie and contacts police. As Keechie looks on in horror, Bowie is gunned down, and as the film ends, she poignantly reads a letter penned by Bowie during his last hours: "I'm gonna miss you. I'll send for both of you when I can. No matter how long it takes. I've gotta see that kid. He's lucky. He'll have you to keep him squared around. I love you."

In what was perhaps her best screen performance, O'Donnell offered a striking portrait of a character who is toughened by her dismal upbringing but redeemed by love. Despite the hopelessness of her life with Bowie, Keechie continues to dream of a happy future, and in one of the film's most touching scenes, she conveys this fantasy to her husband: "I thought maybe we'd be lucky — they wouldn't find us. And after a while we'd go away and live like other people. And live that way maybe nine or ten years — it's happened to other men who've escaped. After a while they go back and tell the police and they let them go free, because they've proved they can live right like other people."

Both O'Donnell and Granger were hailed by critics for their first-rate performances, with the reviewer for *Motion Picture Herald* noting their "exceptional skill," and the critic for *Variety* terming the duo "a gifted team of young players" who stand out as "making the performances thoroughly realistic." However, while the film would later achieve status as a minor classic, it received a cool reception from audiences upon its release. According to Granger, the feature was doomed from the start because of its handling from studio heads at RKO: "Working on it was a wonderful experience. After it was done, I went to New York and when I returned to Hollywood a couple of weeks later, everyone was talking about the picture," he said. "Then Dore Schary, who had been running the studio, left to go to MGM and Howard Hughes bought RKO. Hughes hated our picture. It had no tits and ass, so he put it on the shelf. By the time *They Live by Night* finally sneaked out, the bloom was off the rose. We were all so upset ... no one at RKO really understood it."

Seeking to capitalize on the chemistry between O'Donnell and Granger, MGM re-teamed the pair in *Side Street* (1950). A tautly directed film noir offering, this picture tells the story of Joe and Ellen Norson (Granger and O'Donnell), financially strapped newlyweds with a baby on the way. A part-time letter carrier, Joe is desperate to provide his loving spouse with life's finer things, and finds such an opportunity when he steals a file folder from the office of Attorney Victor Backett (Edmon Ryan), believing that it contains

$200. After his impulsive theft, however, Joe is stunned to find that the folder holds $30,000 in cash. Telling Ellen that he has secured a high-paying job out of town, Joe stashes the money with a friend, Nick, then seeks refuge in a cheap hotel, where he comes to regret his crime. Unaware that the money is actually a blackmail payoff involving the murder of a local "B" girl, Lucille "Lucky" Colner (Adele Jergens), Joe decides to return the money to Backett, but the attorney denies any knowledge of it, suspecting that Joe has been sent by police.

Later, Joe learns that Nick has absconded with the money and he tracks him to a run-down apartment, discovering to his horror that Nick has been murdered. Before fleeing, however, Joe is spotted by a neighbor and soon finds himself wanted by police for the murders of both Nick and Lucky. Joe confesses his crime to Ellen, but he disregards her pleas to turn himself in to the authorities and instead goes in search of the real criminals. His hunt leads him to Harriet Sinton (Jean Hagen), the ex-girlfriend of George Garsell (James Craig), who was Backett's partner in the blackmail scheme. But in her quest to reunite with Garsell, Harriet double-crosses Joe and takes him to an apartment where George is waiting. Beaten and abducted by Garsell and his sidekick Larry Giff (Harry Bellaver), Joe is taken on a high-speed chase, with police in close pursuit. After a shoot-out, Garsell and Giff are killed, and Joe is injured, but he is reunited with Ellen in the final scene and the film's narrator intones: "This is the story of Joe Norson. No hero. No criminal. Just human like all of us. Weak, like some of us. A bit foolish, like most of us. Now that we know some of the facts, we can help him. He's going to be all right."

Although *Side Street* did brisk business at the box office, it was labeled in the *New York Times* as "respectable but somewhat tedious," and the critic for *Variety* wrote that its semi-documentary style "never reaches that emotional pitch whereby the spectator can settle back and become engrossed in it." O'Donnell was next seen in MGM's *The Miniver Story* (1950), the ill-advised sequel to the wildly popular *Mrs. Miniver* (1942), followed by her third film noir, *Detective Story* (1951), produced and directed by her brother-in-law, William Wyler. A fascinating film, *Detective Story* focuses on 24 hours at a New York City police precinct, and includes a melange of characters including Lou Brody (William Bendix), a tough but soft-hearted detective; Arthur Kindred (Craig Hill), who is arrested for embezzling company funds in his effort to gain the affections of a high-priced model; Mrs. Farragut (Catherine Doucet), a precinct "regular" who stops in to complain that her neighbors are making an atom bomb; and Karl Schneider (George Macready), an unscrupulous abortionist whose methods frequently result in the deaths of his desperate patients. Central to the film is James McLeod (Kirk Douglas), an inflexible, highly principled detective whose persona is best revealed through his violent treatment of Schneider and his determination to have Kindred prosecuted in spite of his employer's plan to drop the charges against him.

Cathy O'Donnell

When McLeod demonstrates an uncommon drive to nab Schneider for murder, his superior officer becomes suspicious, and learns that McLeod's wife Mary (Eleanor Parker) had obtained an abortion from the physician several years before her marriage. McLeod, however, was unaware of the incident and, despite a valiant effort, is unable to forgive Mary's misdeed when she tearfully confesses. In response to McLeod's reaction, Mary informs her husband that she is leaving him: "Let's have the truth for once. You think you're on the side of the angels. Well, you're not. You haven't even a drop of ordinary human forgiveness in your whole nature. You're a cruel and vengeful man." Devastated by the collapse of his marriage, McLeod recklessly endangers his life when a prisoner grabs an officer's gun and tries to escape, and is mortally wounded before the criminal can be apprehended. Before he dies, McLeod orders the release of Arthur Kindred and, in a heart-rending scene, recites the Act of Contrition as his horrified coworkers look on.

O'Donnell, who frankly admitted that she appeared in *Detective Story* because "William Wyler is producing and directing," played Susan Carmichael, the sister of the extravagant model who Arthur was striving to impress. While her role was a small one, O'Donnell nonetheless turned in a memorable performance, and the film itself was hailed by Bosley Crowther of the *New York Times*, who called it "hard-grained entertainment, not revealing but bruisingly real."

Unfortunately, *Detective Story* would be one of the last of O'Donnell's first-class pictures, and she next appeared in a series of clunkers. In the first, Columbia's *Never Trust a Gambler* (1951), she played the ex-wife of a murderer on the run; the film's only excitement was provided through a dramatic chase scene that culminated atop a massive shipyard crane. It was then announced that O'Donnell would star in Cecil B. DeMille's circus extravaganza *The Greatest Show on Earth* (1952), but the promised role was later played by Betty Hutton. Instead, after a three-year absence from the screen, O'Donnell starred in a British production, *The Woman's Angle* (1954), a trite romantic drama in which the actress portrayed a music critic who tames a philandering musician. This box office bomb was followed by a laughable French-Italian film, *The Loves of Three Queens* (1954), starring Hedy Lamarr and produced by her newly-formed company.

O'Donnell rebounded somewhat with her next two releases, *The Man from Laramie* (1955), a critically acclaimed Western starring James Stewart, and *Eight O'Clock* (1955), a better-than-average British courtroom drama, which featured O'Donnell as the wife of a taxi cab driver wrongly accused of murdering a little girl. And in the summer of 1955 she took a break from Hollywood, appearing to rave reviews in the title role of *Gigi* at the Falmouth Playhouse in Cape Cod, Massachusetts. But, back on screen, O'Donnell's next two films would be among the worst of her career. In *Mad at the World* (1955), a quickie exploitation feature, O'Donnell played a mother whose infant son is killed after being hit by a whiskey bottle thrown by a teenage hood, and *The Story of Mankind* (1957), a dreary Irwin Allen–directed bomb that endeavored to illustrate a half-million years worth of history. In addition to O'Donnell, who portrayed an Early Christian Woman, the film's star-studded cast included Ronald Colman (in his last screen appearance) as the Spirit of Man, Hedy Lamarr as Joan of Arc, Harpo Marx as Sir Isaac Newton, Peter Lorre as Nero, Virginia Mayo as Cleopatra, Edward Everett Horton as Sir Walter Raleigh, Francis X. Bushman as Moses and Dennis Hopper as Napoleon.

In her second film of 1957, O'Donnell fared slightly better, starring with Lex Barker and Rita Moreno in *The Deerslayer*, a loose adaptation of James Fenimore Cooper's novel, but the following year, she was seen in *Terror in the Haunted House*, a talky, offbeat horror film that promised not only to communicate with the audience visually, but also "subconsciously throughout your brain." With her appearance in MGM's blockbuster *Ben-Hur* (1959), as the title character's sister Tirzah, O'Donnell would be cast in a vehicle equal to the efforts of her early career. But this Best Picture Oscar winner would be O'Donnell's last feature film appearance. Ironically, it was directed by her brother-in-law William Wyler, who had helmed O'Donnell's first screen performance.

Having made her television debut in the early 1950s, O'Donnell now turned her talents to the small screen, guesting on a variety of programs, including *The Detectives, The Rebel* and *Cheyenne*. But soon after her role on the latter series, O'Donnell faded from public view, and in the mid–1960s she was diagnosed with cancer. After struggling with the illness for several years, O'Donnell died in Los Angeles on April 11, 1970, her 22nd wedding anniversary. Nine months later, her husband Robert Wyler suffered a massive heart attack and followed his wife in death. A friend would later note that throughout his wife's illness, Wyler "was a sick man pretending that he was well. And he did a magnificent job. He stood by her for years, always festive and acrobatic in his talk, always the lighthouse grin of youth and confidence on his face."

With the gentle beauty and shining talent that Cathy O'Donnell exhibited in her best movies, it is regrettable that most of her films were barely mediocre offerings. Although she appeared in only 17 films over a brief 14-year period, the fragile actress earned a place in Hollywood history with her most memorable roles — Wilma in her film debut and Keechie in *Side Street*. And, more importantly, the actress enjoyed a close and loving union off-screen — often a rarity in the Hollywood community — which was typified by one of the actress' favorite quotes, from Kahlil Gibran's *The Prophet*: "Think not you can direct the course of love, for love, if it finds you worthy, directs your course."

Film Noir Filmography

THEY LIVE BY NIGHT (Original release title: *The Twisted Road*) *Director:* Nicholas Ray. *Producer:* John Houseman. Released by RKO, June 1948. *Running time:* 95 minutes. *Cast:* Cathy O'Donnell, Farley Granger, Howard da Silva, Jay C. Flippen, Helen Craig, Will Wright.

SIDE STREET *Director:* Anthony Mann. *Producer:* Sam Zimbalist. Released by MGM, March 1950. *Running time:* 83 minutes. *Cast:* Farley Granger, Cathy O'Donnell, James Craig, Paul Kelly, Edmon Ryan, Paul Harvey, Jean Hagen, Charles McGraw, Ed Max, Adele Jergens, Harry Bellaver, Whit Bissell.

DETECTIVE STORY *Director and Producer:* William Wyler. Released by Paramount, November 6, 1951. *Running time:* 105 minutes. *Cast:* Kirk Douglas, Eleanor Parker, William Bendix, Cathy O'Donnell, George Macready, Horace McMahon,

Gladys George, Lee Grant. *Awards:* Academy Award nominations for Best Actress (Eleanor Parker), Best Supporting Actress (Lee Grant), Best Director (William Wyler), Best Original Screenplay (Philip Yordan and Robert Wyler).

References

"Bama Beauty." *American Magazine*, October 1949.
Crichton, Kyle. "Girl with a Poetic Touch." *Collier's*, October 30, 1948.
Goodman, Dean. "Cathy O'Donnell." *Films of the Golden Age*, Fall 1996.
Graham, Sheilah. "Practically Kidnapped by Sam Goldwyn." *The Baltimore Sun*, February 18, 1946.
"Meet Miss Cathy O'Donnell." *PM*, December 1, 1946.
Roberts, John. "Cathy O'Donnell — Her Daydreams Came True." *Classic Images*, October 1990.
Wechsberg, Joseph. "Dear Mr. Goldwyn..." *New York Herald Tribune*, September 1, 1946.
Wilson, Earl. "Mr. Goldwyn Presents." *Silver Screen*, August 1946.

Dorothy Patrick

Dorothy Patrick should have been a star. Assigned to lead roles from the start of her career, she appeared with some of Hollywood's best-known personages, including Joan Crawford, Loretta Young, Robert Taylor and Wallace Beery. With her classical features and blue eyes once described as "electric," Patrick was a welcome addition to a wide variety of pictures, but the quality of her vehicles declined after her promising start. She retired from the screen after just 12 years, and she is now all but forgotten. During her heyday, however, Patrick was seen in such highly regarded films as *Till the Clouds Roll By* (1946) and *Come to the Stable* (1949), and was featured in three examples from the era of film noir: *The High Wall* (1947), *Follow Me Quietly* (1949) and *711 Ocean Drive* (1950).

Patrick was born Dorothy Davis on June 3, 1924, in St. Boniface, Manitoba, a Canadian province near Winnipeg, where her father worked as a conductor on the Canadian Railway. As a child, Dorothy made her professional debut on a local radio station, and at the age of 12, while attending Mulvy Grammar School in Winnipeg, Dorothy's natural beauty earned her a job modeling children's clothing. The following year, the teen won her first beauty pageant, a contest sponsored by the city.

After graduating from Winnipeg's Kelvin High School with top honors in dramatics, biology and history, Dorothy enrolled at a local business college, and in 1937, while a student there, she entered and won her second beauty contest, earning the title "Miss Winnipeg." Presented with a set of luggage as her prize, Dorothy decided to travel to New York, where she combined business with pleasure and landed a modeling job with John Robert Powers. Before long, she was gracing billboards and magazine covers nationwide, and became a familiar face as a Chesterfield Girl, one of the many models used by the cigarette company in its advertising. But the exciting life associated with being a Powers model wasn't enough for Dorothy, and she quickly grew restless and dissatisfied. As a lark, she entered Jesse Lasky's *Gateway to Hollywood* radio contest, and out of 2,000 entrants in the New York region, Dorothy emerged the winner.

Dorothy's triumph in Lasky's annual contest earned her a movie contract offer, but by now she had become involved with New York Ranger hockey star (and future Hall-of-Famer) Lynn Patrick, and she turned down the contract in order to get married in 1939. The couple would later have a son, Lester Patrick, but the union would not last. After her divorce, using her married name, Patrick set out for California, determined to take Hollywood by storm, but after making the rounds at the major studios, she came up empty. The only role Patrick was able to secure was a bit part as one of a bevy of Goldwyn Girls (along with future stars Virginia Mayo and Linda Christian) in RKO's lavish musical comedy *Up in Arms* (1944). Disappointed but not disheartened, Dorothy returned to her Canadian home, where she gained experience by working in radio and little theater.

In 1945, Patrick decided to give Hollywood another try. Once back in Tinseltown, she auditioned for a little theater group in Los Angeles, the Geller Workshop, where she won the title role in *The Last of Mrs. Cheyney*. During her well-received run in the play, she was spotted by MGM talent scout Billy Grady, who invited her to the studio for an interview. "I was so amused when he started giving me directions how to get to Culver City," Patrick said later. "For I'd been there two years before and had been interviewed, but the talent report on me was, 'We like this girl. She has a certain maturity about her, though she's only 19. Advised her to get some experience, then see us again. She will be back.' They looked that up in the files, and how I loved it, for there I was back again, but this time they'd sent for me. And meantime, I'd gotten a little experience, so they took me."

After signing with MGM, Patrick was assigned to a lead role in *Boys' Ranch* (1946), which costarred James Craig as a baseball player who rallies a group of Texas ranchers in order to create a retreat for juvenile delinquents. Patrick next starred in MGM's successful musical *Till the Clouds Roll By* (1946), playing opposite Robert Walker as the wife of composer Jerome Kern. In her third picture of the year, she appeared with Wallace Beery in *The Mighty McGurk* (1946), which the critic for *Variety* said "varies little from the basic theme of all Wallace Beery starrers." The following year, on loan-out to United Artists, Patrick played the employer of Billie Holiday in *New Orleans* (1947), the only film made by the legendary jazz singer. Of her performance in this film, the critic for *Variety* found that Patrick "scores neatly on appearance and thespically." And in her second film of 1947, Patrick returned to MGM for a small but pivotal role in her first film noir, *The High Wall* (1947).

At the start of this picture, Patrick's character, Helen Kenet, is found murdered, and her husband, Steven (Robert Taylor), is held by police. But after being examined at a psychiatric hospital, it is discovered that Steven suffers from a subdural hematoma, which has caused excruciating headaches and blackouts. Reluctantly consenting to an operation to relieve his condition, Steven realizes that he cannot remember the circumstances surrounding his wife's death, and undergoes drug therapy in order to recall the events.

Injected with sodium pentathol, Kenet reveals that he had spent the last two years as a flier in Burma, while his wife worked as secretary to Willard Whitcombe (Herbert Marshall), an ambitious executive in a publishing company. Upon his return from Burma, Kenet found his wife at Whitcombe's apartment, where her overnight bag was seen on the bed. Ignoring her attempts to rationalize the situation, Kenet began strangling his wife, but blacked out and awoke later to find her dead. Later, Kenet forces a hospital physician, Ann Lorrison (Audrey Totter), to take him to Whitcombe's apartment, where he remembers that his wife's overnight bag was missing after he awakened from his blackout, and realizes that she was killed by Whitcombe. Unable to prove his innocence, Kenet breaks out of the hospital and heads for Whitcombe's apartment, joined

by Ann. Kenet subdues Whitcombe and Ann injects him with sodium pentathol, after which he admits his guilt in the death of Kenet's wife.

Although Patrick played only a minor role in the film, she made the most
of her screen time, particularly in the scene in which her character is murdered by Whitcombe. After learning that her lover plans to end their affair in
an effort to avoid a scandal, Helen first tries to shrewishly bully Whitcombe
into acquiescence: "You're not walking out on me. We're in this together," she
says. "What you've worked 20 years for I'll smash in 20 minutes. He'll divorce
me all right and you'll be named in every newspaper in town." Although Patrick
was overlooked by most critics, the film itself earned favorable reviews, with
Ray Lanning of *Variety* labeling the picture "chilling entertainment," and the
critic for the *New York Times* calling it "a likely lot of terrors."

After a featured role in *Alias a Gentleman* (1948), a fairly entertaining comedy which re-teamed Patrick with Wallace Beery, the actress starred with
William Lundigan and Jeff Corey in her second film noir, *Follow Me Quietly*
(1949). Here, Patrick played Ann, a reporter for a sleazy magazine who is
determined to get the inside story about a serial killer who is plaguing a small
town. The killer, who always strikes in the rain, is known only as The Judge
(Edwin Max), and after six months and seven murders, he continues to elude
police. Stymied by their inability to secure a description, Lt. Harry Grant
(Lundigan) and his partner, Sgt. Art Collins (Corey) use clues left behind by
The Judge to construct a life-size model of the killer. After showing photos
of the faceless model, the detectives manage to track The Judge to a local
bookstore, and later to a restaurant where he is identified by a waitress. Stak-
ing out the apartment where The Judge lives, Grant corners the killer and captures him after a chase in an abandoned gas plant. But as he is led away, the
handcuffed criminal is unnerved by water dripping from a large canister and
tries to escape. During a struggle with Grant on a high platform, The Judge
slips out of his handcuffs and falls to his death.

Follow Me Quietly was dismissed in *Motion Picture Herald* as a "routine
murder opus" and panned in the *New York Times* as an "utterly senseless little
thriller." Patrick had better luck with her next feature, 20th Century–Fox's
Come to the Stable (1949). This delightful film, starring Academy Award nom-
inees Loretta Young and Celeste Holm, focused on the efforts of two French
nuns to establish a children's hospital in New England, and was applauded by
critics and audiences alike. However, after this first-rate film, Patrick left
MGM and signed with Republic Studios, based on a never-kept promise of
a starring role opposite John Wayne. Instead, her new studio kept her busy
with prominent roles in such forgettable features as *Tarnished* (1950), the tale
of an ex–Marine shunned because of his shady past; *Lonely Hearts Bandits*
(1950), where Patrick played one-half of a husband and wife team that goes
on a killing spree; *Federal Agent at Large* (1950), featuring Patrick as a female
gangleader who falls for a treasury agent; and *Belle of Old Mexico* (1950), a

Western in which Patrick portrayed the snooty fiancée of a college president. Patrick's best feature of the year was her sole non–Republic appearance, in Columbia's *711 Ocean Drive* (1950), her final film noir.

Focusing on the world of book making and wire services, this film begins with an intriguing foreword: "Because of the disclosures made in this film, powerful underworld interests tried to halt production with threats of violence and reprisal. It was only through the armed protection provided by members of the police department in the locales where the picture was filmed, that this story was able to reach the screen." The plot of *711 Ocean Drive* focuses on Mal Granger (Edmond O'Brien), a technology-savvy telephone repairman who unsuccessfully strives to increase his income through frequent bets on the horse races. Referred by his bookie, Chippie Evans (Sammy White), Granger gets a job with a local wire service run by Vince Walters (Barry Kelley), and uses his technical know-how to expand Walters' wire service throughout the state of California. When Walters is murdered by a disgruntled bookie, the ambitious Granger takes over the operation, turning it into a gold mine.

Granger's operation is so lucrative that it attracts the attention of an East Coast syndicate run by Carl Stephans (Otto Kruger) and his right-hand man Larry Mason (Donald Porter). Granger accepts the syndicate's offer of 50 percent of the proceeds in exchange for a take-over of his operation, but his position is threatened when he has an affair with Mason's wife, Gail (Joanne Dru). Infuriated to discover that the syndicate is cheating him out of his share of the wire service profits, Granger is pushed to the breaking point when he learns that Mason has savagely beaten his wife because of her infidelity. Granger pays a local hood, Gizzi (Robert Osterloh), to murder Mason, but Granger himself later kills Gizzi when the hit man threatens him with blackmail. With police now on his trail, and with the syndicate head suspecting him of Mason's murder, Granger flees to Las Vegas with Gail and Chippie. When Chippie is murdered by syndicate thugs, Granger and Gail try to skip town, but they are cornered by police at Hoover Dam and Granger is riddled by bullets as he tries to cross the dam on foot.

As Trudy Maxwell, the secretary who loves and loses Granger, Dorothy Patrick was shown to good advantage in *711 Ocean Drive*, and was included in *Variety's* praise of the "standout" supporting characters. But by now, the actress had grown weary with her steady filmmaking routine, and briefly abandoned her acting career in favor of a job as a personnel interviewer and counselor for industrial concerns. This new venture, however, would not last. "They talk about heartaches in films," Patrick said, "but there are more and deeper heartaches in the commercial world. I have seen people with enormous records for accomplishment and superior schooling, real experts, who were completely and even ignominiously ignored. It's not like that in pictures, no matter what they say. People are kind for the most part in their treatment of the individual."

Around this time Patrick also experienced a change in her personal life

Dorothy Patrick

when she married Beverly Hills dentist Sterling Bowen, with whom she later had a son, Sterling T. Bowen. But like her first marriage, this one, too, would be a failure, and Patrick focused her energies on her screen career. After appearing in 1951 with Wayne Morris and Preston Foster in a standard oil field yarn, *The Big Gusher*, Patrick returned to her non-stop film schedule the following year, starring in a mediocre Western with Tim Holt and Noreen Nash, *Road Agent* (1952), and again with Holt in his last of 46 oaters for RKO, *Desert*

Passage (1952). She also returned to MGM for bit parts in two big-budget films, *Scaramouche* (1952), an entertaining swashbuckler starring Stewart Granger and Janet Leigh, and MGM's blockbuster musical, *Singin' in the Rain* (1952), in which Patrick had a tiny part as an audience member.

Patrick continued playing minor roles in MGM's *Torch Song* (1953), which starred Joan Crawford as a Broadway star in love with a blind pianist, and *Half a Hero* (1953), a domestic comedy with Red Skelton and Jean Hagen. She was also seen in featured roles in Allied Artists' *Tangier Incident* (1953), a run-of-the-mill spy thriller; *Savage Frontier* (1953), another routine horse opera at Republic; and *Man of Conflict* (1953), an Atlas production costarring Edward Arnold as a tyrannical industrialist who tries to force his son into his footsteps. The actress also found time to accept a stage role, portraying the flashy part of Crystal in *The Women* at the Sombrero Playhouse in Phoenix, Arizona.

Despite Patrick's rather disappointing experiences at MGM and Republic, and her numerous appearances in less-than-stellar productions, the actress remained optimistic about her chances for stardom in Hollywood. "There have been both ups and downs in both the pictures and the assignments I've had," she told the *Los Angeles Times* in 1954. "I have yet to experience that perfect coordination which means complete success — the ideal assignment in the smash hit. Once you have that good fortune, you may face other troubles, but you are bound to be in great demand." But none of the actress's three films of 1954 offered her that "perfect coordination." For Lippert, she starred with Dane Clark and Raymond Burr in yet another routine oater, *Thunder Pass*, followed by a Western for Columbia, *The Outlaw Stallion*, in which she portrayed a widowed mother living with her son on a remote ranch. And returning to MGM for her last film for the studio, Patrick played a superfluous role in the otherwise all-male war film *Men of the Fighting Lady*, starring Van Johnson, Walter Pidgeon, Louis Calhern and Keenan Wynn.

After minor parts in 20th Century–Fox's *Violent Saturday* (1955), a crime drama starring Victor Mature, and Allied Artists' *Las Vegas Shakedown* (1955) with Dennis O'Keefe and Coleen Gray, Patrick jumped into the matrimonial pool again, this time with television producer J. Hugh Davis. In her next film, Fox's *The View from Pompey's Head* (1955), the actress had another small role, and was billed under her new name, Dorothy Patrick Davis. The following year, she was seen briefly in the United Artists Western *The Peacemaker* (1956), starring James Mitchell (who would later gain a new generation of fans as Palmer Courtlandt on the ABC-TV soap opera *All My Children*).

Following her appearance in *The Peacemaker*, Patrick retired from films and moved with her new husband to New York. Their union, however, would not last, and Patrick later returned to Hollywood, married her fourth husband Harold Hammerman and once again found work as a personnel counselor. Over the next two decades, Patrick was out of the public eye, as she focused her energies on philanthropic and liberal causes. But during those years, her fourth marriage, too, would end. Patrick later continued her business interests by becoming vice president of her son's consulting firm, but in the mid–1980s she was diagnosed with cancer, and on May 31, 1987, just days before her 66th birthday, she died at the UCLA Medical Center. At the time of her death, Patrick had been working on her memoirs.

Appearing in more than 30 films during her relatively brief career, Dorothy Patrick demonstrated that she possessed the physical beauty and acting talent that should have ensured her success. But with her frequent roles as wholesome wives or devoted sweethearts in a series of mostly forgettable films, she never achieved the level of stardom that had seemed inevitable at the start of her promising career. Still, the actress seemed to view her celebrity status with realism and, even toward the end of her prolific career, she expressed satisfaction with her stay on the silver screen: "I am not the flashy type who can click with the public immediately. I have never wanted to zoom to success," she said. "Even when conditions are difficult, Hollywood is still fun, and working in films always holds the promise of dreams that may be fulfilled, and they are wonderful dreams."

Film Noir Filmography

THE HIGH WALL   *Director:* Curtis Bernhardt. *Producer:* Robert Lord. Released by MGM, December 1947. *Running time:* 100 minutes. *Cast:* Robert Taylor, Audrey Totter, Herbert Marshall, Dorothy Patrick, H.B. Warner.
FOLLOW ME QUIETLY   *Director:* Richard Fleischer. *Producer:* Herman Schlom. Released by RKO, July 1949. *Running time:* 59 minutes. *Cast:* William Lundigan, Dorothy Patrick, Jeff Corey, Nestor Paiva, Charles D. Brown.
711 OCEAN DRIVE   *Director:* Joseph M. Newman. *Producer:* Frank N. Seltzer. Released by Columbia, July 1950. *Running time:* 102 minutes. *Cast:* Edmond O'Brien, Joanne Dru, Donald Porter, Sammy White, Dorothy Patrick, Barry Kelley, Otto Kruger, Howard St. John, Robert Osterloh.

References

"Actress Dorothy Patrick; Featured in '40s, '50s Films." *Los Angeles Times*, June 6, 1987.
"Dorothy Patrick, Model, Actress." *Newsday*, June 8, 1987.
Gebhart, Myrtle. "Films Let Her Go, Then Sent for Her." *Boston Sunday Post*, July 20, 1947.
Lieber, Perry. Biography of Dorothy Patrick. RKO Radio Studios, Hollywood California, circa 1947.
Muir, Florabel. "Lead in Three Pictures, Dorothy's Still Unseen." *Citizen News*, October 26, 1946.
Schallert, Edwin. "Actress Would Rather Climb Than Zoom." *Los Angeles Times*, June 13, 1954.

Jean Peters

A green-eyed brunette whose film debut catapulted her to stardom, Jean Peters is perhaps more often recognized for her marriage to eccentric billionaire Howard Hughes than for her considerable acting talents. During the peak of her popularity in Hollywood, Peters appeared opposite some of the top Hollywood stars of the day, including Tyrone Power, Marlon Brando, Joseph Cotten and Burt Lancaster, and was unique in that she seldom, if ever, played less than a leading role. But soon after her appearances in such box office hits as *Three Coins in the Fountain* (1954) and *A Man Called Peter* (1955), the actress abruptly quit the screen and has not returned since. Before her departure, however, Peters displayed her talents in a variety of top-notch productions and starred in three fine examples of film noir: *Niagara* (1953), *Pickup on South Street* (1953) and *Vicki* (1953).

Elizabeth Jean Peters entered the world on October 15, 1926, in Canton, Ohio, the oldest of two daughters born to Gerald Morris Peters, an engineer and accomplished pianist, and Mary Elizabeth Peters, who was a talented painter. When Peters was ten years old, her father died following a lengthy illness, and her mother bought a seven-acre chicken farm near East Canton, where she and her sister Shirley were raised. While attending high school in the tiny Ohio town, Peters decided to pursue a career as a teacher, and was in the process of completing the requirements for her educational degree when the course of her life changed forever.

In 1945, a college chum of Peters', Arlen Hurwitz, entered a picture of the young beauty in a "Miss Ohio State Contest" and, to her surprise, Peters was selected the winner out of a pool of 400 hopefuls. The first prize for the contest was $200 in cash and a trip to Hollywood for a screen test at 20th Century–Fox Studios. Although Peters promptly set out for California, she had no acting ambitions and, according to a studio biography, was more concerned about missing her college classes than landing a contract.

Stories differ on the specific circumstances that led to Peters' contract with 20th Century–Fox, but according to the most intriguing version, studio executives were initially unimpressed with the screen test of the college beauty, and after her two-week stay, she boarded a train back to Ohio. But at one of the stops on the way back to college, Peters received a wire from the studio, offering her a contract. Reportedly, executives had experienced a change of heart after footage of her test had been seen by a major stockholder at Fox, billionaire Howard Hughes.

Regardless of the manner in which Peters inked a deal with Fox, it is a fact that she settled in Hollywood in 1946, a fresh-faced brunette who was such a novice that her own mother reportedly told her, "Well, you can have fun for six months and then come back and finish college." But before long, Peters was offered the lead in her first film, *Captain from Castile* (1947), playing the peasant wife of a young Spanish nobleman. Later, the actress would admit that she was stunned when she was given the part: "I made the test [for the movie] and shortly after that, Mr. Zanuck called me into his office," Peters recalled. "When he told me I had won the role, I could do little but stare blankly. I'd never expected any such a thing as this, never in my wildest dreams." The film was a box office hit and, virtually overnight, Peters was a star. Years later, the actress would credit costar Tyrone Power with helping her through her debut performance: "I'd envisioned Ty as something like a great god and was afraid he wouldn't be very interested in what I did in the picture. But he did so many things that made my job easier."

In response to fans clamoring for details about Fox's promising new star, movie magazines began printing a surfeit of details about Peters' life. Famed columnist Hedda Hopper, for instance, reported that Peters was "a nine days' wonder" on the set of *Captain from Castile* because she took along a portable sewing machine and made her own clothes. While filming on location in Mexico, Hopper further disclosed, Peters visited the local public schools because "the idea of being a schoolmarm was still in her blood." Other articles revealed such tidbits as Peters' love for hamburgers, hot dogs and peanuts, her "highbrow" taste in music, and the fact that "the unspoiled Miss Peters does her own washing and is as proud of her washing machine and steam iron as [Lana Turner] is proud of her new convertible."

Although these popular publications also stressed that Peters was a private, home-loving type who was seldom seen on the town, they linked her romantically with a number of men, particularly Howard Hughes. Peters admitted that she frequently dated the wealthy bachelor, but she emphatically stated, "I have no intention of marrying now.... I don't see why I should rush into anything as serious as marriage right now. I'm only 20 and I don't think I'm emotionally mature enough to take such a step. Besides, I've only been out of school a year and I think every girl should take a long time deciding whom she wants to marry before she actually settles down."

Meanwhile, after her auspicious debut in *Captain from Castile*, Peters was cast opposite Dana Andrews in *Deep Waters* (1948), in which she portrayed a state welfare worker who encourages a friendship between her lobster man boyfriend and a wayward orphan. But following this run-of-the-mill melodrama, Peters stunned studio brass by refusing her next two assignments, *Yellow Sky* (1948) and *Sand* (1949). Of the latter, she outspokenly told the press: "I frankly thought *Sand* was a very poor script. I think anyone who plays it will be sorry afterward." (The roles would be played by Anne Baxter and Coleen Gray, respectively.) To punish the young "upstart," studio executives placed her on suspension but relented when she accepted the lead in her third film, *It Happens Every Spring* (1949). Costarring Ray Milland and Paul Douglas, this entertaining comedy told the story of a scientist who develops a formula that helps him become a star baseball player. Next, in Peters' sole film of 1950, she starred opposite Paul Douglas in *Love That Brute*, portraying a recreation director who falls in love with a soft-hearted racketeer, followed in

Jean Peters

1951 with *Take Care of My Little Girl*, which offered a dramatic criticism of college sorority and fraternity life, and *As Young as You Feel*, a Monty Woolley starrer about a senior citizen who impersonates a company president after he is dismissed from his job.

Becoming increasingly disenchanted with her film assignments, Peters went after her next part with a vengeance and won the title role in *Anne of the Indies* (1951). In this feature, Peters portrayed the merciless captain of the

Spanish Main who valiantly dies after a battle with her rival, Blackbeard the Pirate. "I would have died if I'd lost the part of Anne," the actress said. "It took a lot of fortitude to go after a big part. If I am a flop, I thought — and a woman pirate is a difficult role to play because women in the audience won't be able to create any identity with her — then I have brought about my own downfall. However, if you sit back and let life pass you by, you have only yourself to blame if you are overlooked."

In the first of Peters' four releases of 1952, she portrayed the daughter of a Mexican merchant in *Viva Zapata!*, which starred Marlon Brando as the legendary Mexican revolutionary. This critically acclaimed film was followed by *Wait 'Til the Sun Shines, Nellie*, a poignant turn-of-the-century drama about the life and loves of a small town barber, *Lure of the Wilderness*, a mediocre melodrama about a fugitive hiding out with his daughter in the Okefenokee swamps of Georgia, and *O. Henry's Full House*, a grouping of five separate stories by the famed author. Peters was featured in the third segment, "The Last Leaf," about an invalid who recovers due to the sacrifices of an elderly painter.

In 1953, Peters entered the realm of film noir, starring with Marilyn Monroe and Joseph Cotten in *Niagara*, a tale of murder and betrayal. Here, Peters portrayed Polly Cutler who, along with her husband, Ray (Casey Adams), visits Niagara Falls for a "delayed honeymoon." At the famed Falls, the couple meet an alluring guest, Rose Loomis (Monroe), and her husband, George (Cotten), who has been recently released from a veteran's mental hospital. Although Rose expresses concern to the Cutlers about her husband's illness, her duplicitous nature soon becomes apparent when Polly spots her kissing another man during a sightseeing junket to the Falls.

Before long, it is revealed that Rose and her lover, Patrick (Richard Allan), plan to murder George, and when her husband later turns up missing, Rose puts on a convincing show of insisting that police find him. But when she is asked to identify a body at the morgue, Rose is horrified to find that not George, but Patrick, has been killed. Meanwhile, Polly realizes that George intends to murder Rose, but her warning to police comes too late, as George hunts Rose down and strangles her. Later, George steals a boat, not knowing that Polly is aboard, but the boat runs out of gas and is caught in the current leading to the Falls. Unable to reverse the boat's inevitable course, George manages to help Polly to safety, and moments later, plunges over the Falls to his death.

Although Marilyn Monroe was *Niagara's* top attraction, Peters was commended in the *New York Times* as "a believable honeymooner who is as comely as they come," and by the reviewer for *Variety*, who wrote, "Miss Peters portrays the honeymooning wife with a wholesome quality and generally makes a favorable impression." After this box office smash, the actress offered a memorable performance in her second film noir, *Pickup on South Street* (1953).

As this fast-paced, gritty film begins, Peters' character, Candy, is on a crowded subway train, being carefully observed by two fellow passengers. When Candy's wallet is stolen by a skillful pickpocket, Skip McCoy (Richard Widmark), it is revealed that Candy was unknowingly transporting microfilm containing military secrets, as a favor to her former boyfriend, Joey (Richard Kiley), a Communist spy. The two men watching Candy are federal agents, and the remainder of the movie involves their efforts, along with local police, to track down the microfilm. In trying to locate Skip, the police turn to Moe (Thelma Ritter, in an Academy Award–nominated performance), who supplements her tie-selling business by selling information to the authorities. A colorful character, Moe's major concern in life is saving enough money to buy a decent burial plot: "If I was to be buried in Potter's Field, it would just about kill me," she says. "I got a hole picked out on Long Island — it's private. You got to be screened before they'll let them put you in there, that's how exclusive it is."

Like the police, Candy also learns Skip's whereabouts from Moe, but the pickpocket has discovered the value of his plunder, and demands a $25,000 payoff, despite his attraction to Candy. When Candy fails to recover the film, Joey pays a visit to Moe, seeking Skip's whereabouts, but he kills her when she refuses to give the information to a "Commie." Later, Candy manages to retrieve the film from Skip but, in a frighteningly realistic scene, Joey discovers a frame missing from the film and savagely beats and shoots Candy when she tries to escape. Transformed by his love for Candy, Skip tracks Joey down and turns him into police, but not before first avenging the death of Moe and the shooting of Candy by giving the spy a much-deserved thrashing. As the film ends, Candy has recovered from her injuries, and she and Skip prepare to start a life together.

After earning praise in the *New York Times* for "doing very well" in her role as Candy, Peters next starred with Joseph Cotten in *A Blueprint for Murder* (1953), a mystery about a man who falls in love with his sister-in-law, only to discover that she is guilty of murder. The film's director, Andrew Stone, later said of Peters, "Jean was a charming girl. I don't think she had the greatest screen personality but she was a very competent actress. I'll never forget a Friday afternoon when she read for a part and wasn't good. I was concerned. She said, 'Don't worry. Monday I'll be in and I'll be a different girl.' Monday came and you wouldn't know it was the same actress."

Next, in her last film of 1953 and her final film noir, Peters starred with her old friend Jeanne Crain in *Vicki*, playing the title role of a ruthlessly ambitious model. A remake of 1941's *I Wake Up Screaming*, this film opens with the murder of Vicki Lynn, a famous model whose face graces the cover of countless magazines and billboards nationwide. When New York police detective Ed Cornell (Richard Boone) hears of the crime, he cuts short his vacation and insists on running the investigation. From the start, Cornell's prime suspect is Steve Christopher (Elliott Reid), a publicity agent who'd discovered Vicki working nights as a waitress and skillfully transformed her into a star. Steve, Cornell suggests, was angered when Vicki secretly negotiated a Hollywood film contract, and murdered her on the morning of her departure for the West Coast. Despite circumstantial evidence against Steve, Vicki's sister Jill (Crain) insists that Steve is innocent and suggests that the killer might be a man who frequently spied on Vicki during her days as a waitress. But when Vicki later identifies Cornell as the man, the detective explains that surveillance of the restaurant was part of his job.

Steve is released from custody when police focus their investigation on the switchboard operator of Vicki's apartment building, Harry Williams (played by Aaron Spelling, later the successful producer of such programs as *Charlie's Angels, Dynasty* and *Melrose Place*). However, Cornell later clears Williams of guilt and continues his blatant harassment of Steve, at one point even handcuffing him and planning to beat him into a confession. But Jill helps Steve to escape and, after conducting his own probe into the murder, Steve realizes that the switchboard operator, Williams, is the guilty party. After notifying police, Steve tricks Williams into a confession, but is shocked to learn that Cornell had known of his guilt all along. Confronting Cornell later, Steve discovers that the detective was obsessed with Vicki and finds his home set up as a shrine to the dead model. "You're the one who took her away from me, not him," Cornell says. "I used to hang around that cafeteria at night, just to make sure she got home safe. We had a cup of coffee together. I started to hope we'd get to know each other better — I might even get up the courage to ask her to marry me some day. Why didn't you leave her alone?"

Although Peters' character dies before the film begins, she was a forceful presence throughout, as the technique of flashback first shows Vicki as a rather sweet waitress, then follows her transformation into a callous star. Her altered personality is particularly evident in the scene in which she informs Steve of her plans to move to Hollywood: "I know what you're thinking — you gave me my start and all that. But it was me they were interested in. I've got what it takes and you didn't invent it." Although the film itself earned mixed reviews, Peters and her costars were singled out in the *New York Times* for making "the best of Harry Horner's brisk direction to make it look as though they're playing a tingling film."

After *Vicki*, Peters starred with Dorothy McGuire and Maggie McNamara in *Three Coins in the Fountain* (1954), the story of three American girls searching for love in Rome. The popularity of this glossy soaper was enhanced by the title song by Sammy Cahn and Jule Styne, which became a standard. The film was also a favorite with Peters, who later said, "I loved the picture and it gave me a chance to smile for a change. I was usually beaten to death in pictures. *Three Coins* was full of life and living and love. I think I first began to understand love in that picture."

Coincidentally, soon after the release of this film, Peters' personal life took center stage. Since her arrival in Hollywood, Peters had been involved in an off-and-on relationship with Howard Hughes, but over the years, the actress reportedly had become increasingly disillusioned with Hughes' frequent absences and his well-publicized affairs with such stars as Ava Gardner and Mitzi Gaynor. In 1954, Peters began dating Stuart Cramer III, an oil man from Charlotte, North Carolina, and after several dates, Cramer proposed, telling the press, "I found Jean had a beautiful, compelling, unhappy quality. Not only did I think this, but I talked to two or three other men who had gone with Jean and it seemed everyone was interested in doing things for her. Anything, just to make her happy." On May 29, 1954, in Washington, D.C., Peters and Cramer were married, but they lived together for only three months, and by 1956, they were divorced. Cramer later told reporters, "After our marriage she was busy doing pictures, and I was busy with my own work, and we didn't spend much time together. Frankly, I don't think she knew what she wanted to do or how important movies were to her." (Ironically, Cramer would later marry actress Terry Moore who, after the death of Howard Hughes, would claim that she had been the wife of the eccentric billionaire.)

Professionally, Peters was next seen in *Broken Lance* (1954), which starred Spencer Tracy as a wealthy cattle baron who rules his home and his four sons with a ruthless hand, followed by her only non–Fox film, United Artists' *Apache* (1954), a better-than-average Western about a lone Indian chief's last stand against the encroaching U.S. army. Peters was well-received for her role as the chief's devoted squaw, and later recalled: "I had a wonderful part in *Apache*, but no one will ever know me. It took ages to get the makeup on and two full hours at night to become white again. I had a disreputable, scroungy old wig and my clothes were assorted rags. The makeup and wardrobe woman came to pick me up in the morning and I'd be made up before I went to the studio. We'd go to work in a long black limousine, driving through Bel-Air. People must have wondered what such a horrible looking creature was doing in such a car."

Back at Fox, Peters starred in *A Man Called Peter* (1955), playing the devoted wife of Peter Marshall, the real-life Scotsman who became a clergyman and U.S. Senate chaplain. The role was one of Peters' favorites, and the film is often considered to be her best. But it would also be her last. In 1956, soon after her divorce from Stuart Cramer, the actress resumed her relationship with Howard Hughes and the following year, the two secretly wed in Tonopah, Nevada, giving their names as G.A. Johnson and Mary Ann Evans. After the marriage, at age 31, Peters retired from filmmaking and almost completely disappeared from both social and professional life.

During most of her marriage to Hughes, Peters lived separately from her husband in a heavily guarded mansion near Beverly Hills, visiting him on weekends at his home in Las Vegas. After her abrupt disappearance from the public eye, she spent much of her time taking art courses at UCLA, conducting door-to-door political polling, and shopping, but always incognito and frequently accompanied by guards. During this time, Peters also read textbooks for taping by the Braille Institute, but stopped when, she said, "I couldn't stand the sound of my own voice any more." In all the years they were married, not a single photograph was ever published of the couple, and only one appeared of Peters alone, in 1969 at an opera in Los Angeles.

Little is known about the unusual marriage of Peters and Hughes, but famed newspaper columnist Jack Anderson said that Hughes kept his wife "on a yoyo string. He would disappear for long stretches and send her endearing but false messages through his aide, William Gay." Anderson related several stories that illustrated the couple's odd relationship, including a 1965 Thanksgiving Day dinner, during which Hughes insisted that Peters sit across the room from him "because of his fear of germs." And the following year, Anderson said, Hughes convinced Peters to join him in Boston, "but again he kept her at across-the-room distance. She put up with it for three days."

When the marriage finally broke up in 1971, Anderson said that Hughes placed the blame on his aide William Gay, quoting the billionaire's complaint that "Bill's total indifference and laxity to my pleas for help in my domestic area ... have resulted in a complete, I am afraid, irrevocable loss of my wife." The details of the divorce settlement were not released, but one columnist speculated that Peters received $120 million from Hughes, while another source suggested that she was awarded $70,000 annually for the next 20 years, an amount that could double, depending on the consumer price index. For her part, Peters has declined to discuss Hughes since their divorce; when asked by a television talk show host what it was like being married to the eccentric billionaire, Peters firmly replied, "That was and shall remain a matter on which I will have no comment." Shortly after her divorce, Peters married former 20th Century–Fox production executive Stanley L. Hough, whom she had first met in 1947 during the filming of her screen debut. By all accounts, the third time was the charm for Peters, and she remained married to Hough until his death in 1990.

Meanwhile, after an absence from performing of nearly two decades, Peters made her return to acting in 1973 for the PBS production of *Winesburg, Ohio*. After receiving good notices for her portrayal of a neurotic, middle-aged woman, Peters told a *TV Guide* reporter, "I don't know if I would want to do a film or anything else that would require me to be separated from my husband, but this is perfect. Only a few weeks long, right here in Los Angeles and a marvelous role." Three years later, Peters was seen in a small role in the four-part TV special *The Moneychangers*, and in 1989, she was featured on an episode of the popular CBS-TV series *Murder, She Wrote*. After her appearance on this show, Peters said: "It was my mother's very favorite program. She passed away two years ago and I figured she'd be very angry if I didn't do it. It was fun going back to work.... It's the first acting I've done in some time but I'd do it again if it was something I liked." Off-screen, Peters has donated much of her time in recent years to various charitable causes, including working with the National Autistic Society fund-raising campaign and volunteering in the Screen Smart Shop, which sells items for the benefit of the Motion Picture and Television Country House and Hospital.

Although she made only 19 pictures during an eight-year film career, Peters displayed an innate acting ability and a unique screen presence that more than hints at the potential superstardom that could have been hers had she continued acting. As described by Buddy Adler, one-time head of 20th Century–Fox, "Jean Peters was an excellent actress. She had a great deal of fire that she kept under control and you could feel it."

Film Noir Filmography

NIAGARA   *Director:* Henry Hathaway. *Producer:* Charles Brackett. Released by 20th Century–Fox, January 1953. *Running time:* 92 minutes. *Cast:* Marilyn Monroe, Joseph Cotten, Jean Peters, Casey Adams, Dennis O'Dea, Richard Allan, Don Wilson, Lurene Tuttle.

PICKUP ON SOUTH STREET   *Director:* Samuel Fuller. *Producer:* Jules Schermer. Released by 20th Century–Fox, June 1953. *Running time:* 83 minutes. *Cast:* Richard Widmark, Jean Peters, Thelma Ritter, Murvyn Vye, Richard Kiley. *Awards:* Academy Award nomination for Best Supporting Actress (Thelma Ritter).

VICKI   *Director:* Harry Horner. *Producer:* Leonard Goldstein. Released by 20th Century–Fox, September 1953. *Running time:* 85 minutes. *Cast:* Jeanne Crain, Jean Peters, Elliott Reid, Richard Boone, Casey Adams, Alex D'Arcy, Carl Betz, Aaron Spelling.

References

"Back in Filmdom." *New York Daily Mirror*, November 4, 1954.
Biography of Jean Peters. 20th Century–Fox Studios, 1956.
Borg, Louis. "Jean Hits the Top." *New York Herald Tribune*, June 6, 1954.
Cassa, Anthony. "Pete, the Reluctant Movie Star." *Hollywood Studio Magazine*, September 1980.
"Change of Address." *TV Guide*, March 3, 1973.
"Co-Ed from Ohio." *American Magazine*, circa 1947.
Crosby, Joan. "A 17-Year Hiatus for Jean Peters." *TV Scout Entertainment News and Features*, February 26, 1973.
Hall, Gladys. "Exploding the Myth of the Mysterious Miss Peters." *Photoplay*, October 1954.
Hopper, Hedda. "Hollywood's Gorgeous." *Chicago Tribune Magazine*, July 11, 1954.
_____. "Hollywood's Mystery Girl." *Photoplay*, March 1952.
"Jackpot!" *Modern Screen*, June 1948.
"Jean Peters." *Boston Sunday Post*, November 13, 1949.
Muir, Florabel. "Hughes Secretly Signs Jean Peters as Bride." *New York Daily News*, March 16, 1957.

"New Star Over Hollywood." *Coronet*, April 1952.

Peters, Mary E., as told to Robert Peer. "She Never Left Home." *Modern Screen*, June 1949.

"Rules Out Glamour Boys." *New York Morning Telegraph*, May 29, 1954.

Scott, Vernon. "Glamour Out for Peters." *New York Morning Telegraph*, October 10, 1953.

Strait, Raymond. *Mrs. Howard Hughes*. Los Angeles, Calif.: Holloway House, 1970.

Wallace, Rosalie. "Halfway to Heaven." *Photoplay*, November 1948.

Ella Raines

Ella Raines was one of the few Hollywood actresses to almost literally become "an overnight sensation." But with a film career that spanned less than 15 years, and only 22 films to her credit, Raines was rarely cast in the sleek, mysterious roles in which she excelled, and is frequently all but forgotten by modern audiences. However, she managed to display a talent for comedy as well as drama, and was used to good advantage in her four film noir appearances: *Phantom Lady* (1944), *The Strange Affair of Uncle Harry* (1945), *Brute Force* (1947) and *Impact* (1949).

The sultry beauty with the striking green eyes was born Ella Wallace Raubes on August 6, 1921, in Snoqualmie Falls, a small town in Washington with a population of less than 800 inhabitants. An only child, Ella was an outgoing, adventurous youngster who spent much of her time engaged in such outdoor activities as swimming, horseback riding, skiing, archery and fishing. Taught by her engineer father Ernest, the actress could also expertly handle a shotgun by the age of ten.

In addition to her athletic abilities, Ella was also a top student in school and displayed a flair for acting during her high school years, joining the drama club and participating in several school plays. Winning a dramatic scholarship to the University of Washington in 1939, she continued her theater work there, becoming somewhat of a local celebrity through her appearances in a variety of productions, including *Hay Fever, The Tempest* and *Mr. and Mrs. North*, as well as number of dramatic programs on Seattle radio stations. A popular student whose radiant beauty earned her such titles as "Navy Queen" and "Cinderella Girl," it appeared that Ella's acting ambitions might be forever thwarted when a stove exploded in her face in 1941. Luckily, although the actress was in serious condition for a time, with burns to her hair, face and hands, she suffered no permanent damage.

By now, Ella's acclaimed performances in her college productions had caught the attention of Hollywood agent Charles Feldman, who convinced the young beauty to come to California following her graduation. But fate intervened on the day prior to her commencement, when Ella received a telegram from her long-time beau, Army Air Force Lt. Kenneth Trout, asking her to fly to Palm Beach, Florida, and marry him before he went overseas with the Army Air Force. Without waiting to graduate, Ella married the handsome bomber pilot on August 11, 1942, in a formal ceremony featuring 200 invited guests. But the marriage would not last. Two weeks later, Trout departed for duty in India and Burma and the couple's near-constant separation led to their divorce after only three years.

Meanwhile, shortly after her wedding, Ella traveled to Hollywood, meeting with Feldman and famed director Howard Hawks, who had recently formed a production company with actor Charles Boyer. Hawks and Boyer were entranced by the beautiful young girl and promptly signed her to a unique contract with their B & H Productions that earned her the title "the million-dollar actress." Changing her last name to Raines, the future star debuted in *Corvette K-225* (1943), the story of life on board one of the compact escort warships of the British and Canadian naval forces, known as corvettes. Produced by Hawks through Universal Studios, the film was a box office hit and Raines was hailed by critics for her role as the love interest of Randolph Scott. After the film's release, Universal bought Raines' contract from B & H Productions and immediately loaned her to MGM for *Cry Havoc* (1943). In this well-received wartime film, Raines appeared in an all-female cast that included Joan Blondell, Ann Sothern and Margaret Sullavan.

Back at Universal, Raines was next cast in the picture for which she is perhaps best remembered, *Phantom Lady* (1944), starring Franchot Tone and Alan Curtis. In this highly acclaimed example of film noir, Raines portrayed Carol Richman, the loyal secretary of a successful engineer who has been accused of murdering his wife. On the night of the murder, the engineer, Scott Henderson (Curtis), had been in the company of a young woman whom he had met in a local bar. The woman, who wore a large, distinctive hat, refused to tell Scott her name: "No names, no addresses — just companions for the evening." Later, police learn that everyone Scott came in contact with on the night of the murder — the bartender, a cab driver, the star of a musical revue and a drummer from the show — all deny that he was with a woman. Unable to locate the woman, Scott is convicted and sentenced to die. But Carol, who is secretly in love with Scott, refuses to accept the verdict and, assisted by a police inspector, Burgess (Thomas Gomez), sets out to find the real killer. She first pursues the bartender, but he is struck by a car and killed before he can reveal any information. Next, Carol tries to get information by cozying up to the drummer from the musical revue (Elisha Cook, Jr.). He reveals that he was paid $500 to deny any recollection of the "phantom lady," but when Carol returns to his apartment with Inspector Burgess, she finds that he has been murdered.

By now, Scott's best friend, Jack Marlow (Franchot Tone), has returned from a trip to South America to offer his help, and with just weeks remaining before Scott's execution, Carol finally tracks down the "phantom lady." But when she and Jack return to his studio to celebrate, Carol realizes that Jack is the killer. Jack admits his guilt, revealing that he had been having an affair with Scott's wife, but she had broken off their relationship: "She laughed at me," he says. "I had to stop her laughing.... I'm fond of Scott. We're friends. But what's his life compared to mine? What's any life compared to mine?" As Jack prepares to make Carol his third victim, Burgess arrives at the door, and Jack falls to his death from a window while trying to escape. Later, Scott is released from prison and, via a message left for Carol on his dictaphone, he reveals his plans for their future together.

For her portrayal of Carol Richman, Raines was praised in the *New York Journal American*, whose critic stated that she "checked in an excellent performance," and she was honored with a photo on the cover of *Life* magazine. Soon after, the actress was loaned to Paramount for *Hail the Conquering Hero* (1944). This classic comedy, written and directed by Preston Sturges, told the story of a hapless Marine recruit (hilariously portrayed by Eddie Bracken) who is rejected for war service because of a hay fever condition, but is mistakenly acclaimed as a hero upon his return to his hometown. As the recruit's girlfriend, Raines showed a flair for comedy and was singled out by one reviewer for her "perfect" performance.

In her third film of 1944, Raines was again loaned out, this time to RKO for her first Western, *Tall in the Saddle*, a rip-roaring hit starring John Wayne. Next, for Universal, she starred as the love interest of newcomer Charles Korvin in *Enter Arsene Lupin* (1944), a mildly successful picture that focused on the exploits of a dashing jewel thief, followed by *The Suspect* (1944), a first-rate thriller set in Victorian London. Starring Charles Laughton, this box office hit told the story of an unhappily married man who murders his shrewish wife and weds his beautiful stenographer. While critics seemed more focused on Raines' physical appearance in this film, labeling her "most appealing" and "beautiful," her performance served to add to her popularity with the public.

In another offering from the film noir era, Raines next appeared in Universal's *The Strange Affair of Uncle Harry* (1945). Set in the small New Hampshire town of Corinth, this story focuses on the lives of Harry Quincy (George Sanders), a mild-mannered, unassuming factory worker, and his two sisters, the possessive and subtly domineering Lettie (Geraldine Fitzgerald) and the slightly neurotic Hester (Moyna McGill). Harry enjoys a pleasant, if dull, life with his sisters, but when he falls in love with Deborah Brown (Raines), a fashion consultant from New York City, Lettie only barely manages to mask her displeasure. When Harry and Deborah decide to marry and move to New York, Lettie feigns a heart attack, forcing Harry to choose between his sister and his would-be bride. Harry insists on caring for his sister, but when Deborah leaves town, Harry is devastated to not only learn that Deborah plans to wed the owner of the town mill, but that Lettie purposely faked her illness. Angered by her interference, Harry puts poison in a cup of cocoa that Lettie is to drink, but Hester drinks it instead, and dies. Lettie is accused of murdering her sister and Harry allows her to be convicted and sentenced to death for the crime.

Later, Harry has a change of heart and admits the truth, but the district attorney does not believe him, and Lettie herself refuses to incriminate her brother. Once alone with Harry, she reveals her motivation: "Ever since we were children I've wanted to do something for you, to give you something. Something worthy of your talent and imagination. Seems strange, doesn't it, that I should choose this peculiar moment to give you this peculiar present.... Your future, my dear. You'll not be good company for yourself all the long years that stretch ahead. When you can't think or sleep or eat or read. Poor Harry." Lettie is returned to her cell to await her execution, and in the next scene, Harry is seen disposing of the vial of poison. As he sits in his room alone, Deborah suddenly enters, informing Harry that she didn't get married after all, and she is closely followed by a delighted Hester. As it turns out, the entire situation was a dream.

For her portrayal of Deborah, Raines received mixed reviews. While Bosley Crowther of the *New York Times* noted her "weak" performance, William R. Weaver of *Motion Picture Herald* found the actress "capital." She was next cast with Broderick Crawford and Rod Cameron in *The Runaround* (1946), a tedious comedy that was clearly inspired by Frank Capra's *It Happened One Night*. Raines didn't fare much better in her next feature, *White Tie and Tails* (1946), a fantasy-comedy that suffered primarily from the miscasting of the unctuous Dan Duryea as a light-hearted butler.

While Raines' career appeared temporarily stagnant, her personal life took center stage when, on February 6, 1946, she married another military man, Major Robin Olds of the Army Air Force. Olds, who had more than 20 aerial victories to his wartime credit, was working as a jet aircraft test pilot at the time of his wedding to Raines. The "fairy tale" marriage of the beautiful actress and the war hero, which produced two daughters, Christina and Susan, was later described by actress Audrey Totter: "This town is full of men who look the handsome hero type, but they're only actors. This guy that Ella landed was the real thing. Talk about good-looking and dashing!" But after 28 years, the marriage ended, and Raines would candidly admit: "The man had no heart. So macho all the time, but when he testified at our divorce he had to admit that he'd had a free ride financially all the years we were together. I spent over 30 years of my life with a man whom I must admit I dislike. But my two daughters ... more than compensate for him."

Career-wise, Raines was next cast in another box office disappointment, *Time Out of Mind* (1947), a tiresome drama about a young musician whose seafaring father disapproves of his vocation. But she rebounded with her next two features, *The Web* (1947), in which she was top-billed as the secretary of a wealthy industrialist suspected of murder, and her third film noir, *Brute Force* (1947).

A gritty drama set in a federal penitentiary, *Brute Force* tells the story of a group of convicts — including Joe Collins (Burt Lancaster), Soldier (Howard Duff) and Tom Lister (Whit Bissell) — who are planning to escape from prison. In flashback scenes, each of the men remember the women they left behind and reveal the circumstances that led to their lives of crime. Joe recalls a sweet, wheelchair-bound girl (Ann Blyth) who is unaware that he is committing crimes to pay for her medical expenses, while Soldier dreams of returning to his Italian wife (Yvonne DeCarlo), for whom he nobly took the blame after she shot and killed a military policeman. And Tom remembers the funds he embezzled from his job in order to buy a fur coat for his money-hungry wife, Cora (Raines). Later, in prison, after learning that Cora is divorcing him, Tom is found hanging in his cell.

Ella Raines

Along with Gallagher (Charles Bickford) and Freshman (Jeff Corey), the other men continue planning their break from prison, but their well-designed scheme is thwarted when a sadistic guard, Capt. Munsey (Hume Cronyn), learns of the plot. The film's violent climax sees the death not only of each of the men, but of Munsey, as well, who is tossed from a tower into a swarm of convicts.

After the release of *Brute Force*, Raines was singled out in *Variety* for her brief but "excellent" performance, and she was next seen in another small role, this time in *The Senator Was Indiscreet* (1947), a mildly entertaining comedy that flourished at the box office on the strength of its star, William Powell. Following this picture, Raines' contract with Universal lapsed and, although her parting was an amicable one, she would never make another film for the studio. Off-screen for the next year, she turned to freelancing as the 1940s came to a close, appearing in Columbia's *The Walking Hills* (1949), a solidly crafted programmer about a group of treasure hunters looking for buried gold, and *Impact* (1949), her final film noir.

Impact opens by introducing Walt Williams (Brian Donlevy), a successful San Francisco businessman, and his beautiful wife, Irene (Helen Walker). Despite Irene's seeming devotion to her husband, however, it is soon revealed that she is having an affair with a local man, Jim Torrance (Tony Barrett), and that the two are plotting Walt's demise. Irene and Jim plan an elaborate scheme to make it appear that Walt was murdered by a hitchhiker. Jim is killed in an auto accident after bludgeoning Walt with a tire iron and leaving his unconscious body on the side of a road. Ironically, Jim's charred body is identified as Walt.

Meanwhile, Walt manages to make his way to a small town in Idaho, but when he reads of his death in a local newspaper, he decides to remain in hiding. Giving a false name, he gets a job as a mechanic in a small service station owned by Marsha Peters (Raines), and after several months, he and Marsha fall in love. Back in San Francisco, however, Irene is indicted for murder, and Walter is convinced by Marsha to exonerate his wife. The couple return to San Francisco together, but when Irene learns that it was her lover who died in the crash, she accuses Walt of murder. With evidence now pointing to him, Walt is arrested and tried for the crime, while Marsha works with a police detective (Charles Coburn) to establish Walt's innocence. They discover proof that they need, the charges against Walt are immediately dropped, and Irene is arrested for conspiring to kill her husband.

Upon its release, *Impact* received high marks from critics — it was labelled as a "better-than-average melodrama" in the *Los Angeles Examiner* and in *Variety* as "a well-paced mix of crime and romance encased in a glossy production." Most of Raines' notices were good as well, with the possible exception of Bosley Crowther, who wrote in the *New York Times*: "Ella Raines as the Idaho small town girl reminds one of that state's most famous crop." However, the reviewer for the *Los Angeles Examiner* said that "with plenty of competition ... Raines comes through with the best acting of the lot," and *Variety's* critic found that she "registers nicely with an easy-going performance."

But by now it seemed that Raines' best screen offerings were behind her, a fact that was clearly demonstrated in her next film, RKO's *A Dangerous Profession* (1949). Starring George Raft and Pat O'Brien as partners in a bail bond firm, this would-be mystery suffered from a confusing screenplay and left

Raines with little to do as the widow of a robbery suspect. Signing with Republic Studios in 1950, Raines' career continued to flounder, as she was cast in such drivel as *Singing Guns* (1950), a dreadful musical-Western starring Vaughn Monroe; *The Second Face* (1950), a low-budget programmer featuring Raines as a "plain Jane" who is transformed into a great beauty through plastic surgery; and *Fighting Coast Guard* (1951), a film that was notable only for its real-life film footage from World War II battles in the Pacific. After *Ride the Man Down* (1952), a plodding Western starring Rod Cameron (with whom Raines was reportedly having a romance), the still-stunning actress took a break from filmmaking, and would not be seen on the silver screen for another three years.

Instead, Raines turned to the medium of television. Having made her debut on *Robert Montgomery Presents* in 1950, and subsequently performing on *Ides of April* and *The Pulitzer Prize Playhouse*, in 1953 she formed Cornwall Productions with William Dozier, then supervising producer in charge of dramatic programs at CBS-TV. The following year, Raines hired Joan Harrison (who would later produce the acclaimed *Alfred Hitchcock Presents*) to develop a television vehicle for her, resulting in *Janet Dean, Registered Nurse*. Although the popular series lasted only one season, it attracted considerable attention for its handling of such social issues as anti–Semitism, and was the first television program to feature a nurse as the principal character. "Many people were afraid when we started filming the show that it would be just another soap opera," Raines said during the run of the program. "But I think we've succeeded in getting a mature, adult approach to our stories." Still, the actress seemed to quickly tire of playing the sedate young nurse who had little time for personal entanglements, and said in a 1954 interview: "I'm so tired of being sweet and pure all the time. I can't wait to get back to Hollywood … and get a chance to do a couple of romantic scenes. I guess I just like men."

In 1955, after the end of the short-lived series, Raines returned to her roots on the stage, appearing on Broadway with veteran actress Helen Hayes in *The Wisteria Trees*. Later that year, she moved to England, where her husband was stationed, and in 1956 gave her final feature film performance in *The Man in the Road*, a British suspenser that was released to mixed reviews. Several years later, during the Vietnam War, Raines moved with her family to Washington, D.C., where she penned articles for various newspapers, including one in which she wrote about service wives who maintain "a home that is as normal as possible for the children, while keeping their worries to themselves." And the actress herself made the news in 1967 when she chased a would-be prowler off her estate by firing at him with a shotgun. Given the familiarity with firearms that she'd acquired during her childhood, it can only be surmised that Raines missed the criminal on purpose.

In the 1980s, now divorced from Olds, Raines taught drama courses at her alma mater, the University of Washington, then returned to Los Angeles where she provided private tutoring for actors. Briefly resuming her television career, she also guested on a handful of popular programs, including *Police Story* and *Matt Houston*. Soon after her appearance on the latter series, however, Raines was diagnosed with throat cancer, and on May 30, 1988, she died in Sherman Oaks Hospital in Los Angeles. She was 66 years old, and at the time of her death she was reportedly working on her autobiography.

Although Ella Raines never managed to achieve the potential that seemed so promising upon her arrival in Hollywood, she leaves behind a number of fine performances in classic productions that will forever attest to her contribution to the annals of cinema. And unlike many a film star, she managed to keep her career in perspective and appeared to relish her personal happiness as well as her professional triumphs. As the actress herself stated at the peak of her fame, "I am naturally captivated with the rewards that Hollywood bestows on those who are successful. But I'm going to do my best to see these [rewards] never disturb the essential values in my life — love of husband, family, home — the things that really count."

Film Noir Filmography

PHANTOM LADY   *Director:* Robert Siodmak. *Producer:* Milton Field. Released by Universal, February 1944. *Running time:* 87 minutes. *Cast:* Franchot Tone, Ella Raines, Alan Curtis, Thomas Gomez, Elisha Cook, Jr., Fay Helm, Aurora.

THE STRANGE AFFAIR OF UNCLE HARRY   *Director:* Robert Siodmak. *Producer:* Joan Harrison. Released by Universal, August 1945. *Running time:* 80 minutes. *Cast:* George Sanders, Geraldine Fitzgerald, Ella Raines, Sara Allgood, Moyna MacGill, Samuel S. Hinds, Harry Von Zell.

BRUTE FORCE   *Director:* Jules Dassin. *Producer:* Mark Hellinger. Released by Universal-International, June 1947. *Running time:* 95 minutes. *Cast:* Burt Lancaster, Hume Cronyn, Charles Bickford, Ann Blyth, Ella Raines, Anita Colby, Sam Levene, Howard Duff, Art Smith, Roman Bohnen, John Hoyt, Richard Gaines, Frank Puglia, Jeff Corey, Whit Bissell.

IMPACT   *Director:* Arthur Lubin. *Producer:* Leo C. Popkin. Released by United Artists, April 1949. *Running time:* 108 minutes. *Cast:* Brian Donlevy, Ella Raines, Charles Coburn, Helen Walker, Anna May Wong, Mae Marsh, Tony Barrett.

References

Becklund, Laurie. "Ella Raines: Sultry Star of '40s-Era Films." *Los Angeles Times*, June 7, 1988.
Carle, Teet. Biography of Ella Raines. Paramount Studios, July 1943.
Cheney, Carlton. "Ella Moves Up in a Hurry." *Milwaukee Journal*, November 21, 1943.
"Ella Raines Gets Divorce." *Boston Post*, December 14, 1945.
"Ella Raines' RX for TV." *TV Guide*, July 17, 1954.
Ghidalia, Miriam Alberta. "Gal with a Glint." *Modern Screen*, December 1945.
Graham, Sheilah. "Boyer Turns Drama Coach for Newcomer." *Dallas Morning News*, June 1, 1943.

"Holiday with Ella Raines." *Life*, July 30, 1945.
"If I Had One Wish." *Photoplay*, October 1946.
James, Caryn. "Ella Raines, a Star of Westerns and Dramas of the 40s Dies at 67." *New York Times*, June 9, 1988.
"Janet Dean, Registered Nurse." *TV Guide*, June 25, 1954.
Lieber, Perry. Biography of Ella Raines. RKO Radio Studios, May 13, 1949.
MacPherson, Virginia. "It Never Raines — It Pours." *New York Morning Telegraph*, May 5, 1950.
"Meet the Cover(all) Girls." *Lions Review*, January 1944.
"Million-Dollar Baby." *American Magazine*, December 1943.
Parsons, Harriet. "Keyhole Portrait." *New York Journal American*, March 12, 1944.
"Pretty Young Star." *Life*, February 28, 1944.
Scott, John L. "Ella Raines Will Sail to Join Mate." *Los Angeles Times*, November 14, 1948.
Van Neste, Dan. "Ella Raines: A Striking Beauty." *Classic Images*, November 1995.
"The Warrior's Wife." *New York Sunday News*, August 20, 1967.
Wilson, Earl. "I Say What I Think." *Silver Screen*, September 1945.

Ruth Roman

While she never achieved the ranks of movie superstardom, Ruth Roman possessed cool, elegant good looks and a versatile acting style that catapulted her to brief but solid fame. In nearly 50 feature films, the actress appeared opposite some of Hollywood's biggest stars, including Gary Cooper, Kirk Douglas and James Stewart, but hers was a career fraught with missed opportunities and forgettable supporting roles. Still, she provided some of her most successful performances in three films noirs: *The Window* (1949), *Beyond the Forest* (1949) and *Strangers on a Train* (1951).

The striking brunette with the soulful eyes was born in Lynn, Massachusetts, on December 22 (most sources agree that her year of birth was 1923, although it has variously been reported as 1922 and 1924). Originally christened Norma, the actress was renamed Ruth after a fortune teller predicted that her original moniker would bring bad luck. And encounters with fortune tellers was a run-of-the-mill occurrence in the family household — Roman's parents, Anthony and Mary Gold Roman, were owners of a carnival sideshow in Boston. Years later, Roman recalled that while the sideshow wasn't "very big or very fancy ... it was the most exciting thing in the world to me. I would hang around it hour after hour. I even hated to take the time to go home to lunch. I still get weak with nostalgia whenever I look at a merry-go-round."

Before Roman was five years old, her father died and Mary Roman was forced to move her family to a tenement in the West End of Boston, sell the sideshow business and make ends meet by working as a cleaning woman, seamstress or waitress. Her mother was frequently unable to pay the rent, necessitating a number of moves to residences throughout the West End, but Roman would later recall that her early years were joyous ones: "It wasn't dreary at all. When you start out poor, you don't know what you're missing. I've never met a family, rich or poor, that had a happier life than we did together."

Roman's acting ambitions were fostered at an early age, when she began to participate in after-school productions at a community settlement house. Although she won a scholarship for painting while a student in junior high school, Roman turned it down, knowing even then where her true interests lay. Only a few years later, while a high school sophomore, the already-striking Roman dropped out to pursue an acting career. After securing a job as a movie theater usherette, she worked nights with the New England Repertory Company, a semi-professional group. During the next three years, she performed in walk-on roles, served as a stage hand in a variety of New England summer theaters and spent a semester at the Bishop Lee Drama School.

When Roman was 16, her professional ambitions were briefly sidetracked when she impulsively married Jack Flaxman, a young man who worked in a Boston art store. The newlyweds lived with Roman's mother and sister, but after only six months, the marriage was over. The following year, Roman moved to New York with two classmates from the Bishop Lee School, each in search of fame and fortune on Broadway. But the actress spent the next three years futilely hounding producers' offices and making a living by posing for crime magazine covers and working as a baby-sitter, sales clerk and waitress. Years later Roman would admit that the experience was a "real frustration for me. It still makes me shudder. Most people don't know how many heartbreaking years there are behind a success in this business."

Just when it appeared that her dreams of stardom would never be realized, Roman was selected for a brief appearance as a WAVE in *Stage Door Canteen* (1943), a huge money-making morale booster filmed at New York's famed Stage Door Canteen with an all-star cast that included Tallulah Bankhead, Helen Hayes, Paul Muni, Merle Oberon, George Raft, Ralph Bellamy and Ethel Merman. After four days' work, Roman had earned enough money to pay off her creditors and purchase a one-way coach ticket to Hollywood: "I was going to conquer the world," Roman recalled years later. "I had about a hundred bucks on me."

A short time after her arrival in California, a friend arranged for Roman to have a screen test at Warner Bros. But while executives took note of her potential, they concluded that the young hopeful was in need of extensive training, "and not at our expense." Undeterred by this rejection, the strong-willed actress proceeded to make the rounds at each of the Hollywood studios until she was granted one-day bit parts in Universal's *Ladies Courageous* (1944), starring Loretta Young, and David O. Selznick's wartime hit, *Since You Went Away* (1944), with Claudette Colbert, Jennifer Jones and Shirley Temple. She also logged additional screen time and earned extra money by appearing in several WAC training films and as the title character in Universal's 15-week serial *Jungle Queen* (1945). It looked as if Roman was making real headway when she was given the lead in *White Stallion*, a low-budget quickie Western for Astor Pictures, but the film was never released.

In addition to her unflagging determination, Roman was beginning to demonstrate that she possessed a bold brashness as well. While appearing as a cigarette girl in Republic's *Storm Over Lisbon* (1944), she fearlessly approached the studio's president, Herbert Yates, informing him that she had written a movie story, *Whip Song*, whose heroine was a female Robin Hood-type. Yates purchased the synopsis from Roman for $100, later turning it into a serial entitled *Zorro's Black Whip*. The story was "a piece of junk," Roman recalled with amusement more than 50 years later. "It was a little Western, and I was killing off everybody."

Aside from selling story ideas and appearing in bit parts, Roman also garnered funds by posing for various local magazines. In October 1944, she appeared on the cover of *Police Gazette*, photographed in a two-piece bathing suit beside a swimming pool. While Roman was touted in the publication as "one of Hollywood's shapeliest beauties," she was misidentified as "Ruth Roland." In her continuing efforts to break into the ranks of Hollywood fame, Roman lightened her brunette locks to blonde, but she was still able to secure only walk-ons in a series of films including *The Affairs of Susan* (1945), starring Joan Fontaine; *Incendiary Blonde* (1945), a Betty Hutton vehicle; and the classic Rita Hayworth starrer, *Gilda* (1946).

In 1946, the promise of a big break beckoned to Roman again when she was given the role of a harem girl in the Marx Brothers' *A Night in Casablanca*. In the poster advertising the film, Roman's picture was used alongside Groucho Marx, and in Manhattan, a 50-foot cutout of the actress in her harem garb was displayed above a Broadway movie theater. But the expected benefits from this exposure did not materialize — Roman's bit part in the film wound up on the cutting room floor.

Next, the struggling actress lost out on a series of roles that could have provided the boost that her fledgling career sorely needed. Roman tested for *Crossfire* (1947) but Gloria Grahame won the part instead, earning an Academy Award nomination for Best Supporting Actress. She was given a shot at a role opposite George Raft in *Outpost in Morocco* (1949), but the part was given to Marie Windsor. And when she was spotted by David O. Selznick and signed to an 18-month contract, she was used only to pose for publicity shots advertising the famed producer's latest film, *Duel in the Sun* (1947). Roman then inked a six-month contract with Paramount, but she only earned bit roles in *The Big Clock* (1948), with Charles Laughton and Ray Milland, and *Night Has a Thousand Eyes* (1948), starring Edward G. Robinson. "I got enough breaks for half the actors in Hollywood," Roman would later quip, "but nothing happened."

In her biggest role to date, Roman portrayed a sales clerk in *Good Sam* (1948), a bland comedy starring Gary Cooper, followed by the title role in *Belle Starr's Daughter* (1948), a forgettable Western with George Montgomery and Rod Cameron. But Roman's long-awaited shot at the big time was just around the corner. Having befriended Dore Schary, then a production manager at RKO, Roman was given a role in a low-budget picture about a little boy who witnesses a murder committed by a neighbor and his wife. The picture, *The Window* (1949), was Roman's first film noir.

Set in the tenements of New York's Lower East Side, *The Window* opens with an introduction to Tommy Woodry (Bobby Driscoll), an imaginative youngster who is frequently chastised by his parents (Arthur Kennedy and Barbara Hale) for his tall-tale weaving. One night, while on the fire escape of his building, Tommy witnesses a murder in an upstairs apartment. Tommy tells his parents about the incident, identifying their neighbors Mr. and Mrs. Kellerton (Paul Stewart and Ruth Roman) as the killers, but in typical "boy-who-cried-wolf" fashion, his parents do not believe him. The Kellertons realize that their crime was witnessed when Tommy is forced by his mother to apologize, and the remainder of the film involves the couple's attempts to permanently silence the youngster. Left alone by his parents and locked in his bedroom by his father, Tommy is stalked by the murderous couple, who

Ruth Roman

eventually chase the boy to a nearby abandoned building. After a suspenseful chase, Mr. Kellerton falls to his death, Mrs. Kellerton is apprehended, and Tommy promises never to lie again.

Along with Paul Stewart, Roman won praise in *Motion Picture Herald* for her "excellent" performance, and in the *New York Times* for playing her role "with just the right show of fear and desperation." Hailed as a "gripping suspense-filled film," the modestly budgeted hit not only resulted in a miniature

Academy Award for Bobby Driscoll for outstanding juvenile actor, but was also voted best mystery film of the year by the Mystery Writers of America. Despite its success, however, Roman later recalled that she did not initially realize the impact the picture would have. "I saw a rough cut of *The Window* without the music — I remember seeing it in a projection room all by myself," she said. "I left crying and thinking, 'They'll never let me perform again.' I later saw it in Westwood with a full audience and with all the sound, and the people were screaming! Goes to show you, doesn't it?"

Roman's appearance in *The Window* was just the beginning. When director Stanley Kramer viewed a pre-release showing of the picture, he instantly decided to cast the actress in his new film for United Artists, *Champion* (1949), starring Kirk Douglas. Roman would later say that her "happiest 26 days in the movies" were spent during the production of this film, and stated that Douglas told her the film would made her a star. "I couldn't believe that, but Kirk insisted and even offered to make a bet on it," Roman recalled. "If I had taken the bet, I would have lost, for the role of Emma did more for my career than any other role." This engrossing tale about a ruthless boxer turned out to be a box office smash, and when *The Window* was released a few weeks later, it became the sleeper of the year.

Suddenly, after six years in Hollywood, Roman was an "overnight sensation," and found herself courted by several studios. After weighing her options, she signed a seven-year contract with Warner Bros. and was quickly cast in her second film noir, *Beyond the Forest* (1949), starring Bette Davis. The film would be Davis' last film under her Warners contract, and Roman recalled that the famed star despised her role of the frustrated adultress who turns to murder. "She didn't want to do it, and there was a story around that, if Bette walked [out on the picture], I would get the part — which would have been great!" Roman said. "But Bette didn't walk!"

A dark tale of lust, greed and murder, *Beyond the Forest* takes place in Loyalton, Wisconsin, an ugly, dull milltown with one movie theater, one bank and one doctor, Lewis Moline (Joseph Cotten), the husband of the picture's heroine, Rosa (Davis). Although she lives in the nicest house in town, Rosa is far from content — it is in this film, in fact, that Davis delivered her much-repeated line, "What a dump!" On a daily basis, she treks to the town's depot, watching longingly as the train departs for Chicago. During one of these visits, Rosa encounters Carol (Roman), the long-lost daughter of Moose (Minor Watson), a hunting buddy of her husband's. Later, it is revealed that Rosa is having an affair with Neil Latimer (David Brian), a wealthy Chicago manufacturer who owns a lodge in Loyalton. After collecting long overdue debts from her kindly husband's patients, Rosa uses the money to visit Latimer, only to be informed that he has decided to marry a socialite.

Defeated, Rosa returns home, and when she later discovers that she is pregnant, she reconciles herself to a bland life of normalcy with her husband.

But later, at a party given by Carol for her father, Latimer reappears, telling Rosa that he has broken his engagement and urging her to return with him to Chicago. Rosa, of course, agrees, but fails to tell Latimer about the pregnancy. When Moose overhears their plans, he threatens to expose Rosa and during a hunting party the following day, she shoots Moose, fatally wounding him. After an inquest, the shooting is judged accidental, but Rosa, anxious to join Latimer in Chicago, is still faced with her burdensome pregnancy. In desperation, she throws herself down a steep embankment, suffering a miscarriage, but developing peritonitis in the process. Despite her worsening condition, she insists on going to Chicago, but as she staggers toward the depot in a feverish state, she collapses and dies beside the train tracks.

Although *Beyond the Forest* was almost unanimously blasted by critics, Roman's performance was singled out in *The Hollywood Reporter*, whose reviewer said that she "comes across splendidly and beautifully," and by the critic for *Variety*, who wrote, "Ruth Roman's part means little to the story but she graces it nicely." And while Davis was criticized for her overacting, Roman later said that her costar was "great" in the film, and she fondly remembered the veteran actress for her assistance during production: "I kept blowing my lines in one scene with her because they were so awful to try to say. I finally told the director that and Bette immediately came to my rescue," Roman recalled. "Later she told me: 'Ruth, never forget what you did today — never be afraid to fight for what you know is right.' And I never did forget."

After *Beyond the Forest*, Roman starred in a comedy, *Always Leave Them Laughing* (1949), in which she played the mistreated girlfriend of Milton Berle. The picture was moderately successful, and gave Roman's new fans an opportunity to see her talent for singing and dancing. During the next two years, Roman was cast as the female lead in eight films — a shooting schedule that she later likened to "a stretch at hard labor." Her first of these pictures was *Barricade* (1950), a fist-flying drama about a sadistic mine owner. Two decades after her appearance in this film, Roman recalled that she heartily disliked the production and asked to be released from her contract. Her studio bosses refused, however, telling Roman, "'You'll work or we'll suspend you from salary,'" the actress related. "I had maybe five cents at the time, so I worked. Brother, how I worked!"

But her non-stop filming schedule did not put a damper on Roman's personal life. After being romantically linked with several notables — including actor Ronald Reagan; Bill Walsh, a top cartoonist at Disney Studios; and Herb Caen, a San Francisco newspaper columnist — in 1950 Roman met Mortimer Hall, a television and radio executive and son of the publisher of the *New York Post*. After a courtship of only a few months, Roman and Hall were married in a pre-dawn ceremony in Las Vegas on December 17, 1950, just days before the actress's 27th birthday. The couple had a son, Richard, but by April 1955, the marriage was over. Several years later, in 1956, Roman would give marriage another try, with agent Bud Moss, but after two years, this union, too, would end in divorce.

Meanwhile, the up-and-coming star had one of her best roles in *Three Secrets* (1950), a taut drama in which, along with Eleanor Parker and Patricia Neal, she played an anxious mother waiting to learn whether her son has survived an airplane crash. Although gossip columnists of the day reported friction between the three stars of this film, Roman later denounced the rumor: "Never believe that we didn't get along — we liked each other as persons and we respected each other's talents. There was no scene stealing. Amateurs compete with each other; real pros never do. That's how you tell the difference."

Roman's next two films were fairly forgettable. In *Dallas* (1950), she was seen as the love interest of an ex–Confederate guerrilla, played by Gary Cooper, and in *Lightning Strikes Twice* (1951), she was an actress who falls in love with an accused murderer. But in *Strangers on a Train* (1951), her final film noir, Roman appeared in one of the best thrillers of the decade.

Directed by Alfred Hitchcock, this gripping picture tells the story of Guy Haines (Farley Granger), an unhappily married professional tennis champion, and Bruno Antony (Robert Walker), a self-professed fan, who meet on a train bound for New York City. Although they are strangers, Bruno knows a great deal about Guy's personal life, including his plans to divorce his wife and marry Anne Morton (Roman), the daughter of a powerful senator. Before long, Bruno is sharing with Guy his theory for the perfect murder: "Two fellows meet accidentally, like you and me ... each has somebody that he'd like to get rid of. So, they swap murders. Each fellow does the other fellow's murder — then there's nothing to connect them. Each one has murdered a total stranger. For example, your wife, my father!"

Although Guy blithely dismisses Bruno's hypothesis, he later has cause to regret the encounter when his wife turns up dead and Bruno expects him to complete his part of the "bargain." Lacking a plausible alibi, Guy discovers that he is suspected of his wife's murder, and is horrified when Bruno continues to stalk him. Guy eventually confesses the truth to Anne and, in an attempt to clear her fiancé's name, she appeals to Bruno's mother for help. When this fails, the couple learns that Bruno intends to plant evidence at the scene of the murder, a small-town amusement park, that will clearly implicate Guy for the crime. Guy and Anne hatch an elaborate plot to stop Bruno, and with the police hot on his trail, Guy catches up to his tormentor on a merry-go-round. An accident causes the ride to spin out of control, crushing Bruno in the process, but even with his last breath, he insists that Guy is guilty: "They got you at last, huh, Guy?" he says while police listen in. "I'm sorry, Guy, I want to help you, but I don't know what I can do." But as Bruno dies, his clenched hand opens to reveal the evidence he planned to leave behind — Guy's inscribed cigarette lighter — proving that the tennis player was innocent.

Although Roman's role in *Strangers* was a secondary one, she was applauded by reviewers, including the critic for *Variety*, who wrote, "Miss Roman's role of a nice, understanding girl is a switch for her, and she makes it warmly effective." However, although the actress later viewed her experience on the film as a positive one, she revealed that director Alfred Hitchcock did not originally want her for the role of Anne Morton. "He wanted some cool blonde," Roman told *Scarlet Street* magazine. "It wasn't because he thought I was a bad actress; he just didn't think I was right for it — and I don't believe I *was* right for it. He had some woman come on the set and give me the English pronunciations of certain words. [Hitchcock's daughter] has a slight English accent, and he wanted me to be a very proper Bostonian. Of course, I do come from Boston. So, that's the way that went. It didn't matter, really, because we got along beautifully after we got to know each other."

Roman was now at the peak of her fame. She was receiving an estimated 500 letters a week from fans worldwide, and her countless magazine features included an alluring photo on the cover of *Life*. At the time, reviewers were comparing her with the screen's top stars, including Myrna Loy, Rosalind Russell and Irene Dunne. While an article in *Collier's* acknowledged that Roman's films had not "presented any spectacular scope for acting," it went on to reveal that the actress had "built up one of the widest and most avid fan followings in the movie world." And in another magazine feature, this time in *Photoplay*, Roman appeared to accept her newfound celebrity with humility: "It's strange how you dream about how great it will feel when you finally get on top, all the things you'll do, yet when it happens you're so involved with new problems, new struggles, that you don't have the time or the energy to wallow in your success."

Extra time and energy were certainly luxuries that Roman did not enjoy. Continuing her back-to-back filming activities, she was seen in *Tomorrow Is Another Day* (1951), a formulaic melodrama about an ex-con wrongly accused of a crime; *Starlift* (1951), a feeble wartime musical whose star-studded cast included Doris Day, James Cagney, Gary Cooper and Jane Wyman; *Invitation* (1952), a moving soaper starring Van Johnson; and *Mara Maru* (1952), described in *Variety* as a "deep-sea treasure hunt with whodunit overtones."

Roman's best film by far during this period was an amusing Mitchell Leisen–directed comedy, *Young Man with Ideas* (1952). Of her performance in this picture, Bosley Crowther wrote in the *New York Times*, "A sad sack in her previous deploys, [Roman] cuts some adroitly agile capers."

After a 17-month absence from the screen, during which her son was born, Roman returned to films in *Blowing Wild* (1953), but this picture about bandits in the Mexican oilfields could not be salvaged by a top-notch cast that included Gary Cooper, Barbara Stanwyck and Anthony Quinn. While Roman fared no better in her next role, playing a Toronto school teacher in the box office bomb *Tanganyika* (1954), her cinematic fortunes improved slightly with *Down Three Dark Streets* (1954), a well-paced crime thriller starring Broderick Crawford. But she ended the year on a down note, portraying a slinky lady of the world in *The Shanghai Story* (1954).

Roman began 1955 with a bang, costarring in a first-rate Western, *The Far Country*, as a saloon keeper with a yen for costar James Stewart. This rugged and entertaining box office success provided Roman with a much-needed boost, but the actress experienced a close call during production that threatened to end her career. While filming in northern Canada, Roman found herself in the midst of an avalanche caused by electric power generators: "Let me tell you, the earth trembled! It was all we could hear. I ran like hell over a glacier, which was a stupid thing for me to do. But thankfully, it all stopped within about three minutes."

Following this brush with danger, Roman appeared in a series of near-hits and definite misses, including *Joe Macbeth* (1955), a dreadful underworld drama loosely based on Shakespeare's famed Scottish tragedy; *Great Day in the Morning* (1956), a slightly above-average Western that again featured Roman as a saloon keeper; and *Rebel in Town* (1956), a low-budget horse opera that was greatly improved by good performances and a sensitive script.

In 1956, Roman faced a dramatic personal scenario to rival her on-screen plots when she took her son Richard on a trip to Europe. Returning to New York aboard the S.S. *Andrea Doria*, the actress was enjoying a shipboard party on the night of July 22, 1956, when the 647-foot cruiseliner was struck by a Swedish motorship, the *Stockholm*. Hearing the collision, which Roman said sounded "like a firecracker," the actress gathered her sleeping son from his stateroom and "handed him to a sailor on a lifeboat that was going over the side. I figured if one of us gets out, let it be him." Richard was placed on the *Stockholm* and Roman later boarded a rescue ship, the *Île de France*. She was reunited with her son 24 hours later, after the *Andrea Doria* had sunk, killing 51 passengers.

In 1958, Roman accepted a rare stage role and won the Sarah Siddons Award for Best Actress for her portrayal of a kooky, uninhibited character in *Two for the Seesaw*, but by now, her best films were unquestionably behind her. The actress herself considered the foreign *Desert Desperadoes* (1959) as one of her worst pictures: "It was made in Italy—it should have stayed there!" she quipped several years later. "Today it would be high camp." After this stinker, Roman was away from the screen for two years, returning for the all-but-forgotten *Look in Any Window* (1961) with Paul Anka, and *Miracle of the Cowards* (1961), filmed in Spain.

She would make a memorable appearance several years later, however, in *Love Has Many Faces* (1965), starring Lana Turner. Although this glossy soaper was a bit laughable, Roman was noted for her role as a wealthy, hard-bitten femme by *Variety*, whose critic noted that she "hits just the right chord as the woman who knows she's being taken by [Hugh] O'Brian but plays it his way."

With her film career on its last legs, Roman turned more and more to television, a medium in which she had worked since the early 1950s. Roman appeared on many of the small screen's most popular series, including *Route 66, Dr. Kildare, Ironside, Mannix, Knots Landing* and *Murder, She Wrote*. She also was featured in a number of made-for-TV movies, most notably *The Old Man Who Cried Wolf* (1974), starring Edward G. Robinson, and *Go Ask Alice* (1973), with William Shatner and Andy Griffith.

Although Roman continued to act sporadically in feature films, they were mostly a mishmash of such bizarre pictures as *The Baby* (1973), which Roman termed a "horrible thing! I'm sorry I made it. Oh, it was a terrible piece.... I was surprised it came out at all." Other films in later years included *Day of the Animals* (1977), *Echoes* (1980) and *Silent Sentence* (1983).

While Roman has expressed a willingness to accept occasional television or movie roles, she maintains that she is content with her current life out of the spotlight: "A lot of people want to work just to work, but ... I'm happy. I have a lovely home; I live on the water and I love the water, and I have a fine son and no problems." Looking back on her career that spanned 60 years, Roman has said that she has no regrets; as she stated in an interview conducted during her heyday, "If I never do anything else from here on in, I have the satisfaction of knowing I did exactly what I set out to do when I came out here — to stay until I proved myself, no matter how tough it got to be."

And she did just that.

Film Noir Filmography

THE WINDOW   *Director:* Ted Tetzlaff. *Producer:* Frederic Ullman, Jr. Released by RKO, August 1949. *Running time:* 73 minutes. *Cast:* Barbara Hale, Bobby Driscoll, Arthur Kennedy, Paul Stewart, Ruth Roman. *Awards:* Best Mystery Film of the Year award from the Mystery Writers of America, Academy Award for Outstanding Juvenile Actor (Bobby Driscoll) (miniature statuette), Academy Award nomination for Best Editing (Frederic Knudtson).

BEYOND THE FOREST   *Director:* King Vidor. *Producer:* Henry Blanke. Released by Warner Bros., October 1949. *Running time:* 97 minutes. *Cast:* Bette Davis, Joseph Cotten, David Brian, Ruth Roman, Minor Watson, Dona Drake. Academy Award nomination for Best Score (Max Steiner).

STRANGERS ON A TRAIN   *Director and Producer:* Alfred Hitchcock. Released by Warner Bros., June 1951. *Running time:* 101 minutes. *Cast:* Farley Granger, Robert Walker, Ruth Roman, Leo G. Carroll, Patricia Hitchcock, Laura Elliott, Marion Lorne, Jonathan Hale. *Awards:* Academy Award nomination for Best Cinematography (Robert Burks).

References

"Actress of the Year." *Theatre Arts*, April 1960.

Asher, Jerry. "Until It Happens to You." *Silver Screen*, February 1954.

"Hollywood's Roman Candle." *Collier's*, March 17, 1951.

Hopper, Hedda. "The Sexiest Girl in Town." *Photoplay*, September 1950.

Kantor, Shirley. "Roman History." *Photoplay*, January 1951.

Lilley, Jessie. "The Woman in the Window: Ruth Roman." *Scarlet Street*, Fall 1993.

"Lovely Ruth." *American Magazine*, November 1949.

Meyer, Jim. "Passing Time Has Left Ruth Roman Untouched." *The Miami Herald*, January 10, 1971.

"The Progress of a Rising Star." *Life*, May 1, 1950.

"Rapid Rise of Ruth Roman." *Life*, May 1, 1950.

Rayfield, Fred. "'I Haven't Arrived Yet,' Ruth Insists." *Sunday Compass*, July 23, 1950.

Roman, Ruth. "It's My Life — or Isn't It?" *Silver Screen*, February 1952.

"Roman Holiday." *Modern Screen*, May 1952.

"Ruth Roman." *Hollywood Studio Magazine*, May 1982.

"Ruth Roman, Glamorous Starlet, Has Hollywood Agog." *Dallas Morning News*, November 19, 1950.

"Second Self." *American Magazine*, October 1950.

Stanke, Don. "Ruth Roman." *Film Fan Monthly*, April 1973.

"Turned Down for a Chorus Job, So —" *Sunday Mirror Magazine*, December 24, 1950.

Gail Russell

Of all the actresses who rose to fame during the film noir era, Gail Russell's story is perhaps the most tragic. Although critics and audiences alike were bewitched by her delicate beauty and aura of vulnerability, Russell's personal demons were apparent from the start of her career and, sadly, she is remembered more for her descent into alcoholism than for her considerable on-screen talent. Still, the dark-haired lovely with the dreamy sapphire eyes was a standout in such pictures as *The Uninvited* (1944) and *Angel and the Badman* (1947), and she was seen to good advantage in four films from the realm of noir: *Calcutta* (1947), *Moonrise* (1948), *Night Has a Thousand Eyes* (1948) and *The Tattered Dress* (1957).

A native of Chicago, Illinois, Gail Russell was born on September 21, 1924, the second child of George and Gladys Russell. While her brother George was an outgoing sort who later became an accomplished musician, Russell was shy and self-conscious as a child, spending most of her free time engaging in such solitary pastimes as painting or sitting in darkened movie theaters. Years later, Russell would recall that there were weeks when she would go to the movies "every single afternoon.... I'd walk blocks to my favorite picture house and sit there often right through dinner, seeing a film two and three times. My father would have to come and find me." Because of her bashful, retiring nature, Russell had few friends during these early years, a fact that was no doubt sustained by the fact that her father, an auto bond salesman, frequently moved his family from place to place, beginning with a relocation to California in 1936. Despite this instability, Russell managed to become a top art student in high school and was well on her way to pursuing a career as an artist when a chance occurrence thwarted this dream forever.

According to the much-publicized story, a classmate of Russell's, Charlie Bates, hitched a ride one fateful day to Balboa, California, bragging to the driver about the beautiful girl at his school who looked "just like Hedy Lamarr." The driver turned out to be William Meiklejohn, a Paramount executive, who later dispatched a studio talent scout, Milton Lewis, to contact Russell and set up an appointment at the studio. Although Russell objected to the idea, she said that her mother, herself a frustrated actress, "practically dragged me there." And Lewis himself later recalled Russell's reluctance, calling her "a lovely girl who didn't belong in the movie industry. I believe she would have had a happy life had she become a commercial artist instead of a movie actress."

Still, after a screen test, Russell was signed to a contract and just days later was assigned to her first film, *Henry Aldrich Gets Glamour* (1943), one of an eight-picture series starring Jimmy Lydon. To help acquire her screen presence, the inexperienced 17-year-old was instructed by Paramount coach William Russell (no relation), who not only worked to develop her dramatic abilities, but also taught her how to walk and aided her in bringing out her soft, velvety voice.

In her debut, Russell played a high school girl who briefly steals the title character from his steady girl (portrayed by Diana Lynn, who would become one of Russell's few close friends). For her performance, Russell was singled out by the critic for *The Hollywood Reporter*, who noted: "A flash that will count is registered by Gail Russell as the town belle.... You'll be hearing from Gail Russell." Despite this praise, Russell would later reveal that filming the picture was a terrifying experience: "I can hardly remember it," she said. "When I went over [the role] with Mr. Russell, it seemed possible — well, almost possible. But, on the set, with the director shouting, and the lights blazing, and the cameras threatening, I'd go deaf. Really. They'd tell me what to do and I simply couldn't hear. I'd try desperately to listen and all I did was wish I were dead."

Russell had only a small role in her next picture, *Lady in the Dark* (1944), but she was thrilled to be working with the film's star, Ginger Rogers, whom Russell had idolized since her movie-going days in Chicago. But upon her first meeting with the famed actress, Russell later admitted, "I was frantic. I thought, I am going to faint; I thought, I will run away and hide. Then Ginger Rogers came over to me, put her arm around me, took me into her dressing room, gave me tea, and went over the script with me. Best of all, she told me how scared she had been when she first got into pictures.... Ginger was, so to speak, the turning point in relaxing me."

It was Russell's third feature, *The Uninvited* (1944), that catapulted the reluctant starlet to national prominence. An unnerving story starring Ray Milland and Ruth Hussey, the film focused on a young girl (Russell) who is haunted by the ghost of her dead mother. For the role, Russell had to acquire an English accent, and she later stated that her coach helped in this area by locking her in a projection room: "I saw *Pygmalion* four times, *Rebecca* twice, and *Young Mr. Pitt* twice. I finally fell asleep," she recalled. "When I came out I had a British accent thicker than a London fog." Once she'd mastered this task, however, Russell was still hampered by her innate shyness and on-set fears. But as with Ginger Rogers in Russell's second film, the budding star found an ally in costar Ray Milland. It was the veteran actor who taught Russell to face the camera, rather than shying away from the lens, and whenever he sensed that Russell was succumbing to her nervousness, Milland would deliberately flub his lines to put her at ease. "When he saw I was scared," Russell recalled, "he'd say, 'Come on, you can do it.'"

However, in addition to the support she received from her costars, it is believed that Russell began finding courage during this period in another form. Actress Yvonne DeCarlo, then another Paramount starlet, wrote of the sensitive actress in her 1987 biography, "I felt I had much in common with her, but she was much more vulnerable than I. [Russell] confided in hushed tones how she wished her mother, Gladys, had never dragged her to Paramount for her screen test. She despised acting and everything it entailed, especially being put on display before executives and film crews. I sympathized with her misery, but had no soothing words for her.... There was an actress on the lot, however, who would show Gail how to cope, the good-natured but tough-talking Helen Walker. She took Gail under her wing and introduced her to the tranquilizing benefits of vodka."

Regardless of the source of her newfound confidence, Russell was almost unanimously hailed for her performance in *The Uninvited*, with the reviewer for *Variety* stating that she "has youth, beauty, loveliness of a kind the screen is crying for, and she possesses the presence of a veteran actress," and Archer Winsten of *The New York Post* raving: "Any man who would not fight a couple of ghosts for Gail Russell, and thank her for the privilege, is missing something." This film was followed by *Our Hearts Were Young and Gay* (1944), a comedy based on the memoirs of actress Cornelia Otis Skinner and Emily Kimbrough during their sailing trip to Europe. Costarring Diana Lynn, this charming romp was a smash hit, and Russell surprised critics and audiences alike with her flair for comedy. Still, Russell continued to be plagued by self-doubt, stating, "I find comedy harder to play. There's less involvement in what you're doing. I'm not sure enough of myself to find fun in it yet."

Of Russell's three 1945 releases, the best was *The Unseen*, in which she played opposite Joel McCrea as a governess who is haunted by the murder of her predecessor. But her next two features of the year failed to further her burgeoning career — in the Alan Ladd starrer *Salty O'Rourke*, Russell had little to do except stand around and look pretty, and *Duffy's Tavern* was a cheerless musical despite an all-star cast that included Bing Crosby, Betty Hutton, Veronica Lake, Alan Ladd, Barry Fitzgerald and Paulette Goddard. And Russell's 1946 releases weren't much better. The first, *Our Hearts Were Growing Up*, was a sequel to the popular *Our Hearts Were Young and Gay*, but it lacked the nostalgic appeal of the original; the second, *The Bachelor's Daughters*, a loan-out to United Artists, was a rather silly comedy starring Claire Trevor, Ann Dvorak, and Jane Wyatt.

By now, Russell had become increasingly reliant on alcohol to boost her sagging self-esteem. Reportedly, she began drinking during scene breaks at a café across the street from her studio, and before long she kept her dressing room equipped with a bottle of vodka. Paramount executives were fully aware of Russell's habit, however, and rather than guide her toward treatment, they closed her sets to outsiders and rarely allowed the actress to conduct interviews with the press. But at this point in her career, Russell's growing dependence on alcohol had affected neither her looks nor her acting capabilities, and she was seen to good advantage in her first Western, Republic's *Angel and the Badman* (1947). In this film, delivering what is often her best-remembered performance, Russell portrayed a strong-willed Quaker girl who reforms outlaw John Wayne. The chemistry between the costars was noted in the *Los Angeles Reader*: "Wayne and the hauntingly beautiful Russell have a wonderful rapport, and the most interesting sequences are the intimate ones." The actress also earned accolades in *Variety*, whose reviewer raved, "Gail Russell has never been seen to better

Gail Russell

advantage as the fresh and honest Quaker girl who falls in love and actually pursues the gunman. Role is played with an intelligent interpretation of the attraction between the sexes. It should advance her career immeasurably."

Next, Russell entered the realm of film noir in a re-teaming with Alan Ladd for *Calcutta* (1947). Set in India, this picture focuses on three commercial pilots, Neale Gordon (Ladd), Pedro Blake (William Bendix) and Bill

Cunningham (John Whitney). Shortly after Bill announces his plans to get married, he is found murdered, and Neale and Pedro set out to find the killer. Neale is initially suspicious of Bill's fiancée, Virginia Moore (Russell), but soon finds himself attracted by her innocent, vulnerable demeanor. But after an Indian smuggler is killed, Neale realizes that Virginia is not as virtuous as she appears. Viciously slapping her, Neale tries to force her into a confession: "I know you think you're too beautiful to hit," he says. "You've always counted on that with guys, haven't you? Even when you're shooting them down in cold blood." Finally, Virginia reveals that she was part of a jewelry smuggling ring and that, while only indirectly responsible for Bill's death, it was she who murdered the smuggler. At the film's end, Neale ignores Virginia's pleas and turns her into police.

Unable to accept Russell as an unflinching murderess, most critics complained that the actress was miscast in *Calcutta*—in a typical review, the critic from *Cue* magazine griped: "Who do you think [the killer] turns out to be, but pretty, baby-faced, apple-cheeked, lisping, teenage Gail Russell. It's quite a job trying to palm off this wide-eyed bobby soxer as a cold-blooded killer and brains of a giant international jewel smuggling ring and Paramount doesn't quite manage it."

Russell's last picture of 1947 was *Variety Girl*, another all-star jamboree featuring such notables as Bob Hope, Bing Crosby, Gary Cooper, Barbara Stanwyck, Dorothy Lamour and Ray Milland. After her appearance in this box office hit, Russell was chosen as one of the "Stars of Tomorrow," based on a poll of exhibitors, and her popularity continued to rise with her appearance in her second film noir, *Night Has a Thousand Eyes* (1948).

This film centers on the relationship between Russell's character, Jean Courtland, and John Triton (Edward G. Robinson), a mentalist who has foreseen Jean's death. In flashback, it is revealed that 20 years earlier, Triton had starred in a phony-mindreading act on the vaudeville circuit, assisted by his fiancée, Jenny (Virginia Bruce), and Whitney Courtland (Jerome Cowan). During one night's act, Triton had a premonition that the son of an audience member was in danger, and later learned that the boy was injured in a fire. Thereafter, Triton began having more visions, including one that predicted Jenny's death while giving birth to her first child. Attempting to save Jenny's life, Triton disappeared and became a virtual recluse. Years later, he learned that Courtland and Jenny had married, and that Jenny died giving birth to a daughter, Jean.

After experiencing a premonition that Courtland would die in a plane crash, Triton emerged from his hermit-like existence to warn Jean, but he was too late. During another encounter with Jean, Triton reveals that he has also seen into her future, and predicts that she will die within the next few days. Over the objections of her fiancé, Elliott Carson (John Lund), Jean invites Triton to move into her home. But Elliott, doubting the validity of Triton's claims, contacts police, who set up camp in Jean's house to protect her. Later, Triton's predictions come true and he saves Jean from being murdered by a business associate of her late father's. Ironically, police mistake Triton's intentions, and fatally shoot him while he is struggling with Jean's would-be killer.

After the preview of the film, Ray Lanning wrote in *Variety* that audience members were "audibly anxious about Miss Russell's fate," but Bosley Crowther dismissed her performance in the *New York Times*, saying that she appeared "in a mood of distinct melancholia, with her face all the way down to here." Her mixed reviews notwithstanding, Russell frankly acknowledged that she'd enjoyed the role because it aided in boosting her self-esteem: "I like to play in these spooky stories, and it was the ghosties that gave me my break," she told the press. "I've analyzed it this way, maybe to bolster my inferiority complex: I'm still scared every time I face the camera and that helps the characterization. If I'm nervous, no one scolds me. I get away with it because they think I'm acting."

Next, in an acclaimed performance, Russell starred opposite Dane Clark in *Moonrise* (1948), her third film noir. Set in a small Southern community, *Moonrise* follows the life of Danny Hawkins (Clark), whose father was hanged for murder in Danny's boyhood, prompting years of physical and emotional torture. Chief among Danny's tormentors was Jerry Sykes (Lloyd Bridges), who has continued baiting Danny as an adult. During one episode of harassment, a fight breaks out between the two adversaries and Danny kills Jerry in self-defense, burying his body in the swampy marsh. Meanwhile, Danny romances Jerry's ex-fiancée, Gilly Johnson (Russell), a schoolteacher who seems to be the one person in the small town who understands his temperamental nature: "I was just thinking about a little boy in one of my classes," she tells Danny. "All the kids pick on him. Give him milk, he breaks the glass — hand him a toy, he smashes it. He gives me a lot of trouble. You see, Danny, he's unhappy."

When Sykes' body is found, the town sheriff (Allyn Joslyn) suspects a local singer to whom Sykes had owed a large sum of money, but he later realizes that Danny is responsible. When Danny learns that the police are closing in, he plans to flee, but stops first at the mountain home of his grandmother (Ethel Barrymore), who provides him with insights regarding his father's life and death. After confronting his past, Danny decides to turn himself in to police and finds Gilly waiting for him as he faces his future.

Although one critic found *Moonrise* to be "well made, but too drab," Russell earned praise in the *New York Times* for her "convincingly compassionate" performance, and in *Variety*, whose critic wrote, "Gail Russell comes through best as the schoolteacher, honestly in love and troubled by her man's moody fear." But she followed this film with a series of mediocre loan-outs, including Republic's *Wake of the Red Witch* (1948), a South Sea saga in which she was re-teamed with John Wayne; Columbia's *The Song of India* (1949), an amateurish production that featured Russell as an East Indian princess on a tiger hunt; and United Artists' *The Great Dan Patch* (1949), a so-so saga about horse racing. And she had no better luck in her two Paramount features during this period, *El Paso* (1949), a routine Western, and *Captain China* (1949), a tedious programmer about a sea captain who seeks revenge on his conspirators. As her drinking both on and off the set escalated, Hollywood insiders began speculating that Paramount was loaning Russell out for unimportant pictures because she was becoming increasingly difficult to handle.

But Russell's professional problems briefly faded to the background when, on July 31, 1949, she became the wife of handsome teen idol Guy Madison, who was perhaps best known for his debut in United Artists' *Since You Went Away* (1944). The attractive duo had first met soon after Russell's arrival in Hollywood, and were, according to the gossip columnists of the day, "mad about each other." Still, after just six months, the couple separated, and although they later reconciled, the marriage seemed doomed for failure.

Professionally, however, Russell's career was on the upswing. In her first screen appearance after her much-ballyhooed wedding, she starred in Paramount's *The Lawless* (1950), a riveting drama about the neglected problems of Mexican-Americans. Portraying a crusading newspaper reporter who attempts to aid a falsely accused immigrant, Russell was hailed by critics, with the reviewer for *Time* magazine declaring that she was "so good ... that filmgoers may feel they are seeing her for the first time," and *Variety's* critic reporting, "Miss Russell unveils a fiery temperament and a hitherto unsuspected disregard for flattering camera angles."

Sadly, her highly acclaimed performance in *The Lawless* would mark a turning point in Russell's film career. During the next five years, she would appear in only one feature, Universal's *Air Cadet* (1951), a plodding drama about three fledgling pilots. After this film, Russell was placed on suspension by Paramount for refusing the lead in *Flaming Feather* (1951), a Western starring Sterling Hayden, and a short time later, her contract was terminated. Russell was considered for several other films, including *Loan Shark* (1952) and *Fair Wind to Java* (1953), but with reports about her heavy drinking on the rise, no studio seemed willing to take a risk on the actress.

Meanwhile, Russell's personal life had taken a turn for the worse. Again separated from her husband, she made news in October 1953 when Esperanza Baur, the notoriously jealous wife of John Wayne, sued her husband for divorce, naming Russell in the suit. Among other charges, Baur claimed that Russell and Wayne had spent a night together several years earlier, and that Wayne had given the actress a car "for services rendered." (Wayne later denied the charge, stating that he had merely given Russell the down payment for an automobile after discovering the low salary she was receiving on her Paramount loan-outs.) Around this time, Russell entered a sanitarium in Seattle for intensive psychotherapy, but she was arrested shortly after her release on the first of a series of drunk driving charges. The following year, Russell filed for divorce, charging mental cruelty, and Madison counter-sued, claiming that Russell had no concern in keeping up their home, would not allow servants, discouraged visitors, and showed no interest in his career. Russell subsequently dropped her charge and the divorce was granted later that year. Although Madison remarried the following year, Russell would never wed again.

In 1955, Russell's personal life continued to plummet when she was involved in a hit-and-run accident and, for the first time, she admitted that she had a drinking problem: "I'll have to use the word alcoholic," she told the press, "because that's what I am." A year after this public confession, Russell returned to the silver screen in *Seven Men from Now* (1956), a better-than-average Western produced by John Wayne's production company, Batjac. Although the 32-year-old actress now appeared to be haggard and thin, she did a more than passable job in the film and showed a depth that had been lacking in many of her previous performances. And she continued to display this talent in her next picture, *The Tattered Dress* (1957), her final film noir.

This picture centers on James Gordon Blane (Jeff Chandler), an unprincipled criminal attorney known for his successful defenses of society's most infamous criminals. Traveling to a resort town in the California desert to defend a wealthy resident accused of murder, Blane continues to improve his track record when he wins an acquittal, primarily due to his hostile cross-examination of the town sheriff, Nick Hoak (Jack Carson). Humiliated by Blane's savage treatment, Hoak arranges for his mistress, Carol Morrow (Russell), a juror in the trial, to claim that Blane bribed her to insure a not guilty verdict. Although Carol is reluctant to carry through with the farce, she is desperate to hang on to her lover, and complies with his demands.

Now accused with bribery, Blane defends himself, but finds that his usual courtroom tactics backfire, especially during his examination of Carol Morrow, who hysterically maintains Blane's guilt while on the stand. But after Carol's effective performance, Hoak cruelly informs her that their relationship is over: "From here on out you'll be lucky if I tip my hat to you on the street," he says. Ultimately, Blane is acquitted of the bribery charges, but as he and his wife (Jeanne Crain) triumphantly emerge from the courthouse, Hoak prepares to shoot the attorney. Instead, Hoak himself is shot and killed by Carol Morrow.

Although Russell played only a minor part in *The Tattered Dress*, she made the most of every scene, and was singled out in the *New York Times*, whose reviewer wrote, "Gail Russell has an effective scene or two as [Jack Carson's] partner in double-dealing." Despite her well-received performance, however, the actress continued to suffer setbacks off screen. In 1957, she was again arrested for drunk driving when her car crashed through a café window, pinning the night janitor under the wheels. During a hearing on the incident, Russell was unable to recall the amount of alcohol she had consumed, telling a Los Angeles judge that she'd had "a few, maybe two [drinks]. Maybe four.

I don't know how many. It's no one's business but my own." After receiving a 30-day suspended jail sentence and put on three years' probation, Russell told the press that she had stopped drinking. "I've beat it, I've beat it," she said of her alcoholism. "If I could give advice to others who might get into the tangle I found myself in, I'd say get back to nature ... there is no medicine in the world as great as God and nature."

With her drinking apparently under control, Russell was seen in 1958 in a low-budget Republic film, *No Place to Land*, and appeared in 1960 on a daytime television series, *Here's Hollywood*, on which she exhibited her oil paintings and discussed her plans for resuming her career. Then, in 1961, she received top billing in *The Silent Call*, but the 20th Century–Fox feature was a box office bomb and would turn out to be Russell's last appearance on the big screen. Later that year, she portrayed a cynical Southern belle in an episode of TV's *The Rebel*. The creator and writer of the program, Andrew Fenady, recalled that although Russell was initially nervous on the set, she later regained her confidence and "was just fine. We finished the [program] on time and Gail Russell was absolutely radiant."

This television episode would be Russell's last performance. Less than a month before her 37th birthday, on August 27, 1961, she was found dead on the floor of her furnished apartment in West Los Angeles by two neighbors. The exact date of her death could not be determined — police could only estimate that she had died some time between 6 P.M. Thursday (August 24) and 11 P.M. Saturday (August 26). Although it was ruled that Russell had died from natural causes, the once-promising star was found with an empty vodka bottle beside her and several other empties scattered throughout the room. A neighbor would later tell the press that Russell had expressed a sincere desire to stop drinking, "but she couldn't. It's a tragic thing.... She would go through periods where she wouldn't drink, and then the bad periods when she couldn't stop. The pressures to take a drink must have been enormous."

While Gail Russell served as a captivating addition to several highly-acclaimed films throughout her career, she suffered a tragic life characterized by an unfulfilled romantic life, unimaginable professional stress and an ongoing battle with alcohol that she was powerless to overcome. In her own frank assessment, it was Russell herself who best described the circumstances that led to her downfall and her inability to overcome them: "Everything happened so fast. I was pushed into it. I was a sad character. I was sad because of myself. I didn't have any self-confidence. I didn't believe I had any talent. I didn't know how to have fun. I was afraid. I don't exactly know of what — of life, I guess.

"I'm just a hard-luck girl."

Film Noir Filmography

CALCUTTA   *Director:* John Farrow. *Producer:* Seton I. Miller. Released by Paramount, May 1947. *Running time:* 83 minutes. *Cast:* Alan Ladd, Gail Russell, William Bendix, June Duprez, Lowell Gilmore.

MOONRISE   *Director:* Frank Borzage. *Producer:* Charles Haas. Released by Republic, March 1949. *Running time:* 90 minutes. *Cast:* Dane Clark, Gail Russell, Ethel Barrymore, Allyn Joslyn, Rex Ingram, Henry Morgan, David Street. *Awards:* Academy Award nomination for Best Sound (Republic Sound Department).

NIGHT HAS A THOUSAND EYES   *Director:* John Farrow. *Producer:* Endre Bohem. Released by Paramount, October 1948. *Running time:* 81 minutes. *Cast:* Edward G. Robinson, Gail Russell, John Lund, William Demarest, Virginia Bruce, Jerome Cowan, Richard Webb.

THE TATTERED DRESS   *Director:* Jack Arnold. *Producer:* Albert Zugsmith. Released by Universal-International, March 1957. *Running time:* 93 minutes. *Cast:* Jeff Chandler, Jeanne Crain, Jack Carson, Gail Russell, Elaine Stewart, George Tobias, Edward Andrews, Philip Reed, Edward C. Platt.

References

"Actress Gail Russell Found Dead at Home." *Los Angeles Times*, August 28, 1961.

Balch, Dave. "Through a Glass Darkly, Her Epitaph." *New York World Telegraph and Sun*, August 28, 1961.

Benjamin, George. "Dark Angel." *Modern Screen*, November 1946.

Biography of Gail Russell. Paramount Studios, January 1950.

Ciaccia, Maria. "Gail Russell: Hollywood's Hard Luck Girl." *Hollywood Studio Magazine*, February 1989.

Colby, Anita. "Her Beauty Program." *Photoplay*, May 1947.

Crivello, Kirk. "Gail Russell." *Classic Film Collector*, Winter 1971.

"Death Beside a Bottle Ends Gail's Alky Fight." *New York Daily News*, August 28, 1961.

"Death Closes Gail Russell's Battle of Bottle." *New York Journal American*, August 28, 1961.

Dreier, Hans. "Home of Gail Russell." *Photoplay*, November 1949.

Fenady, Andrew J. "Gail Russell by Candlelight." *Hollywood Studio Magazine*, April 1983.

"Filmland's Gail Storms at Cops; Jailed as Tipsy." *New York Daily News*, November 26, 1953.

"Gail Russell in Smash-Up." *New York Herald Tribune*, July 5, 1957.

"Gail Russell, 36, Actress, Is Dead." *New York Times*, August 28, 1961.

Graham, Sheilah. "Madison-Russell: More in Sickness Than in Health." *Sheilah Graham's Hollywood Romances*, 1954.

Hopper, Hedda. "Gail Russell." *Chicago Tribune*–New York News Syndicate, Inc., 1955.

Jacobson, Laurie. "The Final Bow: Suicide in Hollywood." *Hollywood: Then and Now*, November 1990.

"Never Intended to Be a Star." *New York Hearld Tribune*, August 28, 1961.

Russell, Gail. "My Kind of Guy." *Photoplay*, August 1946.

_____. "Why I Waited Four Years to Marry Guy." *Silver Screen*, February 1950.

Vermilye, Jerry. "Gail Russell." *Films in Review*, October 1961.

Waterbury, Ruth. "Gail Russell: A Woman Reborn." *Photoplay*, March 1956.

Jane Russell

Jane Russell rose to fame as the busty, lusty love interest of Billy the Kid, and struggled for years before proving herself as an adept singer and comedienne. Often remembered by modern audiences for her commercial hawking of brassieres for the "full-figured" woman, Russell's highly touted physique was her ticket to stardom, but her sex symbol status actually prevented her from achieving recognition for her performing talents. Although her career consisted of roles in mostly minor films, Russell was a standout in such pictures as *Gentlemen Prefer Blondes* (1953), and starred in three films noirs: *His Kind of Woman* (1951), *The Las Vegas Story* (1952) and *Macao* (1952).

Ernestine Jane Geraldine Russell was born in Bemidji, Minnesota, on June 21, 1921, the only girl and the oldest of five siblings. Russell may have inherited her love for the performing arts from her mother, Geraldine Jacobi Russell, a minor stage actress who was the subject of a portrait exhibited at the 1915 Panama-Pacific Exposition in San Francisco (and later displayed at the White House during the Woodrow Wilson administration). While attending high school in Van Nuys, where the family settled in 1932, Russell performed the lead in *Shirt Sleeves*, and also played the piano in her family's "orchestra," which frequently gave neighborhood concerts. Still, acting was not her original career choice: "The subjects at school in which I was any good were art, drama and music," the star later recalled. "My mother was an actress, so to rebel from the start, I decided on being a designer."

When her father, Roy William Russell, died following a gall bladder operation in 1937, Russell abandoned her ambitions for fashion design and briefly worked as a chiropodist's receptionist. She also earned money by folding small boxes in a packaging plant, and later by modeling dresses, hats and coats for photographer Tom Kelley (who would go on to achieve a measure of fame as the man behind the camera for Marilyn Monroe's famed nude calendar shots). After a bit of urging from her mother, Russell decided to try her hand at acting, and studied drama at Max Reinhardt's Theatrical Workshop and Maria Ouspenskaya's School of Dramatic Arts. But her training failed to pay off when she took screen tests at two studios — Paramount, whose executives found that at five feet, seven inches, Russell was "too tall," and 20th Century–Fox, where she was judged "unphotogenic."

But Russell didn't have long to wait for her big break. When her photograph was seen by RKO head Howard Hughes, the eccentric billionaire tested Russell for a role in his upcoming film, *The Outlaw*, a turgid tale about the life of Billy the Kid. Based on her performance of a haystack fight scene, Russell was given the part of the "half-breed" girlfriend of the famed bandit, and she signed a seven-year contract with RKO at a starting salary of $50 dollars a week. In her autobiography, Russell recalled: "[I was] on cloud nine. I was 19 years old; I had a new car, a beautiful new wardrobe, a contract to star in a motion picture ... I thought I was in heaven."

The filming of Russell's first picture, however, was somewhat less than heavenly. A week after production began, director Howard Hawks quit the picture after a confrontation with Howard Hughes, and in a 1996 interview with Robert Osborne, Russell recalled: "Hughes was giving [Hawks] his opinions over the phone, and Hawks finally says, 'Howard, why don't you direct the picture?' And he got in his plane and flew home." As a director, the inexperienced Hughes proved to be relentlessly exacting, sometimes requiring more than 100 takes on a single scene, and spending an estimated $3.4 million on a film originally budgeted at $440,000. "He was very polite and very sweet," Russell said, "but I don't think he really knew what he wanted, or he didn't know how to tell you what he wanted. So you did it over and over and over."

While she wasn't busy filming, Russell was the focus of a massive publicity campaign that included posing for countless photographs and participating in such activities as judging baby contests and christening boats. She was touted by famed publicist Russell Birdwell as "the new Jean Harlow" and before ever appearing on screen, the actress had been featured in more than 60 magazine articles, voted "the girl we'd most like to have waiting for us in every port" by the U.S. Navy, and selected as Miss Anatomy of the first half of the 20th century by the Anthropology Club of Harvard College.

The Outlaw was finally released in February 1943, but it was promptly withdrawn after censors objected to revealing shots of Russell's cleavage in the film and in its print ads. Refusing to cut any of Russell's scenes, Hughes would spend the next three years fighting all attempts to censor the movie. In the midst of the controversy, on April 24, 1943, Russell eloped to Las Vegas with her high school sweetheart, Robert Waterfield, who later became a star quarterback for the Cleveland Rams football team and head coach of the Los Angeles Rams. The couple would adopt three children, Thomas, Tracy and Robert, but after 23 years, the marriage ended in divorce.

After completing *The Outlaw*, Russell was loaned to United Artists for the title role in *Young Widow* (1946), touted by Howard Hughes as "the best woman's part in ten years." But Russell was obviously not up to the challenge. The picture was a flop and the actress was unanimously panned by critics, including Wanda Hale of the *New York Daily News*, who said that the film's lead "should have been handed to a more experienced actress. Or to one who has, at least, a couple of changes of facial expression." Decades later, in a 1996 documentary for Turner Classic Movies, Russell herself recalled the film with amused disdain: "Young widow should have died with her husband," she quipped, "and that story would never need be told."

Meanwhile, following a limited release of *The Outlaw* in 1946, Howard Hughes was forced to appeal to the courts in each state. In nearly every case, the film was banned; a Baltimore judge, in disallowing the film in his state, said that Russell's breasts "hung over the picture like a summer thunderstorm spread out over a landscape. They were everywhere." Until he was able to secure the nationwide release of the five-year-old film, Hughes refused to assign Russell to any pictures, instead sending her on public appearance tours that she said made her feel "ridiculous ... they always gave me some corny speech to make." But by now, Russell had discovered that she had a talent for singing and the previously passive starlet began to assert herself, declining any further tours unless she was allowed to perform as a songstress. When Hughes relented, Russell appeared for a week at the Latin Quarter Club in Miami Beach, and was signed in 1947 to a 12-week stint on *Kay Kyser's Kollege of Fun and Knowledge*. She also recorded two singles and an album for Columbia Records.

In 1948, Hughes loaned Russell again, this time to Paramount for the Bob Hope starrer *The Paleface*, a Western spoof in which the actress first demonstrated her comedic talents. The film did brisk business at the box office, and Russell was better received this time around, with one reviewer reporting that the actress "does not exactly act in the part of Calamity Jane, but she is extremely effective in underlying the ludicrous quality of the show." But Russell's two other films of the year, *Montana Belle* with George Brent, and *It's Only Money* with Frank Sinatra and Groucho Marx, were of such poor quality that both were shelved. The latter film would finally be released by Howard Hughes in 1951, with a new title —*Double Dynamite*— that obviously referred to Russell's buxom assets, and *Montana Belle* would not be released until 1952. The years that both films spent gathering dust in the RKO vaults did not save them from being critical and financial disasters.

Nearly nine years after its completion, *The Outlaw* was finally permitted a general release in 1950, and while the public flocked to see the much-bally-hooed film, the reviews for Russell's performance ranged from benign to cruel. The critic for the *New York Herald Tribune* found that Russell's "sultry advances ... are more amusing than licentious"; while the *New York Times* reviewer acknowledged that the starlet was "undeniably decorative," he further stated that she was "hopelessly inept as an actress." Russell herself would later admit that her performance in the film was less than stellar, stating: "I thought the picture was ghastly and that I looked like a wooden dummy. I don't know how I ever got another part." Still, she forged ahead with her singing appearances, including a stint at the Princess Theatre in London in 1949, and an engagement with Bob Hope in March 1950 at New York's Paramount Theatre.

In 1951, Russell returned to the big screen, starring in the first of three consecutive films noirs, *His Kind of Woman*, with Robert Mitchum. This complex picture centers on a plot to have Nick Ferraro (Raymond Burr), a syndicate boss exiled in Italy, assume the identity of Dan Milner (Robert Mitchum), a professional gambler who has been recently released from jail. Dan is offered $50,000 to leave the United States for a year and travels to Mexico to await further instructions, unaware that Ferraro's henchmen plan to murder him so that Ferraro can return to America. While in Mexico, Dan meets a mixed bag of colorful characters, including Lenore Brent (Russell), a singer posing as a wealthy heiress, Mark Cardigan (Vincent Price), a pretentious film star, and Martin Krafft (John Mylong), a former Nazi who wiles away the hours by playing games of chess with himself.

Tipped off by Bill Lusk (Tim Holt), a federal agent with the U.S. immigration service, Dan learns of Ferraro's scheme, but Lusk is later found murdered and Dan is forced aboard Ferraro's nearby yacht. Lenore, who has fallen for Dan, seeks help from Mark Cardigan, who views the entire situation as a movie plot and employs the assistance of local police and hotel guests to rescue Dan. ("I must rid the seas of pirates," he says dramatically. "Survivors will get parts in my next picture!") On board the ship, Martin Krafft, who is in league with Ferraro, prepares to inject Dan with an anesthetic that can destroy the memory and induce death within a year. Before this plan can be carried out, Dan manages to escape and Mark storms the boat, killing several of the men on board. Dan gets hold of a gun, kills Ferraro and winds up with Lenore in the final reel.

As the "his kind of woman" to which the film's title refers, Russell had little to do in the picture except exhibit lavish, form-fitting gowns and bestow coy looks upon the admiring gents in the area. Dismissed in the *New York Herald Tribune* as "nonsensical melodramatic hodgepodge," the picture did only moderate business at the box office and was blasted in the *New York Times* as "one of the worst Hollywood pictures in years."

Russell's second film noir, *The Las Vegas Story* (1952), fared little better at the box office. Here, the actress portrayed Linda Rollins, a former Las Vegas singer and the wife of Lloyd Rollins (Vincent Price), a wealthy businessman who is desperate to raise a large sum of money to cover his role in an embezzlement scheme. Traveling to Los Angeles, Lloyd insists on stopping in Las Vegas, where he attempts to establish a line of credit by using Linda's expensive necklace. While Lloyd tries his hand at the gaming tables, Linda visits the city's Last Chance casino, where she'd worked as a singer. Shortly after her arrival, she encounters her former lover, David (Victor Mature), now a lieutenant with the sheriff's department. But David is bitter about the abrupt end of their love affair years before: "You've got everything you've always wanted," he tells Linda. "And whatever you came back to Vegas for, find it quick and get out. I have to live in this town."

Lloyd and Linda are being trailed by Tom Hubler (Brad Dexter), a private detective who works for the company that has insured Linda's necklace. Before long, Tom discovers that Lloyd has given the necklace to the owner of the Last Chance casino in exchange for a $10,000 credit line. When the casino owner is found murdered the following morning, Lloyd is suspected of the crime and jailed. Assigned to the case, David later learns that Hubler is the real murderer, but before he can capture the detective, Hubler kidnaps Lenore. Chasing the couple in a helicopter, David traps Hubler in the tower of an abandoned airfield and kills him. Having settled his past differences with Lenore,

David learns that Lloyd is facing multiple embezzlement charges and he and Lenore face their future together.

Like Russell's first film noir, *The Las Vegas Story* was a box office disappointment, and she was almost unanimously slammed by critics. The reviewer for the *New York Herald Tribune* claimed that the actress looked "as though she had been first carved out and then lacquered," and Bosley Crowther of the *New York Times* criticized Russell's "petulant pout and twangy whine" and stated, "Miss Russell's figure, which is the sole prop of her acting career, seems to be the one consistent point of reference to which director Robert Stevenson turns throughout the film."

Playing a similar role in her third and final film noir, Russell was again teamed with Robert Mitchum in *Macao* (1952), set in a "quaint and bizarre" colony off the coast of China. In this feature, Russell portrayed a singer, Julie Benton, who has recently arrived in Macao along with Nick Cochran (Mitchum), an ex–GI wanted for a minor criminal offense in the United States, and Lawrence Trumble (William Bendix), a New York detective posing as a salesman. Although Julie steals Nick's wallet shortly after their meeting, the two soon fall in love.

Julie gets a job singing at a gambling house owned by Vincent Halloran (Brad Dexter), the man Trumble has come to Macao to arrest. Halloran, having disposed of three previous detectives from America, wrongly suspects that Nick is a lawman and offers him money to leave town. Exploiting this misconception, Trumble seeks Nick's assistance in luring Halloran outside the borders of the colony where he can be captured by authorities. When Halloran discovers the scheme, he orders Nick killed, but his underlings accidentally murder Trumble instead. Before dying, Trumble informs Nick that his criminal record will be purged if he can aid in securing Halloran's arrest. With help from Halloran's mistress (Gloria Grahame), Nick manages to trap the gambling house owner aboard his own boat, and drives him outside the borders of Macao, where he is collared by police.

Yet another box office flop, *Macao* was labeled in *Variety* as a "routine formula pic" and Bosley Crowther wrote in the *New York Times*: "It is remarkable how often Miss Russell, in an assortment of low-cut sweaters and gowns, is directed to lean toward the camera — quite by accident, of course — and how often and how casually Mr. Mitchum is surprised with his manly chest bared. For those who delight in such glimpses, *Macao* is generous to a fault. Certainly the principal performers do not reveal much more." Interestingly, Crowther's assessment was bolstered by a memorandum from Howard Hughes to studio manager C.J. Devlin, in which he addressed a 26-pound lamé dress that Russell wore in the film: "The fit of the dress around her breasts is not good and gives the impression, God forbid, that her breasts are padded or artificial. They just don't appear to be in natural contour." Hughes went on to decree that the bulk of Russell's wardrobe in *Macao* consist of "low-necked" dresses so that "the customers can get a look at the part of Russell which they pay to see."

After *Macao*, Russell was re-teamed with Bob Hope in the box office smash, *Son of Paleface*, followed by a guest appearance in *Road to Bali* (1952), the sixth of the *Road* pictures starring Hope and Bing Crosby. Then, in 1953, she starred in the film that would turn out to be the highlight of her career, the 20th Century–Fox production *Gentlemen Prefer Blondes*. Costarring Marilyn Monroe, the picture was a hit with audiences and critics alike, and Russell's favorable notices indicated that her flair for musical comedy was finally beginning to be appreciated. In connection with the film's release, Russell and Monroe embedded their hand and footprints in the forecourt at Grauman's (now Mann's) Chinese Theater in Hollywood and Russell recalled in her autobiography that she was "thrilled beyond words" to be involved in the ceremony.

By now, the media was showing interest in something else besides Russell's physical dimensions — her religious convictions. Russell's mother had become a self-ordained minister and conducted religious services at her own church, Chapel in the Valley. In addition to Jane Russell, other regular attendees at the church included actresses Gail Russell and Chili Williams, better known as the "Polkadot Girl." Russell even convinced Marilyn Monroe to visit the church, and while Monroe admitted that the services "didn't happen to turn me into a deeply religious person, if anybody could do that, Jane could." In years to come, Russell would combine her devout beliefs with her singing talent, forming a quartet with three other singers and releasing several singles as well as an album of high-spirited religious numbers. To the press, Russell straightforwardly explained her religious beliefs: "Look, it's very simple. God gave me certain physical attributes that made it possible for me to become a star. But that didn't change the kind of person I am — deep down. The church and show business are all the same to me — part of my life."

After witnessing Russell's success in *Gentleman Prefer Blondes*, Howard Hughes decided to produce his own musical comedy vehicle for his well-endowed star. But instead of an entertaining romp that highlighted Russell's singing and comic skills, *The French Line* (1953) became another scandalous footnote in the star's career. Because of a vulgar bump-and-grind dance number that Russell performed in a skimpy black satin costume, the Motion Picture Association refused to give the picture its Production Code seal of approval. A spokesperson from the Association specifically objected to the focus on Russell's anatomy in several scenes, stating: "Some glaring breast shots of Jane Russell ... will certainly bring the cops to any theater where it is shown." To make matters worse, *The French Line* was filmed in the new three-dimension process, leading to the picture's barely-subtle advertising of "Jane Russell in 3-D ... it'll knock both your eyes out!" But in contrast to her acquiescence regarding *The Outlaw* a decade earlier, Russell was vocal in her objections to the "accent on sex" in *The French Line*: "I don't object to the dance scene itself, but some of the camera angles are in horrible taste," Russell said. "I had an awful time with some of the things they wanted me to wear — hardly anything at all. I fought and beefed and argued over several scenes. I hope and pray the studio will see the light and make the cuts required."

Still, RKO proceeded with plans to release the picture as filmed, despite a $25,000 fine from the Motion Picture Association, and in late 1953, *The French Line* opened in St. Louis. After the archbishop of the St. Louis Archdiocese banned the film, it was withdrawn, slightly re-edited, and re-released in mid-1954. Although the picture finally received a Code approval a year later, the end result failed to live up to the hoopla, and the film was universally panned, with the *New York Times* decreeing it a "cheap exhibitionist thing" and *Time* magazine concluding that the picture was "long on notoriety and short on entertainment."

Russell fared no better in her next film, *Underwater* (1955), which she herself labeled a "turkey." The premiere for this standard sea-adventure was far more exciting than the story itself— it was held in a specially built underwater theater in Silver Springs, Florida, with Russell and the other attendees donned in swimsuits, aqua-lungs and flippers. "I've had to do everything else," Russell told reporters, "I might as well do this!" The picture was slammed by critics, but it was a box office smash and boasted the distinction of having more theatrical bookings than any other RKO film in the previous decade.

After *Underwater*, Russell's contract with Howard Hughes expired and, acting on rumors that Hughes planned to sell RKO, Russell formed Russ-Field Productions, with her husband Robert Waterfield as executive producer. But soon after, she inked a new contract with Hughes that committed her to five pictures at a salary of $1,000 a week for 20 years. When Hughes sold RKO to General Teleradio, Inc., the billionaire retained the rights to the unique contract and began loaning Russell out to other studios. The first film under this agreement was Universal's *Foxfire* (1955), a mildly entertaining soaper with Jeff Chandler and Dan Duryea. Russell next starred with Clark Gable in the big-budget Western *The Tall Men* (1955), receiving a number of favorable reviews, including one noting that "with each film, Russell seems to grow in power and surly confidence." Russell's final picture of 1955 was the first produced by Russ-Field, *Gentlemen Marry Brunettes*. Costarring Jeanne Crain, it served as a follow-up to Russell's successful *Gentlemen Prefer Blondes*, but it suffered in comparison to the earlier film. Russell later praised Crain's acting ability, calling her a "darling girl," but admitted: "At the box office she wasn't a Marilyn Monroe."

Although Russell was still a popular draw with the public, her best roles were obviously far behind her, and she continued to appear in a series of forgettable pictures. But the actress has maintained that her career suffered primarily because of the "sex symbol" image she acquired with the release of *The Outlaw*. "*The Outlaw* typed me and set a pattern that I could never break,"

Jane Russell

she stated in a 1971 interview. "I never had a chance to do really good movies. I never had any choice in my pictures. When you are under contract, you must do the movies they order you to do."

Between films, Russell was busying herself with a cause close to her heart — the adoption of "unwanted" children. In 1955, along with fellow stars Irene Dunne, Loretta Young, June Allyson and Marie Windsor, she founded WAIF (Women's Adoption International Fund), which was originally dedicated to assisting American couples in adopting foreign-born babies. WAIF, which later merged with the International Social Services, has been responsible for providing homes in the United States for more than 20,000 orphans worldwide and currently focuses on the needs of American homeless children. In her autobiography, Russell stated that she is "grateful and amazed" at the organization's successes: "The Lord gave me the idea and asked me to obey," she said. "I simply put one foot in front of the other and started knocking on doors."

On screen, Russell next starred in Columbia's *Hot Blood* (1956), a rather mindless rendition of gypsy life, followed by *The Revolt of Mamie Stover* (1956), a bland drama in which she portrayed a hard-luck whore with a heart of gold, and *The Fuzzy Pink Nightgown* (1957), a dreadful comedy about a kidnapped movie star. The latter film would be her last screen appearance for seven years. Instead, with no suitable film offers coming her way, the 36-year-old actress turned to other performing media. In 1957, she debuted with a solo act at the Sands Hotel in Las Vegas, and later appeared in nightclubs throughout the United States, as well as Mexico, South America, Europe and Canada. She also appeared on NBC's *Colgate Theatre* in 1958, on CBS's *Desilu Playhouse* in 1959, and in guest spots on a number of television variety programs.

Still faced with a dearth of film offers as the 1960s rolled around, Russell tried her luck on the stage, appearing in 1961 in a New England tour of *Janus*, followed by a run of *Skylark* in Chicago and *Bells Are Ringing* in Yonkers, New York. In 1963, plans were announced for Russell's return to the screen in MGM's *Never Enough*, and a British production, *A Talent for Loving*, but both projects fell through. Still, Russell insisted that she didn't mind her absence from films: "I never got a charge about seeing myself up there on the screen. I never took any of it seriously.... Who wants to work in films when you've got a loving husband and family at home? Who needs it?"

But in 1964, she finally did return to films, playing herself in a cameo role in *Fate Is the Hunter*, a drama starring Glenn Ford and Rod Taylor. Two years later, Russell appeared in two low-budget Paramount Westerns, *Johnny Reno* (1966), in which she portrayed a saloon owner, and *Waco* (1966), playing the wife of a corrupt preacher. And Russell sunk even lower with her 1967 portrayal of a trashy waitress in *Born Losers*, a cheap exploitation picture about the evils of motorcycle gangs.

Also in 1967, Russell was in the news when she filed for divorce from her husband Robert Waterfield, charging him with physical abuse. In his cross-complaint, Waterfield cited his wife's frequent drunkenness, and Russell later admitted: "We were both drinking and we'd been drinking for years. I think if we hadn't been drinking we'd probably still be together. Everything got out of proportion." The divorce was finalized in July 1968, with Russell awarded custody of the couple's two oldest children, and Waterfield winning custody of 12-year-old Robert. Soon after, Russell married actor Roger Barrett, whom she had met a year earlier while both were appearing in Chicago in *Here Today*. But three months after their lavish Beverly Hills wedding, Barrett died of a heart attack and Russell later recalled, "I went into one of those darling depressions and couldn't care less about anything. Nothing mattered. Nothing at all.... I didn't care if I lived or died. I just wanted to drown myself in a bottle."

Gradually, Russell emerged from her depression and began to publicize her desire to return to acting: "I'm begging to be a character actress, to play parts with some depth to them," she told the press. "I'm willing to try anything! I'm ready to be my age and look like hell, if necessary." In 1970, Russell did return to the screen, appearing in a small role in *Darker Than Amber*, starring Rod Taylor. But the part was hardly the comeback vehicle that Russell might have envisioned — her screen time amounted to less than two minutes, and in her autobiography she stated, "The less said about that cameo, the better." *Darker Than Amber* has been Russell's last feature film to date.

After her disappointing experience with *Darker Than Amber*, Russell appeared on Broadway, replacing actress Elaine Stritch in the Tony award–winning musical, *Company*. She received mostly favorable reviews for her performance, including one from *Variety*, whose critic noted that Russell was "still a knockout looker whose first entrance is met by silent whistles from the men and envious sighs from the women in the audience." Playing the part of Barbara, a dipso-nymphomaniac, Russell had finally hit on a role that fit her talent and maturity: "I played a character I could identify with because she was my age and I was no longer Jane Russell, sex idol," After a five-month run in *Company*, Russell returned to California, and occupied her free time by designing the rough sketches for an 80-unit luxury apartment complex in the San Fernando Valley. Around this time, Russell also became known to a new generation as the pitch woman for the Playtex 18-hour bra, touting the garment as ideal for "us full-figured gals." Of her long association with the commercials, Russell would later say that the job was "easy and it was something I've always believed in — bras!"

Between these varied activities, Russell managed to find time for her personal life and on January 31, 1974, she married John Calvin Peoples, a real estate executive. Russell had first met her third husband when he was dating a friend of hers: "Then one night, a long time after he broke up with her, he asked me to dinner," she explained. "And then our romance just sort of happened.... John is the sweetest, dearest man in the world!"

But Russell's happy married life did not mean an end to her personal struggles. In 1976, her youngest son, Robert — known as Buck — spent six months in jail for an involuntary manslaughter conviction in the death of a Mexican farmhand. "Buck had been to a party and gotten smashed," Russell recalled. "He and his friends decided to shoot at a neon sign as a game. To this day, I don't think Buck knows if he hit the man or whether it was one of the others." And two years later, Russell herself was jailed for four days on a drunk driving conviction, her second. In this incident, she hit a truck and, on the advice of her attorney, refused to take submit to a blood alcohol test. She has since stopped her long-time drinking habit, but stated in a 1984 interview,

"I used to be able to drink and it wouldn't affect me.... But because of age or all the trauma I went through, it came to the point where I'd have a few glasses of wine and somehow end up blotto."

In 1984, Russell returned to television, accepting the recurring role of Sam Elliott's mother in the NBC series *The Yellow Rose*. The following year, her autobiography, *Jane Russell: My Path and My Detours*, was published. A year after the book's release, she explained its title in an interview with *Drama-Logue*: "It's like I think the Lord has a path for all of us and I was born a rebel and will die a rebel — so every time I went on a detour the Lord would let me go — gave me enough rope to hang myself, then he would lovingly get me back on the path." In recent years, Russell has remained out of the public eye, but she did make a rare television appearance in 1996 when she was interviewed with Robert Mitchum on *Private Screenings*, a feature on the Turner Classic Movies cable channel.

The actress who was once billed as "Mean! Moody! Magnificent!" will probably be remembered more for her wildly publicized film debut in *The Outlaw* than for any other film, but during her lengthy career, she demonstrated that she possessed far more than a pretty face and a well-endowed physique. It was perhaps costar Robert Mitchum who best summed up the actress' innate charisma and lasting appeal when he simply stated: "Jane Russell is an authentic original."

Film Noir Filmography

HIS KIND OF WOMAN   *Director:* John Farrow. *Producer:* Robert Sparks. Released by RKO, August 1951. *Running time:* 120 minutes. *Cast:* Robert Mitchum, Jane Russell, Vincent Price, Tim Holt, Charles McGraw, Marjorie Reynolds, Raymond Burr, Jim Backus, John Mylong.

THE LAS VEGAS STORY   *Director:* Robert Stevenson. *Producer:* Robert Sparks. Released by RKO, 1952. *Running time:* 87 minutes. *Cast:* Jane Russell, Victor Mature, Vincent Price, Hoagy Carmichael, Brad Dexter, Jay C. Flippen, Gordon Oliver.

MACAO   *Director:* Josef von Sternberg. *Producer:* Alex Gottlieb. Released by RKO, April 1952. *Running time:* 81 minutes. *Cast:* Robert Mitchum, Jane Russell, William Bendix, Thomas Gomez, Gloria Grahame, Brad Dexter, Edward Ashley.

References

Berg, Louis. "They Didn't Like Jane." *This Week*, September 18, 1955.
Biography of Jane Russell. Paramount Studios, October 1965.
Connelly, Sherryl. "The Reluctant Sex Symbol." *New York Daily News*, June 11, 1984.
Deford, Frank. "Jane Russell." *People*, October 18, 1985.
Galligan, David. "Sex Symbol Jane Russell." *Drama-Logue*, February 13–19, 1986.
"The Girl the Sailors Like." *New York Post*, October 11, 1947.
Hagen, Ray. "Jane Russell." *Films in Review*, April 1963.

Hyams, Joe. "Sex and Salvation." *Cue*, June 26, 1954.

"Jane Russell Invites the Censors." *New York Inquirer*, June 27, 1955.

Leon, Richard. "Handle with Care." *Photoplay*, January 1954.

Maxwell, Elsa. "The Girl in *The Outlaw*." *Photoplay*, September 1946.

_____. "Jane Russell's Right for Her British Tommy." *Photoplay*, September 1952.

"1941's Best New Star Prospect." *Life*, January 20, 1941.

Ott, Beverly. "Jane Russell's Happiest Year." *Photoplay*, June 1954.

Peary, Gerald. "Russell." *Film Comment*, July-August 1992

"Poses for Pin-Up Photos." *Life*, January 29, 1945.

Reid, Ashton. "Jane Does a Movie." *Collier's*, June 13, 1945.

Robbins, Fred. "Jane Russell's Naughty, Gaudy Facts of Life." *50 Plus*, July 1988.

Russell, Jane. "Gentlemen Prefer Brains." *Photoplay*, December 1954.

_____. *Jane Russell: My Path and My Detours*. New York: Franklin Watts, 1985.

St. Johns, Elaine. "Do Lord ... Do Lord!" *Cosmopolitan*, October 1954.

Skolsky, Sidney. "Tintypes — Jane Russell." *New York Post*, December 12, 1965.

Spiegel, Penina. "Outlaw Grandmaw." *Us*, March 12, 1984.

"This Week: Jane Russell." *Time*, March 25, 1946.

"Tomboy." *American Magazine*, April 1941.

Wheeler, Lyle. "Skytop House." *Photoplay*, January 1952.

Wilson, Earl. "How Jane Russell Got That Way." *Liberty*, June 1949.

Zeitlin, Ida. "Just Plain Jane." *Photoplay*, September 1950.

Documentary

"Private Screenings: Jane Russell and Robert Mitchum." Copyright 1996, Turner Classic Movies.

Lizabeth Scott

Lizabeth Scott, a tawny-haired beauty with a smoldering gaze and a distinctively throaty voice, was best known for her on-screen portrayals of the duplicitous dame who more often than not received her comeuppance in the last reel. Labeled as "The Threat," Scott had a starring role in her film debut, but after only a decade she had lost most of her public appeal, and rapidly receded into obscurity. During the pinnacle of her career, however, Scott was one of the quintessential bad girls of film noir, starring in seven pictures from the era: *The Strange Love of Martha Ivers* (1946), *Dead Reckoning* (1946), *I Walk Alone* (1947), *Pitfall* (1948), *Too Late for Tears* (1949), *Dark City* (1950) and *The Racket* (1951).

Scott was born Emma Matzo on September 29, 1922, the eldest of six children of an English-born father and a mother of Russian descent. A native of Scranton, Pennsylvania, an industrialized mining town, Emma was raised in a culture-filled home and participated for several years in a variety of lessons, including piano and elocution. By her own account, however, the future star was frequently rebellious and outspoken: "As a child, my mother used to tell me to keep my emotions subdued, to be 'a lady.' Instead of which I was a noisy, screaming little brat, definite about everything."

Working in her father's grocery store, Emma fostered many ambitions, including becoming an opera singer, a journalist or a nun — a notion that was promptly vetoed by her mother. During the summer after her graduation from Central High School, Emma worked with May Desmond's stock company at Lake Ariel, New York, and the following fall, she enrolled at Marywood College, a Catholic school near Scranton. However, after only six months, she left the school, later recalling: "I never wanted to finish college because of the feeling I had ... that life was very short and there were so many more important aspects of life to be explored."

Instead, Emma turned her sights toward an acting career, moving to Manhattan to attend the Alvienne School of Dramatics. Residing at the Ferguson Residence for Girls, a boarding house for young students of dance, art and drama, Emma won her first professional job in the national company of *Hellzapoppin'*, at a salary of $50 a week. Of her role in this Olsen and Johnson production, the actress later told reporters that she'd competed with several hundred girls and "when Olsen and Johnson selected me, I was overjoyed. Do you wonder why? Because I was going to be a great actress and here was my first chance." After a year-long tour, she did summer stock at the 52nd Street Stock Company Theatre in New York. Among her many roles with the company was the lead in *Rain*, for which she was billed in the program as "Elizabeth Scott." The actress explained that she chose the first name "just because I always liked [it]," and the last name in honor of one of her favorite plays, *Mary of Scotland*.

It appeared that the aspiring actress may have gotten her big break when she was hired for a walk-on in Thornton Wilder's *The Skin of Our Teeth*, and was asked to serve as understudy to the star of the play, Tallulah Bankhead. But for the next seven months, Scott remembered, she "waited for the Long Island train to break down or for Tallulah to get a cold. But the train ran and she remained robustly healthy." Later, after Bankhead had been replaced by Miriam Hopkins, Scott quit the play, making ends meet by landing several modeling assignments, including a full-page spread in *Esquire* and a number of appearances in *Harper's Bazaar*. Coincidentally, three months after leaving *The Skin of Our Teeth*, Scott received a call from the play's producer, who requested that she step in for a one-night replacement of Miriam Hopkins, who was ill. "I felt it was an impossibility," Scott said, "but I went over the text of the script, and with a friend cueing me, I found that I knew every line."

Several months later, Scott was again asked to fill in for Hopkins, this time for a three-week run. She received favorable notices for her performance but when the play closed, she was forced to resume her modeling activities. Before long, her four-photograph layout in *Harper's Bazaar* caught the eye of agent Charles Feldman, who asked her to come to Hollywood for a screen test. Of the request, Scott later said: "I wanted to be a great stage actress. I never once thought of movies. But, it was off season on Broadway ... and since I wasn't able to find a job there, I thought it might be a good experience to come to Hollywood and find out what it was all about." (Ironically, two years later Scott would be quoted in a *Citizen News* article as saying that "the movies are more legitimate than the stage will ever be!")

Upon her arrival in Los Angeles, Scott was given a room at the Beverly Hills Hotel, but for two months she did little except collect a weekly paycheck from the office of Charles Feldman. When, in frustration, she informed Feldman that she could no longer "just sit here and get paid for it," the agent immediately arranged for a screen test with Warner Bros. However, studio head Jack Warner was unimpressed with Scott's performance, and reportedly predicted: "She'll never be a star, only a second leading lady." Feldman next arranged a screen test for Scott at Universal-International, but this test, too, was not favorably received. After these back-to-back disappointments, Scott decided to return to New York. Feldman attempted to console the actress, telling her that Warners producer Hal B. Wallis had been interested in signing her but that "circumstances" had prevented him from doing so. Nonetheless, Scott informed her agent: "Thanks, but ... I don't think I'm a motion picture actress."

But Scott was wrong in this self-assessment. In August 1944, Feldman wired Scott that Hal Wallis, now head of his own production company through Paramount Studios, wanted to sign her to an exclusive contract. Three months later, Scott returned to Hollywood, where Wallis immediately cast her in a starring role in her first film, *You Came Along* (1945). Playing a part that had been turned down by Barbara Stanwyck, Scott stated that her "sudden boost to the heights of filmland frightened me. But the story was good, the script was well-written, and my role was realistic." Despite Scott's characterization, critics did not regard the film favorably, with an especially caustic review coming from the *New York Times'* Bosley Crowther: "To a new and quite clearly inexperienced little actress is given the job of making the girl in the story seem real. Except that Miss Scott has a fragile and appealingly candid face, she had little else, including script and direction, to help her toward that end." Soon after reading the review, the unreserved and often brash actress reportedly telephoned Crowther to berate him about what she termed his "unfair" criticism of the film.

But Scott struck gold with her next film, *The Strange Love of Martha Ivers* (1946), described by one reviewer as a "forthright, uncompromising presentation of evil, greedy people and human weaknesses." The film, Scott's first entry in the realm of film noir, opens in 1928 in a small industrial city where a rebellious adolescent inadvertently kills her hated aunt with a blow on the head. A friend of the girl's, who was present at the time, substantiates her cunning lie that her guardian was killed by an intruder, and the girl goes on to inherit her aunt's vast fortune. The film fast-forwards to nearly 20 years later to find that the girl, Martha Ivers (Barbara Stanwyck), and the friend, Walter O'Neill (Kirk Douglas), are married. But the union is an unhappy one, characterized by Martha's frequent dalliances with other men and Walter's alcoholism, and is bound not only by the lie surrounding the murder of Martha's aunt, but also by the execution of an innocent vagrant that Martha later accused of the crime.

When Sam Masterson (Van Heflin), a boyhood friend of the pair, returns to town after a lengthy absence, Martha and Walter incorrectly assume that he knows the truth about the murder and is intent on blackmail. Meanwhile, Sam becomes acquainted with Toni Marachek (Scott), a derelict girl in trouble with the police, and appeals to Walter to help his new friend with a recent scrape with the law. Instead, Walter uses the girl to set Sam up for a violent beating, designed to scare him out of town. Angered, Sam refuses to leave, and through an unthinking statement by Martha, he learns the truth about her aunt's death. Despite a growing attraction to Toni, Sam is drawn by Martha's alluring wiles and nearly yields to her scheme to kill Walter. At the last minute, though, Sam comes to his senses and leaves the unhappy couple in their empty house alone, where their former crimes are finally punished when they both commit suicide. As the film ends, Sam returns to his room to find Toni waiting for him: "I missed a bus once and I was lucky," she tells him. "I wanted to see if I could be lucky twice." A short time later, Sam and Toni are making plans to marry, leaving behind the town and its atmosphere of death, greed and betrayal.

The majority of critics were kinder this time around, although Scott was dismissed in *Time* magazine as "no worse, and not noticeably better, than the other delectable, deadpan ex-models who are currently being peddled to the public as dramatic actresses." But typical of most reviews was that of *The Hollywood Reporter*, whose Jack D. Grant reported that Scott "justifies her quick ascent to stardom with another of her strangely haunting portrayals.... Miss Scott has all it takes to write her own ticket in Hollywood." After the film's release, the actress was named a Star of Tomorrow by *Motion Picture Herald*, along with several others, including Zachary Scott and Don DeFore.

Scott followed her success in *Martha Ivers* with her second film noir, *Dead Reckoning* (1946), costarring Humphrey Bogart. In this dark tale, Bogart portrayed Rip Murdock, a paratrooper whose army buddy Johnny Drake (William Prince) disappears shortly before he is slated to receive the Congressional Medal of Honor. Murdock tracks Johnny to his hometown, only to find that his friend has been killed in a fiery auto crash. Suspecting murder, Murdock sets out to find the truth, and his quest leads him to Coral Chandler (Scott), a sultry former torch singer whom Johnny had loved. Murdock soon learns that, before the war, Johnny had been accused of murdering Coral's wealthy husband, and that Coral is now inexplicably bound to Martinelli (Morris Carnovsky), a powerful gangster and the owner of the nightclub where Coral used to sing.

Against his better judgment, Rip finds himself falling for the beautiful Coral: "I didn't like the feeling I had about her," he says in an early scene. "The way I wanted to put my hand on her arm. The way I kept smelling that jasmine in her hair. The way I kept hearing that song she'd sung. Yeah, I was walking into something all right." After first revealing that Johnny had accidentally killed her husband, Coral later admits to Rip that she was the killer, and that Martinelli possesses the gun that can prove her guilt. But when Rip goes to Martinelli's office to retrieve the evidence, he learns the truth — that Coral's husband had been murdered for his money and that the singer and Martinelli have been secretly married for years. When Rip tries to turn Coral into police, she shoots him, causing a car crash that proves fatal for the ill-fated singer.

Although *Dead Reckoning* did vigorous box office business, reviews for Scott were mixed. Some critics compared her unfavorably to Lauren Bacall, while others praised her portrayal. The reviewer for *Variety* hailed her "persuasive, sirenish performance," and Jack D. Grant of *The Hollywood Reporter* concluded that "her role is likely to do her career more than passing good."

After only three films, Scott was becoming known as an outspoken, opinionated actress. In 1946, following a trip to London at the end of World War II, she told the *Los Angeles Times* that "Americans are living in the lap of luxury compared with the hardships being undergone today by the people of England," and in an October 1946 column by Lowell E. Redelings in *Motion Picture*, she was labeled as having "definite ideas about definite things."

Desert Fury (1947), Scott's next picture, was her first to be filmed in Technicolor. Of her role as a brothel owner's daughter, critics were almost universally disdainful in their assessments — she was complimented in *Variety* only for being a "wonderful clotheshorse," and panned in the *Baltimore Sun* for "a too-ready smile which she switches on and off like an electric sign and nothing more to offer than a set of innocuous mannerisms." Scott's second film of 1947 was the Paramount musical feature *Variety Girl*, whose all-star cast included Gary Cooper, Alan Ladd, Barbara Stanwyck, Paulette Goddard, Pearl Bailey and Veronica Lake (with whom Scott had also been compared). Scott appeared in a circus production number, offering a weak smile as Burt Lancaster prepared to shoot a cigarette out of her mouth. Of her brief appearance, H.B. Darrach of *Time* magazine wrote that Scott offered "a Milton Caniff version of the Mona Lisa."

The following year, Scott starred in two film noir features — *Pitfall* (1948) with Dick Powell, and *I Walk Alone* (1948) with Burt Lancaster and Kirk Douglas. The first begins with an introduction to Johnny Forbes (Powell), an insurance agent bored with his middle class existence: "You were voted the prettiest girl in class. I was voted most likely to succeed," Johnny tells his wife (Jane Wyatt). "Something should happen to people like that." Before long, Johnny gets more than he has bargained for when he meets Mona Stevens (Scott), the girlfriend of a hapless embezzler, Bill Smiley (Byron Barr), who has been jailed for his crime. Dispatched to retrieve stolen items from Mona's apartment, Johnny falls for her instead, and is caught in a triangle rounded out by Mack MacDonald (Raymond Burr), a psychotic insurance investigator.

Even after Johnny ends his brief affair with Mona, he is drawn deeper into her life when she seeks his protection from Mack's unwanted advances. Later, Mack visits Smiley in jail, angering him with news of Mona's affair with Johnny, and when the embezzler is released, Mack plies him with liquor and furnishes him with a gun. Forewarned by Mona of Smiley's intentions, Johnny kills the embezzler and reveals the entire story to his wife. Meanwhile, Mona fatally wounds Mack as he tries to force her to run away with him, and is arrested for the crime. Johnny is exonerated, but faces an uncertain future with his wife, who tells him: "I'd almost made up my mind [to divorce you]. And then I got to thinking — if a man has always been a good husband except for 24 hours, how long should he be expected to pay for it? I'm not sure if it will ever be the same, but we've weathered other things, maybe we can handle this."

For her performance, Scott was hailed by reviewers, including the *New York Times* critic who called her "provocative and acting better than she has ever done before." By now, Scott was a top box office draw, and her popularity continued to rise with her next film noir, *I Walk Alone* (1948).

As this picture opens, Frankie Madison (Burt Lancaster) is being released from prison after a 14-year stretch for bootlegging. He soon learns that his former partner Noll Turner (Kirk Douglas) now owns a swank nightclub and has no intention of honoring the profit sharing agreement made before Frankie was jailed. Frankie also discovers that his brother Dave (Wendell Corey) works as Noll's accountant, and that the nightclub is operating under an intricate corporate structure that prevents Frankie from sharing in its success.

Noll's faithful, longtime girlfriend Kay Lawrence (Scott) is forced to acknowledge Noll's true nature when he suddenly announces his intention to marry a wealthy society matron. Frankie, meanwhile, is unsuccessful in his attempt to take over the club, and when Dave stands up to Noll, he is killed. Later, Frankie forces Noll to confess to the crime, and Noll is gunned down by police when he tries to escape. As the film ends, with both their lives altered by Noll's machinations, Frankie and Kay face a future together.

This time around, critics were unimpressed by Scott's performance, and a particularly mean-spirited appraisal was offered by Bosley Crowther in the *New York Times*: "As the torch singer jilted by [Douglas] and thereafter inclined towards revenge, Lizabeth Scott has no more personality than a model in the window of a department store." But she bounced back with her third consecutive film noir, *Too Late for Tears* (1949), playing a conniving housewife who lets nothing stand in the way of satiating her avaricious desires.

This picture begins when Jane Palmer (Scott) and her husband Alan (Arthur Kennedy) are driving to a dinner party given by the "diamond-studded wife" of one of Alan's business associates. Citing the other woman's "patronizing" manner, Jane convinces her husband to cancel their plans, but on the return trip home, a mysterious suitcase is tossed into their car by a passing vehicle. Discovering that the bag contains $60,000 in cash, Alan intends to turn it over to police, but Jane has other plans: "You've got to let me keep that money. I won't let you just give it away," she tells him. "Chances like this are never offered twice. This is it. I've been waiting for it, dreaming of it all my life."

Alan, however, is unmoved by his wife's plea, and Jane is further dismayed when the rightful owner of the money, Danny Fuller (Dan Duryea), appears at her door demanding its return. Determined to keep the cash, Jane joins forces with Danny to bump off her husband, then poisons Danny and flees to Mexico. But just as it appears that Jane has successfully gotten away with her crimes, Jane is thwarted by the brother (Don DeFore) of her first husband, whom she had driven to suicide. While trying to escape, Jane falls from a balcony to her death, with the coveted bills fluttering around her lifeless body.

More so than any of Scott's other film noir characters, her Jane Palmer was a femme fatale in every sense of the expression, displaying a complete lack of conscience as she murdered anyone who got in her way. For her riveting performance, Scott was applauded by a number of critics — Charles J. Lazarus wrote in *Motion Picture Herald* that she "does a fine job in building the characterization of a woman who is pathologically unable to understand the enormity of her crimes," and the reviewer for the *New York Times* called her "a taut, seductive, husky-voiced schemer who is fascinatingly convincing in a completely unsympathetic role." But not all critics were impressed by her

Lizabeth Scott

performance — the reviewer for *Variety*, who labeled the film a "meandering, slow-paced melodrama that fails to come off," found that Scott "has a good moment or two as the heavy, but overall effect is below her usual level."

In her second film of 1949, Scott starred with Victor Mature and Lucille Ball in *Easy Living*, portraying the ambitious wife of a professional football player. But this plodding drama did not click with audiences and Scott was labeled in *Cue* magazine as "utterly inadequate to her role." After this picture,

Scott returned to stage work, playing the title role in *Anna Lucasta* at the McCarter Theatre in Princeton, New Jersey. She also busied herself by guesting in several plays for *Lux Radio Theatre*, including *Saigon* with John Lund in 1949 and *California* with Ray Milland and Raymond Burr in 1950.

Back on screen, Scott next appeared in *Paid in Full* (1950), a melodramatic soaper in which she played her first "good girl" role in several years. Despite the film's implausible plot, Scott was labeled "warm and restrained" in the *New York Times*, and the critic for *Variety* wrote that she "turns in a capital performance as the unselfish sister." In her second release of the year, she returned to film noir with *Dark City* (1950), costarring Charlton Heston in his film debut.

Here, Scott portrayed Fran, a nightclub singer who is in love with Danny Haley (Heston), a bitter, small-time gambling racketeer whose dissatisfaction with life keeps Fran at arm's length. When his gambling operation is shut down following a police raid, Danny joins with his partners, Augie (Jack Webb) and Barney (Ed Begley), to fleece unsuspecting salesman Arthur Winant (Don DeFore) out of $5,000 in a poker game. Distraught over losing the money, Winant commits suicide, and the three gamblers suddenly find that they are being stalked by the man's psychotic brother, Sidney (Mike Mazurki). After Barney and Augie are both found hanged, Danny tries to locate Sidney, but instead encounters Winant's widow, Victoria (Viveca Lindfors). Danny's inflexible exterior is softened after he spends time with Victoria and her son and, admitting his role in Winant's death, he travels to Las Vegas with plans to raise money to give to Victoria. Sidney Winant follows him there, as does the still-faithful Fran. Danny wins more than $10,000 for Victoria, then works with police to set a trap for Sidney, who is gunned down while trying to murder Danny. The film closes with Danny realizing his love for Fran: "You're my kind of girl, Fran," he admits. "I don't want to be alone anymore."

Unlike most of her previous film noir roles, Scott's character in *Dark City* was self-sacrificing and weak-willed. Despite Danny's often-cruel treatment, and in spite of his culpability in Winant's death, Fran continues to pursue him. "You need me almost as much as I need you, Danny," she says in one scene. "I know I could make you happy." Scott received widely varying reviews for her performance. While she was commended in *Variety* for her "fine portrayal," Bosley Crowther of the *New York Times* found her "frighteningly grotesque."

In her next role, Scott again departed from her usual femmes fatale, playing a probation officer bent on reforming parolee Jane Greer in *The Company She Keeps* (1951). While Scott's performance could not rise above the picture's flimsy plot and modest budget, she was, according to the *New York Times'* Bosley Crowther, "the least of [the film's] absurdities." She then appeared in the well-received *Two of a Kind* (1951), playing a larcenous dame who schemes to claim a $10 million inheritance, followed by *The Racket* (1951), her final foray into the realm of film noir.

This picture focuses on Capt. McQuigg (Robert Mitchum), an honest cop determined to expose corruption in his town, and his nemesis, Nick Scanlon (Robert Ryan), a middle-level gangster who is characterized by his violent, vengeful nature. After a police informant is murdered, McQuigg enlists the help of one of his brightest officers, Johnson (William Talman), but Scanlon learns of the investigation and has a bomb planted at McQuigg's home as a warning. McQuigg's wife is slightly injured, further increasing the police captain's determination to catch Scanlon. In an effort to get to Scanlon, McQuigg orders the arrest of his younger brother Joe on an auto theft charge, and holds Joe's girlfriend Irene (Scott) as a material witness against him.

Later, Scanlon goes to see McQuigg, but he winds up killing Johnson after a scuffle. Scanlon is identified as the murderer by a police reporter who has taken a liking to Irene, and it is Irene herself who baits Scanlon into confessing his guilt: "Joe didn't think much of you, but at least he always bragged about how tough you were," she tells him. "That was one thing he never apologized for. And now it looks like you're not even tough." Scanlon is later killed during an escape attempt, and Irene leaves with the police reporter, having transformed from a selfish, greedy B-girl to an honest and selfless citizen.

With her relatively small role in *The Racket*, Scott's femme fatale roles came to an end and her career began to diminish. Despite her claim that she would "rather starve than perform in a picture just for the money," she began to appear in a series of mediocre films, including *Red Mountain* (1951), of which the reviewer for the *Chicago Daily Tribune* wrote that she "performs with all the animation of a chunk of cement"; *Scared Stiff* (1953), a silly Martin and Lewis starrer; *Bad for Each Other* (1953), which *Variety* noted "hardly helps the careers" of its stars; and *Silver Lode* (1954), a dull Western that was Scott's sole release of the year.

Already falling from favor with the public, Scott suffered a blow in September 1954 that nearly ended her career as an actress. A scandalous exposé in *Confidential* magazine suggested that Scott was leading a lesbian lifestyle and included a number of frivolous accusations, including Scott's own admission that she "always wore male colognes, slept in men's pajamas, and positively hated frilly feminine dresses." The article also pointed out that the actress had "never married and never even gets close to the altar," that she "was taking up almost exclusively with Hollywood's weird society of baritone babes," and that she had been seen in the company of a notorious Paris lesbian. The following year, through famed Hollywood attorney Jerry Geisler, Scott sued the publication for $2.5 million, claiming that she had been portrayed in a "vicious, slanderous, and indecent" manner. Although the result of the suit was never publicized, it is believed that it was settled out of court.

Scott's first film after the *Confidential* scandal was *The Weapon*, a 1955 British-made Western. Although the picture would not released in the United States until four years later, it was praised by *Variety* for its "top-rate" acting.

After a two-year screen absence, Scott completed her contract with Hal Wallis by appearing with Elvis Presley in *Loving You* (1957), portraying a publicist who transforms a hillbilly singer into a superstar. The financially successful film would mark Scott's last screen appearance for nearly 15 years. "I never thought of it as retiring," Scott later explained. "I simply decided there was more to life than just making films. And I proceeded to explore all of life's other facets. The most important thing to me is my personal life. To be content, happy, and to be at peace — these are the top requisites. I'm terribly interested in being creative, but, for me, time is not of the essence."

During her years away from filmmaking, Scott explored a number of creative avenues, which included recording an album entitled *Lizabeth Sings* in 1959. Of the album, which led to a three-year contract with RCA Records, Scott remarked: "I got the notion I wanted to do some singing some three years ago, but my studio wasn't too excited about the idea. Then a year or so ago, I just made up my mind I was going to take singing lessons and this is what's come of it. After all, the worst that could happen is that people won't play my records." She also guest-starred on such television programs as *Adventures in Paradise* and *The Third Man*, appeared on several TV game shows and did voice-overs for television commercials advertising cat food and juice. When Scott returned to the silver screen, it was for an offbeat British-made film, *Pulp* (1972), starring Michael Caine, Mickey Rooney and Lionel Stander. It has been her last film to date.

With a career that produced only 22 films, Lizabeth Scott nonetheless remains a uniquely talented product of Hollywood's Golden Age, and one of film noir's archetypal femmes. She was a nonconformist, an outspoken rebel, and a consummate individualist whose character was best described by Scott herself when she said: "My personal life — my development as a human being — is the most important thing."

Film Noir Filmography

THE STRANGE LOVE OF MARTHA IVERS   Director: Lewis Milestone. *Producer:* Hal B. Wallis. Released by Paramount, July 1946. *Running time:* 115 minutes. *Cast:* Barbara Stanwyck, Van Heflin, Lizabeth Scott, Kirk Douglas, Judith Anderson, Roman Bohnen.

DEAD RECKONING   *Director:* John Cromwell. *Producer:* Sidney Biddell. Released by Columbia, January 1947. *Running time:* 100 minutes. *Cast:* Humphrey Bogart, Lizabeth Scott, Morris Carnovsky, Charles Cane, William Prince, Marvin Miller.

I WALK ALONE   *Director:* Byron Haskin. *Producer:* Hal B. Wallis. Released by Paramount, January 1948. *Running time:* 98 minutes. *Cast:* Burt Lancaster, Lizabeth Scott, Kirk Douglas, Wendell Corey, Kristine Miller, Marc Lawrence, Mike Mazurki.

PITFALL   *Director:* André De Toth. *Producer:* Samuel Bischoff. Released by United Artists, August 1948. *Running time:* 86 minutes. *Cast:* Dick Powell, Lizabeth Scott, Raymond Burr, Jane Wyatt.

Too Late for Tears   *Director:* Byron Haskin. *Producer:* Hunt Stromberg. Released by United Artists, August 1949. *Running time:* 98 minutes. *Cast:* Lizabeth Scott, Dan Duryea, Don DeFore, Arthur Kennedy, Kristine Miller.

Dark City   *Director:* William Dieterle. *Producer:* Hal Wallis. Released by Paramount, October 1950. *Running time:* 98 minutes. *Cast:* Charlton Heston, Lizabeth Scott, Viveca Lindfors, Dean Jagger, Don DeFore, Jack Webb, Ed Begley, Henry Morgan, Mike Mazurki.

The Racket   *Director:* John Cromwell. *Producer:* Edmund Grainger. Released by RKO, December 1951. *Running time:* 88 minutes. *Cast:* Robert Mitchum, Lizabeth Scott, Robert Ryan, William Talman, Ray Collins, Joyce MacKenzie, Robert Hutton, Virginia Huston, William Conrad.

References

Agan, Patrick. "Lizabeth Scott: The Blonde Who's Great to Remember." *Hollywood Studio Magazine*, April 1985.

Callin, Owen. "Movies Far More Legitimate Than Stage, Says Lizabeth." *Citizen News*, August 4, 1945.

Campbell, Kay. "Intensely, Lizabeth Scott." *Photoplay*, November 1946.

DeBona, Joe. "Liz Scott Takes It Out on Her Helpless Helpers." *Sunday Herald*, November 13, 1949.

Deere, Dorothy. "The Saga of Liz." *Photoplay*, April 1946.

"First 100 Pictures to Be Her Hardest." *Paramount News of Hollywood*, July 29, 1946.

"Golden Lizzie." *Photoplay*, May 1948.

Hopper, Hedda. "Lizabeth Scott Sparked by Electric Personality." *Los Angeles Times*, October 14, 1951.

"Liz Scott Is Now Legally — Liz Scott." *Los Angeles Daily News*, November 20, 1949.

"Lizabeth Scott." *After Dark*, September 1981.

"Lizabeth Scott." *New York Sunday Mirror*, August 24, 1947.

"Lizabeth Scott Is Star of First Film." *Paramount News of Hollywood*, circa 1944.

"Lizabeth Scott Will Be at Back-to-School Show." *Los Angeles Times*, September 3, 1951.

"Lizabeth Scott Won't Be Emma Matzo Any More." *Los Angeles Times*, October 21, 1949.

Marshall, Jim. "Not Like the Movies." *Collier's*, August 18, 1946.

Novak, Mickell. "A Kiss Isn't Just a Kiss." *Philadelphia Bulletin*, June 18, 1950.

Parsons, Louella O. "Liz Scott Ill, Has Operation; Rest Ordered." *Los Angeles Examiner*, February 10, 1949.

Reed, Rex. "Pulp Surprise Crackles with Familiar Faces." *New York Daily News*, February 9, 1973.

Scott, John L. "Summer Stage Circuit Again Proves Lure for Alluring Blond Star Lizabeth Scott." *Los Angeles Times*, April 30, 1950.

Scott, Lizabeth. "Don't Misunderstand Me." *Photoplay*, January 1948.

Squires, Harry. "Lizabeth Scott: Sexy Siren." *Classic Film Collector*, Winter 1977.

Stanke, Don. "Lizabeth Scott." *Film Fan Monthly*, November 1971.

"Sweet Role Sought by Liz Scott." *Los Angeles Times*, January 18, 1948.

Wilson, Earl. "Siren from Scranton." *Silver Screen*, August 1945.

Barbara Stanwyck

Barbara Stanwyck was a survivor. Orphaned at a young age, raised in foster homes, and a working girl by the age of 13, her early years were an unending blur of poverty, disappointment and pain. But the invincible nature of this talented beauty led her to become one of the most highly acclaimed actresses in the history of the movies. With a larger-than-life presence, Stanwyck offered stellar performances in nearly every cinematic undertaking, from such little-known films as *Forbidden* (1932) to classics including *Stella Dallas* (1937) and *Meet John Doe* (1941). And as one of film noir's busiest actresses, Stanwyck was a standout in seven movies from this era: *Double Indemnity* (1944), *The Strange Love of Martha Ivers* (1946), *Sorry, Wrong Number* (1948), *The File on Thelma Jordon* (1949), *Clash by Night* (1952), *Witness to Murder* (1954) and *Crime of Passion* (1957).

Stanwyck was born Ruby Katherine Stevens on July 16, 1907, in Brooklyn, New York, the youngest of five children (her siblings were Maude, Mabel, Mildred and Malcolm). The family lived in a poverty-stricken environment, and although the actress was usually reluctant to discuss her childhood, she would admit late in her life: "All right, let's just say I had a terrible childhood. Let's say that 'poor' is something I understand." In 1910, Ruby's mother Catherine, pregnant with her sixth child, was knocked off a trolley car by a drunken passenger and struck her head against a curb. She never recovered from her injury and two weeks after her death, her widower signed up with a crew working on the Panama Canal. His family would never see him again.

Because Ruby's two oldest sisters were married, the care of the family's youngest children fell to Mildred, the third-oldest sibling, known as the "beauty of the family." But Mildred was busy pursuing a career as a chorus girl, and during road trips she placed her brother and sister in a variety of foster homes. Ruby often ran away from these dwellings, only to be found by her brother sitting on the steps of the house where she'd spent her first years, "waiting for Mama to come home."

For the next several years, Ruby and her brother clung to each other, developing a close and mutually protective relationship. But Ruby suffered a crushing blow at the age of eight when Mildred decided that the 11-year-old Malcolm was old enough to live with her. Later, the actress would recall the day her sister came to take Malcolm away: "I screamed and I cried as though my heart would break. I fought and yelled at them. I tried to lock Malcolm up so they couldn't get him…. I couldn't believe they were taking him, and that I was being left behind."

Without the companionship of her beloved brother, Ruby became resentful and rebellious. She was a poor student, used foul language and had no close girlfriends, preferring to spend her time at the local matinee where she would lose herself in the trials of Pearl White in *The Perils of Pauline*. "Her courage, grace, daring and spirit lifted me right out of the world," she would later say. The high point of her adolescence came when she was allowed to accompany

Mildred on tour during the summers of 1916 and 1917. It was during these trips that Ruby began to develop her passion for performing. She loved watching the dancers and longed to be one herself, mastering their routines as she viewed their performances.

By the time Ruby was 13, she'd had enough of her dreary education. She quit school, lied about her age and got a job wrapping packages at a local department store. The following year, she answered an ad for telephone operators, earning $14 a week. Later, in search of a higher salary, she secured a job cutting patterns for *Vogue*, but this position wouldn't last. After ruining the pattern of almost every patron, she was fired. Years later, the actress declared: "I hated those three little jobs. I knew there was no place but show business that I wouldn't hate."

Moving in with her sister Maude in Flatbush, the closest that Ruby could come to show business was a typing job for the Jerome H. Remick Music Company in Manhattan. But her dream of performing was just around the corner. It is believed that the manager at Remick's arranged for Ruby to audition for Earl Lindsay, manager of the Strand Roof nightclub in Times Square. Although she was not yet 16, Ruby borrowed her sister's dress, made up her face and won a $40-a-week job in the nightclub's chorus. Ruby's new boss was a no-nonsense director whose gruff manner and drive for perfection endeared him to the young chorine: "I'll always love Earl Lindsay … I owe everything to his teaching," the actress later said. "I started in the back of the chorus where it was easy to give something less than your best. He never let me get away with that."

At long last, Ruby was happy. She was finally a real performer, and she began to make friends with her fellow chorines, including Walda Mansfield and future actress Mae Clarke, with whom she took a small apartment on 46th Street. For Ruby, it was her first real home. When the show at the Strand closed, Ruby and her roommates found work in *Keep Kool*, another Earl Lindsay show, which opened at the Morosco on May 22, 1924. Ruby appeared as one of 16 "Keep Kool Cuties" and also had a specialty number in a skit called "A Room Adjoining a Boudoir (Apologies to Avery Hopwood)." The show was well-received and the "Cuties" were termed in *Variety* as "the hoofiest chorus seen in ages … [they are] pips, lookers, and dancers."

When *Keep Kool* closed after three months, portions of the Lindsay show, including Ruby's skit, were incorporated into the touring company of the *Ziegfeld Follies*, and Ruby was offered $100 a week to join the show. In addition to her Hopwood sketch, she sang and danced in two numbers and appeared in the famous Ziegfeld Shadowgraph, in which she performed a strip tease behind a white screen. Ruby's tour with the *Follies* ended in 1925, but she was not out of work for long. Along with Mae Clarke, she took a job dancing in the chorus at Anatole Friedland's Club on 54th Street, and six months later, the girls appeared in a Shubert revue, *Gay Paree*. In January 1926, the roommates also took on a job at the Everglades Café, and they raced nightly between the two gigs: "We worked like dogs," the actress would later say. "And we were as strong as horses."

Among the haunts frequented by the young hoofers was the Tavern on 48th street, where Ruby and Mae mingled with other show business types. It was the Tavern's owner, Billy LaHiff, who was indirectly responsible for initiating Ruby's path to stardom. In 1926, he introduced the 18-year-old to Willard Mack, the producer, director, playwright and actor, who was casting for his play *The Noose*, a death row drama. Mack hired Ruby on the spot for a small part as a cabaret girl. For Ruby, this was the beginning of her career as a true actress: "This was the big time. Willard Mack ... directed me right out of a dancing yen and into a dramatic one. I was all Bernhardt from that time forth." In addition to providing Ruby with her dramatic debut, Mack was also responsible for her transformation into Barbara Stanwyck. While leafing through old theater programs, Mack found a title that caught his eye: "Jane Stanwyck in *Barbara Frietchie*." By combining the two names, Barbara Stanwyck was "born."

Although the play flopped in its Pittsburgh tryout, Stanwyck was mentioned by the reviewer for the *Pittsburgh Gazette*, who noted her "unexpected bit of genuine pathos." Mack revised the play's script, expanding Stanwyck's role, and when the play opened on Broadway in October 1926, it was a hit. Stanwyck was hailed by a number of critics, earning praise in *Billboard* for achieving "real heights in her brief emotional scene," and in the *New York Telegram* for her "uncommonly fine performance."

It was during her run in *The Noose* that Stanwyck fell in love for the first time, with costar Rex Cherryman. The 28-year-old actor was attracted to Stanwyck's brash innocence, and the young actress was flattered by the attention she received from the handsome, mature Cherryman. "I adored him," Stanwyck said years later. "Everything about him was so vivid." And while her love life was heating up, Stanwyck's career appeared to be taking a new direction. She was invited by producer Bob Kane to make a screen test at the Cosmopolitan Studios for the lead in the silent film *Broadway Nights*. But the experience was not a pleasant one. During the test, she was unable to cry on cue — despite the director's use of a raw onion and plaintive violin strains — and instead of the lead, Stanwyck was given the smaller role of the heroine's friend. The film was released on June 28, 1927, but Stanwyck never listed it among her credits.

In June 1927, after 197 performances, *The Noose* closed, and soon afterward, Stanwyck was cast as a vaudeville performer in *Burlesque*. The play, which opened at the Plymouth Theater on September 1, 1927, was a smash hit, and Stanwyck's portrayal was again favorably noted by critics. Alexander Woollcott reported in *The World* that Stanwyck's performance was "touching and true," while Brooks Atkinson of the *New York Times* remarked that the actress "plays with genuine emotion and kicks her way skillfully through the chorus numbers."

While Stanwyck played her triumphant run in *Burlesque*, Rex Cherryman was enjoying his own success in *The Trial of Mary Dugan*. The two were considered the golden couple of Broadway, and many expected them to marry. But in the summer of 1928, Cherryman fell ill, and doctors recommended a complete rest. To recuperate, Cherryman set sail on the S.S. *DeGrasse*, but he would not live to see the end of the voyage. He died aboard the ship on August 10, 1928, and Stanwyck was left alone again. The young actress was devastated by the unexpected death of her first love, and later recalled: "I nearly died getting over the loss of him." But her grief would soon be assuaged by another man — vaudeville comedian Frank Fay.

Stanwyck first met Fay in 1926, when the actor was at the peak of his career. Fay was unlike any man Stanwyck had ever met — the twice-married comedian was a heavy drinker and gambler, was notorious for being either flat broke or basking in wealth, and was disliked by his fellow comedians ("Fay's friends could be counted on the missing arm of a one-armed man," Milton Berle once remarked). From the start, Stanwyck and Fay shared a mutual animosity, with Stanwyck deriding the vaudevillian's enormous ego, and Fay showing little respect for the budding actress. But when Fay heard of Cherryman's death, he rushed to Stanwyck's side, and she found in him the comfort and solace she so desperately needed.

According to actor Oscar Levant, who introduced the couple: "Barbara fell madly in love with [Fay]. She went for Fay in such a complete way — I never saw anything to equal it." And on August 25, 1928, after a whirlwind courtship, and just over two weeks after the death of Stanwyck's first love, she and Fay were married in St. Louis. Hours after the small wedding, Stanwyck boarded a train for New Jersey, where she began the *Burlesque* tour, and her new husband remained behind in St. Louis, where he was appearing as master of ceremonies at the Missouri Theater. But this career-related separation would not last for long. Both Stanwyck and Fay were being courted by Hollywood, and six months after their marriage, Stanwyck and Fay were on their way to California.

Stanwyck signed with United Artists, whose head, Joseph Schenck, had spotted her in *Burlesque*, and Fay was contracted to host several musicals with Warner Bros. Stanwyck's first film was *The Locked Door* (1929), the adaptation of the popular 1919 play *The Sign on the Door*. In her portrayal of a young wife who tries to save her husband by assuming the guilt for a murder, Stanwyck was singled out by the *New York Herald Tribune*, who noted her "honest and moving" performance. But *The Locked Door* was panned by most critics, and Stanwyck herself later quipped: "They never should have unlocked the damned thing!" And the actress fared little better in her next film, *Mexicali Rose* (1929), in which she was miscast as a cheap bordertown temptress.

After these two films, Stanwyck began to doubt her future in motion pictures and spent the next six months out of work: "Nobody in Hollywood wanted any part of me," she recalled. "I sat around … working myself into a panic of self-doubt. My confidence had almost been destroyed." But her career received an unexpected boost when a screen test she had made for Warner Bros.—performing her heart-rending scene from *The Noose*—found its way into the hands of director Frank Capra. In his autobiography, the veteran director recounted his reaction after viewing the three-minute test: "I got a lump in my throat as big as an egg…. Never had I seen or heard such emotional sincerity. When it was over, I had tears in my eyes. I was stunned." Capra convinced Columbia Pictures head Harry Cohn to sign Stanwyck for the lead in his upcoming picture *Ladies of Leisure* (1930), and Stanwyck finally got the break she needed.

As Kay Arnold, a wisecracking party girl, Stanwyck offered a moving and sensitive portrayal that was unanimously hailed by critics. The *New York Review* reported that the film "gives Barbara Stanwyck an excellent opportunity to show that she is as good an actress in the talkies as she is on the stage," and the *New York Times* topped its review with the banner headline: "Miss Stanwyck Triumphs." But the most effusive praise came from *Photoplay*, which claimed that *Ladies of Leisure* was "a really fine picture because of the astonishing performance of a little tap-dancing beauty who has in her the spirit of a great artist. Her name is Barbara Stanwyck. Go and be amazed by this Barbara girl."

After her success in *Ladies of Leisure*, Stanwyck became one of the most sought-after actresses in Hollywood. She signed non-exclusive contracts with Columbia and Warner Bros. and appeared next in Warners' *Illicit* (1931), the first film in which she received star billing; *Ten Cents a Dance* (1931), directed by veteran actor Lionel Barrymore; *Night Nurse* (1931), costarring Clark Gable (of whom Stanwyck later enthused, "He was just the kind of guy who made you look at him all the time"); and *The Miracle Woman* (1931), her second of five films under the direction of Frank Capra.

With each cinematic undertaking, Stanwyck's popularity soared. But her home life with Frank Fay was crumbling—as her star rose, his was rapidly descending. The musicals that Fay had hosted for Warner Bros. had been successful, but not necessarily because of his role, and after he appeared in two disastrous films for the studio, his contract was canceled in June 1931. Fay began drinking more heavily, his colleagues began to whisper that he was a has-been, and it was reported in the press that his marriage to Stanwyck was in trouble. Despite the flurry of rumors, Stanwyck staunchly defended her husband, insisting to reporters: "I am Mrs. Frank Fay first, and Barbara Stanwyck second. He's old-fashioned. He thinks a woman's place is in the home but he wants me to be happy."

Struggling to save his dying career, Fay moved back to New York, and insisted that his wife accompany him. Although Stanwyck was scheduled to begin work on *Forbidden* (1932), her third film with Frank Capra, she decided to put her marriage first and informed Columbia head Harry Cohn that she would be unavailable — unless he increased her salary from $30,000 to $50,000. Cohn was furious and sued Stanwyck for failing to fulfill the terms of her contract. Reactions to this course of events were mixed. Many movie magazines of the day hailed Stanwyck's devotion to her husband, labeling her as "the girl who finds no sacrifice too great for love," but columnist Louella Parsons flatly stated: "I do not mean to imply that Frank Fay is selfish and self-centered, but from all I can gather it is Barbara who is making all of the sacrifices." On September 11, 1931, Columbia won an injunction that barred Stanwyck from working for any other studio until she had honored her obligation, and four days later, she agreed to return to work.

Stanwyck was again commended by critics for her work in *Forbidden*, which was loosely based on the Fannie Hurst novel *Back Street*. She described her next film, *Shopworn* (1932), as "one of those terrible pictures they sandwiched in when you started," but she was still applauded for her role as a girl from the other side of the tracks. *The London Times* critic stated that Stanwyck "does what she can with a thankless part," and the reviewer for the *New York Herald Tribune* reported: "There is something about the simple, straightforward sincerity of Miss Stanwyck which makes everything she does upon either stage or screen seem credible and rather poignant."

On the home front, Stanwyck was still striving to save her rocky marriage. After her work on *Forbidden*, she appeared in a successful two-week run with her husband at the Palace Theatre, but behind the scenes, the couple's violent arguments continued. Stanwyck and Fay returned to California, and in December 1932, in perhaps a last-ditch effort to mend their ever-worsening union, Stanwyck and Fay adopted a ten-month-old boy, whom they named Dion Anthony. But the addition of a child to the volatile relationship could not solve its many problems, not least of which was Fay's rapidly failing career. In June 1933, he was panned by reviewers for his appearance in *Tattle Tales*, a stage revue that had been financed by Stanwyck. One critic was particularly brusque, writing: "Frank Fay does not know where to draw the line.... If he is funny for a minute he jumps to the childish conclusion that if he keeps going for ten minutes he will be ten times as funny. He never knows when to go home." The production closed after one month, and Stanwyck lost almost $200,000. In public, Stanwyck continued to maintain the facade of a stable marriage, telling reporters: "We're going to be happy in spite of everybody." But during the summer of 1935, the masquerade crumbled and Stanwyck filed for divorce.

While Stanwyck's marriage was on the decline, her popularity had continued to soar. After *Shopworn*, she had starred in *So Big* (1932), based on Edna Ferber's Pulitzer Prize–winning novel, earning the now-familiar raves for her portrayal, including one from William Boehnel in the *New York World Telegram*: "By her performance in *So Big* Barbara Stanwyck definitely establishes herself … as being a brilliant emotional actress." She followed this success with *The Purchase Price* (1932), as a torch singer who becomes the mail order bride of a North Dakota farmer, then starred in another Frank Capra film, *The Bitter Tea of General Yen* (1933), in which she portrayed an American missionary who falls in love with the Chinese warlord who kidnaps her. While the film was commended for its aesthetic beauty, its interracial theme was a bit much for audiences to accept, and the movie was not a financial success.

During the next few years, Stanwyck continued her nearly non-stop shooting schedule, appearing in such well-received films as *Ladies They Talk About* (1933), *Baby Face* (1933), *Ever in My Heart* (1933) and *Gambling Lady* (1934), the first of her six successful teamings with Joel McCrea. She also starred in several productions that did little for her professional resumé, including *The Secret Bride* (1935), a slow-moving mystery, *The Woman in Red* (1935), her last film under her Warners contract, and United Artists' *Red Salute* (1935), her first comedy. But the actress offered her fans a top-notch production in *Annie Oakley* (1935), and was praised by in the *New York Sun* for her "curious quality of sincerity, strikingly rare on the screen."

In 1936, Stanwyck starred in five films of varying quality, but the year would be significant for more than her on-screen accomplishments — it would be the year that saw her introduction to her future husband and, some say, the love of her life, actor Robert Taylor. Stanwyck and Taylor met at a dinner dance at the Café Trocadero, and the two clicked almost immediately, despite their divergent backgrounds. Stanwyck was born and bred in the city, while Taylor was raised in small towns in Nebraska and Missouri. Taylor loved hunting, but Stanwyck found the sport to be cruel and inhumane. While Taylor had been schooled at the Neely Dixon Dramatic School and Pomona College, Stanwyck barely had a grammar school education. And Stanwyck, four years Taylor's senior, was a divorcée with a young son. In short, as Taylor told the press: "Miss Stanwyck is not the sort of woman I'd have met in Nebraska."

While her romance with Taylor continued to heat up, Stanwyck appeared in *Internes Can't Take Money* (1937), again with Joel McCrea; *This Is My Affair* (1937) with Taylor; and *Stella Dallas* (1937), a highly acclaimed tearjerker that would send critics scrambling for new accolades for the actress. For her outstanding performance of a low-class mother who makes the supreme sacrifice for her daughter's happiness, Stanwyck received her first Academy Award nomination. (The award would later go to Luise Rainer for her portrayal of a Chinese peasant woman in *The Good Earth*, and Stanwyck would bitterly remark: "My life's blood was in that picture — I should have won.")

Despite her cinematic successes, Stanwyck was not faring well in her role as a mother. She reportedly showed little affection toward young Dion and rarely spent time with him, and in 1937 Frank Fay filed contempt-of-court

Barbara Stanwyck

charges against her, claiming that Robert Taylor was Stanwyck's "consort," and charging that Stanwyck had denied Fay the right to see his son for more than a year. Stanwyck countered by calling Fay an unfit guardian; she revealed that Fay had once tossed Dion into the family swimming pool, and on another occasion had left a smoldering cigarette on the carpet beneath their infant son's crib. Despite Stanwyck's charges, the court granted Fay the right to visit Dion twice weekly and on alternating Saturdays, as long as he was completely sober and under the supervision of the child's nurse. But although both Stanwyck and Fay had fought bitterly over their young son, neither seemed to show much interest in the child. In fact, a friend of the couple's remarked: "If she wanted a broken cup worth a penny and [Fay] had thrown it in the garbage, she'd fight him and vice versa. Frank was not much better than Barbara as far as their son was concerned. He took advantage of his visitation rights and got bored soon after. That was that." Soon after the court decision, the six-year-old Dion was sent by Stanwyck to a military school, where he remained during weekends and holidays, even though the school was only six miles from Stanwyck's San Fernando Valley ranch (adjacent to which, incidentally, Robert Taylor had built a home). During the summers, Dion was sent to a camp on Catalina Island, and he would spend only two weeks a year living under the same roof as his mother. In later years, Dion would state that Stanwyck "threw me away like so much garbage."

Career-wise, Stanwyck followed her triumph in *Stella Dallas* with a light comedy, *Breakfast for Two* (1937), costarring Herbert Marshall; a screwball comedy with Henry Fonda, *The Mad Miss Manton* (1938); and a tearjerker, *Always Goodbye* (1938), again with Marshall. In 1939, she starred with Joel McCrea in the well-received Western *Union Pacific*, directed by Cecil B. DeMille, who would later call Stanwyck "one on whom a director can always count to do her work with all her heart." Later that year, she triumphed again in *Golden Boy*, costarring with William Holden in his first major role. Stanwyck was extremely helpful to the inexperienced actor, offering valuable coaching tips, going to bat for him when Holden was nearly fired by the film's producer, and reading lines with him each night. The result was a polished, highly acclaimed performance and, until his accidental death in 1981, Holden showed his gratitude to Stanwyck by sending her two dozen red roses and a white gardenia each year on the anniversary of the film's starting date.

Stanwyck's relationship with Robert Taylor continued to heat up, despite her reluctance to accept his proposals of marriage. But in January 1939, *Photoplay* magazine printed a scandalous story, "Hollywood's Unmarried Husbands and Wives," which discussed the relationships of five Hollywood couples, including Stanwyck and Taylor, Clark Gable and Carole Lombard, and Charles Chaplin and Paulette Goddard. The article's author, Kirtley Baskette, revealed that Stanwyck and Taylor lived in adjoining ranch homes, and stated: "All in all, it's an almost perfect domestic picture. But no wedding rings in sight!" A month after the article appeared, Stanwyck and Taylor announced their formal engagement, and on May 14, 1939, they were married in San Diego.

After *Golden Boy*, Stanwyck starred in a variety of films, from light comedy to heavy drama, including *The Lady Eve* (1941), a classic satirical farce directed by Preston Sturges; *Meet John Doe* (1941), her final film under the direction of Frank Capra; *Ball of Fire* (1941), a screwball comedy that brought Stanwyck her second Academy Award nomination (she lost to Joan Fontaine in *Suspicion*); *The Great Man's Lady* (1942), again costarring with Joel McCrea, and *Flesh and Fantasy* (1943), which offered three separate stories dealing with the supernatural. In these films, playing parts that included a ruthless newspaper reporter, a wily card sharp and a wise-cracking strip-tease dancer, Stanwyck continued to prove that she was one of Hollywood's preeminent talents. But in 1944, she entered a new phase of her career when she starred in the film version of the James M. Cain tale of lust, greed and murder: *Double Indemnity*.

Initially, Stanwyck was reluctant to play the role of Phyllis Dietrichson, a character she termed "an out-and-out, cold-blooded killer." Fortunately, she was convinced to play the part by director Billy Wilder, and it resulted in one of the most highly acclaimed examples of film noir on record. *Double Indemnity* offers a dark masterpiece of murder that is loosely based on the notorious 1927 case of Ruth Snyder and Judd Gray, who conspired to kill Snyder's husband for $100,000 in insurance money. Like this case, *Double Indemnity* centers on an intricately constructed and flawlessly executed plot by Phyllis Dietrichson and her lover — insurance man Walter Neff (Fred MacMurray) — to kill Phyllis' oil man husband and collect the money from his accident insurance. The plan begins to unravel, however, when Neff's boss, claims investigator Barton Keyes (Edward G. Robinson), figures out the scheme, and the fate of the murdering couple is sealed when they turn on each other as a result of their mutual paranoia and suspicion.

Stanwyck's Phyllis is the epitome of icy, calculating, murderous intent, and she delivers a blood-chilling performance of a beautiful, thoroughly evil woman who knows what she wants and doesn't hesitate to eliminate anyone who gets in her way. In certain scenes, her eyes are like black marbles, glacial and devoid of feeling. Her only emotions are passion and greed — she uses one to satisfy the other. Despite Stanwyck's initial misgivings, audiences and critics alike accepted her as the unrelenting villainess, and she received her third Academy Award nomination (losing again, this time to Ingrid Bergman in *Gaslight*). Reviewers unanimously hailed her performance — Howard Barnes of the *New York Herald Tribune* called her "vibrantly malignant and attractive," and the critic for the *Citizen News* stated that Stanwyck "will chill your blood. Hers is a difficult assignment enacted with rare skill."

While Stanwyck's career was reaching new heights, her home life was not nearly as promising. The busy filming schedules of Stanwyck and Taylor kept them apart a great deal of the time, and when the couple moved to Los Angeles to shorten their daily commute, Taylor felt stifled by city living. Taylor was also growing resentful of Stanwyck's domineering nature. The strained marriage neared the breaking point in 1941, when Taylor fell for 20-year-old Lana Turner, his costar in *Johnny Eager* (1941), admitting to reporters: "I have never seen lips like hers, and though I was never known to run after blondes, Lana was the exception." Although Turner would write in her autobiography that she and Taylor never consummated their relationship, she did admit that they were "attracted to each other from the beginning." Taylor reportedly went so far as to ask his wife for a divorce, but a short time later, Stanwyck squelched rumors by telling the press, "Bob and I are building a house in Beverly Hills. Does that sound like we're getting a divorce?" And in a show of solidarity, Stanwyck and Taylor placed their hand and footprints together in the forecourt of Grauman's (now Mann's) Chinese Theater in June 1941, becoming the only married couple to share a square at the famed attraction. For a time, it appeared that all was well with the popular twosome. But it was a facade that would soon crumble.

Meanwhile, after her triumph in *Double Indemnity*, Stanwyck was eager to star in a film based on another James M. Cain story: *Mildred Pierce* (1945). "I desperately wanted the part," Stanwyck would later say. "I went after it. I knew what a role for a woman it was, and I knew I could handle every facet of Mildred." But the role would go to Joan Crawford, who walked away with that year's Academy Award. Instead, Stanwyck accepted the lead in *My Reputation* (1946), portraying a woman freeing herself from her children and her overbearing mother. The film, directed by William Wyler, was one of the year's top-grossers and would remain one of Stanwyck's favorites. After next starring as a horsewoman in the lightweight comedy The *Bride Wore Boots* (1946), Stanwyck accepted the title role in her second film noir, *The Strange Love of Martha Ivers* (1946), described by one critic as offering a "stealthy plot of murder, false witness, assault, lust, perfidy and tender love."

This compelling film introduces a variety of characters, including the young, rebellious Martha Ivers (Janis Wilson), her cruel aunt (Judith Anderson) and Martha's childhood friends, the adventuresome Sam Masterson (Darryl Hickman) and the quiet, bookish Walter O'Neill (Mickey Kuhn). During a bitter confrontation one stormy night, Martha strikes her aunt with a cane, inadvertently causing her death, and is supported by Walter in her quick lie that the deed was committed by an intruder. Nearly 20 years later, a chance automobile accident causes the now-adult Sam Masterson (Van Heflin) to return to his home town, where he discovers that Martha has inherited her aunt's vast fortune, and that Walter (Kirk Douglas), now the local district attorney, is Martha's husband. Later, Sam also learns the truth about the death of Martha's aunt, and that a local vagrant was eventually executed for the crime, based on Martha's accusation.

Meanwhile, Sam befriends Toni Marachek (Lizabeth Scott), a worldweary drifter who was recently released from jail for theft. When Toni is arrested for violating her probation, Sam appeals to Walter to secure her release. Fearing that Sam knows the truth about Martha's aunt and is intent on blackmail, Walter uses the girl to set Sam up for a violent beating, designed

to scare him out of town. Angered, Sam refuses to leave, but despite a growing attachment to Toni, he is helplessly attracted by Martha's captivating
charms. During a confrontation over Martha's affections, Walter drunkenly falls
down a flight of stairs and Sam is nearly coerced by the beguiling Martha into
finishing him off. Sam ultimately comes to his senses, only to find his own life
threatened by Martha: "You said I didn't know the difference between right
and wrong. What's right for Walter and myself? For us to tell the truth? And
hang for it?" Martha asks as she holds Sam at gunpoint. "For what? What am
I guilty of? What were their lives compared to mine? What was she? A mean,
vicious, hateful old woman who never did anything for anybody. What was
he? A thief, a drunk, someone who would have died in the gutter anyway.
Neither one of them had any right to live." Realizing that Walter will not support her story of shooting Sam in self-defense, Martha allows Sam to leave.
Moments later, Martha turns the gun on herself, and Walter, holding her lifeless body in his arms, shoots himself as well. As the film ends, Sam is seen
leaving town with Toni Marachek, warning her not to look back.

As the philandering murderess of this riveting film, Stanwyck received
enthusiastic notices from critics, including the reviewer from *The Hollywood
Reporter*, who raved, "No one but Barbara Stanwyck could have gotten all she
does from the part of Martha Ivers. Elusive fascination was required and what
Miss Stanwyck does with her assignment is not to be readily defined. Whatever it is is unforgettable." This successful venture was followed by a variety
of mostly mediocre features, including *California* (1946), a Western about California's bid for statehood; *The Two Mrs. Carrolls* (1947), a thriller costarring
Humphrey Bogart; *Variety Girl* (1947), a star-studded tribute to the work of
the Variety Clubs, whose cast included Bing Crosby, Bob Hope, Gary Cooper
and Paulette Goddard; and *B.F.'s Daughter* (1948), which told the story of a
woman who rises to fame without knowing that she is the child of a wealthy
industrialist. But Stanwyck scored again in late 1948 when she starred in *Sorry,
Wrong Number*, her third excursion into film noir.

In this film, Stanwyck portrayed Leona Stevenson, a possessive, imperi-
ous heiress who is confined to her bed because of a heart condition and continuously refers to herself as "a terribly sick woman" and a "helpless invalid."
For several years, Leona has dominated her weak-willed husband, Henry (Burt
Lancaster), using her condition to keep him ensconced in an unfulfilling position in her father's pharmaceutical company. One evening, while placing
numerous telephone calls in an effort to locate her husband, Leona overhears
two men discussing the murder of a woman. Startled by this discovery, Leona
attempts to ascertain more about the plot, but as the night wears on, she learns
more than she bargained for. Via a series of phone calls, she discovers that her
husband has been involved in a lucrative scheme to steal drugs from the company, but that he is being blackmailed by a former partner for $200,000. Believ-
ing that Leona's heart ailment would soon result in her death, Henry agreed

to pay the money, but when he learned from a specialist that Leona's condition was psychosomatic, he was forced to plan her murder.

When Henry contacts Leona later that night, planning to establish his alibi, she realizes that she is the subject of the murder plot she had overheard. Experiencing a change of heart, Henry tells Leona to escape from the house, but it is too late. In anguish, Henry listens to Leona's horrified screams as the murderer enters her bedroom. Seconds later, the telephone connection is broken, and when Henry calls back, a man answers, saying, "Sorry, wrong number."

Following the release of *Sorry, Wrong Number*, Stanwyck was acclaimed by critics, with the reviewer for *Time* magazine stating that she "makes the most of the pampered, petulant, terrified leading character" and *Cue*'s critic claiming that she gave the best performance of her career. For her taut, believable performance, she was awarded her fourth Academy Award nomination, and before the ceremony, she told the press: "[It's] not that I wouldn't like to have an Oscar, but I've lost three times before and it's hard to get your expectations up and not win. It's bad luck to discuss it." Stanwyck's superstitions proved to be correct, as she lost yet again, this time to Jane Wyman, who portrayed a deaf mute in *Johnny Belinda*. After the ceremony, Stanwyck commented: "If I get nominated next year, they'll have to give me the door prize, won't they? At least the bride should throw me the bouquet."

In 1949, Stanwyck starred as a loving wife who becomes addicted to gambling in *The Lady Gambles*, and as a long-suffering woman who tolerates her husband's infidelity in *East Side, West Side*. In her third film of the year, *The File on Thelma Jordon*, she returned to the realm of film noir, again portraying a murderess, but one who is reformed by love.

As this film begins, the title character (Stanwyck) visits the office of Miles Scott (Paul Kelly), the chief investigator for the district attorney's office, intent upon reporting an attempted burglary at the home of her wealthy aunt. Instead, Thelma encounters Cleve Marshall (Wendell Corey), the assistant district attorney, who invites her for a drink. Before long, Thelma and Cleve are involved in a passionate affair, despite the fact that Cleve is married with two young children. Thelma later reveals to Cleve that she is married as well, to a gambler named Tony Laredo (Richard Rober), but she insists that their union is over.

Just before Thelma and Cleve are to depart on a weekend jaunt, her aunt is murdered and an expensive emerald necklace is stolen from her safe. Thelma tells Cleve that she was preparing to meet him when she heard the shot, and points to her husband as the possible culprit. But when police arrive, all evidence points to Thelma's guilt and she is arrested for the crime. With Cleve assigned to prosecute Thelma, he purposely bungles the high-profile case and Thelma is acquitted. Later, Cleve finds Tony Laredo at Thelma's home, and learns that Thelma actually had killed her aunt. "I'd like to say I didn't intend to kill her. But when you have a gun, you always intend if you have to," Thelma confesses. "But you were the fall guy, Cleve. Right from the beginning." Thelma leaves with Tony but she later causes their car to crash. Tony is killed instantly, but Thelma survives long enough to confess her crimes to police and tell Cleve: "I couldn't go on with him. You did that for me. I'm glad it's over."

Stanwyck again scored with critics as Thelma Jordon — Kay Proctor of the *L.A. Examiner* stated that she "comes through with a hard-hitting, clean-cut performance, beautifully paced to the dimensions and requirements of the equivocal role." She triumphed as well in her next picture, *No Man of Her Own* (1950), as a pregnant woman who assumes the identity of a train crash victim. As with most actors and directors who worked with Stanwyck, her costar Lyle Bettger had nothing but praise for the talented actress: "Throughout the ten weeks of shooting, my admiration and respect for Barbara Stanwyck grew each day," Bettger said. "She is a lady with guts, consideration, kindness and great good humor and integrity — a real pro. There are not many like her left."

During the remainder of the year, Stanwyck slowed down her shooting schedule, appearing in only two films: the Western soaper *The Furies* (1950), starring Walter Huston in his final role, and *To Please a Lady* (1950), a slow-moving melodrama with Clark Gable as a race car enthusiast. While both films received mixed reviews, Stanwyck, typically, rose above her material to deliver solid performances. But Stanwyck's career would soon take a back seat to the drama unfolding in her own life.

During Robert Taylor's service in World War II, and in the years that followed, his marriage to Stanwyck had continued to quietly deteriorate. While the couple managed to maintain the public image of the perfect couple, Stanwyck had become increasingly domineering and controlling, while Taylor grew steadily more unhappy. Their problems were complicated by their long separations, and matters worsened in the late 1940s when rumors flared about Taylor's dalliances with Ava Gardner and Elizabeth Taylor. But the final blow came in 1950, while Taylor was on location in Rome shooting *Quo Vadis*. Italian newspapers of the day reported rumors of several women who Taylor was involved with, particularly bit player Lia De Leo. When the news reached Stanwyck in Hollywood, she flew to Rome and threatened her husband with divorce. Stanwyck admitted later that she was only trying to frighten Taylor, but to her astonishment, he took her up on the offer. A week before Christmas 1950, the couple issued a joint statement that read in part: "In the past few years, because of professional requirements, we have been separated just too often and too long. Our sincere and continued efforts to maintain our marriage have failed. We are deeply disappointed that we could not solve our problems. We really tried." Two months later, on February 21, 1951, the couple's divorce decree was granted.

Shortly after ending her marriage to Taylor, Stanwyck would see the end of her relationship with her son Dion as well. The now 20-year-old young man had been drafted for a two-year army tour of duty, and he and his mother met for lunch prior to Dion's departure for boot camp. Dion would later recall: "When I met her, she just stuck out her gloved hand. She didn't kiss me, she didn't hug me." It would be the last time Stanwyck ever saw her son. Years later, in the 1980s, Dion would sell a story to the *National Enquirer* detailing his unhappy relationship with his mother and stating that Stanwyck "never touched, kissed or held me — except when cameras flashed." Although Dion expressed in the article his desire to meet with his mother again — "even for just half an hour, and experience just once more what it feels like to be a son" — Stanwyck refused to see him. A friend of the actress later stated that Stanwyck "wouldn't talk about [Dion]. She kept a picture of him in a closet. She had a way of shutting off things, to close the door behind her."

To rise above the pain of her divorce, Stanwyck focused her energies on her career. As her friend Jack Benny stated, "Maybe it's hammy, but that old line, 'the show must go on' — that's Barbara." In 1951 she portrayed a housekeeper trying to murder her employer for his money in *The Man with a Cloak*, and the following year she starred in her fourth film noir, *Clash by Night* (1952), starring Robert Ryan, Paul Douglas and Marilyn Monroe.

Clash by Night opens with the return of Mae Doyle (Stanwyck) to her home town Monterey, California, after a lengthy absence. Before long, she has attracted the attentions of Jerry D'Amato (Paul Douglas), a hard-working, honorable fisherman she knew in her youth, and Jerry's best friend, Earl Pfeiffer (Robert Ryan), a cynical, bitter man who works as a film projectionist. Mae is initially drawn to Earl, but she decides to accept the marriage proposal of Jerry, telling a friend: "I want to be looked after ... I want a man to give me confidence — somebody to fight off the blizzards and the floods. Somebody to beat off the world when it tries to swallow you up." Soon after her marriage, Mae gets pregnant and gives birth to a baby girl, Gloria. But over time, she grows bored with "pushing a baby carriage, and shopping in the market, and changing the curtains on the bathroom window," and begins an affair with Earl. When Jerry learns of the affair, his reactions range from forgiveness, to rage, to bitter acceptance, but when he discovers Mae's plan to leave him, he takes his infant daughter and hides her aboard his fishing boat. But Mae soon realizes that she cannot envision a future with Earl, and returns home to her family.

By now, Stanwyck's finest roles were behind her, but she continued to offer her captivating presence to a series of films that included the action-packed *Jeopardy* (1953), in which Stanwyck's character allows herself to be attacked by a psychopath in order to gain his aid in saving her drowning husband; the ridiculous *The Moonlighter* (1953), a Western filmed in 3-D; *Executive Suite* (1954), whose star-studded cast included Stanwyck's old friend William Holden, Fredric March, Walter Pidgeon and Shelley Winters; and *Witness to Murder* (1954), Stanwyck's fifth film noir.

Here, Stanwyck portrays Cheryl Draper, who looks through her bedroom window one night and sees a man strangling a young woman in an apartment across the street. She immediately telephones police, but the man, writer Albert Richter (George Sanders), hides the body in a nearby vacant apartment; when police arrive, they find nothing amiss. One of the investigators, Lt. Lawrence Matthews (Gary Merrill), wants to believe Cheryl, but finds no evidence to support her claims. Learning that Cheryl has witnessed his crime, Richter breaks into her apartment, types several threatening notes on her typewriter, then mails them to himself and shows them to police as proof that Cheryl is mentally unbalanced. Confronted with the letters, Cheryl becomes hysterical, believing that she may have written them unconsciously. She is physically restrained by police, and briefly committed to a mental hospital, but upon her release, she continues to believe in Richter's guilt.

When Cheryl confronts him at his apartment, Richter tells her the truth: "Of course I admit it," he says smugly. "I have nothing to fear from you — you're insane. It's recorded in the police files and in hospital reports. Anything that you might foolishly say concerning my admission would merely corroborate their findings.... They'd put you in an asylum, most likely." Meanwhile, Lt. Matthews has unearthed evidence that points to Richter as the killer, but Richter is now planning to murder Cheryl and make it appear a suicide. Cheryl escapes, but Richter pursues her into a building under construction, where he chases her onto the wooden scaffolding. Matthews arrive just as Richter has Cheryl cornered at the top of the building, and after a fight, Richter falls to his death.

Although critics applauded Stanwyck's performance in *Witness to Murder*, they were unimpressed with the film itself— the reviewer for *Variety* labeled it a "standard melodrama that varies little from countless others," and the *New York Times* critic called it "a sensibly executed but hardly inspired exercise in premeditated murder and mental torture." Stanwyck continued to appear in undistinguished films. In 1954 she played the title role in her 71st film, *Cattle Queen of Montana*, a rather slow-moving Western. She then starred in another oater, *The Violent Men* (1955); *Escape to Burma* (1955), a poorly received "B" picture; *There's Always Tomorrow* (1956), a remake of the 1934 Frank Morgan–Binnie Barnes film; *The Maverick Queen* (1956), a Western that would later be remade into *Butch Cassidy and the Sundance Kid*; *These Wilder Years* (1956), Stanwyck's only film with veteran actor James Cagney; and *Crime of Passion* (1957), her final film noir.

In *Crime of Passion*, Stanwyck portrays Kathy Ferguson, an advice columnist for a San Francisco newspaper who is known for her ambitious nature and independent spirit: "For marriage I read life sentence, for home life I read T.V. nights, beer in the fridge, second mortgage — not for me," she says in an early scene. "For me, life has to be something more than that." But when she meets Bill Doyle (Sterling Hayden), a handsome Los Angeles police officer, Kathy abandons her opinions about wedlock and before long, she and Bill are married and living in Los Angeles. Despite her best efforts, Kathy soon becomes bored with the monotonous gatherings with the other police officers' wives, and transfers her innate ambition into furthering Bill's career. She skillfully befriends the wife of Bill's boss, Inspector Tony Pope (Raymond Burr), influencing Pope to promote her husband to a higher position in the department.

Later, after learning that Pope is planning to retire, Kathy succumbs to a one-night dalliance with him, then uses the incident to gain his promise that he will appoint Bill as his replacement. But when Pope informs Kathy of his plans to select a more qualified successor, she fatally wounds him with a gun pilfered from the police station. Working around the clock to solve the case, Bill soon discovers evidence pointing to Kathy's guilt and at the film's end, he is seen taking her into the station to answer for her crime.

After what one critic termed her "rafter-rattling" portrayal in *Crime of Passion*, Stanwyck starred in two more Westerns: *Trooper Hook* (1957), her sixth film with Joel McCrea, and *Forty Guns* (1957), costarring Barry Sullivan. She would not appear on film again for another four years. In the meantime, she turned her talents to the medium of television, where she had appeared sporadically for several years on such shows as *The Jack Benny Show* and Dick Powell's *Zane Grey Theater*. In 1960, she starred in *The Barbara Stanwyck Theater* for NBC-TV, telling the press, "I wasn't working in the movies and I wanted to work. What else is there for me to do?" Featuring half-hour teleplays, most starring Stanwyck, the program received only mildly positive reviews, but Stanwyck was awarded with an Emmy at the end of its first season. Despite this, NBC canceled the program two weeks later, and Stanwyck bitterly said, "I don't know who 'they' are, but they've decreed no more women on television. The only woman who will be left next year is Donna Reed. The rest of us have been dropped: Loretta Young, June Allyson, Dinah Shore, Ann Sothern and me. And we all had good ratings."

After this disappointing stint on television, Stanwyck returned to the big screen in *Walk on the Wild Side* (1962), portraying the madam of a New Orleans bordello who lusts after one of the women in her employ. Although Stanwyck delivered a typically fine performance, audiences and critics were put off by the torrid drama, and Stanwyck herself later said that *Walk on the Wild Side* "could have been a damn good picture, but it just didn't work out." Stanwyck then guested on several television series, including *Rawhide* and *The Untouchables*, before making her next film, *Roustabout* (1964), starring Elvis Presley. In working with one of the nation's top music stars, Stanwyck told reporters that she'd accepted the role "because I want to be exposed to the younger generation who probably never heard of me.... And I thought it would be fun."

Although critics enthusiastically received Stanwyck in *Roustabout*, she suffered a personal blow after the film's release when her beloved brother Malcolm died of a heart attack. Throughout the years, Stanwyck had used her prestige to aid her brother in a career as an extra, and he had gone on to become director of the Screen Extras Guild. Although devastated by his loss, the veteran actress, in typical Stanwyck fashion, used her work to keep her going. She next accepted a role opposite her ex-husband, Robert Taylor, in *The Night Walker* (1964), portraying a sleepwalker who is terrorized by nightmares. The film's impact was summed up by *New York Times* critic Bosley Crowther, who wrote: "The whole thing would not be worth reporting if it didn't have Barbara Stanwyck in the role of the somnambulist and Robert Taylor as her husband's lawyer who tries to help. Miss Stanwyck, silver-haired and seasoned, does lend an air of dignity to the otherwise unbelievable tale."

Her appearance in *The Night Walker* would mark Stanwyck's last portrayal on the big screen. Instead, she rejuvenated her career by starring in a new series for ABC-TV, *The Big Valley*, which served to bring her a new generation of fans. As the matriarch of a family, Stanwyck appeared in all but seven of the 112 episodes that aired over the series' four-year run from 1965 to 1969. For her performance, she won the Emmy Award and the Screen Actors Guild Award in 1966, and was nominated again for an Emmy in 1967 and 1969.

Stanwyck was bitterly disappointed when *The Big Valley* was cancelled in the spring of 1969, but she suffered a deeper heartbreak when, several months later, Robert Taylor died of lung cancer. Stanwyck, who declined an invitation by Taylor's widow to sit with the family at his funeral service, sobbed uncontrollably during the eulogy delivered by then-governor Ronald Reagan. Her life with the man she once referred to as the only man she would ever love was given final closure when Stanwyck later received several items that Taylor had requested she be given after his death. The items included a photo album of pictures taken during the couple's 1947 European vacation, two money clips and a gold cigarette lighter inscribed: "To Lt. Robert Taylor with my admiration and my love from Mrs. Robert Taylor."

Again, Stanwyck was rescued by her work. In 1970, she starred in *The House That Wouldn't Die*, and the following year in *A Taste of Evil* (1971), both ABC Movies of the Week. In November 1971, she began filming *Fitzgerald and Pride*, the pilot for a potential television series, but had to back out when it was discovered that she was suffering from a ruptured kidney wall. She underwent emergency surgery for removal of the kidney and was replaced in the pilot by Susan Hayward, who stated that it was a "hell of a job" trying to fill Stanwyck's shoes. In 1973, Stanwyck had recovered sufficiently to appear in *The Letters*, another ABC Movie of the Week, and later that year was inducted into the Hall of Fame of Great Western Performers in the Museum of the National Cowboy Hall of Fame in Oklahoma City. She was presented with her award by her old friend, actor Joel McCrea, and later stated that the evening was one of the most memorable of her entire career.

Stanwyck would not work again for nearly a decade, stating, "I've had my day and you have to know when to quit." Instead, she filled her days reading books, redecorating her home, visiting friends and traveling. In 1978, she was a highlight of the Academy Awards when she presented an award with former costar William Holden, who told the audience, "Thirty-nine years ago this month, we were working in a film together called *Golden Boy*. It wasn't going well because I was going to be replaced. But due to this lovely human being and her interest and understanding and her professional integrity and her encouragement and above all, her generosity, I'm here tonight." Stanwyck appeared overwhelmed by Holden's impromptu speech as the former stars tearfully embraced.

Three years later, on April 13, 1981, Holden would again express his gratitude to Stanwyck when she was honored by the Film Society of Lincoln Center, New York. The two-hour long tribute featured 43 film clips from Stanwyck's long career; in addition to Holden, accolades were offered by such screen notables as Anne Baxter and Joan Bennett. But the night would be the high point of an otherwise grim year for the aging actress. In October 1981, a masked burglar broke into Stanwyck's home, hit her in the head with a gun and forced her into a closet. The thief made off with $5,000 in money and jewelry, as well as a platinum and gold cigarette case that had been given to her by Robert Taylor. Less than a month later, Stanwyck was devastated by the news that her old friend William Holden had been found dead in his Santa Monica apartment.

Early in 1982, Stanwyck was rushed to the hospital with pneumonia, and was also found to be suffering from an enlarged liver. Originally in serious condition in the intensive care unit, she rallied sufficiently in three days to tell reporters: "I've made the turnaround in my recovery. Now I want to work again." Several months later she accepted the role as Mary Carson in *The Thorn Birds*, starring Richard Chamberlain and Rachel Ward. For her portrayal of the wealthy and ruthless matriarch, Stanwyck won her third Emmy award. That year, Stanwyck also received the honor that had eluded her throughout her stellar career: an honorary Academy Award.

After her triumph in *The Thorn Birds*, Stanwyck worked only sporadically. Now suffering from emphysema and cataracts in both eyes, she was forced to turn down appearances in TV's *Hotel* and *The Love Boat*. In 1985, she starred with Charlton Heston in the ABC-TV series *The Colbys*, but later requested to be released from her contract, stating: "I say the same line every week. The only thing different is my dress."

In 1986, Stanwyck was honored again for her outstanding career, this time by the American Film Institute, which presented her with its Lifetime Achievement Award. By now, the 79-year-old actress was plagued by illness, and checked out of St. John's Hospital only hours before attending the AFI tribute dinner. A sprained back had left her wheelchair bound and her lungs were weakened by chronic emphysema and pulmonary obstruction. In 1988 she suffered another bout with pneumonia and was not expected to live.

Although she rallied yet again from the illness, she finally succumbed to her chronic lung condition on January 9, 1990. According to her wishes, her body was cremated and her ashes scattered over Lone Pine, a stretch of California desert where she had filmed several Westerns.

With a career that spanned nearly seven decades, Barbara Stanwyck was one of the few stars of Hollywood's Golden Age whose talent lived up to her fame. Despite her humble beginnings, and an often disappointing private life, she was a shining luminary whose lasting appeal was perhaps best summed up by Roddy McDowall: "As with all radiant, in-depth stars, they carry an individual stamp," the actor said in a 1997 documentary on Stanwyck. "And perhaps the best thing is that it cannot be defined — they are unique. Stanwyck, because of the versatility of the canon of work, is one of the most valuable of those creatures.... And right up until the end, everything that she performed was full out, and with style, and stamina."

Film Noir Filmography

DOUBLE INDEMNITY   *Director:* Billy Wilder. *Producer:* Joseph Sistrom. Released by Paramount, September 1944. *Running time:* 106 minutes. *Cast:* Fred MacMurray, Barbara Stanwyck, Edward G. Robinson, Jean Heather, Tom Powers, Byron Barr, Porter Hall. *Awards:* Academy Award nominations for Best Picture, Best Director (Billy Wilder), Best Actress (Barbara Stanwyck), Best Cinematography (John Seitz), Best Original Screenplay (Raymond Chandler, Billy Wilder), Best Score (Miklos Rozsa), Best Sound (Loren Ryder).

THE STRANGE LOVE OF MARTHA IVERS   *Director:* Lewis Milestone. *Producer:* Hal B. Wallis. Released by Paramount, July 1946. *Running time:* 115 minutes. *Cast:* Barbara Stanwyck, Van Heflin, Lizabeth Scott, Kirk Douglas, Judith Anderson, Roman Bohnen. *Awards:* Academy Award nomination for Best Original Screenplay (Jack Patrick).

SORRY, WRONG NUMBER   *Director:* Anatole Litvak. *Producers:* Hal B. Wallis, Anatole Litvak. Released by Paramount, September 1948. *Running time:* 98 minutes. *Cast:* Barbara Stanwyck, Burt Lancaster, Ann Richards, Wendell Corey, Harold Vermilyea, Ed Begley, Leif Erickson, William Conrad. *Awards:* Academy Award nomination for Best Actress (Barbara Stanwyck).

THE FILE ON THELMA JORDON   *Director:* Robert Siodmak. *Producer:* Hal B. Wallis. Released by Paramount, January 1950. *Running time:* 100 minutes. *Cast:* Barbara Stanwyck, Wendell Corey, Paul Kelly, Joan Tetzel, Richard Rober, Stanley Ridges.

CLASH BY NIGHT   *Director:* Fritz Lang. *Producer:* Harriet Parsons. Released by RKO, June 1952. *Running time:* 104 minutes. *Cast:* Barbara Stanwyck, Paul Douglas, Robert Ryan, Marilyn Monroe, J. Carrol Naish, Keith Andes.

WITNESS TO MURDER   *Director:* Roy Rowland. *Producer:* Chester Erskine. Released by United Artists, April 1954. *Running time:* 81 minutes. *Cast:* Barbara Stanwyck, George Sanders, Gary Merrill, Jesse White, Harry Shannon.

CRIME OF PASSION   *Director:* Gerd Oswald. *Producer:* Herman Cohen. Released by United Artists, January 1957. *Running time:* 85 minutes. *Cast:* Barbara Stanwyck, Sterling Hayden, Raymond Burr, Fay Wray, Royal Dano, Virginia Grey.

References

Asher, Jerry. "The Amazing Mrs. Taylor." *Silver Screen*, March 1940.
Baskette, Kirtley. "Hollywood's Unmarried Husbands and Wives." *Photoplay*, January 1939.
Blees, Robert. "Barbara Stanwyck." *American Film*, April 1987.
Deere, Dorothy. "Date with Bob and the Queen." *Photoplay*, September 1947.
Dickens, Homer. *The Films of Barbara Stanwyck*. Secaucus, N.J.: Citadel Press, 1984.
DiOrio, Al. *Barbara Stanwyck: A Biography*. New York: Coward-McCann, 1983.
Farber, Stephen. "Role Models: Barbara Stanwyck in *The Strange Love of Martha Ivers*." *Movieline*, December, 1993.
"The Girl on the Cover." *Cue*, January 10, 1942.
Hall, Gladys. "The Poison Gas of Gossip." *Photoplay*, June 1956.
Holland, Jack. "Mind Your Own Business." *Silver Screen*, July 1946.
Madsen, Axel. *Stanwyck*. New York: Harper Collins, 1994.
Nugent, Frank S. "Stanwyck." *Collier's*, July 12, 1952.
Peary, Gerald. "Barbara Stanwyck." *American Film*, July-August 1989.
"Raring to Go." *TV Guide*, November 22, 1958.
Rhea, Marian. "The Law of Averages." *Photoplay*, March 1941.
Ringgold, Gene. "Barbara Stanwyck." *Films in Review*, December 1963.
Rozgonyi, Jay. "The Making of *Double Indemnity*." *Films in Review*, June-July 1990.
St. Johns, Adela Rogers. "The Story Behind the Stanwyck-Fay Breakup." *Photoplay*, January 1936.
Skolsky, Sidney. "She Frightened Herself." *New York Post*, August 26, 1944.
Smith, Ella. *Starring Miss Barbara Stanwyck*. New York: Crown, 1985.
"Stanwyck, the Frustrated Stunt Woman." *TV Guide*, January 21, 1961.
Sullivan, Ed. "Time of Their Lives." *Modern Screen*, July 1947.
Vermilye, Jerry. *Barbara Stanwyck*. New York: Pyramid, 1975.
Waterbury, Ruth. "Secrets Behind Hollywood Heartbreaks." *Photoplay*, November 1952.
Wayne, Jane Ellen. *Stanwyck*. New York: Arbor House, 1985.
Wilson, Earl. "Catching Up with Barbara." *Silver Screen*, July 1942.
_____. "Elusive Barbara." *Silver Screen*, December 1945.
_____. "Gypsy Rose Stanwyck." *Silver Screen*, May 1943.
_____. "Projections." *Silver Screen*, December 1936.
Wilson, Elizabeth. "Honest Working Girl." *Liberty*, August 11, 1945.

Documentaries

"Barbara Stanwyck: Fire and Desire." Copyright 1991, Turner Pictures, Inc. A Lorac Production.
"Barbara Stanwyck: Straight Down the Line." Copyright 1997, Wombat Productions. Produced in Association with Janson Associates and A&E Network. As seen on *Biography*, a presentation of the Arts & Entertainment cable network.

Jan Sterling

Jan Sterling began her life as a socially registered blue-blood, honed her acting craft for ten years on the stage, then made a name for herself in Hollywood by playing a series of hapless tramps, gangsters' molls, high-class floozies and husband-stealers. Never considered among the ranks of the film capital's glamour girls or superstars, Sterling was nonetheless a top talent, exhibiting her capabilities in stage, screen and television in a wide variety of roles. Sterling, who was happily married to burly actor Paul Douglas until his untimely death, enjoyed a lengthy screen career that spanned more than 30 years, and was seen in six features from the film noir era: *Caged* (1950), *Mystery Street* (1950), *Union Station* (1950), *Appointment with Danger* (1951), *The Big Carnival* (1951) and *The Harder They Fall* (1956).

The first of two girls, Jane Sterling Adriance was born in New York City on April 3, 1923 (some sources say 1921), into a family whose impeccable bloodlines earned them a place in the New York Social Register. With ancestors that included presidents John Adams and John Quincy Adams, Sterling's grandfather was a manufacturer of harvesting machinery who sold out to the Deere company after the turn of the century, and her father, William Allen Adriance, was a well-known New York advertising executive. (Out of deference to her father, who disapproved of her acting aspirations, Sterling would later drop her last name, and after a suggestion from actress Ruth Gordon, would eliminate the "e" from her first.)

Soon after Sterling's birth, her family moved to Roslyn, Long Island, but her parents divorced in 1928. That same year, Sterling's mother married Henry James White, an executive in the foreign branch of the Socony Vacuum Oil Company. Because Henry White's job required frequent travel, Sterling saw a great deal of the world at an early age, including Denmark, Brussels and the Riviera. As a result, she received her only formal schooling during two years at the Nightingale-Bamford private school in Manhattan, with the bulk of her education being provided through a governess.

By now, Sterling had been bitten by the acting bug, and when the family moved to London in June 1935, the budding thespian prevailed upon her mother to enroll her at Fay Compton's School of Dramatic Art. Two years later, after White's transfer to Rio de Janeiro, Sterling used her powers of persuasion once again, convincing her mother to let her remain in London with a friend, Sylvia Kissel, so that she could appear in Fay Compton's annual school play. Before departing for Brazil, White purchased tickets for Sterling and her schoolgirl chum aboard the *Hindenburg*, but in the first of many fortuitous circumstances that would occur in Sterling's life, she spent so much money on clothes that she exchanged the tickets for the less pricey *North German Lloyd*. While at sea, Sterling learned of the tragic crash of the *Hindenburg* at Lakehurst and later said that she "wondered which coat I bought tipped my budget and saved my life."

After spending the summer of 1937 in Brazil, Sterling was dismayed to learn that her mother had enrolled her at Miss Porter's, an exclusive finishing school in Farmington, Connecticut. Desperate to get her acting career underway, Sterling sought her mother's permission to go to New York instead, with the agreement that if she didn't land an acting job within a month, she would willingly enter Miss Porter's. "Thinking I was just having a teenage dream, Mother gave her consent," Sterling said. But after a few weeks, she found that "my time was running out and I hadn't had any luck."

But Sterling's fortunes changed while waiting in the rain for a friend outside the offices of the famed Schubert brothers. "I ducked into a producer's reception room to get out of the rain," she recalled. "[The producer] came out of his private office, looked at me, and next thing I knew I had my first part, in the American production of *Bachelor Born*, an English play. I discovered later that he had been attracted by my hair. So my career actually was hanging by a hair." Using her British accent to her advantage, Sterling portrayed the role of a well-brought-up English girl, and, debuting on Broadway at the tender age of 14, the future Hollywood star was on her way.

After a year at the Morosco Theater in New York, Sterling went on the road with *Bachelor Born*, then returned to Broadway for brief roles in *When We Are Married* (1939) and *Grey Farm* (1940), frequently supplementing her income by modeling. Then, in May 1941, just months after her 18th birthday, Sterling married Jack Merivale (son of stage stars Philip Merivale and Gladys Cooper), who had been a member of the *Bachelor Born* road company. After vacationing during the summer with the senior Merivales, Sterling and her husband returned to New York, but were unable to secure a job until her agent, Louis Shurr, called the actress on New Year's Day 1942 with some heartening information. Virginia Field, the agent reported, was leaving the cast of *Panama Hattie* to marry an actor by the name of Paul Douglas. Thrilled after months of inactivity, Sterling accepted the role, not knowing that she would some day replace Field off screen as well.

Shortly before Sterling started work on *Panama Hattie*, Jack Merivale enlisted with the Royal Canadian Air Force, but his frequent absences would lead to the couple's separation in 1946 and their divorce a short time later. Meanwhile, when *Panama Hattie* closed, Sterling was invited by veteran stage actress Katherine Cornell to go on the road as an understudy for Gertrude Musgrove in Chekhov's *Three Sisters*. Although she was reproached by her friends for accepting the $85-a-week job, Sterling would come to appreciate the training she received from the other members of the company, which included such stellar talents as Ruth Gordon, Judith Anderson, Edmund Gwenn and Alexander Knox.

In April 1944, Ruth Gordon cast Sterling in *Over 21*, a comedy Gordon had written about officer candidates and their wives. After a ten-week run in this comedy, Sterling seldom found herself without work and appeared during the next three years in a number of Broadway productions, including *The*

Rugged Path (1945), *Dunningan's Daughter* (1945), *This, Too, Shall Pass* (1946) and *Present Laughter* (1946). "I've probably been in more flops than anybody," Sterling said later. "But you keep trying."

Then, after years of playing ingenue roles, Sterling was cast in the role of Billie Dawn, the empty-headed mistress of a corrupt junk tycoon, in the Chicago production of Garson Kanin's hit play *Born Yesterday* (1947). (In another of the intriguing coincidences of Sterling's life, the role of the tycoon was played on Broadway by Paul Douglas.) "Kanin was the first to see the tramp in me," Sterling later said. "I was scared because I'd never played anyone like that but he said I could do it because I had the dumbest face he'd ever seen. It wasn't a flattering remark, but at that moment, it was the nicest thing he could have said."

As Billie Dawn, Sterling took Chicago by storm, and the role turned her into an "overnight" star. "I had a big suite at a hotel cheap, because they wanted me to stay there," she remembered. "Taxi cab drivers and other people began to recognize me on the street. I got the best tables at restaurants. The press made a circus about me." And Hollywood was not far behind. Six months after opening in *Born Yesterday*, Sterling took a two-week vacation in Los Angeles, where she learned that Garson Kanin had sold the rights to his play to Columbia Pictures and was cutting short the Chicago run. Sterling's agent promptly contacted producer Jerry Wald, who had seen the actress' performance in *Born Yesterday*. After a screen test, the producer promptly signed Sterling to a contract for his upcoming film, *Johnny Belinda* (1948).

This highly acclaimed film starred Jane Wyman as a deaf-mute girl who is molested by a local villager, bears his child, kills him when he tries to take the baby, and is put on trial for murder. Although Wyman, who would receive an Academy Award for her performance, earned the highest reviews, critics also noted Sterling's portrayal of the rapist's mean-spirited wife who is redeemed by the film's end. Still, returning to New York after the film's release, Sterling would philosophically state, "There are at least 20 actresses on the Warner lot who could have played my part. The only reason I got it was because of my theatrical training. Out there anybody who's worked in the theater is considered great. Honestly. They made a big fuss over me just because I came from Broadway. Anyway, I had fun."

Her "fun" experience in Hollywood notwithstanding, Sterling didn't waste time returning to her roots on the stage. She was next seen in *John Loves Mary* in Chicago and *Two Blind Mice* on Broadway, opposite Melvyn Douglas. And in May 1948, she took over the role of Billie Dawn in the Broadway version of *Born Yesterday*, after learning that Judy Holliday was withdrawing from the production. (Contrary to popular belief, however, Sterling did not appear opposite Paul Douglas — he had already quit the play for Hollywood.)

After just two months in *Born Yesterday*, Sterling was lured back to Hollywood when Jerry Wald asked her to portray a convict in *Caged* (1950), his film about a women's prison. In this picture, Sterling's first film noir, she portrayed Smoochie, a good-natured prostitute who, like most of the inmates, blames her troubles on men, but cheerfully admits, "I'd hate to see 'em abolished."

The women's prison that serves as the setting for *Caged* is operated by a compassionate warden, but her kindly intentions are undermined by a sadistic matron who delights in tormenting the women under her charge. In addition to Smoochie, the prison's assortment of inmates includes Marie Allen (Eleanor Parker), a pregnant first-offender, Kitty Stark (Betty Garde), the tough leader of a shoplifting ring, and Georgia (Gertrude Michael), a socialite accused of check forgery. During the course of the film, Georgia is transferred to a mental ward after trying to escape, another inmate commits suicide when her parole is denied, and Kitty murders their matron after she is driven mad by a period of solitary confinement. And by the film's end, Marie has seen her baby removed to the care of the state and has metamorphosed from a naive innocent to a hardened adult. When Marie is paroled, the warden sorrowfully watches her departure and directs a clerk to keep her file active, saying: "She'll be back." For her appearance in the film, Sterling was included in *Variety*'s praise of the supporting cast's "good" performances.

By the time *Caged* was released on May 19, 1950, Sterling had undergone a transformation in her personal life. A week earlier, she had married Paul Douglas, the beefy, imposing actor who excelled in such features as *A Letter to Three Wives* (1949), *Clash by Night* (1952) and *The Solid Gold Cadillac* (1956). The two had first met while Sterling was dining at Romanoff's with her agent, Louis Shurr, who also represented Douglas. Years later, the actor recalled that he had been sitting in a nearby booth at the famed eatery, and although he had never met Sterling, "I waited until Louis paid the check and then I joined them." Sterling and Douglas began dating after that night, but given Douglas' matrimonial track record — he'd divorced his third wife, Virginia Field, in 1946 — Sterling was not overly intrigued. The relationship remained at a standstill until the night Sterling saw Douglas in *Everybody Does It* (1949): "An actor can't really manufacture an emotion he has never felt," Sterling said. "In that picture Paul showed a sensitive sort of warmth and humor that made me ask myself why I was leaving this man around loose."

Despite an age difference of 15 years, Sterling and Douglas seemed ideally suited, and boasted one of Hollywood's rare successful marriages. After their wedding, they rented from actress Marion Davies (for the paltry sum of $500 a month) a gigantic pink mansion, which came equipped with a ballroom, 360-foot swimming pool and 100-foot waterfall. Five years later, on October 20, 1955, in a widely publicized natural delivery at her home, Sterling would give birth to a son, named Adams after his presidential ancestors. "I wouldn't have missed this wonderful experience — motherhood in every sense of the word — for anything in the world," Sterling would tell the press just one day after Adams' birth. "Babies have been born this way for years and years. No other experience can be quite as satisfying. A woman who is not fully conscious when her baby comes is missing three-quarters of the joy of motherhood."

Soon after her marriage to Douglas, Sterling underwent plastic surgery to alter her "broad, flat" nose and, unlike most stars of the day, made no secret of the operation. Extolling the virtues of corrective surgery, Sterling reported in a number of newspapers and magazines that the procedure had boosted her confidence and heightened her understanding of the dissatisfaction faced by others. "There still seems to be something shameful associated with changing ourselves from the way God made us," she said. "Well, God made us naked. Does that mean we have to go around without clothes? Also there is a good old saying that 'God helps those who help themselves!'"

Career-wise, Sterling was next seen in her second film noir, MGM's *Mystery Street* (1950), in which she played Vivian Heldon, her third consecutive "shady lady." Vivian, a flashy, low-class cocktail waitress, learns at the film's beginning that she is "in a jam" and sets up a meeting to inform her married lover, James Harkley (Edmon Ryan), that she is pregnant. When Harkley fails to show, Vivian steals the car of a drunken customer, Henry Shanway (Marshall Thompson), leaving him stranded in the road while she drives to Harkley's home. Catching up to her lover, she informs him of her condition, sneering, "Don't think you're going to walk out on me — not now. It isn't as easy as all that." But Vivian meets an unexpected end when Harkley shoots her, dumping the car containing her lifeless body in a nearby lake.

When Vivian's body is found, Shanway is arrested for her murder, but arresting officer Peter Morales (Ricardo Montalban) later learns of Vivian's involvement with Harkley. Meanwhile, Harkley is being blackmailed by Vivian's landlady, Mrs. Smerrling (Elsa Lanchester), who stole Harkley's gun after realizing that he murdered Vivian. Harkley visits Mrs. Smerrling's apartment, but she refuses to produce the claim check needed to retrieve the gun from the local train station. During a struggle, Harkley kills the landlady, then cons a baggage claim attendant into turning over the suitcase that contains the gun. But before he can escape, Harkley is cornered and arrested by Morales.

Although Sterling's role in *Mystery Street* was a minor one, she was singled out in several publications; in the *New York Times* she was noted as offering "solid support" to the film's principal players, and the critic for *Variety* wrote, "Jan Sterling spots an excellently done small part as the murder victim." Next the actress appeared with Robert Walker, Joan Leslie and Edward Arnold in *The Skipper Surprised His Wife* (1950), a bright domestic comedy about an ex-sea captain who runs his home in the same manner that he operated his ship. Meanwhile, Columbia had announced that it was casting the role of Billie Dawn in its film version of *Born Yesterday* (1950). Although Harry Cohn, head of Columbia, wanted Judy Holliday for the role, Holliday balked at Cohn's request that she sign a contract with the studio for her future services. Reportedly announcing that he "wouldn't use Holliday now if she came crawling on her knees," Cohn took an option on Sterling for the part and began photographic and dialogue tests. But when word leaked to the press that Sterling was a virtual shoo-in, Holliday relented and Cohn signed her for the role, leaving Sterling with what she termed "egg on my face."

But the actress would later view the situation with her typical good humor: "It really was Judy's part," she said philosophically. "She had created it and the studio favored her, naturally. I always thought it was a gamble as far as I was concerned. If some other actress had been chosen, I would have been terribly disappointed. But Judy deserved it." And Sterling had one consolation — Paramount executives decided they wanted her to play a gangster's moll in their upcoming feature *Union Station* (1950), and to sweeten the deal, they offered her a seven-year contract. Sterling signed.

Union Station, Sterling's third film noir, told the story of a wealthy blind girl, Lorna Murchison (Allene Roberts), kidnapped by a trio of ruthless hoods, and the efforts of the Union Station police force to secure her safe return. Led by Lt. William Calhoun (William Holden) and Inspector Donnelly (Barry Fitzgerald), the station police work feverishly to track down the kidnappers with the aid of Joyce Willecombe (Nancy Olson), who saw two of the criminals aboard a train. In quick fashion, the police nab one of the men, Gus Hadder (Don Dunning), but during a chase in the Chicago stockyards, he is killed by stampeding cattle. The officers next apprehend Vince Marley (Fred Graff) and frighten him into revealing the whereabouts of the third member of the gang by threatening to toss him in front of a speeding train. But when the cops close in, they find that the gang's leader, Joe Beacom (Lyle Bettger, in a brilliantly perverse performance), has already fled.

Meanwhile, Beacom and his money-hungry moll Marge Wrighter (Sterling) conceal Lorna in the back seat of their car. When a patrol officer recognizes their license plate number, Beacom shoots him. Helping her man by grabbing the officer's gun, Marge gets in the way of Beacom's hail of bullets, and the cold-hearted hood leaves her to die in the street. Planning to kill Lorna later, Beacom stashes her 40 feet underground in the city's municipal tunnel, but he is spotted by Calhoun after he picks up the $100,000 ransom. After a dramatic chase through the winding tunnel, Beacom is shot and Lorna is safely returned to her grateful father.

In a small role as the cruel gangster's girlfriend, Jan Sterling offered a memorable portrayal, and the critic for *Variety* wrote that she "shows up neatly in a brief spot." The film itself was released to mixed reviews, however; while it was praised in *Variety* for its "overall excellent effect," the *New York Times* critic found that "despite its occasional excitements, the goings-on in *Union Station* only add up to the muscular derring-do likely to turn up in any standard cops-and-robbers adventure."

After appearing in a small role as a jealous stenographer in *The Mating Season* (1951), Sterling returned to film noir in *Appointment with Danger* (1951).

Jan Sterling

This feature stars Alan Ladd as Al Goddard, a United States postal inspector investigating the murder of fellow inspector Harry Gruber. Goddard's quest is aided when he learns that a local nun, Sister Augustine (Phyllis Calvert), is able to identify the man's killers, Joe Regas and George Soderquist (portrayed by Jack Webb and Harry Morgan, several years before their teaming on TV's *Dragnet*). Fearing his partner's weak nature, Regas kills Soderquist, and makes an unsuccessful attempt to murder Sister Augustine. Later, it is revealed that Regas works for Earl Boettiger (Paul Stewart), a gang leader planning a $1 million heist of a postal truck.

Goddard manages to infiltrate the gang by convincing Boettiger that he is a crooked government agent. But the robbery is nearly botched when Regas fails to carry out his role in the scheme and, instead, kidnaps Sister Augustine from the local train station. The men manage to escape with the stolen money and meet at an abandoned shack, where Regas insists on killing the nun. Goddard convinces Boettiger to let her live, but when Sister Augustine accidentally reveals that she knows Goddard, the hoods realize that he is working with the authorities. During a gun battle, police arrive, and Boettiger is gunned down just as he is about to kill Goddard.

As Paul Stewart's wise-cracking girlfriend, Sterling was applauded by for her performance, with her best notices coming from the critic for the *New York Times*: "Credit must be given to Jan Sterling. As the seemingly dumb blonde moll of that criminal crew, she has more than a modicum of the film's funny lines, which she delivers with professional casualness."

Next, Sterling played her most unsavory "bad girl" to date, in the fascinating film noir *The Big Carnival* (1951). Originally released as *Ace in the Hole*, this film stars Kirk Douglas as Charles Tatum, an unprincipled reporter who, after being fired from 11 newspapers, finds himself seeking employment at a small publication in Albuquerque, New Mexico. Tatum manages to talk himself into a spot on the staff, but after a year he is still searching for the big story that will catapult him back to the big time. On the way to cover a rattlesnake hunt, he finds it in an old Indian cavern where a curio shop owner, Leo Minosa (Richard Benedict), has been trapped by a cave-in. Tatum wastes little time in taking advantage of the accident. He first meets with the small town's corrupt sheriff, Gus Kretzer (Ray Teal), promising him favorable coverage for his upcoming election in exchange for exclusive rights to Minosa's story. Next, learning that the rescue efforts will have Minosa freed in less than 24 hours, Tatum insists that the men drill from the top of the mountain, an endeavor that will take at least a week.

Meanwhile, Minosa's slovenly wife Lorraine (Sterling) plans to use her husband's predicament as an opportunity to leave him, but Tatum, needing a "grieving spouse" to spice up his stories, convinces her to stay by pointing out the money-making possibilities. Before long, in response to Tatum's moving stories, a throng of curiosity-seekers and reporters from around the country descend on the area. As the site takes on a circus-like atmosphere (complete with carnival rides and concession stands), Lorraine starts raking in the cash and, as the only journalist allowed access to Minosa inside the cavern, Tatum becomes a celebrity. Tatum eventually uses his sudden success as a tactic to regain his position at a top New York newspaper, but while awaiting his rescue, Minosa grows gravely ill from pneumonia. Fulfilling a request by the dying man, Tatum gives Lorraine a fur piece that Minosa had purchased for their wedding anniversary, choking her with it after she haughtily tosses it on the floor. In desperation, Lorraine stabs Tatum with a pair of scissors, but he manages to return to the mountain, where Minosa later dies. Conscience-stricken by his role in the man's demise, Tatum ruins his chances for an exclusive story by announcing Minosa's death to the horde of onlookers, then returns to the newspaper in Albuquerque with plans to reveal his hoax in an article. But before the story can be written, Tatum succumbs to the injury inflicted by Lorraine.

Sterling, whose performance won her the National Board of Review Award as best actress of 1952, was a standout in the film, bringing to life a self-centered slattern whose lust for money far outweighed her concern for her husband's life. In one scene, when her father-in-law suggests that the onlookers be forced to leave, Lorraine airily explains, "They won't go home. They'll just park on the other side of the highway and eat someplace else. Why shouldn't we get something out of it?" And her persona is perhaps best illustrated when Tatum orders her to attend a religious service for her husband: "I don't go to church," Lorraine drawls. "Kneeling bags my nylons." After the film's release, critics were nearly unanimous in their praise of Sterling's performance, with Bosley Crowther writing in the *New York Times* that she "fills with venom the role of the victim's trampish wife," and *Newsweek*'s critic claiming, "The surprise of the film is Jan Sterling's petulant, uneasy characterization of Minosa's wife, Lorraine. Miss Sterling has been drab and desperate on screen before this, but with *Ace in the Hole* she becomes a star."

After three years in Hollywood, Sterling had played eight successive "baddies," including two gangster's molls, a secretary hopeful of busting up her boss's marriage, and a married woman prowling after men other than her husband. But although she was developing a "bad girl" reputation on screen, Sterling seemed to prefer it that way. "I enjoy these roles," she said. "I was fed up with the ingenues and glad to get the chance to switch. Any straight part is dull — those parts are like paper dolls, not real. The ingenue gets her feelings hurt and cries, she has no sense of humor — no sense, either — whereas the bad girl at least has spirit." But the actress got a change of pace when she starred opposite Ray Milland in *Rhubarb* (1951), a comedy about a cat who inherits the estate of an eccentric millionaire and becomes the owner of a baseball team.

Next, on loan-out to Universal, Sterling returned to the other side of the tracks, starring in *Flesh and Fury* (1952) as a sexy but thoroughly unscrupulous blonde out to exploit a deaf-mute prizefighter, followed by MGM's *Sky Full of Moon* (1952), a pleasant comedy in which she played a Las Vegas dame having a fling with an guileless cowboy. But these films were followed by a succession of barely passable features, including two Paramount Westerns, *Pony Express* (1953), with Charlton Heston and Forrest Tucker, and *The Vanquished* (1953) with John Payne.

But the actress rebounded with her first film of 1954, *The High and the Mighty*, in which she portrayed Sally McKee, a beat-up, world-weary mail order bride. Although the role was one of the best of Sterling's career, the actress later recalled being warned against it: "Even William Wellman, who directed *The High and the Mighty*, told me to think twice before saying yes," Sterling said. "But I grabbed that role of Sally as though it were a parachute. After all, I'm gunning for a career that's going to last — and if Sally's big moment came when she looked ugliest, so what? How long can a girl be fresh, dainty and young enough to play glamour roles? The only people who last in Hollywood are those who can act." Taking place aboard an airplane bound to San Francisco from Honolulu, *The High and the Mighty* was a box office smash, and resulted in Sterling's only Academy Award nomination of her career (for Best Supporting Actress). Most of the Hollywood community expected Sterling to win, but the award went instead to Eva Marie Saint for *On the Waterfront*. "It was the longest minute of my life," Sterling said later. "And when the envelope was opened and it was Eva Marie Saint who had won, my heart sank. I really believed then that my place on Earth would be complete if only I could have an Oscar."

In addition to her triumph in *The High and the Mighty*, Sterling also embarked on a highly successful television career during this period. During the next three decades she would appear in a wide variety of roles on programs that included *Alfred Hitchcock Presents, Wagon Train, Playhouse 90, Burke's Law, The Name of the Game, The Untouchables, Bonanza, Mannix, Medical Center, Kung Fu* and *Three's Company*, as well as the daytime soap opera *The Guiding Light* and such made-for-television movies as *My Kidnapper, My Love* (1980). Meanwhile, on the silver screen, Sterling continued her shady lady roles over the next two years, portraying a nightclub stripper in Allied Artists' *The Human Jungle* (1954), a crafty murderess in Universal's *Female on the Beach* (1955) and her second go-round as a prison inmate in *Women's Prison* (1955). But in her final film noir, *The Harder They Fall* (1956), she played a rare good girl: "I'm finally getting out of the gutter. I've been a tramp for years, but from now on I'm going to be respectable," Sterling joked after the film's release. "I think my son will be proud of me. At last I play an honorable woman."

The Harder They Fall stars Humphrey Bogart as Eddie Willis, an out-of-work sportswriter who is hired as a press agent by a ruthless sports promoter, Nick Benko (Rod Steiger, in another of his patented evil roles). Eddie's task is to promote Benko's latest acquisition, a huge South American fighter named Toro Moreno (Mike Lane), but Eddie quickly discovers that the massive foreigner is "as strong as a bull but green as a cucumber, with a powder puff punch and a glass jaw." Still, with the promise of regaining his former prominence, Eddie takes the job, setting up a series of highly publicized bouts against fighters paid to lose against the inept "Wild Man of the Andes." Over the strenuous objections of his wife Beth (Sterling), and despite his own growing misgivings, Eddie continues to effectively guide Toro's route to the heavy-weight championship, but he is thrown a curve when punch-drunk ex-champion Gus Dundee (Pat Comiskey) suffers a brain hemorrhage and dies after a fight with Toro.

The simple-minded, soft-hearted Toro is devastated by the incident, unaware that Dundee's injury had actually been caused by a previous fight with heavyweight champion Buddy Brannen (played by real-life fighter Max Baer, Sr.). Scheduled next to fight Brannen for the championship, Toro insists on returning to his country, but Eddie convinces him to stay by telling him the truth: "You couldn't kill anybody unless you had a gun," he cruelly announces. "You can't punch — you're a fake. If you go home now, you go home broke — if you fight Brannen, you'll have money." Toro decides to proceed with the bout, but once in the ring, he disregards instructions to stay away from Brannen, and after landing a few good punches he winds up being beaten to a pulp. For his efforts, Eddie is paid $26,000 by Benko, but is stunned to learn that Toro's contract has been sold for $75,000 to an unscrupulous manager, Jim Weyerhause (Edward Andrews), who plans to continue exploiting the hulking fighter. When Eddie is further disillusioned by the discovery that Toro's profits for his journey to the championship is a mere $49.07, he gives the fighter his $26,000 and puts him on a plane back to South America. Benko is incensed by Eddie's disloyalty and threatens his life, but Eddie is unfazed, revealing that he plans to write a series of articles exposing Benko's tactics: "You can't scare me and you can't buy me," he tells him. After Benko leaves, Eddie begins writing his first story, which begins: "Boxing should be outlawed in the United States if it takes an Act of Congress to do it."

Although Sterling was panned in *the New York Times* for her "listless" portrayal of Eddie's moralistic wife, the film itself was acclaimed by critics and was a box office smash. The success of the picture was no doubt assisted by publicity from a $1.5 million lawsuit filed against Columbia Pictures just days before the film's release by Primo Carnera, a former heavyweight boxing champion on whom the story was reportedly based. Carnera, who became a wrestler after his failed boxing career, claimed that certain elements of the movie paralleled his rise and fall in the boxing ring and charged that he was "subjected to ridicule" as a result of the film. Three months later, however, a Santa Monica Superior Court judge threw out the case, ruling that "one who became a celebrity or public figure waived the right of privacy and did not regain it by changing his profession."

After starring with Edmond O'Brien in *1984* (1956), the first screen version of George Orwell's prophetic book, Sterling played another sympathetic character in Universal's *Slaughter on Tenth Avenue* (1957), a hard-hitting drama about criminal activities along New York's waterfront. But she followed this top-notch feature with two clunkers, *The Female Animal* (1958), in which Sterling and costars Hedy Lamarr and Jane Powell are in love with a movie extra

played by George Nader, and *High School Confidential!* (1958), a sleazy melodrama about teenage dopers. She did better, however, in her third film of
1958, *Kathy O'*, which starred Patty McCormack (of *The Bad Seed* fame) as a
famous child star who is "loved by millions yet loved by no one."

Then, on September 11, 1959, Sterling's world was shattered when Paul
Douglas suffered a heart attack and died, two months before his 57th birthday. Left to raise their son on her own, Sterling would tell a New York reporter
nearly a year later: "I never before realized what taking care of someone else
means. I find playing the role of a man is sometimes subtle but very heavy.
Every day there's a new responsibility. Since Paul died I've learned how selfish
I was before and I've suddenly discovered a sense of mortality. I've got to keep
alive because of our son." And in 1961, she revealed to columnist Joe Hyams
that she was grateful for the ten years she spent with Douglas, but she ruefully added, "The trouble is, after Paul, everybody else is kind of dull — they're
so pallid — you're kind of bored with just ordinary people."

Off screen for two years after Douglas' unexpected death, Sterling resumed
her film career with Paramount's *Love in a Goldfish Bowl* (1961), a lighthearted
romp that served as the forerunner of the popular 1960s "beach party" movies.
But following this box office smash, she would be away from the big screen
for six years, concentrating instead on her frequent television appearances and
roles in such stage productions as *The Perfect Setup* (1962), *Once for the Asking*
(1963) and *Friday Night* (1965). She returned to feature films with a small role
in *The Incident* (1967), a gritty drama about two hoodlums who menace a
group of commuters on a New York subway train, then was seen two years
later in *The Minx* (1969), an independently produced film that was actually
finished in 1967, but reportedly could not get a distributor until ten minutes
of sexually explicit scenes were edited in.

Around this time, Sterling became involved with actor-director Sam
Wanamaker, whom she referred to as "my fella," and settled with him in the
Knightsbridge area of London. But she returned to America for various television and stage appearances throughout the 1970s, beginning with the revival
of the Ben Hecht–Charles MacArthur play *The Front Page* (1970), in which
she replaced Peggy Cass in the role of Mollie Malloy. Later in the decade, she
also appeared in *Come Back, Little Sheba, Hot l Baltimore*, and *The November
People*. During her role in the latter production, the 54-year-old actress told
a New York columnist: "I know I'm a different person from the girl I was 20
years ago. My waist is 24 and the bosoms are still there but not pointed up,
and I don't wear platinum hair. I used to think people wouldn't pay any attention to me if I didn't look gorgeous. And it's been such a release to play things
like *Come Back, Little Sheba*. I find I function better in relation to an audience
and I don't have to feel put together with sticks just to look sexy."

As the 1980s approached, Sterling was seen in fewer productions, but in
1981 she starred in *Eleanor of Aquintaine* in Salt Lake City, and made a rare

feature film appearance playing Walter Matthau's wife in *First Monday in October*. And the following year she was seen in a made-for-television movie on CBS, *Dangerous Company*. Most of her time, however, was devoted to working, without pay, for the Royal Voluntary Service in London. "I feel needed and useful," Sterling said. "In London, I'm just Mrs. Douglas, working at St. Pancras Hospital in my mulberry and green uniform and pork-pie hat, or at Brixton Prison. Sometimes at the prison, I feel as though I'm back in Hollywood making *Caged* or *Women's Prison* and that the girls and I will take off our uniforms and go home. I do, but they can't."

Although in 1966 it had been reported in *The Hollywood Reporter* that Sterling and Wanamaker would "tie the knot" when Wanamaker's divorce became final, Sterling never married the actor-director, and after his death in 1993, she returned to California, moving to an apartment in Chula Vista. She has not resumed her performing career, however, attributing her inactivity to "my almost total lack of ambition and the fact that I enjoy my life now very much. I'm not aware that I'm missing anything."

Film Noir Filmography

CAGED *Director:* John Cromwell. *Producer:* Jerry Wald. Released by Warner Bros., May 1950. *Running time:* 97 minutes. *Cast:* Eleanor Parker, Agnes Moorehead, Ellen Corby, Hope Emerson, Betty Garde, Jan Sterling, Lee Patrick, Olive Deering, Jane Darwell. *Awards:* Academy Award nominations for Best Actress (Eleanor Parker), Best Supporting Actress (Hope Emerson), Best Original Screenplay (Virginia Kellogg, Bernard C. Schoenfeld).

MYSTERY STREET *Director:* John Sturges. *Producer:* Frank E. Taylor. Released by MGM, July 1950. *Running time:* 94 minutes. *Cast:* Ricardo Montalban, Sally Forrest, Bruce Bennett, Elsa Lanchester, Marshall Thompson, Jan Sterling, Edmon Ryan, Betsy Blair. *Awards:* Academy Award nomination for Best Original Screenplay (Leonard Spigelgass).

UNION STATION *Director:* Rudolph Maté. *Producer:* Jules Schermer. Released by Paramount, October 1950. *Running time:* 80 minutes. *Cast:* William Holden, Nancy Olson, Barry Fitzgerald, Lyle Bettger, Jan Sterling, Allene Roberts, Herbert Heyes.

APPOINTMENT WITH DANGER *Director:* Lewis Allen. *Producer:* Robert Fellows. Released by Paramount, May 1951. *Running time:* 89 minutes. *Cast:* Alan Ladd, Phyllis Calvert, Paul Stewart, Jan Sterling, Jack Webb, Stacy Harris, Henry Morgan.

THE BIG CARNIVAL (original release title: *Ace in the Hole*) *Director and Producer:* Billy Wilder. Released by Paramount, June 1951. *Running time:* 119 minutes. *Cast:* Kirk Douglas, Jan Sterling, Robert Arthur, Porter Hall, Frank Cady, Richard Benedict, Ray Teal, Lewis Martin, John Berkes. *Awards:* Academy Award nomination for Best Original Screenplay (Lesser Samuels, Walter Newman).

THE HARDER THEY FALL *Director:* Mark Robson. *Producer:* Philip Yordan. Released by Columbia, May 1956. *Running time:* 108 minutes. *Cast:* Humphrey Bogart, Rod Steiger, Jan Sterling, Mike Lane, Max Baer, Sr., Jersey Joe Walcott, Edward Andrews, Nehemiah Persoff. *Awards:* Academy Award nomination for Best Cinematography (Burnett Guffey).

References

Alpert, Don. "Film Life Begins at 40 for Jan." *Los Angeles Times*, January 14, 1968.

Berg, Louis. "Shipshape Sterling." *This Week*, September 28, 1952.

_____. "Silver Sterling." *This Week*, circa 1951.

Biography of Jan Sterling. Warner Bros. Studios, 1955.

Bolton, Whitney. "Jan Sterling Offers Revealing Commentary." *New York Morning Telegraph*, March 8, 1965.

Boswell, Chaim. "You Can Make Yourself Over!" *Movieland*, April 1954.

Brady, Thomas F. "That Sterling Character." *Collier's*, May 26, 1951.

"Broadway Ballyhoo." *The Hollywood Reporter*, September 18, 1980.

Buttitta, Tony. Biography of Jan Sterling. New York, New York, circa 1958.

Cameron, Gledhill. "Child of Divorce Cites Its Rewards." *New York World Telegram*, May 17, 1946.

Cleary-Strauss & Irwin. Biography of Jan Sterling. Los Angeles, California, circa 1961.

Denton, James. Biography of Jan Sterling. 20th Century–Fox Studios, January 26, 1968.

Douglas, Paul. "Take My Wife." *Photoplay*, February 1952.

Gebhart, Myrtle. "Best Moll in Movies." *Boston Post Magazine*, March 12, 1950.

Graham, Sheilah. "Hollywood." *New York Daily Mirror*, February 19, 1955.

Heard, Roby. "Film Actress Stays Home to Bear Son." *Mirror-News*, October 21, 1955.

Hopper, Hedda. "Husky Paul and Gorgeous Jan." *Chicago Sunday Tribune*, circa 1951.

Hyams, Joe. "Jan Douglas a 'Family Man' Now." *New York Herald Tribune*, May 17, 1960.

_____. "Jan Sterling Has New Nose, Outlook." *New York Herald Tribune*, October 19, 1956.

_____. "Stars, Too, Have Troubles." *New York Herald Tribune*, December 24, 1956.

"Jan Sterling for Broadway." *The Hollywood Reporter*, September 7, 1960.

Kraft, Daphne. "Jan Sterling: One More Racy Role." *The Newark New Jersey Evening News*, January 16, 1970.

Miller, John J. "Millerdramas." *New York Inquirer*, February 18, 1957.

Peper, William. "Jan Sterling 'Gets Out of Gutter.'" *New York World Telegram*, May 5, 1956.

Quinn, Frank. "Jan Sterling Makes the 'Honor' Roll." *New York Daily Mirror*, March 15, 1956.

Service, Faith. "Completely Nuts About the Guy." *Silver Screen*, September 1951.

Skolsky, Sidney. "She Can't Cook." *New York Post*, July 8, 1951.

Sterling, Jan, as told to Liza Wilson. "My Baby Was Born at Home." *The American Weekly*, February 19, 1956.

Wahls, Robert. "Sterling Oldie." *New York Daily News*, December 11, 1977.

Wilson, Earl. "Cast as a Star." *New York Post*, August 13, 1961.

_____. "Wives 'Selfish, Aggressive' Charges Jan Sterling (Wife)." *New York Post*, March 17, 1954.

Gene Tierney

Like many a Hollywood glamour girl, Gene Tierney was beloved by fans and praised by critics more for her radiant green eyes and luminescent skin than for her dramatic talents. But no amount of glamour could cloak Tierney's failed marriages, the tragedy of her first-born daughter, and the mental illness that threatened to overpower her life. It was only Tierney's inner strength that allowed her to rise above her adversities and emerge on the other side.

Tierney, a capable performer in comedy as well as drama, frequently saw her professional life overshadowed by her personal romances, which included a highly publicized relationship with Prince Aly Khan, and a turbulent union to fashion designer Oleg Cassini. Still, her life on the silver screen was a triumphant one and she was not only a mesmerizing presence in a variety of successful films, but she also made a striking impact in five films noirs: *The Shanghai Gesture* (1941), *Laura* (1944), *Leave Her to Heaven* (1945), *Night and the City* (1950) and *Where the Sidewalk Ends* (1950).

Unlike many film stars, who began their lives in less than moneyed conditions, Gene Eliza Tierney was born into an affluent Brooklyn, New York, family on November 19, 1920, the second of three siblings. Tierney would later recall that her childhood was happy and secure, filled with "love and gaiety." When she was still in her pre-teens, Tierney's family moved from New York to a large estate in Green Farms, Connecticut, and the unusually beautiful adolescent was educated at private schools in nearby Farmington and in Lausanne, Switzerland. Although she had no ambitions to become a film star, Tierney said that she had always been a great movie fan and went "religiously" to the movies, along with her father Howard and her mother Belle. "My goal at the time was far from becoming an actress," Tierney said in a 1972 interview in *After Dark*. "When I was young, I had a very idealistic viewpoint; I wanted to do good and I wanted to be something like a social worker."

But Tierney's lofty plans changed when she was 17. Touring Warner Bros. studio during a family vacation in Hollywood, Tierney's striking green eyes and delicate features attracted the attention of famed director Anatole Litvak, who delivered the well-worn line that she "ought to be in pictures." Following a screen test, Tierney was offered a standard contract for $150 a week. But Howard Tierney refused to let his daughter sign the agreement — he considered Hollywood "the moral equivalent of purgatory," the actress later recalled — but he struck a bargain with her. Tierney would make her society debut, as planned, and if after three months she still wanted to pursue an acting career, Howard would assist her in finding work on the Broadway stage.

Tierney agreed to her father's proposal. On September 24, 1938, she was presented to society at the Fairfield Country Club, and then entered a seemingly endless routine of attending country club parties and dating "boys whose chief virtue was that they looked well in tails," the actress said. But after three months, Tierney's ambitions had not abated. True to his word, Howard Tierney began accompanying his daughter to New York each Wednesday, where they visited the offices of various agents and producers. After only a few weeks, Tierney won a small role as an Irish orphan in George Abbott's production *Mrs. O'Brien Entertains*. To improve the stage presence of the neophyte actress, Abbott gave her a walk-on part in another play, *What a Life*, and when *Mrs. O'Brien Entertains* opened on February 8, 1939, Tierney received a number of favorable reviews. The show itself, though, was not a success, and closed after only 37 performances.

But Tierney had received enough exposure to bring Hollywood calling again, and she received contract offers from Warner Bros. and Columbia. Although she preferred to remain on the stage, even telling reporters that she "wasn't ready for Hollywood," Tierney followed the advice of her father and signed with Columbia at a salary of $350 a week for the first six months, increasing to $500 a week if her contract was renewed.

Once in Hollywood, Tierney later recalled, she did little but wait for a film assignment and spend long afternoons taking lessons in how to walk, talk and sit. Although her career was being handled by Leland Hayward, Tierney received scant attention from the famed agent, who "collected his ten percent, but seemed to have little interest in his clients until one broke out of the pack." Finally, Tierney was cast in *Coast Guard* (1939), starring Ralph Bellamy and Randolph Scott, but after a nerve-wracking first day during which she frequently forgot her lines, she was replaced by actress Frances Dee. Still, this painful incident did not deter the strong-willed starlet: "I was hurt and began to have doubts, but ... people went out of their way to encourage me," Tierney said in her memoirs. "I became all the more determined to work hard, and study, and develop as an actress."

At the end of six months, Columbia offered to renew her option, but without the promised raise to $500 a week. After consulting with director George Abbott, Tierney rejected Columbia's offer and returned to New York, accepting a role in Abbott's new play, *Ring Two*. After two months of rehearsal, the play opened on November 22, 1939, and closed two days later. But Tierney was again singled out by critics, including Richard Watts, Jr., of the *New York Herald Tribune*, who wrote: "I don't see why Miss Tierney shouldn't have an interesting theatrical career — if the cinema doesn't kidnap her." And just a few weeks later, Tierney received what she described as "one of those famous show business breaks." When the actress portraying the ingenue in *The Male Animal* became pregnant, Tierney was hired for the role, and for her performance in the small but showy part, she was praised by Brooks Atkinson of the *New York Times*, who proclaimed that Tierney "blazes with animation in the best performance she has yet given."

After appearing in two flops, Tierney was finally in a successful vehicle, and she began to receive national media attention, including a four-page feature in *Life* magazine and photographs in *Harper's Bazaar* and *Vogue*. Before long, Hollywood was beckoning again, and after turning down an offer from MGM, Tierney signed with 20th Century–Fox. Unlike most standard contracts at the time, Tierney's was unique. Her starting salary was $750 a week, with a raise every six months, and the terms of the agreement provided that she would not be kept idle between film assignments, that she would be allowed each year to appear on Broadway, that she would not be required to alter the length or the color of her hair, and that her slightly crooked teeth would not be straightened. At the time of Tierney's signing, her father — who had helped negotiate the contract — established a family-owned corporation, Belle-Tier, which was designed to develop and promote the future star, and which contractually owned the majority of her cinema income.

Accompanied by her mother, Tierney returned to Hollywood, and was promptly given the female lead in her screen debut, *The Return of Frank James* (1940), starring Henry Fonda. But while this Technicolor horse opera offered shots of breathtaking Western scenery, it provided little in the way of entertainment, and Tierney was noted by critics only for her rather stiff and "colorless" performance. The budding star fared no better in her next film, *Hudson's Bay* (1940), after which the *Harvard Lampoon* voted her "The Worst Female Discovery of 1940." Tierney herself did not disagree with the distinction, later recalling that she sounded on screen like "an angry Minnie Mouse." Next, Tierney was assigned to the minor but eye-catching role of a dim-witted Georgia farm girl in *Tobacco Road* (1941). As Ellie May, Tierney had little dialogue and was clad in what she described as a "dismal calico dress which looked as if it had been fried in grease and then rolled in a dustpan." But her performance showed for the first time that she was more than just a pretty face.

Meanwhile, Tierney was enjoying a busy social life, dating a number of such notables including Howard Hughes, Eddie Albert, Mickey Rooney, Rudy Vallee and Desi Arnaz (who, the actress recalled, spent most of their dinner date discussing his love for future wife Lucille Ball). But in late 1940, Tierney's lighthearted dalliances came to an end. While at a dinner party at the home of actress Constance Moore, Tierney met Paramount dress designer Oleg Cassini, who was eight years her senior. Tierney was instantly attracted to the slender, mustachioed designer, finding him "not handsome, but dangerous in a seductive way." The two had their first date on New Year's Eve and six months later, on June 1, 1941, they eloped to Las Vegas. But Tierney's happiness was short-lived. Her parents were furious about their daughter's action and Belle Tierney sounded off in the press, telling reporters, "Gene is a misguided child who has been carried away ... by this suave man."

A short time later, Tierney learned that her father had been having an affair with his wife's best friend, whom he later married. The rift that resulted from this discovery grew even wider when Tierney drew up a new contract with 20th Century–Fox that no longer assigned a portion of her salary to the

Belle-Tier Corporation. Howard Tierney responded by suing his daughter for $50,000, charging her with breach of contract and contending that Belle-Tier should still be recognized as her agent. Tierney ultimately won the suit, only to find out that her father had been stealing from the company. This knowledge led to a final split in their relationship and Tierney saw her father only once in the next 16 years. When informed of Howard Tierney's death from cancer in 1962, the actress would say that she "felt no pain, no shock, nothing. I felt I had lost my father all those years ago."

Prior to Tierney's marriage, it was announced that she would star in *Man Hunt* (1941) and *Swamp Water* (1941), but the parts ultimately went to Joan Bennett and Anne Baxter, respectively. Instead, Tierney was cast in the title role of *Belle Starr* (1941), a romanticized biography of the 1860s outlaw. This time, Tierney's reviews were mixed, with one critic noting that the actress was "almost breathtaking in her loveliness," and another sniping that her "youth and fancy finishing school background betray her as Belle." Next, Tierney portrayed the daughter of an Arab trader in *Sundown* (1941), a desert story set in East Africa, followed by *The Shanghai Gesture* (1941), her first film noir.

Based on a highly successful Broadway play from the 1920s, this early noir entry has as its focal point a cavernous casino operated by the ruthlessly cunning and elegantly self-assured Mother Gin Sling (Ona Munson). Within the walls of this gambling den exist a unique mélange of characters, including Dr. Omar (Victor Mature), a handsome hustler who admits that he is "a doctor of nothing — it sounds important and hurts no one," Dixie Pomeroy (Phyllis Brooks), a showgirl who is hired to work in the casino after being rescued from a certain jail sentence by Omar, and Poppy (Tierney), a wealthy socialite seduced by the decadence that dwells within the casino. "It smells so incredibly evil," she says upon her first visit. "I didn't think such a place existed except in my own imagination. It has a ghastly familiarity, like a half-remembered dream. Anything can happen here. Any moment." And something does. Gin Sling learns that she is being forced by a local financier, Sir Guy Charteris (Walter Huston), to close her gambling hall, and she grimly sets about unearthing information that will compel Charteris to abandon his efforts. Meanwhile, despite a promise that she will never return to the casino, Poppy becomes a regular patron, drinking heavily and mounting a considerable debt.

Later, it is revealed that Poppy is the only daughter of Charteris, who is informed of his daughter's gambling losses and insists that she leave the city. But at a New Year's Eve dinner at the casino, attended by Shanghai's most prominent citizens, Gin Sling confronts Charteris with a series of damaging revelations: Although he no longer recognizes her, Charteris had married Gin Sling many years before, placed their child in an orphanage, and stolen money from her family estate, leaving Gin Sling penniless and alone. And Gin Sling's final blow comes when she reveals that Poppy did not fly to Singapore, as her father had instructed but, instead, had returned to the decayed world of the casino. "Your daughter is no good for anything," Gin Sling savagely informs Charteris. "Wherever you take her she'll be no good. I would have torn down the whole world to get at you, but it wasn't necessary. It was made easy for me. Because her soul was hollow. Her emotions were cheap. She had no more control than her father had. She had no more honor than he had. Her blood is no good." Despite Charteris' shock at these disclosures, he has news of his own: Gin Sling is Poppy's mother. But Poppy refuses to accept this truth, hysterically telling Gin Sling: "I have no more connection with you than with a toad out in the street." Moments later, Gin Sling silently picks up a gun and kills Poppy, saying with a touch of irony to one her employees: "This time we'll not bribe [the police], will we?"

After its release, *The Shanghai Gesture* was almost universally panned by critics, including one who said Tierney gave "a fair imitation of a second lead in a boarding school play." And Tierney herself would say, "What had seemed dramatic and crisp to us, at the time, struck the critics as hollow and absurd. I don't know that I ever went into a movie more excited, with what turned out to be less cause, than I did for *The Shanghai Gesture*." Despite its initial reaction, however, this Josef von Sternberg–directed picture has since become recognized as a stylishly brilliant example from the film noir era.

Tierney followed *The Shanghai Gesture* with a series of mostly forgettable films, including *Son of Fury* (1942), a Tyrone Power vehicle in which she played the peripheral role of a South Sea island native; *Rings on Her Fingers* (1942), her first screen comedy, playing opposite Henry Fonda; and *China Girl* (1942), a lame action picture in which she was top-billed as the daughter of a Chinese patriot. But in her sole film of 1943, *Heaven Can Wait*, Tierney's cinematic fortunes began to change for the better. In this costume comedy, Tierney portrayed the long-suffering wife of a philandering middle-class citizen, played by Don Ameche. Reviews for Tierney's performance were mixed, but the film was a box office smash.

During the filming of *Heaven Can Wait*, Tierney discovered that she was pregnant with her first child. The actress later recalled that she was "thrilled at the idea of starting a family," but during her first month of pregnancy, shortly after a public appearance at the Hollywood Canteen, Tierney contracted German measles. At the time, little was known about the effect of the disease on the nervous system of an unborn child, and when Daria Cassini was born on October 15, 1943, Tierney had no reason for concern. But a year later, the child was diagnosed as mentally retarded, a direct result of Tierney's German measles exposure. Although the actress said that she "kept hoping and hoping that something could be done, that some miracle would make her whole," Daria was eventually institutionalized and, as Tierney later said, "she has never talked or seen clearly, and has heard few sounds.... But on my visits she is always aware of my presence. She sniffs at my neck and hugs me."

The tragedy of her daughter's retardation was compounded when Tierney discovered that she had contracted the German measles from a female marine who had broken quarantine to meet the actress at the Hollywood Canteen. Tierney stated in her memoirs that it wasn't until years later, after the birth of her grandchildren, that she "really accepted the finality of Daria's condition.... At last, I was able to tell myself that life does go on." But the reality of young Daria's diminished mental and physical condition placed a strain on the marriage of Tierney and Cassini, which had already been weakened by the couple's mutual jealousies and Cassini's constant frustration of being viewed as what Tierney described as "the consort of a movie actress." By 1946, shortly before Daria was institutionalized in the Langhorn School in Pennsylvania, the couple had separated.

Meanwhile, in 1944, before the extent of her daughter's affliction was known, Tierney would play the part for which she is perhaps best associated — the title role in *Laura*. Ironically, while labeling the character as "the kind of woman I admired in the pages of *Vogue* as a young girl," Tierney later admitted that she was initially unenthusiastic about the part. In addition, the actress objected to the fact that the role had first been offered to Jennifer Jones, and later recalled asking Fox head Darryl Zanuck: "If Jennifer Jones doesn't want it, why should I?" But Zanuck convinced Tierney that the role would be good for her career — and he was right.

Selected by *Film Daily* as one of the year's best motion pictures, this mesmeric film noir begins with an investigation into the brutal murder of the title character, who was supposedly felled by a single shotgun blast to the face. Headed by police detective Mark McPherson (Dana Andrews), the investigation focuses on the two men closest to Laura: her would-be fiancé, Shelby Carpenter (Vincent Price), and her mentor, noted newspaper columnist and radio personality Waldo Lydecker (Clifton Webb). As the investigation proceeds, it is revealed that Carpenter, despite his relationship with Laura, has also been secretly involved with both Laura's aunt, Ann Treadwell (Judith Anderson), and Diane Redfern, a young model from the advertising office where he and Laura work. And the sharp-witted Lydecker, arguably one of the most fascinating characters in film noir, proves himself to be a calculating, intolerant manipulator who not only was in love with Laura, but also came to regard her as his sole possession, using various methods to fend off her potential suitors.

As he learns more about Laura, McPherson finds himself developing an attraction to the dead woman, a sentiment that is recognized by Lydecker: "Did it ever strike you that you're acting very strangely?" Lydecker asks. "It's a wonder you don't come here like a suitor, with roses and a box of candy. You'd better watch out, or you'll end up in a psychiatric ward. I don't think they've ever had a patient who fell in love with a corpse." In the midst of the investigation, however, Laura returns unharmed from a weekend trip to the country, and it is learned that the dead woman is actually Diane Redfern, who had been taken to Laura's apartment by Carpenter. As McPherson's feelings for Laura continue to grow, he also reluctantly suspects her of the crime. Later, McPherson realizes that the culprit was Waldo Lydecker who, unable to prevent Laura's upcoming marriage to Carpenter, had been compelled to end her life and mistakenly murdered Diane Redfern instead. In the film's thrilling climax, Lydecker returns to Laura's apartment to finish his original plan, but is gunned down by police before he can complete the deed.

Although the reviewer for the *New York Times* stated that Tierney "plays at being a brilliant and sophisticated advertising executive with the wild-eyed innocence of a college junior," most critics applauded the actress' performance in the film. Still, the actress herself would state years later that she never considered her portrayal of Laura to be "much more than adequate. I am pleased that audiences still identify me with Laura, as opposed to not being identified at all. Their tributes, I believe, are for the character — the dream-like Laura — rather than any gifts I brought to the role. I do not mean to sound modest. I doubt that any of us connected with the movie thought it had a chance of becoming a kind of mystery classic, or enduring beyond its generation."

Tierney's appearance in *Laura* turned her into a major star, and in her next film, the prestigious *A Bell for Adano* (1945), she was hailed for her "unobtrusive and sensitive" portrayal of an Italian peasant who falls in love with an American officer. But Tierney's biggest triumph was just ahead of her. In her second picture of 1945, she played the lead in *Leave Her to Heaven*, a haunting film noir that would be the most successful picture of her career. Portraying a possessive, calculating murderess, Tierney would later describe her role as "a plum, the kind of character Bette Davis might have played, that of a bitchy woman. I don't think I have such a nature, but few actresses can resist playing bitchy women."

Tierney's character, Ellen Berent, is revealed early on to be a woman who "loves too much," as evidenced first by her smothering devotion to her father and then her all-encompassing attachment to her new husband, writer Richard Harland (Cornel Wilde). Soon after their impromptu wedding, Ellen works to ingratiate herself with Richard's brother, Danny (Darryl Hickman), an invalid who is hospitalized at a clinic in Georgia. But Ellen's unreasonable possessiveness is soon revealed — at Richard's family lodge, called Back of the Moon, she refuses to hire a housekeeper or cook ("I don't want anybody but me to do anything for you," she tells her husband), she objects when Richard works on his latest book ("I hate your chapter, I hate all your chapters — they take up too much of your time"), and she is consumed with a jealous rage when the newlyweds are visited not only by Danny, but also by Ellen's mother (Mary Phillips) and her adopted sister Ruth (Jeanne Crain).

Later, while boating with Danny on the lake at Back of the Moon, Ellen tries to convince the boy to travel alone to Bar Harbor, Maine, to live with Mrs. Berent and Ruth, but Danny declines the offer. Thwarted, Ellen soon finds another way to have her husband all to herself. When Danny gets a cramp while swimming in the cold lake, Ellen remains in the boat, her face a emotionless mask as she listens to Danny's screams for help and allows him to drown. After the "accident," the couple moves to Maine, where Richard's grief over his brother's death is finally relieved when Ellen becomes pregnant, but her jealousy extends even to her unborn child: "This baby's making a prisoner out of me," she complains to Ruth. "I hate the little beast — I wish it would die. I never wanted it. Richard and I never needed anything else." Finally, jealous of Richard's preoccupation with the birth of his first baby, and insecure over his growing friendship with Ruth, Ellen flings herself down a flight of steps, causing a miscarriage. Devastated by the death of the baby, Richard confronts Ellen, who admits not only to willfully killing their child, but also that she'd purposely allowed Danny to die. Richard promptly leaves Ellen, but she exacts a final revenge when she takes a lethal dose of arsenic and cleverly makes it appear that she was murdered by Ruth. After a court trial, Ruth is ultimately acquitted, but Richard is sentenced to two years in prison for failing to report Ellen's guilt in the death of his brother. The film's end finds Richard being released after serving his sentence and returning to an eagerly waiting Ruth.

Critics were in stark disagreement over Tierney's performance in this Technicolor film; *Film Daily*'s reviewer wrote that the actress "has never shown to finer advantage," and Edwin Schallert, of the *Los Angeles Times* said, "Tierney enacts this sordid virulent role in a manner that will prove strangely arresting for those who look on." But in contrast, Howard Barnes reported in the *New York Herald Tribune* that Tierney "acts with a supreme lack of variety or intensity," and the critic from *Cue* completely panned her performance, saying that the role of Ellen Berent "requires acting of a high order. Miss Tierney fails to provide it ... [Her] efforts at depicting on-screen a murderously jealous woman are ludicrous." Despite these divergent opinions, however, Tierney's performance was judged good enough to earn the actress her only Academy Award nomination for Best Actress. Although she lost to Joan Crawford (for *Mildred Pierce*), Tierney would later state: "My own disappointment was lessened by the conviction, new to me, that I had developed a difficult character and not just a pretty face on the screen. I had been challenged by the role, and to have been nominated for an Oscar was excitement enough."

Tierney followed *Leave Her to Heaven* with a decidedly more sympathetic portrayal in *Dragonwyck* (1946), in which her Connecticut farm girl marries an elegant but demented landowner. The actress later stated that this picture was notable only because during its filming, she met future president John F. Kennedy. After her first encounter with the dashing young congressman, Tierney stated that "my reaction was right out of a ladies' romance novel. Literally, my heart skipped." The two began dating and Kennedy reportedly wanted to marry the beautiful star who was, at the time, still separated from her

Gene Tierney

husband. But according to Otto Preminger, director of *Laura*, the future president's family disapproved of Tierney, feeling that she was "unsuitable," and the relationship ended after several months. The actress later said that "ours was a sweet but short-lived romance [but] from the beginning I should have known our situation was hopeless."

While her personal life was in turmoil, however, Tierney's career continued

to thrive. In her second film of 1946, *The Razor's Edge*, she was cast as a predatory society girl who futilely pursues a spiritually bereft war veteran (Tyrone
Power). Overall, critics were not impressed with Tierney's performance, but
the film was a box office hit and was nominated for an Academy Award for
Best Picture (losing to *The Best Years of Our Lives*). The following year, the
actress starred in *The Ghost and Mrs. Muir* (1947), a charming comedy starring Rex Harrison as the ghost of a sea captain who falls in love with Tierney's strong-willed widow. Critics were mixed in their opinions of the film;
while the reviewer for *Variety* found that the actress turned in "what undoubtedly is her best performance to date," another critic merely noted Tierney's
"customary inexpressive style." Nonetheless, audiences went to the theaters in
droves and the picture would later serve the basis for the late 1960s television
series starring Hope Lange. Also that year, Tierney made her television debut
on Sir Charles Mendl's live video program, but her performance did not sit
well with her bosses at Fox, who objected to one of their top stars appearing
on a rival medium.

After the filming of *The Ghost and Mrs. Muir*, Tierney reconciled with
Oleg Cassini, who had started his own company in New York and was beginning to make a name as a top-notch couturier. Although the couple now faced
a commuter marriage, with separations of up to six weeks at a time, Tierney
soon became pregnant again and gave birth to her second daughter, Christina,
on November 19, 1948. Tierney later said she was fascinated by the infant's
"perfection and alertness," and that she "knew at last that we had a healthy
child." But the birth of young Christina could not salvage the couple's rapidly
deteriorating marriage. According to Tierney, the separations caused by their
careers became "more frequent and less painful," and the couple's efforts to
sustain their marriage were further undermined by newspaper photographs of
Cassini in the company of "slinky models." Tierney and Cassini even made
an ineffectual attempt at normal suburban living by purchasing a house in
Connecticut, but by 1952, the marriage was over. Many years after their
divorce, Cassini would tell an interviewer, "I was guilty of many breaches of
our marital vows. Mostly, I believe in retrospect, because she was the big star
and I was the nothing guy. I had to get even with the world because I was not
recognized. There was a recurring, negative pattern."

Professionally, Tierney next portrayed the wife of a Russian defector in
The Iron Curtain (1948); a publicity-shy heiress opposite Tyrone Power in *That
Wonderful Urge* (1948); and a wealthy kleptomaniac who is trapped into murder in *Whirlpool* (1949). Although these films were not among Tierney's most
popular, she earned a number of favorable notices. Of her role in *That Wonderful Urge*, the critic for *Variety* proclaimed, "This is one of Miss Tierney's
most successful performances ... she polishes off her role with considerable
grace," and for *Whirlpool*, Howard Barnes of the *New York Herald Tribune*
labeled her portrayal as "brilliantly bemused." The following year, Tierney

starred in back-to-back films noirs, *Night and the City* (1950) and *Where the Sidewalk Ends* (1950).

In *Night and the City*, which is set in London, Tierney portrays Mary Bristol, the long-suffering girlfriend of Harry Fabian (Richard Widmark). Harry ekes out a meager living by luring gullible tourists to the nightclub where Mary works as a singer, but he is constantly involved in unsuccessful get-rich-quick schemes and suffers from what one character calls "a highly inflamed imagination, coupled by delusions of grandeur." Finally, Harry stumbles upon what appears to be a sure-thing — the opportunity to become a top sports promoter by gaining the trust of a famous Greco-Roman wrestler Gregorius (Stanislaus Zbyszko) and his talented protégé Nikolas (Ken Richmond). But Harry's scheme angers Gregorius' son Kristo (Herbert Lom), who controls the wrestling game in the city and suspects that Harry will eventually betray Gregorius.

Harry's success appears to be certain when he arranges a bout between Nikolas and a wrestler known as the Strangler (Mike Mazurki), but while preparing to sign the contract at Harry's gym, the Strangler gets drunk and begins taunting Nikolas and Gregorius. The verbal attack results in an impromptu battle between the Strangler and Gregorius, and although the older wrestler prevails, the exertion causes him to suffer a fatal heart attack shortly after Kristo arrives on the scene. Enraged, Kristo offers a reward of £1,000 for Harry's capture, and the luckless hustler spends the rest of the night on the run. Finally, Harry is found at a waterfront shack by Mary, who offers him money to finance his escape. But by now, Harry has grown weary of running and, spotting Kristo waiting for him on a nearby bridge, comes up with one final scheme — to allow Mary to collect Kristo's sizable reward for his capture. Harry runs toward Kristo, screaming that Mary has betrayed him, but before he can reach the bridge, he is stopped by the Strangler, who kills him and tosses his body in the river.

Although *Night and the City* was hailed as an "exciting, suspenseful melodrama," the reviewer for *Variety* found Tierney's part rather superfluous, writing that the actress "is brushed off on her role." After this picture, she starred opposite Dana Andrews in *Where the Sidewalk Ends*, her final film noir. Here, Andrews portrayed Mark Dixon, a police officer with a reputation for brutality. "You don't hate hoodlums, you like to beat them up," Mark's commanding officer tells him. "You get fun out of it. You like to read about yourself in the newspapers, as the tough cop who isn't afraid to wade in anywhere. Your job is to detect criminals, not to punish them." Mark's harsh methods result in his demotion, but soon after, he accidentally kills a suspect, Ken Paine (Craig Stevens), during questioning about a murder case. Afraid for his job, Mark covers up the crime, attempting to blame the murder on a local gangleader, Scalisi (Gary Merrill). Instead, circumstantial evidence points to Jiggs Taylor (Tom Tully), whose daughter Morgan (Tierney) was Paine's estranged wife.

Working to absolve Jiggs Taylor from guilt, while concealing his own,

Mark falls in love with Morgan, and ultimately hatches a scheme that puts his own life in danger. He pens a note to his commander admitting his guilt, then confronts Scalisi, attempting to badger the gangster into murdering him. Scalisi realizes Mark's plan and refuses to rise to the bait, but is later captured by police and charged with Paine's murder. Mark is praised for his detective work but, overwhelmed by his conscience, he confesses his crime and goes to jail, content with the realization that Morgan has forgiven his misdeeds and will be waiting for him.

After earning praise for being "her usual fetching self" in *Where the Sidewalk Ends*, Tierney was next loaned to Paramount for a delightful comedy of errors, *The Mating Season* (1951), in which she plays an upper-class wife who unknowingly hires her mother-in-law as a maid. This was followed by *On the Riviera* (1951), a mildly amusing tale where she portrayed the wife of a French aviator hero; *The Secret of Convict Lake* (1951), a psychological Western that was dominated by the performances of Ethel Barrymore and Ann Dvorak; and *Close to My Heart* (1951), a clever soaper about a couple (Tierney and Ray Milland) who discover that the father of their adopted child is a convicted murderer. Tierney called her part in this film her "best role in half a dozen years."

But by now, Tierney's best films were mostly behind her. In her first picture of 1952, she played the society girlfriend of an Argentinian revolutionary in *Way of a Gaucho* (1952), but was overshadowed by the performances of Richard Boone and newcomer Rory Calhoun. Tierney did have better luck when she was cast opposite Spencer Tracy in *Plymouth Adventure* (1952) and with Clark Gable in *Never Let Me Go* (1953). From there, however, Tierney's career went downhill. The British-made *Personal Affair* (1954) was a boring would-be thriller; *Black Widow* (1954) offered the best role to Ginger Rogers as a temperamental stage star who murders her husband's mistress; the box office hit *The Egyptian* showed Tierney playing the peripheral role of the Pharaoh's sister; and in *The Left Hand of God* (1955), starring Humphrey Bogart, Tierney was panned as "practically stony."

Off screen, Tierney's romantic life was again in the news. In 1952, while filming *Way of a Gaucho* in Argentina, she met Prince Aly Khan, the former husband of Rita Hayworth. While initially unimpressed with the renowned playboy (she labeled him an "Oriental super-stud" and thought he resembled a "thinner version of Orson Welles"), Tierney soon succumbed to Aly Khan's charms and the two became nearly inseparable. With Aly Khan presenting her with a six-carat diamond ring and rumors swarming about their impending marriage, Tierney pointedly ignored warnings from such friends as international party-giver and writer Elsa Maxwell, who penned an article in the *American Weekly* cautioning that "such an alliance ... cannot help but mean eventual disillusionment and despair." But over time, the highly publicized romance became stormy, and when the prince's father, the Aga Khan, objected to his son's marriage to another Hollywood film star, the relationship ended.

The break-up with Aly Khan was the least of Tierney's problems. Since the early 1950s, the actress had suffered from sudden personality swings and frequently struggled to remember her lines; by 1955, the actress later recalled, she was, "so ill, so far gone, that it became an effort every day not to give up." A New York newspaper columnist provided an illuminating image of Tierney's behavior during this period, describing the actress as she fidgeted with her gloves in a local nightclub: "It was quite a performance and probably an unconscious one. She takes them off with great care and deliberation, one finger at a time. Then, just as meticulously, she puts them back on, smoothing each finger before moving on to the next. I tried counting how many times she did it one night, but after a while it made me nervous just to watch."

Cast in the lead role of a television version of Ibsen's *A Doll's House*, Tierney abruptly withdrew from the production and fled to New York, where her condition worsened. She became depressed and paranoid, and would sleep for unusually long stretches or spend hours at a time sitting motionless in a chair. "Suddenly I couldn't use my mind," the actress said in 1972, "and when I realized I was crippled, it frightened me terribly that I might not get my mind back." After consulting several psychiatrists, Tierney was admitted to the Harkness Pavillion in New York, where she was given a series of electric shock treatments. But a week after the last treatment, Tierney's depression returned, and she signed herself into the Institute for Living in Hartford, Connecticut. She remained at the Institute for nearly a year, undergoing a total of more than 30 additional shock treatments: "Pieces of my life just disappeared," Tierney recalled, terming the treatments "a barbaric practice I would never wish upon anyone else."

In early 1958, Tierney was released into the custody of her mother, but she soon suffered a relapse that culminated when she stood for 20 minutes on the fourteenth story ledge of her New York apartment. In her memoirs, Tierney stated that it was her own vanity that saved her: "The thought struck me," she recalled, "I don't want to end up on the pavement like so much scrambled eggs, my face and body broken. If I was going to die, I wanted to be in one piece, a whole person, and look pretty in my coffin." On the day following this incident, Tierney was admitted to the Menninger Clinic in Topeka, Kansas.

Tierney later stated that her first days at the famed clinic were "filled with feelings of hopelessness, of resignation," and while she received no further shock treatments there, she was subjected to a form of therapy known as "the cold pack," in which she was wrapped from the neck down in icy wet bedsheets, with her arms strapped to her sides. "It was like being buried in a snowbank," Tierney said. "I was so shocked, so affected mentally by being enshrouded like a mummy in those chilly, clammy sheets, I walked for days with my arms out from my sides, bent at the elbow, like wings.... My arms would not dangle or relax against my body."

Through intensive therapy with a female psychologist, Tierney gradually improved, and was released from the clinic in August 1958, eager to resume her film career. But on Christmas Day of that year, just three months after both *Time* and *Life* magazines had published features touting the actress's triumphant recovery, Tierney readmitted herself to the Menninger Clinic, stating that she was "sicker than I had ever been. I felt lost, without hope, less than childlike. I could not perform any task more complicated than having to feed myself." Tierney spent the next year at the clinic, where her therapy included painting, needlework and working in a local dress shop. In November 1959, Tierney was discharged from the clinic, and the following year, on July 11, 1960, she married Howard Lee, a Texas oil man whom Tierney had met while vacationing in Aspen, Colorado, shortly after her first release from the Menninger Clinic. Lee, who at the time was in the midst of divorcing actress Hedy Lamarr, visited Tierney during her second stint at the clinic and remained "wonderfully loyal throughout all those turbulent days," the actress recalled.

Eager to resume her film career, Tierney was signed in 1961 for the role of Constance MacKenzie in *Return to Peyton Place*, but she withdrew from the film when she learned that she was pregnant. But Tierney's "happy discovery" would turn into yet another tragedy when the actress suffered a miscarriage at four and a half months. The following year, she appeared in her first film in nearly a decade, portraying a small but glamorous role as a Washington hostess in Otto Preminger's *Advise and Consent*. Tierney revealed in her memoirs that the insurance company for Columbia balked at her association with the film, considering her "uninsurable" because of her mental history, but the company relented when Preminger threatened to cancel his coverage. Faced with the challenge of acting in a film after a seven-year absence, Tierney recalled that Preminger's firm stance "spurred me on even more."

In 1963, Tierney portrayed the mother-in-law of Dean Martin in *Toys in the Attic*, Lillian Hellman's story of a neurotic Southern family, followed the next year by *The Pleasure Seekers* (1964), a glossy soaper in which she played a cameo-sized role as the distraught wife of Brian Keith. Filming the latter picture, which satisfied her contract with Fox, was a "melancholy" experience, Tierney stated: "I had not made it for the money, or for pride, or even a final taste of glory. I had wanted to make the picture to finish the cycle and close the book, and recapture for one last time the fun that making movies had been for me ... but the Hollywood I knew was gone." The film would be Tierney's last big screen appearance.

In the late 1960s, the actress began writing a society-gossip column for a local newspaper in Houston, Texas, where she lived with her husband, and in 1969, she appeared on the hit television series *The FBI*, and in a made-for-TV movie, *Daughter of the Mind*, in which she played the crippled wife of Ray Milland. Her only other role would come more than a decade later, as a lesbian gossip columnist in *Scruples*, a 1980 mini-series starring Lindsay Wagner.

Away from the glamour of Hollywood, Tierney enjoyed a quiet, contented existence in Houston with her husband, occupying her time by attending parties, playing bridge, reading and raising funds for several causes, including mental health and retarded children's charities. In 1979, her frank and moving autobiography *Self-Portrait* was published; it revealed that the actress still occasionally suffered from "periods of odd behavior," and concluded with her judgment that "life is not a movie ... but if my life had been a movie, would a director have cast Gene Tierney to play the part? The bitter with the sweet makes for a better part." Her beloved husband Howard Lee died in 1981, and ten years later, on November 6, 1991, Tierney succumbed to emphysema at her home in Houston. She was 70 years old.

As an on-screen persona, Tierney will be remembered for her sleek elegance and classic beauty, but as a woman who endured life's harshest realities and emerged unbowed, she should forever be admired for her strength of character and the inner force that propelled her through the worst of times. Her existence was one that witnessed the most electrifying highs and the most devastating lows, but as the actress herself stated: "I had given up, fought back, shrunk from people, reached out, been overwhelmed by petty things, looked into a bottomless pit and found hope."

Film Noir Filmography

THE SHANGHAI GESTURE   *Director:* Josef von Sternberg. *Producer:* Arnold Pressburger. Released by United Artists, December 1941. *Running time:* 106 minutes. *Cast:* Gene Tierney, Walter Huston, Victor Mature, Ona Munson, Phyllis Brooks. *Awards:* Academy Award nominations for Best Score (Richard Hageman), Best Art Direction (Boris Leven).

LAURA   *Director and Producer:* Otto Preminger. Released by 20th Century–Fox, October 1944. *Running time:* 88 minutes. *Cast:* Gene Tierney, Dana Andrews, Clifton Webb, Vincent Price, Judith Anderson, Dorothy Adams. *Awards:* Academy Award for Best Cinematography (Joseph LaShelle). Academy Award nominations for Best Director (Otto Preminger), Best Supporting Actor (Clifton Webb), Best Screenplay (Jay Oratler), Samuel Hoffenstein, Betty Reinhardt), Best Art Direction (Lyle Wheeler, Leland Fuller, Thomas Little).

LEAVE HER TO HEAVEN   *Director:* John M. Stahl. *Producer:* William A. Bacher. Released by 20th Century–Fox, December 1945. *Running time:* 110 minutes. *Cast:* Gene Tierney, Cornel Wilde, Jeanne Crain, Vincent Price, Mary Phillips, Ray Collins. *Awards:* Academy Award for Best Cinematography (Leon Shamroy). Academy Award nominations for Best Actress (Gene Tierney), Best Art Direction (Lyle Wheeler, Maurice Ransford, Thomas Little), Best Sound (Thomas T. Moulton).

NIGHT AND THE CITY   *Director:* Jules Dassin. *Producer:* Samuel G. Engel. Released by 20th Century–Fox, June 1950. *Running time:* 95 minutes. *Cast:* Richard Widmark, Gene Tierney, Googie Withers, Hugh Marlowe, Francis L. Sullivan, Herbert Lom, Stanislaus Zbyszko, Mike Mazurki.

WHERE THE SIDEWALK ENDS   *Director and Producer:* Otto Preminger. Released by 20th Century–Fox, July 1950. *Running time:* 95 minutes. *Cast:* Dana Andrews, Gene Tierney, Gary Merrill, Bert Freed, Tom Tully, Karl Malden, Ruth Donnelly, Craig Stevens.

References

"Career Climaxed by *Shanghai Gesture*." *Life*, November 10, 1941.

Cassa, Anthony. "Gene Tierney: A Star Reborn." *Hollywood Studio Magazine*, December 1980.

Catsos, Gregory J.M. "Remembering: *Laura*." *Hollywood Studio Magazine*, March 1987.

"Debutante Makes Her Entrance in Broadway Success." *Life*, February 19, 1940.

Dudley, Fredda. "Laugh or Go Mad." *Silver Screen*, November 1948.

Hall, Gladys. "My Gene Tierney." *Silver Screen*, December 1946.

_____. "Practical but Provocative." *Silver Screen*, February 1946.

"Haunted Beauty." *People*, November 25, 1991.

Holland, Jack. "Must You Step on People's Toes?" *Silver Screen*, April 1951.

Keith, Don Lee. "Because She's Laura..." *After Dark*, July 1972.

Lambert, Gavin. "Beverly Hills Backdrop for the Enigmatic Star of *Laura*." *Architectural Digest*, April 1992.

Maxwell, Elsa. "The G.E.T. Girl." *Photoplay*, July 1947.

Parsons, Harriet. "Gene Tierney in 1940." *Hollywood Studio Magazine*, December 1980.

"Poetess." *American Magazine*, May 1941.

"Reborn Star." *Time*, September 29, 1958.

Rizzo, Frank. "Glimpse of a Troubled Life." *The Hartford Courant*, July 3, 1994.

"She Was Laura." *Newsweek*, January 29, 1968.

Shields, Jonathan. "Gene Tierney." *Films in Review*, November 1971.

Skolsky, Sidney. "The 'Get' Girl." *Photoplay*, April 1943.

Tierney, Gene, with Mickey Herskowitz. *Self-Portrait*. New York: Simon and Schuster, 1979.

"Welcome for a Troubled Beauty." *Life*, September 29, 1958.

"Whatever Happened to Gene Tierney?" *Silver Screen*, October 1971.

Wheeler, Lyle. "Treasure House." *Photoplay*, October 1950.

Wilson, Earl. "Cause for Complaint." *Silver Screen*, April 1945.

_____. "Tips About Aly for Gene." *Silver Screen*, October 1952.

Zacharek, Stephanie. "Gene Tierney: Behind the Glamorous Mask." *American Movie Classics Magazine*, February 1990.

Audrey Totter

A sleek blonde with pouty lips and soulful, ice-blue eyes, Audrey Totter began her film career as an MGM starlet and became, during her heyday in the 1940s, one of the studio's most versatile performers. Her sexual magnetism and acting talents notwithstanding, the petite beauty was perhaps best known for her distinctive voice, once described as "fairly dripping with allure." While she was adept as drama as well as comedy, Totter excelled at playing tough, hard-boiled dames who were cold as ice on the outside and equally glacial within, making her a standout in six films noirs: *The Postman Always Rings Twice* (1946), *Lady in the Lake* (1946), *The Unsuspected* (1947), *The High Wall* (1947), *The Set-Up* (1949) and *Tension* (1949).

Audrey Totter entered the world on December 20, 1918, in Joliet, Illinois, the eldest of five children born to John Michael Totter, a streetcar conductor who was born in Vienna, and Ida Totter, a native of Sweden. As a youngster, Totter showed a remarkable talent for mimicry and quickly learned to imitate the accents of her mother and father, sometimes earning a spanking for her accuracy. She was determined from an early age to pursue an acting career, despite the objections of her parents, and her decision was confirmed at the age of 12 when she was enthralled by the performances at a visiting circus. "Of course, later, MGM publicity changed this to read that I ran away as a child and joined the circus," Totter said in a 1988 interview in *Films in Review*. Although the tale of Totter packing "a comb and a few undies in a scarf and heading for the big top" was fiction, it cannot be denied that the determined youngster was bound for Hollywood. "My mother wanted to make me into a home girl," Totter admitted years later, "but I knew I was destined to be a star!"

After appearing in several school plays and local theater productions, Totter began her career when she joined the Chicago Repertory Theatre following her high school graduation. In her first professional role, she played the lead in *The Copperhead*, and was later seen in several summer stock productions, including *Stage Door* and *Night Must Fall*. Her experience in these plays led to radio work in Chicago in 1939, where she was heard on numerous commercials and such soap operas as *Bright Horizon* and *Road of Life*. She also landed the showy role of the streetwalker in *My Sister Eileen* and toured the country with the production, winding up in New York. Once there, Totter continued her radio career, starring in such programs as *Inner Sanctum, Reader's Digest Show, Cisco Kid* and *Uncle Walter's Doghouse*. On some occasions the actress was heard on as many as three shows a day and, by using her talent for imitating a wide variety of dialects, she eventually earned the title "the girl with the thousand voices."

By now, Totter's intriguing voice had enticed a number of Hollywood talent scouts, and after screen tests with two studios brought no contract offers, she signed in 1944 with MGM at a salary of $300 a week. The actress would later praise her apprenticeship in radio, and while she admitted that she "wouldn't have wanted to continue much longer with it," her last day on the air was a memorable one. Rushing into the studio for her final commercial before boarding a train for Los Angeles, Totter mistakenly announced into the live mike, "Use Ponds skin cream, tissue it off, and leave a light film of skin on your face overnight," she recalled. "The announcer doubled over with laughter and I ran out mightily embarrassed."

Once in Hollywood, Totter spent the bulk of her time undergoing a series of tests, participating in dramatic lessons and posing for publicity layouts. "MGM really believed in the value of a low build-up, and for that I was deeply grateful," Totter said. Finally, the starlet was given the first of her "bad girl" roles in her film debut, *Main Street After Dark* (1944), starring Edward Arnold, Selena Royle and Hume Cronyn. In her next feature, *Bewitched* (1945), Totter was unseen and unbilled — she portrayed the "evil voice" of the film's star, Phyllis Thaxter. "Phyllis wasn't too happy that I was hired," Totter said. "Later she told me, 'I could have done it, and wanted to, but they said no.' Maybe she could have, but she was very young at the time, and as a former radio actress, I naturally had a lot of experience with different voices. So I guess that's why MGM ... got me to do it."

Totter failed to make much of a splash in her next film, *Her Highness and the Bellboy* (1945), a box office bomb in which she did not speak a single line. But she was able to put her ability with accents to good use through her roles as a Viennese nightclub singer in *Dangerous Partners* (1945) and a dark-haired Rumanian siren trying to lure Robert Walker away from June Allyson in *The Sailor Takes a Wife* (1945). Soon after, while lunching in the studio commissary, Totter was spotted by famed director Victor Fleming, who insisted on casting her in a bit part in the Clark Gable–Greer Garson epic *Adventure* (1945). The actress later that said she balked at accepting the minor role, fearing that it would be a setback to her budding career, but Fleming insisted. "He was quite vicious to me so I thought I'd teach him a lesson," Totter said. "I played my scene with my head partly turned from the camera so no one would notice me!"

In Totter's next feature, the lavish *Ziegfeld Follies* (filmed in 1944 but released in 1946), she again was only a voice, this time playing a switchboard operator talking to Keenan Wynn. But this brief appearance was followed by the picture in which Totter finally made her first significant impact, the film noir classic *The Postman Always Rings Twice* (1946).

This riveting feature focuses on the doomed love affair between Frank Chambers (John Garfield) and Cora Smith (Lana Turner), who plot and carry out the murder of Cora's husband, Nick (Cecil Kellaway). When the couple are suspected of the crime, Frank is coerced into signing a complaint against Cora, but due to the efforts of a crafty district attorney (Hume Cronyn), Frank is set free, and Cora is given a suspended sentence after being found guilty of manslaughter. Later, Frank and Cora marry, but Cora is still bitter over Frank's betrayal, and when she discovers that he has been unfaithful, she threatens to reveal his role in the crime. When Cora learns that she is pregnant, the couple reconcile, but in an ironic turn, their car crashes while returning home from a midnight swim. Cora is killed, and Frank is sentenced to death for her murder.

As Madge Gorland, the woman with whom Frank has a brief dalliance, Totter's role in *The Postman Always Rings Twice* was small but flashy. The two first meet in a train station parking lot where Frank offers his help with Madge's stalled car. "I'm going to wait standing up. It's a hot day and that's a leather seat," Madge says suggestively. "And I've got on a thin skirt." Although Totter's two-minute appearance was overlooked by most critics, she earned high praise in *The Hollywood Reporter*: "Audrey Totter, doing the small part of a rather loose pick-up ... proves again that she has a great future, with easy command of what made our top screen sirens stars."

After *The Postman Always Rings Twice*, Totter played the only ingenue role of her career, in *The Cockneyed Miracle* (1946), a fantasy-comedy starring Frank Morgan as an Earth-bound ghost. But it was her next film, *Lady in the Lake* (1946), that became one of her best-remembered, and would be counted among the actress' personal favorites. Billed as "the most unusual film since talkies began," this picture would be the first to use the unique "camera I" method of filming, in which the camera served as the eyes of director and star Robert Montgomery. In casting the role of the leading lady, Montgomery recalled seeing Totter's bit role in *The Hidden Eye* and, defying MGM executives who thought Totter was too young and inexperienced for the part, Montgomery had her tested and, ultimately, cast her in the crucial role.

This complex film noir begins as Montgomery's character, Philip Marlowe, faces the camera, explaining that the audience will view the "Lady in the Lake" case "just as I saw it. You'll meet the people, you'll find the clues, and maybe you'll solve it quick and maybe you won't." The case opens when Marlowe is hired by Adrienne Fromsett (Totter) to find the missing wife of her boss, Derace Kingsby (Leon Ames). Before Marlowe is finished, he will encounter an unscrupulous gigolo (Richard Simmons), a crooked cop (Lloyd Nolan), and a murderous ex-nurse (Audrey Meadows)—and still find time to fall in love with Adrienne. At the film's end, after it is revealed that the former nurse had murdered both Kingsby's wife and the gigolo, Marlowe and Adrienne prepare to start their life together.

Totter later said that the film's original ending left it up to the audience to decide whether Marlowe and Adrienne wind up as a couple. After the sneak preview, however, audiences indicated that they wanted to see "the old-fashioned boy-girl clinch at the end," Totter recalled. "Bob was happy with the film the way it was ... but the studio insisted we go back and film that silly, pasted-on scene at the end. It took us longer to do that scene than anything else, because we began to giggle — we both thought it was ridiculous! The studio thought we were trying to wreck it, but that wasn't so, and finally we got it."

For the most part, reviews for *Lady in the Lake* were favorable — the film was described in *Time* magazine as "unusual, effective and clever," and the reviewer for the *New York Times* stated: "You do get into the story and see things pretty much the way the protagonist, Philip Marlowe does, but you don't have to suffer the bruises he does. Of course, you don't get a chance to put your arms around Audrey Totter, either." And Totter's portrayal was hailed in *Variety*, whose critic wrote, "Audrey Totter … looms as another major star on the Metro horizon. She's fine in this, in both her tough-girl lines and as the love interest."

Totter's next film was a rather syrupy comedy, *The Secret Heart* (1946), with Claudette Colbert and Walter Pidgeon, followed by *The Beginning or the End* (1947), an engrossing drama about the development of the first atom bomb, and *The Unsuspected* (1947), her third film noir. As this stylish feature begins, the body of Roslyn Wright (Barbara Woodell) is found hanging from a chandelier in the study of her employer, Victor Grandison (Claude Rains). A popular radio personality who specializes in the dramatic re-telling of true-life crimes, Grandison lives in a lavish mansion along with an assortment of quirky characters, including his trampy niece Althea Keane (Totter), her alco-holic husband Oliver (Hurd Hatfield) and his wealthy ward Matilda Frazier (Joan Caufield). Into this mix of personalities comes Steven Howard (Michael North), who insists that he married Matilda just days before she was involved in a fiery shipwreck, and tries to convince the confused young woman that she has suffered a nervous breakdown.

It is later revealed, however, that Howard had actually been engaged to Roslyn Wright and is determined to prove that she was murdered by Gran-dison. But Grandison has plans of his own. When Althea learns that he has been secretly spending Matilda's vast fortune in order to maintain his opulent lifestyle, Grandison shoots her, places the blame on Oliver, then arranges for Oliver to die in an automobile accident. Next, Grandison blackmails a fugi-tive into disposing of Howard, and attempts to poison Matilda, making it appear as if she committed suicide. But Grandison's seemingly perfect crimes are exposed when Matilda is found by police and Howard is rescued, just moments before he was to be killed. As he delivers his nightly radio program, Grandison watches as the studio fills with policemen, joined by Matilda and Howard. "Ladies and gentlemen, you are about to experience something unprecedented in the history of radio," he says calmly. "You are listening to my last broadcast."

Although *The Unsuspected* is today viewed as a brilliant example of film noir, the picture received mixed reviews at the time of its release. Dismissed by some critics as a second-rate *Laura*, William R. Weaver of *Motion Picture Herald* termed it "a bit too complicated for its own good," and John McCarten of *The New Yorker* called it "a seedy mystery in which the corpses of murdered people are piled around like buns in a bakery's day-old shop." And Totter met with equally dismal notices; in the *New York Times*, Bosley Crowther labeled her "as patly artificial as the plot." In one of the film's few favorable notices, however, the critic for *Variety* found that the picture was "loaded with thrills and suspense," and that "Audrey Totter and Hurd Hatfield show up well as the murdered pair."

The Unsuspected was Totter's first film on loan-out; ironically, the picture was produced by Warner Bros., one of the studios that had tested and rejected the actress during her radio days in New York. Back at MGM after *The Unsuspected*, Totter starred in her fourth film noir, *The High Wall* (1947), with Robert Taylor and Herbert Marshall.

Here, Totter portrayed Ann Lorrison, a doctor in a psychiatric hospital whose most recent inmate, Steven Kenet (Taylor), has admitted to strangling his wife, Helen (Dorothy Patrick). After being examined, it is discovered that Kenet has a subdural hematoma, which has caused him to suffer from excruciating headaches and blackouts. After undergoing a successful operation to alleviate his condition, Kenet realizes that he cannot remember the circumstances surrounding his wife's death, and undergoes drug therapy in order to recall the events.

Under the influence of sodium pentathol, Kenet reveals to Ann that he had spent two years as a flier in Burma, while his wife worked as secretary to Willard Whitcombe (Herbert Marshall), an ambitious executive in a publishing company. Returning home from Burma, Kenet found his wife at Whitcombe's apartment, where her overnight bag was seen on the bed. Ignoring her attempts to rationalize the situation, Kenet began strangling his wife, but blacked out and awoke later to find her dead. Later, Kenet forces Ann to take him to Whitcombe's apartment, where he recalls that his wife's overnight bag was missing after he awakened from his blackout, and realizes that she was killed by Whitcombe. Unable to prove his innocence, Kenet subdues Whitcombe and Ann injects him with sodium pentathol, after which Whitcombe admits his guilt in the death of Kenet's wife.

Upon its release, *The High Wall* was labeled "a likely lot of terrors, morbid and socially cynical" by the reviewer for the *New York Times*, and by Ray Lanning of *Motion Picture Herald* as "a somber, sobering melodramatic story." Totter made an abrupt change from the dark drama of this film with her next assignment, *Tenth Avenue Angel* (1948), a sappy Margaret O'Brien starrer, but all of the actress's scenes were cut from the final print. But she rebounded from this disappointment when she was loaned out for a series of top-notch films, starting with Universal's *The Saxon Charm* (1948), a riveting drama starring Robert Montgomery (he also directed) as a ruthless stage producer. Playing Montgomery's hapless girlfriend, Totter made her singing debut in this film, warbling "I'm in the Mood for Love." Next, she played a sultry seductress in Paramount's *Alias Nick Beal* (1949), a fantasy-drama about an honest politician who is corrupted by the Devil. Totter would later fondly speak of

Audrey Totter

her costar in this film, Ray Milland, saying, "Ray was a gentlemen. I remember telling him I was supposed to meet with a director who, unbeknownst to me, had a bad reputation with the ladies. 'Oh, no!' said Ray. 'You're not going alone!'"

Next, in her fifth film noir appearance, Totter starred opposite Robert Ryan in RKO's *The Set-Up* (1949), considered by many to be the highlight of her career, as well as one of the best fight pictures ever filmed. Based on a poem by Joseph Moncure March, the action in this fast-paced drama takes place during a single night at Paradise City, where boxing matches are held. One of the boxers is Stoker Thompson (Ryan), an aging fighter whose manager, Tiny (George Tobias), has accepted $50 from a local gangster (Alan Baxter) to insure that Stoker will lose the night's upcoming match. Confident that the washed-up Stoker will be beaten, Tiny does not tell him about the deal.

Meanwhile, as Stoker prepares for the evening's bout, his wife, Julie (Totter), expresses her increasing unhappiness with his career: "It ain't I want to hurt you, but what kind of life is this? How many more beatings do you have to take? It makes no difference to me if you go back to the docks, or drive a garbage truck, or go on relief, even. It's better than having you with your brains knocked out. It's better than having you dead." But Stoker is confident that he will win the match, and later, after fighting three of the four scheduled rounds, it appears that he will. In desperation, Tiny tells Stoker about the prearranged deal, but the boxer refuses to "take a dive," and knocks out his opponent in the final round. Afterward, Stoker is cornered in an alley behind the arena by the gangster and his henchmen, who beat him mercilessly and break his hand. As he staggers from the alley, Stoker is met by Julie, and he tells her with pride that he won his fight. "We both won tonight," Julie says, realizing that her husband's boxing career has come to an end. "We both won tonight."

Robert Wise, who directed *The Set-Up*, later said that Totter was "a lady, real quality, very professional. A pleasure for a director to work with." Wise recalled that she was a last-minute choice for the role of Julie, because Howard Hughes, then head of RKO Studios "wanted beautiful models for the role of Stoker's wife — just the absolute wrong types," Wise said. "Finally, Audrey was on one of the lists of suggestions that Hughes' office sent along. I hadn't known her work but after seeing some of her films I was happy to cast her in the role. I thought Audrey caught just the right measure of genuine love for her boxer and sadness in the role he found himself in. She had a most expressive face and great eyes that said a lot." Reviewers of the film agreed with Wise's assessment — the critic for *Variety* noted the "moving quality" of the scenes between Totter and Ryan, and the actress was noted in the *New York Times* for her "crisp, believable performance."

Back at MGM, Totter appeared in *Any Number Can Play* (1949), a lackluster drama starring Clark Gable as the boss of a gambling hall. The film didn't do much business at the box office, but it did lead to a relationship between Totter and her famous costar, a widower since the 1942 death of his wife, Carole Lombard. "We dated a bit and I could tell he was terribly lonely," Totter said. "He was a nice man, a gentleman, and he talked about Carole Lombard the whole time. Gable was madly in love with Carole — he never got over her. Most of the girls he dated had at least a slight resemblance to Carole Lombard, including me." After *Any Number Can Play*, Totter turned in a first-rate femme fatale performance in *Tension* (1949), her final film noir.

Here, Totter starred as Claire Quimby, whose husband Warren (Richard Basehart) is the bespectacled, unassuming night manager of a drug store. Frustrated with the couple's modest living quarters over the store, and bored with her stodgy mate, Claire spends most of her nights stepping out with other men while claiming to be at the local picture show. Finally, Claire cruelly announces that she is leaving Warren for Barney Deager (Lloyd Gough), who has enticed Claire with his wealth: "I've got what I'm looking for and I'm gonna grab it while I've got the chance. A real man," Claire tells her husband. "There's nothing to talk about. It was different in San Diego — you were kind of cute in your uniform. You were full of laughs then. Well, you're all laughed-out now." In an effort to win his wife back, Warren visits Claire at Deager's beachfront home, but earns only a humiliating beating for his troubles. Afterward, he vows revenge, and comes up with a scheme for the perfect murder. Adopting the name Paul Sothern (after looking at a magazine cover featuring MGM star Ann Sothern), Warren exchanges his glasses for contact lenses, rents an apartment, buys new clothes and claims that he is a traveling salesman for a cosmetics company.

Assuming his new identity on weekends, Warren falls in love with his wholesome neighbor Mary Chanler (Cyd Charisse), but he ignores his growing feelings in favor of his plans to do away with Deager. When he goes to Deager's home to kill him, however, Warren changes his mind, realizing that Claire isn't worth the effort: "If it hadn't been you it would've been some other guy," he says. But the following day, Claire returns to Warren, informing him that Deager has been killed and subtly enticing her husband to let her stay. The couple are questioned by two detectives, Collier Bonnabel (Barry Sullivan) and Edgar Gonsales (William Conrad), who soon begin seeking Paul Sothern in connection with the murder. Meanwhile, Mary reports Paul to police as a missing person, and when she shows them a photo, they realize that Warren and Paul are one and the same. Bonnabel, however, suspects that Claire is actually responsible for Deager's death and after he tricks her into revealing where she hid the murder weapon, Claire is taken to jail.

In *Tension*, Totter did an outstanding job in portraying the sullen murderess whose passions were fueled by greed. The actress was a particular standout in her scenes with Richard Basehart, including one where Warren happily shows his wife a new house he is planning to purchase. Claire refuses to even emerge from the car, rudely drowning out Warren's enthusiastic ravings by repeatedly honking the horn: "I think it's a miserable spot — it's 30 minutes from nowhere," she remarks. And later, after she and Warren are questioned by police, Claire shrewishly berates him for his nervous reaction: "What's the matter with you anyway?" she asks. "You want the cops to move in here and live with us? If you haven't got enough brains to agree with me, then keep your mouth shut. From here on in, I'm answering all the questions. Got it?" But critics disagreed in their appraisals of the film: The reviewer for

Motion Picture Herald said that Totter "does very well, making an unpleasant woman almost monstrous," and *Variety*'s critic wrote: "Miss Totter gets all the meaning of her character into her portrayal." But Bosley Crowther dismissed the entire production in the *New York Times*, saying that it "rambles from one thing to another in a most unsuspenseful way and ends with a shattering revelation which you can see coming a half-hour in advance.... A much better title for this picture would be 'Patience.'"

After her starring role in *Tension*, Totter was honored by *The Saturday Evening Post* (along with Jane Greer, Ava Gardner, Ruth Roman, Elizabeth Taylor and Shelley Winters) as one of the six promising actresses of the future. Despite this distinction, however, MGM farmed out the actress for three more loan-outs: Universal's *Under the Gun* (1950), Lippert's *FBI Girl* (1951) and RKO's *The Blue Veil* (1951), a film that Totter considers one of her least favorites. Returning to MGM for *The Sellout* (1951), Totter delivered a fine performance as a sympathetic honky tonk singer, but this crime drama would be her last picture at Metro. The actress later maintained that the quality of her assignments had declined since Dore Schary had joined the studio in the late 1940s and, eventually, edged Louis B. Mayer out as studio head. "Old L.B. Mayer ran a tight ship — he always knew what was going on. He was like an uncle to me," Totter said. "I'd been over to [Dore's] house and we were friends but it seemed there was little work for me."

After her departure from MGM, Totter returned to her roots in radio, beginning a long run as the star of CBS's *Meet Millie*. In January 1952, she inked an agreement with Columbia, but her best days on film were behind her. To entice the actress into signing, Columbia executives had promised her a number of coveted roles, including the part later played by Deborah Kerr in *From Here to Eternity* (1953). Instead, she was cast in *Assignment Paris* (1952), a far-fetched melodrama starring Dana Andrews and George Sanders. "I remember George stopped me and said, 'My dear, whatever are we doing this tripe for?'," Totter said years later.

Still, Totter's sudden dearth of quality film roles did not disturb the actress as much as one might imagine. In the same month she joined Columbia, she also met Dr. Leo Fred, chief physician at the Los Angeles Veterans Hospital, and later that year, she became his wife. "I'm psychic, and on our first date, I knew I was going to marry him," Totter recalled in 1988. "Thirty-five years later, I'm just as in love with him as I ever was. Don't let anyone tell you there's not such a thing as love at first sight!" Two years after her highly publicized wedding, Totter gave birth to a daughter, Elizabeth.

Meanwhile, the actress continued to appear in a series of mediocre productions, including *Man in the Dark* (1953), a plodding melodrama filmed in 3-D; *Cruisin' Down the River* (1953), a thinly plotted, low-budget musical starring Dick Haymes; and *Massacre Canyon* (1954), a "B" Western with Philip Carey and Jeff Donnell. By now, though, the actress was more focused on her husband and family than furthering her film career. "Before I got married I considered myself a very ambitious actress," she said years later. "But once I made the commitment [to marriage] it was very easy to keep." However, during the next ten years, she continued to maintain a presence on-screen, and while few of her films of this period effectively showcased the full range of Totter's talents, she did manage to shine in *Women's Prison* (1955) as an inmate jailed for gun possession. After a role in Republic's humdrum Western *Man or Gun* in 1958, Totter would not be seen in a feature film for six years.

Having debuted on television in 1953 in *Ford Theatre's* "Ever Since the Day," Totter appeared on the small screen throughout the decade, guesting on such shows as *Four Star Playhouse, Zane Grey Theatre* and *Climax*. In 1958, she signed on as a regular in her first series, CBS's *Cimarron City* with George Montgomery, but the experience was a disappointing one. "I was supposed to star as Beth Purcell every third week, but wound up waving from balconies in crowd scenes," Totter said. "I had a 40-week contract and they had changed producers, so they paid me off." Totter made another attempt at a regular series in 1962, playing Alice MacRoberts in ABC's *Our Man Higgins*, but the show aired against the popular *Dick Van Dyke Show*, and was cancelled after 13 weeks.

After a brief return to the big screen for cameos in *The Carpetbaggers* (1964), *Harlow* (1965) and *Chubasco* (1968), Totter continued her numerous guest spots on television, appearing in such top-rated programs as *Alfred Hitchcock Presents, Route 66, Perry Mason* and *The Virginian*. Then in 1972, the actress was offered another recurring television role, the tough but tender head nurse of *Medical Center*. The part, which had been recently vacated by actress Jayne Meadows, would prove to earn Totter a new generation of fans. "I jumped at the opportunity," Totter said later. "Nurse Wilcox is my kind of character, meaning she's got a heart under her hard exterior." She remained with the show until its cancellation in the mid–1970s, then made her final feature film appearance in Disney's *The Apple Dumpling Gang Rides Again* in 1978.

In recent years, Totter has continued to make occasional television appearances, including the telefilm *The Great Cash Giveaway Getaway* (1980) and such series as *Murder, She Wrote*. But she is mostly content to spend time with her family, and looks back fondly on her days on the silver screen: "I honestly loved every minute of my career," she has said. "I fell for a doctor and married him and lived happily ever after. My life away from the cameras has been one of complete normalcy."

Film Noir Filmography

THE POSTMAN ALWAYS RINGS TWICE   *Director:* Tay Garnett. *Producer:* Carey Wilson. Released by MGM, May 1946. *Running time:* 113 minutes. *Cast:* Lana Turner, John Garfield, Cecil Kellaway, Hume Cronyn, Leon Ames, Audrey Totter, Alan Reed.

LADY IN THE LAKE   *Director:* Robert Montgomery. *Producer:* George Haight. Released by MGM, January 1947. *Running time:* 105 minutes. *Cast:* Robert Montgomery, Audrey Totter, Lloyd Nolan, Tom Tully, Leon Ames, Jayne Meadows.

THE UNSUSPECTED   *Director:* Michael Curtiz. *Producer:* Charles Hoffman. Released by Warner Bros., October 1947. *Running time:* 103 minutes. *Cast:* Joan Caulfield, Claude Rains, Audrey Totter, Constance Bennett, Hurd Hatfield, Michael North, Fred Clark.

THE HIGH WALL   *Director:* Curtis Bernhardt. *Producer:* Robert Lord. Released by MGM, December 1947. *Running time:* 100 minutes. *Cast:* Robert Taylor, Audrey Totter, Herbert Marshall, Dorothy Patrick, H.B. Warner.

THE SET-UP   *Director:* Robert Wise. *Producer:* Richard Goldstone. Released by RKO, March 1949. *Running time:* 72 minutes. *Cast:* Robert Ryan, Audrey Totter, George Tobias, Alan Baxter, Wallace Ford, Percy Helton.

TENSION   *Director:* John Berry. *Producer:* Robert Sisk. Released by MGM, January 1950. *Running time:* 95 minutes. *Cast:* Richard Basehart, Audrey Totter, Cyd Charisse, Barry Sullivan, Lloyd Gough, William Conrad, Tom D'Andrea.

References

Andrews, Pauline. "Eager Beaver." *Motion Picture*, October 1945.

"Audrey Totter Does Her Bit." *New York Morning Telegraph*, August 23, 1952.

Bawden, James. "Audrey Totter." *Classic Film Collector*, Summer 1977.

Charles, Arthur. "Audrey Faces Life." *Modern Screen*, May 1948.

Gebhart, Myrtle. "Husky Voice Won Soap Opera Queen First Movie Contract." *Boston Sunday Post*, January 20, 1946.

Hall, Gladys. "Leo the Lion's New Love." *Silver Screen*, February 1947.

Hamilton, Sara. "Bubble Blonde." *Photoplay*, April 1947.

Lieber, Perry. Biography of Audrey Totter. RKO Radio Studios, circa 1951.

Mank, Gregory. "Audrey Totter." *Films in Review*, October 1988.

Martinez, Al. "It Pays to Marry a Doctor." *TV Guide*, September 28, 1974.

McClelland, Doug. "Audrey Totter." *Film Fan Monthly*, January 1969.

"Picture Plays and Players." *New York Sun*, October 16, 1946.

Skolsky, Sidney. "Hollywood Is My Beat." *New York Weekend Post*, April 12, 1947.

"Soap to Cinema." *American Magazine*, October 1945.

Totter, Audrey. "I Laugh at Wolves and It Works." *Silver Screen*, October 1952.

Wilson, Elizabeth. "Little Audrey." *Liberty*, July 5, 1947.

Claire Trevor

Claire Trevor was the quintessential hard-bitten floozy with a heart of gold, whose on-screen persona was typified by her portrayals of nearly every conceivable type of "bad girl," from hooker to gun moll. While her busy film career spanned a half century and consisted of more than 60 movies, Trevor was inexplicably relegated to mostly supporting roles in primarily "B" movies. But this husky-voiced performer possessed a talent that could not be denied and, perhaps more than any other actress, she represented the classic film noir femme in seven pictures from the era: *Street of Chance* (1942), *Murder, My Sweet* (1944), *Johnny Angel* (1945), *Crack-Up* (1946), *Born to Kill* (1947), *Raw Deal* (1948) and *Key Largo* (1948).

The gifted actress with the brassy blonde locks was born Claire Wemlinger on March 8; sources disagree as to whether she entered the world in 1909 or 1912. (In a 1992 *Architectural Digest* article, the actress proclaimed, "I'm 83 and I don't care who knows it," which would make 1909 the correct year.) This discrepancy notwithstanding, Claire was born into a life of comfort, the only child of Edith Morrison Wemlinger, a native of Belfast, Ireland, and her Paris-born husband, Noel B. Wemlinger, who owned a successful custom-tailoring business on Fifth Avenue. Soon after Claire's birth, the family moved from Bensonhurst, Long Island, to suburban Larchmont, New York.

Claire's first acting experience came during her high school years in nearby Mamaroneck but, expressing a sentiment that would come to characterize her Hollywood career, the actress said that she appeared in school and church plays "just for fun." Rather than drama, Claire's interests were focused on drawing and painting, in which she'd shown early promise, and after high school she took art courses at Columbia University. Before long, however, she decided to enroll with a close friend at the American Academy of Dramatic Arts, quickly finding that she enjoyed the challenge of studying diction, memorizing lines and responding to new stimuli. But she only stayed at the Academy for the first six months of the school term: "The second half is when you do all the Shakespearean plays," the actress said in a 1983 *Films in Review* article. "Instead of doing that, I felt that if I got out and worked and got a job, I'd learn more." And that is what she did.

Her first order of business was changing the rather ungainly last name of Wemlinger. While driving one day to make the rounds at the offices of Broadway agents, Claire was inspired: "There was a sign along the way — Sinclair Oil. I decided to call myself Claire Sinclair. Then I started using Claire St. Claire. Later, I was in some agent's office and he took a telephone book and put his finger down randomly on a page and it was Trevor." After playing a number of bit roles in stock companies, Trevor finally landed a job in the summer of 1929 with Robert Henderson's Repertory Players at the annual Theatre Festival in Ann Arbor, Michigan. While with the company, she was seen as a member of the Greek chorus in *Antigone*, followed by a minor role in *Lady Windemere's Fan* and a slightly larger part as Nina in Chekhov's *The Sea Gull*.

After the run of *The Sea Gull*, Trevor returned to New York and was cast by a Warner Bros. talent scout in a series of Vitaphone shorts being filmed at Warners' studios in Flatbush. She was next employed by Warners' stock company in St. Louis where, along with future film actors Lyle Talbot and Wallace Ford, she appeared in a new show each week. In the summer of 1931, Trevor was the leading ingenue of the Hampton Players in Southampton, Long Island. The actress earned five dollars a week, plus room and board, and the company split the profits at the end of the season. "We all did everything, even made the scenery," Trevor said, "and it was one of the best summers I ever had in my life. It was fabulous."

While appearing with the Hampton Players, Trevor was spotted by producer Alexander McKaig and in January 1932 he cast her opposite Edward Arnold in *Whistling in the Dark*, her Broadway debut. The show was a smash hit, running a year on Broadway and later going on tour. While performing in Los Angeles, Trevor was courted by several studios, but her sights were firmly set on the Broadway stage and she next accepted a role in *The Party's Over*. But despite good reviews, Trevor's second Broadway production was not successful, and when Fox Studios offered her a five-year contract, she quickly accepted. On May 7, 1933, Trevor arrived in Hollywood: "My father was so strict he insisted that my mother accompany me to Hollywood and live with me there," the actress said. "Well, she was ready for anything — she was full of Irish humor and love and excitement. She adored being on the set. When we had to work until two or three in the morning, she was thrilled — it was a party."

After only two days in Hollywood, Trevor was cast in the female lead in *Life in the Raw* (1933), a Western starring George O'Brien, followed by another O'Brien starrer, *The Last Trail* (1933), and *The Mad Game* (1933) with Spencer Tracy. In the latter film, Trevor received excellent notices for her role as a cigarette-rolling newspaperwoman, and she later said that her costar was "very, very impressed by me. This sounds braggadocio, but it was the truth.... He liked the way I delivered lines, tossed my lines away. He really liked my style."

During the next four years, Trevor worked almost non-stop in 20 films, most of which were fast-paced action melodramas for Fox that rounded off a double bill, earning her the title of "Queen of the B's." Of these films, her only top-drawer productions were *To Mary—With Love* (1936), a marital yarn starring Warner Baxter and Myrna Loy, and *Second Honeymoon* (1937), a popular comedy in which Trevor played the best friend of Loretta Young. But on loan to Samuel Goldwyn for *Dead End* (1937), Trevor delivered a performance that made Hollywood sit up and take notice. Playing a downtrodden streetwalker, Trevor logged less than ten minutes of screen time, but her powerful portrayal earned her an Academy Award nomination for Best Supporting Actress (she later lost to Alice Brady in *In Old Chicago*). Years later, Trevor acknowledged William Wyler's contribution to her performance, recalling that the famed director instructed her to report to the set with her hair uncombed, wearing stockings with runs and broken-down shoes. "I wore no makeup, just some eye makeup and some lipstick, that was it," Trevor said. "I felt dirty and run-down and awful, and it was marvelous. He gave me a wonderful feeling of the whole thing. I wish that scene had gone on forever."

Still, Trevor's home studio failed to capitalize on the new-found respect generated by her Oscar nomination. "That was kind of disappointing to me," she said. "I thought, 'Maybe *now* I can get into "A" pictures,' because *Dead End* was an 'A' picture, a very big picture." Instead, she was immediately cast in two low-budget quickies, *Big Town Girl* (1937), in which she portrayed a showgirl who becomes a singing sensation, and *Walking Down Broadway* (1938), which told the story of six Broadway dancers and their respective fates. The latter film concluded Trevor's contract with Fox; she later said that studio head Darryl F. Zanuck "never had faith in me. Why, I don't know. The point is, however, that if he hadn't confidence in a player, said player might just as well up and leave at the outset. And that's what I did."

However, while Trevor's performance in *Dead End* failed to make an impact at Fox, it did lead to her casting in a new CBS radio series called *Big Town*, which starred Edward G. Robinson as a crusading newspaper editor. Trevor was cast in the show as Lorelei, the editor's "girl Friday." Although the show was an instant hit, Trevor would quit after three years because Robinson, who had script control, was reportedly cutting the actress' part in order to boost his own. Still, Trevor gained something other than increased fame and income from her work on the series: In July 1938 she married the show's producer, Clark Andrews. By 1942, however, the marriage was over.

After ending her association with Fox, Trevor appeared as a jewel fence in Warner Bros.' *The Amazing Dr. Clitterhouse* (1938), a clever gangster-comedy starring Edward G. Robinson and Humphrey Bogart. Later that year, she was featured in *Valley of the Giants* (1938) as a shady saloon girl who is reformed by a lumberjack, then returned to Fox for *Five of a Kind* (1938), a programmer whose sole purpose was to exploit the famous Dionne quintuplets from Canada.

But one of Trevor's most memorable roles was just ahead. In 1939, she portrayed a trollop with a heart of gold in *Stagecoach*, starring John Wayne, Thomas Mitchell and Andy Devine. Receiving rave reviews for her performance, Trevor would later attribute her success in the film to the coaching of legendary director John Ford. On the set one day, the actress recalled, Ford "took Duke Wayne's chin and yanked it—in front of 200 people. He said, 'Duke, whaddya doin' with your chin, with your mouth? Acting is in the *eyes!*' I never forgot that." After this top-notch film, Trevor played the worldly-wise wife of a big-time criminal in *I Stole a Million* (1939), then appeared in *Allegheny Uprising* (1939) and *Dark Command* (1940). But the latter two films, both costarring John Wayne, were box office disappointments or, as Trevor termed them, "just crummy."

In 1941, Trevor made two Westerns, *Texas*, an agreeable horse opera that successfully combined action and comedy, and *Honky Tonk*, starring Clark Gable and Lana Turner. While *Honky Tonk* was a smash hit at the box office, Trevor remembered it with bitterness, revealing that most of her role as a hard-boiled barroom broad was cut from the final production. "I was so heartbroken when I went to see it, that I started to cry," she said in a 1983 *Films in Review* interview. "I don't cry easily. I started to cry and couldn't stop crying. I thought, 'I hate this business, I hate it, I'm through with it, I don't want to do it anymore.'" The next year she starred opposite Glenn Ford in *The Adventures of Martin Eden* (1942), a maritime melodrama that was poorly adapted from a stirring Jack London story, followed by *Crossroads* (1942), a diverting suspenser with William Powell and Hedy Lamarr.

Then, in *Street of Chance* (1942), Trevor entered the realm of film noir, portraying the first of the deadly, double-dealing femmes that she would play so convincingly throughout the remainder of the decade. As this picture begins, Frank Thompson (Burgess Meredith) is walking along a busy street and is briefly knocked unconscious by a piece of wood from a building under construction. When Thompson awakens, he is disconcerted to find himself in an unfamiliar section of town and possessing a cigarette case and hat with the initials D.N. He returns home to find that his wife Virginia (Louise Platt) has moved away. When he tracks her down, he learns that he has been missing for more than a year.

Determined to find out what happened to him during the missing year, Frank returns to the area where he'd been struck by the falling beam. Before long he is recognized by a girl, Ruth Dillon (Trevor), who calls him by the name of Dan Nearing and quickly spirits him to her apartment. Once there, Frank learns that, as Dan Nearing, he is being sought for the murder of Harry Diedrich, a wealthy landowner for whom Ruth worked as a maid. Over Ruth's objections, Frank insists on returning to the Diedrich mansion and later discovers that the murder was witnessed by Diedrich's paralyzed mother (Adeline de Walt Reynolds). Although the woman's paralysis prevents her from naming the killer, Frank creates a system of communicating with her, and it is ultimately revealed that Diedrich was killed by Ruth. When Frank divulges the truth about his past and his plans to return to his wife, Ruth pulls a gun, but she is shot and killed by the detective who has been tailing Frank.

In her first film noir appearance, Trevor delivered a fine performance of a deadly femme motivated not by greed, but by love, to murder. As she explains to Frank, she'd killed Diedrich when he discovered her robbing his safe: "I was trying to get that money for you — for us! You always said that you would never marry me unless we had some money. I didn't mean to kill him. I'm not bad. I'm not a killer." After being singled out as "sufficient" in the *New York Times*, Trevor next appeared in Columbia's big-budget horse opera *The Desperadoes* (1943) with Glenn Ford and Randolph Scott; *Good Luck, Mr. Yates*

Claire Trevor

(1943), a fanciful story of an Army reject's efforts to prove himself to his hometown; and *The Woman of the Town* (1943), a Western about Bat Masterson's ill-fated love for Dora Hand.

But the actress' career took a back seat to her personal life in 1943 when she married Lt. Cylos William Dunsmoore. The following year, on December 1, 1944, Trevor gave birth to a son, Charles Cylos, realizing one of her greatest ambitions: "From childhood on, I wanted children," she said in a 1982 interview. "Even babies in strangers' baby carriages appealed to me. If the maternal part of my nature hadn't been satisfied, I'd have felt like a failure in life. I consider myself lucky." Like her first union, however, Trevor's marriage to Dunsmoore would not last—the couple divorced in 1946, with Trevor charging her husband with being morose and sulky, failing to seek employment after leaving the service, and using profanity. Trevor was granted custody of their son but, tragically, Charles would die at the age of 34 in a 1978 commercial airplane crash.

After an absence from films of more than a year, Trevor returned to the big screen with a bang in a series of films noirs, the first of which, *Murder, My Sweet* (1944), is considered to be one of the quintessential films from the era. This exceedingly complex picture begins as private detective Philip Marlowe (Dick Powell) is hired by Moose Malloy (Mike Mazurki), a hulking, dim-witted ex-convict, to find his former girlfriend, Velma Valento. During the course of his search, Powell encounters a foppish playboy (Douglas Walton), a self-described "quack" psychologist (Otto Kruger), an aging millionaire (Miles Mander), his sexy young wife (Trevor) and her bitter stepdaughter (Anne Shirley). The missing person case grows more intricate when Marlowe is employed by the millionaire to locate a stolen jade necklace and later finds himself suspected by police in a series of murders. Ultimately, Marlowe not only learns that the millionaire's wife is responsible for the killings but that she is also the missing woman whom he'd initially been hired to find. In the film's explosive climax, the millionaire kills his wife and Moose Malloy, then turns the gun on himself.

Termed "pulse-quickening entertainment" by one critic, *Murder, My Sweet* received rave reviews upon its release and Trevor earned unanimous acclaim for her portrayal of the beautiful but deadly Mrs. Grayle, with Dorothy Manners of the *Los Angeles Examiner* calling the actress "a knockout in more ways than one," and the critic for *Motion Picture Herald* stating that her role "calls for considerable dramatic effort, which Miss Trevor supplies." Ironically, actress Anne Shirley would recall years later that she'd originally wanted the role played by Trevor: "I was dying to play a heavy. Then Claire told me she was sick of doing heavies and would love to do the role assigned to me," Shirley said. "Claire and I put our heads together and conspired to reverse the female casting.... But it all did us no good. Claire went back to being bad and fascinating and I went back to being good and dull."

Trevor's next film noir, *Johnny Angel* (1945), reunited her with George Raft, her costar in *I Stole a Million*. Here, in the title role, Raft portrayed a New Orleans ship captain seeking to unearth the circumstances behind the mysterious death of his father, also a ship captain, and his crew. Angel quickly finds, however, that he will receive no assistance in his quest from Gustafson (Marvin Miller), the head of the shipping line where he works, and that

Gustafson's indifference is matched by his secretary and devoted former nurse, Mrs. Drumm (Margaret Wycherly). The only party who appears to be concerned about Angel's plight is Gustafson's young, beautiful wife Lilah (Trevor).

From a young Frenchwoman, Paulette (Signe Hasso), Angel learns that $5 million in gold had been removed in the middle of the voyage by smugglers. During the transfer of the gold from the ship, Angel's father and the crew were murdered, but as the smuggler's boat pulled away, the smugglers were killed by a man whom Paulette could not identify. Ultimately, Angel discovers that Gustafson stole the money and committed the murders in a desperate effort to secure his wife's affections. The avaricious Lilah later double-crosses her husband and stabs him, but when he tries to shoot her during a confrontation in an abandoned shack, he is stopped by Mrs. Drumm, who kills him.

After her "convincing" performance in *Johnny Angel*, Trevor appeared in yet another film noir entry, *Crack-Up* (1946), in which she portrayed her only sympathetic noir femme. This picture begins as George Steele (Pat O'Brien), an expert on art forgeries, breaks into the museum where he delivers lectures and tells a crazed story about being involved in a train wreck. With no recollection of the events immediately following the accident, and later informed by police that no such wreck occurred, Steele determines to unravel the mystery. Before long, Steele uncovers a devious plot to substitute museum artwork with forgeries, but when a colleague is murdered, Steele finds that he is the chief suspect. With the help of his girlfriend Terry (Trevor), Steele manages to avoid capture and secure proof of the forgery scheme. But before he can contact authorities, he is abducted and taken to the home of Dr. Lowell (Ray Collins), the man behind the operation. "Perhaps you don't understand how much these paintings mean to me," Lowell explains. "Museums have a habit of wasting great art on dolts who can't differentiate between trash and these masterpieces that mean everything in life to me." Just as Lowell prepares to carry out his plot to kill Steele, an inspector with Scotland Yard (Herbert Marshall) arrives with police and Lowell is gunned down.

Upon its release, *Crack-Up* was hailed in the *New York Times* for its "competent performances" and in *Motion Picture Herald* as a "surprisingly suspenseful melodrama." Following this film, Trevor returned to her stage roots, performing in *Dark Victory, Tonight at 8:30* and Noël Coward's *Family Album*. She also contracted to play opposite Keenan Wynn in the Broadway-bound comedy *Out West It's Different*, but the play closed in Princeton, New Jersey, before reaching New York. The following year, the actress did appear on Broadway, costarring with Philip Dorn in *The Big Two*, but this production was another flop, folding after 21 performances. Trevor later said that the disappointing experience was "the finest thing that could have happened to me. The Broadway mirage was gone. I had always said I didn't want to be a movie star, and I had meant it. I woke up to the truth, and decided to try to be a Hollywood star. You have such advantages."

Back on screen, Trevor next played a rare comedic role in *The Bachelor's Daughters* (1946), a lightweight romp about four salesgirls who cook up a wild scheme to attract wealthy suitors. But she was back at her "bad girl" best in *Born to Kill* (1947), her fifth film noir entry, delivering a hard-bitten performance of a depraved woman driven by passions that she is powerless to withstand.

Described as a "homicidal drama strictly for the adult trade" and a "sexy, suggestive yarn of crime with punishment," *Born to Kill* tells the doomed story of Helen Trent and Sam Wild (Lawrence Tierney), who meet on a train platform on their way to San Francisco. Helen is returning home after her divorce, while Sam is hightailing it out of town after murdering his girlfriend and the man he found her with. Although Helen is engaged to one of Frisco's wealthiest bachelors, she is strongly attracted to Sam, who ingratiates himself into her family and winds up marrying Helen's affluent foster sister, Georgia (Audrey Long). Over the course of the film, Sam continues to pile up corpses — he kills his best friend Marty (Elisha Cook, Jr.) after mistakenly suspecting him of having an affair with Helen, and he winds up murdering Helen as well, just before he himself is shot and killed by police.

As Helen Trent, Trevor portrayed perhaps her most perverted noir femme; her lack of virtue is revealed early on when she discovers the dead bodies of Sam's first victims and quickly decides not to contact the authorities. ("It's a lot of bother — coroner's inquests and all that sort of stuff," she later explains.) And although she soon learns of Sam's crimes, she seems inescapably drawn to him, viewing the psychotic murderer as the personification of "strength and excitement and depravity ... a kind of corruptness." It is Helen's attraction to this corruptness that ultimately becomes her ruin.

The film's director, Robert Wise, would later praise Trevor for her top-notch performance in *Born to Kill*, stating that she "contributed very much to any scene she was in, was very professional, took direction very well. I particularly appreciated her patience and understanding in working with Lawrence Tierney, who tended to be a bit unstable at times. Claire and I always hoped to work together again but the right project never came along." Trevor and Wise appeared to belong to a mutual admiration society; in a 1983 interview, she stated that Wise was still somewhat of a novice when he directed *Born to Kill*, but "boy was he good," she said. "I was thrilled to work with him."

Next, continuing her spate of appearances in first-rate films noirs, Trevor starred with Dennis O'Keefe and Marsha Hunt in *Raw Deal* (1948), her sixth picture from the era. Here, Trevor played Pat Regan, narrator of the film and devoted girlfriend of Joe Sullivan (O'Keefe), a gangster who has been convicted for a crime actually committed by his underworld boss Rick Coyle (Raymond Burr). During his stint in prison, Joe is visited by a stranger who had become interested in his case, Ann Martin (Hunt). Despite his attraction to Ann, Joe ignores her advice to await his parole, and breaks out of prison with

Pat's help, planning to collect a $50,000 payoff from Rick and leave the country. On the way to retrieve the money, Joe abducts Ann from her home and Pat soon realizes that her lover is becoming affected by Ann's principled moralizing: "Chiseling little doll face," Pat sneers. "What is she to you that I'm not? She's got her hooks into you good. She's wormed her way into you so that you don't know what you're saying, where you're going."

Managing to avoid a four-state dragnet, Joe arrives as scheduled at a remote fishing shop to meet with Rick, but instead is met by one of Rick's underlings, Fantail (John Ireland), who tries to kill him. During a struggle, Ann shoots Fantail and later realizes that she is in love with Joe. Although he returns her feelings, Joe knows he is no good for Ann, and nobly sends her home in a rented car and continues his plans to flee to South America with Pat. Later, waiting in a San Francisco motel before boarding the ship, Pat learns that Ann has been kidnapped by Rick, but fails to tell Joe. But as their ship is preparing for departure, Pat realizes that Joe will always be in love with Ann: "Suddenly I saw that every time he kissed me, he'd be kissing Ann. Every time he held me, spoke to me, danced with me, ate, drank, played, sang — it would be Ann." Realizing this, Pat tells Joe about Ann's abduction, and he immediately departs the ship. After a gun battle leaves Rick dead, Joe is able to rescue Ann, but he has been mortally wounded, and Pat arrives with police in time to see Joe die in Ann's arms.

Hailed by one critic as a "well-performed and exceptionally well photographed rough and tumble melodrama," *Raw Deal* met with favorable notices upon its release and Trevor earned praise in *Variety* for her "first-rate interpretation of a gangster moll, maintaining a steady sense of strain without going to pieces." After her appearance in the film, Trevor made a another try at matrimony, this time with realtor and sometime-movie producer Milton Bren. It appeared that, for the actress, the third time was the charm — in a 1992 *Architectural Digest* interview, a neighbor of the couple claimed that their union was "one of Hollywood's truly good marriages. I mean, they shared the sea, the kids, parties, travel. On their last boat they must have traveled 50,000 miles. Milton used to say that Claire was the most intellectual person he ever met." The couple had one son, Peter, and remained married until Bren's death in 1978.

Meanwhile, Trevor's professional life was about to reach new heights. In her last film noir, *Key Largo* (1948), she played the alcoholic mistress of a vicious hoodlum, Johnny Rocco (Edward G. Robinson), whose gang takes over a hotel in one of the Key Islands off the coast of Florida. Held hostage are the hotel's owner James Temple (Lionel Barrymore), his widowed daughter-in-law Nora (Lauren Bacall) and Frank McCloud (Humphrey Bogart), an ex–war hero and a friend of Nora's late husband. After murdering a local policeman, Rocco successfully sells a stack of counterfeit bills to an associate, then forces Frank to pilot a boat to Cuba. But once aboard, Frank manages to kill Johnny's four henchmen and Johnny himself.

As Gaye Dawn, Trevor all but stole the picture away from her more famous costars, portraying a pathetic boozer who would do almost anything for a drink. In what is perhaps the film's best scene, Gaye shakily warbles "Mean as Can Be," a tune from her glory days as a nightclub chanteuse, then collapses in horror when the sadistic Rocco refuses to give her the drink promised in return for her performance. For her portrayal, Trevor deservedly won the Academy Award for Best Supporting Actress, beating out Ellen Corby and Barbara Bel Geddes in *I Remember Mama*, Agnes Moorehead in *Johnny Belinda* and Jean Simmons in *Hamlet*.

On the heels of her triumph in *Key Largo*, Trevor turned in another of her magnificent performances in *The Velvet Touch* (1948), portraying an acid-tongued Broadway actress falsely accused of murder, followed by a rare "normal" role as the wife of the legendary baseball player in *The Babe Ruth Story* (1948), and a breezy portrayal of a befuddled secretary *in The Lucky Stiff* (1949). With the advent of the 1950s, the actress continued to offer stellar portrayals in a wide variety of characterizations, but she frequently had to rise above the less-than-stellar material in such films as *Best of the Badmen* (1951), yet another big budget Western roundup; *Hard, Fast and Beautiful* (1951), the Ida Lupino-directed tale of a tennis champion exploited by her ambitious mother; *Stop, You're Killing Me* (1952), the unsuccessful remake of the 1938 Edward G. Robinson starrer *A Slight Case of Murder*; and *The Stranger Wore a Gun* (1953), a Randolph Scott vehicle filmed in 3-D. During this period, Trevor also made her television debut, appearing in the 1953 production of "Alias Nora Hale" for NBC's *Ford Theatre*. The actress would later say that she enjoyed working in this new medium, explaining that it allowed her to do "what I can't do in pictures — play sympathetic, normal roles."

Then in 1954, Trevor won accolades for her portrayal of a warm-hearted kept woman in *The High and the Mighty*, an air disaster film costarring John Wayne, Robert Stack, Jan Sterling and Laraine Day. Along with Sterling, the film earned Trevor another Academy Award nomination for Best Supporting Actress, but the statue would be won that year by Eva Marie Saint for *On the Waterfront*.

In 1955 Trevor played yet another hard-boiled saloon keeper with a heart of gold in *Man Without a Star*, followed by the wise-cracking pal of the title character in *Lucy Gallant*. But in her sole film of 1956, Trevor appeared in a real clunker, *The Mountain* (1956), which starred Spencer Tracy and Robert Wagner as two brothers feuding over the loot contained in a downed airplane. Years later, Trevor would leave no doubts as to her impressions of this film, describing it as "a horrible picture. Oh, God, that was a terrible picture! It goes on forever and it's bad. Robert Wagner ... looked like he was 12 years old and Spence had already gotten heavy and old-looking. It was ludicrous." Still, the actress compensated for this rather absurd film with her appearance that year opposite Fredric March in *Dodsworth*, an NBC-TV Producers Showcase Production. For her role as Fran, Trevor won an Emmy Award for Best Actress in a Single Performance.

By now, Trevor's screen career was nearing its end. Of the five films she appeared in during the next decade, the best were *Marjorie Morningstar* (1958), in which she turned in a fine performance as the title character's mother, and *The Capetown Affair* (1967), with Trevor portraying a bag lady who gets mixed up with a Communist ring. The latter film would be her last appearance on the big screen for nearly 20 years. Instead, she was seen in numerous roles on television, including appearances on *Ford Theatre, G.E. Theatre, Playhouse 90, Desilu Playhouse, The Untouchables, Dr. Kildare, Alfred Hitchcock Presents* and, more recently, *The Love Boat* and *Murder, She Wrote*. She also returned to the stage in 1968 after a 14-year absence, playing a cigar-smoking lesbian in *The Killing of Sister George*, and eight years later, she costarred with Rock Hudson and Leif Erickson in a 21-week national tour of *John Brown's Body*, a narrative poem adapted by actor Charles Laughton.

In 1982, at age 73, Trevor was cast as Sally Field's tart-tongued mother in her last feature film, *Kiss Me Goodbye*, stating that she accepted the role because "I get to be glamorous and I get to be funny." But this mildly amusing romantic comedy was a box office dud and Trevor later expressed her disappointment over the reviews: "It was only meant for entertainment. The critics killed the picture. Why did they take the axes and slaughter it? I don't understand ... I really don't. I thought it was a darling picture."

Trevor's most recent appearance was in a 1987 television movie, *Breaking the Waves*, and the actress has since devoted much of her time renewing her love for painting: "To me, acting and painting are closely related. You need imagination for both. I don't know how good the paintings are, nor do I care. I'm filling my hours with pleasure, and you can't take that away. Painting is a lot cheaper than going to a psychiatrist."

Although she was most often associated with the numerous "B" movies in which she appeared, Claire Trevor was much more than a "B" movie actress. As she demonstrated in stellar performances in such films as *Dead End, Murder, My Sweet* and *Key Largo*, hers was an acting gift that could not be denied. Her innate talent was perhaps best summed up by Robert Wise, her director in *Born to Kill*, when he said, "She was a fine actress and a lady of quality. Although she didn't attain the big 'star' name of some others in that period, she certainly deserved to be a big star from an acting standpoint."

Film Noir Filmography

STREET OF CHANCE   *Director:* Jack Hively. *Producer:* Burt Kelly. Released by Paramount, November 1942. *Running time:* 74 minutes. *Cast:* Burgess Meredith, Claire Trevor, Louise Platt, Sheldon Leonard, Frieda Inescort, Jerome Cowan, Adeline de Walt Reynolds.

MURDER, MY SWEET (Original release title: *Farewell, My Lovely*)　*Director:* Edward Dmytryk. *Producer:* Adrian Scott. Released by RKO, December 1944. *Running time:* 95 minutes. *Cast:* Dick Powell, Claire Trevor, Anne Shirley, Otto Kruger, Mike Mazurki, Miles Mander, Douglas Walton.

JOHNNY ANGEL　*Director:* Edwin L. Marin. *Producer:* Jack Gross. Released by RKO, December 1945. *Running time:* 76 minutes. *Cast:* George Raft, Claire Trevor, Signe Hasso, Lowell Gilmore, Hoagy Carmichael, Marvin Miller, Margaret Wycherly.

CRACK-UP　*Director:* Irving Reis. *Producer:* Jack J. Gross. Released by RKO, October 1946. *Running time:* 93 minutes. *Cast:* Pat O'Brien, Claire Trevor, Herbert Marshall, Ray Collins, Wallace Ford.

BORN TO KILL　*Director:* Robert Wise. *Producer:* Herbert Schlom. Released by RKO, May 1947. *Running time:* 92 minutes. *Cast:* Claire Trevor, Lawrence Tierney, Walter Slezak, Philip Terry, Audrey Long, Elisha Cook, Jr., Isabel Jewell, Esther Howard.

RAW DEAL　*Director:* Anthony Mann. *Producer:* Edward Small. Released by Eagle-Lion, July 1948. *Running time:* 79 minutes. *Cast:* Dennis O'Keefe, Claire Trevor, Marsha Hunt, John Ireland, Raymond Burr, Curt Conway, Chili Williams.

KEY LARGO　*Director:* John Huston. *Prodcuer:* Jerry Wald. Released by Warner Bros., July 1948. *Running time:* 100 minutes. *Cast:* Humphrey Bogart, Edward G. Robinson, Lauren Bacall, Lionel Barrymore, Claire Trevor, Thomas Gomez, Harry Lewis. *Awards:* Academy Award for Best Supporting Actress (Claire Trevor).

References

Aronson, Steven M.L. "Claire Trevor: A Spacious New York Apartment for *Key Largo*'s Best Supporting Actress." *Architectural Digest*, April 1992.
Christy, George. "The Great Life." *The Hollywood Reporter*, May 27, 1982.
Dreier, Hans. "Star in Your Home." *Photoplay*, August 1949.
Gallagher, John. "Claire Trevor." *Films in Review*, November 1983.
Gebhart, Myrtle. "Tired of Being Typed." *Boston Sunday Post*, June 27, 1948.
Hagen, Ray. "Claire Trevor." *Films in Review*, November 1963.
Holland, Jack. "What a Wife Can Learn from the 'Other Woman.'" *Silver Screen*, June 1945.
_____. "What Can a Man Teach a Woman?" *Silver Screen*, September 1949.
Rainey, Buck. "Claire Trevor: A Provocative Femme Fatale." *Classic Images*, November 1989.
Rosenfield, Paul. "Claire Trevor: A Movie Star with a Real Life." *The Los Angeles Times*, July 18, 1982.
Service, Faith. "My Black Lace Moments." *Silver Screen*, March 1947.
Skolsky, Sidney. "Trevor the Trouper." *New York Weekend Post*, August 8, 1948.
Trevor, Claire. "The Company Remembers *Stagecoach*." Action, September-October 1971.
Wilson, Earl. "It's More Fun to Be Bad." *Silver Screen*, September 1941.

Lana Turner

Lana Turner was a star in the true sense of the word — billed early in her career as "The Sweater Girl," and alternately touted as the successor to Crawford, Harlow, Loy and Colbert, she was the epitome of the Hollywood glamour girl. She was a luminary whose private exploits frequently eclipsed her on-screen performances, and whose talent was usually overshadowed by her striking looks, glamorous charisma and steamy sensuality. Nonetheless, in a diversity of roles that ranged from the tragic *Ziegfeld Girl* (1941) to the frigid mother in *Peyton Place* (1957) to the ambitious actress in *Imitation of Life* (1959), Lana Turner left behind a body of celluloid that has made her a legend. While she only appeared in two films noirs, one, *The Postman Always Rings Twice* (1946), represents the noir experience at its dark and desperate best.

Lana Turner was born Julia Jean Mildred Frances Turner on February 8, 1921, in Wallace, Idaho. (Although a number of her biographers have stated that she was born in 1920, Turner consistently maintained that the 1921 date was the correct one, stating, "Why would I lie for one year?") Judy, as she was called, frequently moved from town to town with her mother Mildred and her father Virgil, who worked a variety of jobs, including selling insurance, working in the mines or on the docks, and even bootlegging. At the beginning of the Depression, the family moved to San Francisco; the Turners separated soon after, and in December 1930, Virgil was found dead on the streets of San Francisco, the victim of a robbery.

Over the next several years, Mildred and Judy moved to Sacramento, back to San Francisco and finally to Los Angeles, where Mildred worked in a beauty shop and her daughter enrolled at Hollywood High School. One of her classmates was actress Nanette Fabray, who later described the 15-year-old as "the most incredibly beautiful girl we had ever seen. Even the teachers stared at her ... even then she had the bearing of a princess. We all knew she would be a movie star."

It was in January 1936, shortly after her move to Los Angeles, that the legend of Lana Turner was born. Although she was not "discovered" at Schwab's Pharmacy, as Hollywood mythology long held, Turner herself said that she was indeed seated at a soda fountain in a drug store across from her high school when she was introduced by the store's manager to Billy Wilkerson, publisher of *The Hollywood Reporter*. Wilkerson got Turner an agent and, after working as an extra in David O. Selznick's *A Star Is Born* (1937), she was interviewed by director Mervyn LeRoy for a role as a murder victim in Warner Bros.' *They Won't Forget* (1937). LeRoy hired her and suggested her name change to Lana. On February 22, 1937, Lana Turner signed a contract with Warner Bros. with a starting salary of $50 a week.

In *They Won't Forget*, Turner had a brief but pivotal role as Mary Clay, a sexy schoolgirl. Although Turner was seen only in the film's opening reels, the actress made a tremendous impact on the moviegoing public. She was dubbed "America's Sweater Girl" and, as one columnist noted, "more sheep were shorn for wool in the years that followed than in all history, for sweaters became the rage."

Turner next played a bit part in *The Great Garrick* (1937), then was loaned out to United Artists to play a Eurasian dancer in *The Adventures of Marco Polo* (1938). But neither film made much of an impact on her budding career. When Mervyn LeRoy moved to MGM, he requested Turner's release from her Warners contract, which was granted. At MGM, Turner was cast as Mickey Rooney's love interest in *Love Finds Andy Hardy* (1938), and then appeared in a series of programmers, including *Rich Man, Poor Girl* (1938), *Dramatic School* (1938) and *Calling Dr. Kildare* (1939).

During this time, Turner lightened her auburn hair to a bright red and took part in MGM's rigorous series of elocution, dramatic and dancing lessons. Hundreds of her still photographs were distributed to movie magazines and newspapers nationwide and the public showered her with enthusiastic devotion. After leading parts in minor films including *Dancing Co-Ed* (1939), the first movie in which she received top billing, MGM began to groom her for the stardom she would ultimately attain.

Dancing Co-Ed was also notable for being the film on which Turner met the first of her seven husbands, bandleader Artie Shaw, who costarred. The two eloped in 1940, but the union would only last a few months. In the movie magazines of the day, Turner claimed that Shaw found fault with everything about her, including her makeup and clothes, but the musician later insisted that the split was amicable and said that the two maintained a friendly and "occasionally intimate" relationship in the years that followed.

The turning point in Turner's career came with her 1941 role in *Ziegfeld Girl*, in which she portrayed an ill-fated showgirl. Of her role in this film, the actress stated, "For once I studied my part long and faithfully, determined to make my Ziegfeld girl not merely a clotheshorse and decoration but, if possible, a human being." Turner obviously succeeded in her mission, for she won critical acclaim, including one reviewer's praise of her "vital, memorable, glamorous and appealing performance." Within the span of only one year, she was cast in films opposite three of Hollywood's top leading men — Spencer Tracy in *Dr. Jekyll and Mr. Hyde* (1941), Clark Gable in *Honky Tonk* (1941), and Robert Taylor in *Johnny Eager* (1942), her first film noir.

In *Johnny Eager*, Turner is Lisbeth Barr, an idealistic sociology student who falls in love with the title character (Taylor), an ex-convict working as a taxi driver. Lisbeth later discovers, however, that Eager's reformed appearance is merely a front for his real occupation as a mob leader who is behind an effort to open an illegal dog track. Meanwhile, Eager discovers that his new girl is the stepdaughter of the district attorney, John Farrell (Edward Arnold), who has issued an injunction to prevent the opening of the dog track. Despite his growing feelings for Lisbeth, Eager implicates her in a staged murder so that he can blackmail Farrell into lifting the injunction. Lisbeth suffers a mental breakdown because of the scheme, and when Eager visits her, he unwillingly admits that he has fallen in love with her. "I've told that to other women, see, but I never meant it before. Never meant it until now." But when Eager tells Lisbeth the truth about the phony murder, she refuses to believe him. Eager risks his life to prove it, and after he nobly turns her over to her ex-fiancé, he is gunned down by police.

Although the highlight of the film was Van Heflin's Oscar-winning portrayal of Eager's alcoholic sidekick, Turner was praised by a number of reviewers, including the critic for *Photoplay*, who stated, "Her performance here is proof La Turner can act." And of working with Turner, costar Robert Taylor later recounted the effect that the budding star had on him: "Lana wasn't as 'busty' as her pin-up pictures, but her face was delicate and beautiful. I have never seen lips like hers, and though I was never known to run after blondes, Lana was the exception. I couldn't take my eyes off her, and there were times during *Johnny Eager* that I thought I'd explode. Her voice was like a breathless child. I don't think she knew how to talk without being sexy. When she said, 'Good morning,' I melted."

In 1942, less than a year after her divorce from Shaw became final, Turner married Josef Stephen Crane, whom she had known for only a short time. Turner frankly explained the rationale behind her impulsive second marriage: "There is nobody so charming as Steve Crane when he wants to be charming. I am lonely unless I have someone to love, and there was Steve. I married him." In December of that year, Turner announced that she was expecting a baby, but this joyous news was marred by the disclosure that Crane's divorce from his first wife, a society girl from Indianapolis, would not become final until January 1943. Turner and Crane were remarried in May 1943 and two months later, their daughter, Cheryl, was born. But this marriage, too, was doomed for failure. Turner later stated that her husband was "unhappy. Nothing had gone right for him. He had to work and he undoubtedly resented my carrying the whole load. Obviously, being remarried in desperation, having no life together, this was an alliance that couldn't last." And it didn't. In April 1944, Turner sued for divorce and custody of baby Cheryl.

Between 1943 and 1946, Turner appeared in seven films, including *Slightly Dangerous* (1943), as a small-town soda fountain clerk; *Marriage Is a Private Affair* (1944), her first film after the birth of her daughter; and *Week-end at the Waldorf* (1945), a box office record-breaker which was an updated version of the star-studded *Grand Hotel* (1932). But Turner's most memorable film during this period was the unforgettable noir classic *The Postman Always Rings Twice* (1946).

Based on James M. Cain's hard-hitting romance, *Postman* focuses on the ill-fated relationship between Cora Smith (Turner) and Frank Chambers (John Garfield), a charming drifter who accepts a job at the roadside café owned by Cora and her husband Nick (Cecil Kellaway). After an aborted attempt to run away together, Frank and Cora murder Nick, but they are instantly suspected of the crime and Frank is coerced by the district attorney into signing a complaint against his lover. But due to the efforts of a wily defense attorney (Hume Cronyn), Frank is set free, and Cora is given a suspended sentence after being convicted of manslaughter. Though the couple marry, Cora is still bitter over Frank's betrayal, and she threatens to expose his role in the crime after she discovers that he engaged in a brief affair while she was out of town attending her mother's funeral.

Cora discovers that she is pregnant and the couple reconcile, renewing their love for each other in a midnight ocean swim. But in an ironic twist, their car crashes while returning home from their swim and Cora is killed. Although he is innocent, Frank is convicted for her murder and sentenced to death. Frank accepts his fate, realizing that Cora paid for Nick's death with hers, and that he must now do the same. As he awaits his execution, Frank tells the district attorney, "You know, there's something about this which is like expecting a letter you're just crazy to get, and you hang around the front door for fear you might not hear him ring. You never realize that he always rings twice."

With the exception of two scenes where Turner wore black, the stunning actress was clad in nothing but white in the film, a wardrobe that *Life* magazine predicted would become historic. Director Tay Garnett later recalled the reasoning behind this device: "At that time there was a great problem of getting a story with that much sex past the censors. We figured that dressing Lana in white somehow made everything she did seem less sensuous. It was also attractive as hell. And it somehow took the stigma off everything that she did."

As Cora, Turner offered a memorable performance as a scheming murderess who is at once immoral and vulnerable, but while the picture is viewed today as one of film noir's finest offerings, the critics were mixed in their reviews. Bosley Crowther wrote in the *New York Times* that both Turner and Garfield played their roles in "an extraordinarily honest way," and Turner was hailed in *Variety* for giving "the role of the femme lead an interpretation that will hold the women of the audience and the other Turner attributes guarantee attention from the male contingent." But the critic for *The Commonweal* found that the film "lacks conviction and even fails to hold one's interest" and the reviewer for *Time* claimed that "Lana Turner is a very highly charged and appealing girl but too much in this role is far beyond her experience, her understanding, and even her sincerely overworked imagination." Still, it is this role that Turner remembered as her favorite: "[It] gave me something to work with. Cora was not the usual heroine, but a woman who was willing to involve herself in murder to get what she wanted." The actress would also later condemn the 1981 remake starring Jessica Lange and Jack Nicholson: "They are such fools to play around with something that's still a classic. I'm a little heartsick. Jack Nicholson just isn't John Garfield. The chemistry we had just crackled. Every facet [was] so perfect."

While her career continued to soar, Turner dated a variety of well-known men, including actors Peter Lawford, John Hodiak and Turhan Bey and millionaire Howard Hughes. She was also involved in a highly-publicized affair with 20th Century–Fox heartthrob Tyrone Power, whom many expected her to make husband number three. But this much-touted union would never be. Although Turner later claimed that Power was "the only man I ever really loved," in 1948 she wed Henry J. "Bob" Topping, a wealthy playboy. Years after this union, Lana stated, "Bob felt that I would learn to care more deeply for him and I must say that when things were right he was a joy to be with. But things went wrong pretty fast." The couple separated in September 1951 and were divorced a little over a year later.

Meanwhile, Turner starred in *Green Dolphin Street* (1947), an epic production that was a huge hit with moviegoers, *Cass Timberlane* (1947), which focused on a May-December romance, *Homecoming* (1948), her third of four teamings with Clark Gable, and *The Merry Widow* (1952), costarring Fernando Lamas, with whom Turner had another steamy affair. And her popularity reached new heights in 1953, when she starred in *The Bad and the Beautiful*. The winner of five Academy Awards, this film is considered to be one of the best dissections of the movie industry, and Turner was hailed by critics for her portrayal of a glamorous but neurotic movie star.

The Bad and the Beautiful was followed by a series of mostly forgettable films, including *The Flame and the Flesh* (1954), which showcased Turner as a brunette but offered little else; *The Prodigal* (1955), a Biblical spectacle in which Turner appeared as a scantily-clad temptress; and *Diane* (1956), Turner's last costume drama and her final film under her MGM contract. But her career was resuscitated with her 1957 role in *Peyton Place*, for which she received an Academy Award nomination for Best Actress (losing to Joanne Woodward in *The Three Faces of Eve*). Playing the mother of a teenager, Turner was a standout in this film that was filled with one scandal after another, including incest, suicide, rape and murder.

Although Turner had been quoted following her third divorce as saying that she would "never, never marry again," in September 1953 she married Lex Barker, the tenth actor to play Tarzan on screen. This union, Turner's only "Hollywood" marriage, would end in 1958, soon after Turner became involved with another man — small-time racketeer Johnny Stompanato.

Turner had first met Stompanato in 1957, and the two appeared to be wildly in love, with Stompanato wearing Turner's picture suspended from a gold chain and carrying a lock of her hair. But while the relationship initially seemed blissful, Stompanato's jealousy, social ambitions and penchant for physical violence caused the relationship to take a downward spiral following Turner's divorce. The worst was yet to come. According to reports, on April 4, 1958, 14-year-old Cheryl Crane overheard her mother and Stompanato engaged in a heated argument in Turner's bedroom, during which the gangster threatened to beat and disfigure the beautiful star. Cheryl grabbed a butcher knife from the kitchen, entered the bedroom and, as she later explained, "Johnny ran on the blade. It went in. He looked straight at me and said, 'My God, Cheryl, what have you done?'" Stompanato died before reaching the hospital.

The press had a field day following Stompanato's death. *The Los Angeles Herald-Examiner* printed a series of torrid love letters from Turner to Stompanato, in which she referred to him as "My dearest darling love." Other articles reported that Turner feared retribution from Mickey Cohen, the notorious mobster with whom Stompanato was affiliated. There were even hints that Cheryl may have been intimately involved with Stompanato and that she stabbed him in a jealous rage. After a sensational court trial in which newspapers claimed Turner "played the most dramatic and effective role of her long screen career," a jury took only 25 minutes to reach a verdict of justifiable homicide. In the trial's aftermath, Cheryl was made a ward of the court until her 18th birthday, and Turner was sued for $752,500 by the family of Johnny Stompanato, who claimed that Turner "incited Cheryl to inflict the wound." The suit was settled two years later for $20,000.

Despite fears that the Stompanato case would damage Turner's career, the actress survived and even thrived on the scandal; in fact, her latest film, *Another Time, Another Place* (1958), was rushed into the theaters ahead of schedule in order to capitalize on her notoriety. And she next starred in *Imitation of Life* (1959), a glossy soaper that became one of Universal Pictures' top-grossing films, and *Portrait in Black* (1960) which, despite critics' disparaging comments, proved to be another smash at the box office.

But at this point, Turner's stellar film career began its final descent. Her subsequent films, including *Bachelor in Paradise* (1961), featuring Turner as straight man to comedian Bob Hope; *Who's Got the Action?* (1962), another comedy, this time costarring Dean Martin as Turner's horse-betting husband; and *Love Has Many Faces* (1965), a sleek drama noted primarily for Turner's extensive wardrobe, were panned by critics and unpopular with audiences. And while her 1966 remake of *Madame X* is favorably viewed today, it had a poor theatrical showing when first released, with one critic sneering: "If you haven't seen a movie since 1930, you may think it's great."

As her career began to wane, Turner's matrimonial entanglements continued. In November 1960, she married Fred May, a millionaire rancher. While the cultured May seemed genuinely in love with Turner, the marriage ended less than two years later, with May declaring, "Real life can't be lived as if it were a movie script." Turner's next marriage was in June 1965, to Robert Eaton, a businessman who was 11 years her junior. By April 1969, this marriage, too, was over. Her seventh and final marriage was to Ronald Dante, a 39-year-old nightclub hypnotist whom Turner had dated for approximately three weeks before their May 1969 wedding. This coupling, considered to be the worst of

Lana Turner

Turner's marriages, only lasted until December 1969, with Turner charging that Dante had defrauded her of $34,000. Turner would later explain her many marriages by saying, "I was so gullible, so vulnerable, so believing that this person doesn't want anything from me but my complete love, and he will return his complete love … when I fell in love, I fell hook, line and sinker, and took the boat with me."

Professionally, Turner would only make five more movies, including

Persecution (1974), a British-made horror film that Turner herself labeled as "a bomb"; *Bittersweet Love* (1976), another box office flop; and *Witches' Brew* (1980), which was never released, due to legal entanglements involving the film's producer. Off screen, Turner made her stage debut in *Forty Carats* in 1971, and also appeared in stage productions of *Bell, Book and Candle* in 1976 and *Murder Among Friends* in 1978. She also starred in a television series for ABC, *The Survivors*, which debuted in September 1969, was cancelled three months later, and was described in *Variety* as "one of the most expensive flops in television history." Her last major role was on the CBS prime-time soap opera *Falcon Crest* in 1983.

After years of declining to write her memoirs, Turner penned her autobiography in 1982, the best-selling *Lana: The Lady, the Legend, the Truth*. In promoting the book, she attended numerous book signings, at which her fans proved their continuing fascination with the blond sex goddess by standing in long lines for her autograph. And six years later, Turner's daughter Cheryl wrote her own autobiography, *Detour*, in which she openly discussed her homosexuality, Johnny Stompanato's death, her troubled adolescence and her sexual abuse at the hands of Turner's fourth husband, Lex Barker. This book, too, was an enormous success. Meanwhile, Turner adopted a somewhat reclusive existence, reportedly telling friends that she wanted her fans to "remember me as I was."

In June 1992, it was revealed that Turner was undergoing treatments for throat cancer, which had spread to her lungs and jaw. Although her prognosis was grim, Turner beat the odds, reporting in 1993 that she was completely recovered. But two years later, she succumbed to the disease, leaving behind a legacy of professional achievements and private dramas which insure that her name will not soon be forgotten. Her legendary status is doubtless best rendered in a quote by columnist Adela Rogers St. Johns, who once said, "The *real* Lana Turner *is* Lana Turner. She was a movie star and loved it. Her personal life and movie star are one."

Film Noir Filmography

JOHNNY EAGER *Director:* Mervyn LeRoy. *Producer:* John W. Considine, Jr. Released by MGM, February 1942. *Running time:* 102 minutes. *Cast:* Robert Taylor, Lana Turner, Edward Arnold, Van Heflin, Robert Sterling, Patricia Dane, Glenda Farrell. *Awards:* Academy Award for Best Supporting Actor (Van Heflin).

THE POSTMAN ALWAYS RINGS TWICE *Director:* Tay Garnett. *Producer:* Carey Wilson. Released by MGM, May 1946. *Running time:* 113 minutes. *Cast:* Lana Turner, John Garfield, Cecil Kellaway, Hume Cronyn, Leon Ames, Audrey Totter, Alan Reed.

References

"All-Time Female Superstar." *Look*, August 9, 1955.

Atwood, Toni. "Lana Turner on Life, Love and the MGM Glamour Factory." *Hollywood Studio Magazine*, May 1980.

"Bad and Beautiful." *Time*, April 21, 1958.

Brown, Peter. "Great Hollywood Love Scenes." *Hollywood Studio Magazine*, May 1980.

Colby, Anita. "About Face!" *Photoplay*, August 1950.

Considine, Shaun. "What Becomes a Legend Most?" *After Dark*, January 1972.

Crane, Cheryl, with Cliff Jahr. *Detour: A Hollywood Story*. New York: Arbor House, 1987.

Crichton, Kyle. "Campus Sweetheart." *Collier's*, March 23, 1940.

"Drama vs. Glamour." *Lions Review*, October 1941.

Garner, Jack. "For Lana Turner, Art Imitated Life." *Chicago Sun-Times*, July 2, 1995.

Hall, Gladys. "Her Advice to All the School Girls." *Silver Screen*, January 1940.

"Her Love Affairs." *Time*, January 12, 1948.

"Hollywood — The Bad and the Beautiful." *Newsweek*, April 14, 1958.

Hopper, Hedda. "If Ty Had His Way." *Modern Screen*, July 1947.

"Lana: Star-Crossed Life." *New York Daily Mirror*, April 6, 1958.

"L-A-N-A Spells Glamour." *Lions Review*, December 1944.

"Lana Turner's Fourth and Positively Last Time." *Life*, May 10, 1948.

"Lana's Plea for Daughter Is a Real-Life Triumph." *Life*, April 21, 1958.

"Life of a Sweater Girl." *Time*, November 26, 1951.

Maslin, Janet. "The Story Is the Same, but Hollywood Has Changed." *New York Times*, April 26, 1981.

"Miss Turner." *Lions Review*, September 1941.

Morella, Joe, and Edward Z. Epstein. *Lana: The Public and Private Lives of Miss Turner*. New York: Citadel Press, 1971.

O'Dowd, Brian. "Lana Turner on Book Trip — Fans Stand in Line." *Hollywood Studio Magazine*, circa 1982.

Parsons, Louella O. "And So, Goodbye." *Photoplay*, February 1946.

_____. "Diamonds and Diapers." *Photoplay*, January 1949.

_____. "I've Waited All My Life." *Photoplay*, July 1948.

_____. "Lana and Ty." *Photoplay*, June 1947.

_____. "Lana Talks About Turhan." *Photoplay*, April 1945.

"The Pinup Girls." *Screen Greats*, Summer 1971.

St. Johns, Adela Rogers. "Lana." *Photoplay*, September 1945.

St. Johns, Elaine. "Bringing Up Lana." *Photoplay*, October 1946.

"Sweater Girl Lana's Build-Up to a Tragedy." *Life*, April 14, 1958.

Thompson, David. "A Life of Imitation." *Film Comment*, May-June 1988.

"Tragic Life of a Star." *Newsweek*, April 14, 1958.

Turner, Lana. *Lana: The Lady, the Legend, the Truth*. Boston: G.K. Hall, 1983.

_____. "The Role I Liked Best." *Saturday Evening Post*, October 4, 1947.

Valentino, Lou. *The Films of Lana Turner*. Secaucus, N.J.: The Citadel Press, 1976.

Waterbury, Ruth. "The Lady Said Yes." *Photoplay*, December 1953.

Wayne, Jane Ellen. *Lana: The Life and Loves of Lana Turner*. New York: St. Martin's Press, 1995.

Helen Walker

Helen Walker's life was a roller coaster ride of dizzying highs and devastating lows, fortuitous breaks and tragic misadventures. After struggling for years to gain a foothold as an actress, she made a promising start on Broadway, was courted by Hollywood, and appeared to be on her way to becoming one of filmdom's most talented luminaries. But over the years, her shining light was eclipsed by an addiction to alcohol, her involvement in an auto accident that resulted in the death of a serviceman, and the loss of all her belongings in a mysterious house fire. Ultimately, her screen career would span only 13 years, but during the height of her fame, the square-jawed beauty starred opposite such stars as Tyrone Power, Charles Boyer and Fred MacMurray, and provided a memorable contribution to four films noirs: *Nightmare Alley* (1947), *Call Northside 777* (1948), *Impact* (1949) and *The Big Combo* (1955).

The second of three daughters, Helen Marion Walker was born on July 17, 1920, in Worcester, Massachusetts, on "the very far side of the railroad tracks," the actress said. Walker's father, Russell, a grocery store manager, died when Walker was four years old, and the rearing of the family was left to her mother Irene. "I came up the hard way, since we never had a dime when I was a child," Walker said. "My family was always poor. You'd say we didn't have a biscuit. [But] my mother, who raised the family all by herself, is a wonderful woman. She worked hard to raise us properly, to give us good educations. She has always accepted fate, and has never counted on anything, so she has never been disappointed. Long ago she passed that philosophy on to me."

A tomboy as a child, Walker was bitten by the acting bug while a student at Worcester High School, where she played the female lead in school productions for three successive years. Following her graduation, Walker performed in several plays for a summer stock company in Boylston, Massachusetts, then won a scholarship to the Erskine School of Dramatics in Boston. But her experience at the school nearly caused the aspiring actress to abandon her dreams. "I absorbed so many different theories about acting, and was so mixed up by the time I finished one term, I felt I could never act again," Walker said. "I knew how to breathe correctly and how to speak a sentence so that it had a dramatic climax, but my acting was self-conscious. I decided to give it up, be sensible, and go to work in an office."

Instead of a stage, Walker found herself working in the dog license bureau at the Boston City Hall: "If that job hadn't been so horrendously dull, I might still be a Boston civic employee, and not a very efficient one at that." Before long, she resumed her acting pursuits, working in everything from Shaw to musical comedies with a variety of area stock companies, playing in an eight-week run of *Pygmalion* at the Copley Theater in Boston, and touring with Helen Twelvetrees in *Personal Appearances*.

Convinced that she was ready for Broadway, Walker moved to a tiny apartment in New York ("It cost $3.50 a week and I got cockroaches and bedbugs for free," she quipped). But her plans to take the town by storm failed to materialize, and the only stage work Walker was able to find was a four-week appearance with a stock company in Montclair, New Jersey. "Somehow, Broadway couldn't summon the courage to try me," she wryly recalled years later. "Even modeling, the old standby of young actresses out of work, wasn't for me. I'd march in, and they'd look me over and say, 'You have possibilities; get yourself a stunning wardrobe and a batch of good photos.' Since I never had the cash for either, it would always stop right there!"

Desperate for money, Walker took an office job pasting clippings in the advertising department of a shirt manufacturer, and was eventually promoted to writing copy for the company. "I really was considering becoming a young businesswoman," Walker told a reporter from the *New York Journal American*. "Only the guy I worked for started chasing me around the room every night. I didn't mind, personally, but I figured that the poor chap was paying me $24 a week and not getting his money's worth. I quit and went to Cape Cod to play summer stock." Following this latest stock experience, Walker returned to New York and finally landed a job on Broadway, playing understudy to Dorothy McGuire in *Claudia*. Although McGuire remained in excellent health and Walker never got a chance to perform in the play, her association with *Claudia* led to the opportunity she been seeking for so long. The play's author, Rose Franken, recommended Walker to playwright Samson Raphaelson for a role in his new play *Jason*, and the rest, as they say, is history. Even before the comedy was sold to the play's producer, George Abbott, Raphaelson had selected Walker for the role of Lisa, a critic's seductive wife who ambitiously raises herself to a position of importance in literary circles. "I don't suppose I'll ever get as great a compliment again in my life," Walker said after winning the part. "Every young girl thirsting for a Broadway career dreams of such luck, but when it happens, you just can't believe it is true."

Walker's performance in *Jason* was hailed by critics, including Brooks Atkinson, who called her "lovely and intelligent," and Richard Watts, Jr., who wrote: "Although inexperienced, the attractive Miss Helen Walker handles many of the scenes of the wife admirably, despite the fact that the part of the Southern millhand girl who pretends to be an aristocratic Virginian is difficult and is but intermittently well written." Walker's performance also attracted the attention of Hollywood talent scouts and after four months, she withdrew from the production and signed with Paramount Pictures.

The actress did not have to wait long for her screen debut — in her first film, she was assigned to costar with Alan Ladd in *Lucky Jordan* (1942), a financially successful comedy-drama about a killer who turns patriot in order to outwit a Nazi spy ring. The attractive blonde also wasted no time in her personal life. In a secret marriage that was not revealed in the press until a year later, she wedded Lt. Robert Blumofe, then an attorney in Paramount's legal department and later a production chief for United Artists who would produce such features as *Yours, Mine and Ours* (1968) and *Bound for Glory* (1976).

But three years after her Tijuana marriage, Walker announced her plans to seek a divorce, and on January 22, 1946, obtained an interlocutory divorce decree.

Meanwhile, in Walker's second picture, *The Good Fellows* (1943), the actress was featured as a dutiful daughter who takes over the family real estate business while her father, played by Cecil Kellaway, concentrates on the activities of his fraternal lodge. Next, on loan-out to United Artists, Walker starred with William Bendix and Dennis O'Keefe in *Abroad with Two Yanks* (1944), a broad slapstick comedy that scored big at the box office, then returned to her home studio for *The Man in Half Moon Street* (1944), a slightly above-average melodrama about an aging scientist who murders young men in order to obtain a youth-preserving gland. This was followed by another loan-out to United Artists, *Brewster's Millions* (1945), the third — and best — of six film versions of the 1905 Winchell Smith-Brian Ongley play about a man who must spend $1 million in 60 days in order to inherit his uncle's $7 million estate.

After *Brewster's Millions*, Walker was cast in Paramount's *Murder, He Says* (1945), costarring Fred MacMurray as an insurance salesman who encounters a family of homicidal hillbillies. This hilarious slapstick farce offered the actress one of the best roles of her career, but she followed it with a small, unbilled part in *Duffy's Tavern* (1945), a lifeless musical featuring Paulette Goddard, Alan Ladd, Veronica Lake, Barry Sullivan, Dorothy Lamour and Brian Donlevy.

Faced with yet another proposed loan-out after *Duffy's Tavern*, Walker refused the role, confidently expecting to be placed on suspension. "Instead," the actress recalled, "I got fired. So for four months I didn't work." When she did, it was in Republic's *Murder in the Music Hall* (1946), a better-than-average programmer starring William Marshall and Vera Ralston. After this film, Walker signed with 20th Century–Fox and replaced newcomer Peggy Cummins (who won and later lost the title role of *Forever Amber*) in *Cluny Brown* (1946), a sophisticated Ernst Lubitsch comedy that was praised in the *New York Times* as "a delectable and sprightly lampoon." In her two remaining films of the year — the busiest of her brief career — Walker was back on loan-out, first to Universal for *Her Adventurous Night* (1946), a rather juvenile comedy-drama about an imaginative teenager whose exploits land his parents in jail, and then in Paramount's *People Are Funny* (1946), a pleasant musical starring Jack Haley and Rudy Vallee.

By now, Walker had become known, according to one movie magazine, as "a soft touch for a pal in need" who, during the war, had made four bond selling tours and entertained regularly at the weekly Masquers' parties for servicemen. She also had reportedly developed an affinity for alcohol and was a fun-loving party girl who loved to entertain. "Like last Christmas, when I invited two or three people to drop in for egg nog," Walker herself recalled. "It grew into a party. Forty to sixty people all afternoon, until finally the only standing room was on the ceiling."

But the actress' big-hearted nature would come back to haunt her on New Year's Eve 1946 when, while driving from Palm Springs to Los Angeles, Walker gave a lift to a soldier, Pfc. Robert E. Lee, and two other hitchhikers, Philip Mercado and Joseph Montaldo. Near Redlands, California, Walker's car hit a dividing island and turned over six times, killing the soldier and leaving Walker with a fractured pelvis and collarbone and several broken toes. Manslaughter charges against the actress would later be dismissed for "insufficient and uncertain evidence," but in February 1947 she was sued for $150,000 by Mercado, who charged that Walker had been intoxicated and traveling at more than 90 miles an hour when the accident occurred. Later, the third passenger, Montaldo, would also file a civil suit against the actress.

Several months after the lawsuits were filed, Walker told Valerie Sloan of *Modern Screen* magazine that she'd been driving only 45 miles an hour when her car struck the dividing island and "without warning, seemed to jackknife into the air." She also denied that she had been drinking and appeared to view the accident philosophically: "I think this happened to me for a reason. I don't know why Robert Lee wasn't spared and I was, but I believe that there is something I was meant to do," she said. "Perhaps I can express what I mean by imagining how much I would have to account for if I had been drinking or careless. I hope that by reading about my misfortune, some folks will be more careful."

Ultimately, Walker was absolved of all guilt in the tragic incident, but it had an immediate effect on her career. Confined for several weeks to the hospital, she was replaced by Marjorie Reynolds in the picture she'd just started work on, United Artists' *Heaven Only Knows* (1947), at a cost of approximately $100,000 to producer Seymour Nebenzal. Her first release after the accident was *The Homestretch* (1947), a mildly entertaining race track picture starring Cornel Wilde and Maureen O'Hara, followed by Walker's first entry in the realm of film noir, *Nightmare Alley* (1947).

This fascinating film focuses on the experiences of Stanton Carlisle (Tyrone Power in one of his greatest performances), an unscrupulous but ambitious carnival barker. After marrying Molly (Coleen Gray), one of the carny sideshow performers, Stan becomes a great success in Chicago as "The Great Stanton," dazzling his audiences with what appears to be an uncanny mind-reading gift. During one performance, Stan meets Dr. Lilith Ridder (Walker), a psychologist who is fascinated by his act. Later, Stan seeks Lilith's professional help after experiencing an anxiety attack brought on by his lingering guilt over the death of Pete (Ian Keith), who'd operated a mind-reading act at the carnival. But before long, Lilith is providing Stan with confidential details about the lives of her patients, which he uses for financial gain by making them believe he is in contact with their deceased loved ones.

Seeking the promise of still greater rewards, Stan even persuades his reluctant wife to portray the long-dead sweetheart of one of the patients, but his fortunes topple when Molly breaks down, unable to continue the charade. With his profitable hoax now exposed, Stan sends Molly back to the carnival and, before fleeing town, returns to Lilith to collect a cache of money he'd given her for safe keeping. But Lilith has no intention of returning the cash and chillingly employs blackmail to convince Stan of her plans: "The police records show that a carnival employee by the name of Peter Crombine actually died of wood alcohol poisoning in Burleigh, Texas. Self-administered. You told me you gave him that bottle of wood alcohol yourself," Lilith says coolly. "Speaking of records, would you like to hear a playback of the recital you made to me that night?" Destitute, Stan becomes a hopeless alcoholic, and later accepts the job as "the geek" at a traveling carnival, receiving payment in liquor for the degrading duty of biting the heads off live chickens. Unaware that his wife also works at the carnival, Stan later goes wild, running through the grounds in a state of near-madness, but he is saved from his final destruction by Molly, who assures him: "Everything's going to be all right now."

For her first-rate performance in *Nightmare Alley*, Walker was praised by a number of critics, including the reviewer for the *New York Times*, who said the actress was "cool and poised as the role demands," and the critic for *Variety*, who wrote: "Helen Walker comes through successfully as the calculating femme who topples Power from his heights of fortune." Walker followed this triumph with a smaller role in her second film noir, *Call Northside 777* (1948).

In this highly acclaimed feature, Walker portrayed the understanding and sensitive wife of Jim McNeal (James Stewart), a Chicago newspaper reporter who is assigned to investigate a newspaper advertisement offering a $5,000 reward for the killers of a police officer 11 years before. McNeal learns that the ad was placed by Tillie Wiecek (Kasia Orzazewski), who believes that her son Frank (Richard Conte) was wrongly imprisoned for the crime. McNeal is touched by Tillie's faith, but he doubts Wiecek's innocence and is interested only in "mass appeal" and "a good angle." After writing a well-received human interest article, McNeal writes several follow-up stories, interviewing Wiecek himself, as well as his ex-wife and school-age son.

McNeal soon becomes disturbed by his growing ambivalence over Wiecek's case, and it is his wife Laura who helps to resolve his conflict: "Why don't you let go?" she urges. "You want him to be innocent. You want him to be free. Admit it." After Wiecek passes a lie detector test, McNeal vigorously goes to work on securing his freedom, setting up a parole hearing with the governor, compiling a substantial amount of circumstantial evidence pointing to Wiecek's innocence, and locating Wanda Skutnik (Betty Garde), a tavern owner who had identified Wiecek as the murderer. However, the hard-bitten Skutnik stubbornly refuses to admit that she was coerced by police into the identification, and McNeal is nearly forced to admit defeat. As time runs out, however, he employs a new police technique to magnify a photograph taken of Wiecek and Skutnik, resulting in solid proof that refutes Skutnik's testimony.

Helen Walker

McNeal's efforts lead to Wiecek's favorable review from the parole board and as the film ends, he is released from prison, announcing: "It's a good world outside."

Although Walker's brief appearance attracted little attention from critics, the film itself was praised in *Motion Picture Herald* as "among the best" of 20th Century–Fox's series of semi-documentary dramas, and in the *New York*

Times as "a slick piece of modern melodrama [that] combines a suspenseful mystery story with a vivid, realistic, pictorial style." And after a small role in United Artists' unfunny comedy *My Dear Secretary* (1948), Walker returned to film noir with a knockout bad girl performance in her sole film of 1949, *Impact.* Here, Walker played Irene, the captivating wife of successful San Francisco businessman Walt Williams (Brian Donlevy). Although Irene appears to be the very image of the loving, devoted wife, she is actually carrying on a torrid affair with Jim Torrance (Tony Barrett), with whom she has plotted Walt's murder. But the carefully designed murder scheme goes awry after Jim strikes Walt with a tire iron on a winding mountain road; fleeing the scene in Walt's car, he crashes head on into a large gasoline truck, resulting in a fiery accident that leaves him burned beyond recognition.

The charred body in the car is identified as Walt Williams, and Irene is later indicted for the murder of her husband. Meanwhile, Walt makes his way to a small town in Idaho, where he reads of the news of his death and decides to remain in hiding. Giving a false name, he gets a job as a mechanic in a small service station owned by Marsha Peters (Ella Raines), and after several months, he and Marsha fall in love. When Walt learns of Irene's indictment, Marsha convinces him to return home but, discovering that it was her lover who died in the crash, Irene turns the table on her husband: "You killed him," she says nastily. "You wait all these months to tell this story. You let me rot in this filthy jail. You let everybody think you're dead. Pretty convenient, wasn't it? A dead man can't be tried for murder." Walt is subsequently arrested, but Marsha and a police detective (Charles Coburn) discover the proof they need to establish Walt's innocence. The charges against Walt are immediately dropped and, instead, Irene is again arrested, this time for conspiring to kill her husband.

After the film's release, Walker would tell columnist Louella Parsons that she had initially been considered for the part of Marsha Peters: "But when the nice girl role was offered me, I turned it down," she said. "I wanted the other role, which had more guts." And Walker was right. She was applauded for her portrayal of the ruthless wife by several critics, including Ann Helming of *Citizen News*, who wrote that the actress "combines saccharine and venom most effectively."

Walker was absent from the screen in 1950, but she made the news in April of that year when she announced her impending wedding to Edward Nicholas DuDomaine, a department store executive whom she had met eight months before. "Edward and I met in front of the Goldwyn studio and he asked me if I'd like to go to the beach," Walker told the press. "I told him I would." But just two years later, the marriage was over; according to newspaper accounts, Walker said DuDomaine "resented her friends, her career, and the movie industry," and that her husband's attitude had forced her to relinquish all her connections with the acting profession.

Walker returned to films in 1951, but her career was rapidly deteriorating.

Appearing considerably older than her 31 years, she played a convicted jewel thief in *My True Story*, but this box office disaster was notable only for being the directorial debut of film veteran Mickey Rooney. After another year-long absence, the bloated and weary-looking actress starred in *Problem Girls* (1953), a tawdry melodrama in which she portrayed the owner of a private school for mentally ill girls.

Then, in 1955, Walker appeared in her final film noir and the last big-screen feature of her career, *The Big Combo*. This complex film centers on a ruthless mobster known only as Mr. Brown (Richard Conte), Susan Lowell (Jean Wallace), the weak-willed socialite who is sexually drawn to Brown despite his brutal treatment, and Leonard Diamond (Cornel Wilde), a police detective who is in love with Susan and obsessed with bringing Brown to justice. A fascinating character, Brown's personality is illuminated early in the film when he compares himself with one of his underlings, Joe McClure (Brian Donlevy): "He used to be my boss. Now I'm his," Brown says. "What's the difference between me and him? We breathe the same air, sleep in the same hotel. He used to own it. Now it belongs to me. We eat the same steaks. Drink the same bourbon. Same manicure. Same cufflinks. But there's only one difference. We don't get the same girls. Why? Because women know the difference. They got instinct. First is first and second is nobody."

After constantly harassing Brown and using such tactics as false arrests of the mobster's henchmen, Diamond is beaten and tortured, which only serves to strengthen his resolve to nab his nemesis. And Diamond is further spurred when a botched attempt on his life results in the death of his sometime lover Rita (Helene Stanton). Diamond finally appears to be closing in when he learns that Brown murdered his first wife Alicia (Walker), leaving her body at the bottom of the sea. But he later discovers that Alicia has been placed in a mental institution and that the body in the sea is actually that of Brown's former boss, Grazzi. Unsure of his henchmen's continued loyalty, Brown begins systematically eliminating them, planning to flee the country with Susan, but he is betrayed by Alicia, who reluctantly reveals Brown's getaway plans. In the film's climax, Diamond corners the mobster in an isolated airplane hangar and, as Susan helps by constantly turning a large spotlight on Brown, Diamond finally places him under arrest.

As the mentally feeble Alicia, Walker turned in a sensitive performance, infusing her character with both emotional instability and pitiable resentment, as demonstrated in her final scene. "I wouldn't raise a finger to help that girl," she says of Susan. "Let her go through what I went through. I hate her. Her and every other woman that had anything to do with him. I don't want to help you. But I will." Critics were mixed in their reviews of the film, with Howard Thompson of the *New York Times* dismissing it as "a shrill, clumsy and rather old-fashioned crime melodrama," and the critic for *The Hollywood Reporter* terming it "grim, sordid, sexy and candid." Walker, however, earned mostly favorable notices, including one that labeled her performance "dandy."

But by now, it was apparent that Walker's life, both professionally and personally, was on the downslide. Soon after the release of *The Big Combo*, she reportedly arrived at a friend's birthday party bearing gifts wrapped in her old movie stills, bitterly announcing: "They're not good for anything else." During this period she also told a reporter: "I was at a party the other night and a little man I had never met came up to me and exclaimed, 'Betty Hutton! You were in that funny old movie about the whip-cracking hillbilly mother with the half-wit twin sons — where everyone glowed in the dark before they died. What was it called?' Well, I told him *I* wasn't called Betty Hutton — that much I knew," Walker said. "I finally thought of it this morning: *Murder, He Says* — that was also the name of a song Betty Hutton sang in another Paramount picture. I've been in Hollywood for 15 years, and have done almost 20 pictures, and all they remember me for is *Murder, He Says* — and they don't really even remember that, or me!"

Little seen during the next several years, Walker resurfaced in the late 1950s, appearing opposite Fernando Lamas in *Once More, with Feeling*, a California Playhouse Production in La Jolla, California, and in the television series *Lock Up* with Macdonald Carey. But when the press next carried news of her, it was to report in 1960 that she had lost all her possessions in a house fire. To help the actress recoup some of her losses, several friends from the film industry, including Ruth Roman, Vivian Blaine, Hugh O'Brian and Dinah Shore, staged a benefit for her.

Purportedly plagued by a growing dependency on alcohol that pushed her toward paranoia and emotional collapse, Walker would again disappear from the public eye during the 1960s. Her next appearance in the press would be the news of her death from cancer on March 10, 1968. Sadly, by the time of her death at age 47, Walker had been all but forgotten. With a personal life that was ravaged by alcohol and a career that never quite recovered after her 1946 auto accident, Helen Walker never fulfilled the potential that looked so promising when she first arrived in Hollywood as a fresh-faced, luminous 22-year-old. Still, although she appeared in only 22 feature films, Walker left behind a body of work that leaves no doubt to her beauty and talent.

Film Noir Filmography

NIGHTMARE ALLEY   *Director:* Edmund Goulding. *Producer:* George Jessel. Released by 20th Century–Fox, October 1947. *Running time:* 110 minutes. *Cast:* Tyrone Power, Joan Blondell, Coleen Gray, Helen Walker, Taylor Holmes, Mike Mazurki, Ian Keith.

CALL NORTHSIDE 777   *Director:* Henry Hathaway. *Producer:* Otto Lang. Released by 20th Century–Fox, February 1948. *Running time:* 111 minutes. *Cast:* James Stewart, Richard Conte, Lee J. Cobb, Helen Walker, Betty Garde, Kasia Orzazewski.

IMPACT   *Director:* Arthur Lubin. *Producer:* Leo C. Popkin. Released by United

Artists, April 1949. *Running time:* 108 minutes. *Cast:* Brian Donlevy, Ella Raines, Charles Coburn, Helen Walker, Anna May Wong, Mae Marsh, Tony Barrett.
THE BIG COMBO   *Director:* Joseph H. Lewis. *Producer:* Sidney Harmon. Released by Allied Artists, February 1955. *Running time:* 89 minutes. *Cast:* Cornel Wilde, Richard Conte, Brian Donlevy, Jean Wallace, Robert Middleton, Lee Van Cleef, Earl Holliman, Helen Walker, Jay Adler.

References

"Actress Hurt as Car Upsets, Killing Soldier." *Los Angeles Times*, January 3, 1947.
Biography of Helen Walker. 20th Century–Fox Studios, circa 1946.
Carroll, Sidney. "Worcester Girl a Star." *Boston Sunday Post*, circa 1942.
Coons, Robbin. "Lowdown on Cinderella." *Motion Picture*, March 1947.
Gebhart, Myrtle. "Worcester's Helen Walker Steps Into Star Film Roles." *Boston Sunday Post*, October 18, 1942.
Heimer, Mel. "Escape from a Dog Tag." *New York Journal-American*, November 11, 1944.
"Helen Walker, 47, Dies on Coast; Film Actress in '40s and '50s." *New York Times*, March 12, 1968.
"Helen Walker Gets Lead in *Brewster's Millions*." *New York Times*, circa 1944.
"Helen Walker Plodded Into Films the Methodical Way." *New York Daily Mirror*, October 23, 1944.
"Hitchhiker Seeks Damages from Helen Walker." *Los Angeles Times*, February 6, 1947.
McClelland, Doug. "Helen Walker." *Film Fan Monthly*, March 1968.
Obituary. *New York Post*, March 12, 1968.
Obituary. *Variety*, March 13, 1968.
Parsons, Louella O. "Helen Walker." *Photoplay*, circa 1949.
Sloan, Valerie. "The Truth About Helen Walker." *Modern Screen*, July 1947.
Thirer, Irene. "Don't Count Screen Roles Before They're Yours, Says Helen Walker." *New York Post*, October 14, 1944.

Marie Windsor

Whether she was portraying a gangster's moll, a barbarous lady pirate or a tough-as-nails outlaw, Marie Windsor proved that she was one of cinema's best "bad girls." Although once labeled "The Wasted Queen of the Bs," Windsor managed to sustain successful careers in both movies and television that spanned more than half a century. Of her nearly 80 feature films, she is perhaps best remembered for her femme fatale roles in some of film noir's most riveting offerings: *Force of Evil* (1948), *The Narrow Margin* (1952), *The Sniper* (1952), *City That Never Sleeps* (1953) and *The Killing* (1956).

The actress who has been described as "looking like Loretta Young with touches of Edmond O'Brien" was born Emily Marie Bertelson on December 11, 1922, in Marysvale, Utah, a small town with a population of less than 500 residents. One of three children born to Lane Joseph and Etta Marie Long Bertelsen, Emily was drawn to acting at an early age, later recalling, "At the age of eight, after going to a movie with my grandmother, I wanted to be another Clara Bow. No one in the family ever said, 'Oh, don't be silly' or 'You can't.' If that's what I wanted, they were going to help me." Emily's supportive parents drove her each week to nearby Richfield, a 30-mile trek over dirt roads, so that she could participate in dancing and drama lessons, and the youngster's earliest performances came in the form of shows she staged herself on the porch of her Utah home.

After completing her high school studies, the statuesque beauty studied drama for two years at Brigham Young University, where she appeared in several upper-class plays. During this time, she also entered a number of beauty contests, earning the titles of "Miss Covered Wagon Days" and "Miss D. & R.G. Railroad." In the latter contest, the top prize was 99 silver dollars, with which Emily purchased a set of luggage to be used for her next destination — Hollywood.

Arriving in California in 1940, Emily took a room at the Hollywood Studio Club, a boarding house for young movie hopefuls, and was accepted as a student at the Maria Ouspenskaya School of Drama. She would later recall that the famed veteran actress was "a strange little creature who wore silver Indian rings and bracelets that jingled all the time, especially when she was giving a critique. She seemed to like me very much, but was always working on me to deliver more 'inner energy.'" Because her parents were only able to afford tuition for one nine-month semester, Emily paid for her room and board by working as one of the first cigarette girls at the newly opened Mocambo nightclub. But the job was not a pleasant one, as the actress later remembered: "The concessionaires wouldn't let us keep our tips unless we made over $10— then we were allowed to keep half. I'd gotten friendly with some of the girls there who were very social, and through them I'd met several people in the industry. It embarrassed me to be selling cigarettes to them."

Still, it was this "embarrassing" nightclub stint that would lead to the future star's first big break. "I was crying [one night] and helping people on

Femme Noir

with their coats," the actress said in a 1986 interview, "and then I helped Arthur Hornblow, a producer, with his. He asked me, 'Are you working at this job because you want to be an actress?' I sobbed, 'Yes.' Hornblow responded, 'You don't belong here — call my secretary in the morning, and I'll see if I can help you.'" True to his word, Hornblow arranged for an audition, and the newly named Marie Windsor made her screen debut as "Miss Carrot" in *All American Co-ed* (1941), starring Frances Langford.

Over the next two years, Windsor appeared in bit parts in numerous films, including RKO's *Call Out the Marines* (1942) and *The Big Street* (1942), Columbia's *Parachute Nurse* (1942) and Paramount's *Let's Face It* (1943), starring Bob Hope. She also appeared during this period with the East Side Kids in *Smart Alecks* (1942): "It was obvious that I was naive and green. I seemed to favor Stanley Clements and Leo Gorcey because they helped put me at ease," she said in a 1992 interview in *Filmfax*. "In the picture I played the part of a nurse in a hospital where one of the kids was a patient. It was publicized that I gave Leo Gorcey his first screen kiss."

But with only brief appearances in eight pictures to her credit, Windsor decided that she might fare better on stage and was cast in a vaudeville show, *Henry Duffy's Merry-Go-Rounders*. Although the show closed after 13 weeks, Windsor moved to New York and promptly earned a part as Gloria Grahame's understudy in *Stardust*. This play, too, was a flop, but before long, Windsor landed a running role on the popular radio soap opera *Our Gal Sunday*, and during the next three years she would appear in more than 300 radio shows. The stage beckoned again when Windsor replaced Karen Stevens in *Follow the Girls*, and during her eight-month stint in this hit play, she was noticed by an MGM executive who flew her to Hollywood for a screen test and signed her to a two-year contract.

At MGM, Windsor was given daily lessons in dancing, singing, and acting, but she went all but unnoticed in 15 films, including *The Hucksters* (1947), starring Clark Gable and Ava Gardner; *The Romance of Rosy Ridge* (1947), a rousing post-Civil War drama with Van Johnson; *On an Island with You* (1948), a big-budget musical starring Cyd Charisse and Ricardo Montalban; and *The Kissing Bandit* (1948), a box office flop starring Frank Sinatra. Perhaps Windsor's primary disadvantage at the prestigious studio was executives' attempt to transform her into "the new Joan Crawford." As Windsor later recalled, studios in the 1940s and 1950s "always signed up people to keep the stars in line. Audrey Totter was the 'new' Lana Turner and I was the second Joan Crawford. Imagine! Miss Crawford didn't like the idea and thought I'd started it. Later, we became good friends and she realized I'd had nothing to do with it. Actually, it was a detriment because when the public hears you're a second anybody, they're already prejudiced against you."

Windsor did manage to attract some attention, though, with slightly larger roles as a gun moll in *Song of the Thin Man* (1947), the final entry in the long-running William Powell–Myrna Loy series, and a treacherous lady-in-waiting in *The Three Musketeers* (1948), with Lana Turner and Van Heflin. But during this period, Windsor didn't fare well in her personal life — she married orchestra leader Ted Steele, an old friend from her soap opera days, but after only eight months, the union was over. And in 1948, when her MGM contract expired, Windsor was dropped by the studio.

Next, at the request of producer-director Otto Preminger, Windsor made a test of a 13-minute condensed version of Jean Cocteau's one-woman play, *The Human Voice.* At the time, 20th Century–Fox had a six-week option on the actress to determine if she would be placed under contract, but studio head Darryl F. Zanuck was skiing in Sun Valley and Ben Lyon, Fox head of talent, was in London. "There was no one with any power around, no one who could do anything for me," Windsor said. The six-week option ran out, and Windsor's agent obtained permission to show the test outside the studio, which led to her most significant picture to date and her first film noir, *Force of Evil* (1948).

In this film, Windsor portrayed Edna, the predatory wife of a syndicate king, Ben Tucker (Roy Roberts), who has developed a scheme to "legalize" a large-scale numbers racket by forcing the smaller bookies to join his organization. Tucker's plan is carried out by Joe Morse (John Garfield), an attorney whose estranged brother Leo (Thomas Gomez) is an operator of one of the small-time bookie joints that would be affected by the plan. Despite Leo's reluctance, Joe convinces him to go along with the strategy, placing him in charge of the newly formed organization, but the situation later spirals out of control. Hunted by police and berated by his innocent, would-be girlfriend, Joe unsuccessfully strives to extricate himself and Leo from the organization. Later, Joe learns that Leo has died at the hands of Tucker's rival, and he confronts his boss, killing him. At the film's end, Joe has reunited with his girl, and the two head together to expose the syndicate to authorities.

Upon release, *Force of Evil* received mixed reviews. Although it was described in the *New York Times* as "a dynamic crime-and-punishment drama, brilliantly and broadly realized," the critic for *Variety* said that the film "fails to develop the excitement hinted at in the title," and Red Kann of *Motion Picture Herald* dismissed it as "so excessively talky and so loaded down with mumbo jumbo that it appears to run far beyond its length." Still, Windsor's performance was almost unanimously praised, and after this film she began landing more noticeable roles in a variety of pictures, including *Outpost in Morocco* (1949), in which she played the love interest of George Raft; *The Fighting Kentuckian* (1949), where she starred opposite John Wayne as a schemer striving to cheat land grants from French settlers; and *Hellfire* (1949), an above-average Republic Western which Windsor later recalled as one of her three favorite pictures. In this film, Windsor portrayed Doll Brown, a lying, thieving murderess who dies in the arms of the preacher who tries to save her. The actress would later call the role a "fabulous part for a woman," adding that it "gave me a chance to ride and shoot and be tough, but softly feminine and pathetic too. I dearly loved that role." As in her subsequent pictures, Windsor performed her own stunts in *Hellfire* and demonstrated her uncommon skill as a horsewoman. "I was given my first horse, Silver Queen, when I was about six," Windsor said. "At the time, we couldn't afford a saddle, so I learned to ride bareback."

It was believed that *Hellfire* would be Republic's big picture of the year and that Windsor's role would be a star-making vehicle, but it was not to be. According to the actress, studio boss Herbert J. Yates "suddenly got involved in trying to get the Communists out of our industry." As a result, Yates spent huge sums of money promoting an anti–Communist picture, *The Red Menace* (1949), which Windsor termed "a well-intentioned film, but a bomb." Despite this disappointment, Windsor continued her busy filming schedule in 1950, starring in *Dakota Lil*, a fairly entertaining Western with George Montgomery and Rod Cameron; *Frenchie*, a dull reworking of Universal's *Destry Rides Again* (1939); *Double Deal*, an aimless RKO programmer; and the best of the bunch, *The Showdown*, a gambling house drama in which, Windsor said, "the producer decided I was such a bad girl that the hero shouldn't be seen kissing me. So they took out the kiss!"

Windsor expanded her repertoire of "bad girl" roles in the next two years, playing a small-time criminal in *Two-Dollar Bettor* (1951); one of the screen's most fearsome lady pirates in *Hurricane Island* (1951); a Western wildcat called "Iron Mae" in *Outlaw Women* (1952); and the trouble-making sister-in-law of an army officer in *Japanese War Bride* (1952). In her efforts to heighten the realism in the latter film, however, Windsor got more than she bargained for: "I asked [costar Cameron Mitchell] to slap me hard in a scene to make it more believable," Windsor recalled. "One of us miscalculated and he hit me with the butt of his hand rather than the 'faking-it' way of letting the fingers go over the face. I got a slight fracture of the jaw."

Next, Windsor was seen in two back-to-back film noir offerings, *The Sniper* (1952) and *The Narrow Margin* (1952). In the first, Windsor portrayed Jean Darr, a nightclub pianist who is the first of a series of sniper victims. The murderer, Edward Miller (Arthur Franz), is a mentally disturbed laundry service employee who recognizes his sickness and endeavors to stop his killing spree, first by purposely burning his hand on an electric stove, and later by mailing a note to police that indicates his desire to be caught. The police manhunt for the killer, led by Lt. Frank Kafka (Adolphe Menjou) and police psychiatrist James Kent (Richard Kiley), eventually leads to Miller's home, where he is surrounded by authorities and curiosity-seekers in his one-room apartment. When police break into his room, they find Miller sitting on his bed with his rifle, a single tear running down his cheek.

Although Windsor was praised for her "very good portrayal" in *The Sniper*,

Marie Windsor

the film itself received mixed reviews, with the critic for *Variety* terming it "an effective suspense melodrama" and Bosley Crowther writing in the *New York Times*: "*The Sniper* develops, as it casually gets along, into nothing more forceful or impressive than a moderately fascinating chase." The film's writers, Edna and Edward Anhalt, received an Academy Award nomination for best original screenplay, but the picture did only moderate business at the box office and

Windsor would later say that *The Sniper* was "way ahead of its time. Today it'd be a huge hit."

In *The Narrow Margin*, Windsor's second film noir offering of 1952, she portrayed Mrs. Neil, a racketeer's widow, described by one character as "a dish, 60-cent special. Cheap, flashy, strictly poison under the gravy." As the film begins, two detectives, Walter Brown (Charles McGraw) and Gus Forbes (Don Beddoe), arrive in Chicago to escort Mrs. Neil by train to Los Angeles, where she is scheduled to testify before a grand jury regarding her late husband's "payoff list." But the murdered gangster's organized crime associates are endeavoring to insure that Mrs. Neil never makes it to Los Angeles alive. Although the hoods are unaware of what Mrs. Neil looks like, they have been tailing Brown and Forbes and when the detectives exit Mrs. Neil's apartment, Forbes is gunned down.

Brown, who views Mrs. Neil with contempt, manages to safely spirit her aboard the train to Los Angeles, where he ensconces her in the compartment adjoining his. Before long, however, he learns that he has been followed by two gangsters who unsuccessfully try to bribe Brown into turning over Mrs. Neil. Even Mrs. Neil suggests selling the "payoff list" to the hoods, scornfully telling Brown, "You're a bigger idiot that I thought. When are you gonna get it through your square head that this is big business? Wake up, Brown — this train's headed straight for the cemetery. But there's another one coming along. The gravy train. Let's get on it." Meanwhile, with Mrs. Neil safely inside the locked compartment, Brown finds himself attracted to a fellow passenger, Ann Sinclair (Jacqueline White), who is traveling with her young son and his nanny. When a third gangster boards the train, they gain entry to Mrs. Neil's room and, as she reaches for a gun, she is killed. It is only later that Brown, along with the audience, learns that Ann is the actual gangster's widow, and that the woman in the compartment was a policewoman planted to insure the safety of the real Mrs. Neil. Before the train reaches its destination, Brown captures the hoods and later escorts Mrs. Neil to the Hall of Justice.

After its release, *The Narrow Margin* was expected to catapult Windsor and costar Charles McGraw to choice roles, but this never occurred. In a 1988 interview in *Classic Images*, Windsor recalled, "Everyone appeared enthused about the picture, but no one seemed more enthused than [Howard] Hughes. He was so crazy about the little movie he wouldn't let any other studio screen it." According to the actress, Hughes delayed the release of the film for 18 months, attempting to put it into an "A" category. Before he could accomplish this, however, the eccentric billionaire became interested in purchasing airplanes. "As a result, *Narrow Margin* was released by other executives as a second bill, with absolutely no fanfare," Windsor said. "It was booked with multimillion dollar movies which usually got bad reviews while ours got raves. I had thought, like others, this movie would thrust me into big stardom. But, it took several years for the word-of-mouth to prove it was a great little picture."

Despite its poor marketing, *The Narrow Margin* received favorable notices and Windsor was singled out for her performance by several critics, including one who noted her "splendidly incisive" portrayal and said that she "looked capable of halving a railroad spike with her teeth." In one of her best scenes, in which she is roughed up by the gangsters in the cramped train compartment, Windsor said "one of the heavies threw me against the seat in the train and my head was supposed to bounce off the upholstered part. Instead, my head hit the wood frame. I had asked him to really hit me, but we misjudged where I would fall. It really stunned me, but it was good for the scene."

Critics were not the only ones to praise Windsor's portrayal of Mrs. Neil. Director Richard Fleischer hailed her performance as well, stating that he had "vivid recollections" of the actress, "probably because of the flamboyance of the role and the brilliance of her performance. It was a great part for any actress to play, but it fitted Marie perfectly and she was able to give it the bite and the high tension performance it required. I was fortunate to have such a talented actress in the picture."

Windsor's features in 1953 included *Trouble Along the Way*, an entertaining comedy in which she portrayed the ex-wife of costar John Wayne; *So This Is Love*, which starred Kathryn Grayson as soprano Grace Moore and marked the film debut of Merv Griffin; and *The Eddie Cantor Story*, a routine rags-to-riches biopic starring Keefe Brasselle in the title role. She also starred in what she termed "one of the worst pictures I've been involved in," the 3-D sci-fi cult classic, *Cat Women of the Moon*. "No wonder film buffs love to poke fun at it," Windsor said. "I think we made it in two weeks. In the last few days of production we were told we were over schedule and filming just stopped. Several pages of the script never got shot!" But Windsor's best offering of the year was *City That Never Sleeps*, her fourth film noir.

This film takes place on a single night in Chicago, and begins by introducing several characters, including Johnny Kelly (Gig Young), a police officer dissatisfied with his life both at home and on the job; Johnny's mistress, Sally (Mala Powers), a showgirl determined to escape the seamy world of the nightclub; Gregg Warren (Wally Cassell), who works as a "mechanical man" in a store window and carries an unrequited love for Sally; Hayes Stewart (William Talman), a former magician turned burglary expert; Penrod Biddell (Edward Arnold), a ruthless, high-powered criminal attorney, and Lydia (Windsor), Biddell's glamourous wife, who is having an affair with Hayes.

With fascinating skill, the lives of each of the characters are woven together, beginning when Johnny informs Sally that he is leaving his wife, resigning from his job and agreeing to her request to move to California. Johnny is then summoned by Biddell, who offers him $5,000 to prevent a robbery of his office by Hayes Stewart. But Hayes craftily eludes Johnny and later demands a $100,000 payoff from Biddell in exchange for damaging papers he has stolen. Hayes' plans are foiled, however, when Biddell pulls a gun and he is forced to shoot the attorney. Later, Hayes tries to locate Johnny at Sally's nightclub, but he instead encounters Johnny's father, a police sergeant. In his effort to escape, Hayes shoots and kills the sergeant and outside the club, he murders Lydia as well. Hayes then realizes that his crime has been witnessed by the "mechanical man" in the nearby store window, but his attempt to shoot the man misses and he flees, with Johnny in close pursuit. Johnny follows Stewart atop the elevated train tracks and after a struggle, Stewart falls onto the electrified "third rail" and plunges to his death. The film's end finds Johnny withdrawing his resignation from the police force and reuniting with his wife.

Although *City That Never Sleeps* stands up today as a fascinating drama, critics were divided; a particularly scathing review was offered by the *New York Times'* Howard Thompson, who panned the picture's "cardboard cops-and-robbers style, with dialogue to match," and claimed that its "general, pat flabbiness of action and the hollow dialogue smack consistently of pulp corn."

Of Windsor's three films in 1954, the best was *The Bounty Hunter*, a Western starring Randolph Scott. But her career took a back seat to her personal life that year when she married realtor Jack Hupp, the son of silent picture star Earl Rodney. Unlike Windsor's brief first attempt at matrimony, this union would be a lasting one, and in 1963, the actress would give birth to her only child, Richard. The success of their marriage could be attributed in part to Hupp's support of Windsor's career: "Even when we first got married, he was never the kind of man to want me to stay home and scrub and iron shirts," Windsor said in 1986. "He likes the vitality of my life." Meanwhile, having become typecast as a "bad girl" on screen, Windsor played a series of such roles in *Abbott and Costello Meet the Mummy* (1955), *No Man's Woman* (1955), *Two-Gun Lady* (1955) and *The Killing* (1956), her final film noir.

The action in *The Killing* focuses on a race track robbery, meticulously devised by Johnny Clay (Sterling Hayden), a petty criminal who has recently been released from prison. To carry out the job, Johnny assembles a mixed bag of characters, none of which, he tells his girlfriend (Coleen Gray), "are criminals in the usual sense. They've all got jobs, they all live seemingly normal, decent lives. But they've got their problems and they've all got a little larceny in them." Johnny's co-conspirators include Randy Kennan (Ted deCorsia), a police officer who owes money to the mob; George Peatty (Elisha Cook, Jr.), a spineless race track cashier whose wife Sherry (Marie Windsor) is a flashy gold digger; and Mike O'Reilly (Joe Sawyer), a tender-hearted bartender with an invalid wife.

Despite Johnny's carefully designed plan, the race track heist ultimately falls apart, starting when a sharpshooter hired to create a distraction at the race track by killing a horse is gunned down by police. Later, after the gang meets to split the stolen cash, Sherry Peatty's lover (Vince Edwards) attempts to steal the money, setting off a horrific shootout that leaves all the men dead except Johnny, who had been delayed, and George Peatty. Mortally wounded,

George manages to live long enough to lurch back to his home and kill Sherry as she is packing her clothes to leave him. And the downfall of the scheme is complete when Johnny and his girlfriend prepare to board a flight out of town with a suitcase stuffed with the stolen money. As he waits for his plane, Johnny is forced to watch in helpless despair when the suitcase falls from a luggage cart and breaks open, the loose bills scattering in the wind. In the film's final reel, Johnny waits with resignation as the police close in, glumly asking his girl, "What's the difference?"

As Sherry Peatty, Windsor offered one of her most memorable portraits, bringing to life a character who is sexy but slovenly, quick-witted and immoral. Her personality is brought into startling focus early in the film when her short, balding husband returns home from the race track and inquires about dinner. "There's all sorts of things," Sherry responds. "Steak and asparagus and potatoes..." But George looks perplexed; "I don't smell nothin'," he says, and his wife archly replies, "Well, that figures, 'cause you're too far away from it.... You don't think I had it all cooked, do you? It's all down at the shopping center." And later, like a platinum blonde Lady Macbeth, Sherry craftily convinces her reluctant husband to go through with the job: "Not that I really care about such things, understand — not when I have a big, handsome, intelligent brute like you. [But] think how disappointed I'd be if you didn't get that money. I'd feel like you didn't really love me. I don't see how I could feel any other way."

Windsor, who counts *The Killing* as one of her favorite films, said she found the character of Sherry Peatty to be "not just vicious, but rather sad too, and very mixed-up about what she wants." The actress also later addressed the phenomenon of film noir: "When we were making those movies, there was no special name for them," she said in 1995. "Obviously we weren't thinking anything special was happening. To me, it was just another job and I was happy to do them because most of them were good parts and fun to do. I had already established myself as being good at playing heavies, so I guess that's why I got those parts."

Many Hollywood insiders believed that Windsor deserved an Academy Award nomination for her outstanding performance as Sherry, but the film was not heavily promoted by United Artists. "[The studio] just didn't believe in the film and sold it as a second feature," Windsor recalled. "By the time they realized what a gem it was, it was too late to get better bookings." She did, however, win the *Look* magazine award for best supporting actress, one of a series of honors given annually at a large ceremony at the Cocoanut Grove restaurant. Windsor later said that she "anxiously awaited the fanfare and publicity" generated by the lavish event but, as luck would have it, the highly touted celebration was not to be. "It was the last time *Look* magazine gave out awards because they'd decided to stop publishing the magazine," Windsor said. "They also didn't have the huge award party at the Cocoanut Grove because

George Stevens, Ingrid Bergman and another awardee were out of the country. Moss Maby the designer, had designed a dress for me to wear to the Awards, which I never got to wear. A couple of weeks later, the editor of *Look* magazine called and said, 'I have your award here in the office. I always drive near your house on my way home. Would it be all right if I dropped it off?' And, so he did. I gave the man a drink. He toasted my winning and went on his way. Some ceremony indeed!"

After *The Killing*, Windsor appeared in a series of pictures of varying quality, including the dreadful *Swamp Women* (1956), costarring Beverly Garland, Jil Jarmyn, Carole Mathews and Susan Cummings. Although this movie is one of her least favorites, Windsor later viewed her filming experience with humor, noting that director Roger Corman took "so many shortcuts it's no wonder he's made so many movies on low budgets. We five women had to do most of the stuff that stunt women should have been doing, but there weren't any stunt women there! We gals waded through the Louisiana swamps with snakes and other live things all around us. The picture was very hard, but some of it was fun!"

Windsor was kept busy throughout the remainder of the decade, receiving her best notices for *The Unholy Wife* (1957), which starred Diana Dors as a murderous party girl, and *The Girl in Black Stockings* (1957), an entertaining whodunit with Lex Barker, Anne Bancroft and, in bit parts, Windsor's real-life siblings Jerry and Louise. By now Windsor had also begun to make frequent guest appearances on a variety of television shows, beginning with *Las Vegas Theater* in 1953. By the end of the 1950s, she would be seen in numerous television programs, and over the next three decades, would have more than 100 shows to her credit, including such top-rated series as *Maverick, Bonanza, Lassie, 77 Sunset Strip, Hawaiian Eye, Adam 12, Gunsmoke, Hawaii Five-0, Mannix, Barnaby Jones, Marcus Welby, M.D., Fantasy Island, Lou Grant* and *Murder, She Wrote*. As with her film career, many of her television roles were of the "bad girl" type, and Windsor estimated in a 1959 *TV Guide* article that she had sabotaged 75 marriages and 50 engagements in her television parts alone: "People remember the bad girl more clearly than the good girl," Windsor said. "When I get 'arrested' on TV, I can't work again in that series. People write in and say, '*That* girl is in *jail!*'"

In addition to her frequent television appearances, Windsor continued to appear in feature films, including such well-received pictures as *Critic's Choice* (1963) with Bob Hope and Lucille Ball; *Bedtime Story* (1964), starring Marlon Brando and David Niven; *Support Your Local Sheriff* (1969) and *Support Your Local Gunfighter* (1970), both starring James Garner; and *Cahill: United States Marshall* (1973), her third and final screen appearance with John Wayne. Some of Windsor's more recent pictures have included *Freaky Friday* (1976), *Lovely but Deadly* (1983) and *Commando Squad* (1987).

After several decades away from the stage, Windsor returned to the theater in the 1980s, starring in a number of Los Angeles productions, including *The Vinegar Tree*, Michael Cristofer's Pulitzer Prize-winning play *The Shadow Box* and *The Bar Off Melrose*. In the latter production, Windsor won the coveted L.A. Critics Award, and was highly acclaimed in reviews, with Ruth E. Maier of the *New Californian* stating that the actress "achieves a truly accurate balance of honest fragility and hesitant triumph," and the *Evening Outlook*'s Terry Fisher claiming: "It's ultimately veteran actress Marie Windsor who steals the show.... Without trying to overshadow the rest of the cast, Windsor does a marvelous self-parody." In addition to the L.A. Critics Award, Windsor has also received numerous other honors in recent years, including four *Drama-Logue* Awards, the Bronze Halo Award for her outstanding contributions to the motion picture industry, and the Motion Picture and Television Fund's Golden Boot Award. In 1983 she was bestowed with a star on the Hollywood Walk of Fame.

Between her screen, television and stage appearances, Windsor has managed to find time for a variety of civic activities. She is a cofounder of the Thalians, an organization dedicated to helping mentally troubled children, and WAIF (Women's Adoption International Fund), which was originally dedicated to assisting American couples in adopting foreign-born babies and currently focuses on the needs of American homeless children. She also served on the board of the women's auxiliary of the John Tracy Clinic, which teaches hearing-impaired children to speak, as well as the Screen Actors Guild (SAG), for which she cofounded the SAG Film Society. Upon her retirement from the Guild, she was awarded the prestigious Ralph Morgan Award for her 25 years of distinguished service on the SAG board. Windsor is also a well-respected artist, having sold more than 100 paintings, and holds California licenses entitling her to sell real estate and practice interior decoration. And, as if these activities weren't enough, Windsor has also continued her studies throughout the years, taking a year-long refresher course at the Lee Strasberg Theatre Institute, studying each summer for nine years with Stella Adler, and enrolling for two years with the Harvey Lembeck Comedy Workshop. "It's all a part of me," Windsor said of her numerous interests. "Just different colors. So when I sit down at my easel, or do enameling in my studio, or play tennis or go to the theater, it's all the same — just a different location, a different task."

Although Windsor never achieved the ranks of superstardom, she views her lengthy career with satisfaction, admitting that she wouldn't have had it any other way. In a 1986 interview, she admitted: "I would like to have become a bigger star, because I wish I could have done a lot more for my mother and father — they were wonderful people, loving and supportive parents. But as far as happiness goes, I'm about as happy as anybody can be. I don't know how it could have gone better as far as my personal life is concerned. Maybe, if it had gone the other way, I might not be as happy as I am now — and that's something to consider."

Film Noir Filmography

FORCE OF EVIL   *Director:* Abraham Polonsky. *Producer:* Bob Roberts. Released by MGM, December 1948. *Running time:* 78 minutes. *Cast:* John Garfield, Beatrice Pearson, Thomas Gomez, Howland Chamberlain, Roy Roberts, Marie Windsor, Paul McVey.

THE SNIPER   *Director:* Edward Dmytryk. *Producer:* Stanley Kramer. Released by Columbia, May 1952. *Running time:* 87 minutes. *Cast:* Adolphe Menjou, Arthur Franz, Gerald Mohr, Marie Windsor, Frank Faylen, Richard Kiley, Mabel Paige. *Awards:* Academy Award nomination for Best Original Screenplay (Edna Anhalt, Edward Anhalt).

THE NARROW MARGIN   *Director:* Richard Fleischer. *Producer:* Stanley Rubin. Released by RKO, May 1952. *Running time:* 71 minutes. *Cast:* Charles McGraw, Marie Windsor, Jacqueline White, Gordon Gebert, Queenie Leonard, Don Beddoe. Academy Award nomination for Best Original Screenplay (Martin Goldsmith, Jack Leonard).

CITY THAT NEVER SLEEPS   *Director and Producer:* John H. Auer. Released by Republic, August 1953. *Running time:* 90 minutes. *Cast:* Gig Young, Mala Powers, William Talman, Edward Arnold, Chill Willis, Marie Windsor, Paula Raymond, Otto Hulett.

THE KILLING   *Director:* Stanley Kubrick. *Producer:* James B. Harris. Released by United Artists, May 1956. *Running time:* 84 minutes. *Cast:* Sterling Hayden, Coleen Gray, Vince Edwards, Jay C. Flippen, Marie Windsor, Ted deCorsia, Elisha Cook, Jr., Joe Sawyer, Timothy Carey, Jay Adler.

References

Anhalt, Edna, and Edward Anhalt. "*The Sniper*—From Research to Shooting." *New York Times*, May 4, 1952.

Arkatov, Janice. "Windsor's 'Star' Label Still Intact." *Los Angeles Times*, April 23, 1986.

Gebhart, Myrtle. "Re-discovered When She Won Riding Contest." *Boston Sunday Post*, December 22, 1946.

Masse, Cheryl. "Persistence." *Beverly Hills*, July 23, 1986.

Meyer, Jim. "Marie Windsor Invites Me to Her House." *Filmograph*, 1972.

_____. "Marie Windsor Talks About Some of Her Films." *Filmograph*, 1971.

_____. "Marie's Family Comes First." *Miami Herald*, March 7, 1971.

_____. "A New Nose, a New Series." *Miami News*, January 20, 1962.

_____. "She's a 'Wildcat' on Screen — And an 'Owl Mother' at Home." *Miami Herald*, June 19, 1969.

Miller, Mark A. "Marie Windsor: This Actress Knew How to Survive ... with Style." *Filmfax*, December 1991–January 1992

Pontes, Bob. "Interview with Marie Windsor." *Classic Images*, June 1988.

Swisher, Viola Hegyi. "Marie Windsor: Stretches Beyond the 'Shadow' of a Doubt." *Drama-Logue*, September 6–12, 1984.

Thirer, Irene. "Screen Views." *New York Post*, December 16, 1950.

"When She's Bad, She's Good." *TV Guide*, May 2, 1959.

Shelley Winters

Shelley Winters may be best known to modern audiences as the overweight former swimming champion who valiantly died halfway through *The Poseidon Adventure* (1972), or as the irreverent grandmother of the title character on television's *Roseanne*, but in her heyday, she was a striking blonde with a tremendous acting talent that earned her two Academy Awards. Winters, who has proven that she is equally at home in lightweight comedy as well as heavy drama, appeared in six films noirs: *A Double Life* (1947), *Cry of the City* (1948), *He Ran All the Way* (1951), *The Big Knife* (1955), *I Died a Thousand Times* (1955) and *Odds Against Tomorrow* (1959).

The actress who, it was once stated, "wasn't discovered — she scratched and clawed her way," was born Shirley Schrift in St. Louis, Missouri, on August 18, 1922. The second daughter of Jonas Schrift, a Jewish tailor cutter, and Rose Winter Schrift, who before her marriage had performed with the St. Louis Municipal Opera Company, Shirley would later say that she couldn't remember a time when she didn't want to be an actress. Her performance debut took place at the tender age of four, when the future star won a prize for singing "Shortnin' Bread" after sneaking into an amateur contest at a neighborhood theater. Years later the actress recalled, "The more they tried to get me off, the louder I sang. Finally, in desperation, the master of ceremonies gave me a size 14 knitted sweater that hung down to my feet."

When Shirley was still a child, her family moved to Long Island, New York, and later to Brooklyn, where her favorite activity was frequenting the city's movie theaters. Never particularly fond of school, she stated in her autobiography that she was "the most undisciplined kid in the school and failed everything. It was no doubt a relief to the teachers whenever I played hookey." But her fun-filled childhood was abruptly shattered when her father was convicted of the arson fire of his Long Island haberdashery and sentenced to ten-to-twenty years in prison. Although Jonas Schrift only spent a year in Sing Sing prison, and was later cleared of all charges, he was, the actress recalled, "a destroyed man." To help the family make ends meet, Shirley sold magazines door to door, and struggled to escape the grim reality of her life by developing a "whole fantasy world ... fantasy was necessary to my lonely ghetto existence.... This ability to fantasize has been a powerful tool in my acting."

In the late 1930s, Shirley made her first attempt to break into motion pictures when she tried out for the role of Scarlett O'Hara in David O. Selznick's classic *Gone with the Wind* (1939). For her interview with Selznick, director George Cukor and MGM talent scout Bill Grady, the future star donned her sister's high heels, her mother's large straw hat and an off-the-shoulder violet dress with the bra cups stuffed with powder puffs. Although Selznick and Grady dissolved into laughter at Shirley's pronouncement of "Lawdy, folks, I'm the only goil to play Scarlett," the actress recalled that George Cukor suggested that she study speech and acting and try her hand on the stage. "I walked out of that office on air," she stated in her autobiography. "I didn't get the part, true, but Mr. Cukor made me feel as though I had — he was the first person to treat me as if I were really an actress."

Soon after, Shirley began acting in school plays, including *Good News* and *The Mikado*. But in 1939, several months before she would have graduated from Thomas Jefferson High School, Shirley left school to become a model in New York's garment district and attend drama classes at the New Theatre School ("The drama school that was to change my life, my art, my politics, and, I think, my soul," she recalled). That summer she earned $100 for a ten-week season in summer stock, and the following fall she found work as what she called "probably the world's worst chorus girl" at the La Conga nightclub. Around this time, Shirley registered with Actors Equity and changed her professional name to Shelley (after her favorite poet) and adopted her mother's maiden name of Winter. Several years later, in 1947, Universal Studios would add the "s" to her last name, officially making her Shelley Winters.

After haunting the offices of theatrical managers for the better part of a year, Winters began appearing in a number of stage productions, including her Broadway debut in *The Night Before Christmas, Rio Rita* and *Meet the People*. During the tour of the latter production, Winters met Mack Paul Meyer, a salesman from Chicago. According to Winters, she "promptly fell in love," and after a three-week whirlwind romance, the two were married on January 1, 1943. The first months of the couple's marriage were happy ones, but before long, Meyer entered the Army, and four years later, the couple divorced. "We were both too young," Winters explained. "We were together for six months and when he returned from the Army we were strangers to each other."

Meanwhile, during her run in Max Reinhardt's hit play *Rosalinda*, Winters was spotted by Harry Cohn, head of Columbia Pictures, and after a screen test, the famed mogul signed her to a seven-year contract starting at $100 a week. Her screen debut was an unbilled bit part in the Rosalind Russell vehicle *What a Woman!* (1943), followed by larger roles in *Sailor's Holiday* (1944), a lightweight comedy starring Arthur Lake, and United Artists' *Knickerbocker Holiday* (1944), a musical with Charles Coburn and Nelson Eddy. But after failing to attract much notice in such well-received films as *A Thousand and One Nights* (1944) and the Rita Hayworth starrer *Tonight and Every Night* (1945), Winters was informed that she didn't fit in with the Columbia "Love Goddess image," and was dropped from her contract.

Never one to let a setback get her down, Winters got braces to fix her "overlapping eyeteeth," took lessons in dance, speech and acting (including a class taught by Charles Laughton), appeared in such stage productions as *The Taming of the Shrew, Of Mice and Men* and *Oklahoma!*, and was seen in bit parts in *The Gangster* (1947), starring Barry Sullivan; *New Orleans* (1947), featuring jazz greats Louis Armstrong and Billie Holiday in her only feature film appearance; and *Red River* (1948), with John Wayne and Montgomery Clift. Her persistence paid off when she was cast as a lonely waitress in her first film noir, Universal's *A Double Life* (1947), starring Ronald Colman. According to Winters, ten actresses, including Lana Turner and Kim Stanley, tested for the part: "I was very lucky. I rehearsed it and then I barely made the test."

In preparation for the role, Winters took a job for a week working as a waitress, but she later recalled that her first day of filming was a disaster, with her initial scene requiring a whopping 96 takes: "Everything imaginable went wrong. I stumbled in. I poured coffee on Ronald Colman's hands. I poured coffee in his lap. I dropped my pad. I broke my pencil.... It wasn't funny; it was a nightmare." But Colman managed to calm Winters' nerves, and the actress stated that she has "always been eternally grateful" to him.

This George Cukor–directed feature focuses on Anthony John (Colman), a highly respected actor who is known for his ability to completely submerge himself in his characters, "becoming someone else, every night ... so completely." Against the wishes of his ex-wife and leading lady Brita (Signe Hasso), Tony agrees to star in *Othello*, the Shakespearean tale of murder and betrayal. Shortly before beginning the production, Tony meets a young waitress, Pat Kroll (Winters), who makes no secret of her instant attraction to the debonair actor. "You wanna know something? You're cute," she boldly informs him. "I'll be through here in three quarters of an hour. We could tell each other our troubles. I like you ... you gonna say you like me?"

After a year, *Othello* is still enjoying a well-received run, but Tony has become so obsessed with his character that he actually chokes Brita during one performance, nearly killing her. And as Tony becomes further enmeshed with the life of his character, he returns one night to Pat Kroll's home and, confusing her with his unfaithful on-stage wife, he strangles her. Before long, Tony's press agent Bill Friend (Edmond O'Brien) begins to suspect that Tony is guilty of Pat's murder and arranges for a local actress to disguise herself to closely resemble the dead waitress. Confronted by the waitress in a restaurant, Tony reacts so frantically that Bill's suspicions are confirmed. Later, at the evening's performance of *Othello*, Bill arrives at the theater with a police detective, who plans to place Tony under arrest. Realizing that his guilt has been unearthed, Tony plunges a dagger into his heart during the performance and dies in the wings.

Winters, who later described *A Double Life* as a "wonderful ... truly scary movie," was critically acclaimed for her small but showy role in her first film noir, including a mention in the *New York Times* for her "intriguing" portrayal. She followed this triumph with a part as a gun moll in *Larceny* (1948), a gangster melodrama starring John Payne and Dan Duryea. Critics were mixed in their reviews for this film, but Alton Cook of the *New York World Telegram* hailed Winters as "one of the definitely important actresses of the year," and the critic for *Time* magazine said she gave her role "a strong blend of sex, humor, loneliness and desperation." After her standout performance, Winters received contract offers from no less than four studios, finally signing a seven-year agreement with Universal. The studio immediately loaned the budding star to 20th Century–Fox for a small role in *Cry of the City* (1948), her second film noir.

As this film begins, Martin Rome (Richard Conte) is in a hospital receiving last rites after being wounded during a restaurant hold-up that left a policeman dead. As Rome is being taken to surgery, an unscrupulous attorney, Niles (Berry Kroeger), urges Rome to confess to a recent jewel robbery that involved the torture and murder of an elderly matron. Martin refuses, and later recovers from his injuries, but he learns that both police and Niles are searching for his young, innocent girlfriend Teena (Debra Paget), trying to pin the jewel heist on the couple. Martin convinces a night nurse to hide Teena from police, then uses a trustee at the hospital to help him escape. Paying a visit to Niles' office, Martin learns that the attorney was actually behind the jewel heist and forces him to turn over the jewels, as well as disclose the name of the couple who committed the crime. When Niles tries to shoot Martin, he stabs the attorney and escapes. Later, suffering from his leg wound, Martin convinces his former girlfriend Brenda (Winters) to find an unlicensed doctor who will treat his injuries, then locates Rose Given (Hope Emerson), the woman involved in the heist. He offers to trade the jewels for $5,000 in cash, tickets to South America and a car, but he double-crosses Rose and she is arrested by police while trying to collect the jewels from a subway station locker.

Meanwhile, Martin is being fiercely hunted by Lt. Candella (Victor Mature), who finally catches up to Martin at a neighborhood church, where he has gone to meet Teena. Martin reveals that the virtuous young girl is leaving the country with him, but Candella tries to dissuade her: "She knows that you killed two men. But does she know about the others? Does she know about the poor little crack trustee, who'll get five years for helping you break jail? Does she know about Brenda, the girl that shuttled you? She'll serve time, Marty. So will that doctor with the sick wife. You forgot all about them, didn't you? No, he didn't forget them. He didn't even think about them. He used them and brushed them aside, just like he's used everybody's he's ever known." Faced with her boyfriend's past, Teena leaves. Martin tries to escape, but Candella guns him down in the street outside the church.

Despite her minor role in *Cry of the City*, Winters' performance caught the notice of more than one critic, including the reviewer for the *New York Times* who incorporated her in his praise of the film's "fine supporting roles." Around this time, Winters was also named by *The Saturday Evening Post*, along with Jane Greer, Ava Gardner, Ruth Roman, Elizabeth Taylor and Audrey Totter, as one of the six promising actresses of the future. This distinction notwithstanding, Universal next cast Winters in such forgettable pictures as *Take One False Step* (1949), which tried unsuccessfully to combine drama with lightweight comedy, and *Johnny Stool Pigeon* (1949), a weak cops-and-robbers tale. After a loan-out to Paramount for a small role in *The Great*

Shelley Winters

Gatsby (1949), Winters had her first leading role, a cabaret singer in Universal's *South Sea Sinner* (1950). But the film, described by one critic as "having about as much South Sea flavor as a roadside papaya bar," did little for Winters' career, and was notable only for its distinction as the screen debut of the flamboyant pianist, Liberace.

    After the laughable *South Sea Sinners*, Winters was seen in *Winchester '73* (1950), a well-received Western starring James Stewart, and was praised by the critic for *Variety* as "just sufficiently hard-boiled and cynical" in the role of a dance hall floozie. Next, during the summer of 1950, she appeared in a variety of East Coast theaters, portraying the role of Billie Dawn in *Born Yesterday*. On the heels of her success in this play, Winters settled in New York, vowing (as she recalled in her autobiography), "I'm never coming back [to Hollywood]. I'm going to be a great theater actress." Upon her arrival in the Big Apple, Winters began studying acting, singing and dancing at the Actors Studio, the famed training institution whose students included Marlon Brando, James Dean, Geraldine Page and Montgomery Clift. But when Universal suspended her salary, Winters resumed her film career, appearing in her third film noir, the United Artists production *He Ran All the Way* (1951).

In her second autobiography, *Shelley II*, Winters relayed an interesting anecdote regarding the manner in which she secured the role in *He Ran All the Way*. Universal had originally refused to loan the actress to United Artists for the film, instead planning to star her in what she called "some cockamamie film" entitled *Little Egypt*, a lightweight tale of a phony Egyptian princess. In order to avoid suspension by refusing *Little Egypt*, Winters instead "began eating as if it was going out of style," gaining 12 pounds within one week. Seeing that the actress was unable to fit into her skimpy Egyptian-style wardrobe, Universal consented to the loan-out, whereupon Winters embarked on a crash weight-loss regime consisting of fasting, diet and water pills and frequent steam baths. She quickly lost 15 pounds and triumphantly reported to the set of *He Ran All the Way*, but the rapid weight gain and loss would start a life-long process of "ruining my metabolism," Winters stated.

Starring John Garfield in his last film role before his untimely death, *He Ran All the Way* covers three days in the life of Nick Robey (Garfield), a petty thief who lives with his cold-hearted, beer-guzzling mother (Gladys George). The quality of Nick's home life is revealed early in the film when his mother chides him: "If you were a man, you'd be out looking for a job." And Nick rejoins with hostility, "If you were a man, I'd kick your teeth in." Against his better judgment, Nick is talked into committing a payroll robbery with an associate, Al Molin (Norman Lloyd). Before they can escape, they are surprised by a police officer, who shoots Al and is, in turn, wounded by Nick. Fleeing to a nearby public swimming pool, Nick meets Peg Dobbs (Winters), later escorting her home where she lives with her parents (Wallace Ford and Selena Royle) and her younger brother Tommy (Bobby Hyatt). When Nick mistakenly believes that Peg's parents know about his crime, he holds the family hostage.

The following morning, Nick learns of the death of the policeman he shot and that he is being sought for murder. He remains holed up in the apartment and later, convinced that Peg has fallen in love with him, plans to run away with her. Later, Nick sends Peg to buy a car for their escape, but when the car fails to be delivered as expected, Nick becomes increasingly paranoid and forces Peg from the apartment: "Last night, coming home all dolled up — making a big play. You thought it would work, didn't you? Thought you had me all tied up. Like a knot. You got me to trust you, didn't you? You don't love me. You never loved me. Nobody loves anyone." As the couple reach the front door of the building, Nick is shot at by Peg's father and drops his gun. Nick begs Peg to return his gun to him, but she picks it up and shoots him. As he staggers into the street, the car he had been waiting for pulls up to the curb, but Nick collapses in the gutter and dies.

After earning unanimous praise for what one reviewer called Winters' "first full-length part that makes adult sense," the actress offered one of her most powerful and memorable performances in *A Place in the Sun* (1951). In an excellent cast that included Montgomery Clift and Elizabeth Taylor, Winters was a standout as the drab factory girl who gets pregnant by her social-climbing boyfriend. Her highly acclaimed performance earned Winters her first Academy Award nomination, but she would later lose to Vivien Leigh in *A Streetcar Named Desire* (1951). She also lost the New York Film Critics Award to Leigh that year, but she did receive the *Holiday* award for "the woman in the motion picture industry who has done the most in the past year to improve standards and to honestly present American life to the rest of the world."

Winters followed this picture with a series of films of varying quality, including *Behave Yourself!* (1951), a lightweight comedy with Farley Granger; *The Raging Tide* (1951), a confusing waterfront melodrama; *Meet Danny Wilson* (1952), a Frank Sinatra vehicle that Winters said "began shooting in chaos and ended in disaster"; *Untamed Frontier* (1952), a boring Technicolor Western with Joseph Cotten; and *My Man and I* (1952), in which Winters earned high praise from the critic for *Variety*, who wrote: "Miss Winters turns in another standout job as the wise-cracking but warm-hearted dipso, and her appealing play gives the film most of its warmth."

While maintaining her busy acting schedule, Winters managed to keep up an active social life, engaging in brief relationships with a number of well-known actors, including Marlon Brando, Burt Lancaster, William Holden and Farley Granger, to whom she was reportedly briefly engaged. But Winters' free-wheeling love life came to an abrupt halt when, during a trip to Europe, she met the man who would become her second husband, Italian actor Vittorio Gassman. Upon first spotting Gassman, Winters later recalled, she imagined that he might be her "adolescent Prince Charming come to life," and although the actor spoke little English, the two experienced an instant mutual attraction. On April 28, 1952, just hours after Gassman obtained a divorce from his first wife, he and Winters were married in Juarez, Mexico. Although Winters gave birth to a daughter, Vittoria Gina, the following year, the marriage was a stormy one, with the final straw coming when Gassman had a brief affair with a 16-year-old Italian actress. On June 2, 1954, the couple divorced, and Winters would later say of Gassman: "I was in love with him and he was in love with him."

During her two-year marriage to Gassman, Winters was seen in a variety of films that included *Saskatchewan* (1954), a big-budget Western starring Alan Ladd; *Executive Suite* (1954), an absorbing star-studded drama with Barbara Stanwyck, June Allyson, Walter Pidgeon and William Holden; and her final film under her Universal contract, *Playgirl* (1954), which Winters described as a "gangster film [that] nobody remembers ... and I have never even seen."

In 1955, Winters appeared in a whopping six films — the first, *Mambo*, was notable primarily because it costarred her then-husband, Gassman. It was filmed during the final days of their relationship. Winters followed this picture with a touching performance as a German girl too cowardly to marry a Jew in *I Am a Camera*, then had a small but memorable role in *The Night of the Hunter*, portraying a countrified widow who is murdered by her psychopathic preacher-husband (Robert Mitchum). After being somewhat miscast as an American idealist caught up in the Mexican revolution in *The Treasure of Pancho Villa*, Winters finished the year with back-to-back films noirs, both costarring Jack Palance: *The Big Knife* and *I Died a Thousand Times*.

Based on a play by Clifford Odets, *The Big Knife* focuses on Charlie Castle (Palance), a womanizing film star who is unhappily separated from his wife Marion (Ida Lupino). The chief obstacle in the couple's relationship is Charlie's plan to sign a seven-year contract with his studio which, Marion fears, will turn him into "one of the witless, sold-out guys sitting around a gin table, swapping phone numbers and the latest dirt." The couple reconcile when Charlie agrees to leave Hollywood, but the luckless actor is later forced into the contract agreement by his sadistic studio head, Stanley Hoff (Rod Steiger), who threatens to expose Charlie's guilt in a drunk driving accident in which a child was killed. Tormented over his situation, Charlie has a one-night dalliance with the wife of his press agent Buddy Bliss, who had taken the blame and been briefly imprisoned for the driving accident.

Charlie sinks further into despair when Dixie Evans (Winters), a heavy-drinking starlet who was with him on the night of the car accident, reveals her plans to disclose the truth as a payback for her shabby treatment by studio execs. "They hired me for my figure, not to act. They hire girls like me to entertain the visiting exhibitors. I'm a deductible item," Dixie bitterly tells Charlie. "They'd drown me if they could, that studio." When Hoff's associate (Wendell Corey) hatches a scheme for Charlie to permanently silence Dixie by poisoning her, Charlie refuses, insisting, "That pathetic little girl is my friend." Charlie's refusal incurs the wrath of Hoff, but ironically, Dixie is killed in a freak car accident while crossing the street. Unable to face his future, Charlie commits suicide, and the film ends with the heart-rending sounds of Marion screaming desperately for help.

Although *The Big Knife* won third prize at the Venice Film Festival in late 1955, the film was a critical disaster, with one reviewer writing that the picture had a "dull cutting edge," and another dismissing it as "too unrelentingly morbid to appeal to a sizable viewing audience." After this feature, Winters starred in her second film noir of the year, *I Died a Thousand Times*.

A remake of *High Sierra* (1941), *I Died a Thousand Times* features Jack Palance as ex-convict Roy Earle, who joins two small-time hoods in a scheme to rob a resort hotel in California. When he arrives at the gang's mountain hideout, Roy is dismayed to learn that one of the men, Babe (Lee Marvin), is accompanied by his girlfriend Marie (Winters). Over time, however, Roy comes to respect and admire Marie and allows her to remain. Meanwhile, Roy encounters an elderly couple (Ralph Moody and Olive Carey), whose grand-daughter Velma (Lori Nelson) suffers with a crippling clubfoot. Drawn to the girl's virtuous demeanor, Roy finances an operation to correct her condition, but after the successful surgery she rejects his plans to marry her. Roy later comes to realize his love for Marie, but their dreams of a future together are doomed. During the heist at the resort hotel, Roy shoots a security guard and during the getaway, Roy's co-conspirators are killed in a fiery auto crash. Before long, Roy becomes the focus of a statewide manhunt and is later gunned down by police in the High Sierra mountains.

Unfavorably compared to its predecessor, *I Died a Thousand Times* was panned by critics, including Bosley Crowther who wrote in the *New York Times*: "Somehow it isn't quite as touching as it was 14 years ago." Crowther was equally unimpressed with Winters' performance in the film, calling her "piteously without skill." And the actress herself later recalled asking the film's director Stuart Heisler, "Why is Warners remaking [*High Sierra*]? Why don't they just re-release this great picture as is?"

After next appearing in an unappealing comedy, *Cash on Delivery* (1956), Winters turned her back on Hollywood and fled to the Broadway stage, telling reporters: "For every good film like *A Place in the Sun* or *Executive Suite*, you have to do a Technicolor Western like *Saskatchewan*.... I hate the rotten pictures they put me in. Out of all the pictures I've made, I'm proud of four. Think of it. Seven years of my life thrown away — for what?" She would be absent from the big screen for the next three years, instead starring in a number of highly acclaimed plays and television dramas, including the television versions of *A Double Life* and *The Women* and such Broadway productions as *The Girls of Summer* costarring Pat Hingle and George Peppard, and *A Hatful of Rain*, with Ben Gazzara. For her performance in the latter production, Winters was lauded by critics, including Brooks Atkinson of the *New York Times*, who wrote, "As the bewildered wife, Miss Winters could hardly do better. She is simple, aware of all that is going on around her, good-humored and full of compassion and decision when the last scene comes around. She has the taste as well as the craft for a lucid and disarming character portrait."

During the run of *A Hatful of Rain*, Winters became involved with co-star Anthony Franciosa, and on May 4, 1957, the couple were married in Carson City, Nevada. But, like her previous unions, this marriage would be a

turbulent one, and Winters would later state, "I have never been able to understand my affair with and subsequent marriage to Tony. It was a kind of obsessive compulsion." The talented but volatile Franciosa was prone to violence
and frequently in trouble with the law, including an incident shortly after the
couple's wedding when the actor assaulted a photographer and was sentenced
to ten days in jail. Franciosa also reportedly engaged in several extramarital
affairs, including one with Judy Balaban, the wife of a top Hollywood agent,
and Winters herself had a fling with actor Sean Connery of "James Bond"
fame. In 1960, following an argument in which Winters injured her husband
with a heavy perfume bottle, she filed for divorce. Franciosa would go on to
marry and subsequently divorce Balaban, but Winters has since steered clear
of the matrimonial altar.

Meanwhile, Winters triumphantly returned to pictures in 1959, in the
film that would earn the actress her first Academy Award for Best Supporting Actress — *The Diary of Anne Frank*. In this gripping story, Winters portrayed Mrs. Van Daan, a slobbish, frightened neighbor who hid for two years
from Nazis in an Amsterdam attic with the real-life title character and her
family. Fifteen years after winning the Oscar (beating out Susan Kohner and
Juanita Moore for *Imitation of Life*, Hermoine Baddeley in *Room at the Top*
and Thelma Ritter in *Pillow Talk*), Winters donated her award to the Anne
Frank Museum in Amsterdam, where it remains to this day.

After her successful performance in *Anne Frank*, Winters appeared in her
final film noir, *Odds Against Tomorrow* (1959). Here, Winters played Lorry
Slater, who selflessly supports her ex-convict husband Earl (Robert Ryan): "I
knew you were in trouble when I fell in love with you," Lorry assures Earl. "I
knew it would be rough for us, and it would take time, but I didn't care. You
don't have to be the great big man with me." But Earl's pride forces him back
into a life of crime, and he agrees to participate in an intricate scheme to rob
an upstate New York bank, as planned by ex-cop David Burke (Ed Begley).
To carry out the plot, Burke also solicits the help of Johnny Ingram (Harry
Belafonte), a black singer, in spite of Earl's objection to "the third man being
a nigger."

Typified by the underlying racial tension between Earl and Johnny, the
well-designed plans for the robbery fall apart. After the men successfully steal
the cash, Burke is gunned down by police, and Slater and Ingram escape with
the authorities close behind. Climbing atop a pair of oil storage tanks, the
two men turn on each other and both die in an explosive blaze. The following day, with the corpses laid out side by side, one fireman asks another,
"Which is which?" In a reply tinged with irony, his colleague tells him, "Take
your pick."

The director of *Odds Against Tomorrow*, Robert Wise, later praised Winters' performance, pointing out that, during filming, the actress was preoccupied with her failing marriage to Anthony Franciosa. "I had worked with

Shelley earlier in *Executive Suite*, so this was a return engagement," Wise said in 1994. "Shelley is basically a very warm and generous person and certainly was a very experienced actress by the time of *Odds*. But she was particularly high strung on the picture — not temperamental, I hasten to add — so it took extra time to get the right performance from her. I always appreciated the amount of patience Robert Ryan displayed in the scenes he had with Shelley. But when we got the scenes right they were good and she was quite effective."

Winters next delivered a powerful portrayal of a drug-addicted widow in *Let No Man Write My Epitaph* (1960), played the childhood sweetheart of a crusading district attorney in *The Young Savages* (1961), and gave what she considered "one of the best performances I ever gave in any medium" in *Lolita* (1962), the tale of a middle-aged man attracted to a 14-year-old nymphet. Although plumper and more mature, Winters continued to act steadily, easing comfortably into supporting character roles such as the whorehouse madam in *The Balcony* (1963), the Bible's "woman-of-no-name" in the star-packed *The Greatest Story Ever Told* (1965), and the amoral mother of a blind girl in *A Patch of Blue* (1965), which earned the actress her second Academy Award for Best Supporting Actress (beating out Ruth Gordon for *Inside Daisy Clover*, Joyce Redman and Maggie Smith for *Othello* and Peggy Wood for *The Sound of Music*).

Although the films in which Winters appeared varied in merit, she consistently turned in highly acclaimed performances, including her greedy ex-child star in *Harper* (1966), starring Paul Newman; the prototype Jewish mother in Carl Reiner's *Enter Laughing* (1967); and the mother of the youngest president of the United States in *Wild in the Streets* (1968). Between film roles, Winters continued performing in other media, winning an Emmy Award for her role in the television drama *Two Is the Number* with Martin Balsam, and appearing in such stage productions as *Two for the Seesaw*, *Invitation to a March*, *The Country Girl* and *Night of the Iguana*. During this period, Winters also managed to find time for political activism, working on the campaigns of Adlai Stevenson and John and Robert Kennedy.

Demonstrating her versatility, Winters wrote a play in the early 1970s, *One Night Stands of a Noisy Passenger*, which was presented on Broadway with a cast that included Robert DeNiro, Will Geer, Sally Kirkland and Joanna Miles. The actress also earned her third Academy Award nomination for Best Supporting Actress for her performance in *The Poseidon Adventure* (1972), in which she played an overweight survivor of an ocean liner disaster who dies while courageously struggling to help her remaining fellow passengers. (The award that year would go to Eileen Heckart for *Butterflies Are Free*.) The actress continued to work steadily throughout the 1970s and 1980s, appearing in such films as *Cleopatra Jones* (1973), *Journey Into Fear* (1975), *The Magic of Lublin* (1979), *Fanny Hill* (1983), *Witchfire* (1984), *The Delta Force* (1986) and *An Unremarkable Life* (1989). Winters also penned two autobiographies during the 1980s — the first, *Shelley: Also Known as Shirley* (1980), covered her life from birth through her divorce to Vittorio Gassman, and *Shelley II: The Middle of My Century* (1989), spanned the mid–1950s through the 1960s, and concluded with the words: "To Be Continued, I Hope!" Currently, the actress is reportedly working on her third autobiography.

In the 1990s, Winters maintained her busy performing schedule, appearing in such films as *Silence of the Hams* (1992), a satire on *Psycho* and *The Silence of the Lambs*; *The Pickle* (1993); *Raging Angels* (1995); *Jury Duty* (1995); *Backfire!* (1995); *Portrait of a Lady* (1996) and *Heavy* (1996). She also was seen in a recurring role on the long-running ABC-TV sitcom *Roseanne*, and was nominated in 1997 for a Cable Ace award for her performance in Showtime's *Mrs. Munck*.

With a phenomenal career consisting of more than 100 films, Shelley Winters is truly one of Hollywood's most durable stars. She exhibited an exceptional talent and versatility in such films as *A Double Life*, *A Place in the Sun*, and *The Diary of Anne Frank*, and even as she approaches her 80s, she is showing no signs of stopping. The actress once stated that her beloved mother Rose was the source of her "strength, talent, chutzpah and ingenuity" — perhaps it is these qualities that have kept her on top after more than a half-century.

Film Noir Filmography

A DOUBLE LIFE   *Director:* George Cukor. *Producer:* Michael Kanin. Released by Universal-International, December 1947. *Running time:* 103 minutes. *Cast:* Ronald Colman, Signe Hasso, Edmond O'Brien, Shelley Winters, Ray Collins, Philip Loeb, Millard Mitchell.

CRY OF THE CITY   *Director:* Robert Siodmak. *Producer:* Sol Siegel. Released by 20th Century–Fox, September 1948. *Running time:* 96 minutes. *Cast:* Victor Mature, Richard Conte, Fred Clark, Shelley Winters, Betty Garde, Berry Kroeger, Tommy Cook, Debra Paget, Hope Emerson.

HE RAN ALL THE WAY   *Director:* John Berry. *Producer:* Bob Roberts. Released by United Artists, July 1951. *Running time:* 77 minutes. *Cast:* John Garfield, Shelley Winters, Wallace Ford, Selena Royle, Bobby Hyatt, Gladys George, Norman Lloyd.

THE BIG KNIFE   *Director and Producer:* Robert Aldrich. Released by United Artists, November 1955. *Running time:* 111 minutes. *Cast:* Jack Palance, Ida Lupino, Wendell Corey, Rod Steiger, Jean Hagen, Shelley Winters, Ilka Chase, Everett Sloane, Wesley Addy, Paul Langton.

I DIED A THOUSAND TIMES   *Director:* Stuart Heisler. *Producer:* Willis Goldbeck. Released by Warner Bros., November 1955. *Running time:* 109 minutes. *Cast:* Jack Palance, Shelley Winters, Lori Nelson, Lee Marvin, Earl Holliman, Perry Lopez, Gonzalez Gonzalez, Lon Chaney, Jr., Howard St. John, Ralph Moody.

ODDS AGAINST TOMORROW   *Director and Producer:* Robert Wise. Released by United Artists, October 1959. *Running time:* 96 minutes. *Cast:* Ed Begley, Harry Belafonte, Robert Ryan, Shelley Winters, Gloria Grahame, Will Kuluva, Mae Barnes, Carmen DeLavallade.

References

Buckley, Michael. "Shelley Winters." *Films in Review*, March 1970.

"The Day Shelley Winters Returned to Her Old Studio and TV in a Rented Car." *TV Guide*, July 3, 1965.

Fuller, Graham. "A Winters Tale." *Interview*, May 1996.

Gassman, Vittorio. "Let Me Tell You About My Shelley." *Silver Screen*, February 1954.

"Green-Eyed Movie Madcap." *Collier's*, June 30, 1949.

Haspiel, Jim. "The Mensch Behind the Myth." *Films in Review*, June-July, 1980.

"Hit and a Miss." *Newsweek*, November 21, 1955.

Holland, Jack. "What's Good About Being a Bachelor Girl?" *Silver Screen*, November 1949.

Lilley, Jessie. "Chilling Winters." *Scarlet Street*, Summer 1993.

Maxwell, Elsa. "Latins Are Lousy Lovers." *Photoplay*, July 1952.

"Method Madam." *Newsweek*, October 8, 1962.

"Shelley Winters." *Life*, August 7, 1950.

Spines, Christine. "Shelley Winters." *Premiere*, January 1995.

"That Wonderful, Deep Silence." *Theatre Arts*, June 1956.

Wilson, Liza. "Stormy Winters." *Photoplay*, June 1951.

Winters, Shelley. "The Man I Married." *Photoplay*, May 1953.

_____. "Next Time I Want to Be a Man." *Silver Screen*, August 1950.

_____. *Shelley: Also Known as Shirley*. New York: Ballantine, 1980.

_____. *Shelley II: The Middle of My Century*. New York: Simon and Schuster, 1989.

_____. "You Can't Help Loving That Man." *Photoplay*, November 1950.

"Winters Steps into Harlow's Shoes." *Cue*, June 17, 1950.

Zeitlin, Ida. "Their Love Is Like This." *Photoplay*, August 1951.

Loretta Young

The recipient of a wide range of descriptions, from a "kind and loving woman" to "Attila the nun" and a "chocolate-covered black-widow spider," Loretta Young was a durable screen legend with a career that spanned seven decades, including nearly 100 feature films and a popular, long-running television show. Never considered a great talent, Young nonetheless possessed what can best be described as "star quality," and made an impressive impact in three films noirs: *The Stranger* (1946), *The Accused* (1948) and *Cause for Alarm* (1951).

The dark-haired actress with the distinctive features was born Gretchen Michaela Young in Salt Lake City, Utah, on January 6, 1913. Her parents, John Earl Young, a railroad auditor, and Gladys Royal Young, separated when Gretchen was three years old — the actress stated in her autobiography that her father "went away one day and never came back." Soon after, with Gretchen and her three other children, Polly Ann, born in 1908, Elizabeth Jane (better known as actress Sally Blane), born in 1910, and John Royal, born in 1915, Gladys Young moved to Los Angeles, where she had a married sister, and supported her family by operating a boarding house at 9th and Greer. (Following her divorce in 1920, Gladys married a Los Angeles businessman, George Belzer, with whom she had a daughter, Georgiana, who would later wed actor Ricardo Montalban.)

Gretchen was bitten by the acting bug when she was not yet five years old. Her uncle, Ernest Traxler, an assistant director at Famous Players–Lasky, arranged for the Young children to appear as extras in a variety of films, and at the age of four, Gretchen was paid $3.50 a day to portray a child weeping on an operating table in *The Only Way* (1917). Among the films in which the Young siblings appeared was the Rudolph Valentino starrer *The Sheik* (1921), where they were seen as a quartet of Arab children. The meager funds that the children received for their extra work was, Young recalled, "very welcome in the family kitty."

By all accounts, Gretchen was a natural performer and she would later say, "I'd thought of myself as a great big motion picture star from the time I was six. I didn't like being lost in a crowd of kid extras, so I started to pretend I was a star." But despite her youngest daughter's aspirations, Gladys Young objected to the full-time devotion of her children to the motion picture industry, and enrolled the girls in Ramona Convent in Alhambra, temporarily ending their brief film careers. Although Gretchen was disappointed with her mother's decision, she wrote in her autobiography that she "coped with it by withdrawing into dreams of what and where I'd be when I'd survived it and this kind of learning."

By 1926, Gladys Young allowed her two eldest daughters to resume their film aspirations. But it was Gretchen who got the big break when Mervyn LeRoy, then an assistant director at First National Pictures, telephoned the Young house to ask if Polly Ann was available for a role in a Colleen Moore vehicle, *Naughty but Nice* (1927). Polly Ann was already at work on another film, but the quick-thinking Gretchen informed LeRoy, "I'm an actress, too, and I'm available," and was hired for the part. On the set of the film, Colleen Moore was impressed by the conscientious demeanor of the 14-year-old actress, and urged the studio to sign her to a contract. Moore, declaring that the name Gretchen sounded "too dutchy," also ordered the youngster's moniker changed to Loretta, after a favorite doll from her childhood. Four decades later, Moore would recall her impressions of the teenager: "She had huge gray eyes and seemed to be watching everyone the director was talking to. In between scenes she kept to herself. She was never underfoot. She was all business."

After a minor role in *Whip Woman* (1928), Young attracted the attention of MGM director Herbert Brenon, who borrowed the novice to star as a tightrope walker opposite Lon Chaney in *Laugh, Clown, Laugh* (1928). Of her performance in the film, Louella Parsons of the *Los Angeles Examiner* wrote, "Little Miss Young, who plays Simonette, is still inexperienced and a trifle self-conscious, but she will overcome that in time. She is a promising little actress with a screen personality that is different from the average bobbed-hair flapper."

Her favorable reviews notwithstanding, Young recalled that her first star-ring role was a "terrible" experience because of the film's director, Herbert Brenon: "He was the first director I ever worked with where I had a leading role, and he picked up a chair and threw it at me. If it had hit me, it would have killed me.... At lunch he'd put me up in front of everybody and for half an hour he bawled me out.... Why he did this I don't know. But he did it every single day." This heartless treatment might have left a lasting scar on a more fragile type, but even at age 15, Young was strong-willed and deter-mined, and refused to be deterred from her goals of movie stardom. For sev-eral years after making *Laugh, Clown, Laugh*, Young's pride compelled her to assume a posture of self-confidence, and she would later reveal: "I had to make believe I had it — I knew I couldn't be a star without it." Young's air of assur-ance also extended to her home life, where she displayed a haughtiness that led her sisters to frequently refer to her as "Your Highness" or "The Princess."

After *Laugh, Clown, Laugh*, Young was seen in *The Magnificent Flirt* (1928), a comedy in which she played the daughter of Florence Vidor; *The Head Man* (1928), an implausible story about an alcoholic ex-senator; and *Scarlet Seas* (1928), a pirate yarn starring Richard Barthelmess, with whom she performed her first love scene. Of this eventful occasion, Young later recalled: "The first time I did a love scene, I was so self-conscious I could hardly stand it. [Barthelmess'] mere proximity was enough to set me shaking, to say noth-ing of his taking me in his arms and kissing me." But in a fashion that was coming to typify Young's professionalism, she added, "I suppose every begin-ner goes through the same thing and lives to see the scenes as part of the busi-ness of acting and nothing else."

Now under contract to Warner Bros., which had taken over First National, Young worked almost non-stop in 1929, appearing in six films — *The Squall* (her talkie debut), a box office flop that was widely criticized for its direction, script and performances; *The Girl in the Glass Cage*, a flimsy yarn about the misfortunes of a movie house cashier; *Fast Life*, the first of her six teamings with Douglas Fairbanks, Jr.; *The Forward Pass*, a college musical in which the actress displayed her pleasant soprano voice; *The Careless Age*, a melodrama concerning a medical student who strangles his actress-lover; and *The Show of Shows*, a part-Technicolor musical revue whose all-star cast included Noah Beery, Myrna Loy, Dolores Costello, Ann Sothern and Chester Morris. Also that year, Young was named one of the Wampas Baby Stars of 1929; this group of promising starlets also included Jean Arthur, Anita Page, Helen Twelvetrees and Young's sister Sally Blane. Despite this honor, however, Young received little critical praise for her acting ability, instead being noticed primarily for her striking features, and she continued to be cast in a series of mediocre films.

Young continued her fast-paced film schedule the following year, doing her best work in two well-received comedies, *Loose Ankles* (1930) with Douglas Fairbanks, Jr., and *The Man from Blankley's* (1930), starring John Barrymore. But her other efforts that year were in forgettable programmers, including *Road to Paradise* (1930), a flimsy piece of business in which Young played a dual role of twin sisters, and *The Second Floor Mystery* (1930), memorable primarily for its teaming of Young with contract player Grant Withers. A rising matinee idol, Withers was a dashing ladies' man who, at the age of 26, was divorced with a five-year-old son and reported to be a heavy drinker. But Young was drawn to the handsome actor's charming personality and aura of excitement, and after a brief romance, the two secretly eloped to Yuma, Arizona, less than three weeks after Young's 17th birthday.

Young's mother was strongly opposed to the union and initiated annulment proceedings, but soon afterward she dropped the suit and her daughter blithely announced to the press: "I am extremely happy. I love my mother, but I love Grant and he loves me, and that's all that matters…. Grant and I are married and are going to stay married." But Young's defiant proclamation would soon be disproved. The couple argued frequently and Young discovered that her handsome spouse was unpredictable and irresponsible, with little concept of the value of money. "I wanted to understand him," Young has said, "because I was so anxious to prove to my family and the rest of the world that I had not been impulsive in my marriage. But every day I realized that understanding him was more difficult than I had thought." Less than a year after their impromptu wedding, Young and Withers separated, and on September 15, 1931, Young obtained a divorce. In a 1986 interview, Young would admit: "I was playing at being married in my mind, for as a young actress it was difficult to know where movie acting stopped and the realities of life started. In your own life it's hard to know when to stop acting, because you get so wrapped up in it, so involved in the role." (Nearly three decades later, in March 1959, Withers would be found dead from an overdose of sleeping pills. Young's only comment to the press would be that Withers was "the most bewildered man I ever met.")

Professionally, while Young did not lack for film assignments, she continued to appear in rather humdrum fare in 1931, appearing as a young woman who nurses an amnesiac back to health in *Right of Way*, one of a trio of girls who travels to Chicago for fortune and romance in *Three Girls Lost*, and as the girlfriend of costar (and soon-to-be-ex-husband) Grant Withers in the ironically titled *Too Young to Marry*. Her best film of the year was *Platinum Blonde*, in which she is in love with a fellow newspaper reporter who marries a shallow socialite (Jean Harlow). In the end, it is Young's character who gets her man.

In Young's six films in 1932, she still failed to break into the ranks of stardom, but the pictures were of higher quality, and she began to appear with some of Hollywood's top actors, including James Cagney in *Taxi!*, George Brent in *They Call It Sin* and Edward G. Robinson in *The Hatchet Man*, of which the critic for *Picturegoer* wrote that Young had "never appeared to better advantage ... she is almost unbelievably different from her normal screen self." She also appeared that year in an all-star two-reel comedy, *The Slippery Pearls*, with a cast that included Norma Shearer, Joan Crawford, Gary Cooper, Warner Baxter and Douglas Fairbanks, Jr. The following year, in which Young appeared in a whopping ten films, one of her best was a loan-out to Fox, *Zoo in Budapest* (1933). Receiving top billing as an escaped orphan who finds refuge with a zookeeper, Young was praised by Richard Watts, Jr., of the *New York Herald Tribune*, who wrote that "Miss Young as the heroine is properly wide-eyed, shy and childlike."

While filming another picture that year, Columbia's *A Man's Castle* (1933), Young became romantically involved with costar Spencer Tracy, who was then separated from his wife. Rumors teemed about the couple's impending marriage, and gossip columns frequently included items about Young and Tracy's "cozy, intimate luncheons" or nights on the town. Finally, after enduring a year of innuendo and slurs on her sterling reputation, Young informed the press: "Since Spence and I are both Catholic and can never be married, we have agreed not to see each other again."

In June 1933, frustrated with the quality of her roles at Warners, Young signed a contract with former Warner Bros. executive Darryl F. Zanuck, who had recently formed 20th Century Productions with Joseph Schenck. Her first assignment under Zanuck was *The House of Rothschild* (1934), starring George Arliss. Although critics again only acknowledged Young for her decorous appearance, the prestigious film was a hit with audiences. After her auspicious beginning with Zanuck, Young starred in a series of films that ranged from such hits as *Bulldog Drummond Strikes Back* (1934), a witty and fast-moving film starring Ronald Colman, to flops like *Born to Be Bad* (1934), in which she portrayed an unwed mother who is determined to survive on any terms. The original script of this film called for Young to be a model who tries to entice potential buyers by posing without her underclothes, but this scandalous element had to be dropped because of censorship problems, resulting in a number of confusing scenes. Audiences also objected to the rather seedy part being played by the usually wholesome Young, and the actress herself would later state, "I hated it so, and disapproved of it."

In her autobiography, Young wrote that by age 25, she was certain that she was not going to find what she called her "prince," but she admitted, "I did love someone very much and I had to learn the lesson of self-denial. The man I loved could not love me." According to rumors of the day, that man could have been actor Clark Gable, with whom Young starred in the entertaining adventure yarn *Call of the Wild* in 1935. Rumors spread throughout Hollywood that the two were having a romance, but after the completion of the film, Young's press agent announced that she was ill and had gone to Europe to recuperate. Of the "mysterious" illness, *Photoplay* columnist Dorothy Manners explained: "Hard work ... the physical strain of making one picture immediately following another, capped by the climax of two strenuous roles ... has aggravated an internal condition from which Loretta has suffered since maturity." Despite this rationale, gossip abounded that Young was pregnant with Clark Gable's baby, and a *Photoplay* article would later allude to a "secret child." Two years later, in June 1937, it was announced in the press that Young had adopted a 23-month-old girl, Judy, from a nearby Catholic orphanage. (Judy would grow up to write a book, *Uncommon Knowledge*, claiming that Loretta Young and Clark Gable were her natural parents. To this day, Young has refused to confirm this allegation, and has been estranged from her daughter since 1986.)

The gossip about Young faded into the background as she zealously resumed her professional career, starring with Franchot Tone in *The Unguarded Hour* (1936), a box office hit about a prosecutor who finds himself on trial for murder; *Private Number* (1936), a contrived melodrama about a servant girl who marries the wealthy son of her employers against their wishes, and *Ramona* (1936), the first 20th Century–Fox film in full Technicolor, which featured Young as a half–Indian girl in love with an Indian chief's son. In the latter film, Young's growing knowledge of all aspects of the motion picture business was noted by costar Don Ameche, who remarked, "Loretta knew more about the technical end of moviemaking than almost any other actress I ever worked with." And although she exuded an aura of gentility and polite elegance, Young was fast developing a reputation as a disciplined professional with the demeanor of what her former husband termed a "steel butterfly."

In her last picture of 1936, *Ladies in Love*, Young portrayed a character attracted to a wealthy nobleman portrayed by rising star Tyrone Power. Audiences enjoyed the pairing of Young and Power, and the following year the two were teamed in three popular comedies, *Love Is News* (1937), *Café Metropole* (1937) and *Second Honeymoon* (1937). By now, Young had become one of the major personalities of the 20th Century–Fox lot, along with Sonja Henie, Shirley Temple and Alice Faye, and was earning close to $300,000 a year.

But as Young's popularity continued to rise, she faced a scandal that threatened her stellar career. The star had been involved for nearly a year with William Buckner, a handsome, seemingly wealthy attorney whose uncle was chairman of the board of the New York Life Insurance Company. On December 1, 1938, Buckner was arrested by federal agents after returning from a European cruise, charged with mail fraud in connection with Philippine Railway bonds, which had been under investigation by the Securities and Exchange Commission. Authorities confiscated Buckner's luggage and briefcases and among the items seized were letters and cables from Loretta Young, to whom, according to the *New York Daily Mirror*, Buckner was engaged. Tabloids nationwide were filled with reports of the scandal, including one headline which proclaimed: "Loretta's Darling Buck Held in Swindle." And while one account claimed that Young "had no notion of the extracurricular activities of her self-styled fiancé," there were suggestions that the star not only knew about the scheme, but had been a party to it herself. As the days passed, it was revealed that Buckner had previously been charged with embezzlement and had resigned from the bar because of his inability to defend himself against the charge. Although Young had loaned Buckner money, it was ultimately concluded that she was not involved in the incident. "He did not ask me to invest any money and I certainly didn't invest any," Young declared.

After this brush with scandal, Young emerged virtually unscathed, and went on to star in four entertaining and diverse films in 1938: *Four Men and a Prayer*, a murder mystery costarring David Niven and George Sanders; *Three Blind Mice*, a love comedy about three girls in search of wealthy husbands; *Kentucky*, a horse-racing story that won an Academy Award for co-star Walter Brennan; and *Suez*, a well-mounted historical romance in which she was again teamed with Tyrone Power. However, the actress was growing dissatisfied with her film roles, especially her relatively unimportant stints in *Suez* (according to reports, she ordered the studio wardrobe department to create a huge hooped skirt so that she could make her presence known) and her next film *The Story of Alexander Graham Bell* (1939), in which she had the rather peripheral role of the inventor's wife. (This picture was notable primarily for Young's appearance with her three sisters, Polly Ann, Sally Blane and Georgiana, the only occasion that the four siblings would appear on screen together.) But Young did have a good role in her next picture, *Wife, Husband and Friend* (1939), playing a woman who has delusions about becoming a great singer, and demonstrated her comedic timing to good advantage.

But the well-received *Wife, Husband and Friend* was Young's last film for 20th Century–Fox for a decade. When she left in 1939, many said it was due to her desire for more money, but the actress revealed years later that she had turned down the studio's $7 million contract offer because of her inability to work with Darryl Zanuck. The studio executive, Young said, did not "know anything about women.... Zanuck was great in his way, but not in *my* way!" Her first freelance film after leaving the studio was United Artists' *Eternally Yours* (1939), an entertaining comedy with David Niven about a magician who causes his wife to disappear.

Throughout the years following her divorce from Grant Withers, Young had been romantically linked with a variety of Hollywood notables, including James Stewart, Ricardo Cortez, Gregory Ratoff, David Niven and Joseph Mankiewicz, but in 1939, she met the man who would become her second husband, radio-advertising executive Thomas H.A. Lewis. The following year, on July 31, 1940, the two were married. (Most sources state that Young's daughter, Judy, was adopted by Lewis, but in her 1994 book, Judy herself claimed that although she assumed Lewis' last name, the adoption never took place.) On August 1, 1944, Young would give birth to her first son, Christopher Paul, and less than a year later, on July 15, 1945, her second son, Peter Charles, was born.

Meanwhile, after her first freelance assignment, Young was finding it hard to secure film roles, having been labeled as "difficult" following her defection from Fox. After several months of inactivity, Young accepted an offer from Harry Cohn of Columbia to make three pictures at $75,000 each, which was half her normal fee. In her first film for Columbia, *The Doctor Takes a Wife* (1940), Young was slammed in the *New York Herald Tribune*, whose critic stated that she "has to be guided carefully through the comical aspects of the plot." Young followed this film with *He Stayed for Breakfast* (1940), a sophisticated comedy with Melvyn Douglas; *The Lady from Cheyenne* (1941), her first Western; and *The Men in Her Life* (1941), in which she portrayed a former circus rider who becomes a famous ballerina. Her performance in the latter was viciously panned by a *New York Times* reviewer, who wrote: "She poses outrageously and her lack of resemblance to a dancer is almost laughable."

Young next starred in *Bedtime Story* (1942), an amusing little comedy about a successful actress who wants to abandon her career for life on a Connecticut farm, followed by *A Night to Remember* (1942), a forgettable comedy-thriller costarring Brian Aherne. In director John Farrow's *China* (1943), a wartime adventure yarn with Alan Ladd, Young continued to illustrate her behind-the-scenes know-how and steel-willed character, and according to an observer on the film's set, should have been "given directorial credit along with John Farrow." Over the next two years, Young made *Ladies Courageous* (1944), a patriotic and sentimental tribute to the WAF; *And Now Tomorrow* (1944), a melodramatic soaper about a deaf woman who falls in love with her doctor; and *Along Came Jones* (1945), a Western spoof with Gary Cooper.

Loretta Young

Young's first film of 1946 was also her first entry in the realm of film noir, *The Stranger*. Considered to be one of her most impressive films, *The Stranger* offers the gripping tale of a Nazi war criminal, Franz Kindler (Orson Welles), who is masquerading as a college professor in Hartford, Connecticut. To complete his portrait of normalcy, Kindler marries Mary Longstreet (Young), the daughter of a Supreme Court judge, but his facade begins to crumble when he is tracked to the small town by Wilson (Edward G. Robinson), a member of the Allied War Crimes Commission. After ingratiating himself with Mary's family, Wilson learns that Kindler is not only guilty of wartime atrocities, but has also recently murdered a former underling who turned up in Hartford, threatening to expose him.

Despite the evidence presented to her by Wilson, Mary initially refuses to believe the truth about her husband: "He's good. You have nothing to link my husband with this man Kindler except a wild suspicion. It's a lie," she hysterically insists. "He wouldn't hurt anybody except to help somebody he loves. He's not a Nazi. He's not one of the those people!" But before long, she is forced to face facts and as the townspeople close in on her husband, she follows him to a clock tower where she confronts him with his past. Her earlier distress now subsided, she calmly tells Kindler, "I came to kill you." After a struggle, Mary shoots her husband and he falls to his death, impaled on a mechanism connected to the tower.

Although the *New York Times'* Bosley Crowther claimed that Young turned in "another silly performance," and another critic dismissed her as "more decorative than dynamic," the actress offered a well-rounded portrait of a small-town woman blindly in love with a man responsible for acts that are almost beyond her comprehension. In demonstrating Mary's transformation from a gullible, naive housewife to one with the righteous courage needed to take her husband's life, Young managed to deliver a believable portrayal that remains one of her most riveting.

By now, Young had added a number of philanthropic activities to her filmmaking schedule, including serving as president of the board of trustees for St. Anne's Maternity Hospital, an institution for unwed mothers. In the early 1940s, the big-hearted star was responsible for helping to raise nearly $50,000 for a new building for St. Anne's, and along with Irene Dunne and the wives of John Wayne and Bob Hope, was considered to be one of the leading benefactresses of Catholic charities in Los Angeles.

On screen, Young followed her role in *The Stranger* with *The Perfect Marriage* (1946), a comedy with David Niven that suffered from a flimsy plot and an overly wordy script. But her next picture, *The Farmer's Daughter* (1947), would be the one for which she is perhaps best remembered. In this delightful comedy, Young portrayed a Swedish girl from a Minnesota farm who gets a job as a domestic in a large midwestern city, falls in love with her Congressman boss and winds up running for Congress to beat the crooked political machine. The film was a box office hit and Young's much-praised performance earned the actress her first Academy Award nomination, along with Susan Hayward for *Smash Up, the Story of a Woman*, Rosalind Russell for *Mourning Becomes Electra*, Dorothy McGuire for *Gentleman's Agreement* and Joan Crawford for *Possessed*. Although Russell was the odds-on favorite to win the gold statuette, Young was awarded the Oscar, exclaiming "At long last!" at the start of her acceptance speech. Ironically, Young would later say that she had voted for Susan Hayward because "I was absolutely stunned by this performance, and when I saw it, I knew I couldn't do it as well. I knew that woman had done that part magnificently.... But I got that award playing a straightforward, honest, factual, good girl."

Young's next film, *The Bishop's Wife* (1947), was a wholesome tale about an angel who is sent to Earth to help a bishop in raising money for a new church. A box office smash, the film was included in many critics' lists of the top ten films of the year. She followed this success with *Rachel and the Stranger* (1948) starring Robert Mitchum and William Holden, and it was on the set of this top-grossing film that Young's famed "swear box" may have first come into play. According to all accounts, Young abhorred profanity and one source quotes her as saying, "Cussing is the one thing I dislike about making pictures. Every time I hear a cuss word it jars me. I just decided to do something about it." Young's solution was to establish a box to contain fines exacted from anyone who used profanity in her presence. According to a legendary story, Robert Mitchum shoved several bills in the box each morning and told Young, "This should cover me for the day." Thereafter, the swear box was present on each of Young's films.

After delivering what many consider to be one of her best performance in *Rachel and the Stranger*, Young starred in her second film noir, *The Accused* (1948), a riveting drama about a college psychology professor who accidentally kills one of her students. As the film opens, Dr. Wilma Tuttle (Young) is shown as a spinsterish, tightly controlled woman whose composure is rattled by the suggestive comments of a handsome student, Bill Perry (Douglas Dick). Against her better judgment, Wilma accepts a ride from Perry, who takes her to a cliff where he indulges his passion for diving. Before long, Perry is kissing the professor, arrogantly telling her, "You little firecracker — don't pretend you don't like it." Panic-stricken, Wilma strikes the boy with a steel bar, killing him, then makes his death appear as a diving accident.

Despite an inquest which rules that Perry died by drowning, police detective Ted Dorgan (Wendell Corey) suspects murder and goes about finding the killer. Meanwhile, Wilma meets and falls in love with Warren Ford (Robert Cummings), an attorney and Perry's guardian. For a time, Wilma manages to effectively mask her inner terror at being found out, but Dorgan — despite his own growing feelings for Wilma — doggedly pursues the case until the truth is exposed. After a court trial in which she is defended by Ford, Wilma is ultimately acquitted.

Despite the rather lukewarm ending of the film, *The Accused* offered a tale of mounting suspense as it followed the efforts of the professor to conceal her guilt from the two men who love her. In addition to the fine performances by Wendell Corey and Sam Jaffe, as a callous criminologist, the film was highlighted by Young's depiction of Wilma Tuttle, which earned the actress praise from *Motion Picture Herald* for her "first-rate performance," and in the *New*

York Times for bringing "a high degree of conviction to her portrayal." Perhaps her best notices came in *Variety*, whose critic raved, "Miss Young's portrayal of the distraught professor plays strongly for sympathy. It's an intelligent delineation, gifting the role with life. She gets under the skin in bringing out the mental processes of an intelligent woman who knows that she has done wrong but believes that her trail is so covered that murder will never out."

Following *The Accused*, Young signed a multi-picture contract with Darryl Zanuck of 20th Century–Fox, stating that she had ended "a silly feud with the man I thought was my one big enemy." But this professional triumph was overshadowed by the news that Young's father, who had deserted his family three decades earlier, had died in a county hospital. Although newspapers of the day reported that John Earle Young had been a pauper, he had actually been sent monthly checks by his daughter for several years. Nonetheless, Young stayed away from the funeral services, and years later would admit, "I'm sorry now that I sat in judgment on him. This was one of those things I wish I could do over again. Frankly, I brushed him off and I think this was unforgivable of all of us."

Under her new Fox contract, Young appeared in *Mother Is a Freshman* (1949), a pleasant comedy with Van Johnson and Rudy Vallee, and *Come to the Stable* (1949), the story of two nuns who raise funds for a children's hospital. For her performance, Young would win her second Academy Award nomination, and would later say that *Come to the Stable* was a picture she was "crazy to do. It was a nun story but not at all sticky sweet. These nuns were battlers. Darryl Zanuck had bought the story for Irene Dunne, then shelved it because he thought it was uncommercial.... But *Come to the Stable* won me an Oscar nomination and very definitely made a lot of money. It's revived on television every Christmas. So I knew what suited me better and Darryl still did not." Although Young would lose the Academy Award to Olivia de Havilland in *The Heiress*, the role would remain her favorite.

Young next inked a deal with MGM, starring in *Key to the City* (1950), her first film with Clark Gable since their teaming in *Call of the Wild* more than a decade earlier. But despite high expectations, the film was a failure at the box office, and Bosley Crowther of the *New York Times* panned Young's performance, saying that she was "reduced very largely to uttering double-entendres and batting her eyes." But the actress rebounded from this disappointing venture with a top-notch performance in her final film noir, *Cause for Alarm* (1951), produced by her husband, Tom Lewis.

Cause for Alarm takes place during one 24-hour period in July, described by Young's character Ellen Jones as "the most terrifying day of my life." Ellen's unreasonably jealous husband George (Joseph Cotten), who is recuperating from a heart ailment, believes that his wife is having an affair with his doctor and that the two are plotting his murder. George goes so far as to detail his suspicions in a letter to the district attorney, which he gives to Ellen to mail. Soon after George reveals the contents of the letter, he collapses from a fatal heart attack, and Ellen begins a frantic effort to regain the incriminating correspondence.

As the day progresses, Ellen's life becomes a nightmarish existence, filled with encounters and actions that further point to her guilt, including her irrational attempt to convince the postal authorities to return the letter, her refusal to admit a visitor who'd had a scheduled appointment with George, and her questionable placement of a refill for her husband's medicine. "I did everything wrong," she realizes. "They'll all think I'm guilty." But just as it appears that Ellen will completely break down under the pressure, the postman returns the letter to her — the thick envelope did not have enough postage.

After the release of *Cause for Alarm*, Young was hailed for her "well-modulated portrayal" in the *New York Times*, in which Howard Thompson wrote: "Under her husband's astute sponsorship the picture is Miss Young's — lock, stock, and barrel.... Sporting an admirably skimpy wardrobe and a shiny nose now and then, she does splendidly as the desperate housewife, avoiding all the pitfalls, even in her hysterical breakdown at the end." Labeled by one critic as a "stimulating thriller," this film is especially notable given the fact that it was filmed on a modest budget in exactly 14 days, proving, according to Howard Thompson, that "superior writing, directing and acting — and some imagination — can go a long way."

In her second film of 1951, Young completed her commitment to Fox playing a woman with a split personality in *Half Angel*. In this film, Young decisively embodied her "steel butterfly" image when she had the original director, Jules Dassin, removed from the production. Of the incident, columnist Harold Heffernan wrote, "Loretta's girlish face and extreme femininity of manner conceal a strong will, which comes as quite a surprise to those who attempt to cross her. When she and director Jules Dassin disagreed on her interpretation of the role in *Half Angel*, Loretta smilingly had him yanked off the picture. She'd do the same to anyone whose method of working didn't coincide with her own."

Next, Young starred in *Paula* (1952), a four-hanky soaper about a woman who adopts a child whom she injures in an automobile accident, and *Because of You* (1952), an overly sentimental tale about a former gangster's moll who becomes a nurse's aid and falls in love with a wounded pilot. In 1953, she starred with John Forsythe in *It Happens Every Thursday*, about a couple who try to revive a run-down newspaper. This picture would be her last feature film.

By now, television had become a booming medium, with such hits as *I Love Lucy* dominating the small screen. With what she would later call "absurdly lucky" timing, Young launched *The Loretta Young Show* (originally titled *A Letter to Loretta*) in 1953, produced by her husband Tom Lewis. Each show began with Young's trademark entrance, in which she swept through a door and executed a graceful twirl, showing off an elegant gown. Following her introduction, the program featured a half-hour drama, many of which starred Young in a variety of character roles. Of her dramatic entrance, Young said, "After the audience has seen me well groomed, I can wear horrible clothes, ugly makeup or even a false nose during the show, without anyone wondering whether I've aged overnight, or something." Although Young assured columnist Louella Parsons that she intended to maintain her film career and that her venture into television was "just a sideline," the actress remained with the series for eight seasons, winning three Emmy awards and becoming the first Oscar winner to be awarded television's highest honor. Although the popular series was frequently lambasted by critics who labeled it "corny" and "sentimental," Young insisted, "What, for the record, is wrong with being sentimental? I love it. I couldn't live without it. When people say our shows are sentimental, we feel complimented."

Young's strong-willed persona continued to be evidenced as she made the transition from movies to television. Dubbed the "Iron Madonna," she was in charge of nearly every aspect of her show, and writer-director Richard Morris explained: "It's simply that Loretta is in absolute control. The fact that she's both star and owner doesn't make for the usual director-actress relationship. But you're aware of this when you take the job." After a year on the series, rumors began circulating about problems in the marriage of Young and Tom Lewis, and an item in Walter Winchell's column hinted about their imminent breakup. In an attempt to salvage their relationship by separating their business and personal lives, Young took over the producing responsibilities for the show in 1955, but the couple separated later that year. They would remain separated for nearly 15 years, finally divorcing in 1969.

After the cancellation of her series in 1961, Young published her autobiography, *The Things I Had to Learn*. Actually, the book is less autobiographical in nature than a series of isolated reminisces, homespun philosophies and religious views, as well as tips on fashion, charm and glamour. In one chapter, for instance, entitled "God Said Yes," Young stresses that prayer is the "infallible line of communication to all-powerful God," and "You can't try to outsmart God as though He were the other half of a business deal." In another chapter, she tells readers that "glamour is something no woman can be born with," and extols the virtues of good posture, graceful use of the hands and effective makeup application. Although critics were unimpressed with the book, *The Things I Had to Learn* was popular with Young's fans and became a best-seller.

The year after *The Loretta Young Show* went off the air, Young was back on the small screen with her second series, *The New Loretta Young Show*, which premiered in September 1962. Although Young maintained her patented introduction, viewers did not take to the predictable sitcom format that followed, and after a year of poor ratings the program was cancelled. Young philosophically told the press, "As an actress I have learned that you can't fly every

day, that someday you have to fall on your face." She retired from performing, instead spending her time traveling and donating her energy to charitable causes: "I honestly have trouble finding the time to do all the things I like
to do," she was quoted as saying. "I don't feel any compulsive drive to be acting again."

But after several years, Young's activities appeared to be continually interrupted by litigation. In 1965, she was sued by Pamela Mason, wife of actor
James Mason, who charged that her daughter Portland had been eased out of
Young's second television series prior to its cancellation. The suit was later
settled when Portland was awarded $2,800. A year later, Young herself sued
NBC for $2.5 million, claiming that the network had violated its agreement
with her when it failed to delete the introduction portion of her long-running
television series when it was shown abroad. "Most of the gowns, hairstyles
and makeup, which the plaintiff wore in said openings, were outmoded, out-
dated and out of style," the suit charged. After years of legal wrangling, the
case was decided in Young's favor and she was awarded nearly $600,000 from
the network. And in 1970, brief scenes from two of Young's films were shown
in *Myra Breckenridge*, a sex fantasy starring Mae West and Raquel Welch which
was the first 20th Century–Fox production to receive an "X" rating. Young,
objecting to the film's lurid content, obtained a restraining order demanding
that her film clips be removed from the picture. Fox quickly complied and
Young's lawsuit was dropped.

After an absence from television of nearly 25 years, it was announced in
1985 that Young would star in *Dark Mansions*, an hour-long dramatic series
for ABC-TV, portraying the domineering head of a family-owned shipping
company. But just six weeks after the project was announced, Young dropped
out of the show. She declined to comment on her abrupt departure, but E. Duke
Vincent, executive supervising producer of the show, revealed that it was Young's
take-charge nature that led to her exit: "Basically, the show is meant to be an
ensemble piece. I think Loretta wanted to be more important in the scheme
of the overall series. You have to remember that she is not only an actress and
a star, but a producer-director-owner of a television series. She is not a lady
who is opinionless." Young was replaced in the program by Joan Fontaine. A
year later, Young appeared in the television drama *Christmas Eve*.

In 1993, more than two decades after her divorce from Tom Lewis, Young
married again, this time to costume designer Jean Louis, who had designed
the gowns worn by the actress on her long-running television show. Louis, an
Academy Award winner for his work, was perhaps best known for his creation
of the strapless black gown worn by Rita Hayworth in *Gilda* (1946); he also
designed the white sequined gown worn by Marilyn Monroe when she sang
her rendition of "Happy Birthday" to President John F. Kennedy in 1962.
Young and Louis remained married until the designer's death in April 1997.

In recent years, Young has remained out of the limelight, continuing to devote her energies to charitable causes, including the Loretta Young Youth Project of Phoenix, Arizona, which is dedicated to helping financially and emotionally deprived youth. As she focuses her time on such philanthropic concerns, one can only assume that she continues to display the same strong-willed purposefulness that governed her film and television careers. The tenacious determination that seems to have been innate with the glamourous actress has been best described by the actress herself: "I would like to think of myself as a gutsy broad, but, in all honesty, I can't think of myself that way. I do have an ambition to do something with this talent that I have been given, and I want to put it to good use. So it does take tenacity, or guts, or fortitude, or stubbornness, or perseverance. You can use all sorts of fancy words for it. Yes, I have survived..."

Film Noir Filmography

THE STRANGER   *Director:* Orson Welles. *Producer:* Sam Spiegel. Released by RKO, July 1946. *Running time:* 95 minutes. *Cast:* Edward G. Robinson, Loretta Young, Orson Welles, Philip Merivale, Billy House, Richard Long. *Awards:* Academy Award nomination for Best Original Screenplay (Victor Trivas).

THE ACCUSED   *Director:* William Dieterle. *Producer:* Hal B. Wallis. Released by Paramount, January 1949. *Running time:* 101 minutes. *Cast:* Loretta Young, Robert Cummings, Wendell Corey, Sam Jaffe, Douglas Dick, Suzanne Dalbert.

CAUSE FOR ALARM   *Director:* Tay Garnett. *Producer:* Tom Lewis. Released by MGM, January 1951. *Running time:* 74 minutes. *Cast:* Loretta Young, Barry Sullivan, Bruce Cowling, Margalo Gillmore, Bradley Mora, Irving Bacon, Georgia Backus.

References

"Back in Working Clothes." *TV Guide*, January 14, 1956.
Bowers, Ronald L. "Loretta Young." *Films in Review*, April 1969.
Colby, Anita. "Her Blueprint for Beauty." *Photoplay*, February 1947.
Crichton, Kyle. "Young Idea." *Collier's*, November 18, 1939.
Dudley, Fredda. "Swell People." *Silver Screen*, March 1945.
"Ex-Wife Who Went Back to Girlhood." *Silver Screen*, January 1932.
Hall, Gladys. "Recipe for Happiness." *Silver Screen*, May 1941.
"How Does Loretta Do It?" *TV Guide*, November 5, 1960.
"I'm Still a Ham." *TV Guide*, October 19, 1957.
"Innocent Abroad." *Life*, February 16, 1948.
"Just Take It Out of My Salary," *TV Guide*, May 7, 1959.
Lewis, Judy. *Uncommon Knowledge*. New York: Pocket Books, 1994.
"Loretta Lost an Argument." *TV Guide*, November 8, 1958.
"Loretta Young in *The Accused*." *Coronet*, February 1949.
"Loretta's Gowns." *TV Guide*, April 20, 1957.
Manners, Dorothy. "Fame, Fortune, and Fatigue." *Photoplay*, January 1936.
Marshall, Jim. "Reasonable Miss Young." *Colliers*, December 27, 1947.

Maxwell, Elsa. "The Young Idea." *Photoplay*, May 1948.
"No Shrieks, No Screams." *Newsweek*, December 8, 1958.
Pollock, Louis. "Her Heart Stood Still." *Modern Screen*, June 1948.
"'The Queen' Stakes Her Crown on Television." *TV Guide*, December 4, 1953.
Spoto, Donald. "Loretta Young: *The Farmer's Daughter* Heroine on Sunset Boulevard."
    Architectural Digest, April 1994.
"Television's Number One Messenger Girl." *TV Guide*, December 26, 1959.
"A Visit with Loretta Young." *Photoplay*, January 1936.
Williams, Lena. "Life Waltzes On." *New York Times*, March 30, 1995.
Wilson, Earl. "Loretta Tries an Experiment." *Silver Screen*, January 1944.
"Winner of Academy Award for 1947." *Life*, April 26, 1948.
"Winning Smile." *American Magazine*, October 1948.
Young, Loretta. *The Things I Had to Learn*. New York: Bobbs-Merrill, 1961.

Bibliography

Agan, Patrick. *The Decline and Fall of the Love Goddesses*. Los Angeles: Pinnacle Books, 1979.
_____. *Is That Who I Think It Is?* Vol. 1. New York: Ace, 1975.
_____. *Is That Who I Think It Is?* Vol. 3. New York: Ace, 1976.
_____. *Whatever Happened to—*. New York: Ace, 1974.
Alleman, Richard. *The Movie Lover's Guide to Hollywood*. New York: Harper and Row, 1985.
Amberg, George. *New York Times Film Reviews, 1913–1970*. New York: Arno, 1971.
Barraclough, David. *Hollywood Heaven*. New York: Gallery Books, 1991.
Barris, Alex. *Hollywood's Other Women*. New York: Barnes, 1975.
Basinger, Jeanine. *A Woman's View: How Hollywood Spoke to Women, 1930–1960*. New York: Knopf, 1993.
Bloch, Jeff, ed. *The Women's Book of Movie Quotes*. Secaucus, N.J.: Citadel, 1993.
Boller, Paul F., and Ronald L. Davis. *Hollywood Anecdotes*. New York: Morrow, 1987.
Bookbinder, Robert. *Classics of the Gangster Film*. Secaucus, N.J.: Citadel, 1985.
Briggs, Colin. "Republic Heroines." *Hollywood Studio Magazine*, September 1989.
Brode, Douglas. *The Films of the Fifties*. Secaucus, N.J.: Citadel, 1976.
_____. *The Films of the Sixties*. Secaucus, N.J.: Citadel, 1980.
_____. *Lost Films of the Fifties*. Secaucus, N.J.: Citadel, 1988
Brown, Peter Harry, and Pamela Ann Brown. *The MGM Girls: Behind the Velvet Curtain*. New York: St. Martin's, 1983.
Brunette, Peter, and Gerald Peary. "Tough Guy: James M. Cain Interviewed." *Film Comment*, May-June 1976.
Buller, Richard. "James M. Cain: The Hollywood Years, 1944–1946." *Hollywood Studio Magazine*, November 1985.
Connor, Edward. "Cornell Woolrich on the Screen." *Screen Facts*, 1963.
Copjec, Joan, ed. *Shades of Noir*. London: Verso, 1993
Crivello, Kirk. *Fallen Angels: The Lives and Untimely Deaths of 14 Hollywood Beauties*. Secaucus, N.J.: Citadel, 1988.
Crowther, Bosley. *The Great Films: Fifty Golden Years of Motion Pictures*. New York: Putnam, 1967.
Crowther, Bruce. *Film Noir: Reflections in a Dark Mirror*. London: Columbus, 1988.
Da, Lottie, and Jan Alexander. *Bad Girls of the Silver Screen*. New York: Carroll and Graf, 1989.
Dooley, Roger. *From Scarface to Scarlett*. New York: Harcourt Brace Jovanovich, 1979.
Dorian, Bob, with Dorothy Curley. *Bob Dorian's Classic Movies*. Holbrook, Mass.: Adams, 1990.

Eames, John Douglas. *The MGM Story*. New York: Crown, 1982.
_____. *The Paramount Story*. New York: Crown, 1985.
Endres, Stacey, and Robert Cushman. *Hollywood at Your Feet*. Los Angeles, Calif.: Pomegranate, 1992.
Finch, Christopher, and Linda Rosenkrantz. *Gone Hollywood*. Garden City, N.Y.: Doubleday, 1979.
Fox, Patty. *Star Style: Hollywood Legends as Fashion Icons*. Santa Monica, Calif.: Angel City, 1995.
Fox–Sheinwold, Patricia. *Gone but Not Forgotten*. New York: Bell, 1982.
_____. *Too Young to Die*. New York: Crescent, 1991.
Gelman, Barbara, ed. *Photoplay Treasury*. New York: Crown, Inc., 1972.
Griffith, Richard. *The Movie Stars*. Garden City, N.Y.: Doubleday, Inc., 1970.
Hadleigh, Boze. *Hollywood Babble On*. New York: Berkley, 1994.
Haskell, Molly. *From Reverence to Rape: The Treatment of Women in the Movies*. New York: Holt, Rinehart and Winston, 1973
Herbert, Ian, ed. *Who's Who in the Theatre*. 16th ed. Detroit: Gale, 1981.
Higham, Charles, and Joel Greenberg. *Hollywood in the Forties*. New York: Barnes, 1968.
Hirsch, Foster. *The Dark Side of the Screen: Film Noir*. New York: Da Capo, 1981.
Hoberman, J. "B Bop." *Village Voice*, May 21, 1991.
Holden, Anthony. *Behind the Oscar: The Secret History of the Academy Awards*. New York: Simon and Schuster, 1993.
Hubbard, Linda S., and Owen O'Donnell, eds. *Contemporary Theatre, Film and Television*. Vol. 7. Detroit: Gale, 1989.
Katz, Ephraim. *The Film Encyclopedia*. New York: Crowell, 1979.
Kleiner, Dick. *Hollywood's Greatest Love Stories*. New York: Pocket, 1976.
Kobal, John. *People Will Talk*. New York: Knopf, 1985.
Lamparski, Richard. *Whatever Became Of... ?*, 2nd ser. New York: Crown, 1968.
_____. *Whatever Became Of... ?*, 3rd ser. New York: Crown, 1970.
_____. *Whatever Became Of... ?*, 5th ser. New York: Crown, 1974.
_____. *Whatever Became Of... ?*, 8th ser. New York: Crown, 1982.
_____. *Whatever Became Of... ?*, 9th ser. New York: Crown, 1985.
_____. *Whatever Became Of... ?*, 10th ser. New York: Crown, 1986.
_____. *Whatever Became Of... ?*, 11th ser. New York: Crown, 1989.
Levin, Martin, ed. *Hollywood and the Great Fan Magazines*. New York: Harrison House, 1970.
Lloyd, Ann, and Graham Fuller, eds. *The Illustrated Who's Who of the Cinema*. New York: Macmillan, 1983.
Lyons, Barry. "Fritz Lang and the Film Noir." *Mise-en-Scène*, circa 1970.
McCarty, John. *Hollywood Gangland*. New York: St. Martin's, 1993.
_____. *Thrillers: Seven Decades of Classic Film Suspense*. Secaucus, N.J.: Citadel, 1992.
McClelland, Doug. *Forties Film Talk*. Jefferson, N.C.: McFarland, 1992.
McClure, Arthur F., and Ken D. Jones. *Star Quality*. New York: Barnes, 1974.
MacPherson, Don, and Louise Brody. *Leading Ladies*. New York: Crescent, 1986.
Maltin, Leonard, ed. *Leonard Maltin's Movie Encyclopedia*. New York: Penguin, 1994.
Maxfield, James F. "Out of the Past: The Private Eye as Tragic Hero." *New Orleans Review*, Fall and Winter 1992.
Maxwell, Roger. *Love Goddesses of the Movies*. New York: Crescent, 1975.
Miller, Rex. "Film Noir." *The Big Reel*, August 1995.
Mordden, Ethan. *The Hollywood Studios*. New York: Fireside, 1988.

O'Donnell, Monica M., ed. *Contemporary Theatre, Film and Television.* Vol. 4. Detroit: Gale, 1987.

_____, and Owen O'Donnell, eds. *Contemporary Theatre, Film and Television.* Vol. 5. Detroit: Gale, 1988.

Ottoson, Robert. *A Reference to the American Film Noir.* Metuchen, New Jersey: Scarecrow, 1981.

Palmer, R. Barton. *Hollywood's Dark Cinema: The American Film Noir.* New York: Twayne Publishers, 1994.

Parish, James Robert. *The Fox Girls.* New York: Arlington House, 1971.

_____. *Good Dames.* New York: Barnes, 1974.

_____. *Hollywood Character Actors.* New York: Arlington House, 1978.

_____. *The Paramount Pretties.* New York: Arlington House, 1972.

_____. *The RKO Gals.* New York: Arlington House, 1974.

_____, and Ronald L. Bowers. *The MGM Stock Company: The Golden Era.* New York: Bonanza, 1972.

_____, and Lennard DeCarl. *Hollywood Players: The Forties.* New York: Arlington House, 1976.

_____, and Don E. Stanke. *The Forties Gals.* New York: Arlington House, 1980.

_____. *The Glamour Girls.* New York: Arlington House, 1975.

_____. *The Leading Ladies.* New York: Arlington House, 1977.

Peary, Danny, ed. *Close-Ups: The Movie Star Book.* New York: Simon and Schuster, 1978.

Pickard, Roy. *The Hollywood Story.* Secaucus, N.J.: Chartwell, 1986.

Polan, Dana. "Film Noir." *Journal of Film and Video,* Spring 1985.

Pratley, Gerald. *The Cinema of Otto Preminger.* New York: Barnes, 1971.

Quinlan, David. *The Illustrated Encyclopedia of Movie Character Actors.* New York: Harmony, 1985.

_____. *Wicked Women of the Screen.* New York: St. Martin's, 1987.

Quirk, Lawrence J. *The Great Romantic Films.* Secaucus, N.J.: Citadel, 1974.

Ragan, David. *Movie Stars of the '40s.* New Jersey: Prentice Hall, 1985.

_____. *Movie Stars of the '30s.* New Jersey: Prentice Hall, 1985.

_____. *Who's Who in Hollywood, 1900–1976.* New Rochelle, N.Y.: Arlington House, 1976.

Rothe, Anna, ed. *Current Biography, 1951.* New York: H.W. Wilson, 1952.

Sattin, Richard. "Joseph H. Lewis: Assessing an (Occasionally) Brilliant Career." *American Classic Screen,* November-December 1983.

Scheuer, Steven H. *The Movie Book.* Chicago, Ill.: Playboy, 1974.

Schickel, Richard. *The Stars.* New York: Bonanza, 1962.

Schrader, Paul. "Notes on Film Noir." *Film Comment,* Spring 1972.

Schultheiss, John. "The Noir Artist." *Films in Review,* January 1989.

Selby, Spencer. *Dark City: The Film Noir.* Jefferson, N.C.: McFarland, 1984.

Sennett, Ted. *Hollywood's Golden Year,* 1939. New York: St. Martin's, 1989.

Shipman, David. *The Great Movie Stars: The Golden Years.* New York: Bonanza Books, 1970.

_____. *The Great Movie Stars: The International Years.* New York: St. Martin's, 1972.

Silden, Isobel. "It's No Crime When Yesterday's Stars Get Into 'Murder.'" *Los Angeles Times,* August 17, 1989.

Sills, Claire. "Stars of the Late Show." *TV Radio Mirror,* December 1971.

Silver, Alain, and James Ursini, eds. *Film Noir Reader.* New York: Limelight, 1996.

_____, and Elizabeth Ward, eds. *Film Noir.* 3rd ed. New York: Overlook, 1992.

Springer, John, and Jack D. Hamilton. *They Had Faces Then.* New York: Citadel, 1974.

Stephens, Michael L. *Film Noir: A Comprehensive, Illustrated Reference to Movies, Terms and Persons.* Jefferson, N.C.: McFarland, 1995.

Thomas, Nicholas, ed. *International Dictionary of Films and Filmmakers. Volume Three—Actors and Actresses.* 2nd ed. Detroit: St. James, 1992.

Thomas, Tony. *The Films of the Forties.* Secaucus, N.J.: Citadel, 1975.

_____, and Aubrey Solomon. *The Films of 20th Century–Fox.* Secaucus, N.J.: Citadel, 1985.

Tims, Hilton. *Emotion Pictures.* London: Columbus, 1987.

Truitt, Evelyn Mack. *Who Was Who on the Screen.* New York: Bowker, 1977.

Twomey, Alfred E., and Arthur F. McClure. *The Versatiles: A Study of Supporting Character Actors and Actresses in the American Motion Picture.* New York: Barnes, 1969.

Vermilye, Jerry. *The Films of the Thirties.* Secaucus, New Jersey: Citadel, 1982.

_____. *More Films of the Thirties.* Secaucus, N.J.: Citadel, 1989.

Wilson, Ivy Crane, ed. *Hollywood in the 1940s: The Stars' Own Stories.* New York: Ungar, 1980.

Zinman, David. *Fifty Classic Motion Pictures.* New York: Crown., 1970.

Documentaries

"American Cinema: Film Noir." Copyright 1994, NYCVH. A New York Center for Visual History Production, in co-production with KCET and the BBC.

"Hollywood: The Golden Years" (Episode Five). Copyright 1987, BBC. A BBC Television Production in association with RKO Pictures.

"Hollywood Diaries." Copyright 1997, Beehive Productions. An American Movie Classics Original Production.

Index